Labor and Urban Politics

THE WORKING CLASS IN AMERICAN HISTORY

A list of books in the series appears at the end of this book.

Labor and Urban Politics

Class Conflict and the Origins of
Modern Liberalism in Chicago, 1864–97

RICHARD SCHNEIROV

UNIVERSITY OF ILLINOIS PRESS
Urbana and Chicago

Publication of this book was supported by a grant from Indiana State University.

Manufactured in the United States of America

1 2 3 4 5 C P 5 4 3 2 1

This book is printed on acid-free paper.

Library of Congress Cataloging-in-Publication Data
Schneirov, Richard.
Labor and urban politics : class conflict and the origins of modern liberalism in Chicago, 1864–97 / Richard Schneirov.
p. cm. — (The working class in American history)
Includes bibliographical references and index.
ISBN 0-252-02374-9 (acid-free paper). —
ISBN 0-252-06676-6 (pbk. : acid-free paper)
1. Chicago (Ill.)—Politics and government—To 1950.
2. Working class—Illinois—Chicago—History—19th century.
3. Trade-unions—Illinois—Chicago—Political activity—History—19th century.
4. Liberalism—Illinois—Chicago—History—19th century.
I. Title. II. Series.
F548.42.S35 1998
977.3'11041—dc21 97-21164
CIP

Contents

Acknowledgments

In the two decades that I have spent studying Chicago labor history I have accumulated many important debts, both intellectual and personal. Martin J. Sklar, Alfred Young, Carl Parrini, and J. Carroll Moody helped guide my graduate work at Northern Illinois University, where I began this project almost two decades ago. My greatest intellectual debt is to Martin J. Sklar, teacher, friend, and mentor, to whom I largely owe my understanding of socialism, liberalism, and political economy. Most important, I learned from Sklar the necessity of systematically relating my research topic to the central social characteristics of a period, both historical and transhistorical, that is, the task of periodization. To Alfred Young, who helped transmit and interpret to me the new labor history in the form of his own seminal work and that of Herbert Gutman, I owe much of my understanding of how the "presence" of the lower classes can influence the larger configurations of politics. My friend Steven Sapolsky generously shared with me his extensive research and, more important, his insights into Chicago labor history. His suggestion that the Chicago police often aided strikers led me to formulate the hypothesis that has largely guided my research. Throughout my work John Jentz has been my friend and colleague in thinking and writing about Chicago labor history; he has shared with me his knowledge of German sources and his balanced judgments on social history matters. Finally, through my work with Thomas Suhrbur, with whom I coauthored an earlier book on the Chicago carpenters' union, I learned the rewards of a painstaking examination of union records.

I would also like to mention longtime friends who have broadened and stimulated my understanding of history and politics, particularly Bill Burr, Keith Haynes, James Livingston, Larry Lynn, Steve Rosswurm, and Paul Wolman. I received assistance from Archie Motley, Linda Evans, and especially Fannia Weingartner at the Chicago Historical Society and from Les Orear and William Adelman at the Illinois Labor History Society. I also appreciate the summer grants from the National Endowment for the Humanities and from Indiana State University.

I greatly benefited from a critical reading of the manuscript by David Montgomery. John Jentz and Martin Sklar also read the manuscript and offered critical comments. Michael Les Benedict, Robert Weir, and Norty Wheeler aided at various stages in the process of revision.

Closer to home, I acknowledge that I could not have even begun this project without Celeste Trevino. I will always be grateful for her support at a critical time in my life. David Alexander was also a source of counsel and support in completing this work. My wife Silvia's love and understanding, from the time she supported my return to graduate school, has been a bedrock source of my perseverance. I hope too that my sons, Zachary and Nathan, will accrue something from the fruits of this work. More than anyone, however, this book must be dedicated to the memory of my parents, Maurice and Ruth Schneirov, for in some sense it is an offering to them.

Labor and Urban Politics

Introduction

This book chronicles the growing self-awareness of workers in Chicago as a class from the formation of the city's first Trades Assembly in 1864 to the founding of the Chicago Federation of Labor in 1896. The maturation of that awareness in the shape of a political consciousness compelled other groups in society and in the economy to take account of its presence. As a result the nature of Chicago politics was transformed, and a modern or new liberalism began to evolve.

Because the rise of labor as a major factor in Chicago's political history structures this book, a word about the rise of class or class formation is necessary. I have examined that process in three dimensions: the horizontal, the vertical, and the longitudinal. By horizontal I mean the way in which workers of different parties, ethnicities, races, religions, genders, skill levels, and trades transcended or sidestepped these identities to constitute a new social identity as a working class, with an awareness of common values and interests. I have examined this process culturally—that is, the way in which class was present in workers' everyday life—but above all in workers' creation of formal institutions, particularly trade unions and trades assemblies, and the way these interacted with political parties and institutions of governance, such as the police force. Formal institutions aggregated divergent and sometimes competing interests and identities among working people, thereby making possible the formulation and public articulation of a more general interest or class interest, referred to then, and in this book as well, as that of "labor." In the early stages of class formation the aggregation and articulation of interests was accomplished primarily by political parties, either working-class reform parties or one or both of the major parties. By the mid-1880s, however, this function was increasingly taken on by permanent labor unions and citywide federations capable of bargaining or lobbying with the parties at least quasi-independently.

I have not assumed that a working-class identity foreclosed the existence and persistence of other identities or that a working-class identity did not have ethnic, gender, trade, or partisan political characteristics. In fact much of this book argues that class formation proceeded in segmented fashion, that is, that workers forged ethnoclass institutions within and through different ethnopolitical cultures and coalesced at various points in classwide institutions.

A special word is necessary about race and gender. Recent work has demonstrated that class has important gendered and racial dimensions. Especially in its manifestations in the 1860s and 1870s class formation must be understood as being virtually equivalent to white male class formation. Not only were African Americans and women largely excluded from the labor movement, but also the very definition of what it meant to be part of the working class—the discourse of class—marginalized these groups and their potential agency.[1] During the era of the Knights of Labor white workers began to accept small numbers of African Americans into their movement. More significant was the entrance of large numbers of women into the labor and civic reform movements, which allowed them to play a critical part in transforming the agenda of urban reform and in rethinking the parameters of class politics to legitimate the concerns of working women.

The quest for class solidarity did not occur in a vacuum. Workers sought to transcend their diverse interests to exercise power vis-à-vis other social strata. Workers realized their capacity for collective action to the extent that they were able to compel other classes, and thereby the political system, to take account of their presence. Politically, this meant the ability to translate their demands into authoritative public policy. The relation between labor and other classes and between these classes and the political system as a whole make up the vertical dimension of class formation. So that this dimension of class formation can be better understood, I have interspersed chapters examining labor in isolation from other strata with chapters examining labor in relations with other strata and within the context of Chicago society, municipal politics, and various reform coalitions. In general workers made their presence felt in and through multi- or cross-class coalitions, sometimes outside of the existing party system but usually within it. There were two kinds of cross-class coalitions in this period. Until the depression of the 1870s labor often joined an antimonopolist coalition of producers based on greenback politics. After that period a different kind of multiclass reform coalition became possible: a progressive coalition with a new liberal agenda.

The third dimension necessary for understanding class formation is the longitudinal one, that is, change over time. Because consciousness is a critical part of the story of class formation, that process was inevitably a contingent and historical one rather than a unidirectional one closely correlated with an inexorable modernization. In different terms class formation was a social movement, rising and falling and taking different forms according to the actions of human agents. Class is therefore best understood as a contingent, multidimensional social construct developing over time within the context of industrial and political change (and this applies to capitalists as well as workers). In sum the coalescence of a collective identity across alternative social lines and the creation of autonomous organizational capacities capable of influencing public authority enabled working people to become a collective actor on the local political stage.

Class formation in Chicago was, of course, never "completed" or triumphant. It proceeded in fits and starts through four great upheavals or moments of class formation, which in turn can be grouped into two stages. In the first stage, between the Civil War and the late 1870s, which included the upheavals of 1864–68 and 1877–79, Chicago workers' new trade unions remained under the political tutelage of labor politicians espousing a labor republican ideology with an antimonopolist emphasis. Beginning in the 1880s, especially during the upheaval of 1886–87 (and in 1894 as well), trade unions grew increasingly independent of third party and major party politicians and could bargain with the two parties from a more autonomous position. In the aftermath of the Haymarket era they adopted important elements of a new liberal politics and began to view themselves as part of a progressive coalition. The Chicago Federation of Labor, formed in 1896, was the first city trades assembly in Chicago history largely committed to new liberal politics.

The central contention of this book is that class formation among late nineteenth-century workers had a profound and transformative impact on the urban political system. That impact, however, is misunderstood and greatly underestimated if it is seen as manifesting itself mainly through the episodic appearance of labor or socialist parties. The more enduring political effect of class formation occurred within the two major parties, particularly the Democratic party, and in the policies of local government. To understand how that process occurred, this book looks beyond the formal outcomes of elections and examines the less formal processes of party coalition-making, electoral appeals, the practical policies of local government, and the complex political relationships among labor leaders, politicians, and officeholders. The growing presence of labor could scarcely be contained within machine-dominated politics, however. After 1886, elite liberal reform thinking and practice began to be rethought. In the course of that process, organized labor, the labor question, and prolabor policies attained political credibility, electoral appeal, and legitimacy in respectable discourse.

Linking labor to liberal reform—a major part of the larger thesis of this book—requires historiographical comment. In the past fifteen years many labor historians have reexamined working-class politics and have contributed much of enormous value. But rather than study the reshaping of America's liberal polity, much work has focused on validating the existence of nonliberal or antiliberal alternatives. Some labor historians have willy-nilly developed a new synthesis of the place of workers in the American political system that views them as fashioning a relatively distinct and autonomous political culture and ideology by the end of the nineteenth century. American working-class activists, it is argued, articulated their grievances and aspirations within a "labor republican" framework that contained key elements of socialism and served as an alternative to a purportedly undemocratic liberalism flourishing among the American middle and upper classes. The movement of labor republicanism, particularly as manifested in the Knights of Labor and associated labor parties of the late nineteenth century, could have provided the rudiments of a viable opposition movement to the emerging but not yet crystallized hegemony of corporate capitalism.

In sum the argument is that highly contingent political events, notably those resulting from the defeat of the Knights in specific strikes in the mid-1880s and the political defeat of the Populists in the mid-1890s, foreclosed a more democratic and emancipatory set of historical possibilities in twentieth-century America. In the words of one scholar American exceptionalism—the belief that American sociopolitical development differed in fundamental ways from a standard established in Europe—was "made" in this period.[2]

The ironic outcome of this argument is that the exceptionalism these historians have challenged for the nineteenth century reemerges in the twentieth century in the tail end of their narratives. Whether it was because of the state-aided defeat of critical strikes, the decline of oppositional movement or ethnic subcultures, the legal interpretations of the federal courts, or the co-optation of independent labor politics by the two major parties that prevented the formation of a labor party, a kind of hegemony of procorporate capitalist liberalism emerged sometime between the fall of the Knights and the fall of the Populists or at the latest by the early twentieth century. It is almost as if American history's "good" possibilities came to an end with the close of the nineteenth century and the fall of "labor republicanism." America, it seems was not born liberal but was made liberal, after which its path diverged—tragically so—from Europe's. At least this is the interpretation many U.S. labor historians have adopted.[3]

The interpretation defended in this book dissents from the notion that the period from the end of the Civil War to the beginning of the Progressive Era—a period commonly known as the Gilded Age—was a tragedy of lost opportunities. Without abandoning the insights and many of the approaches of the cultural turn of the new labor history, this book returns to the historiographical tradition that originated with the progressive historians, one that viewed American liberalism as potentially idealistic, democratic, prolabor, and, above all, progressive. It also builds on recent scholarship that demonstrates liberalism and republicanism were not mutually exclusive and cannot be counterposed.[4]

Not long after World War II two historians in this tradition, Ray Ginger and Chester McArthur Destler, used late nineteenth-century Chicago as a context for treating the transformation of American democratic political thought that eventually came of age during the 1930s. To Ginger, the genesis of modern democratic liberalism was the story of how the "Lincoln Ideal" of universal compassion grounded in individual opportunity and popular government was distorted and undermined by the new social realities of Gilded Age capitalism, how Governor John Peter Altgeld and other reformers sought to restore the power of that ideal through social reform, and how in the course of that work they revised the ideal itself. Working somewhat earlier, Destler examined the pathbreaking but only partially successful attempt by Henry Demarest Lloyd to "cross-fertilize" an indigenous radicalism with "imported proletarian Socialism" to create a "restricted democratic collectivism" comparable with British "new liberalism." To Ginger and Destler, such democratic pioneers as Altgeld, Lloyd, Jane Addams, Clarence Darrow, and Eugene Debs and such thinkers as John Dewey and William James, all of whom matured in the maelstrom of Chicago's labor and political wars of the 1880s and 1890s, were heroic progressive liberals who reinvigorated a stultifying American democracy.[5]

This book covers much the same ground that Ginger and Destler did, and it shares their underlying assumption that the liberalism of that era was capacious and flexible enough to capture much of the best of Continental and British socialist thinking, while retaining the vigor and liberal faith of the American democratic heritage. It differs, however, in several ways. Instead of telling the story primarily from the vantage point of heroic figures like Lloyd and Altgeld, it widens the angle of vision by also connecting the reconfiguration of liberalism to the rise of the trade unions and the broader labor movement and its presence in local politics. From this perspective the labor movement continued its ascent and development into the late 1890s instead of declining and devolving into exceptionalism. In this book the study of labor's rise is grounded in an in-depth investigation of the social and political history of urban Chicago and takes into account the discoveries and approaches of the latest social, political, and urban historical scholarship, without its truncated historiographical perspective. By exploring workers "search for power" in the context of class relations and the American political system, it picks up where the new labor history, pioneered by Herbert Gutman, David Montgomery, and others in the 1960s, left off.[6] This book also differs because rather than limit democratic forces to heroic labor leaders or prolabor reformers, it views liberal development as a cross-class phenomenon (or, more precisely, a movement composed of segments of different classes) rooted as well in the political evolution of leading members of the local "establishment": bankers, merchants, manufacturers, jurists, and journalists, who helped build a new progressive politics.

Finally, this book does not ignore, paper over, or explain away the flaws, limitations, and internal divisions within labor and liberal politics that recent historians have uncovered. Rather than magnify these divisions and thus artificially counterpose purportedly liberal and nonliberal or postliberal forms of thought, this book views liberalism as a historically evolving system of thought capable of including, accommodating to, and being shaped by forms of thought seemingly outside its purview. The purpose of relinking labor and liberalism is not to dismiss the recent focus on paths not taken or resume an outworn celebration of American consensus but to understand better what did happen rather than what "unfortunately" did not happen, that is, to see how liberalism began to accommodate to and be reshaped by popular movements and new social questions to yield what historians acknowledge as modern, twentieth-century liberalism.

The transition from an older to a revised liberalism discussed in this book can best be understood in the context of—though it cannot be reduced to—the larger social transformation in production systems occurring in the United States during the last three-quarters of the nineteenth century. Household labor in the colonial era was characterized by a personal but hierarchical and patriarchal relationship between journeyman and master, farmhand and freeholder, wife and husband and by self-sufficiency and the exchange of products unmediated by money and market. In addition to the household system the colonial and early nineteenth-century economy depended on various forms of unfree labor, from the indentured servitude of most white immigrants and the bound labor of apprentices and servants to the brutally exploited slave labor of African Americans. To be sure, the impersonal relationships that inhered in product markets and wage labor were not unknown by the end of the eighteenth century, but such relations did not structure the everyday lives of the majority of Americans working outside the slave economy until the 1850s, when for the first time the number of wage laborers exceeded the number of slave laborers. In the first half of the nineteenth century a dynamic market economy spread and flowered, especially throughout the American North, disintegrating and reconstituting household relations or relegating them to the margins of social life through outwork or cottage industry. By the mid-nineteenth century commercial agriculture had become the norm in expanding northern agrarian regions, and out-of-home industry spurred by capital accumulation in railroad building had grown up alongside the old artisan workshops, merchant capitalism, and slave labor creating the basis for growing urban-industrial centers linked to a national market.[7]

As these changes transpired, especially in the North, market relations—defined as those involving money exchange where buyer and seller bargain according to the criteria of maximizing utility—became the prevalent matrix of social intercourse. This was a profound transformation, not only economic but also social, cultural, and political in nature. As the nineteenth century proceeded, the United States was becoming a modern rather than a traditional society. In different terms it shed characteristics associated with a gemeinschaft, a communality in which the individual was integrated organically into the group (household, clan, village) and in which social change was the exception rather than the rule. It became a dynamic gesellschaft, a society of independent individuals freely contending and associating with each other, harmonized less by custom and tradition and more by contractual relations and the hidden hand of market competition; innovation, social change, impersonal relationships, and social mobility became the norm.[8] In its American version this market society was, above all, a liberal society, one in which the state's powers were constitutionally defined and limited and did not stand above and command but instead served and protected the rights and liberties of freely associating individuals in an autonomous civil society.

In the period after the Civil War the most intractable conflict in the United States was no longer between tradition and modernity, communality and society, slave labor and free labor but between two different phases in the evolution of a liberal gesellschaft, one in crisis and one emerging. By the 1870s it had become clear that America's expanding market society was not automatically harmonious. The social harmony liberalism had promised was not being realized; social progress had become problematic. Obstacles were being encountered that had not been predicted by liberal theory. First, as Thorstein Veblen, the country's most perspicacious sociologist at the time, put it, the "business enterprise" characteristic of a competitive market society conflicted with the "machine process" that society had generated, a conflict reflected in recurrent financial panics and depressions and a new kind of social inequality. Veblen was hardly the first to notice this. Since the Civil War and especially during the depression of the 1870s America's working men and women were the most avid audience of such theorists and agitators as Henry George and assorted greenbackers and socialists, who exposed the glaring disparity between industrial progress and poverty.[9]

Something else distressed the defenders of liberal society. In the course of competition business proprietors began to combine or associate in such organizations as trusts, employers' groups, and corporations to consciously regulate market competition. The new organizations were an inescapable reaction to the need to accumulate large sums of capital and labor and to protect them in an unpredictable marketplace; more particularly, the new organizations sought to ameliorate the supply-demand disequilibrium that resulted from firms with high fixed capital costs competing with each other in an unregulated market. In regulating, planning, coordinating, and creating predictability according to consciously specified goals, such organizations dramatically contravened a central tenet of market liberalism, that the market's hidden hand was sufficient to harmonize competing individuals and generate the common good.

But the crisis of the legitimacy of the competitive market carried with it the prospects for a reformed liberalism. Freely associating individuals seeking to escape competition created a kind of gemeinschaft within a gesellschaft. Put differently, classes were being formed and reformed as a way of culling a new order from the midst of disorder. Such organizations as Standard Oil and the Pennsylvania Railroad were, in Chandlerian language, "visible hands" that integrated competing proprietary firms into cohesive units able to plan investment and coordinate and speed production. By integrating individual workers into a complex division of labor and subjecting them to the discipline of the machine process controlled by hired managers, they "socialized" labor to a degree hitherto unknown. In the same vein such unions as Eugene Debs's American Railway Union could bring the nation's rail system and virtually the entire interconnected industrial economy to a halt with a majority vote of delegates in a union convention. The organizational thrust of late nineteenth-century market society can be thus understood as a phase in class formation, which in turn proceeded as a function of the socialization of production. The process was reciprocal, for as men and women became more aware of the interdependency of the units of industrial society, they increasingly sought the protection of organizations. This book is about that process of social and class awareness and how it interacted with older conceptions and ideals of liberty to produce new political beliefs and ways of acting.[10]

For workers and those critics and reformers who became aware of the disharmonies in market society, the search for a way out led them to distinguish between two meanings of liberalism that have often been confused. The oldest, most enduring—what Martin J. Sklar calls the "transhistorical" element—in American democratic thought has been the liberal principle of the sovereignty of the people in a constitutionally limited state. In the eighteenth-century guise of the independent producer and the self-governing citizen early liberalism sanctioned and celebrated the liberation of society from the dictates of the state or ruler.[11] By the early nineteenth century Americans adapted and amended their liberalism to take into account the emergence of a bourgeois social order composed of profit-seeking property owners competing in a self-regulated market. By the Jacksonian period market liberalism, deriving much of its legitimacy from classical political economy, came to be seen as a prime condition for the maintenance of a vibrant self-governing society guaranteeing liberty and freedom.[12]

With the appearance of market disharmonies and the rise of labor organizations the mutually reinforcing congruence of these two principles—constitutional liberalism and market liberalism—began to be called into question. The recognition among labor advocates and other critics that market competition among proprietors was not sufficient to implement and guarantee liberty and equality tended to reinvigorate republicanism, which along with liberalism had been part of American democratic thought since the American Revolution.[13]

Instead of sustaining the liberty of the individual in a market society, republicanism was concerned above all with the health of the Republic and specified the conditions for its maintenance. Republicanism was built on the much older belief in Western history that republics were fragile, ephemeral entities, liable to decay and degeneration into monarchies, mob rule, or other forms of tyranny. To prevent the turn of what was known as the Polybian Cycle, republicans felt that the distribution of property and access to power needed to be balanced among the members of the republic, though not necessarily distributed equally. That would allow citizens to exercise public virtue in ascertaining the common good and prevent the takeover of the state by an interested minority or majority seeking to use it in its own behalf in violation of the rights of other citizens. As nineteenth-century workers became aware that they were bearing the social brunt of market failure, they returned to and helped reinvigorate republican thinking in the form of a resurgent "labor republicanism."[14]

Recent scholarship has demonstrated that labor republicanism in the late nineteenth century, as in the previous decades of the century, was far from incompatible with liberalism. The two were not distinct or separable ideologies or languages but were commonly intertwined in the thought of both individuals and movements. Producer or labor republicans thus relied on liberal natural rights language that posited a presocial right of workers or producers to the product of their labor. For propertied liberals natural rights legitimized their title to property, but to workers their claim to the fruits of their labor was no less legitimate than the property rights of their employers, hence the latent critical edge to the cry of "equal rights." Conversely, even propertied or pro-propertied liberals worried that an American republic beset by grasping monopolists, machine politicians, and uneducated freedmen and immigrants would become corrupted and would no longer serve the common or public good. In short what seems to have emerged from the most recent work on American political ideology is that liberalism and republicanism were complementary, often mutually reinforcing political languages, which, though analytically distinct and sometimes in tension, were commonly mixed in the speech and thought of the same people.[15] What predominated in the last half of the nineteenth century was thus something that can be termed republican liberalism.[16] Though the terms *liberalism* and *republicanism* are employed throughout this book, they are used only to emphasize different constituent elements of this larger democratic ideology and are not intended to be understood as constituting opposing and mutually exclusive political philosophies.

If we resist the current tendency to counterpose labor republicanism and liberalism and instead view the labor question as a problematic within, not outside, (republican) liberalism, it is possible to begin to tell the story of how American democratic thought and practice, instead of being stymied in the Gilded Age, began the long transformation into a twentieth-century variant that accepted organizational and state regulation of marketplace activity. In different words this liberalism became America's "via media," great compromise, or merger between market liberalism and socialism.[17]

This book has three parts. Chapter 1 sets the economic, social, and political stage for the initial phase of class formation for Chicago's workers during the Civil War and Reconstruction. In this phase, which culminated in the 1867 eight-hour-day strike, skilled workers drew on developments during the Civil War era to unite for the first time as a class. Organized workers viewed themselves as part of a free-labor coalition of producers, including ethnic leaders, small manufacturers and other businessmen, and soft-money politicians from both parties. Chapter 2 turns to the rise of machine politics and discusses how both the reconstituted working class and the industrialists were able to generate independent organizational capacities in party politics. Chapter 3 examines a major watershed in class formation, the great upheaval of 1877, and how the attempt to mobilize less skilled industrial workers gave rise to the Knights of Labor and the Socialist Labor party. Chapters 4 and 5 recount how a segmented class culture emerged in Chicago's Irish community, which was represented by the Knights of Labor.

The second third of the book centers on the upheaval of the mid-1880s. By 1886–87 trade unions had entered into a quasi-independent political bargaining relationship with Mayor Carter Harrison. Chapter 6 examines the conditions shaping that relationship, while chapter 7 details how, under pressure from mugwump liberal reformers on the one hand and revolutionary anarchists on the other, this relationship fell into crisis, thus creating the preconditions for the eight-hour-day strikes and the Haymarket tragedy. Chapters 8, 9, and 10 survey and analyze the great upheaval itself. The most distinctive feature of the city's strike wave and the associated events surveyed in chapter 8 was not so much the events surrounding the Haymarket affair but the acceptance by large numbers of workers of the need for organization and collective regulation of market activities. Chapter 9 discusses the rise of the United Labor party and how it eventually broke apart on the rocks of political disagreements stemming from class segmentation and internal dilemmas that prevented it from breaking out of its class shell. Chapter 10 details the decline of the Knights and its brand of labor politics and the rise of the trade unions.

The third part of the book, chapters 11 through 13, argues that the impact of the upheaval in the 1880s created the conditions for the emergence—though not yet the triumph—of a new liberalism and a new progressive coalition in local politics. Chapter 11 discusses how new cross-class associations among labor leaders, women and other reformers, politicians, and business leaders created a new social ethics, a new conception of citizenship, and a limited acceptance of collective bargaining in the late 1880s. Chapter 12 details how leading trade unionists in the early 1890s abandoned a static natural rights outlook and replaced it with an evolutionary perspective grounded in a new organizational culture. The final chapter reinterprets Chicago progressivism of the mid- to late 1890s. Labor populism was defeated following the Pullman strike, but the deep social impact of the depression, the need to moderate persistent class conflict, and the growing cross-class acceptance of a moderate version of socialism as part of public discourse combined to create a new urban reform agenda by the late 1890s. That agenda and the cross-class movement that emerged from it incorporated a more formal recognition of labor and its articulated interests than had ever existed and prefigured the National Civic Federation that was so influential in the early twentieth century.

Notes

1. David R. Roediger, *The Wages of Whiteness: Race and the Making of the American Working Class* (London: Verso, 1991); Alice Kessler-Harris, "Gender and Labor History," in *Perspectives on American Labor History: The Problem of Synthesis,* ed. J. Carroll Moody and Alice Kessler-Harris (De Kalb: Northern Illinois University Press, 1989), 55–79; Joan Scott, "Women and the Making of the English Working Class," in her *Gender and the Politics of History* (New York: Columbia University Press, 1988), 68–9; Ava Baron, "Gender and Labor History," in *Work Engendered: Toward a New History of American Labor,* ed. Ava Baron (Ithaca, N.Y.: Cornell University Press, 1991), 1–46; Leon Fink, "Culture's Last Stand: Gender and the Search for Synthesis," *Labor History* 34 (Spring–Summer, 1993): 178–89.

2. Sean Wilentz, "Against Exceptionalism: Class Consciousness and the American Labor Movement: 1790–1920," *International Labor and Working Class History* 26 (Fall 1984): 1–24; Sean Wilentz, *Chants Democratic: New York City and the Rise of the American Working Class, 1788–1850* (New York: Oxford University Press, 1984); Gregory S. Kealey and Bryan D. Palmer, *Dreaming of What Might Be: The Knights of Labor in Ontario, 1880–1900* (New York: Cambridge University Press, 1982), chap. 8; Leon Fink, "The New Labor History and the Powers of Historical Pessimism: Consensus, Hegemony, and the Case of the Knights of Labor," *Journal of American History* 75 (June 1988): 115–36; Kim Voss, *The Making of American Exceptionalism: The Knights of Labor and Class Formation in the Nineteenth Century* (Ithaca, N.Y.: Cornell University Press, 1993) (quote). On labor historians' use of republicanism, see Richard L. McCormick, *The Party Period and Public Policy: American Politics from the Age of Jackson to the Progressive Era* (New York: Oxford University Press, 1986), 89–140. For signs that the study of labor liberalism may be reviving, see Ira Katznelson, "The 'Bourgeois' Dimension: A Provocation about Institutions, Politics, and the Future of Labor History," *International Labor and Working Class History* 46 (Fall 1994): 7–32. For suggestive critiques of labor history's exceptionalist bias, see James Livingston, *Pragmatism and the Political Economy of Cultural Revolution, 1850–1940* (Chapel Hill: University of North Carolina Press, 1994), 124–31; and Terrence McDonald, "The Burdens of Urban History: The Theory of the State in Recent American Social History," *Studies in American Political Development* 3 (1989): 3–29.

3. Fink, "New Labor History and the Powers of Historical Pessimism"; Richard Jules Oestreicher, *Solidarity and Fragmentation: Working People and Class Consciousness in Detroit, 1875–1900* (Urbana: University of Illinois Press, 1986); Gerald Friedman, "The State and the Making of the Working Class: France and the United States, 1880–1914," *Theory and Society* 17 (May 1988): 403–30; William E. Forbath, *Law and the Shaping of the American Labor Movement* (Cambridge, Mass.: Harvard University Press, 1991); Victoria C. Hattam, *Labor Visions and State Power: The Origins of Business Unionism in the United States* (Princeton, N.J.: Princeton University Press, 1993); Voss, *Making of American Exceptionalism.*

4. Richard Hofstadter, *The Progressive Historians: Turner, Beard, Parrington* (New York: Vintage Books, 1968); John Higham, *History: Professional Scholarship in America* (New York: Harper and Row, 1965), 171–211. On recent scholarship, see note 14.

5. Ray Ginger, *Altgeld's America, 1890–1905: The Lincoln Ideal versus Changing Realities* (1958; reprint, Chicago: Quadrangle Books, 1965), 1–14; Chester McArthur Destler, *American Radicalism, 1865–1901: Essays and Documents* (1946; reprint, New York: Octagon Books, 1963), 30–31; Chester McArthur Destler, *Henry Demarest Lloyd and the Empire of Reform* (Philadelphia: University of Pennsylvania Press, 1963). In the same camp are Harry Barnard, *Eagle Forgotten: The Life of John Peter Altgeld* (1938; reprint, Secaucus, N.J.: Lyle Stuart, 1973); and Bessie Louise Pierce, *A History of Chicago,* 3 vols. (New York and Chicago: Alfred A. Knopf and University of Chicago Press, 1939–57).

6. Herbert G. Gutman, "The Workers' Search for Power," in *The Gilded Age,* rev. and enlarged ed., ed. H. Wayne Morgan (Syracuse, N.Y.: Syracuse University Press, 1963), 31–53; David Montgomery, *Beyond Equality: Labor and the Radical Republicans, 1862–1872* (New York: Vintage Books, 1967); Herbert G. Gutman, *Work, Culture, and Society in Industrializing America* (New York: Vintage Books, 1976), 234–92. More recently, see Leon Fink, *Workingmen's Democracy: The Knights of Labor and American Politics* (Urbana: University of Illinois Press, 1983); Iver Bernstein, *The New York City Draft Riots: Their Significance for American Society and Politics in the Age of the Civil War* (New York: Oxford University Press, 1990); and Philip J. Ethington, *The Public City: The Political Construction of Urban Life in San Francisco, 1850–1900* (Cambridge: Cambridge University Press, 1994).

7. David Montgomery, *Citizen Worker* (Cambridge: Cambridge University Press, 1993), 13; Charles Sellers, *The Market Revolution: Jacksonian America, 1815–1846* (New York: Oxford University Press, 1991); Allan Kulikoff, *The Agrarian Origins of American Capitalism* (Charlottesville: University Press of Virginia, 1992); Eric Foner, "The Idea of Free Labor in Nineteenth-Century America," in his *Free Soil, Free Labor, Free Men: The Ideology of the Republican Party before the Civil War* (Oxford: Oxford University Press, 1995), ix–xxxix.

8. Ferdinand Tonnies, *Community and Society,* trans. Charles P. Loomis (East Lansing: Michigan State University Press, 1957); Richard D. Brown, *Modernization: The Transformation of American Life, 1600–1860* (New York: Hill and Wang, 1976); James M. McPherson, *Ordeal by Fire: The Civil War and Reconstruction* (New York: Alfred A. Knopf, 1982); Richard J. Jensen, *Illinois: A History* (New York: W. W. Norton, 1978); Thomas Bender, *Community and Social Change in America* (New Brunswick, N.J.: Rutgers University Press, 1978); Martin J. Sklar, *The United States as a Developing Country: Studies in U.S. History in the Progressive Era and the 1920s* (Cambridge: Cambridge University Press, 1992), chap. 2.

9. Thorstein Veblen, *The Theory of Business Enterprise* (1904; reprint, New York: Mentor Books, 1963); Henry George, *Progress and Poverty* (1879; reprint, New York: Walter J. Black, 1942).

10. Alfred D. Chandler Jr., *The Visible Hand: The Managerial Revolution in American Business* (Cambridge, Mass.: Harvard University Press, 1977); Robert Max Jackson, *The Formation of Craft Labor Markets* (Orlando, Fla.: Academic, 1984), chaps. 2–4. On socialization, see Michael Harrington, *Socialism: Past and Future* (New York: Plume, 1990), chaps. 1 and 7; and Daniel T. Rodgers, "In Search of Progressivism," *Reviews in American History* 10 (Dec. 1982): 124–26. On the organizational synthesis, see Samuel P. Hays, "The New Organizational Society,"

in *Building the Organizational Society: Essays on Associational Activities in Modern America*, ed. Jerry Israel (New York: Free Press, 1972), 1–15; and Louis Galambos, "Technology, Political Economy, and Professionalization: Central Themes of the Organizational Synthesis," *Business History Review* 57 (Winter 1983): 471–93. In the same vein, see William Lazonick, *Business Organization and the Myth of the Market Economy* (Cambridge: Cambridge University Press, 1991), chap. 2.

11. Sklar, *United States as a Developing Country*, chap. 1; Daniel T. Rodgers, *Contested Truths: Keywords in American Politics since Independence* (New York: Basic Books, 1987), 80–111.

12. Joyce Appleby, *Capitalism and a New Social Order: The Republican Vision of the 1790s* (New York: New York University Press, 1984); Hebert Hovenkamp, *Enterprise and American Law, 1836–1937* (Cambridge, Mass.: Harvard University Press, 1991), chaps. 1–9; Sellers, *Market Revolution*.

13. James Kloppenberg, "The Virtues of Liberalism: Christianity, Republicanism, and Ethics in Early American Political Discourse," *Journal of American History* 74 (June 1987): 9–33; Martin J. Sklar, *The Corporate Reconstruction of American Capitalism, 1890–1916: The Market, the Law, and Politics* (Cambridge: Cambridge University Press, 1988), 34.

14. J. G. A. Pocock, *The Machiavellian Moment: Florentine Political Thought and the Atlantic Republican Tradition* (Princeton, N.J.: Princeton University Press, 1975); Bernard Bailyn, *The Ideological Origins of the American Revolution* (Cambridge, Mass.: Harvard University Press, 1967); Lance Banning, *The Jeffersonian Persuasion: Evolution of a Party Ideology* (Ithaca, N.Y.: Cornell University Press, 1978); Drew R. McCoy, *The Elusive Republic: Political Economy in Jeffersonian America* (New York: W. W. Norton, 1980). On the origins of labor republicanism, see Wilentz, *Chants Democratic;* David Montgomery, "Labor and the Republic in Industrial America, 1860–1920," *Le mouvement social* 3 (Apr.–June 1980): 201–16; and James L. Huston, "The American Revolutionaries, the Political Economy of Aristocracy, and the American Concept of the Distribution of Wealth, 1765–1900," *American Historical Review* 98 (Oct. 1993): 1079–1105.

15. Daniel T. Rodgers, "Republicanism: The Career of a Concept," *Journal of American History* 79 (June 1992): 11–38. J. G. A. Pocock argues against a "binary reading of the debate" between liberalism and republicanism in "Between Gog and Magog: The Republican Thesis and the Ideologia Americana," *Journal of the History of Ideas* 48 (Apr.–June 1987): 325–46. Jeffrey C. Isaac advances the view that liberalism required and normally included the virtue offered by republicanism in "Republicanism vs. Liberalism: A Reconsideration," *History of Political Thought* 9 (Summer 1988): 349–77. Michael Les Benedict demonstrates that even laissez-faire constitutionalism was based on republican premises in "Laissez-Faire and Liberty: A Re-evaluation of the Meaning and Origins of Laissez-Faire Constitutionalism," *Law and History Review* 3 (Fall 1985): 293–331. On natural rights republicanism, see Rodgers, *Contested Truths*, 72–79.

16. Kloppenberg, "Virtues of Liberalism," 33.

17. Sklar, *Corporate Reconstruction of American Capitalism;* Sklar, *United States as a Developing Country*, chaps. 1 and 7; Mary O. Furner, "The Republican Tradition and the New Liberalism: Social Investigation, State Building, and Social

Learning in the Gilded Age," in *The State and Social Investigation in Britain and the United States*, ed. Michael J. Lacey and Mary O. Furner (Cambridge: Cambridge University Press, 1993), 197–218; Stuart Hall, "Variants of Liberalism," in *Politics and Ideology*, ed. James Donald and Stuart Hall (Philadelphia: Open University Press, 1986), 145. For "via media," see James T. Kloppenberg, *Uncertain Victory: Social Democracy and Progressivism in European and American Thought, 1870–1920* (New York: Oxford University Press, 1986), 145–60.

CHAPTER 1

Early Class Formation in Chicago, 1864–72

In 1864 the nation's attention was riveted on the progress of the Union army as it broke the military stalemate of the first two years of the war and conducted continuous and intensive offensive operations in the South. The previous year the implementation of President Abraham Lincoln's Emancipation Proclamation, controversial in the North and anathema in the South, had set the nation on a course toward the abolition of slavery and a radical shift in the social basis of wealth and the distribution of power. Lincoln's defeat of the Democrat George McClellen in November's presidential election seemed to be the seal of approval on these developments.

In the midst of that momentous year something else just as critical, though less dramatic and less noticed, was also occurring. Throughout the North, wageworkers were overcoming ethnic and political divisions, organizing trade unions in unprecedented numbers, striking for higher wages, and bringing the class question into public discussion through the actions of their trades assemblies, which were forming in every important city, including Chicago.[1]

During the 1850s Chicago workers had established a variety of associations, though few were large or influential. Least important were the newly formed trade unions of skilled workers formed among the printers, machinists and blacksmiths, iron molders, carpenters, and house painters. Of these, by far the most powerful and long-lived was the typographers' union, formed in 1852. More numerous were the ethnic benevolent societies, primarily among the German-speaking artisans, which provided their members with insurance. The most successful of these was the Schneider (tailors) Verein, which also established a price list in 1854 that their masters accepted for ten years. The Irish had their counterpart to these associations in the benevolent societies of the ship carpenters and caulkers and the horseshoers and laborers. A third type of workers association was the citywide association composed of mechanics of all trades. German-speaking workers formed the Arbeiter Verein in 1857–58 while English-speaking skilled workers found refuge in the smaller and less influential Mechanics Institute. Both associations welcomed artisan employers and middle-level professionals, though their membership remained largely wageworkers seeking mutuality, self-improvement, and benevolence.[2]

On the eve of the Civil War the city had at most ten associations of workers and nothing approaching a modern trade union movement. That situation changed drastically in 1863 with the arrival of runaway inflation, falling real wages, and a severe labor shortage brought about by the war. Together, they created the incentive and the leverage for workers to form "protective" associations or unions. In 1864 workers formed fifteen new unions, seven of them affiliated with national unions in their trade; and the press reported thirteen strikes, more than the total of the previous three years. When employers resisted by forming employers associations, the new unions combined to form the Trades Assembly, which consisted of twenty organizations and replaced the defunct Mechanics Institute. They also established one of the nation's two national labor papers, the *Workingman's Advocate*.[3]

Not only their actions but also the rhetoric of the newly mobilized workers indicated a new and more sharply defined awareness of class divisions rending the city's social fabric. According to one activist, "A general union of all denominations of workingmen must be formed . . . for all workingmen have a common interest." The president of the Trades Assembly, the printer George Hazlitt, asserted that its formation was necessary "to protect ourselves against the present aggressive actions of capital." Also, typical were the words of the journeymen bakers' union, which called on their fellows to join a movement "to emancipate ourselves from the degradation into which, as a craft, we have fallen." The bakers went on to assert that "the degradation of labor is a certain prelude to despotism" and that "if we would maintain a republican form of government . . . we must do so by maintaining the honor, dignity and respectability of labor."[4]

To ascribe the sudden and dramatic emergence of a substantial labor movement in Chicago only to wartime economic conditions would vastly oversimplify the situation. Labor's new prominence was based on a series of complex and interwoven economic, social, and political developments that were transforming the city almost beyond recognition and creating a permanent and distinct working class. Three elements stand out as critical in this process: (1) industrialization and the spread of market relations, (2) immigration and its interaction with class and local political alignments, and (3) workers' reinterpretation of American political traditions to make sense of their class predicament. For the most part, wartime developments only accelerated, highlighted, and intensified these deeper processes of class formation originating in the 1850s and extending into the early 1870s.[5]

Chicago in the 1860s was in the throes of an epic transformation from a regional mercantile center to a diversified metropolitan economy. In the 1840s and 1850s the character of the city's economy and its pace of growth were closely dependent on the explosive growth of the Midwest region. As early as 1840 the Midwest surpassed New England in population, and by 1860 it had surpassed the Mid-Atlantic region. With the completion of the Illinois-Michigan Canal in 1848 and the first great spurt of railroad building in 1857 the economic activities of midwesterners centered largely on Chicago. As early as 1851 the city had become the nation's largest corn market, in 1854 the largest wheat market, in 1856 the largest lumber market, and in 1862 the largest pork market. Chicago thus became a "gateway city," a site for exchanging western primary products for eastern manufactured goods.[6]

In 1850 Chicago was a frontier town with only 30,000 inhabitants, fewer than in Galena, Illinois. By the eve of the Civil War, because of its mercantile activities, it had grown to 112,172 citizens, making it the eighth largest city in the United States. The extent to which the city's economy was given over to wholesaling, retailing, transportation, banking, insurance, and other activities that greased the wheels of trade is measured by the percentage of population engaged in manufacturing, which in 1860 was far smaller than in Cincinnati, Indianapolis, or Galena. The largest capitalized firm was the city's gas works. Only the agricultural implements plant of Cyrus McCormick, the city's second largest capitalized firm and with two hundred workers the largest employer, produced for a regional or transregional market.[7]

During this early period Chicago was guided by a business elite of "boosters." Such men as William Butler Ogden, Jonathan Young Scammon, Walter J. Newberry, and other leading members of the Board of Trade had enormous investments in real estate as well as trade and predicated their fortunes on promoting the virtues of the city to eastern investors and developers. In sponsoring or lobbying for canal and railroad development, free banking, internal improvements, or free-soilism, as they did in the 1850s, the boosters were not only advancing their adopted city but also raising the value of the land they had bought for speculative purposes and expanding the trade they financed.[8]

Though the boosters were developmentally oriented stewards of the city's growth, their horizons were narrow. Apart from real estate, Bessie Louise Pierce points out that "in their overweening eagerness to get rich" they limited their investments to enterprises that offered a quick return and steered clear of manufacturing or railroads. With the exception of the Galena and Chicago Railroad, investment in railroads came from eastern and British capitalists, leading an early exponent of development to write that Chicago in this period grew out of "a junction of Eastern means and Western opportunity. . . . Greatness was thrust upon Chicago as a golden subjugation."[9]

During the Civil War era Chicago's economic infrastructure reoriented itself toward promoting capital accumulation in local manufacturing and distribution. Most important, the continued growth of the city's hinterlands—facilitated by the extension and integration of the rail system in the late 1850s and dramatic local population growth—created a market capable of absorbing the products of indigenous manufacturing. Meanwhile, the federal government during the Civil War undertook a variety of measures that directly and indirectly promoted manufacturing at the expense of trading. Congress created a national banking system that forged a more stable national currency, thereby promoting interregional markets. The printing of greenbacks and the removal of the country from the international gold standard inflated the currency and reduced the value of manufacturers' prewar debt to wholesale merchants. The existence of cost-plus contracts during the war years and the creation of a national capital market helped them accumulate fixed capital. When Congress passed a protective tariff bill in 1862, it erected a wall against British imports, further promoting capital growth.[10]

With few exceptions eastern capitalists were unable to take full advantage of these developments because they had not yet developed the economies of scale that would enable them to undersell Chicago-based competitors, who had the advantage of proximity to their market. During this critical period eastern capitalists, instead of continuing to export their finished products west, increasingly decided to relocate to or invest new capital in Chicago. During the 1860s many industries reached thresholds in sales volume necessary to support optimum-sized factories or greatly expand existing ones. The growth of these industries created multiplier effects in other industries, resulting in the self-sustaining growth of a diversified local economy.[11]

The industries that grew the most were in the transport-sensitive sectors serving the city's hinterlands. For example, in 1857 Detroit's Eber Ward established, with the help of eastern capitalists, the city's first iron mill. At first Ward only rerolled iron rails, but with the growth of the local railroad supply industry and the opening of the Lake Superior iron-ore mining region to development, the conditions were created for a thriving local iron and steel industry. Between 1860 and 1870 the capital invested in iron manufacturing had increased almost sixfold, and by 1873 the industry employed 9,623 men. Iron production furnished the material for thriving industries producing finished goods, the most important of which were agricultural implements and machinery. Between 1860 and 1870 the value of output of the city's four major firms almost quadrupled.[12]

The most dramatic case of industrial growth occurred in meatpacking.[13] Before the war porkpacking was centered in Cincinnati, which was called "Porkopolis." But the wartime closure of Cincinnati's river access to southern markets and the enormous demand of the Union army for salt pork, coming on the heels of the maturing of the western rail network centering on Chicago, led to a relative decline in porkpacking in Cincinnati. By the winter of 1861–62 Chicago was the new Porkopolis. Three years later the city's nine largest railroads, together with members of the Chicago Pork Packers Association, supplied the $1 million in capital necessary for the formation of the Union Stockyards and Transit Company, located south of the city at the terminus of the city's western feeder lines, which conveyed hogs and cattle into the city from the farms in the Midwest and open ranges on the Great Plains. By 1868 Chicago's packing industry made up 25 percent of the city's manufacturing output, up from 12 percent in 1860.

The making of Chicago into a meatpacking colossus was only the start of an important transformation in the industry itself. Early packers had been essentially wholesale merchants, but by the 1860s the stabilization of the demand for pork and the emergence of a national capital market allowed investors with a deeper commitment to innovation in the production process to seize control of the industry. The size of the average firm increased four times, to $200,000; the largest was the Chicago Packing and Provision Company of B. P. Hutcheson. The packing magnates overcame seasonality by storing ice from nearby country lakes, thus allowing plants to operate in the summertime. In the 1870s Gustavus Swift used ice to create the refrigerated railroad car, enabling Chicago meatpacking firms to market chilled beef as well as pork throughout the nation.

The coming of the meatpacking industry spawned a host of auxiliary industries utilizing the by-products of hogs and cattle. Gelatin was manufactured into glue, animal oils and tallow became soap and lard, offal became fertilizer, and hides were worked into leather goods. Between 1855 and 1870 the number of leather manufacturing firms increased from three to nine, helping give rise to a thriving local boot and shoe industry. Overall, between

1860 and 1870 the capital invested in Chicago manufacturing increased sevenfold, from $5.4 million to $39.0 million, while the population increased less than threefold, from 112,172 to 299,000.[14]

The transformation of the packers from commission merchants into industrialists whose investments were in production rather than trade was at the core of a larger social transformation occurring among Chicago businessmen. The hothouse industrial development of this period swamped the old booster elite, creating something approaching a modern capitalist class whose profits depended on its control over the process of labor rather than on speculative investment and mercantile activities. A number of historians have identified the late 1850s and 1860s as the watershed for this development. Frederic Jaher finds that while the new business leaders of the 1860s, like the antebellum elite, were New Yorkers and New Englanders in origin, they tended to be wealthier, partly because of the prodigious growth of the economy but also because many were able to create monopolies in a specialized line of business. The 1860s witnessed the advent of local magnates of renown, such as Marshall Field (dry goods), B. P. Hutcheson (meatpacking), Nathaniel K. Fairbank (soap and lard), Richard T. Crane (iron manufacturing), and William Deering (harvesting). These men no longer viewed their interests as identical with those of the community as a whole as had the boosters. The relationship was quite the reverse; the economic health of the community depended on the prosperity of their enterprises.[15]

The appearance of new leaders of industry focused on obtaining personal wealth more than on building the community coincided with the appearance of a distinct working class defined by its members' need to sell their capacity to work on the market in order to live. One indication of the watershed character of this decade was that by 1870 the portion of the population employed in Chicago—about 38 percent—had reached the approximate level attained earlier by New York, Boston, Brooklyn, and Cincinnati. It was not simply the sheer growth in the number of workers that provided the indispensable condition for a modern labor movement, however. As the city developed a diversified industrial economy, the scale of the workplace grew accordingly. In 1860 there was only one large factory in the city, but ten years later there were three large meatpacking firms, two huge railcar works, and two mammoth furniture firms, each employing hundreds of workers. In 1850 Chicago's average firm was significantly smaller than Philadelphia's. By 1860 Chicago had closed the gap by having 54 percent of its workers in firms of 26 workers or more, compared with the Quaker City's 68 percent. By 1870 Chicago had more than 75 percent of its workers in firms of this size, while Philadelphia had 72 percent. In agricultural implements four firms employed an average of 184 workers, in rolled and forged iron six firms employed an average of 244, and in meatpacking three large firms employed a majority of the industry's 2,119.[16]

The concentration of workers in a small number of firms, approximating a level achieved earlier in the East, was critical to the emergence of the labor movement in Chicago. It decreased prospects for moving into the ranks of employers, weakened the personal tie between employer and employee, and intensified the sense of social distance, dependence, and impersonality in the employment relation. The intermingling of large numbers of workers also helped create an awareness of common predicament and shared interest, which furthered the realization that those who labored constituted a distinct class and that unions were not only possible but necessary.[17] The first bakers' strike occurred in 1864 at the Chicago Mechanical Bakery, the largest and most mechanized firm in the industry and the city. The strike was directed not against a working owner or master baker but the firm's "superintendents." The issue was not the price list for goods, which would indicate a small craft shop, but wages and hours.[18]

Contributing just as much to the objective conditions for class formation was the emergence in the 1860s of an extensive market in labor. The critical factors were the tenfold population increase between 1850 and 1870 and the transformation of Chicago into the nation's rail hub. Employers could now draw on the nation's floating reserve labor force, consisting of recently arrived immigrants, tramping artisans, and the poor and unemployed generally. In describing the formation of "a general labor market" in 1869 the *Chicago Tribune* reported that "a large majority" of this reserve was "without trades and go[es] where the wages are highest."[19] The role of the railroad in integrating the city into a national labor market was felt dramatically after the great fire of 1871, when the demand for workers to rebuild the city more than doubled the manufacturing work force within a few months, thereby swamping trade union efforts to organize and laying the basis for mass unemployment after the panic of 1873.

The evolution of a labor market meant that employers had little choice but to accede to competitive pressures in determining the wages, hours, and working conditions of their employees. The effect was to standardize conditions of work, not only for employees of large-scale manufacturing firms but also for those in industries that resisted or ran counter to the trends of increasing scale and capitalization, such as men's clothing, printing, and many of the building trades. Realization that the market impersonally determined wages and working conditions spread slowly and unevenly in mid-nineteenth-century Chicago. The Civil War era inflation, which affected workers across the labor market, accelerated and evened out this process, imbuing workers with the sense that they faced a common class situation.

The growth in the size of firms, the widening of product markets, and the increase of competition intensified pressures on employers to improve productivity in the workplace, resulting in the dilution of craft traditions. This dilution, however, was accomplished more by the extension of the division of labor than by the introduction of skill-displacing mechanization. For example, the general carpenters, who had fashioned doors, sashes, and trim on the job were displaced in large numbers during this period by lower-paid, less-skilled carpenters who merely installed prefabricated materials and were paid by the piece. Iron molders also found their jobs subdivided, and the simpler tasks were taken over by a flood of helpers they called "berks," who were paid by the piece. Indeed, piecework was the bane of mid-nineteenth-century craftworkers, and ameliorating its effects motivated much of the organizing, workplace rulemaking, and striking in this period.[20]

The prevalence of grievances relating to piecework underlines an important point. Even though steam power was becoming the norm, few local firms could muster the coordination of diverse labor processes that allowed for a significant increase in "the velocity of throughput," which, according to the economic historian Alfred D. Chandler Jr., was the key to creating economies in production. In the rolling and forging of pig iron, in the manufacture of finished iron products from agricultural implements to railroad cars, and in the making of furniture, the production process in this period was still under the control of skilled rollers and heaters, iron molders, patternmakers, machinists, general carpenters, blacksmiths, and cabinetmakers, along with their helpers and unskilled laborers. The closest an industry in Chicago came to mass production methods, in which factory hands operated machines composed of interchangeable parts to produce standardized goods, was the "disassembly line" Chicago packers borrowed from their Cincinnati forebears to specialize the labor employed in dismembering pork carcasses. Even here the division of labor was significantly less developed compared with its elaboration in later years, and those employed to do the work were skilled butchers and their helpers.[21]

The continued importance of skilled workers was critical to the formation of class associations among workers. On the one hand, through their control over the work process and their supervision of helpers, they maintained the culture of artisanal pride, autonomy, and independence that was conducive to organization and collective action. On the other hand, they found themselves in large-scale work settings subject to the impersonal authority delegated to foremen and supervisors by absentee owners, tyrannized over by the workings of the labor market, threatened by a degradation of craft traditions, and in close association with many other workers laboring in similar circumstances. In short they harbored new kinds of grievances, together with the means and motivation to redress them. Not surprisingly these skilled workers initiated organizing attempts and monopolized the leadership positions in the new labor movement. General carpenters, seeking to protect craft traditions, began the first union, which eventually included unskilled pieceworkers; machinists began organizing in the carshops; and iron molders organized in the iron foundries.

Though the "objective" developments in the market and industrial system were necessary to working-class action, the national background of the men and women who constituted the wage-earner class immensely complicated this process, at some points crosscutting it and retarding it and at others reinforcing it. The process of immigration and how it interacted with domestic industrialization is therefore the second critical element of class formation. The work force in almost all urban centers in the United States underwent a dramatic recomposition between 1840 and 1880. By the end of this period in nearly every important city a native-born working-class had been replaced by one whose members were at least 75 percent foreign-born, children of the foreign-born, or African American. Already in Chicago in 1850, 64.5 percent of employed males were immigrants; in 1860, 71.6 percent were foreign-born; by 1870 that figure had fallen slightly, to 69.0 percent. In 1870 the city's male work force was 31 percent native-born, 25 percent German, 19 percent Irish, 8 percent British, and 17 percent other nationalities. Because approximately one-quarter of the native-born population was of foreign-born parentage, over three-quarters of the work force was of foreign-born parentage. Slightly less than 49 percent of the population in Chicago was foreign-born, a figure 20 percentage points less than in the work force.

To say that the working class was predominantly foreign-born does not mean that solidarity existed among immigrant groups on all or even most points of interest. Several kinds of major divisions were possible among immigrants, each one interacting with class cleavages to create a distinct social configuration. One major configuration occurred where workers with foreign-born parents faced American-born employers. Since two-thirds of the city's predominantly immigrant workers were employed in firms owned by capitalists born in the United States, this configuration played a defining role for Chicago society. If immigrant workers faced employers of their own nationality, class antagonisms tended to be moderated, and ethnic or artisanal solidarity was reinforced. This was particularly the case among the Germans. Germans owned 38 percent of Chicago's manufacturing establishments in 1870, slightly more than the percentage for the American-born. Where the average native-owned firm employed forty-six workers, however, the average German firm was a small craft shop employing fifteen workers. Not surprisingly, craft solidarity among masters and journeymen was strong in the German community, which took the form of the Arbeiter Verein (Workers Association). By contrast the Irish owned only 5.6 percent of all firms, whereas they constituted 13.0 percent of the city's population.[22]

Those of foreign parentage often were at odds. A major line of demarcation among the city's workers was between German-speaking immigrants from Central Europe (including Polish, Hungarian, and Bohemian artisans) and English speakers of immigrant background, such as the Irish and British who found a common language with the native-born. This division was important because the German language served as the vehicle of a political culture dating from the 1848 revolutions in Europe, which was congenial to what has been called a "social republican" politics. Social republicanism predisposed many German-speaking workers to support class conflict, state economic activism, and a social revolutionary outlook. English-speaking workers tended to assimilate quickly and easily into America's liberal republican political culture, which stressed the supremacy of an independent citizenry acting within a limited state. Though there were important commonalities between these two political cultures—both chafed at the dependence of the wage-labor system—there were also critical tensions that by 1870s widened into a deep gulf.[23]

Still another dividing line among immigrants pitted pietistic Protestants against liturgical Protestants and Catholics. When sumptuary or temperance laws became a political issue, this religious division became salient electorally in Chicago and other northern cities. It left most English and Scandinavian immigrants on the side of native Evangelical Protestant reformers. Those immigrant Protestants who were liturgical Lutherans and virtually all Catholics—together, probably the majority of voters in the city—were united in defense of the right to drink on Sundays. How this translated into politics was revealed with an astonishing degree of detail in 1877 by the *Chicago Tribune* editor Joseph Medill in an argument against reviving temperance. Of the 68,000 registered voters in Chicago, observed Medill, only 12,000 were affiliated with "orthodox Protestant churches"; they were easily outmatched by 12,000 English-speaking Catholics, 3,000 German-speaking Catholics, 2,000 Jews, and 2,000 unorthodox Protestants. Ethnoreligious categories however, go only so far in explaining the divisions among workers, for according to Medill, 36,000 voters were not affiliated with any church.[24]

These complexities make it clear that the immigrant status of workers by itself tells very little without considering the interaction among diverse ethnic, religious, and class groupings. These complex, historically contingent interactions were critical to the story of the origins of the labor movement, which in turn was an element in class formation. The first political coalescence of the two major immigrant working-class groups in Chicago occurred in 1855 at the height of the anti-immigrant or nativist Know-Nothing movement in the city. Mayor Levi D. Boone and the city council raised the license fee on saloons and attempted to enforce the new law in the face of open defiance among most Germans and Irish Catholics. The two groups united against the city's middle- and upper-class "Puritans" to mount the so-called Lager Beer riot, which was followed by the overwhelming defeat of a prohibition initiative in a city election. In the 1856 municipal election the local issues of temperance and know-nothingism were overshadowed by national politics in the form of widespread antislavery opposition to Senator Stephen A. Douglas's Kansas-Nebraska Act. In this circumstance a significant segment of Germans, under the leadership of exiled leaders of the failed 1848 German Revolution, joined the Republican party crusade to stop the advance of slavery in the West. Irish Catholic workers, however, resisted anything associated with abolitionism and remained firmly attached to the Democratic party.[25]

In Chicago the success of the Republican party extended the political dominance of the Free-Soil movement, which since 1848 had united the Democratic and Whig booster elite behind a program of antislavery, free banking, railroad and commercial development, and government-financed internal improvements. In 1857 the Republican "Long John" Wentworth became mayor, inaugurating a series of Republican victories in the city that would last—with interruptions in 1862–65 and 1873–76—for twenty-two years.

At the start of the Civil War German and Irish workers, constituting almost half the city's work force, were politically divided. Though Democratic leaders supported the war effort, Lincoln's Emancipation Proclamation aggravated the race issue. According to the politically active printer Frederick Cook, "Among the Democratic masses . . . antipathy to the Negro outweighed every other consideration." German workers, led by the Arbeiter Verein, were solidly antislavery and pro-Republican. In 1863 the Arbeiter Verein even offered its services to the federal government to put down expected Irish draft riots, which were widely feared after the revolt of the Irish in New York City, in which many hundreds were killed.[26]

The feared clash between the Irish and Germans over the draft never materialized in Chicago, however. Because the city appropriated $211,000 for bounties and stipends to buy "substitutes," it usually fulfilled its quotas, and the federal government made no draft call until late in the war. Moreover, unlike in New York and Philadelphia, Chicago's booster elite was solidly prowar, and outright antiwar sentiment found no political legitimacy in the city.[27] Another process was also at work in the city, though. When abolition as a war aim became a political issue, Irish and German workers were sharply divided. But, though the course of the war remained in doubt, victories at Vicksburg and Gettysburg greatly diminished the force of Democratic opposition to emancipation.[28] The ebb of slavery as a divisive political issue in the North came at the same time that the labor question rose to prominence because of wartime inflation and the labor shortage. These developments served to detach an important segment of the Irish from their ethnic and political associations and a key segment of the Arbeiter Verein from its moorings in the Republican party.

Among Irish workers the growth before and during the war of the Fenian Brotherhood, a revolutionary nationalist secret society, provided a path away from the antinationalist (at the time) Catholic church and the Democratic party. Unlike many of their urban brethren, the Fenians had no doubts about emancipation, wholeheartedly supported the war, and were in tune with those German groups that favored a secular republican revolution in Europe. In April 1864 the Fenians defied the church hierarchy and held a national fair in the city. The fair won the warm support of not just many nationalist Irish but also the German Turners and the presidents of six unions, including the heavily German tailors' union. The multiethnic shoemakers' union even held a mass meeting in support of the fair. Most important, the Fenians helped assimilate Irish worker activists into a political culture of popular republicanism, which helped Irish worker political activists transcend ethnopolitical barriers. After this event Irish labor leaders, such as Frank Lawler, president of the ship carpenters' union and an officer in the Trades Assembly, were also strong Irish nationalists.[29]

Meanwhile, with antislavery ensured as a war aim, elements of the Arbeiter Verein felt free to dissent from President Lincoln's impending renomination. A group called the Sozial Arbeiter Verein (SAV) supported John Frémont on a radical program to confiscate and redistribute rebel property and to support European revolution. The SAV had backed street workers in a dispute with the Republican mayor and had severely criticized the draft law for allowing draftees to buy substitutes. After Lincoln was renominated, and with Chicago German workers engaged in a wave of strikes, the SAV and much of the rest of the Arbeiter Verein shifted their allegiance to the labor movement. At an August 1864 meeting Arbeiter Verein leaders stressed that though politicians worked to divide people, trade unions "would unite all nationalities, natives and Irishmen and Germans." In September they decided to send five delegates to the Trades Assembly, and the Arbeiter Verein leader Eduard Schlaeger joined Andrew Cameron, a printer, to form the *Workingman's Advocate*.[30]

By 1864 a multiethnic labor movement with a political presence was established in the city. Certainly, ethnic, religious, and political loyalties continued to be significant forces in the electoral system, as evidenced by the fact that in 1864 the labor movement, whose constituency was largely Democratic, supported the antiwar program of the Democratic party. Moreover, racial exclusion would continue to beset the city's organized workers—an issue not to be confronted until large numbers of black migrants began to enter the city's work force at the turn of the century. But the emerging Irish acquiescence in antislavery as a war aim had, for the first time, made class-conscious action an alternative for many workers.

Given the importance of political developments among the Irish and Germans in the making of Chicago's labor movement, it is clear that the process of class formation was not a simple subjective response to the objective process of industrialization and the spread of a market economy. It has become a commonplace of "the new labor history" that insofar as a working class existed, it "made itself as much as it was made." Purposive action or agency was as integral to the emergence of a self-conscious working class as the more familiar socioeconomic developments were. But workers' consciousness is impossible to understand without examining the cultural resources that workers inherited in the form of religious, political, and economic beliefs and that were rooted in informal customs and habits, institutions, and norms of all sorts. Working people used these resources, often in novel ways, to make sense of their new experiences.[31] The third critical element of class formation is thus an ideological one.

For most Chicago workers the relevant cultural resources were the country's Protestant and democratic republican belief systems. These forms of thought constituted the sealike culture within which Chicago workers swam like fish. Workers drew on and reinterpreted several closely related threads of belief within this culture. Critical was the Protestant axiom, embedded in the country's political economic ideology, that work, including physically demanding manual labor, far from being a curse and something from which to escape, was dignified, honorable, and even holy. Abraham Lincoln and other advocates of the "free-labor" ideal that originated in the early nineteenth century proclaimed that the North was superior because, unlike in the South, labor was "not a distinct class" and could aspire to self-improvement and social mobility based on character and talent. According to Lincoln, "The prudent, penniless beginner in the world, labors for wages awhile, saves a surplus with which to buy tools or land, for himself; then labors on his own account another while, and at length hires another new beginner to help him." Those who remained wage earners throughout their lives, according to Lincoln, did so because of "a dependent nature which prefers it, or improvidence, folly, or singular misfortune." Closely allied with the work ethic was the traditional artisan or producer belief that those who worked were entitled by natural right to the fruits of their labor in the form of capital or property; that property was validated and justified by labor; and that the value of property was determined by the labor embodied in it. This, too, was a common belief in 1860s America. It was Lincoln, not Karl Marx, who said that "capital is the fruit of labor and could never have existed if labor had not first existed . . . labor is the superior—greatly the superior—of capital."[32]

Finally, from the nation's corpus of civic teachings—democratic republicanism—came a set of beliefs that related the sphere of work and property to the health and viability of the Republic itself. One belief, dating to Thomas Jefferson and the "country party" ideology of the American Revolution, held that citizens' ability to make free political choices that promoted the good of the commonwealth—civic virtue—required social and economic independence for freeholders. Such self-mastery in turn rested on their ability to claim their right to the fruits of their labor in the form of property. Americans viewed their country, because of the easy availability of western land, as uniquely embodying this ideal, which Jefferson had called "a yeoman's republic." But republican theory also held that republics were susceptible over time to corruption, decay, and overthrow through the concentration of wealth and the abuse of political power. Americans had always worried about the centralization of power in the hands of an aristocracy of birth or wealth. Such "parasites" were a threat because they might rob the laborers or producers of the fruits of their labor and replace the Republic with a tyranny. Whether those abusers of power were the federal bondholders of Thomas Jefferson's era, the Second Bank of the United States that Andrew Jackson assailed, or the southern slaveholding aristocrats against whom the nation under Lincoln's guidance was warring, liberty was always in danger from within.[33]

Unlike any other group, labor leaders, agitators, and journalists of the Civil War era were acutely aware that the social basis of the free-labor Republic was fast disintegrating. By the onset of the Civil War the yeomen and independent artisans of Lincoln's youth were in decline; their central role in the economy was being overshadowed by permanent wage earners, who by 1860 outnumbered self-employed members of the labor force.[34] In the first half of the nineteenth century American law legitimated this relationship by redefining free labor as simply the voluntary wage contract between autonomous individuals in the marketplace. According to this definition wageworkers were "free" when they sold their labor to the owners of capital, even though they did not own property, enjoyed limited autonomy on the job, and lacked the right to collectively organize to redress grievances, which the courts deemed to be a legal "conspiracy" to restrain trade in the market.[35]

Beginning in the 1820s urban labor agitators on both sides of the Atlantic challenged this definition by applying and interpreting republican premises in a different way, one that made more sense of their own experience of wage labor. Labor agitators held that, like businesspeople, workers were propertyholders; the difference was that they held property in the form of a craft skill. From this premise labor leaders claimed the right to regulate the price of their labor in the same way propertyholders set the price for their products. As Jonathan Fincher, a leading labor journalist, argued, "Pray, who is to estimate the price that shall be paid for a day's labor? Is it he who sells the labor or he who buys it? If the latter, why at once give all purchasers the same privilege and we warrant the first to resist would be the [Chicago] Iron Founders Association."[36] Denied this right in law and practice, labor leaders claimed they were being "robbed" of the fruits of their labor. Instead of being accorded dignity and honor, their labor was subject to the coercion of the market and the tyranny of employers. In Illinois an 1863 law defined as a conspiracy any combination of two or more persons for the purpose of depriving employers of the lawful use or management of their property. To labor activists this amounted to an abridgement of their own free-labor rights. In a controversial turn of phrase they coined the term *wage-slavery,* thereby equating slaveholding "lords of the lash" with capitalist "lords of the loom."[37]

Labor agitators went further. They claimed that while the abolition of slavery was a worthy objective, the "money power" had used the war to centralize wealth through the National Banking Act and the concentration of the war debt in the hands of bankers. This power now had a stranglehold on the Republic, which threatened to go the way of Rome. Labor agitators were not, however, revolutionaries; because they thought the Republic could still be redeemed, they styled themselves labor *reformers.* Workers, in the words of Andrew Cameron, the first editor of the *Workingman's Advocate,* "must guard the gates of the Republic and declare to the world that it is a Workingman's Government, and that millions of workingmen and women will bare their right arms to preserve and protect it as such." The first significant national federation of labor organizations, the National Labor Union (NLU), formed in 1866, had as its first plank a plan intended to preserve the Republic from the impact of capital accumulation that was creating an alien money power. Like producer radicals outside their class, those in the NLU wanted to abolish the national banking system and replace it with a system of government-issued greenbacks convertible to federal bonds, with a 3 percent interest rate. The result would be "an equitable distribution of the products of labor between non-producing capital and labor," the liquidation of the national debt, and "the removal of the necessity for excessive toil."[38] Insofar as labor theorists limited their solutions to such antimonopoly schemes as the interconvertible bond system, they did not differ appreciably from other producer radicals in mid-nineteenth-century America.

But dating from the 1830s working-class leaders began to advocate that an ethic of "association" and "cooperation" replace the ethic of competitive and acquisitive individualism that many saw as the moral taproot of wage-slavery. The idea of cooperation was rooted in their own organizing experiences as well as Christian and republican currents of thought. If employees competing in the labor market could overcome their isolation to create functioning trade unions, perhaps they could also unite to form worker-owned businesses and thus end their dependence on the owners of capital. Yet even here labor leaders drew on free-labor axioms, for they viewed cooperative businesses as a means of self-improvement and economic independence. Just as labor leaders incorporated the language of class into their republicanism, they commonly combined their goal of restoring the virtue of the Republic with one of "producers cooperation."[39]

LABOR'S FIRST GREAT UPHEAVAL, 1864–72

During the last two years of the Civil War the rapid growth in the pervasiveness, scale, and impersonality of the wage relation in industry, the political common ground created by the two largest ethnic groups in the new working class, and the labor republican critique of dependence that was given new force by the struggle against southern slavery together created the conditions for the first significant self-conscious working-class action in Chicago's history.

At least nineteen new unions sprang into existence in the city during or immediately following the Civil War. These unions included the sailors (1863), carpenters (1863), painters (1863), cigarmakers (1863), musicians (1864), dockhands and laborers (1864), tailors (1864), stonecutters (1864), sewing women (1864), harnessmakers (1865), bricklayers (1865), plasterers (1866), iron puddlers (1866), engineers (1866), boot and shoemakers (1867), and plumbers (1867). Three important characteristics of these unions indicate the maturation of a class outlook among Chicago workers. First, they were not temporary, makeshift associations. Most lasted into the 1870s, and their demands went beyond wages to include the closed shop and sometimes the establishment of an apprenticeship system. Second, unlike earlier associations, these unions were multiethnic. Though different branches were often based on nationality, language, and neighborhood, the new unions' citywide leadership was ethnically diverse. Of 100 leaders from twenty-eight different unions in 1864, 41 were Anglo-American, 31 were German, and 27 were Irish.[40] Third, these associations were oriented toward conflict, as evidenced by the word *protective* in almost all of their titles. Two years of hothouse industrial growth, inflation, strikes, and employer resistance had unsettled old workplace relations and customary notions of what constituted a fair day's pay for a fair day's work, starkly revealing the power of the market and the need to regulate it collectively. The Trades Assembly was also formed in this crucible of conflict. In a battle for its very existence against the city's organized newspaper proprietors, the typographers' union brought together sister unions to organize a newspaper boycott. The new assembly claimed to represent 8,500 workers organized in twenty-four unions in 1865, about 28 percent of the city's work force.[41]

The issue of the printers' strike, however, highlighted an increasingly problematic feature of the new labor movement. The *Chicago Times* had attempted to break the union by using female typesetters and nonunion male compositors to replace strikers. In the 1850s the gendered division of labor that had limited women to family, domestic service, and teaching had begun to break down as women entered cigarmaking, baking, garment work, bookbinding, and other industries. Because women were now potential low-wage competitors of organized male workers, the labor movement generally tried to exclude women from the trades. Where the employment of women—as in domestic garment work—did not threaten men's wages, labor leaders were willing to tolerate female organization.[42]

Class formation in its political dimension, both in public discourse and in relation to other classes, awaited the flowering of the eight-hour movement in 1866. Andrew Cameron, editor of the *Workingman's Advocate,* which led the movement, noted that "the painful truth is that there is no workingmen's interest [in American politics]. Should we not too be an interest"? During the winter and spring of 1866, in what Cameron called "labor's first contest for political supremacy," workers formed eight-hour leagues and succeeded in electing committed supporters in five of the city's sixteen wards. Throughout the rest of the year they lobbied on the state level for an eight-hour law. The Republicans, who ruled both the city and state governments, blandly endorsed the eight-hour workday, classing it with public improvements and education as part of their program to uplift free labor. By March 1867 both the city and state governments had enacted eight-hour laws. But the new state law, due to take effect on May 1, contained a gaping loophole that allowed workers to labor longer than eight hours if stipulated in a freely arrived at contract. Moreover, the new law lacked any provision for enforcement.[43]

During April 1867 all parties began to think through the consequences of the bill, sparking a debate on the pages of the city's newspapers that revealed the class implications of the reform that Cameron had earlier perceived. The debate began with misgivings voiced by the *Chicago Tribune,* which under the editorship of Horace White spoke for radical Republicans and most city employers. Joined by the *Chicago Times,* the paper argued that according to the rules of political economy and the law of free contract, the eight-hour law could not be enforced and in any case would put local employers at a competitive disadvantage in regional and national markets. Labor leaders grew increasingly impatient. The eight-hour law was "a question of reform, not wages." Arguing from free-labor premises, they portrayed shorter hours as a means to dignify and uplift labor by promoting intellectual, moral, and political self-improvement and preventing the excessive concentration of wealth. According to one worker, "The eight hour system will have a tendency to keep society more upon an equality. It will give the laboring classes more time for study and thinking, and thereby they will become more independent of professional men."[44]

The Arbeiter Verein went further, stating in a resolution that "the eight hour system [is] the first step toward the abolition of the system of hired labor, the entire abolition of which is only a question of time, as it formerly was with slavery." Labor leaders, however, never demanded state enforcement of the law; they only hoped that the prestige conferred by near unanimous political support would legitimate their own attempts to enforce the law. Trade unionists planned a massive parade on May 1 to celebrate passage of the law and to put public pressure on employers who resisted its application.[45]

Not all probusiness Republicans were opposed to eight-hour workdays. The *Chicago Republican,* a party loyalist paper established in 1865, which supported the land redistribution programs of Thaddeus Stevens in Congress and the protectionist arguments of the radical economist Henry Carey, lined up with the city's trade unions. The *Republican* argued that workers' moral rights overrode the right of free contract: "On [the workers'] side a kind of capital is invested which employers ought not to seek to control, viz., the souls of men. . . . Let employers everywhere admit the absolute and perfect of workingmen to fix their own hours of labor as an element in their human freedom." In a more practical vein the paper spoke for skilled workers in arguing that their social uplift would improve labor productivity, compensating for the two-hour loss in production. The stand of the *Republican* demonstrated that the lines of class being etched in the social landscape by the eight-hour issue did not lead all Republican leaders to withdraw from the social implications of reform democracy and human rights. It also helps explain the real stake workers had in upholding the integrity of the radical reform movement of Reconstruction.[46]

With most employers resisting shorter hours, city workers inaugurated an eight-hour strike on May 2, following a large demonstration on May 1. The strike, however, was far from general and highly uneven in its effects.

The largest group of strikers were the building tradesmen, especially plumbers, gasfitters, and painters, and metal trade workers, primarily machinists, iron molders, blacksmiths, and boilermakers. The main arenas of conflict were the large metalworking factories of P. W. Gates and R. T. Crane and the railroad carshops. Here skilled workers, led by British immigrants with trade union experience, held daily strike meetings to uphold morale and organized "vigilance" committees to remonstrate with weaker members.[47]

Standing in stark contrast to the organized and skilled metal and building trades workers were the outdoor laborers and unskilled factory hands, helpers, and laborers in and around the brickyards, lumberyards, planing mills, and furniture factories. Rather than hold meetings, proclaim strikes, and pitch appeals to public opinion couched in republican rhetoric, these workers, beginning on the second day of the strike, gathered in what the *Chicago Tribune* called "committees of the whole" and indiscriminately visited places of industrial employment. Their theaters of action were the streets in and around working-class neighborhoods, most notably Irish Bridgeport. Before they were suppressed by overwhelming police power these "mobs" of predominantly young men had either forcibly expelled the work force or compelled proprietors to close nearly all the brickyards and lumberyards and planing and furniture mills on the South Side and the West Side.[48]

The unexpected and tumultuous intervention of the unskilled and unorganized component of the new industrial working class horrified the city's press, which spoke of "Mob Law Instituted." Strike leaders also condemned the shameful actions of the mob. Yet even though eight-hour leaders attempted to disassociate themselves from the affair and there was little actual violence, the crowd action introduced a new dynamic into the local labor movement. The city's strong trade unions were narrowly based among skilled workers, but they had resorted to a broad class appeal centering on eight hours to sanction their strike. Almost without intending, they had conjured into action a segment of their class that, because it did not share their skills, craft pride, and aspirations to respectability and political influence in the larger community, was willing to broaden the strike into an open-ended general upheaval of all workers. The strike of the unskilled was important in another way. Lacking unions or access to the reform politics, these workers resorted to ethnic and therefore community-based solidarity to supplement class action.

Despite some short-term victories in the construction industry, the eight-hour-day strike failed to achieve its stated goal. But it was a fruitful failure, for it taught important political lessons and pointed the labor movement in a more self-reliant direction. One major outcome of the strike that was immediately apparent was the movement for producers' cooperation. The popular term *cooperation,* which came to symbolize the distinctive ideology of the period's labor movement, had an ambiguous social character. On the eve of the strike the *Chicago Tribune* and the *Chicago Republican* endorsed cooperation, hailing it as a means of uplifting wage labor into economic independence. Within the context of reform, however, there were divergent tendencies.

Horace White's *Chicago Tribune* viewed cooperation as a way of reining in class conflict. On the eve of the strike the paper offered an elaborate plan for joint stock ownership and profit sharing with the express purpose of preventing strikes and inducing employees to take an interest in their firm. White also supported worker ownership as a fulfillment of the free-labor ideal of social mobility, which had nothing to do with abolishing the wage system. For the *Republican* and most labor reformers cooperation was a social, economic, and moral principle that underlay a vision of industrialization and social progress generally. Competition, said the *Republican,* following Henry Carey, was the law of trade that elevated the product of labor above its producer. Cooperation, however, held the producer to be of supreme importance. The paper used this distinction to justify protection over free trade and to argue that "capital represents despotism in the workplace." The paper editorialized that "the drift and current of the time [was] undoubtedly toward the further emancipation of labor by substituting cooperative associations for employment at wages." "Co-operation," said the paper, "is the practical application of Christianity, liberty and true democracy to the labor question. This is the perfect emancipation of the working classes."[49]

The ideological ambiguity that allowed divergent meanings and rationales to coexist within reform and the movement for cooperation was also evident in the plans workers espoused. John Orvis, a leading advocate of Charles Fourier's utopian socialism in Chicago, called on the city's employers to put their capital and their management experience at the service of their workers in the form of joint stock cooperatives in which the economic surplus above that devoted to a sinking fund (a fund to retire debt) would be divided among workers and managers according to their wages and salaries. Though far more in the interest of workers than the *Tribune*'s plan or that of Gates and Crane, it did not meet the standard of the Arbeiter Verein, which resolved at the start of the strike that "in every trade at least one co-operative should be started" with the objective of "abolishing the wage system."[50]

The two divergent views of cooperation were live issues in the city until it became clear that joint stock cooperation would not prevent a strike for the eight-hour day. After eleven days of the strike the *Tribune* reported that small groups of iron molders, machinists, and carpenters were forming their own cooperative businesses. Two weeks later the *Republican* described two large workers' cooperatives capitalized at $100,000 and $150,000. The paper optimistically concluded that workers no longer viewed cooperatives as utopian schemes but as a realistic alternative to working for wages.[51]

Though partly a response to frustration over the defeat of the strike, the cooperative movement of 1867 had enough resilience to continue through the end of the decade. In 1868 the unions of the ship carpenters, iron molders, shoemakers, and tailors and the Chicago branch of the British-based Amalgamated Society of Engineers all boasted worker-owned and operated cooperatives. By 1869, however, most cooperatives were either in difficulty or had failed, and labor reformers lobbied for a bill in the Illinois legislature to incorporate cooperatives and joint stock companies on different bases. Still optimistic, in July 1869 Cameron urged that cooperation become "the objective point of every labor organization, whenever or wherever possible." Given the admitted failures of most individual cooperatives, however, Cameron called for unions to contribute to a cooperative central sinking fund—a striking anticipation of the Knights of Labor plan a decade later. Though there is no evidence that the joint sinking-fund proposal was put into effect, it was an indication that the initial failure of cooperative experiments impelled labor leaders not to abandon the idea but instead to search for more inclusive, classwide forms of cooperation. Perhaps the most ambitious cooperative proposal in postbellum Chicago was posited after the 1871 Chicago fire, when building trades unions unsuccessfully sought to rebuild the city under the auspices of a mechanics' building company.[52]

Notwithstanding the repeated failures attending workers' cooperative experiments, they were of social and ideological significance. The labor movement had broken from the antebellum idea of cooperation as an experimental community formed away from urban areas by social reformers. They had also abandoned their reliance on reform-minded businesspeople to furnish the brains and capital for cooperation through joint stock companies or profit sharing. Though each of these approaches would continue to have some influence, the new and most typical form of cooperative became the producers' cooperative initiated by wage earners, and the formation of cooperatives became a weapon in the arsenal of trade unions. Cameron summarized the emerging labor movement consensus on cooperation: "To combine and cooperate effectually labor should have all the profits and so long as we are continually aiming merely to get an equal division of the profits we will wander in the dark." He even advocated that the forming of cooperatives by unions be "the next step" in the labor movement. During this period the national unions of the iron molders and the Knights of Saint Crispin adopted Cameron's view of cooperation, setting an important precedent for the Knights of Labor in the 1880s.[53]

The poststrike cooperative movement marked the high point for the labor reform movement of Chicago during Reconstruction. From then on the trade union basis of labor reform suffered a fitful but persistent decline. The years from 1867 through 1870 were characterized by mild but rising unemployment, and though this trend was interrupted by prosperity in the early 1870s, conditions worsened with the onset of the 1873–79 depression.[54]

Besides inhibiting organizing and striking, the economic climate exacerbated two problems that afflicted the city's new trade unions. First, most could claim the allegiance of only a minority of workers in their particular trade; and few of these, beyond a core of loyalists, had more than a tenuous commitment to unionism. Second, the movement as a whole remained isolated from the fast-growing sector of unskilled laborers and factory hands.

Throughout the 1863–76 period there were few unions powerful enough to control wages and conditions in their own trade. Judged by three criteria—long-term stability of membership, the existence of a closed shop, and the ability to enforce work rules—there were only two strong unions in Chicago. Typographical Union No. 16 and the stonecutters' union both maintained a fairly constant membership of four to six hundred members between 1867 and 1876. Each union boasted a closed shop in almost all the firms of their industry, and both had written agreements with their employers. The stonecutters had the most effective union in the city, enjoying the highest wages and basking in the prestige of being the only union to have retained the eight-hour day from the 1867 strike.[55]

Unions of intermediate strength included the iron molders, machinists and blacksmiths, cigarmakers, tailors, and shoemakers. Though these unions were able to maintain their organizational identity throughout the period, their memberships and bargaining strength fluctuated according to seasonal and business cycles. The weakest unions, most notably the carpenters, painters, sailors, and coopers, underwent periodic reorganizations, usually in preparation for a strike. Motivated by short-term goals, they relied heavily on spontaneity and the enthusiasm of the moment.[56]

The decline of the city's trade unions greatly undermined the effectiveness of the Trades Assembly. When the 1868 depression impelled labor reform leaders toward political action, only seven unions attended the convention called for that purpose. In April 1869 the *Workingman's Advocate* admitted that the Trades Assembly was "in a dilapidated condition." In October 1870 the paper reported that the Trades Assembly had "died a natural death." The decline of unionism was strongest among English-speaking workers. Unions divided into language and ethnic branches—the building trades, tailors, and shoemakers unions for example—found their citywide union apparatuses rendered defunct and their German-speaking branches orphaned. In September 1868 these branches formed the German Trades Assembly, claiming 2,000 members.[57]

The organizational decline of the English-speaking protective societies led local labor leaders to turn to immigrant unions for new ideas. The Chicago branches of the British-based Amalgamated Society of Engineers (1866) and the Amalgamated Society of Carpenters (1870) set an example for floundering unions during this period. Though both unions were small, their ethnic homogeneity and cohesiveness allowed them to transplant key features of English "new model unionism." Both unions were composed of highly committed skilled workers willing to pay high dues, both began thriving cooperatives, and both boasted extensive benefit systems. Above all it was the beneficial feature that attracted the attention of beleaguered American unionists, almost all of whose unions were solely protective in character. One local activist argued that "when the benevolent is combined with the protective . . . selfishness, if no more honorable instinct, prompts to active and continued membership." Cameron marveled at how the Chicago branch of the British carpenters' union, with only ninety-seven members, could control its trade, while the undisciplined Americans, with their larger but unwieldy and evanescent unions, remained powerless. As a result, between 1869 and 1872 such unions as the iron molders, sailors, shoemakers, bricklayers, tailors, printers, stonecutters, painters, and ship carpenters adopted benefits, along with high dues, to shore up their organizations.[58]

Yet the turn toward new model unionism—which in New York City was pioneered by Samuel Gompers and Adolph Strasser of the cigarmakers' union—further reinforced the other weakness of Chicago's labor movement: its isolation from lower-paid laborers and factory workers. Hardly any of the unions organized factory hands, helpers, or semiskilled workers. The unions of the heaters, rollers, and catchers and the iron molders, for example, organized only skilled workers in the North Side Rolling Mills and McCormick's Reaper Plant, though other workers followed their lead during strikes. The large railroad carshops proved impervious to the organizing efforts of the machinists and blackmiths' union, and there is no evidence of organization of any kind in the packinghouses. The notable exception was the Knights of Saint Crispin, organized in 1869, which enrolled factory shoemakers.[59]

Skilled workers had little motivation to promote unionization of lesser-skilled workers during this period because for the most part they did not face the kind of threats to their craft that would drive them to make common cause with those who might replace them. The expansion of productive capacity normally occurred without undermining existing skill levels. Between 1850 and 1870 the proportion of skilled and unskilled workers in the local work force remained stable, except among the craft-oriented Germans. Few skilled unionists protested the effects of the introduction of de-skilling machinery, though they often complained about sweating (subcontracted labor paid below generally acceptable rates) and lowering of craft standards resulting from prison contract labor.[60]

To say that class formed in this period among workers is not to deny that those who sold their labor on the market were a diverse lot—from helpers, laborers, and factory hands to skilled workers and subcontracting craftworkers—or that workers often identified themselves as Democrats, Irish, or craft artisans. Nor is it to imply that all or most workers identified with the labor movement. It is to say that for the first time a significant number of Chicago workers were able to build durable institutions distinguished by class. It also meant that as other members of the community found themselves compelled to confront, take account of, and respond to questions and demands raised by these institutions—such as the demands for the eight-hour day or the end to prison contract labor—the very nature of society and politics was redefined by and began to revolve around these issues.

The evolution of class formation did not proceed evenly but came about through moments of partial making and partial unmaking, the first of which occurred between 1863 and 1867. During this first moment helpers, factory hands, outdoor laborers, and the unskilled, easily replaced workers, such as women, for the most part did not find a place in the organizations of craftworkers. Instead they tagged along behind the unions and political leadership of craftworkers and sometimes resorted to their own informal mechanism of mobilization, the crowd action. The building of more inclusive class institutions, both among workers and the upper class, awaited the next great moment of class formation during the 1870s depression.

Notes

1. According to *Fincher's Trade Review,* the number of local trade unions in northern states rose from 79 in December 1863 to 270 in December 1864. See John R. Commons, David J. Saposs, Helen L. Sumner, E. B. Mittelman, M. E. Hoagland, John B. Andrews, and Selig Perlman, *History of Labour in the United States* (1918; reprint, New York: Macmillan, 1946), 2:19, 72.

2. Bessie Louise Pierce, *A History of Chicago,* vol. 2, *From Town to City, 1848–1871* (New York: Alfred A. Knopf, 1940), 160, 165–68, 179–80, 187.

3. *Chicago Tribune,* Mar. 4, 1861, Mar. 8, 1864. Data on strikes based on a daily reading of the *Tribune* from 1861 to 1864, see esp. Mar.–Apr. 1864. On affiliation with national unions, see *Workingman's Advocate,* Oct. 8, 1870, Jan. 28, 1871, Mar. 11, 1871, Apr. 8, 1871, May 10, 1873, Dec. 13, 1873.

4. *Fincher's Trade Review,* Apr. 2, 1864; *Chicago Tribune,* Aug. 21, 1864; *Fincher's Trade Review,* July 23, 1864.

5. In contrast to Chicago, eastern cities witnessed significant class division during the antebellum period. For a survey, see Sean Wilentz, "The Rise of the American Working Class, 1776–1877: A Survey," in *Perspectives on American La-*

bor History: The Problems of Synthesis, ed. J. Carroll Moody and Alice Kessler-Harris (De Kalb: Northern Illinois University Press, 1989), 83–151.

6. David R. Meyer, "Midwestern Industrialization and the American Manufacturing Belt in the Nineteenth Century," *Journal of Economic History* 59 (Dec. 1989): 921–35; William Cronon, *Nature's Metropolis: Chicago and the Great West* (New York: W. W. Norton, 1991), 60–61, 307–8; Pierce, *History of Chicago*, 2:77–117.

7. U.S. Department of the Interior, Census Office, *Eighth Census of the United States: 1860*, vol. 2, *Report on Manufactures* (Washington, D.C.: Government Printing Office, 1865), 86–87; Carl Abbott, *Boosters and Businessmen: Popular Economic Thought and Urban Growth in the Antebellum Middle West* (Westport, Conn.: Greenwood, 1981), 19–20, 65; Elmer Riley, "The Development of Chicago and Vicinity as a Manufacturing Center prior to 1880" (Ph.D. diss., University of Chicago, 1911), 114.

8. Rima Lunin Schultz, "The Businessman's Role in Western Settlement: The Entrepreneurial Frontier, Chicago, 1833–1872" (Ph.D. diss., Boston University, 1985), esp. chap. 7; Frederic Cople Jaher, *The Urban Establishment: Upper Strata in Boston, New York, Charleston, Chicago, and Los Angeles* (Urbana: University of Illinois Press, 1982), 453–72.

9. Pierce, *History of Chicago*, 2:51, 52, 148–49 (first quote on 149); Abbott, *Boosters and Businessmen*, 138 (second quote); *Industrial Chicago*, vol. 3, *The Manufacturing Interests* (Chicago: Goodspeed, 1894), 699–703; Harry H. Pierce, "Foreign Investment in American Enterprise," in *Economic Change in the Civil War Era*, ed. David T. Gilchrist and W. David Lewis (Greenville, Del.: Eleutherian Mills-Hagley Foundation, 1965), 42–61.

10. Glenn Porter and Harold C. Livesay, *Merchants and Manufacturers: Studies in the Changing Structure of Nineteenth-Century Marketing* (1971; reprint, Chicago: Ivan Dee, 1989), 116–30; Robert Sharkey, *Money, Class, and Party: An Economic Study of Civil War and Reconstruction* (Baltimore, Md.: Johns Hopkins University Press, 1959); Jeffrey G. Williamson, "Watersheds and Turning Points: Conjectures on the Long-Term Impact of Civil War Financing," *Journal of Economic History* 34 (Sept. 1974): 636–64.

11. Meyer, "Midwestern Industrialization"; Allen R. Pred, *The Spatial Dynamics of U.S. Urban-Industrial Growth, 1800–1914* (Cambridge, Mass.: M.I.T. Press, 1966), 24–37.

12. Pred, *Spatial Dynamics of Urban Growth*, 70; Pierce, *History of Chicago*, 2:113–14; Riley, "Development of Chicago as a Manufacturing Center," 109–17.

13. The following discussion is based on Cronon, *Nature's Metropolis*, 207–59; Margaret Walsh, *The Rise of the Midwestern Meat Packing Industry* (Lexington: University Press of Kentucky, 1982); and Pierce, *History of Chicago*, 2:90–102.

14. U.S. Department of the Interior, Census Office, *Eighth Census of the United States: 1860*, vol. 2, *Report on Manufactures*, 86–87; U.S. Department of the Interior, Census Office, *Ninth Census of the United States: 1870*, vol. 3, *Statistics of Wealth and Industry of the United States* (Washington, D.C.: Government Printing Office, 1872), 649.

15. Jaher, *Urban Establishment*, 453–75; Robin Einhorn, *Property Rules: Political Economy in Chicago, 1833–1872* (Chicago: University of Chicago Press, 1991), 226–

27; Kathleen D. McCarthy, *Noblesse Oblige: Charity and Cultural Philanthropy in Chicago, 1849–1929* (Chicago: University of Chicago Press, 1982), 254–66; Schultz, "Businessmen's Role in Western Settlement," chap. 8.

16. Pierce, *History of Chicago,* 2:150; figures compiled by the Chicago Working-Class History Project from the 1850, 1860, and 1870 federal manuscript manufacturing censuses; Bruce Laurie and Mark Schmitz, "Manufacture and Productivity: The Making of an Industrial Base, Philadelphia, 1850–1880," in *Philadelphia: Work, Space, Family, and Group Experience in the Nineteenth Century; Essays toward an Interdisciplinary History of the City,* ed. Theodore Hershberg (New York: Oxford University Press, 1981), 43–92.

17. Robert Max Jackson, *The Formation of Craft Labor Markets* (Orlando, Fla.: Academic, 1984), esp. chap. 2.

18. *Chicago Tribune,* June 8, 1864, June 10, 1864, June 20, 1864; John B. Jentz, "Bread and Labor: Chicago's German Bakers Organize," *Chicago History* 12 (Summer 1983): 25–35.

19. *Chicago Tribune,* Dec. 5, 1869.

20. Ibid., Mar. 7, 1863, May 4, 1872; Bob Reckman, "Carpentry, the Craft and Trade," in *Case Studies on the Labor Process,* ed. Andrew Zimbalist (New York: Monthly Review, 1979), 78–80; Richard Schneirov and Thomas J. Suhrbur, *Union Brotherhood, Union Town: The History of the Carpenters' Union of Chicago, 1863–1987* (Carbondale: Southern Illinois University Press, 1988), 5–7, 13–16; Jonathan Grossman and William Sylvis, *Pioneer of American Labor: A Study of the Labor Movement during the Era of the Civil War* (New York: Columbia University Press, 1945), 120–51. On piecework in general, see David Montgomery, *The Fall of the House of Labor: The Workplace, the State, and American Labor Activism, 1865–1925* (Cambridge: Cambridge University Press, 1987), 148–54.

21. Alfred D. Chandler Jr., *Visible Hand: The Managerial Revolution in American Business* (Cambridge, Mass.: Belknap, 1977); Montgomery, *Fall of the House of Labor;* David Hounshell, *From the American System to Mass Production, 1800–1932: The Development of Manufacturing Technology in the United States* (Baltimore, Md.: Johns Hopkins University Press, 1984), 152–87; James R. Barrett, *Work and Community in the Jungle: Chicago's Packinghouse Workers, 1894–1922* (Urbana: University of Illinois Press, 1987), 21–31.

22. Chicago figures based on samples taken from the manuscript U.S. Census of Population, 1850, 1860, and 1870. Of the nation's five largest cities only Philadelphia had more native-born than foreign-born workers; still two-thirds of the nation's industrial workers were native-born in 1870. See Ira Berlin and Herbert G. Gutman, "Class Composition and the Development of the American Working Class, 1840–1890: Immigrants and Their Children as Wage Earners," in *Power and Culture: Herbert G. Gutman and the American Working Class,* ed. Ira Berlin (New York: Pantheon Books, 1987), 380–94. Figures on German manufacturers reported in John B. Jentz, "Class and Politics in an Emerging Industrial City: Chicago in the 1860s and 1870s," *Journal of Urban History* 17 (May 1991): 227–63.

23. Richard Schneirov, "Political Cultures and the Role of the State in Labor's Republic: The View from Chicago, 1848–1877," *Labor History* 32 (Summer 1991): 376–400; Stanley Nadel, "From the Barricades of Paris to the Sidewalks of New

York: German Artisans and the European Roots of American Labor Radicalism," *Labor History* 30 (Winter 1989): 47–75.

24. Paul Kleppner, *The Third Electoral System, 1853–1892: Parties, Voters, and Political Cultures* (Chapel Hill: University of North Carolina Press, 1979); Joel A. Tarr, *A Study in Boss Politics: William Lorimer of Chicago* (Urbana: University of Illinois Press, 1971); *Chicago Tribune*, June 24, 1877.

25. Richard Wilson Renner, "In a Perfect Ferment: Chicago, the Know-Nothings, and the Riot for Lager Beer," *Chicago History* 5 (Fall 1976): 161–70; Bruce Carling Levine, "Free Soil, Free Labor, and Freimänner: German Chicago in the Civil War Era," in *German Workers in Industrial Chicago, 1850–1910: A Comparative Perspective*, ed. Hartmut Keil and John B. Jentz (De Kalb: Northern Illinois University Press, 1983), 163–82.

26. Frederick Francis Cook, *Bygone Days in Chicago* (Chicago: A. C. McClurg, 1910), 76; *Chicago Tribune*, July 22, 1863.

27 Einhorn, *Property Rules*, 196–203.

28. James M. McPherson, *Battle Cry of Freedom: The Civil War Era* (New York: Ballantine, 1988), 684–88.

29. *Chicago Times*, Feb. 3, 1864, Feb. 8, 1864, Feb. 23, 1964, Apr. 7, 1864; *Chicago Tribune*, Feb. 8, 1864, Feb. 17, 1864, Mar. 26, 1864, Mar. 28, 1864, Mar. 29, 1864, Dec. 29, 1864, Aug. 13, 1865, Aug. 19, 1865; John B. Jentz and Richard Schneirov, "Chicago's Fenian Fair of 1864: A Window into the Civil War as a Popular Political Awakening," *Labor's Heritage* 6 (Winter 1995): 4–19.

30. *Chicago Tribune*, Mar. 28, 1864, Apr. 4, 1864; *Illinois Staats Zeitung*, Oct. 28, 1863, May 5, 1864, May 26, 1864, June 10, 1864, June 26, 1864; *Chicago Times*, Aug. 19, 1864; *Workingman's Advocate*, Sept. 17, 1864 (quote).

31. Preface to E. P. Thompson, *The Making of the English Working Class* (New York: Vintage Books, 1963); E. P. Thompson, "The Poverty of Theory," in his *The Poverty of Theory and Other Essays* (London: Merlin, 1978), 193–397; Ellen Meiksins Wood, "Class as Process and Relationship," in *Democracy against Capitalism: Renewing Historical Materialism*, ed. Ellen Meiksins Wood (Cambridge: Cambridge University Press, 1995), 76–107; Perry Anderson, *Arguments within English Marxism* (London: New Left Review, 1980), 32 (quote).

32. Eric Foner, *Free Soil, Free Labor, Free Men: The Ideology of the Republican Party before the Civil War* (New York: Oxford University Press, 1970); Richard Current, ed., *The Political Thought of Abraham Lincoln* (New York: Bobbs-Merrill, 1967), 133–34 (quote).

33. Lance Banning, *The Jeffersonian Persuasion: Evolution of a Party Ideology* (Ithaca, N.Y.: Cornell University Press, 1978).

34. Stanley Lebergott, "The Pattern of Employment since 1800," in *American Economic History*, ed. Seymour E. Harris (New York: McGraw-Hill, 1961), 292.

35. Victoria Hattam, *Labor Visions and State Power: The Origins of Business Unionism in the United States* (Princeton, N.J.: Princeton University Press, 1993), 30–75; Robert J. Steinfeld, *The Invention of Free Labor: The Employment Relation in English and American Law and Culture, 1350–1870* (Chapel Hill: University of North Carolina Press, 1991).

36. *Fincher's Trade Review*, July 2, 1864.

37. Earl R. Beckner, *A History of Labor Legislation in Illinois* (Chicago: University of Chicago Press, 1929), 9–10; Sean Wilentz, *Chants Democratic: New York City and the Rise of the American Working Class, 1788–1850* (New York: Oxford University Press, 1984), 61–103; Bruce Laurie, *Artisans into Workers: Labor in Nineteenth-Century America* (New York: Noonday, 1989), 63–73; Foner, *Free Soil, Free Labor, Free Men,* 21 (quote).

38. *Workingman's Advocate,* Nov. 9, 1867, Jan. 8, 1868.

39. Wilentz, *Chants Democratic,* 366–67, 373, 384–85; Bruce Laurie, *Working People of Philadelphia* (Philadelphia: Temple University Press, 1980), 102–3, 193–94.

40. Names and birthplaces of union officers taken from *Chicago Tribune, Illinois Staats Zeitung, Workingman's Advocate,* and *Chicago City Directory, 1864–65* (Chicago: John C. W. Bailey, 1865); ethnicity taken from Elsdon C. Smith, *New Directory of American Family Names* (New York: Harper and Row, 1973).

41. *Chicago City Directory, 1864–65.* I have taken the percent of the manufacturing and mechanical work force for 1870 and applied it to the population of 1865 to calculate union density; see Pierce, *History of Chicago,* 2:151nn4, 5, 499.

42. *Chicago Tribune,* Sept. 8, 1864, Sept. 11, 1864; Pierce, *History of Chicago,* 2:153–54.

43. *Workingman's Advocate,* Apr. 21, 1866; *Chicago Tribune,* Apr. 21, 1867, May 1, 1867; David Montgomery, *Beyond Equality: Labor and the Radical Republicans, 1862–1872* (New York: Vintage Books, 1967), 306–8.

44. *Chicago Republican,* Apr. 30, 1867 ("eight hour system" quote), May 1, 1867, May 2, 1867 ("reform, not wages" quote); *Chicago Times,* May 1, 1867.

45. *Chicago Tribune,* Apr. 9, 1867.

46. *Chicago Republican,* May 1, 1867. On the paper's origins, see ibid., May 15, 1867.

47. *Chicago Tribune,* May 8, 1867; *Chicago Republican,* May 31, 1867.

48. *Chicago Tribune,* May 3, 1867, May 4, 1867.

49. *Chicago Republican,* May 7, 1867.

50. *Chicago Tribune,* Apr. 9, 1867 (quote), Apr. 18, 1867, May 11, 1867.

51. Ibid., May 12, 1867; *Chicago Republican,* May 31, 1867.

52. *Workingman's Advocate,* Jan. 25, 1868, May 23, 1868, Feb. 20, 1869, Mar. 27, 1869, July 3, 1869, Mar. 23, 1872, May 18, 1872, Oct. 12, 1872; Farmers and Mechanics Savings Bank, *The Labor Question* (Chicago: Warden, 1867), 42, 43.

53. Clare Horner, "Producers' Cooperatives in the United States, 1865–1890" (Ph.D. diss., University of Pittsburgh, 1978), 36–41, 219–28; *Workingman's Advocate,* Nov. 13, 1875 (quote).

54. Pierce, *History of Chicago,* 2:159.

55. On the typographers, see *Workingman's Advocate,* Jan. 30, 1869, Feb. 18, 1871, Sept. 5, 1874, Sept. 12, 1874; on the stonecutters, see Feb. 27, 1869, May 21, 1870, Sept. 7, 1872, Sept. 21, 1872, May 10, 1873, July 19, 1873, Jan. 16, 1876.

56. On the iron molders, see ibid., Feb. 18, 1871; on the sailors, see ibid., Apr. 17, 1869; on the coopers, see ibid., Oct. 8, 1870; on the carpenters, see *Chicago Tribune,* May 14, 1872, Sept. 24, 1872.

57. *Workingman's Advocate,* Sept. 19, 1868, Apr. 17, 1869 (first quote), Oct. 8, 1870 (second quote), May 1, 1869. On the decline of English-speaking branches, see ibid., June 19, 1869.

58. Ibid., July 4, 1868 (quote), Sept. 28, 1872, Mar. 30, 1872, June 28, 1873; Pierce, *History of Chicago,* 2:445. For reports of unions adding benevolent features, see *Workingman's Advocate,* Apr. 18, 1869, Mar. 19, 1870, May 21, 1870, Jan. 14, 1871, Mar. 11, 1871, Apr. 6, 1872, June 7, 1873.

59. Selig Perlman, *A History of Trade Unionism in the United States* (New York: Macmillan, 1922), 76–78. The heaters, rollers, and catchers' union, with only thirty-three members, led a strike of eight hundred workers at the North Chicago Rolling Mills. See *Workingman's Advocate,* Aug. 16, 1873. On strikes at McCormick, see Robert Ozanne, *A Century of Labor-Management Relations at McCormick and International Harvester* (Madison: University of Wisconsin Press, 1967), 3–9. On the railcar shops, see *Workingman's Advocate,* May 19, 1866. On the shoemakers, see Don D. Lescohier, "The Knights of St. Crispin, 1867–1874" (Ph.D. diss., University of Wisconsin, 1910), 6.

60. Jentz, "Class and Politics in an Emerging Industrial City," 231–32; David M. Gordon, Richard Edwards, and Michael Reich, *Segmented Work, Divided Workers: The Historical Transformation of Labor in the United States* (London: Cambridge University Press, 1982), 79–92.

CHAPTER 2

Labor and Party Politics, 1868–77

The same economic, social, and political processes that gave rise to Chicago's labor reform movement in the 1860s also created the conditions that produced a crisis in the 1870s. A new politics, known to historians as "machine politics" or "organizational politics," emerged in Chicago in the 1860s at the same time as labor reform.[1] Like labor reform, machine politics grew out of the new problems and opportunities created by industrialization, immigration, and a class-divided society. In the 1860s labor reform and machine politics were interwoven developments, each reinforcing the other. By the 1870s two great social and economic events in Chicago history—the great fire of 1871 and the 1873–79 depression—created a crisis for all classes and their relation to the city's political system. As a result two political reform movements, one at the upper and the other at the lower end of the city's social structure, emerged to challenge machine politics. Among the city's respectable citizens there arose a deep revulsion against machine politics, which eventuated in the formation of the Citizen's Association, while among the city's working people labor reform was updated and superseded by two new formations, which also challenged machine politics. The movements of each strata sought to control, redirect the energies, and incorporate the new immigrant, less-skilled workers spawned by industrialization, who were a core constituency of machine politics.

THE RISE OF MACHINE POLITICS IN CHICAGO

Organizational politics, which emerged in many American cities after the Civil War, was a complex phenomenon. Socially, it entailed the dominance of professional politicians rather than patrician notables and the creation of permanent party organizations rooted in the urban neighborhoods of working people, small propertyholders, and ethnic groups. In the absence of a strong administrative apparatus in government, mass parties propitiated different classes and interest groups by using patronage, the selective enforcement of controversial laws, and behind-the-scenes deals to disburse public revenues, mobilize electoral support, and keep social peace. These parties have been stereotyped as monolithic and all-powerful "machines," but in recent years scholars have replaced this view with one that recognizes that parties in this period were rarely centralized and often were highly fragmented and factionalized. Moreover, in the words of Martin Shefter, they were "easily penetrated by external authorities." Mass parties and organizational politics were therefore as much terrains for the conflict and accommodation between classes and interest groups as they were autonomous political players.[2]

As Robin Einhorn has shown, machine politics was virtually nonexistent in Chicago before the Civil War. Rather than rely on the general taxing and spending power of the municipal government, the city's booster elite financed urban improvements—such as the building of sewers, streets, and bridges—semiprivately, through special assessments initiated by the petitions of propertyholders. Moreover, the boosters themselves directly controlled city government as nonpartisan aldermen and mayors. As a result, the primary function of city government from the late 1840s through the Civil War—the building up of the city's physical infrastructure—was effectively isolated from party politics. City aldermen and mayors refused to appropriate funds for projects in the "public interest" and generally refused to make decisions that might be construed as political.[3]

These features of the local polity began to crumble during the Civil War era as several developments combined to create the underlying preconditions for the rise of mass politics. The period witnessed an explosion of the city's population, which required new and expanded government functions, thus making many new positions available for patronage. It also saw a growth in the scale and scope of the city's industrial, commercial, and financial enterprises, which increasingly monopolized the time and energies of a new industrial upper class, leading them to retreat from office-holding. Finally, the political rise of a working class that rejected older habits of deference meant that people without property could no longer be politically ignored.[4]

What was then called "ring" politics (a group of politicians cooperating for unethical purposes) first appeared during the Civil War, when Chicago politics and government lost their nonpartisan character. National issues related to slavery were injected into the municipal arena, and city government disbursed public monies to encourage enlistments and avert draft riots. After the war the eight-hour movement compelled aldermen to take open political positions and to contemplate using the government to regulate industry. Meanwhile, the wartime growth of the packing industry, which had created a massive pollution problem in the city, forced the city government to abandon the special assessment method of funding. To restore public health, the city government decided to reverse the flow of the Chicago River so that it would carry industrial waste away from the city's drinking water in Lake Michigan. Most important, the city financed the project out of public revenues rather than rely on a special assessment on the packers that might have driven them out of the city. The decision set a precedent for the politicians' disbursement of city revenues to redistribute wealth—in this case upward—in the name of the public interest and was a watershed in the politicization of city government.[5]

The electoral foundation for the new politics lay in the city's neighborhoods. Starting out as labor contractors, ethnic leaders, gamblers, saloonkeepers, small shopkeepers, and other small-time entrepreneurs and promoters, aspiring candidates used their associations to court the votes of the city's workingmen and small propertyholders. The post of alderman most closely reflected the new politics. The office itself was not financially attractive, since there was no salary until a $3 per meeting fee was established in 1881. But as the council began granting corporate franchises for municipal services, as city patronage expanded, and as the regulation of saloons became a partisan political issue, aldermen willing to sell their votes could earn a substantial income in what was popularly termed "boodle."[6]

When the post of alderman became an attractive one, the persistence of aldermen in office rose dramatically. Between 1852 and 1857, when boosters dominated public office, each ward was represented by an average of 7.1 aldermen out of a maximum possible number of 8.0. By contrast, in the 1864–69 period, when they were replaced by ward-based professional politicians, the average fell to 4.4 and rose slightly to 5.2 in the 1870–75 period. Many wealthy Chicagoans still participated in politics, but especially after 1870 those that did were pushed to the margins of party leadership and public office. Gilded Age business magnates with reform pretensions, such as George Pullman, did not enter politics but contented themselves with reforming their factories.[7]

Before the 1880s there were two major periods of "ring" rule, each punctuated by a short reform spurt. The first ring, lasting from 1863 to 1868, was dependent on the political mobilization of Chicago workingmen. During that period there were only three aldermen who were in office every year, and each had the strong support of the *Workingman's Advocate*. Alderman Charles

C. P. Holden not only supported the eight-hour day but in 1868 recommended an appropriation of $250,000 for the new Mechanics Institute. Pat Rafferty, an Irish alderman, was a founder of the Eight Hour League and received labor endorsement for the Board of Police and Fire Commissioners. "If elected," argued Andrew Cameron, the editor of the *Workingman's Advocate*, "he would not allow the police force of this city to be prostituted as it has been too often in the past, to intimidate workingmen. . . ." Another ethnic alderman, Mark Sheridan, a republican nationalist exiled from Ireland in 1848, won election to the police board, where he opposed police brutality, enforcement of a Sunday-closing law, and centralizing governmental reforms.[8]

Though virtually every elected alderman in 1866 was pledged to support the eight-hour day, labor reformers quickly grew disenchanted with the performance of ring aldermen. The failure of the city to enforce its new eight-hour law soured Cameron on aldermen who "wink at its violation." Yet when the city's labor movement nominated an independent slate of union leaders, together with Rafferty and Holden in the spring of 1868, the labor men either withdrew or suffered ignominious defeat. Revulsed at the vote-buying methods of ring politicians, labor reformers adopted an antimachine program in 1869 that called for an end to private contractors' building public works and public officials' receiving their pay in fines and fees; the recall by vote of public officials; and the creation of primaries in place of party caucuses to nominate candidates. But Cameron was disillusioned with the efficacy of independent labor politics. Instead, the *Workingman's Advocate* joined respectable reformers in the nonpartisan Citizens Reform party in a united assault on the dominant ring run by the German Republican boss Anton Hesing. Headed by the mayoral candidate Roswell B. Mason, the reform ticket won a resounding victory, but the city council remained in the grip of a ring known as McCauley's Nineteen.[9]

The reform efforts of 1869 marked the beginning of a ten-year period of party instability in local politics. It was a period characterized by an intermittent electoral conflict that pitted an emergent Anglo-American upper class against party rings drawing their strength from immigrant voters. It also marked the beginning of a second phase of ring politics. Whereas in the 1860s the labor issues of skilled workers were important in local politics, by the early 1870s the declining strength of local trade unions had led to the preeminence of neighborhood-based ethnic-class issues, which appealed to a constituency of lesser-skilled, foreign-born workers and small property owners. Such ethnic appeals alienated labor reformers as well as the "better classes."

The first major occasion where these new issues recast local politics came in the aftermath of the great fire of 1871, which inaugurated a three-year crisis in class relations in the city. Immediately following the fire, Mayor Mason, at the urging of the city's "best men," bypassed the Board of Police and Fire Commissioners, then under the control of politicians sympathetic to the city's workers and small-propertied ethnic elements, and transferred the city's policing to the U.S. Army, under General Phil Sheridan. In the same week the mayor turned over the collection and disbursement of relief aid pouring into Chicago from the rest of the world to the Relief and Aid Society, a private body operated by members of the city's Yankee Protestant establishment. Though the city council, under Holden's leadership, protested the action, there was little it could do.[10]

These two actions effectively placed in the hands of the leading businesspeople and professionals a powerful lever over the labor power of the city's workers and allowed them to bypass professional politicians susceptible to the popular will. These men worried that the "indiscriminate" distribution of charity would dispose unionized building trades workers and unemployed laborers to use the immediate labor shortage to jack up wage rates or avoid the rebuilding effort altogether. This fear dovetailed with civic leaders' larger concern that the absence of social stability would jeopardize eastern insurance money. Not only did burned out Chicago capitalists require the funds from eastern insurance companies to rebuild their own enterprises, but also they were dependent on renewed insurance coverage to attract investment funds from New York, Philadelphia, and European sources. This in turn required a stable social environment and sound investment climate. Accordingly, the *Chicago Tribune* endorsed Henry Greenebaum, a banker, for mayor, pointing out that in addition to being active in relief efforts he had "high standing" with the German banking community. "What the people of Chicago need," editorialized the paper, "in order to rebuild the burnt district and restore matters to their former condition is the abundant use of foreign and Eastern capital."[11]

Andrew Cameron and the city's labor unions, weakened by the absence of the Trades Assembly, did not offer alternatives to these actions. Labor reformers had grown so alienated from "bummer" politicians that the *Workingman's Advocate* endorsed the *Tribune*'s Joseph Medill for mayor on the Union-Fireproof ticket. Though Medill won election easily, ethnic politicians quickly filled the vacuum left by labor in January 1872, when, at the behest of Medill and the insurance companies, the city council began considering an ordinance to outlaw all wooden structures in the city. If passed, the ordinance would drive up rents and the cost of home ownership to levels beyond the means of ordinary working people. Just before the fire 22 percent of all adult males in Chicago owned real estate, and German-born men had the highest rate, 27 percent.[12] The German boss Anton Hesing, owner of the city's second largest planing mill and publisher of the *Illinois Staats Zeitung*, the city's major

German newspaper, intervened. Hesing mobilized a diverse, though largely German, group of ethnic laborers, craftworkers, and small property owners that protested the ordinance by invading city hall. One sign carried by a demonstrator from the German branch of the carpenters' union even depicted a gallows and stated, "This is the lot of those who vote for the fire ordinance." Much to the dismay of the mayor and the press, the council relented by allowing wood structures outside the central city and refusing to attach any enforcement provision to the bill.[13]

Though Cameron had joined the city's press in decrying riotous assemblies, the labor movement soon became a problem for civic leaders. Soaring housing costs and the still existing labor shortage combined to spark a revival of unionism among the building trades. Organizing also occurred among the iron molders, ship carpenters and caulkers, and machinists and blacksmiths. Despite the revival Chicago's labor leaders refrained from staging another strike for the eight-hour day or even for increased wages. Labor reformers feared that a strike would mobilize the thousands of newcomers who had come to Chicago looking for work rebuilding the city and would spark another riot by unskilled and barely organized workers, such as had attended the 1867 strike. Even the prospect of such an incendiary uprising was alarming to the city's business leaders and threatened to undermine the position of labor in civic opinion.

Instead of a strike, which a minority of unions advocated, the existing leadership, backed by Cameron, decided to stage a mass procession "to show the strength of the trade unions to the strange workmen now here and to induce them to unite with their brethren." After the speeches leaders offered resolutions that renounced violence, offering to "put down" unlawful demonstrations; instead of a strike they endorsed arbitration boards and cooperative production.[14] Chicago unions, primarily those in the building trades, finally resorted to sporadic strikes in the fall, and the bricklayers and plasterers won the eight-hour day. When the feared oversupply of labor became a reality in the winter of 1872–73, however, the weakened unions dissolved into their ethnic components and acquiesced to the loss of their short-lived gains.[15]

Meanwhile, elite reformers, at the urging of eastern insurance companies, began an attempt to depoliticize, professionalize, and centralize control over the city's police and fire department. The *Chicago Tribune* complained often and loudly that police selectively enforced the new fire ordinance and might be sympathetic with strikers, and the paper excoriated politically appointed firemen for their incompetence. All at once, however, disaster struck elite reformers. Mayor Medill acceded to the demands of a group of pietistic church leaders that he enforce the Sunday-closing law for saloons, a law ignored since the Lager Beer riot. For the pietists temperance reform, like the attempts to reform city government and channel the flow of relief funds, was a law-and-order issue, a way of reasserting social stability in a city menaced by large numbers of unattached male laborers. Unlike other measures, however, the temperance law stirred up a hornet's nest in the German community, driving Hesing from the Republican party into the arms of former Democratic boss of the city's Irish, Daniel O'Hara. Together they formed a new party, the People's party. Though the party endorsed a soft-money greenback program, the principle theme was a fusion of ethnicity and class. According to Hesing, drinking a glass of beer on Sunday and listening to outdoor music were "privileges of the poor." In November 1873 the party overwhelmed reformers, electing its mayoral candidate, Harvey Colvin, and thirteen out of twenty aldermen. The turnout was twice that of the postfire mayoral election, which suggests the party had mobilized a large sector of the immigrant working class.[16]

The People's party–dominated council of 1873 differed in important ways from the Republican-run council of 1866. In 1866 83 percent of council members were Republican, 65 percent American-born, and 10 percent Irish. In 1873 only 50 percent were Republican, 40 percent American-born, and 42 percent Irish. In 1866 lawyers, professionals, business agents, and commission merchants made up almost half the council, while in 1873 their share had fallen to only 8 percent. The percentage of saloonkeepers and liquor sellers rose from 3 to 14 percent, while there was a dramatic decline in the percentage of aldermen directly beholden to the labor movement, from 14 to 0 percent. The 1873 council also had a decided Democratic flavor and more closely resembled the councils of the 1880s, presided over by Carter Harrison, than those of the 1860s.[17]

Labor reformers' response to the People's party was conditioned by their understanding of temperance. To Anglo-American skilled workers, just as to the foreign-born base of the People's party, temperance was a highly symbolic cultural issue. It symbolized a panoply of nineteenth-century values centering on self-control, frugality, enterprise, perseverance, and foresight, all of which promoted the free-labor ideals of self-mastery and independence. Labor reform, a wage-earner variant of this ideology, posited as the goal of the labor movement the elevation of workers, both as individuals and as a class. Personally a teetotaler, Cameron viewed workers who made up the base of the People's party as men requiring uplift and education. Not surprisingly, he viewed the party as a "canker worm . . . knawing at the city's vitals."[18]

During this period not all labor leaders followed Andrew Cameron in allying with "better class" reformers or the Germans in becoming independent socialists. A small but important group of ambitious Irish labor leaders used their labor connections to enter regular party politics. Three major figures stand out. Frank Lawler, president of the ship carpenters' union, one of the founders of the Trades Assembly, author of the state's eight-hour law, and a Fenian nationalist, decided in 1868 to accept a patronage post with the Republican party as a letter carrier. In 1874 he opened a fruit store and then a saloon; two years later he was elected alderman on the Republican party ticket from an Irish West Side ward, though he soon changed parties. Throughout his years in public office, which included a stint in Congress, Lawler retained his ties with the labor movement and pioneered city labor legislation. Another important labor politician was John McGilvray, president of the stonecutters' union, the most powerful union in the city during the 1870s because of an exclusive agreement with employers. Given the stonecutters' interest in public works, the union was always heavily political and built strong ties with the People's party. McGilvray, labeled a "chronic office seeker" by the *Chicago Tribune,* bid for many jobs under the banner of the People's party. Hugh McLaughlin was an Irish immigrant who organized the first iron puddlers' union in the city in 1866 and rose to president of the national union, the United Sons of Vulcan. In 1873 he won election to the state legislature and in 1874 was appointed warden of Cook County Hospital.[19]

The Birth of the Socialists and the Citizens Association

By replacing informal ring rule with a broader and more organized structure, the People's party challenged both labor reformers and elite municipal reformers. Since party politicians had a grip on the immigrant working class, it is unlikely that reformers in either camp could have penetrated municipal politics without a crisis. Such a crisis presented itself in the winter of 1873–74, when the effects of the financial panic of July 1873 began to be felt in the city.

The impact of the depression in Chicago was greatly magnified because rebuilding after the fire had attracted large numbers of laborers and craftworkers to the city. According to one estimate 50,000 men were engaged in rebuilding work in May 1872. The manufacturing work force in the city had thus grown enormously by the time of the depression, perhaps to as much as three times the number indicated in the 1870 U.S. census. In February 1874 a Relief and Aid Society survey found about 20 percent of the manufacturing work force unemployed. That so many of the out-of-work were recently arrived single male immigrants living in makeshift housing intensified the volatility of the situation.[20]

Into this tinderbox stepped a new group of German-speaking labor leaders, the city's first self-proclaimed socialists. Since the formation of the independent German Trades Assembly in 1868, the establishment of a separate German labor newspaper, the *Deutsche Arbeiter*, and Andrew Cameron's abandonment of independent labor politics in 1869 in favor of an alliance with the Citizens Reform party, German labor reformers and Anglo-American labor leaders had increasingly taken separate political paths. Just as significantly, as John Jentz has shown, exiled revolutionaries like Eduard Schlaeger, who had served to link the German labor movement and the rest of the German community, were by 1869 replaced by open socialists with links to the socialism in the old country and an antagonistic attitude toward German nationalism and German-American capitalists like Hesing. While Schlaeger took a job with Hesing, the most important German labor leader during the first five years of the 1870s in Chicago became Carl Klings, who had arrived in Chicago in 1869 as a forty-four-year-old socialist and had taken up editing the *Deutsche Arbeiter.* Klings helped alienate much of the German labor movement from its ethnic moorings by leading a boycott of the local celebration of the Prussian victory over France in 1871. He also helped form the Sozial-Politischer Arbeiterverein, with links to Karl Marx's First International.[21]

The new Sozial-Politischer Arbeiterverein, called by the press "the internationals," mobilized thousands of unemployed workers, most of them immigrants, during the winter of 1873–74. In late December the socialists led a tumultuous march of at least five thousand workers to city hall, where they pressured the reputedly friendly People's party (less than two months in office) to either provide public works jobs for the unemployed or force the Relief and Aid Society to disburse the remaining fire relief funds. The demonstration, followed by a week in which thousands daily thronged the Relief and Aid Society's offices, electrified the city; the press likened it to the Paris Commune. The local call for jobs or relief echoed demands made by impromptu coalitions of socialists, labor reformers, and trade unionists in many American cities that winter, notably New York. In Chicago, however, where the socialists assumed uncontested leadership of the marches, the demand assumed a highly symbolic aspect to labor reformers.[22]

Cameron had earlier attacked socialism insofar as it meant relying on the state "as a grand machine" to guarantee employment. He was willing to grant European collectivism its legitimate place in Europe and even welcomed the Paris Commune of 1871, but now that a statist-tending socialism had migrated to the United States, he was unwilling to overlook his differences with it. The conflict between labor reformers and socialists was thrown into sharper relief when Klings proposed that the state of Illinois construct huge manufactories and storehouses for agricultural products so that capitalist intermediaries could be eliminated in the exchange of products between Grangers and workers. Meanwhile, the inability of the People's party to meet their demands had led the socialists to form a rival party, the Workingmen's Party of Illinois (WMPI). The WMPI, which by March had 31 sections—16 German, 4 Bohemian, 3 Polish, 4 Scandinavian, 3 American, and 1 Irish—distinguished itself from labor reform by calling for state operation of the railroads, telegraphs, canals, savings banks, and fire insurance companies.[23]

At this point Cameron intervened with a major editorial statement of policy in the *Workingman's Advocate.* For the state to guarantee employment as Klings had proposed, he argued, would deprive the citizen of "the noblest ambition in man, that of independence, and he would become a simple pensioner." Cameron was not, however, endorsing a laissez-faire liberalism that would ratify the existing distribution of wealth. He was reasserting an older free-labor republicanism that viewed dependence in the form of either wage labor or state dictation as incompatible with a democratic citizenship. As he had put it in 1869, "Between communism and property the foundation of new world is to be laid." In his reaffirmation of the self-help tradition, Cameron spoke for Anglo-American labor unionists, who in May had excluded "communist" representatives from a meeting called by the Industrial Congress to secure enforcement of the national eight-hour law.[24]

The new socialists not only antagonized Anglo-American labor reformers but also challenged the People's party head on. As one socialist optimistically put it, the WMPI would have little trouble garnering a local majority, since it was well known that "the united foreign nationalities defeated the whole Yankee crew on the 4th November [1873 election]." When the socialists challenged Hesing in its first electoral contest for minor offices in the spring of 1874, however, they were soundly trounced. Hesing reminded voters of his recent actions on the fire limits and temperance. His free-labor rhetoric urging "industrious laborers" to avoid becoming "miserable proletarians dependent on the mercy of capital, but rather the creators of capital" resonated with his mixed constituency of ethnic propertyholders, professionals, craftworkers, and laborers seeking respectability more than did the socialists' class-conflict language. Moreover, the WMPI could not claim to represent and defend the ethnic customs of the Germans against the "Yankee Puritans" better than the People's party did, since the WMPI consisted not of Germans alone but a slice of German-speaking nationalities, including Bohemians and Poles, who were united by a revolutionary politics.[25]

Despite their rebuff, dating from that turbulent winter the socialists established an ongoing presence in Chicago politics, much of it due to the formation of a movement subculture revolving around independent meeting halls, political celebrations, singing societies, newspapers, and militia groups. The socialist leadership that had superseded the artisan-based Arbeiter Verein, however, was undermined by its electoral failure and was soon replaced by a more consistently Marxist leadership, which established a new paper, *Vorbote,* edited by Carl Conzett. Unlike their electorally oriented predecessors, these leaders were disillusioned with the ballot and focused on workplace issues and strikes by unskilled immigrant workers. During the depression these workers adopted a spontaneous, neighborhood-based method of strike in which they marched in crowds to different workplaces. It was a practice that put them beyond the influence of labor reformers and craft unionists. To those inflamed by what the German socialist Herman Shlueter called "revolutionary romanticism," it portended a proletarian revolution. With this outlook, the WMPI sought to widen its base of support by organizing assistance for the violent strikes by lumbershovers in 1875 and 1876. The most ambitious attempt of the new party to organize immigrant industrial workers would come during the 1877 great railroad strikes.[26]

In the interim the political landscape of the city was shaken and reconstructed by a remarkable series of events beginning in July 1874 that culminated in the first successful civic organization of the upper class since the boosters and the defeat of the People's party. On July 14 another runaway fire hit the city. It was less severe than the 1871 fire, but it had a more lasting political impact. The fire started among the wooden shacks erected south of the 1872 fire limits by poor workers and spread north into the newly built business district. The compromise fire limits and the inability to reform the police and fire departments, which had reflected the political standoff between elite business reformers and ethnic politicians, had become untenable. Mobilizing themselves as never before, business and professional reformers picked up where they had left off when temperance reform had derailed "fireproof reform" in 1872.[27]

That a new consensus had been achieved overnight among the city's large propertyholders was evident by the coming together of George How, president of the Board of Trade; Marshall Field; and, significantly, Anton Hesing. The class spirit was apparent in an editorial in Horace White's *Chicago Tribune:* "We must no longer decide our fire policy by counting noses. Those who have property to lose feel directly interested in the efficiency of the fire department, and there are tens of thousands in this city who have nothing to lose if half the city were reduced to ashes." The pressure to act was reinforced on July 24, when the National Board of Fire Insurance Underwriters demanded (1) the extension of the ban on wooden buildings to the city limits; (2) reform of the fire department; (3) enactment of a stringent building code; (4) improvement in water facilities, supplemented by ward fire patrols;

and (5) removal of lumberyards and other hazardous industries from the city. The alternative was a suspension of insurance coverage, which would have caused a flight of capital from the city.[28]

That the ultimatum occurred during the depression gave it particular force. For ten years following the legal tender act of 1863 manufacturers, particularly western entrepreneurs, had been freed from relying on merchants for financing due to the creation of a national capital market pioneered by Jay Cooke. With the collapse of Cooke's company in July 1873 and the resulting financial panic, western interests faced the prospect of once again having to rely on eastern bankers and investors with their European ties. During the early depression years the city's building trades interests and businessmen in the railroad and railroad supply industries joined their employees and labor reformers in supporting greenback politics and cheap credit. A survey of twenty-six active Chicago greenbackers reveals the sectoral impact of the depression on this brand of money politics. Of these greenbackers 40 percent were workers and labor reformers, almost all iron workers, stonecutters, and printers. Among the businessmen two-thirds were primarily in real estate, building, or the railroads.[29]

By 1875, however, the economic interests of Chicago businesspeople had changed. The depression in manufacturing and the steep decline in real estate values during the depression made the city's economic health more dependent than ever on eastern capital.[30] Furthermore, by this time many manufacturers feared labor and the socialists and no longer identified themselves with debtors. These men, plus the bankers and merchants whose interests inclined them toward sound money politics, supported the federal (gold) resumption act of 1875 on which the health of eastern financiers depended.[31] The vast majority of large propertyholders therefore reacted with panic to the insurance underwriters' ultimatum, believing it threatened the future of the city. As the *Tribune* put it, "Insurance credit is the foundation of commercial credit, as commercial credit is the foundation of our whole commercial system. Take away the insurance companies from Chicago, and our merchants would be compelled to buy in eastern markets for cash. Take away the insurance companies and, despite all the wealth we have here amassed in buildings, we would not be able to compete with Milwaukee, Peoria, and Dubuque, to say nothing of St. Louis and Cincinnati."[32]

With only Cameron and the WMPI in opposition, the city council caved in to business pressure by extending the fire limits, and Mayor Colvin agreed to remove Fire Marshall Mathias Benner, a former officer of the cigarmakers' union and the Mechanics Institute, in favor of a Denis Swenie, favored by business interests. To reformers, however, the deeper problem lay in the People's party's control of city government. The city administration was discussing building a new courthouse as a way of mollifying the demand for jobs as well as providing a lucrative source of boodle. Meanwhile, a coalition of aldermen from immigrant working-class wards held up an appropriation for new water mains for business and industrial districts until the same could be provided for working-class districts. On July 24, in the face of an unresponsive government and the chilling prospect of a limit to the city's economic growth, the city's business leaders established the city's first ongoing political association of upper-class leaders, the one-hundred-member Citizens Association of Chicago.

Franklin MacVeagh, a wholesale merchant who was the first president of the Citizens Association, candidly explained the purpose of the new organization in his first address when he asserted that universal male suffrage had placed "political power in the hands of the baser part of the community," which resulted in binding "hand and foot the best part of the community." The Citizens Association was "a supplemental political organization" that would "represent these disfranchised people."[33] By dividing according to wards—five members were drawn from each of twenty wards—the Citizens Association made clear that its purposes were political and antimachine. About half of the Citizens Association's membership of one hundred consisted of a cross section of the city's new Gilded Age capitalists: manufacturers, merchants, bankers, and corporate lawyers. Approximately a third were small merchants and professionals representing the working-class wards. Decision-making power was concentrated in its executive board, every member of which was a leading merchant or manufacturer.[34] To further unify the city's heterogeneous property interests, the association studiously avoided the divisive issues that had diverted and defeated previous reform efforts. It remained nonpartisan, refused to endorse particular candidates, and, in the words of one leader, avoided "temperance and sumptuary nonsense." Explained another, "The best men differ on these questions."[35]

The first success of the Citizens Association came in early October, when it brought General William Shaler from New York to reorganize the city's fire department by bureaucratizing and depoliticizing it. Over the objections of Mark Sheridan, president of the Board of Police and Fire Commissioners who was backed by the People's party, Shaler had his $10,000 salary paid by the Citizens Association and the insurance companies. The satisfied insurance companies lifted their boycott by the end of the month.[36]

Though the immediate crisis was dissipated, the association pressed ahead with efforts to revamp the entire structure of city government in which authority was fragmented and dispersed. Much of the city's administration was divided among autonomous boards—among them the Board of Police and Fire Commissioners—whose heads were not appointed by the mayor but elected. For other offices the power of appointment and removal lodged in the city council. The various structures of city government coexisted with a township system that divided Chicago into three towns, each with a taxing power and a plethora of offices available for patronage purposes. To render this system less amenable to machine rule, the Citizens Association proposed a number of centralizing remedies that would give more power to the "best men." It pushed a bill inspired by Joseph Medill that would create a cabinet-style executive branch supplemented by a two-house council, one part of which would be elected on a citywide basis. Though this bill never made it through the state legislature, in 1875 city voters decided to reorganize under the state's general incorporation act of 1872, which resulted in abolishing the independent boards and placing the power of appointment and removal in the hands of the mayor.[37]

The same propertied elements that founded the Citizens Association as a counterweight to the People's party lived in trepidation of general strikes, riots, and disorder emanating from immigrant industrial workers. Because state law required militiamen to purchase their own uniforms, contribute to the rental of armories, and drill on their own time, existing militia companies remained private bodies without legal obligation to the state or city. In the wake of the postfire labor demonstration in May 1872 and a renewal of socialist demonstrations at the Relief and Aid Society in April 1874 business leaders made attempts to form a businessmen's militia but were unsuccessful. The formation of the Citizens Association in August provided the first funding for a businessmen's militia: $17,000 for uniforms and equipment. By February 1875, when the socialists threatened another march to the Relief and Aid Society, they were overawed by the presence of police and the newly formed First Regiment, 60 percent of whose rank and file consisted of clerks and bookkeepers. Faced with overwhelming force, WMPI demonstrators stayed home.[38]

The use of the businessmen's militia to intimidate their constituency fed the growing belief among German socialists that the Republic had been irrevocably corrupted by a new oligarchy of wealth. On April 16, 1875, they decided to form their own militia, the Lehr- und Wehr-Verein; Bohemian socialists followed with the Bohemian Rifles. Confronted with what one socialist termed "armed political competition," state legislators, at the urging of the Citizens Association, began deliberations that culminated in the state's first comprehensive military code, passed in May 1877. Two years later the Citizens Association successfully lobbied legislators for a law prohibiting private militia companies and banning armed drilling without the governor's permission. It was perhaps the most stunning triumph of Chicago's top citizens in creating new state administrative apparatus and centralizing political power.[39]

The elite propertyholders who founded the Citizens Association were not unique to Chicago but part of a national political trend during the 1870s, in which a segment of the free-labor coalition that had prosecuted the war against slavery and supported Reconstruction broke off to become "liberals." First and foremost, the liberals recoiled from the corruption that had attended Reconstruction attempts to bring political equality to the freed slaves in the South and increased public spending by federal, state, and local governments to assist economic development. Many feared not only corruption but also "special legislation" or "class legislation" and wanted government to retreat to a less activist role except on questions of law and order. Rather than rely on government, which in response to mass politics might redistribute income and property downward as well as upward, northern liberals affirmed the laws of the market, which they believed were immutable, scientifically valid, and beneficent. Liberals thus opposed tariff protection for domestic industry and the attempts of greenbackers to inflate the currency and make credit easier. In response to the demands of freedpeople for land and wageworkers for unions, they also narrowed the definition of free labor to the freedom to contract in the labor market, thus jettisoning the older goal of climbing out of wage labor into property ownership. Liberal beliefs that the best men, defined by their virtue and character, should rule in place of professional politicians, whom they scorned as demagogues, led many to muse in public about the dangers of universal suffrage; oppose the intrusion of national issues in municipal politics, which they believed should be nonpartisan; and support civil service reform. Taken together, these beliefs positioned liberals to speak for elite northern industrialists, bankers, and merchants, who were also distinguishing themselves from the free-labor coalition.[40]

It should not be assumed, however, that the liberals were mere representatives of northern business interests, because laissez-faire dogma on the tariff often clashed with these interests. Moreover, suspicion of a powerful central government was a longstanding characteristic of American political culture that resonated with all classes. Finally, many liberal advocates of market primacy were also professionalizers and progressives—members of the American Social Science Association, for example—seeking to align society with the latest discoveries of social science.[41] Nonetheless, the liberal advocacy of minimal government reflected the fear of Gilded Age business that big-city taxation and spending would be used under the influence of universal suffrage and the politicization of urban government and politics to redistribute wealth downward. Just as important, liberalism's popularity represented the culmination of a process whereby a politically dominant capitalist class manifested its growing class awareness by discarding the egalitarian and republican strands in free-labor ideology.

Still, the progress in professionalizing government and insulating it from the pressures of popular politics proved curiously self-limiting. As the depression wore on, many city propertyholders found their immediate interests diverging from the long-term political goals actuating those leading the Citizens Association. For one thing, the success of reformers in associating municipal spending with corruption and the downward redistribution of wealth prompted many propertyholders to lose confidence in city government and along with it the policy of spending on fire-related public improvements and expanding and centralizing a government still in the hands of the People's party. The press and other critics pointed out that increasing the mayor's powers had the effect of increasing and centralizing the patronage powers of Mayor Colvin, thus creating a virtual Tammany Hall in Chicago. The loss of confidence in government was reinforced by the continuing decline in real estate values—50 percent by 1877—and a concomitant fall in rents. As a result, many property owners simply refused to pay their local taxes. On July 26 the reforming *Chicago Tribune* published a list of prominent tax evaders, including the bankers W. F. Coolbaugh and Mahlon Ogden. The Colvin administration, however, continued its policy of not enforcing unpopular laws, such as the fire limits, temperance, and now taxation, and instead resorted to expanded short-term borrowing on the New York financial markets to sustain spending.[42]

Seizing an opportunity to discredit the People's party, the reform press announced to the world that because of the city's profligate borrowing and spending, Chicago's best men had lost confidence in city government. The immediate effect was to undermine the confidence of eastern investors in city bonds, creating a fiscal crisis for the city. The irony of the situation was not lost on Mayor Colvin, who pointed out that "the so-called respectable element has fought against the payment of their just indebtedness to the city year after year and at the same time were insisting upon and demanding increased privileges and new improvements."[43]

The crisis was compounded by a political one when a blatant case of ballot box fraud in the spring 1876 election prompted a mass indignation meeting of twenty-five thousand citizens. Speakers compared the outrage and unity of feeling with the response to the firing on Fort Sumter fifteen springs earlier. As in 1874, leading businessmen formed an executive committee to take action, but this time they fielded a bipartisan candidate for mayor and the city council. Both locally and nationally the year 1876 had been one for exposing political corruption. In Chicago a spectacular whiskey ring scandal and trial resulted in the conviction of Anton Hesing, further discrediting the People's party. On the eve of the city election manufacturers and merchants acted to ensure victory by giving their employees the day off to vote. The result was a smashing victory for reform. Colvin went down to defeat and the *Tribune* estimated that 28 of 36 new aldermen elected were "respectable." Though the courts temporarily restored Colvin to power, a judicial decision allowed the new council to call a special election for mayor, which resulted in a victory for a new antimachine candidate, the Republican Monroe Heath.[44]

Despite the seeming victory for reform, in some ways the return of the Republicans to power restored pre-1869 conditions. The submergence of temperance agitation allowed respectable, non-Catholic Germans to return temporarily to their Republican moorings in city politics.[45] A more durable development was that during the election the previous two years' emphasis on structural reform and the expansion of government's administrative capacities gave way to a more popular one of minimizing property taxes and reducing government spending. After 1875 Chicago's tax levy for corporate and school purposes fell precipitously and remained at a low level for much of the 1880s. The reason for the fall in taxes was an open secret in the city: scandalously low and inequitable tax assessments. Chicago propertyholders, particularly those holding corporate property, made their peace with machine politics by utilizing corruption and the selective nonenforcement of laws to minimize their taxes. Partially because of a 1875 state law allowing corporations to be assessed on the local level, state assessment of personal property in Chicago fell drastically after 1873, then leveled off in the 1880s and early 1890s, and did not regain the 1873 level until 1898—all this despite tremendous economic and population growth in the city. By 1885, though Chicago was the nation's third largest city, it ranked last in per capita taxation among the top thirteen most populous cities.[46]

Limited public revenues required low public expenditures, especially because the 1870 state constitution limited Chicago's indebtedness to 5 percent of assessed valuation and an 1879 law limited the city's property tax to 2 percent of the assessed worth of city property. This helps explain why Mayor Heath was not a nonpartisan, Citizens Association–sponsored reformer but rather a solid businessman and a former Republican party alderman, who recognized property owners' desire for low taxes and a retrenchment in spending.[47] Since such a policy could be provided by partisan politicians as easily as by reformers, the 1876 businessmen's council did not last. Indeed, it was the last one not dominated by machine politicians until the Municipal Voters League succeeded in reforming the council two decades later. To state the issue bluntly, as soon as the issues of taxation and spending became disentangled from the corruption issue, much of the business constituency of the Citizens Association lost interest in reform.

When propertyholders made their peace with the political status quo, the Citizens Association lost its capacity to play the role of what E. Digby Baltzell has called "a goal-integrating elite," that is, its ability to translate the economic power of the Gilded Age upper class into political authority, something that could be done only when the interests of the city's new capitalists were made compatible with society's redefined general interest. The Citizens Association had succeeded admirably on issues involving the militia, the centralization of the powers of the mayor, and the professionalization of the fire department. But the ongoing issue of taxing and spending, the redefinition of the public interest as one of low taxes, and a minimal and nonpartisan government worked against an activist, political association, such as the Citizens Association. The well-documented post–Civil War withdrawal of urban capitalists from municipal officeholding—though not politics—thus resumed, and after 1870, in Frederic Jaher's words, the "premier entrepreneurs" in Chicago were "pushed to peripheral places in party leadership and public office." In 1880 and again in 1885, when the Citizens Association called for consolidation of tax districts to centralize assessment of property, few among the city's leading businessmen were interested. By that time the Citizens Association had accepted a less ambitious role as watchdog group.[48]

The successes and the limitations of the Citizens Association were paralleled in the career of the liberals in the city and state Republican party. From 1868 through 1874 pragmatic "Stalwart" Republicans, led by U.S. Senators John A. Logan and Charles B. Farwell and Governor Richard J. Oglesby, dominated party councils because of their ability to win elections by "waving the bloody shirt" and accommodating soft-money sentiment among Grangers and iron manufacturers. But the declining importance of the money question following the 1875 Specie Resumption Act, the growing fear of communism and riots by the dangerous classes, and the general revulsion at corruption in the Ulysses S. Grant administration and the Republican party at all levels helped alter the balance of power in the party from Stalwarts toward the liberals and from free-labor reform toward law and order and retrenchment. Indications of this shift were apparent when state Republicans were able to override Democratic opposition to a strong antitramp law in 1877 and a bill restricting the activities of the workers' militia in 1879.[49]

The rise of the liberals coincided with and drew strength from the unprecedented solidarity in the ranks of the city's business elite during the last half of the 1870s. Business leaders had surmounted divisions in their ranks over soft money, temperance and other ethnoreligious issues, and political partisanship. Yet just as the Citizens Association faded, class solidarity among the city's large propertyholders would be threatened and undermined by events in the rest of the decade. Machine politicians would prove far more resourceful and resilient than the liberals had anticipated.

Notes

1. Morton Keller, *Affairs of State: Public Life in Late Nineteenth Century America* (Cambridge, Mass.: Belknap, 1977), 238–83. The degree to which organizational imperatives, especially corruption, characterized Gilded Age politics has recently been questioned by scholars. See, for example, John C. Teaford, *The Unheralded Triumph: City Government in America, 1870–1900* (Baltimore, Md.: Johns Hopkins University Press, 1984); for a survey, see Charles W. Calhoun, "The Political Culture: Public Life and the Conduct of Politics," in *The Gilded Age: Essays on the Origins of Modern America*, ed. Charles W. Calhoun (Wilmington, Del.: Scholarly Resources, 1996), 185–213.

2. Martin Shefter, "The Emergence of the Political Machine: An Alternative View," in *Theoretical Perspectives on Urban Politics*, by Willis D. Hawley, Michael Lipsky, Stanley B. Greenberg, J. David Greenstone, Ira Katznelson, Karen Orren, Paul E. Peterson, Martin Shefter, and Douglas Yates (Englewood Cliffs, N.J.: Prentice-Hall, 1976), 23; M. Craig Brown and Charles N. Halaby, "Machine Politics in America, 1870–1945," *Journal of Interdisciplinary History* 17 (Winter 1987): 587–612; Terence J. McDonald, "The Problem of the Political in Recent American Urban History: Liberal Pluralism and the Rise of Functionalism," *Social History* 10 (Oct. 1985): 323–45.

3. Robin L. Einhorn, *Property Rules: Political Economy in Chicago, 1833–1872* (Chicago: University of Chicago Press, 1991).

4. Bessie Louise Pierce, *A History of Chicago*, vol. 2, *From Town to City, 1848–1871* (New York: Alfred A. Knopf, 1940), 289–353; Donald S. Bradley and Mayer N. Zald, "From Commercial Elite to Political Administrator: The Recruitment of the Mayors of Chicago," *American Journal of Sociology* 51 (Sept. 1965): 153–67; Frederic Cople Jaher, *The Urban Establishment: Upper Strata in Boston, New York, Charleston, Chicago, and Los Angeles* (Urbana: University of Illinois Press, 1981), 502–4.

5. Robin L. Einhorn, "The Civil War and Municipal Government in Chicago," in *Toward a Social History of the American Civil War: Exploratory Essays*, ed. Maris A. Vinovskis (Cambridge: Cambridge University Press, 1990), 117–38.

6. Pierce, *History of Chicago*, 2:200–201, 291, 297–98; *Workingman's Advocate*, Oct. 9, 1869, Nov. 13, 1869; *Chicago Tribune*, Nov. 8, 1874.

7. The 1850s period was chosen because it marked the beginning of the Republican party; the latter two six-year periods were chosen because each end year marks a dividing line between periods of ring rule and reform. Names of aldermen were taken from Alfred T. Andreas, *History of Chicago from the Earliest Period to the Present Time* (Chicago: A. T. Andreas, 1884–86), 2:49–50; 3:101–2. On changes in officeholding, see Jaher, *Urban Establishment*, 500–505; and Rima Lunin Schultz, "The Businessman's Role in Western Settlement: The Entrepreneurial Frontier, Chicago, 1833–1872" (Ph.D. diss., Boston University, 1985), chaps. 8 and 10.

8. *Workingman's Advocate*, Nov. 2, 1867 (quote), Apr. 18, 1868, Oct. 16, 1869; *Chicago Tribune*, June 1, 1872, Jan. 21, 1874; Michael L. Ahern, *The Great Revolution: A History of the Rise and Progress of the People's Party in the City of Chicago and County of Cook* (Chicago: Lakeside Publishing, 1874), 139–44.

9. *Workingman's Advocate*, Feb. 8, 1868 (quote), Apr. 18, 1868, Oct. 16, 1869; *Chicago Tribune*, Sept. 6, 1869, Sept. 27, 1869; Pierce, *History of Chicago*, 2:297–98.

10. *Chicago Tribune,* Oct. 12, 1871, Oct. 14, 1871, Oct. 18, 1871; Karen Sawislak, *Smoldering City: Chicagoans and the Great Fire, 1871–1874* (Chicago: University of Chicago Press, 1995), chaps. 1 and 2; Carl Smith, *Urban Disorder and the Shape of Belief: The Great Chicago Fire, the Haymarket Bomb, and the Model Town of Pullman* (Chicago: University of Chicago Press, 1995), part 1.

11. *Chicago Tribune,* Oct. 15, 1871, Oct. 20, 1871, Oct. 23, 1871 (quote).

12. Figures drawn from a sample of employed persons in the 1870 federal manuscript census by the Chicago Working-Class History Project.

13. *Workingman's Advocate,* Nov. 11, 1871, Nov. 25, 1871, Feb. 2, 1871; *Chicago Tribune,* Jan. 16, 1872, Jan. 17, 1872 (quote). For a perceptive narrative of this episode, see Sawislak, *Smoldering City,* chap. 3.

14. *Workingman's Advocate,* Jan. 13, 1872, Jan. 20, 1872, Mar. 2, 1872, Mar. 30, 1872, Apr. 27, 1872, July 6, 1872, Sept. 21, 1872; *Chicago Tribune,* May 4, 1872 (first quote), May 14, 1872, May 15, 1872, May 16, 1872 (second quote).

15. *Workingman's Advocate,* Sept. 21, 1872, Sept. 28, 1872, Oct. 5, 1872, Oct. 26, 1872, Nov. 16, 1872, Nov. 23, 1872, Feb. 8, 1873, June 28, 1873, July 19, 1873.

16. *Chicago Tribune,* Oct. 5, 1873 (quote), Nov. 6, 1873; Ahern, *Great Revolution,* 65–99; Sawislak, *Smoldering City,* chap. 5. The People's party was part of a national electoral trend that, according to Paul Kleppner, *The Third Electoral System, 1853–1892: Parties, Voters, and Political Cultures* (Chapel Hill: University of North Carolina, 1979), 97–142, "reinstated" normal Democratic voting strength in the early 1870s.

17. Ahern, *Great Revolution,* 205–49; *Edwards Directory, 1871* (Chicago: Edwards, 1871).

18. *Workingman's Advocate,* June 6, 1865, May 8, 1875 (quote); June 12, 1875, Oct. 23, 1875; Alan Dawley and Paul Faler, "Workingclass Culture and Politics in the Industrial Revolution: Sources of Loyalism and Rebellion," *Journal of Social History* 9 (June 1976): 466–80.

19. On Lawler, see *Chicago Tribune,* Jan. 18, 1896; and *Progressive Age,* June 24, 1882; on McGilvray, see *Chicago Tribune,* Sept. 15, 1877 (quote); and *Workingman's Advocate,* Mar. 4, 1876; on McLaughlin, see *Workingman's Advocate,* Dec. 13, 1873, Dec. 18, 1875.

20. *Chicago Tribune,* Mar. 24, 1872, May 14, 1872, Feb. 18, 1874, Apr. 10, 1875.

21. *Illinois Staats Zeitung,* Sept. 8, 1867; *Deutsche Arbeiter,* Aug. 28, 1869, July 25, 1870, Aug. 1, 1870; *Workingman's Advocate,* June 19, 1869; *Chicago Tribune,* Mar. 28, 1872. I want to thank John Jentz for sharing his translations and interpretations of the above German language articles. See also John B. Jentz, "Class and Politics in an Emerging Industrial City: Chicago in the 1860s and 1870s," *Journal of Urban History* 17 (May 1991): 227–63

22. *Chicago Tribune,* Dec. 23–28, 1873, Jan. 1–7, 1874; Herbert G. Gutman, "The Failure of the Movement by the Unemployed for Public Works in 1873," *Political Science Quarterly* 80 (June 1965): 254–76; Herbert G. Gutman, "The Tompkins Square 'Riot' in New York City on January 13, 1874: A Reexamination of Its Causes and Aftermath," *Labor History* 6 (Winter 1965): 44–70.

23. *Workingman's Advocate,* Oct. 30, 1869 (quote), Nov. 27, 1869, Apr. 29, 1871, July 8, 1871, July 15, 1871; *Chicago Tribune,* Dec. 29, 1873, Jan. 12, 1874, Mar. 5, 1874;

Bruce C. Nelson, *Beyond the Martyrs: A Social History of Chicago's Anarchists, 1870–1900* (New Brunswick, N.J.: Rutgers University Press, 1988), 53–55.

24. *Workingman's Advocate,* Oct. 30, 1869, Jan. 24, 1874.

25. Jentz, "Class and Politics in an Emerging Industrial City," 248 (socialist quote); *Chicago Tribune,* Mar. 17, 1872 (Hesing quote).

26. Jentz, "Class and Politics in an Emerging Industrial City," 249–50; *Chicago Tribune,* Mar. 15, 1875, June 4, 1875, May 5, 1876, May 10, 1876, May 12, 1876; Christine Heiss, "German Radicals in Industrial America: The Lehr- und Wehr-Verein in Gilded Age Chicago," in *German Workers in Industrial Chicago, 1850–1910: A Comparative Perspective,* ed. Hartmut Keil and John B. Jentz (De Kalb: Northern Illinois University Press, 1983), 211 (Shlueter quote).

27. Richard Schneirov, "Class Conflict, Municipal Politics, and Governmental Reform in Gilded Age Chicago, 1871–1875," in *German Workers in Industrial Chicago, 1850–1910: A Comparative Perspective,* ed. Hartmut Keil and John B. Jentz (De Kalb: Northern Illinois University Press, 1983), 183–205; Sidney I. Roberts, "Businessmen in Revolt: Chicago, 1874–1900" (Ph.D. diss., Northwestern University, 1960); Donald David Marks, "Polishing the Gem of the Prairie: The Evolution of Civic Reform Consciousness in Chicago, 1874–1900" (Ph.D. diss., University of Wisconsin, Madison, 1974).

28. *Chicago Tribune,* July 18, 1874 (quote), July 26, 1874.

29. Vincent P. Carosso, *Investment Banking in America: A History* (Cambridge: Cambridge University Press, 1970), 24–26; Glenn Porter and Harold C. Livesay, *Merchants and Manufacturers: Studies in the Changing Structure of Nineteenth-Century Marketing* (Baltimore, Md.: Johns Hopkins Press, 1971), 116–30; Robert Sharkey, *Money, Class, and Party: An Economic Study of the Civil War and Reconstruction* (Baltimore, Md.: Johns Hopkins University Press, 1959), 244–48; greenback leaders compiled from references in *Workingman's Advocate,* 1875 and 1876; *Edwards Directory, 1871;* Hugh S. De Sanatis, "George S. Bowen and the American Dream," *Chicago History* 6 (Fall 1977): 143–54.

30. *Chicago Tribune,* Jan. 1, 1875, July 31, 1875, Aug. 14, 1875, Aug. 20, 1875; Homer Hoyt, *One Hundred Years of Land Values in Chicago* (Chicago: University of Chicago Press, 1929), 117–27.

31. Walter T. K. Nugent, *The Money Question during Reconstruction* (New York: W. W. Norton, 1967), 60–64.

32. *Chicago Tribune,* Aug. 3, 1874.

33. "Address by President Franklin MacVeagh, Sept. 11, 1874," in Citizens Association of Chicago, *Annual Reports, 1874–1901,* 1874 report (Chicago: Citizens Association of Chicago, 1901), 6.

34. Of the ninety-three names of Citizens Association members listed in the *Chicago Tribune,* Aug. 1, 1874, sixty-eight were identified using Andreas, *History of Chicago from the Earliest Period to the Present Time,* vol. 3; and *Edwards Directory of Chicago* (Chicago: Richard Edwards, 1873). Of these, forty-three were prominent businessmen or corporate lawyers.

35. *Chicago Tribune,* July 26, 1874.

36. Ibid., Oct. 21, 1874, Oct. 25, 1874.

37. Ibid., Oct. 7, 1874, Nov. 4, 1874, Mar. 17, 1875, Apr. 24, 1875, June 29, 1875;

Pierce, *History of Chicago,* 2:300–304; Samuel Edwin Sparling, "Municipal History and Present Organization of the City of Chicago" (Ph.D. diss., University of Wisconsin, 1898), 93; Sidney I. Roberts, "Ousting the Bummers, 1874–1876" (typescript, Chicago Historical Society).

38. *Chicago Tribune,* July 10, 1872, Aug. 29, 1874, Jan. 3, 1875, Jan. 15, 1875, Feb. 23, 1875, Feb. 24, 1875, Mar. 5, 1875; Roy Turnbaugh, "Ethnicity, Civic Pride, and Commitment: The Evolution of the Chicago Militia," *Illinois State Historical Society Journal* 62 (May 1979): 111–12; Holdridge O. Collins, *History of the Illinois National Guard* (Chicago: Black and Beach, 1884), 12–14. Figures based on a random sample of one of every three privates in companies A, B, C, and D of the First Regiment. Thirty-eight of fifty-five names were identified for occupation. Of these, seventeen were clerks, six were bookkeepers, and the rest were lawyers, salesmen, proprietors, and real estate men; only one was a skilled craftsman. Collins, *History of the Illinois National Guard,* 7–9, 17, 41–57; Turnbaugh, "Ethnicity, Civic Pride, and Commitment," 114–15; *Edwards Directory of Chicago; Lakeside Directory of Chicago, 1874–75* (Chicago: Williams, Donnelley, 1875); Heiss, "German Radicals in Industrial America".

39. *Chicago Tribune,* Jan. 3, 1875.

40. John G. Sproat, *"The Best Men": Liberal Reformers in the Gilded Age* (1968; reprint, Chicago: University of Chicago Press, 1982); Michael McGerr, *The Decline of Popular Politics: The American North, 1865–1928* (New York: Oxford University Press, 1986), 42–68; Eric Foner, *Reconstruction: America's Unfinished Revolution, 1863–1877* (New York: Harper and Row, 1988), 488–99, 517–19.

41. Michael Les Benedict, "Laissez-Faire and Liberty: A Reevaluation of the Meaning and Origins of Laissez-Faire Constitutionalism," *Law and History Review* 3 (Fall 1985): 293–331; Gerald W. McFarland, *Mugwumps, Morals, and Politics, 1884–1920* (Amherst: University of Massachusetts Press, 1975), 38–52. Mary O. Furner, "The Republican Tradition and the New Liberalism: Social Investigation, State Building, and Social Learning in the Gilded Age," in *The State and Social Investigation in Britain and the United States,* ed. Michael J. Lacey and Mary O. Furner (Cambridge: Cambridge University Press, 1993), 171–241, argues that "the reconstruction of liberalism" (174) began with the academic investigations of the 1870s.

42. *Chicago Tribune,* Mar. 12, 1876, Mar. 24, 1876, Apr. 5, 1876, Apr. 12, 1876, July 19, 1876, July 26, 1876.

43. Ibid., Apr. 17, 1876.

44. Ibid., Apr. 20, 1876, June 6, 1876, July 13, 1876.

45. See translation of *Illinois Staats Zeitung* article in *Chicago Tribune,* Feb. 7, 1877. See also *Chicago Tribune,* Mar. 28, 1877.

46. Hoyt, *One Hundred Years of Land Values in Chicago,* 488; Bennett Stark, "Political Economy of State Public Finance: Illinois, 1830–1970" (Ph.D. diss., University of Wisconsin, Madison, 1982), 75–81, 95, 103, 113; *Eighth Biennial Report of the Illinois Bureau of Labor Statistics* (Springfield: Ed. F. Hartman, 1896); John A. Fairlie, *A Report on the Taxation and Revenue System of Illinois* (Danville: Illinois Printing, 1910); Jaher, *Urban Establishment,* 503; C. K. Yearley, *The Money Machines: The Breakdown and Reform of Governmental and Party Finance in the North, 1860–1920* (New York: State University of New York Press, 1970), 37–74.

47. *Chicago Tribune*, July 2, 1876, July 25, 1876, May 1, 1877.

48. E. Digby Baltzell, *Philadelphia Gentlemen: The Making of a National Upper Class* (New York: Free Press, 1958), 32–68; Jaher, *Urban Establishment*, 503–4; David C. Hammack, "Problems in the Historical Study of Power in the Cities and Towns of the United States, 1800–1960," *American Historical Review* 83 (Apr. 1978): 323–49; Bradley and Zald, "From Commercial Elite to Political Administrator"; Stark, "Political Economy of State Public Finance," 92–97.

49. Gary Lee Cardwell, "The Rise of the Stalwarts and the Transformation of Illinois Republican Politics, 1860–1880" (Ph.D. diss., University of Virginia, 1976), 215–335; David Montgomery, *Beyond Equality: Labor and the Radical Republicans, 1862–1872* (New York: Vintage Books, 1967), 356–60, 384–86.

CHAPTER 3

The Rise of the Knights of Labor and the Socialist Labor Party

On April 24, 1877, Joseph Medill, the publisher of the *Chicago Tribune*, proclaimed the end of an era. "The Negro has been emancipated," the *Tribune* editorialized. "He has been made a citizen and the ballot placed in his hands. . . . The colored men have nothing more to ask. There is nothing which national politics can give them as a class. . . . With the retirement of the Negro from politics, there will be time and opportunity" to wage a reform war, a war on "a scandalous system of politics under which a few men have grasped power and place and assumed dictatorial control over popular elections. . . . "The war on machine politics might have the been the one Medill wanted to wage, but three months later he and other civic leaders would find thrust into their laps a class war carried on in Chicago's streets. Almost as if to respond to Medill's editorial, an Irish Union army veteran, speaking on the first day of the railroad strikes in July, referred to the same subject in bitter tones: "The Black man has been fought for; and we have given him the ballot; the people have shown an interest in him and have done all they can to bring him up to the point where he could compete with the white man. Now why not do something for the workingman. I was through the war. I fought for the big bugs—the capitalists. . . . And what is our reward now? What have the capitalists done for us?"[1]

The railroad strike of July 1877 marked a watershed in American history. Coming on the heels of the "compromise of 1877" that signaled an end to Reconstruction, the 1877 railroad strike in Chicago and elsewhere dramatically highlighted the dawn of a new era, one in which the labor question replaced the slave question, class conflict threatened to overshadow sectional conflict, and urban-industrial issues rivaled rural-agrarian issues. Americans had to rethink their very identity. If class divisions were now inherent in their social fabric, thoughtful Americans began to ask openly whether their country was so different from (and better than) Europe after all.

The Great Upheaval of 1877

Mid-1877 was a year before the end of the contraction phase of the depression. Overcapitalization and cut-throat business competition, especially on the railroads, spurred an unceasing downward wage-price spiral that by 1879 would leave wholesale prices 30 percent below their 1873 level. The Chicago press reported wage cuts in virtually every trade and industry. For those employed work was sporadic and scarce, putting the working poor on the edge of destitution. The destitute and unemployed workers searching for work were called "tramps" and were widely despised and feared by the respectable sort, their presence visible reminders of press stories about crime, bomb-throwing Molly McGuires, skulking communists, and "savages" on the prairies. On July 2 a new state vagrant law went into effect that for the first time allowed police to arrest without warrant "any one who goes about begging; . . . persons who do not support themselves or their families; and those who take lodgings in the open air or unoccupied houses or barns and give no accounts of themselves"; as well as those known as "thieves, burglars and pickpockets."[2]

In February a reporter visited a Polish and Bohemian neighborhood in the Milwaukee Avenue area. He described long rows of shanties and tenements "two, three, and four deep" on each lot, each house or apartment containing "two or more families. There were certainly indications of dire hardship and squalor, and wretchedness—indications that were as apparent as if written on hung-out sign-boards." "Fortunately, these people are not vicious. Some of the men are Communists, but not a large proportion, since," reported the paper in a candid display of prejudice typical of the period but breathtaking to the modern ear, "it requires a certain amount of intelligence to be even a Communist." In one house the reporter met a Polish member of the International, who said someday "there would be trouble."[3]

The first sign that there might indeed be trouble came on July 16, when a spontaneous strike by firemen protesting a recent wage cut shut down the B & O Railroad at Camden Junction near Baltimore, Maryland. The next day the strike drew in other railway workers and spread rapidly west along the B & O line to Baltimore, Reading, and then Pittsburgh. The introduction of federal troops on July 19, followed by the state militias of Maryland and

Pennsylvania, inflamed strikers and their sympathizers, sparking riots, general strikes, and rebellions. In Pittsburgh the militia from Philadelphia fired on a crowd of strikers and killed twenty of them, prompting a huge crowd to burn down the railyard of the Pennsylvania Railroad, the nation's largest corporation. As the Chicago press screamed "Civil War," it seemed only a matter of time before the strike would hit the railroad center of the Midwest. When switchmen from different Chicago railroads met on Monday, July 23, to discuss a walkout against their own pay cut, the *Tribune* only had to headline, "It Is Here."[4]

Hoping to avoid the violence and property damage that had accompanied the Pittsburgh strike, railroad officials in Chicago either restored wage cuts or avoided attempting to break the strike, and Mayor Monroe Heath ruled out the use of police to protect strikebreakers. The avoidance of confrontation at the rail depots and railyards denied railroad workers the central role they had played in the East, but it did not keep Chicago from having its strike and only delayed confrontation.

The most ominous development for authorities was the aggressive role taken by the socialists, now part of the renamed Workingmen's Party of the United States (WPUS). Since 1876 the party had presented a new face to the public. In addition to the German-speakers Carl Klings and Carl Conzett the party could now boast three dynamic, articulate, and charismatic young English-speaking leaders, each of whom had been "converted" by Peter J. McGuire, the peripatetic socialist carpenter, when he had visited the city in March. Now speaking for the party were George Schilling, a bilingual cooper who would later become an anarchist opposed to physical force, an influential Knights of Labor leader, a single-taxer, and an ally of Governor John Peter Altgeld and other local Democrats; Thomas J. Morgan, a combative 5 foot 2 inch British-born machinist, poised to become the city's leading socialist and the most consistent advocate of independent labor politics for over two decades; and the magnetic young orator Albert Parsons, a tramping typographer of old American stock, recently arrived with his African American wife, Lucy, from Texas, where they had been radical Republicans. Joining them in the city was Philip Van Patten, the new American-born president of the WPUS.[5]

Because they could more effectively translate socialist ideas into an American republican idiom, the new WPUS leaders enabled socialists to offer credible leadership to the strike. On Monday the party issued a leaflet that asked Chicago workingmen, "Have You No Rights?—No Ambition? No Manhood"? Using labor reformer rhetoric, the leaflet accused the liberals, whom it called "money lords," of conspiring to restrict the vote to propertyholders and return to a monarchy, and it cast the party in the role of the defenders of the Republic. The leaflet also spoke of the need to protect "the fruits of your labor." On Monday evening the socialists staged an enormous mass meeting that attracted between 10,000 and 30,000 excited and angry workers. The eloquent Albert Parsons was one of four speakers on four different rostrums who addressed the crowd. He began with a pointed metaphor any of his listeners would have understood. In an ironic allusion to the Grand Army of the Republic (the post–Civil War veterans' organization and mainstay of the Republican party) he addressed his listeners as the "Grand Army of Starvation." With a free-labor faith that Andrew Cameron would have shared, he continued, "While we still have the Republic we still have hope." Meanwhile, other speakers, including members of the audience, rallied the crowd and were repeatedly interrupted with chants of "Pittsburgh" and wild applause. The rally ended with Van Patten's calling for workers to organize trade unions, to join the WPUS, and to demand the eight-hour day, a 20 percent wage increase (to make up for recent pay cuts), and government takeover of the railroads and telegraphs. In fusing class militancy and traditional American political language, the demands represented a new appeal that promised to transcend the rift between labor reformers and German socialists.

Without waiting for the socialists the strike began in earnest the next morning. A group of Michigan Central switchmen led by John Hanlon, a discharged railroad hand with "chinwhiskers and a pipe in his mouth," ranged along the lakefront rail tracks calling men out at the different freight yards and depots. At one firm some men did not want to quit because their pay cut had been restored. Hanlon asked if the restoration applied to all the employees on the line. When told that it did not, he gave a response that typified the spirit of the day: "They were working for the rights of all," and work must cease until the wages were restored to all.

By this time the strike had spread beyond the railroads. A group of Bohemian lumbershovers commenced a strike for the third year in a row and tried to shut down the brickyards and stoveworks as well. By the afternoon bands of workers and teenagers roamed up and down the heavily industrialized North Side and West Side, closing factories and shops. Many employees struck of their own volition, but just as often proprietors closed for the day before their employees could call a strike. The crowds were exuberant, like being "out on a holiday" noted one disapproving reporter. One band even stopped at Fortune's Brewery, where an anxious owner dispensed free beer. Press accounts often referred to the crowd as "hordes of ragamuffins, vagrants, saloon bummers, and generally speaking the dregs of the population," but the account of one paper suggested that many crowds were little more than "roaming committees of strikers." Given the sharp decline of trade union organization during the depression, it makes sense that many workers would have resorted to this mode of action. For example, Thomas J. Morgan led a machinist delegation from the Illinois Central Railroad shops, where he worked, to present demands to the company superintendent. George Schilling played the same role for an impromptu delegation of coopers.[6] The striker characterization also applied to many of the teenagers, who made up about half of all crowds.

During the afternoon the WPUS issued a circular that called for something that labor reformers had avoided since 1867: a general strike for the eight-hour day and a restoration of wage cuts. The circular called on workers to appoint delegates to a provisional strike committee and in the meantime to "keep quiet" until an orderly strike could be planned. Though sixty delegates met that evening to form a strike committee, police clubbed, shot at, and dispersed a large outdoor rally of workers. It was the first instance of repression and set a pattern for police violence that intimidated the WPUS and prevented it from organizing an orderly and effective general strike, such as the one socialists directed in St. Louis that week. Meanwhile, Parsons was fired from his job and summoned to city hall, where the police chief and Board of Trade businessmen browbeat and threatened him with lynching if he took an active role in the strike.

That night trade unionists and labor reformers convened for the first and only time. At a meeting of the Labor League, an independent organization of trade unionists, they endorsed the rail strike but, as in 1872, declined to sanction a general walkout, instead advocating repeal of the Specie Resumption Act and free coinage of silver.

On Wednesday, July 25, the strike continued where it had left off on Tuesday, the main industrial areas of the city. By now it was clear that authorities would not refrain from challenging crowds. Responding to pressure from the business community, Mayor Heath mobilized the militia and called on "the better class of citizens" to arm itself and enroll as special police to preserve order. After a large meeting of businessmen in the afternoon, organizers formed two armed companies of Civil War veterans, and well-off citizens formed "patrols" in at least five wards. Police attempted to disperse crowds wherever they appeared, but roving bands of workers seemed to coalesce, disappear, and reappear at random, leaving many police officers with bloody feet by the end of the day for their troubles.

Meanwhile, the city council, perhaps mindful of the 1873 demands for bread or work and the response of the People's party, considered at the urging of Frank Lawler, labor's spokesman in the city council, an ordinance to enable the city to undertake a public works project to employ the unemployed. But any possibility that workers could have been propitiated or that the strike could have been orderly was dashed by the escalating violence. The response of the unskilled laborers, factory hands, and unemployed to the repression was hinted at by the words of one Irish boathand who addressed a crowd of dockworkers. He denied that he was a "loafer" (as the press would have it) by showing the audience his horny hands and then asserted that they were not an aimless mob: "We know what we're fighting for and what we're doing. We're fighting those God damned capitalists. . . . Let us kill those damned aristocrats!" Late in the afternoon two regiments of the U.S. Army arrived fresh from the Dakotas, where they had been battling the Sioux. From a "red war" on the plains, they had returned to fight a different "Red War" in Chicago.[7] The bronzed veterans were cheered by downtown clerks, but as they marched to their armory, they were jeered by a working-class crowd from Canal Street. That evening sixteen policemen exchanged shots for fully two minutes with a crowd of fifteen hundred gathered at the railyards. Then the police fled. The actions of the crowds had gone beyond a strike and had become, in the words of the historian Norman Ware, "almost . . . a revolution without revolutionary intent."[8]

On the third day the scene of confrontation shifted to immigrant working-class neighborhoods along South Halsted Street, where at least five thousand men, women, and children, many of them Bohemian lumbershovers, lined the street. Police chased one crowd south of the Sixteenth Street viaduct; when it turned, they emptied their revolvers into the mass. "Although men were seen to drop away at every minute the mob dragged or carried them away at the instant." Having expended their ammunition, the police fled for their lives. When they were trapped on the south side of the street after a gang of roughs had raised the bridge, they were almost "annihilated"; but a boy lowered the bridge, and the cavalry rode to their rescue. The battle of Halsted Street reached its climax when five hundred stockyard workers, who had begun a strike the previous day, set out from Irish Bridgeport along Archer Avenue to join the Bohemian lumbershovers, behind a Fenian banner and a sign reading "Workingmen's Rights." "When the police called on them to disperse," wrote a reporter, "they vowed they would rather die than return." An hour-long battle ensued for control of the Halsted Street bridge, which ended when a squad of police reinforcements arrived.[9]

A more typical reaction of the ten thousand people that reporters estimated lined Halsted Street that afternoon was guerrilla warfare. When mounted cavalry approached, a crowd might part and then close behind it, many throwing stones and pieces of wood and coal. Women constituted at least one-fifth of every gathering in the neighborhoods that day according to the *Chicago Times*. Called "amazons" by reporters, women brought men stones in their aprons or attacked cavalry themselves by filling their stockings with stones and swinging them over their heads.

That day a number of trades, including the coopers, stonecutters, and tailors, tried to hold meetings. The police, however, were making no distinctions between rioters and the proverbial "honest workingmen." They attacked and dispersed all gatherings, most notably a meeting of three hundred cabinetmakers and their employers at Turner Hall, where police shot and killed one worker. A judge later termed the police action a "criminal riot."[10] For years to come Chicago's labor movement would bitterly recall the "Turner Hall incident."

By Friday the city was an armed camp, and mobile crowd actions had become almost impossible without instant opposition. Though many places of employment, including the railroads, remained closed until the following week, the strike lost its momentum without crowd action to enforce it. Police violence had taken a terrible toll: approximately thirty were killed—the true number could not be reported since many were buried at night in lime pits south of the city—and another two hundred were wounded.[11] Not one policeman or militiaman was killed.

If the casualty lists published in the newspapers can be taken as an indication of the identity of the rioters, at least 45 percent were boys, nineteen and under. A slight majority had Irish names, and almost all the rest were German, Polish, or Bohemian. Virtually all the riot victims whose residences were identified came from three South Side wards around Halsted Street; 42 percent, however, came from the Sixth Ward, and 22 percent of these were from the largely Bohemian portion of the ward, near the lumberyards.

The 1877 strike presented a study in contrast to the 1867 strike. First, the sequence of events in 1877 reversed that of 1867. Instead of beginning as a strike of skilled craftworkers followed by the temporary joining in of unskilled workers, the 1877 strike began with railyard hands and lumbershovers and then mushroomed into a more general walkout, whose backbone included workers from the packinghouses, foundries, iron factories, brickyards, docks, and lake ships. Only in its later stages did the 1877 strike involve the trade unions of skilled workers. Second, the two strikes faced very different reactions from the city establishment. In 1867 employers and civic leaders in both parties sought to propitiate the concerns of labor reformers, whom they recognized as part of a broader free-labor, antislavery coalition. By 1877 a liberal, largely Republican establishment faced a riotous strike led by socialists, a group it hated and feared. By the second day of the strike authorities not only took a confrontational stance toward crowd actions and strikes called by the trade unions but also mobilized many respectable citizens to fight what was almost a class war. This contributed to an unprecedented level of class divisiveness and bitterness in the years to come. Finally, in contrast to the 1867 strike, the strikes of 1877 left the city's workers with a vivid experience of wider solidarity and empowerment as a class, seeming to promise that ethnic and skill divisions would be surmounted. Instead of serving as a high tide from which labor action would recede, 1877 seemed to whet the appetite of Chicago working people for new and more inclusive forms of solidarity and action.

The Rise of the Knights of Labor and the WPUS

The 1877 strikes made it clear to leaders of the local labor movement that new forms of organization were necessary to incorporate the unskilled laborers and factory hands who had taken to the streets and presented demands without formal organization. As a result, by early August many trade union–based labor reformers began joining the more inclusive Knights of Labor; at the same time the socialists, who had been a political force in the city since 1874, began to sink deep roots in the trade unions. As the two organizations competed for the mantle of labor reformers, the socialists were able to appropriate the legacy of 1877 and lead local labor's second great foray into independent politics. The Knights remained a secret, shadowy organization, of little consequence.

The first Chicago Knight was secretly initiated into the order in May 1877, when Charles Lichtman, the grand secretary of the Knights, lectured in the city. The Knights had been founded in Philadelphia in 1869 by nine skilled garment cutters and at first differed little from other craft associations. The fledgling Knights of Labor was distinguished only by its mania for ritual and secrecy (which one of its founders, Uriah Stephens, adapted from fraternal orders) and its willingness to "amalgamate" with other crafts much in the manner of a trades assembly. During the depression years, when the new order began to take in miners in the western coal districts of Pennsylvania, the Knights began a transition—which it never quite completed—from a multicraft organization to a class organization.[12]

When Lichtman arrived in Chicago, he was introduced not as a Knights of Labor officer but as a former chief of the Knights of Saint Crispin. Before he left, Lichtman secretly initiated Richard Griffiths, a local Crispin leader, into the Knights of Labor. That the Crispins should appear as the immediate forerunner of the Knights in Chicago is of the utmost importance, for it stood out among labor organizations of the period for its advanced position on labor solidarity and labor reform. Founded by male shoe workers in 1867, the Knights of Saint Crispin was the first national labor organization to bring together workers of all skill levels. There was also a parallel Daughters of Saint Crispin founded in 1869. In Chicago German custom-shoe workers founded a Crispins' local in 1869. That same year it drew in a large number of shoe workers from factories to form a multiethnic lodge, headed by Griffiths. Despite being involved in a lockout and a strike, the local Knights of Saint Crispin was opposed to class conflict and on three different occasions formed cooperative boot and shoe factories. In 1870 the local Crispins were alone among Chicago unions in supporting an independent labor slate, thus dissenting from Andrew Cameron's policy of presenting names to the candidates of the two parties.[13] Nationally, the shoemakers were the largest single craft to supply members to the Knights of Labor, and David Montgomery tells us that ten Crispin leaders "were renowned" in the Knights.[14]

In the four months following his initiation, Griffiths remained a lonely Knight. But three weeks after the July strikes in 1877, Griffiths assembled "50 leading trade unionists" in the back of the little cigar shop that he had opened following the loss of his job during the 1874 lockout of the Crispins. Those attending the August 19 meeting included John O'Neil, another Crispin leader; John Swerdtfeger, a socialist freethinker; the engineer leader William Ponsonby; and Thomas Kavanaugh, an officer in the machinists and blacksmiths' union and a leader in the Labor League. The result was the formation of Local Assembly 400, the first local assembly of the Knights in Chicago.[15]

Because the press could not report on this secret meeting, it is not clear what prompted the fifty trade union leaders to affiliate with the Knights of Labor that August. There is, however, much evidence that local trade unionists had begun reorienting their thinking as early as 1875, when Andrew Cameron muted his earlier admiration of English new model unions and began to criticize their exclusivity. The adoption of benefit provisions and the affiliation of local unions with national unions—the preferred solutions in the early 1870s—had not been able to stem a drastic decline in union strength during the depression. During the 1877 strikes and crowd actions Chicago trade unions had distinguished themselves primarily by their absence, and trade unionists may have been hurrying to catch up with rank-and-file workers who had conducted rough-and-tumble collective bargaining in the streets.

No doubt many labor leaders viewed the Knights of Labor as a progressive alternative to trade unions. In one of his last editorials in October 1877, before the *Workingman's Advocate* went under, Cameron admitted that "our unions are isolated and consequently are weak and inefficient. They have no common ties, no sympathy in common with each other and are indifferent to each others' success and elevation." The socialist George Schilling echoed Cameron that same month: "Trades organizations in the past had always acted separately, and when one appealed to the others for aid, they were met with a cold shoulder." A local Knights historian recalling that period noted that the "principal feature" of the Knights that "aroused the curiosity of all laboring men was that it embraced all who earned an honest living without distinction of trade. In comparison to the old English system of trade unions, this was a new departure."[16]

The great lesson taught by the strikes seems to have been solidarity, though it went under the name of "amalgamation." *Amalgamation* was actually an English trade union term present in the name of two of its most powerful unions that had Chicago branches. As early as 1866 Cameron had advocated "amalgamation" or consolidation of various trades unions in an industry where an "identity of interest" existed. In 1872 the bricklayers' union spoke of amalgamating different trades in one building trades council. By 1877, possibly because of the absence of a local trades assembly and a national trades congress or federation, amalgamation also came to mean the cooperation or confederation of different trades whether or not they were industrially related.[17] In this instance amalgamation promoted mutual aid during strikes and common legislative interests. Amalgamation was therefore an ambiguous, catchall term whose meaning ranged from a council federating different craft organizations to what was later called "industrial unionism" and even "one big union."

During the late 1870s labor agitators and representatives of unions did not draw these distinctions. Whether socialist or trade unionist, after 1877 they all pronounced in favor of the universal blessings conferred by amalgamation. George Schilling thus argued that wage increases could "never be accomplished by independent trade union action. Amalgamation was essential so that when the bosses made an assault upon one trade, the whole wage class would recognize it as an assault against them." Andrew Cameron editorialized in favor of uniting "all branches of labor" in one "grand organization," with rules and regulations to be made "not by unions but by a 'district council.'" The cigarmakers, led by the socialist Sam Goldwater, proclaimed themselves in favor of "One Grand Union of All Trades."[18] The Knights and socialists did differ on the vehicle for amalgamation, for while the Knights pointed to their own order as the means for achieving solidarity, the socialists from around the country founded the International Labor Union (ILU) in early 1878 to unite the skilled and unskilled and workers of all races and nationalities. The ILU, however, confined its activities to eastern textile workers and was never a factor in Chicago.[19]

Like others at the time, national and local Knights leaders made a grand claim that perfect amalgamation would make strikes unnecessary. As Griffiths put it during an organizing campaign among painters, "Had the men of '77 and the Crispins been part of the [Knights of Labor], the result would have been totally different. The strike of '77 would have never taken place because the men would have obtained their wants without it." It was this belief that prompted the Knights to create a national resistance fund at its first general assembly in January 1878. A year later Uriah Stephens reported that the fund was growing so fast that "in the future strikes that have been the great bane of the former efforts in arbitration matters will be of rare occurrence and irresistible and effectual when they must be resorted to."[20]

Another characteristic the Knights shared with trade unionists, though not with the socialists, was the practice of secrecy. The order's secret ritual was embodied in the Adelphon Kruptos, or AK, which, until published by an enterprising reporter in 1886, remained a well-kept secret. The AK described an elaborate set of signs, handshakes, spoken phrases, and a test of membership that allowed Knights to identify themselves without using the order's name. A further guarantee of secrecy came with the rule that a prospective Knight could not be initiated unless a member had known the individual for at least twelve months, and the candidates' character had to be approved by a three-person investigating committee.[21]

As Norman Ware, the Knights' first great historian, pointed out, the Knights "differed little" from the trade unions in this respect. The Crispins were a secret organization until the 1880s. In 1878–79 one of two carpenter unions in the city used secret signs and passwords. Richard Powers, president of sailors' union and one of the city's foremost trade unionists, advised new unions to keep their meetings secret. Whatever its Masonic origins or religious connotations, secrecy was based on practical trade union needs. Secrecy served to protect the members of a fledgling labor organization from being fired and blacklisted by employers. Ritual complemented secrecy by serving as a cultural glue among the members, binding them together in a special fellowship regardless of background and separating them from nonmembers.[22]

Without doubt the greatest departure of the Knights of Labor from the trade union model lay in the way its characteristic building block, the local assembly (LA), could take different forms. The Knights LA not only enlisted wageworkers but also encouraged farmers, shopkeepers, small manufacturers, and professionals to join. Only lawyers, bankers, and "rum-sellers" were excluded. Because of this rule, the Knights seemed to give form to the unity of the "producing" classes and array them against the "parasitic," or nonproducing, classes. Yet in practice the Knights remained almost wholly a working-class organization, a characteristic enforced by the rule that three-quarters of all LA members must at all times be wageworkers.[23]

In seeking to embody the principle of amalgamation and to overcome the insularity common to craft-specific organizations, the Knights, although they organized workers into locals limited to a single craft, encouraged prospective members to join "mixed local assemblies." Many mixed assemblies consisted of workers of different crafts or occupations whose numbers were too few to form a craft local. In this case, the mixed local assembly served as a temporary "holding tank." Other mixed assemblies were formed on the basis of industry, ethnicity, gender, or political belief. There thus came to be farmer LAs, packinghouse LAs, Bohemian LAs, women's LAs, and anarchist or greenback LAs. Each LA was affiliated with a district assembly. Though in later years some district assemblies were limited to a single craft and covered the nation, thus approximating national trade unions, most were geographically narrow and brought many different LAs under one umbrella. Theoretically, though not always in practice, the LAs were subject to the authority of the district assemblies, while these in turn were subject to the general executive board, which implemented the policies and laws passed by the yearly general assembly.[24]

Knights doctrine enjoined all LAs to "educate" workers, which began with political reform and extended to the oft-repeated injunction to advance "the cause of humanity." Specifically, the Knights' constitution ordered every LA to teach that "the right to life carried with it the right to the means of living," and the 1879 general assembly ruled that all assemblies had to spend at least ten minutes discussing broad labor questions, including "political economy." On the face of it the Knights' commitment to political discussion and action contrasted sharply with the traditional trade union ban on political discussion. But for the Knights politics meant social questions considered on the basis of first principles, not partisan issues. The Knights' constitution thus forbade the conversion of any local or district assembly into a political party. When it is remembered that it was common for trade unions to send delegates to such political reform bodies as the Labor League and to work for such legislative goals as the abolition of prison contract labor and the eight-hour day, the difference in attitude between the Knights and the trade unions was one of a division of labor. Because labor activists viewed the Knights of Labor as an educational organization, it was common for trade unionists (and sometimes socialists as well) to hold dual membership, in both their trade union (or party) and the Knights of Labor. Beyond education, both the Knights and the trade unions shared the distinction between political education and partisan politics, and when Knights and trade union leaders participated in partisan politics, they did so as individuals.[25]

If all their characteristics are considered in historical context, the Knights of Labor can be understood as part of a class response to the 1870s depression and to the 1877 great upheaval. Labor leaders of all stripes sought new ways to induce cooperation among the crafts and incorporate unorganized and unskilled industrial workers. Though their unique organizational form stamped them as a potential rival to the trade unions—a potential realized after 1886—their approach to amalgamation, secrecy, strikes, and politics did not differ from that of most trade unionists.[26]

The Socialists and Chicago's Labor Movement, 1877–79

The roots of the Knights in current trade union and labor reform thought and practice explain why labor activists viewed it as an organizational vehicle that could be used to reorganize and revivify the local labor movement. But the continuing depression, which kept unions weak, and the impact of the July strikes shifted the terrain to electoral politics, which favored the socialists in the WPUS. While the Knights shared with the socialists a commitment to labor politics, their commitment to secrecy and nonpartisanship kept them from openly espousing political positions, much less constituting themselves as a party, as the WPUS did. In addition the socialists enjoyed greater prestige among workers because they had championed the cause of the strikers in July, thus partly enabling them to overcome the impression that they were "un-American." As George Schilling wrote, "Our influence as a party . . . both in Chicago and elsewhere was very limited, until the great railroad strike of 1877." "The labor question," he continued, "rose to a grave and important question and secured us the public ear."[27] On the other hand, many of the union leaders who had founded the Knights of Labor were identified with the People's party and had therefore lost prestige among workers.

Another reason for the relative strength of the WPUS was its grounding in the German crafts and German neighborhoods, where since 1874 they could rely on an increasingly dense network of community institutions to nurture their political action. In 1876 Cameron reported that it was "to the eternal disgrace of our American, Irish, English, and Scotch mechanics" that they owned no buildings of their own, while the Germans had "their lyceums, their reading rooms, their lecture and music halls, their gymnasiums, where they can meet in social concourse, discuss the political situations, enjoy an intellectual treat and improve their physical conditions." By the late 1870s the socialists sponsored a thriving movement culture—paralleling that of the Social Democratic party in Imperial Germany—that included an array of newspapers, periodic parades, picnics, meetings, militia drills, and celebrations of the Paris Commune, which mobilized members and sympathizers in German, Bohemian, and Scandinavian immigrant working-class neighborhoods.[28]

The political implications of 1877 were apparent in August, when the WPUS and the Labor League each held mass meetings to discuss independent political action in the upcoming county elections. For the Labor League, which since 1876 had lobbied for the abolition of prison contract labor and for other labor objectives, the decision to enter electoral politics put them in competition with the Greenback party as well as the WPUS. The Chicago Greenbackers, by then reduced to a handful of labor leaders, small businessmen, politicians, and ideologues, sought an alliance with labor, as did other Greenback parties that were reviving in parts of the United States affected by the strikes. But Labor League trade unionists, led by Thomas Kavanaugh of the Knights and John McGilvray of the stonecutters' union, kept their group—renamed the Workingmen's Industrial party (WMIP)—independent. They hoped to rival the WPUS, their real competitor.[29]

The platforms of the WMIP and the WPUS were remarkably similar. Both advocated passage of an eight-hour law, repeal of conspiracy laws, and abolition of prison contract labor. The WPUS, however, advocated nationalization of the railroads and telegraphs, while the WMIP, though it dropped its support of the Greenbacker's interconvertible bond system, called for repeal of the Specie Resumption Act and free coinage of silver. These were real differences but of minor importance in a local election. Both parties also appealed to 1877 strikers on the basis of class. Kavanaugh spoke openly of wanting "to unite workingmen as a class," described himself before one meeting as an "ablebodied tramp," and attacked the police superintendent for authorizing indiscriminate assaults on workers at the Halsted Street viaduct. The Irish Fifth Ward (Bridgeport) Club, the party's main base, even decided that "no politician nor holder of an office could become a member of the club and that no person who had served as special policemen in the late riot could become a member."[30]

So close were the parties, whose aims Schilling called "identical," that they were on the verge of merging, and it was understood that the WMIP would adopt the socialists' nationalization plank. But underneath it all the WMIP leaders, especially the Irish contingent from Bridgeport, were part of an older tradition of labor politics in which the formation of an independent labor party was simply a tactic to secure a better deal from one of the two major parties before election time. Therefore, instead of merging with the WPUS, the WMIP fused with the Democratic party at its convention on October 24. The convention was packed by twenty-five "strikers" (political thugs) from County Clerk Herman Lieb's office. In the fusion bargain Kavanaugh and another Knight received Democratic nominations, but much of the rest of the WMIP, led by McGilvray, the typographer Andrew Adair, and the manufacturer Charles Dixon, refused the bargain and instead joined a tiny group of Greenbackers led by Cameron to form a Greenback-Labor body, a local branch of the national Greenback-Labor party.[31]

The November election proved a disappointment to labor politicians. Despite the infusion of the labor issue, the anticorruption reform impetus from the early 1870s still predominated in the city as a whole. The press charged that the WPUS would be another version of the People's party in using county funds for a public works project to provide jobs and boodle. The Republicans swept the election, defeating the last of the People's party officeholders. The Greenback-Labor party won 1,673 votes, up from the 251 votes the presidential candidate Peter Cooper had won in 1876 but still far short of the WPUS total of 6,592 votes, 13 percent of the vote.[32]

What did the socialist vote mean asked the press? "In plain English," answered the *Chicago Times,* "it represents the riots." About half of the WPUS votes came from the Fifth, Sixth, and Fourteenth wards, the heart of the riot district. In the Fifth and Sixth wards, along South Halsted Street, the socialists polled, respectively, 21 percent and 21 percent of the total vote; in the North Side's Fourteenth Ward, they polled 41 percent, up from 16 percent in April of 1877. To the *Chicago Tribune,* the only satisfaction was that there was no danger of natives "becoming infected with Socialistic heresies."[33]

The party's vote owed chiefly to German and German-speaking Bohemian immigrants. In the Fifth Ward 63 percent of its votes came from the area east of Halsted Street and north of Thirty-first Street, the only part of the ward with a plurality of German residents. The lowest socialist total, although still high for the city, came from the area adjoining the stockyards, which was about 70 percent Irish.[34] The Sixth Ward's Bohemian community of Pilsen adjoining the lumberyards, which was the quintessential riot district, delivered the highest socialist vote of any precinct in the city. Only months before the strikes and riots the community had turned en masse away from the Catholic church and toward the leadership of prosocialist freethinkers. In 1878 Police Lieutenant Vesey, whose district encompassed Pilsen, reported that "nearly every one" of the workingmen in the area was "a strong socialist."[35]

The socialists' growing strength among German-speaking immigrants implied an acceleration in the transformation of the German political culture in the city that had been going on during the depression. Anton Hesing's People's party had mobilized German workers on the basis of temperance and community issues, and this political tie had proven impervious to the early efforts of the socialists. Voters interested in reform could vote only Republican. The socialists' actions in the 1877 strikes, their resistance to the lure of office, and their firm stand against a deal with the Democrats had won them respect among local workingmen. Their vote for the WPUS in November of 1877 demonstrated that a large segment of German-speaking workingmen could be mobilized behind a program combining anticorruption reform and class demands. That the WPUS did not realize this at first can be seen in their neglect of a county reform program. That lack was soon remedied, and it became the secret of the party's subsequent success.

The newfound strength of the socialists might have also stemmed from a decline in the social base of support for the People's party. Not only had reformers learned to sidestep the temperance and Sabbatarian issues, but during the depression it had proven impossible to appropriate funds for projects, like a courthouse, that would generate political support. Meanwhile, the hopes that poor workers might own a home, which had been given some reality by the speculative mania that had gripped the city in the early 1870s, had been undermined by the shortage of capital during the depression. In early 1877 the largest local savings banks, which had been patronized by workers, collapsed. As the prospect of owning a home receded, so did local community issues on which ward politicians thrived. In their wake came a resurgence of industrial and workplace issues that the socialists and the Knights, each in their own way, sought to mold into a class consciousness. Finally, the makeup of Chicago's German working class was changing significantly with the rise in the percentage of unskilled workers, thus undermining the base of Hesing's People's party.[36]

For all these reasons the socialists began to exercise a loose hegemony over Chicago's labor movement in late 1877, much as in Germany, where even before 1878 the Social Democratic party treated unions as simply training schools for the political tasks of the party. When it was founded, the American WPUS had supported independent trade unions, but with the great strikes of 1877, the party's initial electoral successes, and the continuing difficulty of organizing unions during the depression, the political action socialists gained complete control of the national party apparatus. The new leadership declared that trade unions should be organized "upon socialist principles" and subordinated to the goal of achieving party electoral success.[37]

This position held sway in Chicago, where Thomas J. Morgan and other socialists sought to bring the remnants of the city's trade unions under the wing of the WPUS. At a December 1 meeting of delegates from eighteen unions, Thomas Kavanaugh opposed Morgan by arguing that rather than form a new assembly, unionists should join the Amalgamated Workmen, the public name for the secret Knights of Labor. Morgan countered that since Kavanaugh's organization (specifically, LA 400) did not represent workers by trade, membership in it was "an individual matter." George Schilling, though himself a Knight, opposed secrecy, arguing that "coming out and declaring the rights of labor was the only way to assure success." Other Knights present replied that without secrecy a new trades assembly would be controlled by politicians and that an additional labor body would disunite local labor. After further sparring, the delegates voted 8-7 to establish the open Trade and Labor Council. Two weeks later delegates elected Albert Parsons as the assembly's first president.[38]

The rivalry between the Knights and socialists for allegiance of the city's trade unionists continued through the summer of 1878, by which time the Workingmen's Party of the United States had changed its name to the Socialist Labor party (SLP). In March, at a meeting to reorganize the machinists and blacksmiths' union, Morgan and Kavanaugh clashed again. By the end of the year Morgan held two top offices, his ally was president, and Kavanaugh was left on the sidelines. A more critical test of influence came during the shoemakers' strike of July–August 1878. Crispins Lodge No. 7, consisting of bottomers or peggers of boots, demanded a 20 percent increase in their piece rates to make up for a wage cut in 1877. When large manufacturers responded with a threat to import Chinese labor from the West, John O'Neil, a Crispin officer and a leader of Knights LA 400, promised aid from the Amalgamated Workmen, and apocalyptic rumors emanated from the Knights. "All say that with the organization that is inaugurated all over the country," reported the *Tribune*, "a general strike is liable to break out at any time which will sweep everything before it and all classes of employers who are not paying living wages will suffer the consequences." But it was the socialist-run Trade and Labor Council, not the Knights of Labor, that organized a mass meeting in support of the strike and in condemnation of the Chinese threat.[39]

Throughout the year there was other evidence that socialists were consolidating their hold over the few reviving unions. The largely German Cigarmakers Union No. 14, which had elected the socialist Sam Goldwater as president in 1877, adopted in April 1878 a preamble incorporating the SLP platform calling for abolition of the wage system. The furniture workers' union, another predominantly socialist union, led by German SLPer William Stahlknecht, participated in major strikes in 1878 and 1879, which the *Tribune* blamed on a large contingent of "socialist cabinetmakers." The SLPer George Schilling headed up the coopers' union, and the SLPer Henry Stahl led the upholsterers' union. The silver gilders, clothing cutters, and wood carvers were also probably under socialist influence for they met at SLP headquarters. Even the labor reform–oriented typographers' union selected Albert Parsons as its Trade and Labor Council delegate in 1878, and in 1879 it elected Ed Irwin, an SLPer, as its president.[40]

The prestige of the socialists was such that a small but significant number of other trade unionists and labor reformers, mainly printers, actually joined the SLP in the late 1870s. Among the first to join were Andrew B. Adair, the chief compositor of the *Daily News*, and Charles G. Dixon, both of whom had split from Kavanaugh's WMIP when it joined the Democrats. Darwin Streeter, a printer who was the president of the Trade and Labor Council in 1879, publicly declared himself a "socialist" in favor of government control of all machinery.[41]

Yet it is important to distinguish between the organizational hegemony of the Socialist Labor party and the ideological assimilation of socialist beliefs. According to P. H. McLogan, a local typographers' union leader who was later second president of the Federation of Organized Trades and Labor Unions, the socialists "were reinforced in great measure by the trade unionists, who considered themselves oppressed. . . . I know a great many trade unionists who voted the socialistic party's ticket: I know I did it myself by way of protest." This was particularly true of the Irish, who, according to the socialist leader Benjamin Sibley, constituted at most 10 percent of the party's membership but contributed 25–30 percent of the party's vote. A *Times* survey of the SLP found that even the Irish who joined the party were socialists only "in the sense of office-seeking and not with reference to the principles of socialistic science."[42]

There was also a difference between party leaders' conceptions of socialism and those they conveyed to trade unionists. Such leaders as Morgan, Sibley, and Goldwater were staunch state socialists, advocating that the national government replace capitalists in the ownership and control of the means of production, communication, and distribution. These men saw trade unions as a means of educating and mobilizing members, but, like some Knights, they viewed unions as ultimately incompatible with social reform. When socialists spoke before workers, their version of socialism came out differently. Albert Parsons, speaking before a large picnic in 1878, denied that socialism meant "state sovereignty" and defined it simply as "self-government on the part of individual men and individual women" to control their labor. SLP leaders often used the word *cooperation* as a synonym for socialism or in a phrase, such as "state cooperation." Though strongly criticized by Morgan and Goldwater as futile and diversionary, the goal of cooperative enterprise remained popular among many German as well as American trade unionists, particularly those with strong craft traditions. William Stahlknecht, with the support of the *Arbeiter-Zeitung* editor Paul Grottkau, led a group of socialist furniture workers to found a cooperative furniture factory in 1878, and in 1879 the cabinetmakers formed six more cooperatives. Within the cigarmakers' union those who favored cooperatives openly opposed state socialism.[43]

Despite their victories over the WMIP in local politics and over the Knights in the formation of the Trade and Labor Council, the socialists had only a superficial hold over Chicago's labor movement, particularly its English-speaking sector. In their attempt to dilute the meaning of state socialism, SLP leaders tacitly admitted this. SLP strength was largely dependent on the weakness of local trade unions, which induced trade unionists to turn to electoral methods. It therefore should not be surprising that the SLP's hegemony over Chicago labor was short-lived.

The Decline of the SLP and the Rise of the Trade Unions

For two major reasons the year 1879 marked an important break in the SLP's political leadership in the city's labor movement. The rehabilitation of the Democratic party and the election of Carter Harrison as mayor brought a direct rival to the SLP for the allegiances of union voters. At the same time, the local economy began to revive, and workers' energies found an outlet in trade unionism and the eight-hour agitation, both of which met an accommodating embrace from local government. Together these developments precipitated a split in the labor movement, which then reunified under the auspices of trade unionists friendly to the Knights of Labor.

In the aftermath of the November 1877 election the socialists found themselves the center of public attention. Though the SLP had only about eight hundred members in 1878, the police claimed that the party had ten times as many. To many respectable native citizens, the most menacing development was the growth in numbers and public visibility of armed groups against the background of continuing unemployment and destitution among the city's working people. Taking the Turner Hall incident as its rallying cry, the Lehr- und Wehr-Verein had grown to more than two hundred members in 1878 and had begun drilling in public and protecting socialist picnics. They were joined by the smaller Bohemian Sharpshooters, the Jaeger Verein, and the Irish Guards. Though most English-speaking socialists sought to play down the threat of the workers' militia, Albert Parsons spoke for many German-speaking socialists who distrusted the electoral machinery. "If the police try to break up our meetings as they did at Turner Hall," asserted Parsons, "they will meet foes worthy of their steel. The social revolution began last July. The issue is made and sooner or later it must be settled." The threat was not taken lightly. The Citizens Association began raising $30,000 to sustain the local militia and agitate for the banning of public drilling. "It is useless to disguise the fact," editorialized the *Tribune*, "that the businessmen of Chicago are considerably alarmed at the possibility of trouble with the Communists this coming summer or fall." But the fear was not so much that riots would escalate into an armed confrontation but rather that the socialists would be able to direct the energies of workingmen into "a general strike."[44]

The SLP's public presence reached its zenith in the spring of 1879 when the party nominated the well-known German doctor Ernst Schmidt to run for mayor. A week before the election the attendance of forty thousand mostly German Chicagoans at an SLP anniversary of the Paris Commune testified to the enthusiasm and numbers the party had managed to garner since the great strikes. But Chicago's Democrats had been no less busy since the defeat of the People's party in 1877. Seeking to refurbish the Democrat's tawdry image, the "better elements," or "silk-stocking" wing, took control of the party's nominating process in March by preventing the "strikers" (party sluggers) from entering and stampeding the convention. The convention subsequently nominated the wealthy businessman Carter Harrison for mayor.[45]

Carter Harrison was a man of many contradictions. He had been a soft-money, People's party candidate for Congress in 1874 and had been nominated by the Greenback party for mayor the week before the Democrats endorsed him. But any thoughts of his being economically unsound were overshadowed by the fact that he was a respectable businessman, whose support of retrenchment allowed him to put on airs of being a reformer. His Democratic label, however, won him the backing of the party's ward politicians. Harrison was also on good terms with Mike McDonald, the city's gambling king who used the proceeds from his operation, "The Store," to finance the People's and Democratic parties. Harrison worked with McDonald, but because of his personal wealth he did not need to depend on him for campaign funds. Finally, his aloof stance on the temperance issue allowed him to win support from business moderates while neutralizing opposition from the city's "Puritans." Harrison was, in fact, a broker between most of the city's organized interest groups, and his effectiveness was aided by the fact that he was a charming and flamboyant Kentucky-born gentleman, who could be all things to all people.[46]

The final element in Harrison's coalition fell into place through his appeal to the Socialists, whose growing electoral presence turned into his most important strength. Through the fall of 1878 the SLP city vote maintained itself at 6,500, but the nomination of the respected Schmidt positioned the SLP to take advantage of German voters' concerns about the temperance associations of the Republican candidate. Though Schmidt finished a distant third to Harrison and his Republican opponent, the SLP registered an 85 percent increase of 5,500 votes over its fall total, winning 19 percent of the total vote. The bulk of the new SLP voters were probably many of the same liberal Germans who had become accustomed to bolting the Republican party over ethnoclass issues. If that was the case, these liberal Germans provided most or all of the margin of Harrison's 5,189 vote victory over his Republican opponent in the 1879 election. The German Republican exodus allowed the liberal (former Republican) German-Democratic Irish coalition that had been the basis of the People's party to reassert itself. Sidetracked in the process were the two aspiring goal-integrating elites of their respective classes, the Citizens Association and the Socialist Labor party.[47]

In a short inaugural address Harrison neatly summarized his diverse appeal. Decrying Chicago's "enormous" debt burden, popularly associated with the People's party, he declared at the outset that "I recognize but one science in finance. This is, to collect the revenues and to live within them." He promised businesspeople he would foster public sanitation and would not politicize the police department. Next he spoke of Chicagoans as "a cosmopolitan people aggregated from many nationalities" and made it clear that he would only "execute laws and ordinances" that would "do the greatest good to the greatest number," a veiled promise not to enforce the Sunday-closing law to the detriment of immigrant workers. Finally, the new mayor became the first to publicly grant legitimacy to the socialists by defending their right "to peaceably assemble," "speak," and "to keep and bear arms." "Some persons fear an organized resistance to authority in Chicago," observed Harrison, "I do not."[48]

Because Chicago remained a Republican city in national elections, Harrison realized that to maintain his hold on power he must either bring the German socialists directly into the Democratic fold or foster a strong socialist vote. He also needed the support of four SLP aldermen elected in 1879, because they held the balance of power in the closely divided council. Harrison therefore wooed the Socialists with unconcealed ardor. He appointed the defeated Schmidt to the public library board and the German SLP politico Joe Gruenhut to a position with the city's Health Department. He even gave the city's printing business to the SLP paper, the *Arbeiter-Zeitung*. When the state legislature outlawed public demonstrations by the SLP's militia, he arranged for the Lehr- und Wehr-Verein to march unharassed and for the arrest of one preselected militiaman to facilitate a test case in the courts. When members of the Bohemian Sharpshooters were arrested for firing at Irish toughs who invaded their picnic, Harrison arranged for their early release and defused public clamor for retaliation.[49]

In June 1879 a large faction of the SLP returned these favors by throwing their support to Judge William K. McAllister, a Democrat who had just declared the Vagrant Act unconstitutional. After McAllister was reelected, he decided against the police in a socialist suit arising from the Turner Hall incident. When the entire Democratic ticket was elected in June 1879, many gave credit to the Socialist vote. Within a week office hunters besieged city hall, claiming as their prime qualification that they were socialists. It was graphic evidence of the pull that patronage had on the SLP's constituency and the difficulty party leaders had keeping their members loyal.[50]

While Harrison worked his magic on the SLP and spurred a realignment of German voters into the Democratic party, the end of the depression stimulated a major resurgence of trade unionism. It began after an increase in building activity prompted building trades workers and brickmakers to demand wage increases. A brickmakers' strike was soon followed by walkouts by the cigarmakers, tanners, and coopers and finally a mammoth packinghouse workers' strike (which is discussed in detail in chapter 4). Almost all the strikes involved large numbers of previously nonunion workers, many of them unskilled; all were characterized by impressive unity across ethnic lines. Yet hardly any were aided by socialists.[51]

The decline of SLP influence was most obvious in the strikes of two SLP-run unions, the furniture workers' union and the cigarmakers' union. In June 1879 Albert Parsons led a segment of the party into an alliance with an assortment of labor reformers and trade unionists to form the Eight Hour League. Parsons, a recent convert to the doctrines of Ira Steward, viewed the movement for shorter hours as a prelude to revolution. Morgan and the political socialists, however, opposed heavy socialist involvement in the fight for the eight-hour workday, which they saw as a pedestrian demand and a diversion from more important electoral activity. At the urging of Parsons and the editor of the *Arbeiter-Zeitung*, the skilled cabinetmakers struck in July for the eight-hour day. The strike was weakened from the start by the unwillingness of unskilled machine hands and varnish men to join and by the stiff resistance of employers. Within the month the cabinetmakers resorted to an ill-fated cooperative, and a year and a half later what had been the strongest socialist union in Chicago barely existed.[52]

The SLP met a similar fate among the cigarmakers, who had one of the strongest socialist unions in the city. In 1878 three hundred cigarmakers participated in a socialist picnic. At the international union's convention that year Chicagoan Frank Hirth proposed that "all local unions" form themselves into "labor bodies upon the basis and platform of the Workingman's Party of the United States." Fearing that their local union would be turned into a "political club," Chicago's English-speaking cigarmakers seceded to form Local 14. In October 1878 both locals—which had only 140 members—attempted to provide leadership for a spontaneous strike of a thousand cigarmakers. During the strike the socialists condemned the international as a failure and were suspended. After the strike failed Local 11 dwindled to eleven members and two years later joined Local 14.[53]

Their dwindling base led some SLPers toward closer cooperation with the Knights of Labor, which had begun to grow. Five months after the failure of the Workingmen's Industrial party a group of politically minded, English-speaking labor reformers, including the Greenbackers Benjamin Goodhue and Charles Dixon, joined with English-speaking SLPers, led by Thomas J. Morgan, to create the mixed LA 522. Their goal was to foster labor politics in the city independent of the two major parties. By the end of the year six more assemblies formed, making enough to form District Assembly 24, with Richard Griffiths as its master workman. By January 1879 the Chicago Knights had 629 members, and by October 1879 it had 1,018 members, more than the SLP had. All but one of the Knights LAs were mixed, which suggests that instead of being part of the trade union revival itself, the order served as a nonsocialist political alternative for reform-minded English-speaking trade unionists. From 1878 through 1880 many individual Knights, including Griffiths, offered support for the Greenback-Labor party, though as an organization the Knights of Labor confined itself to lobbying for labor bills in the state legislature.[54]

The trade union revival, the growth of the Knights, and the victory of the union-friendly Harrison administration made possible a brand of interest group politics that left the SLP increasingly isolated from its constituency. Immediately after Harrison's election Frank Lawler, a Democratic alderman, intervened in a local stonecutters' strike by asking the city council to forfeit the city contract of a firm that was resisting the union. Lawler received backing from Greenbackers, out-of-office Democratic politicians, and, very reluctantly, the SLP aldermen. As a party, however, the SLP refused to support Lawler and warned stonecutters against ties with "ring" politicians. The entire affair redounded to the credit of Lawler and the Democrats.[55]

During this period socialists won three notable legislative victories in city and state government. In the midst of the furniture workers' strike the city council, without a murmur of dissent, passed a socialist resolution to enforce the 1866 eight-hour ordinance in the Department of Public Works. At the same time, the state legislature, under the leadership of the SLPer Sylvester Artley, passed a bill establishing the Bureau of Labor Statistics. Finally, in late October the city council passed an ordinance written by Morgan authorizing factory and workshop inspection. Between 1878 and 1882 five SLP aldermen distinguished themselves for relentlessly supporting the expansion of municipal responsibilities and expenditures for the health and education of young children, including construction of new school buildings and the abolition of child labor under the age of twelve; the manufacture of gas by the city; the improvement of safety at railroad crossings; and the establishment of public baths, public water closets, and public reading rooms.[56]

But these victories did little to enhance the political reputation of the SLP, for the city council had acted mainly to accommodate the trade union strike wave of that year. The victories also shifted the political tasks of the labor movement from agitation for legislation to administrative enforcement and created a scramble to fill the new patronage offices. This task required intense lobbying with the city and state and deal making with the party leaders, a job best undertaken by the nonpartisan Trade and Labor Council and the Eight Hour League rather than a minority political party.

Unlike SLPers, trade unionists and labor reformers were not averse to taking jobs with the administration. By the end of the year at least seven prominent leaders in the greenback movement and the Eight Hour League had jobs, including Lars P. Nelson (assessor's office), William V. Barr (milk inspector), Benjamin Goodhue (city clerk's office), Michael Haley (construction superintendent, later election judge), David McGann (clerk), Thomas Kavanaugh (Cook County Hospital engineer), and Dan Gleason (sewer inspector). To Morgan and other SLP leaders this was a sordid betrayal of the working class, but for labor reformers it was an alliance with a friendly soft-money Democrat and a local base from which to pursue Greenback politics and labor legislation.[57]

For trade unionists pragmatic politics with Harrison promised its own benefits. During the state election campaign in the fall of 1879, Darwin Streeter, president of the Trade and Labor Council, publicly endorsed a Democrat rather than an SLPer for county treasurer, because the Democrat had endorsed labor reforms and stood the best chance of winning. In this election the SLP received only 3,913 votes, down from the 11,183 votes Schmidt had received only seven months earlier. When Morgan charged Streeter with prostituting himself to the Democrats, Cornelius McAuliffe, a printer, reportedly shot back that the Trade and Labor Council "had been run as the fag end of the Socialistic Labor Party and he wanted no more of it." Several meetings later Morgan struck back at his enemies by proposing that delegates of secret bodies that were not unions—meaning the Knights' mixed LAs—be banned from the Trade and Labor Council. On this issue Morgan won the support of other delegates who felt that the order acted as a secret caucus within the council and their trade unions. This precipitated a secession of the Knights and other antisocialist trade unions, including those of the typographers, painters, shoemakers, sailors, and butchers. Though Morgan charged his enemies with being Democratic shills, the printers, who led the opposition to him, were actually reverting to an older trade union tradition—adopted by labor reformers after 1869—of shelving independent politics when it promised no returns and working within one or both of the two major parties to win labor legislation, patronage appointments, and police neutrality during strikes.[58]

That SLP leaders could not sustain the party under such circumstances was evident in the deepening dissension in its ranks over whether or how to cooperate with Democrats and Greenbackers. The longstanding dispute over whether to emphasize political or trade union action cut across ethnic lines. Led by Paul Grottkau and supported by a few English-speaking SLPers, such as Parsons, the majority of Germans were restive at the party's support for Judge McAllister and any cooperation with the Greenbackers. Still, Morgan's political action faction, which included most English-speaking members, the small French section, and a minority of the Germans, continued to lead the party. Speaking for this faction when he resigned from the party in October

1879, Benjamin Sibley criticized German members for being ignorant of American institutions, refusing to learn English, yet demanding immediate revolution. Sibley spoke of the need to "Americanize socialism."[59]

Socialist factionalism culminated in 1880 with a series of open defections from Morgan's leadership. In March Tim O'Meara and Dan Sullivan, Irish SLPers from the Sixth Ward, refused to back the SLP candidate. Instead they threw their support to a nonpartisan Democrat who had a chance of defeating the notorious machine alderman Ed Cullerton. Fearing defeat, Democrats in the city council denied SLPers their election judges in that ward—an action that all knew opened the way to unchecked election fraud. This prompted SLP aldermen to walk out of the city council in protest. But with the SLPers gone Democrats were able to deny the party its election judges in all wards except the Fourteenth and Fifteenth, which were former Republican wards where a strong SLP vote aided Democratic candidates. In the spring aldermanic election, the SLP vote was decimated. SLP candidates lost close races in the Sixth Ward and the Fourteenth Ward, leading many Germans to the conclusion that they had been "counted out" by fraud.[60]

The crisis of the SLP created the conditions for a reunification of the two factions into which the Trade and Labor Council had split the previous year. In May the Socialists, Knights, and trade unionists created the Trades and Labor Assembly under the compromise leadership of Albert Parsons, who by this time opposed independent socialist politics. The vice president was P. H. McLogan, a printer who advocated working within the major parties. The dissatisfaction within the SLP came to a head in September, when Morgan and the local leadership sought allies outside the party by deciding to send delegates to the local Greenback-Labor convention. This was the final straw for those opposed to political action. Disillusioned with electoral politics, 70 percent of the party's Germans, led by Paul Grottkau, seceded. Thereafter, the SLP faded into obscurity under the name of the Chicago Labor Union, while its erstwhile membership drifted toward anarchism.[61]

The swift demise of the SLP in Chicago after 1878 followed because its success was premised to a large degree on temporary developments: the carryover of class feeling from 1877; the weakness of trade unionism, especially among English-speaking members; the secrecy of the Knights of Labor; and the corruption of leading labor reformers. All of these factors were absent or much less important by the early 1880s. But another complex of factors, external to the party and to the labor movement, was also critical, what has been called "the structure of political opportunity."[62] In local politics the most implacable obstacle to independent labor politics was not the influence of upper-class businessmen but the rule of machine politicians who packed caucus nominating meetings, stuffed ballot boxes at election time, and offered support for labor's program and immigrant workers' community demands. The victory of business-backed reformers over the People's party between 1874 and 1877 temporarily thwarted the ability of machine politicians to do these things and put in power a more repressive regime that caused those voters animated by both reform and working-class issues to turn to the SLP as the only viable alternative. The resurgence of machine politics under Harrison's leadership destroyed the external opportunity structure for SLP political success at the very time that the return to prosperity and developments internal to the labor movement undermined its social bases.

In the first half of the 1880s the Knights of Labor stepped in to fill the vacuum created by the demise of the SLP. To understand how this occurred requires a shift in focus from the German-speaking crafts and neighborhoods in which the SLP had been based to the Irish neighborhood of Bridgeport and Irish-based labor politics.

Notes

1. *Chicago Tribune,* Apr. 24, 1877 (first quote), July 24, 1877 (second quote).

2. Eric Foner, *Reconstruction: America's Unfinished Revolution, 1863–1877* (New York: Harper and Row, 1988), 512–20; Robert Bruce, *1877, Year of Violence* (1959; reprint, Indianapolis: Quadrangle Books, 1970), 20–26, 28–42; *Chicago Tribune,* June 15, 1877, July 1, 1877 (quote).

3. *Chicago Tribune,* Feb. 23, 1877.

4. Unless otherwise indicated the account of the 1877 strikes and riots comes from a compilation of newspaper accounts in the *Chicago Tribune, Chicago Inter-Ocean, Chicago Evening Journal,* and *Chicago Times* from July 21, 1877 to Aug. 4, 1877. See also Richard Schneirov, "Chicago's Great Upheaval of 1877," *Chicago History* 9 (Spring 1980): 3–17. On the strike nationally, see Bruce, *1877, Year of Violence;* and Philip S. Foner, *The Great Labor Uprising of 1877* (New York: Monad, 1977).

5. George A. Schilling, "A History of the Labor Movement in Chicago," in *Life of Albert R. Parsons with Brief History of the Labor Movement in America, Also Sketches of the Lives of A. Spies, Geo. Engel, A. Fischer and Louis Lingg,* ed. Lucy E. Parsons (Chicago: Lucy E. Parsons, 1903), xxii.

6. *Chicago Inter-Ocean,* July 26, 1877 (quote); Ralph William Scharnau, "Thomas J. Morgan and the Chicago Socialist Movement, 1876–1901" (Ph.D. diss., Northern Illinois University, 1970), 33.

7. For the boathand's quote and the headline "Red War," see *Chicago Tribune,* July 26, 1877; Indians were called "red rebels" by *Chicago Daily News,* July 13, 1877.

8. Norman J. Ware, *The Labor Movement in the United States, 1860–1895: A Study in Democracy* (New York: Vintage Books, 1929), 45.

9. *Chicago Tribune,* July 27, 1877 (quote).

10. *Chicago Legal News,* Mar. 5, 1879.

11. These figures are estimates based on comparing newspaper accounts and names of casualties.

12. *Journal of United Labor,* May 1883; Ware, *Labor Movement in the United States,* 22–50. For an excellent recent summary of the rise of the Knights as a more inclusive organization, see Kim Voss, *The Making of American Exceptionalism: The Knights of Labor and Class Formation in the Nineteenth Century* (Ithaca, N.Y.: Cornell University Press, 1993), 46–63.

13. *Workingman's Advocate,* May 19, 1877, May 14, 1870, Oct. 22, 1870, Oct. 29, 1870, Mar. 11, 1871, Apr. 1, 1874; *Chicago Tribune,* Apr. 18, 1874; Mary H. Blewett, *Men, Women, and Work: Class, Gender, and Protest in the New England Shoe Industry, 1780–1910* (Urbana: University of Illinois Press, 1990), 168. On the antebellum origins of the Knights of Saint Crispin, see Alan Dawley, *Class and Community: The Industrial Revolution in Lynn* (Cambridge, Mass.: Harvard University Press, 1976), 77–78, 93–96, 141.

14. Ware, *Labor Movement in the United States,* 200–201; David Montgomery, *Beyond Equality: Labor and the Radical Republicans, 1862–1872* (New York: Vintage Books, 1967), 199.

15. *Knights of Labor,* Jan. 29, 1887.

16. *Workingman's Advocate,* Oct. 13, 1877; *Chicago Tribune,* Oct. 31, 1877; *Knights of Labor,* Jan. 29, 1887.

17. *Workingman's Advocate,* May 19, 1866, Oct. 26, 1872.

18. *Chicago Tribune,* Oct. 31, 1877, Apr. 29, 1878; *Workingman's Advocate,* Oct. 13, 1877.

19. Philip S. Foner, *History of the Labor Movement in the United States,* vol. 1, *From Colonial Times to the Founding of the American Federation of Labor* (New York: International Publishers, 1947), 500–504.

20. *Progressive Age,* Jan. 21, 1882; *Record of the Proceedings of the Third Regular Session of the General Assembly Held at Chicago, Ill., Sept. 2–6, 1879,* 54, Reel 67, in *Terence Vincent Powderly Papers, 1864–1937, and John William Hayes Papers, 1880–1921: The Knights of Labor* (Glen Rock, N.J.: Microfilming Corporation of America, 1974).

21. Versions of the AK can be found in the Powderly-Hayes Papers. See also Henry J. Browne, *The Catholic Church and the Knights of Labor* (Washington, D.C.: Catholic University of America Press, 1949), 359–62; and Robert E. Weir, *Beyond Labor's Veil: The Culture of the Knights of Labor* (University Park: Pennsylvania State University Press, 1996), 10, 38–39, 43, 60–61.

22. Ware, *Labor Movement in the United States,* 155, 243; *Chicago Tribune,* Sept. 12, 1879, Dec. 24, 1879, July 8, 1879.

23. *Record of the Proceedings of the Third Regular Session of the General Assembly Held in Chicago,* 161; Victoria Hattam, *Labor Visions and State Power: The Origins of Business Unionism in the United States* (Princeton, N.J.: Princeton University Press, 1993), 114, 122–31, argues that the Knights viewed themselves as producers; for a different view with which I concur, see Voss, *Making of American Exceptionalism,* 86–87.

24. *Record of the Proceedings of the Third Regular Session of the General Assembly Held in Chicago,* 181; Ware, *Labor Movement in the United States,* 25–26, 29–

30. Jonathan Garlock, comp., *Guide to the Local Assemblies of the Knights of Labor* (Westport, Conn.: Greenwood, 1982).

25. *Record of the Proceedings of the Third Regular Session of the General Assembly Held in Chicago*, 147.

26. In this interpretation I draw on the most recent scholarship on the Knights of Labor. See most notably Leon Fink, *Workingmen's Democracy: The Knights of Labor and American Politics* (Urbana: University of Illinois Press, 1983), 1–15; Richard Jules Oestreicher, *Solidarity and Fragmentation: Working People and Class Consciousness in Detroit, 1875–1900* (Urbana: University of Illinois Press, 1989), 78–79, 90–92, 108, 188; Voss, *Making of American Exceptionalism*, 73–75, 85–89; and Gregory S. Kealey and Bryan D. Palmer, *Dreaming of What Might Be: The Knights of Labor in Ontario, 1880–1900* (New York: Cambridge University Press, 1982), chap. 3. For a similar contemporary evaluation, see Frederick Engels, *The Labor Movement in America* (New York: Louis Weiss, 1887), 6–8.

27. Schilling, "History of the Labor Movement in Chicago," xxiii.

28. *Workingman's Advocate*, Jan. 8, 1876. On the Socialist Labor party movement culture, see *Chicago Tribune*, June 17, 1878; Bruce C. Nelson, *Beyond the Martyrs: A Social History of Chicago's Anarchists, 1870–1900* (New Brunswick, N.J.: Rutgers University Press, 1988), 146–52; Hartmut Keil and John B. Jentz, eds., *German Workers in Chicago: A Documentary History of Working-Class Culture from 1850 to World War I* (Urbana: University of Illinois Press, 1988), 151–346; and Hartmut Keil, ed., *German Workers' Culture in the United States, 1850 to 1920* (Washington, D.C.: Smithsonian Institution Press, 1988). On Germany, see Vernon L. Lidtke, *The Alternative Culture: Socialist Labor in Imperial Germany* (New York: Oxford University Press, 1985).

29. Foner, *Great Labor Uprising of 1877*, 219–30.

30. *Chicago Tribune*, Aug. 24, 1877, Aug. 26, 1877, Aug. 30, 1877 (quotes).

31. Ibid., Sept. 7, 1877, Sept. 24, 1877 (quote), Oct. 26, 1877, Oct. 27, 1877, Oct. 30, 1877, Nov. 1, 1877; Edward B. Mittelman, "Chicago Labor in Politics, 1877–1896," *Journal of Political Economy* 28 (May 1920): 407–18.

32. *Chicago Tribune*, Sept. 14, 1877, Sept. 16, 1877, Nov. 7, 1877.

33. *Chicago Times*, Nov. 8, 1877; *Chicago Tribune*, Nov. 8, 1877.

34. For ethnic breakdown within wards, see *Chicago School Census, 1884* (Chicago: Board of Education, 1884); on Fifth Ward politics, see *Chicago Tribune*, Sept. 9, 1877.

35. *Chicago Tribune*, Apr. 27, 1878 (quote); Richard Schneirov, "Free Thought and Socialism in the Czech Community in Chicago, 1875–1887," in *"Struggle a Hard Battle": Essays on Working-Class Immigrants*, ed. Dirk Hoerder (De Kalb: Northern Illinois University Press, 1986), 121–42.

36. Homer Hoyt, *One Hundred Years of Land Values in Chicago* (Chicago: University of Chicago Press, 1929), 117–27; *Chicago Tribune*, May 1, 1877; *Progressive Age*, Apr. 16, 1881; John B. Jentz, "Class and Politics in an Emerging Industrial City: Chicago in the 1860s and 1870s," *Journal of Urban History* 17 (May 1991): 232–33.

37. Mary Nolan, "Economic Crisis, State Policy, and Working-Class Formation in Germany, 1870–1900," in *Working-Class Formation: Nineteenth-Century Patterns in Western Europe and the United States*, ed. Ira Katznelson and Aristide R.

Zolberg (Princeton, N.J.: Princeton University Press, 1986), 384–85; Foner, *History of the Labor Movement in the United States,* 1:493–94 (quote); Selig Perlman, *A Theory of the Labor Movement* (1928; reprint, New York: August M. Kelley, 1968), 82–86, 194–95.

38. *Chicago Daily Inter-Ocean,* Dec. 2, 1877; *Chicago Tribune,* Dec. 2, 1877 (quotes), Dec. 16, 1877.

39. *Chicago Tribune,* July 23, 1878, Aug. 7, 1878, Aug. 9, 1878 (quote), Aug. 10, 1878, Aug. 25, 1878.

40. *Cigarmakers Official Journal,* Feb. 4, 1877; *Chicago Tribune,* Sept. 17, 1877, Apr. 29, 1878, May 13, 1878, Sept. 25, 1878 (quote), Sept. 27, 1878, May 21, 1879, Dec. 29, 1879; *Chicagoer Arbeiter-Zeitung,* June 7, 1879; Albert Parsons, "Autobiography of Albert Parsons," in *The Autobiographies of the Haymarket Martyrs,* ed. Philip S. Foner (New York: Monad, 1969), 35.

41. *Chicago Tribune,* July 16, 1880 (Adair); Scharnau, "Thomas J. Morgan and the Chicago Socialist Movement," 107 (Dixon); U.S. House of Representatives, *Investigation by a Select Committee of the House of Representatives Relative to the Causes of the General Depression in Labor and Business; And as to Chinese Immigration,* 46th Cong., 2d sess. (Washington, D.C.: Government Printing Office, 1879), 112–13 (Streeter quote).

42. *Report of the Committee of the Senate upon the Relations between Labor and Capital* (Washington, D.C.: Government Printing Office, 1883–85), 1:585 (first quote); U.S. House of Representatives, *Investigation,* 159–60; *Chicago Times,* June 28, 1879 (second quote). The 10 percent figure for the Irish is the same figure estimated in Nelson, *Beyond the Martyrs,* 87.

43. *Chicago Tribune,* Mar. 11, 1878, June 17, 1878 (Parsons quote), Mar. 31, 1879, Aug. 27, 1879, Sept. 28, 1879, Apr. 2, 1879, July 29, 1879, see esp. editorial, July 30, 1879.

44. Ibid., Apr. 25, 1878, Apr. 26, 1878 (Parsons quote), Apr. 28, 1878, May 12, 1878 (editor's quote); Bessie Louise Pierce, *A History of Chicago,* vol. 3, *The Rise of a Modern City, 1871–1893* (Chicago: University of Chicago Press, 1957), 3:252–55. According to the best membership estimates available, at its height in Mar. 1879 the SLP had 870 members. See Nelson, *Beyond the Martyrs,* 80, 140.

45. *Chicago Tribune,* Mar. 16, 1879, Mar. 23, 1879.

46. Ibid., Mar. 16, 1879, Mar. 22, 1879, Mar. 26, 1879, Mar. 30, 1879 (Puritan quote), Apr. 2, 1879.

47. Ibid., Apr. 3, 1879; on Harrison and Germans, see interview with editor of *Neus Freie-Press,* July 2, 1879.

48. *Chicago Tribune,* Apr. 29, 1979.

49. Ernst Schmidt, *He Chose: The Other Was a Treadmill Thing,* ed. and trans. Frederick R. Schmidt (Santa Fe: Vegara, 1968), 122–23; *Chicago Tribune,* June 7, 1879, June 25, 1879, Oct. 28, 1879, Apr. 18, 1879, Sept. 3, 1880, Sept. 8, 1885; *Chicago Times,* Aug. 28, 1884; Claudius O. Johnson, *Carter Harrison I: A Political Leader* (Chicago: University of Chicago Press, 1928), 150.

50. *Chicago Tribune,* July 7, 1879.

51. Ibid., Mar. 19, 1879, May 19, 1879, May 21, 1879, May 25, 1879, Dec. 16, 1879–Jan. 12, 1880.

52. Ibid., June 9, 1879, July 12, 1879, July 13, 1879, July 19, 1879, Aug. 25, 1879, Sept. 15, 1879, Feb. 21, 1881.

53. *Cigarmakers Official Journal,* June 17, 1878, Sept. 15, 1879, Apr. 10, 1880, May 10, 1880; *Chicago Tribune,* Nov. 4, 1878, Oct. 10, 1879, Oct. 14, 1879; Eric L. Hirsch, *Urban Revolt: Ethnic Politics in the Nineteenth-Century Chicago Labor Movement* (Berkeley: University of California Press, 1990), 47–49 (quote on 48).

54. *Fourth Biennial Report of the Illinois Bureau of Labor Statistics* (Springfield: H. W. Rokker, 1886), 187; *Record of the Proceedings of the Third Regular Session of the General Assembly Held in Chicago,* 115; *Chicago Tribune,* Mar. 18, 1878, Nov. 7, 1878.

55. *Chicago Tribune,* Sept. 17, 1878, Mar. 18, 1879, May 27, 1879, July 30, 1879, Aug. 23, 1879.

56. Ibid., June 11, 1879, July 1, 1879, Oct. 28, 1879; "Ordinances, Resolutions, and Orders Introduced in the Chicago City Council by Socialist Aldermen during the Years, 1878 to 1882," Carter Harrison II Papers, Newberry Library, Chicago.

57. *Chicago Tribune,* June 6, 1879, July 28, 1879, Oct. 27, 1879, Jan. 5, 1880, Oct. 26, 1880, Sept. 25, 1886.

58. Ibid., Oct. 30, 1879, Nov. 6, 1879, Nov. 14, 1879 (quote), Jan. 16, 1880, Jan. 23, 1880, Feb. 27, 1880.

59. The internal lineup relies on a letter by George Schilling quoted in Nelson, *Beyond the Martyrs,* 68–69; *Chicago Tribune,* Oct. 7, 1879 (Sibley quote).

60. *Chicago Tribune,* Mar. 12, 1880, Mar. 13, 1880 (quote), Mar. 16, 1880.

61. Ibid., May 7, 1880, May 22, 1880; John R. Commons, David J. Saposs, Helen L. Sumner, E. B. Mittelman, H. E. Hoagland, John B. Andrews, and Selig Perlman, *History of Labour in the United States* (1918; reprint, New York: Macmillan, 1946), 2:286–90; Nelson, *Beyond the Martyrs,* 70; Paul Avrich, *The Haymarket Tragedy* (Princeton, N. J.: Princeton University Press, 1984), 47–51.

62. J. Craig Jenkins, "Resource Mobilization Theory and the Study of Social Movements," *Annual Review of Sociology* 9 (1983): 546–47; Doug McAdam, *Political Process and the Development of Black Insurgency, 1930–1970* (Chicago: University of Chicago Press, 1982), 40–43.

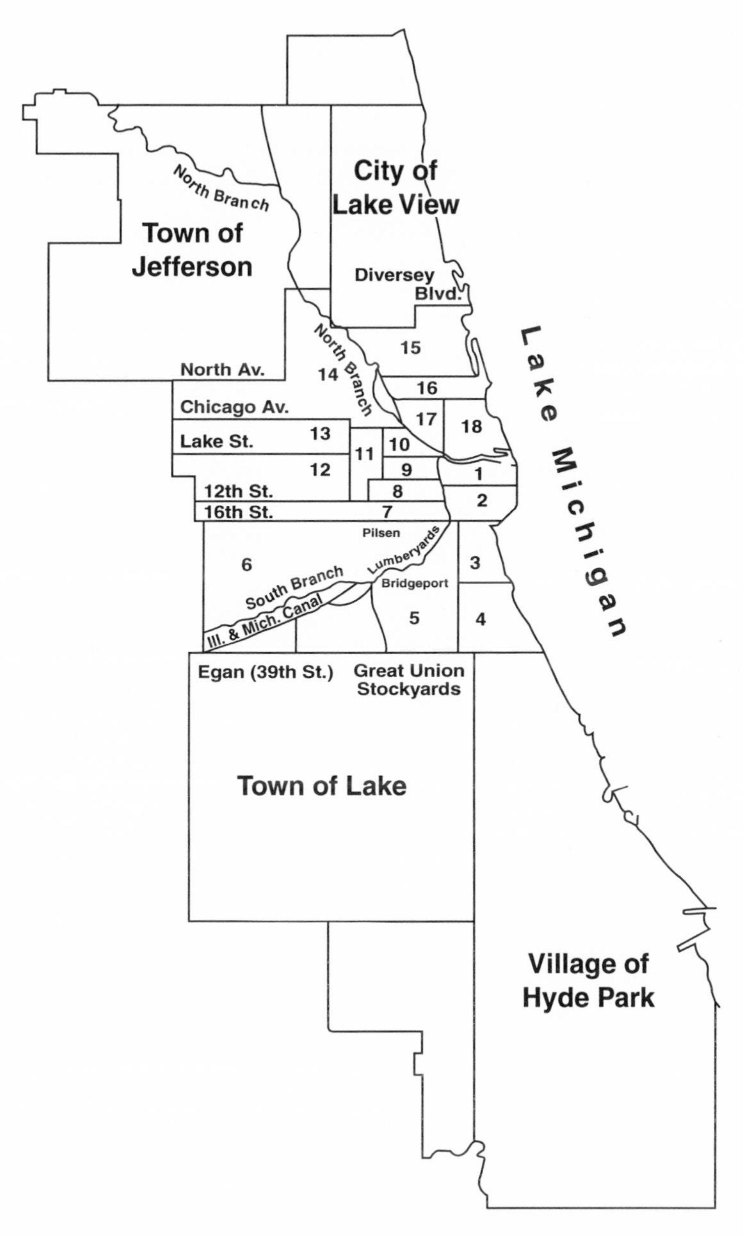

Chicago Wards and Adjoining Towns, circa 1877.

Sketch by C. and A. Sears, which was published in *Harper's Weekly,* August 18, 1877. This depiction of the Battle of the Viaduct during the 1877 railroad strike inaccurately depicts the militia firing on a crowd of workers along Halsted Street. In fact, the police were responsible for almost all fatalities. (Courtesy of the Chicago Historical Society)

WORKINGMEN OF CHICAGO!

HAVE YOU NO RIGHTS?—NO AMBITION?—NO MANHOOD?

Will you still remain disunited while your masters rob you of all your rights as well as all the fruits of your labor? A movement is now inaugurated by the Money Lords of America to allow only property-holders to vote! This is the first step to Monarchy! Was it in vain that our forefathers fought and died for LIBERTY?

They have now passed a law authorizing the arrest, as a vagabond, of any workingman out of employment who may wander in search of work,—no warrant being necessary.

They have passed a law making it a criminal offense for workingmen to combine for an advance of their wages—an offense punishable by imprisonment and fine! The right of employers to combine in reducing our wages and bringing starvation and misery to our homes is protected by all the police and soldiers in the country! These aristocrats refuse to pay their taxes but demand all the improvements!

HOW LONG WILL YOU BE MADE FOOLS OF?

Every day—every hour, that we remain disunited, only helps our oppressors to bind more firmly the chains around us. Throughout the entire Land our brothers are calling upon us to rise and protect our Labor. For the sake of our wives and children, and our own self-respect, LET US WAIT NO LONGER! ORGANIZE AT ONCE!!

MASS MEETING on Market St., near Madison, TO NIGHT!

Let us act while there is yet time!

THE COMMITTEE, Workingmen's Party of the United States.

Handbill issued by the Workingmen's Party of the United States at the start of the 1877 railroad strike. The leaflet plays on the widespread concern that the American Republic was being corrupted by the growing concentration of capital. (Courtesy of the Chicago Historical Society)

Workers of the Horn Brothers Furniture Factory assembled just before the strike for the eight-hour day on May 1, 1886. Note the children in front and the woman in the upper right. (Courtesy of the Chicago Historical Society)

Haymarket Square, 1892, a center of wholesale produce distribution. Note the statue commemorating slain policemen in the center. (Courtesy of the Chicago Historical Society)

LIVING IN BONDAGE.
The Working Women of Chicago.
Read Tomorrow's Times.

The Chicago Times

LIVING IN SLAVERY.
The Working Girls of Chicago.
Read Tomorrow's Times.

VOL. XXIII. SUNDAY MORNING, JULY 29, 1888.—TWENTY PAGES. PRICE 5 CENTS.

Let Romance Rest.

Give Truth a Hearing.

Life Among the Slave Girls of Chicago

NO need to draw upon the imagination nor to indulge in fiction. A dreadful, damnable reality is presented to this community. European methods introduced, developing and expanding here, whereby the marrow is ground out of the bones, the virtue out of the souls, and the souls out of the bodies of the miserable, ill-fed, half-starved, underpaid, insulted, roughly-treated, and unprotected Working Girls.

Shocking Revelations

Resulting from an investigation put on foot by

The Chicago Times

Not a batch of sensational stories, in which names are fictitious and addresses are suppressed, but a series of articles which point to the men who are growing rich at the expense of human life and blood. *The Real Names and Addresses* of Chicago manufacturers who have established a slave trade; who have transformed honest labor into a bondage; who are practicing the arts of the Pharaohs upon the weak and defenseless women of the city; who are running

Organized Hells on Earth.

Places where virtue counts for nothing; where girlhood and womanhood are degraded; where moral and physical rottenness abound; where an ulcer is festering that will eat a hole through society. The entire sickening story will be told in this paper *without regard to persons or places.*

The First Installment Will Appear Tomorrow

The Grinding Process

Women working like slaves for 16c a day.

Long hours of toil with nothing but wretchedness to look forward to.

Rooms so crowded, girls must take short stitches to save elbow-room.

Costs 10 cents to get a seat in a church; can't afford it, and stays at home.

Why a girl of 13 crawled among the rubbish in search of pins.

Seven and a half cents for making a cotton-back Norfolk.

How the Jersey jacket is made and what it costs a girl to make it.

[illegible] to work at [illegible] made by it.

Demanding deposits that are never returned to the girls.

Villainous treatment of unfortunate women in a big factory.

One gets $15 for the work of over six months.

"A concern legally incorporated to grind the lives and souls out of women."

Walking miles to work and working eleven hours for 80 cents.

One cent a gross for cutting dress steels.

Four cents a gross for sewing buckles on bustles.

Three cents per dozen for basting and 4c for springing bustles.

Sixteen cents a day in a box factory.

A little girl who made all of 11 cents in a day.

Where Dr. De Wolf will find some work to do.

A loud and pathetic appeal for the interference of Christian charity and Christian law.

The Grinding Process.

Five cents a yard for making Seal Ball Fringe. Nine hours' work for 16¼ cents.

Working on a cloak two and a half days for 45 cents.

The pale-faced girls cry "If I didn't live at home I'd starve."

Working from June to get enough ahead to buy a pair of shoes.

How one proprietor "pulls the girls" and takes their little away.

Thirty-five cents for making a $35 cloak.

Paying an exorbitant price for a wrap and living three months on tea-dust and [illegible].

Twelve and a half cents a day made at a neck-tie factory.

The girls furnish their own thread and needles and are subjected to fines.

"The good Jew" whom the Rev. Mr. Goss mentioned.

Girls use their underclothing for towels.

The filthy and sickening scenes around and in the "toilet" rooms.

Brutal and cowardly treatment of the overworked employes.

Seventy-five cents per doz. for making overall pantaloons.

Something about 2-cent coffee and 2-cent ice-water.

Twelve cents per week for the use of a sewing-machine.

Blinding tears, but not a sympathetic glance.

Where the Woman's Protective Association might be useful.

THE WHOLE STORY
Beginning Tomorrow in *The Times* and running every day until finished.

And the articles will be published daily until the whole truth is made known to the public.

THE WHOLE STORY
Beginning Tomorrow in *The Times* and running every day until finished.

This front page of the July 29, 1888, *Chicago Times* kicked off a month-long series of exposés in 1888 on the conditions female workers endured in Chicago factories. The series played a critical role in mobilizing cross-class support for social reform in the city.

Cartoon from the *Rights of Labor,* July 16, 1892, depicting labor politicians pestering a bewildered "King Labor" for his vote. "God Pecksniff" is Charles G. Dixon, a perennial candidate for office on Labor party and fusion tickets.

Unlike the regular press, which depicted Eugene Debs and the American Railway Union (ARU) as tyrannizing interstate commerce, this July 4, 1894, *Chicago Times* cartoon portrays the ARU in the role of American revolutionaries battling a George Pullman in the role of King George.

CHAPTER 4

Chicago's Irish and the Knights of Labor

In the 1877–80 period the Knights of Labor in Chicago were still mainly an expression of the labor reform tradition dating to the 1860s. Consisting largely of individual craft union leaders and labor politicians, the order's mixed assemblies represented the political interests of the city's trade unions. Acting as their educational and political arm, the Knights oriented their activities in 1879–80 toward supporting the Greenback-Labor party and lobbying the legislature. When the Socialist Labor party declined, many English-speaking socialists joined the Knights' mixed LAs. By October 1880 the order's Chicago membership had increased 33 percent over a year earlier, and the number of assemblies increased from twelve to nineteen, all of them mixed.[1] The Knights resembled labor reformers in another way. Notwithstanding its professed interest in amalgamation, the order made no consistent attempt to act as the vehicle for the culture and direct action methods of unskilled industrial workers and outdoor laborers.

In the fall 1880 the Greenback-Labor party suffered a great shock when the vote fell from 6,000 in 1878 to 1,043 for the presidential candidate, James B. Weaver. At this point Chicago Knights membership declined by half, and the order entered a minor crisis. By 1883 it emerged from this crisis with a different leadership, a different constituency, and an organization open to industrial workers. How this transformation occurred requires, first, a look at Irish Bridgeport and why it became home to the "mass strike"; second, an examination of several cases of mass strikes and how the Knights related to them; and, finally, the effect of all this on Irish workers' notions of class.[2]

The Emergence of the Mass Strike

The phenomenon of the mass strike may be examined through four dimensions: its characteristic form, the social and economic background of its participants, its community context, and its characteristics in historical perspective.

The term *mass strike* is used here in a more restricted meaning than it had in its European origins.[3] The mass strike can be described as a strike undertaken by unskilled laborers who, in contrast to skilled craftworkers, could not rely on the withdrawal of their scarce skills to shut down their employer's enterprise. Faced with the prospect of thousands of potential strikebreakers, laborers often gathered in large crowds to reinforce their resolve, intimidate strikebreakers, and at times administer exemplary beatings. The mass strike was a transitional phenomenon, following the establishment of large-scale industry but preceding the reliance on unions that could offer access to experienced leadership, sick and death benefits, centralized strike funds, and coordinated tactics. Industrial workers who engaged in the mass strike generally followed an embryonic leadership but relied on the contagion of the moment to spread their strike. Where organization did exist, it was often ethnic- or community-based and was generally temporary and local in character. It was difficult for workers to sustain a mass strike beyond a week, and, especially during the depression, such strikes generally resulted in defeat. Yet, in a favorable business climate, mass strikes sometimes won temporary victories.

There is not an obvious answer to the question of who participated in these struggles. Mass strikers were not just industrial workers, nor was the mass strike simply a response to industrialism. Chicago was still largely a transportation center for the exchange of regional primary products for manufactured goods, and this work required heavy labor. These outdoor laborers were the focal point of the mass strike.

In 1881 the city workshop inspector, Joe Gruenhut, estimated there were twenty thousand "open-air" laborers in the city, working in the building trades; in the lumber, brick, stone, and coal yards; for the streetcars and steam railroads, and as teamsters. He could have added Chicago-based sailors to this group as well. Workers shifted easily from job to job within this constellation. For example, of the 400 members of the salt laborers' union, 250 also held cards in the lumbershovers' union. The brickmakers' union was organized by Pat Carey, president of the Laborer's Benevolent Society. The linchpin of interchangeability was indoor work in the packinghouses. Because most open-air work was seasonal, lasting from the spring through the start of winter, these laborers needed to find work in the winter, and this led them to the packinghouses and stockyards, which doubled their work forces in the peak winter months. According to one reporter nearly all packinghouse laborers were sailors, lumbershovers, and other seasonal workers. The first packinghouse workers' union was organized by Richard Powers, president of the sailors' union, who was joined by Pat Carey of the brickmakers' union.[4]

Many outdoor laborers found employment under the subcontracting system in which a captain contracted with a saloonkeeper or boardinghouse owner, who then paid wages to his men. Workers often felt obliged to spend part of their wages on liquor to keep their position. Those employed in this manner included the lumber vessel unloaders, coal heavers, and the Bridgeport iron-ore shovelers, whose union was actually led by saloonkeepers.[5]

Many aspects of outdoor work—heavy labor, subcontracting, casual labor, and reliance on community institutions—may appear preindustrial, but many outdoor laborers were involved in work processes that were undergoing very modern kinds of changes. For example, a series of labor troubles among coal unloaders led a major coal-yard owner to introduce team-run machinery as early as 1875. Even before this, he attempted to increase output by hiring a timekeeper, who measured the motions of his lead men. By the early 1870s many brickyards, particularly on the South Side, employed steam-run machinery, which had the effect of dividing the labor force into a small group of skilled workers and a larger group of unskilled laborers, who could easily be replaced. The packinghouses pioneered a detailed division of labor. Skilled butchers, whose work was highly specialized, constituted about 25 percent of the work force. As among other workers, the introduction of machinery resulted from labor unrest. In describing a steam-driven hog-scraping machine a reporter noted that "a strike among the scrapers led to the discovery of this handy machine which saves the labor of ten men."[6]

The third characteristic of the mass strike is that it was almost always embedded in an ethnic community in a small neighborhood. Herbert Gutman observed that small industrial towns in the Midwest, instead of dividing along class lines, often supported workers during strikes against the railroads, coal companies, and other outside monopolies. Gutman contrasted the organic unity of small communities with an environment "more often hostile toward workers" in large cities. As the Chicago School of Sociology demonstrated in the 1920s, however, urbanization produced not an undifferentiated city but a collection of distinctive neighborhoods and communities in which immigrants created their own ethnic subcultures based on face-to-face contacts in extended families and leisure, church, and consumption activities. In these semiautonomous ethnic neighborhoods ethnic, class, and sometimes religious identities often fused, allowing them to play the same role in labor conflicts that small towns played during the same period.[7]

The mass strike in particular was very much dependent on these neighborhoods. With poor and high-priced public transportation facilities, nineteenth-century workers tended to live close to their place of employment. In most industries a few absentee-owned large enterprises coexisted with a large number of smaller firms owned and operated by ethnic businesspeople. These firms, located in ethnic neighborhoods, were more responsive to community pressures, were less able to resist the economic pressures of workers, and provided associations that educated and politicized workers.[8]

The absence of strong labor organizations forced workers to rely on their neighborhood ties for support during strikes. Credit from a grocer or a boardinghouse owner became crucially important without a strike fund. Neighborhood saloons provided meeting places for embryonic unions; saloonkeepers, retailers, priests, and other neighborhood leaders functioned as union leaders; and roving teenage gangs aided in intimidating strikebreakers. Mass strikes also attracted significant numbers of women, who transgressed existing gender norms in militant actions against strikebreakers. Such community solidarity, based on ethnicity and neighborhood ties, set limits on the extent to which corporations and governmental bodies could employ force to crush workers' strikes. If the police lived in the community, they were often of little use to employers during a strike that generated community support. Conversely, strikes and social movements that were unable to draw on community loyalties were exceedingly vulnerable to repression and outside public opinion.

The fourth feature of the mass strike is that, as David Montgomery has argued, it was a way station between the community-based, highly political riot or crowd action in defense of popular customs and the deliberate union-called strike for limited economic aims. The mass strike contained elements of both. Its core consisted of wageworkers, whose actions were almost always sparked by work-related grievances that in later years would be articulated by trade unions, but neighborhood leaders and members were also involved. In the same vein of duality the aims of the mass strike were as much political as they were economic. For one thing such strikes usually drew in political authorities in the form of police, local magistrates, and ward politicians. Just as important, during the heyday of the mass strike in the 1860s and 1870s the legitimacy of the "monopolistic" employers and the nature of the national government itself were in question. Under these circumstances mass strikes, such as the draft riots of 1863 or the 1877 strikes, both of which confronted the U.S. Army and the nation's first corporations, bore some similarity to the European affairs in the early twentieth century with which the term *mass strike* is usually associated.[9]

An outstanding instance of the interplay between industrialization, outdoor labor, ethnic community formation, political aims, and leadership and the mass strike was evident among the Bohemian or Czech workers living in Pilsen.[10] Pilsen was a community of Czech and, to a lesser extent, German and Polish laborers and their families who worked in and around the lumber and coal yards and furniture and planing mills on the city's South Side. In 1875 and 1876 thousands of Czech lumbershovers were involved in strikes that included mass crowd actions and confrontations with police. At the same time, a small-scale political revolution was occurring in Pilsen. Many of the Czech intellectual and political leaders who had immigrated to the United States after the failed 1848 revolution in Germany and especially after the repression of workers' protests in the late 1860s were prosocialist freethinkers. With the decline of trade unions during the 1870s depression Czech workers not only resorted to the mass strike but also turned to local benevolent societies, many of which were affiliated with the freethinker-led Czech Slavic Benevolent Society of the United States. By 1877 there were five freethinker-led lodges in Pilsen.[11]

Not long before the July 1877 strikes a social and political upheaval occurred in Pilsen. For some time Catholic priests had refused to bury, baptize, or marry members of freethinker societies. In 1876, after a priest refused to bury a Catholic woman who had not confessed at her death, many local residents revolted against the church. In March 1877 freethinkers led a host of Czech benevolent societies, including some affiliated with the church, in founding the Bohemian National Cemetery. Perhaps 50–70 percent of Pilsen residents shifted their allegiance from the Catholic church to the freethinkers, who, with their control of the burial facilities, the ethnic press, the benevolent societies, and building and loan associations, made up the bulk of the neighborhood's new ethnic elite.[12]

Though several mass strikes occurred in Pilsen in 1875 and 1876, it was only in 1877 that Bohemians rose up as a community. One disapproving Republican wrote, "I was perhaps the only Bohemian in Chicago who opposed the powerful current of the aroused public feeling of my countrymen." Prokop Hudek, a Czech lawyer, freethinker, and WPUS leader who had tried to organize the lumbershovers in 1876, helped bail out rioters during the strike. After the strike the journalist Frantisek B. Zdrubek and other socialist freethinkers successfully organized large numbers of Czechs into the WPUS, and Pilsen, the riot center, became the socialists' stronghold in Chicago. Nonetheless, the demise of the Socialist Labor party and the support given to ethnic institutions by Mayor Carter Harrison led many freethinker leaders and their constituency to switch their affiliation to the Democrats by the early 1880s.[13]

A process very much like that occurring in Pilsen was going on in Irish Bridgeport in the last half of the 1870s. Located south and east of the south branch of the Chicago River, Bridgeport originated as a settlement of Irish and German laborers who had worked on the Illinois-Michigan Canal between 1836 and 1848 and had received their pay partly in land. In those early days most Bridgeport Irish settled between Archer Road—the major highway to Joliet—and the river, where they found unskilled work on the docks, lumber and coal yards, and grain storage houses. When the railroad arrived in the 1860s, the slaughtering and packinghouses moved south past Thirty-ninth Street to the stockyards district in the Town of Lake. As if drawn by that magnet, the shantytown of Bridgeport steadily expanded southward and eastward. By 1880 Bridgeport was bounded on the east by Stewart and on the south by Thirty-first Street (and still later by Thirty-ninth Street).[14]

The growth of Bridgeport paralleled the high tide of Irish immigration to Chicago. In 1860 there were only about 20,000 Irish in the city, but by 1870 this number had doubled. After a decade of depression there were only 44,000 Irish in Chicago in 1880. Ten years later, however, the number of Irish had risen to 70,000. By 1895 Bridgeport had been completely built up. A 1940 city survey concluded that 27 percent of all Bridgeport residences were erected before 1885 and 86 percent before 1895.[15]

The Fifth Ward, in which Bridgeport was located, was by no means exclusively Irish. In 1884 it was 39 percent Irish and 34 percent German. But if the area east of Stewart is dropped and Bridgeport proper is considered, the Irish portion rises to 48 percent, while the German portion falls to 29 percent. In the area closest to the stockyards Irish made up 70 percent of the population.[16]

The growth of Bridgeport in the 1870s and 1880s was closely matched by the expansion of the Catholic church. Irish workers were closely attached to the church, and as long as their labor activity was neighborhood-based, its success or failure rested heavily on the attitude of local priests. The first Catholic church in the community, St. Bridget's, was established in 1847 at Archer and Arch streets. In 1868 a mission from St. Bridget's set up Nativity Church, whose parish encompassed the stockyards district. In 1874 the new parish served only 250 families and 1,800 people. By 1885, however, the boundaries of the old parish included 80,000 Catholics and a set of thriving parochial schools. As a result, the Irish-born pastor of the church, Joseph M. Carten, had his parish broken up into more than a dozen parishes by the early 1880s.[17]

One of the most important parishes was the Town of Lake parish founded by Father Maurice J. Dorney of St. Gabriel's Church, completed in 1881. Known as the "King of the Yards," Dorney epitomized the great influence the church had over Irish Catholic stockyard workers. Famous for his ability to find employment in the stockyards and packinghouses for newly arrived immigrants and respected by both workers and the meatpacking magnates, Dorney was able to arbitrate several strikes. His funeral in 1914 was one of the largest ever witnessed in Chicago.[18]

Bridgeport's growth and much of its character stemmed from three industries: slaughtering and meatpacking, iron and steel making, and brickmaking. In 1860 there were only 146 workers employed in the city's provisions industry, but this number rose to 2,129 in 1870 and 7,180 by 1880. If those who found work only during the winter were added, the total would probably double. By 1885 the city had twenty-nine large packinghouses employing 25,000–30,000 men and boys. In Bridgeport itself there were two slaughterhouses, two packinghouses, a desiccating plant, a glue works, and a large meat-preserving works.[19]

Brickmaking underwent a similar expansion. The number of employees rose from 266 in 1860 to 1,093 in 1870, 1,472 in 1873, and 1,655 in 1880. According to an 1873 survey of the twenty-eight brickyard firms, twenty had been established in 1871 and 1872, during the rebuilding of the city. By 1873 many brickyards were concentrated between Twenty-second Street and the river, but by 1886 a large number were established just west of Bridgeport, especially along Ashland Avenue. Bridgeport also housed two large Chicago iron and steel mills. The Union Rolling Mills, located at Ashland and Thirty-first Street, employed 1,200 men by the early 1880s, while the Joliet Iron and Steel Company, founded in 1871, covered thirty-three acres along the river west of Halsted Street. Of all industries the mills paid the highest wages, leading one worker to recall that "the rolling mills made Bridgeport."[20]

There were many lesser sources of employment in and around Bridgeport. To the west were the lime quarries. Bridgeport laborers also worked as stevedores, or vessel unloaders, on the river docks and in the coal and lumber yards across the river in Pilsen. The Irish made up two-thirds of all railroad yardmen, many of whom worked just east and south of Bridgeport.[21]

More than any other ethnic group, the Irish made up the city's unskilled and reserve labor force. Relief and Aid Society reports consistently placed the Irish at the top of the list of those who required assistance.[22] The better-off "lace-curtain" Irish, many of them Protestants, lived on the North Side. Irish ship carpenters and iron molders and other Irish skilled workers lived in the Irish colonies on the Near West Side, represented by Frank Lawler, an ex-ship carpenter. Bridgeport was home to the "shanty Irish." In 1875 a reporter wrote that "there is probably as much real poverty in Bridgeport as anywhere in the town. It is also the haunt of the roughest characters." According to one resident, "Every kid knee high carries a pistol and it's quite the thing to let it off every now and then just for fun." In 1882 the *Tribune* observed that "Bridgeport has in Chicago become a generic term for smells, for riots, bad whiskey and poor cigars."[23]

The Emergence of the Mass Strike in Bridgeport

It is possible to trace the origins of the mass strike in Bridgeport back to 1867, but the crowd actions of the outdoor laborers in the brick, coal, and lumber yards date to 1875 and 1876. These same workers played a central role in the great railroad strikes of 1877, from which the model of the mass strike gains its fullest articulation. Throughout the strike Bridgeporters played a prominent role in the crowd actions and especially the violent confrontations with police. On the third day of the strike a contingent of Irish stockyard workers led by butchers behind a Fenian banner sought to join the Bohemians along Halsted and fought a ferocious battle with police. Several incidents testify to the community nature of the riots. Police arrested Mollie Cook and her two sons for firing at police from their home. In Bridgeport proper a local grocer, Miles Clynch, led a crowd of several hundred workers against the police. Among the prominent occupational groups of strikers were the brickmakers, coal heavers, sailors, and packinghouse workers, all with a heavy Irish membership. Not surprisingly, a majority of the riot casualties identified by the press had Irish names.

The 1877 strikes had the effect of more sharply distinguishing working-class neighborhoods, notably Pilsen and Bridgeport, from more respectable neighborhoods. These neighborhoods served as a secure base from which workers could undertake a revival, and in many cases a beginning, of union organizing. In the year after the great strikes it is possible to detect in Bridgeport the stirrings of organization among the outdoor laborers who had played so prominent a role in them.

Pat Carey, who worked as a brickmaker in the summer and as a packinghouse worker in the winter, organized the first protective union among the brickmakers on May 4, 1878. It numbered 2,542 members a year and a half later. The sailors' union, which had dissolved during the depression, revived on March 28, 1878. According to Richard Powers, president of the union, the 1877 strikes, "although detrimental to some, gave stability and backbone to others. . . . It was then that many of the unions now existing . . . were organized." In May 1879 the union struck twice, finally winning a uniform wage of $2.50. By then the organization claimed 4,000 men throughout the Great Lakes, and members were required to "wear the union badge." A charismatic speaker, Powers assumed a leading role in organizing local unions among Irish workers throughout the city, among them the freighthouse workers, the horseshoers, and even African American dockworkers. By 1881 Seamen's Hall, located at 99 West Randolph Street, had become to many unions the main alternative meeting place to the socialists' hall at 54 West Lake Street.[24]

A third union, the Butchers Benevolent Society, began among the largely Irish butchers in Bridgeport in 1878, led by a packinghouse foreman, Daniel O'Connell. Though a secret, oath-bound society, it coexisted with the Catholic church (which frowned on such groups) through an arrangement with Father Carten of Nativity Church, whereby the union's secrets could be revealed to the church authorities. Carten in turn allowed the butchers to use the church as a meeting place and supported the union during its first strike.[25]

In the fall of 1879, following the sailors' strike, the butchers organized Chicago's first industrial union of the post-depression era, the Butchers and Packinghouse Workers Benevolent Society. The major reason for the transformation of the craft society of butchers was the fear that sailors, who flocked to the packinghouses to work as laborers during the peak season, would defeat the butchers' attempt to win a wage increase. Since sailors were already organized, O'Connell enlisted Richard Powers's help in forming an industrial union. Using open meetings, the new union mushroomed from 1,200 to 7,000 members within a month, and in November the packers capitulated to the union's demand for a twenty-five-cent wage increase without a strike. When B. P. Hutcheson's Chicago Packing and Provision Company fired O'Connell two weeks later, a thousand union members walked out and won his return.[26]

Solidly entrenched in the community and buoyed with success, the union decided to demand a closed shop. Following the example of the sailors, they required that all union men wear union badges and announced that on December 17 they would no longer work with nonunion men. The union demanded that (1) no nonunion men be employed while union men were out of work; (2) no union men be discharged without cause, and if so discharged, it be by the union at its own agreement; (3) all employer complaints against workers be investigated by the union, with the union having a veto over the discharge; (4) when there was a scarcity of men and nonunion men were employed, the latter were to be discharged as soon as union men presented themselves for work. The demands, though likely distorted by the antilabor *Tribune,* were in close accord with a typical craft union's attempt to establish a union hiring hall and control over the labor market.[27]

It soon became clear that such control could not be easily established in an industry in which large-scale firms employed easily replaceable laborers. Though the smaller firms acceded to union demands, the larger ones, led by Armour and Fowler Brothers, where the union had less strength, declared a lockout. Knowing that the butchers played a strategic role in production and could not be easily replaced, the union responded by assessing those members at work to pay the salaries of the locked-out butchers.[28]

In the midst of the strike Father Carten issued a public letter disavowing support for the strike. Though he had supported the earlier strike for wage demands, he called the closed-shop demands "unreasonable," seeming to echo the *Tribune*'s charge that the strike sought to establish a "Butcher's Commune." With five thousand union men residing in the Nativity parish covering both Bridgeport and the Town of Lake, the church's opposition was a fatal blow. Many of the "winter men," who had joined the union to guarantee their jobs, lost confidence that the strike could succeed, precipitating a near revolt against the union leadership. On December 26 Armour resumed work with a labor force that included five hundred ex-union men. Later, when it became publicly known that laborers were not receiving strike funds, the union lost even more support. From press interviews it was also apparent that many strikers' wives had turned against the strike.[29]

Armour's success encouraged other firms to reopen. With hundreds of special policemen hired by the Town of Lake on guard and the militia being held in readiness, there was little the union could do to prevent the replacement workers from entering the plants. The loss of church support led the union to seek support outside the community. The union accepted an invitation to join a sympathy meeting for Charles Parnell's Irish Land League sponsored by the Socialist Labor party and the Trade and Labor Council. On December 28 three thousand "pig-stickers" marched in a procession out of Bridgeport to join the Lehr- und Wehr-Verein and the sailors' union at a large unity rally. The turn to outside support was also evident in O'Connell's lower visibility and the new prominence of Powers as a strike leader. Powers was a compelling speaker with a citywide reputation, and the fact that he had opposed the strike from the beginning gave him status among the laborers who felt that O'Connell had misled them. At a mass rally of ten thousand workers, Powers claimed that Matthew Cudahy, a packer, had tried to bribe Fathers Carten and Damen to turn their backs on the union. The next speaker, M. J. Downs, another new strike leader, openly identified the union with Irish nationalism and juxtaposed both to the church and the packers. In the "old country," charged Downs, the Irish church had sold out to the British, and he hoped it would not happen in Chicago.[30]

But outside support could not make up for the loss of community legitimacy, and the union turned to violence to enforce its solidarity. The violence differed in important ways from that of 1877 and previous mass strikes. First, as the *Tribune* reported, the union's actions "are not the result of sudden impulse, but are the issue of deliberately laid plans. The victims are spotted, waylaid, and assaulted. Emissaries from the union rowdies visit the packinghouses while they are in operation, find out the names, if possible, of the hands who are doing the expert [butchers'] work, and having followed them from the packinghouses at night, deliver them over to the tender mercies of the gangs of fellow ruffians who are waiting at the various street corners."[31]

Second, the violence of the 1880s was directed against fellow workers rather than against the police. Instead of being an expression of class unity and hostility toward employers, it was an attempt to enforce class in the absence of solidarity. Outside the Town of Lake the police were quite sympathetic to the strike and in Bridgeport took a hands-off approach as committees of strikers beat scabs and visited boardinghouses to remonstrate with the families of strikebreakers.[32]

The kind of organized terrorism practiced by the butchers and their allies against strikebreakers may well have drawn on the tradition of rural peasant violence in Ireland called "Whiteboyism." The Whiteboys (known for the color of their shirts) were the most active and widely known of a number of secret societies organized by poor tenants to prevent their eviction by landlords trying to consolidate their holdings. Described by one historian as "a war of the poor against the poor," Whiteboy violence was directed against fellow tenants who collaborated with landlords. The Whiteboys and other secret societies operated in the face of church stricture, were without middle-class leadership, and were largely immune from British prosecution since British authorities found it difficult to gather witnesses. Irish peasant violence reached its peak between 1806 and the mid-1840s, but it remained strong in Irish memory, as can be seen in its revival in the early 1880s, when the Irish Land League drew on its tradition of resistance but strove to transcend its resort to violence. The nature of the butchers' violence—its targets, its premeditation, its community support, its independence from the church, and its secrecy—suggests a continuity with Whiteboyism.[33]

Just as apolitical peasant terrorism had failed to defeat landlordism in Ireland, it proved ineffective in the butchers' strike. On January 12 the union told its men to return to work. The next day hundreds of wives and mothers of the strikers thronged the packinghouses beseeching employers to take their men back. Eventually, when work revived, many were taken back, but the strong union men faced the blacklist. Residual feelings from the strike festered on the job. Union men were known to pelt nonunion men with pigs' hearts, splattering them with blood.[34]

With the loss of the strike the simmering tension between the butchers and the laborers came to a head. In the wake of charges of misappropriation of strike funds, the unskilled laborers convened a meeting, chaired by the brickmaker president Pat Carey, that attempted to expel the butchers. Though the coup failed, the union was practically dead.[35]

Nonetheless, the butchers' strike and its immediate antecedents were evidence of an important transition occurring in the actions of Bridgeport workers. Beginning as spontaneous, apolitical crowd actions, mass strikes were becoming organized and calculated, taking on a distinct political coloration and developing broader ties of labor solidarity outside the community.

The Rise of the Knights of Labor

In 1880 two small Knights of Labor LAs appeared in Bridgeport, each made up of meatpackers. Little is known of the two assemblies except that LA 1578 was a mixed assembly headed by two Irish labor reformers, while LA 1597 was led by Matthew J. Butler, a blacksmith from Armour who was a member of numerous Irish societies and would become one of the leading Knights of the 1880s. The formation of the two LAs was actually a critical juncture for both the Knights and the Irish laborers, who alternated between doing heavy labor in the packinghouses, unloading vessels, and heaving lumber, coal, and iron ore. For the Knights these were the first assemblies to meet outside the city center in an industrial neighborhood. For the Bridgeport packinghouse workers it represented another step on the road away from the community-based mass strike and toward unity with a broader labor movement.[36]

Another group, the Brickmakers Benevolent Society, paralleled the path of the butchers. In 1880 the brick laborers participated in a demonstration welcoming Charles Parnell, the Irish Land League leader, to Chicago. The following year they engaged in a successful strike using little violence. In February 1882 the Brickmakers Benevolent Society, led by its president, joined the Knights as LA 1771. With 381 members in good standing in 1883 it was the largest Knights of Labor LA in the city that year.[37]

The effect of joining the Knights was evident in the brickmakers' method of striking when they sought a wage increase in April 1882. Instead of congregating in crowds, they posted handbills in three languages at all the yards explaining their reasons for striking and warning all brickmakers to keep away. Then they set up a conference with their employers, where William Halley, a district assembly master workman, offered a no-strike pledge in return for a wage increase. When the employers rejected the offer and appealed to Mayor Harrison for police aid, the LA countered with its own appeal to the mayor. In tones of respectability it renounced "physical force or disorderly conduct" and stated that "we hope to carry our point . . . by good organization and honest persuasion" since "when we lay the case before other workmen, they invariably agree with us, and the bosses cannot get outside labor to aid them." Satisfied with this pledge, Harrison refused the request for police intervention, and the employers eventually gave in to the demands.[38]

The same progression from neighborhood solidarity to class solidarity and from spontaneous crowd action to disciplined and respectable organization and bargaining was evident in two other Bridgeport strikes in 1882. Blast-furnacemen at Bridgeport's Union Iron and Steel Plant customarily worked eight-hour shifts. When a new nonunion superintendent attempted to introduce twelve-hour shifts to conform to practice at the North Chicago Rolling Mills, two hundred blast-furnacemen and their helpers struck. Since the local community was in sympathy with the strikers, the company tried to import Italian strikebreakers. They were met by a crowd of a thousand strikers and "sympathizing men, women, and street arabs." When a small squad of police from the local Deering Street Station commanded by Lieutenant John Byrne allowed the crowd to jeer and taunt the scabs with impunity, the Italians panicked and fled.[39]

According to the company president police inaction was critical to the success of the strike. "What we wanted the police to do," wrote the president in a letter to the *Tribune*, "was to disperse that crowd, just precisely as they would a crowd downtown." Noting that the Deering Street police "were known to and were relatives of the strikers," he asked unsuccessfully to have North Side police transferred to Bridgeport. The backgrounds of the police tend to confirm his judgment. Of thirty-one patrolmen and officers approximately 52.0 percent were Irish-born, far above their 8.8 percent in the city's population. In addition, Lieutenant Byrne was a personal favorite of Mayor Harrison. Though Byrne had resigned from the force in 1877, Harrison reinstated him and elevated him to a lieutenancy. The Irish-born Byrne was a liberal Catholic and a member of the Knights of St. Patrick, and he served as grand marshal for the St. Patrick's Day parade two weeks after the blast-furnacemen's strike. According to a biographical sketch of Byrne, during "many serious strikes among rolling mill employees and . . . other large strikes and threatened riots, Captain Byrne could accomplish better results with masses of determined and excited men by reasoning and persuasion than could be gained by any show of force."[40]

As important as the police were in the conflict, the Knights of Labor played a decisive role in its resolution. Almost from the beginning Myles McPadden and Joseph G. O'Kelley, recently arrived Knights organizers, had been counseling the strikers to abstain from violence and to unite with other organized men at the plant. Soon the bricklayers quit in sympathy with the strike. Meanwhile, the Knights announced a grand ball to benefit the strikers, for which they sold two thousand tickets in all parts of the city. The Knights also requested a sympathy walkout by the Amalgamated Association of Iron and Steel Workers, which represented the skilled workers at the plant, but the union refused to risk its settled relations with the company. McPadden finally effected a compromise settlement in which the men accepted twelve-hour workdays in return for two hours for meals and a pay boost to equal that of the North Side men. At this point the blast-furnacemen voted to join the Knights and later were also accepted into the Amalgamated Association of Iron and Steel Workers. By the end of the year the LA had forced the resignation of the objectionable superintendent and had him replaced by a union-Knight man.[41]

An equally striking incident illustrating the way the Knights broadened the perspective of workers engaged in neighborhood-based strikes can be seen in the iron-ore shovelers' strike. Twenty-four iron-ore workers, nearly all Irish, working on the Bridgeport docks of the Joliet Iron and Steel Company had been organized in a union run by local saloonkeepers. It was an exclusive organization that did not even include the yardmen or helpers and was dedicated to maintaining a kind of ownership or tenure for the shovelers' casual jobs. When the 1882 season opened in May, the company fired the men from their jobs, much as the British landlords had evicted Irish tenants, replacing them with lower-paid sailors. Claiming the work was theirs by custom, the shovelers assaulted the sailors, seriously injuring one of them. They also attacked Italian strikebreakers, guarded in the same half-hearted manner by the Deering Street police.

But nothing outraged the larger Chicago community more than when a body of armed strikers stopped a train carrying Negro strikebreakers just outside of Bridgeport and beat them badly, in the process seriously wounding a state judge. Like peasant violence in Ireland, it seemed to have been "well-planned," and Mayor Harrison admitted that "the men have the sympathy of the men in nearly every other trade and business . . . [and that] there are but small prospects for a squeal." Police support for the strikers was by now notorious, but the affair, which the *Tribune* compared with the exploits of the social bandit Jesse James, proved impossible to cover up, and seven men were indicted.[42]

The ensuing trial was rife with overtones of national and cultural conflict. Emery Storrs, the prosecuting attorney, was a Yankee Protestant, upper-class champion of the city's temperance movement and had served the packers in prosecuting Bridgeport butchers in 1880. For the defense the shovelers retained two leading Irish nationalists, Alexander Sullivan, a national leader in the Clan na Gael, and Richard Prendergast. Meanwhile, the Knights intervened to arbitrate an end to the strike, whereby the company allowed the men back under a subcontractor though at lower pay. The shovelers then joined the order as a local assembly, without saloonkeepers. The report of the Illinois Bureau of Labor Statistics summarized the results by observing that membership in the order "renders their actions less capricious, because they are subject thereby to restraining regulations, and strikes are discountenanced."[43]

The Knights and New Class Norms in Chicago

By 1883 Chicago Knights had facilitated an important transformation in the mass strike as it had developed in Bridgeport in the 1870s. Rather than rely on mass violence against other workers to enforce class norms, the Knights, just as socialist leaders did in Pilsen, taught the importance of persuasion and solidarity based on commitment to universal principles and a perceived common interest.

Yet the Knights would not have been successful had the poor residents of ethnic neighborhoods, like Bridgeport and Pilsen, not begun to take on a distinctly working-class orientation. One indication of new attitudes was the increasing use of the term *scab*. Between 1864 and 1876 the press reports of strikes suggest that *scab* was a little-used epithet. Following the 1877 strikes, however, the term became common during strikes. *Scab* implied a community taboo on behavior that violated class norms. The word evoked community ostracism and redefined strikebreaking as deviant behavior. Though the importance of intimidation and violence in the inculcation of this new norm should not be underestimated, its primary effect was moral. During the blast-furnacemen's strike, the company president observed that not physical harm but "running the gauntlet of abuse was intolerable" to strikebreakers.[44]

In an earlier period the *Workingman's Advocate* used *scab* only in relation to skilled workers—defining it, in part, as "a jack of all trades and master of none." After 1877 the ostracism of scabs seems to have become common among unskilled workers. According to one observer of the packinghouse workers' strike, "Just as in proportion as the labor that composes the trade or union is less skilled, its members are readier in denunciation and more intolerant of . . . fellow workmen who decline to unite with their organization."[45]

The strength of the new class norms was also evident in Bridgeport workers' new attitude toward police. In the midst of fierce fighting in 1877 Irish rioters called the police "peelers," which referred to the Irish constabulary established in 1836 to contain rural Whiteboy violence and included Sir Robert Peel's Peace Preservation Force. Instead of being responsible to local magistrates, as were other police, the Irish constabulary was a semimilitarized strike force, trained professionally and directed by British authorities. With the constabulary increasingly manned by native Irish Catholics, the term *peelers* was used derisively by the Irish to mean that in suppressing peasant terrorism the police were turncoats. Because the Chicago police, who acted so brutally in 1877, were largely Irish as well, when Irish workers used the term *peelers,* they were filtering their American experiences through their cultural heritage grounded in colonized Ireland.[46]

Historians of Chicago have noted that after the 1877 strikes and riots the police, at the urging of the Citizens Association, adopted military ranks and armed themselves with cannons to repel anticipated riots.[47] Yet by 1882 Chicago police, based in one of the former riot strongholds, were acting in concert with workers during strikes, making unnecessary the kind of confrontations that had resulted in riots in 1877. There were no reports after 1877 of the use of the term *peeler,* possibly because it was no longer applicable. Far from becoming professionalized servants of the state, exercising "social control," the police, at least in Bridgeport, were becoming creatures of their own community. Class norms in this instance overrode the trend toward bureaucratization and centralization that marked the Citizens Association's governmental reform movement in the mid-1870s.[48]

Above all it was the Knights of Labor that sought to broaden and systematize the growing class feeling among workers, to rationalize it through its ideology of amalgamation, and finally to consolidate it through membership in an organization that included all branches of labor. Affiliation with the Knights of Labor, which opposed strikes and favored arbitration or conciliation of disputes, also provided unskilled workers with a valuable experience in discipline. Heretofore, local unions had struck openly when supply and demand conditions were favorable. The Knights, however, encouraged them to replace the mass strike with a season-long agreement that had a no-strike pledge.

Most important, the Knights provided a path away from the parochialism of the neighborhood mass strike. Bridgeport's Irish had exhibited strong ethnic hostility toward scabs of another nationality or race who entered firms being struck by local residents. Membership in the Knights encouraged local strikers to rely on the monetary and moral resources of a citywide and national organization of amalgamated trades. On this basis groups outside the community, such as the Italians, could be reasoned with, conciliated, and perhaps brought into the labor fold.

Just as local labor activity had been transformed by the Knights, so the Knights of Labor was transformed by the new presence of unskilled laborers. Before 1882 all but one of the Knights' local assemblies were mixed, and all had meeting places in the central part of the city or just west of it. By the end of 1882 the Knights had at least twenty-two trade-based assemblies, and most of them had meeting places located in Chicago's South Side neighborhoods. The Knights of Labor in Chicago had become more than simply a politically oriented labor reform organization.

Notes

1. *Irish World and American Industrial Liberator,* Oct. 16, 1880; *Chicago Tribune,* Sept. 6, 1880. On the Knights' local assemblies, see *Record of the Proceedings of the Fourth Session of the General Assembly Held at Pittsburgh, Pa., Sept. 7–11, 1880,* 208, Reel 67, in Terence Vincent Powderly Papers, 1864–1937, and John William Hayes Papers, 1880–1921: The Knights of Labor (Glen Rock, N.J.: Microfilming Corporation of America, 1974) (hereafter PHP).

2. *Chicago Tribune,* Oct. 30, 1880, Nov. 1, 1880, Nov. 3, 1880, Nov. 4, 1880; *Record of the Proceedings of the Fifth Regular Session of the General Assembly Held at Detroit, Michigan, Sept. 6–10, 1881,* 300, Reel 67, PHP.

3. See Rosa Luxemburg, *The Mass Strike, the Political Party and the Trade Unions and the Junius Pamphlet* (1906; reprint, New York: Harper and Row, 1971).

4. *Progressive Age,* Nov. 19, 1881, Jan. 7, 1882; *Chicago Tribune,* May 26, 1879; *Irish World and American Industrial Liberator,* Oct. 4, 1879. Outdoor laborers were part of the category "common laborers" discussed in David Montgomery, *Fall of the House of Labor: The Workplace, the State, and American Labor Activism, 1865–1925* (Cambridge: Cambridge University Press, 1987), chap. 2.

5. *Chicago Tribune,* June 1, 1884, June 1, 1875; *Second Biennial Report of the Illinois Bureau of Labor Statistics* (Springfield: H. W. Rokker, 1883), 265.

6. *Chicago Tribune,* June 5, 1875, June 12, 1880 (quote); Alfred T. Andreas, *History of Chicago from the Earliest Period to the Present Time* (Chicago: A. T. Andreas, 1884–86), 3:75; S. S. Schoff, *The Glory of Chicago—Her Manufactories* (Chicago: Knight and Leonard, 1873), 65.

7. Herbert G. Gutman, "The Workers' Search for Power," in *The Gilded Age,* rev. ed., ed. H. Wayne Morgan (Syracuse, N.Y.: Syracuse University Press, 1970), 33. The most notable work of the University of Chicago School of Sociology is Ernest Watson Burgess, *The Urban Community: Selected Papers from the Proceedings of the American Sociological Society, 1925* (Chicago: University of Chicago Press, 1926). For more recent work on communities in relation to labor, see Theodore Hershberg, ed., *Philadelphia: Work, Space, Family and Group Experience in the Nineteenth Century* (New York: Oxford University Press, 1981); and Hartmut Keil and John B. Jentz, eds., *German Workers in Industrial Chicago, 1850–1910: A Comparative Perspective* (De Kalb: Northern Illinois University Press, 1983).

8. The neighborhoods that were home to mass strikes mixed elements of the traditional or communal and the modern or societal. Compare Samuel P. Hays, "Political Parties and the Community-Society Continuum," in *The American Party Systems: Stages of Political Development,* ed. William Nisbet Chambers and Walter Dean Burnham (New York: Oxford University Press, 1967), 152–81; and Thomas Bender, *Community and Social Change in America* (New Brunswick, N.J.: Rutgers University Press, 1978), 31–43, 56–57.

9. David Montgomery, "Strikes in Nineteenth-Century America," *Social Science History* 4 (Feb. 1980): 81–104; George Rude, *The Crowd in History* (New York: Wiley, 1964).

10. Richard Schneirov, "Free Thought and Socialism in the Czech Community in Chicago, 1875–1887," in *"Struggle a Hard Battle": Essays on Working-Class Immigrants,* ed. Dirk Hoerder (De Kalb: Northern Illinois University Press, 1986), 121–42.

11. *Chicago Tribune,* June 14, 1875, May 9, 1876; Karel D. Bicha, "Settling Accounts with an Old Adversary: The Decatholicization of Czech Immigrants in America," *Social History–Histoire Sociale* 8 (Nov. 1972): 45–60; Joseph Chada, *The Czechs in the United States* (Chicago: Czechoslovak Society of the United States, 1981), 89–91, 147–48.

12. J. E. S. Vojan, *The Semi-Centennial of the Bohemian National Cemetery Association in Chicago, Illinois* (Chicago: Bohemian National Cemetery Association, 1927); Josefa Humpel Zeman, "Bohemian People in Chicago," in *Hull-House Maps and Papers: A Presentation of Nationalities and Wages in a Congested District of Chicago by Residents of Hull-House* (New York: Thomas Y. Crowell, 1895), 124; *Chicago Tribune,* Feb. 24, 1886, May 17, 1886; *Svornost* Oct. 18, 1883 (Foreign Language Press Survey).

13. *Chicago Daily Inter-Ocean,* July 28, 1877 (quote); *Chicago Tribune,* July 25, 1877, July 26, 1877; *Svornost,* Mar. 26, 1883 (Foreign Language Press Survey); *Chicago Times,* Aug. 28, 1884.

14. Chicago Historical Society, *Documents: History of the Communities, Chicago,* vol. 6, *Bridgeport* (prepared for the Chicago Historical Society and Local Community Research Committee, University of Chicago, research directed by Vivien M. Palmer), docs. 5, 10.

15. Michael Funchion, *Chicago's Irish Nationalists, 1881–1890* (New York: Arno, 1976), 4; *Housing in Chicago Communities,* Community Area No. 60 (Chicago: Chicago Planning Commission, 1940).

16. *Chicago School Census of the City of Chicago* (Chicago: Board of Education, 1884). The stockyards area was bounded on the east by Stewart, on the south by Thirty-ninth Street, on the west by a canal and by Halsted, and on the north by Thirty-fifth Street and Thirty-third Street.

17. Harry C. Koenig, ed., *A History of the Parishes of the Archdiocese of Chicago* (Chicago: Archdiocese of Chicago, 1980), 1:145–48, 1:200; 2:654–57; *New World,* Nov. 10, 1906; Andreas, *History of Chicago,* 3:776; *Chicago Tribune,* Oct. 30, 1876.

18. Koenig, *History of the Parishes,* 1:302–4; Charles Ffrench, *Biographical History of the American Irish in Chicago* (Chicago: American Biographical Publishing, 1897), 796–801.

19. U.S. Department of the Interior, Census Office, *Eighth Census of the United States: 1860,* vol. 2, *Report on Manufactures* (Washington, D.C.: Government Printing Office, 1865), 87; U.S. Department of the Interior, Census Office, *Ninth Census of the United States: 1870,* vol. 2, *Report on Manufactures* (Washington, D.C.: Government Printing Office, 1872), 649; U.S. Department of the Interior, Census Office, *Tenth Census of the United States: 1880,* vol. 2, *Report on Manufactures* (Washington, D.C.: Government Printing Office, 1883), 393; Andreas, *History of Chicago,* 3:334–36; *Robinson's Atlas of Chicago* (New York: E. Robinson, 1886), 2:plates 19, 20, 22, 25, 26.

20. Schoff, *Glory of Chicago,* 9, 11, 12; Chicago Historical Society, *Documents,* doc. 13 (quote).

21. *Fourth Biennial Report of the Illinois Bureau of Labor Statistics* (Springfield: H. W. Rokker, 1886), 229.

22. Funchion, *Chicago's Irish Nationalists,* 3.

23. *Chicago Tribune*, Feb. 14, 1875, Feb. 6, 1883, May 21, 1882.

24. *Irish World and American Industrial Liberator*, Oct. 4, 1879; *Progressive Age*, Oct. 18, 1879, Jan. 3, 1880, Nov. 12, 1881 (quote); *Western Workman*, Sept. 22, 1883; *Chicago Tribune*, Apr. 29, 1879, Apr. 30, 1879, May 1, 1879, May 8, 1879, Sept. 26, 1879.

25. *Chicago Tribune*, Dec. 24, 1879, May 17, 1882.

26. Ibid., Oct. 25, 1879, Nov. 2, 1879, Nov. 6, 1879, Nov. 15, 1879, Nov. 22, 1879.

27. Ibid., Dec. 16, 1879, Dec. 28, 1879.

28. Ibid., Dec. 18, 1879, Dec. 20, 1879, Dec. 23, 1879, Jan. 1, 1880, Jan. 8, 1880.

29. Ibid., Dec. 24, 1879, Dec. 27, 1879, Dec. 28, 1879, Jan. 1, 1880, Jan. 3, 1880, Jan. 10, 1880.

30. Ibid., Dec. 29, 1879, Dec. 30, 1879, Jan. 2, 1880, Jan. 3, 1879, Jan. 9, 1879 (quote).

31. Ibid., Jan. 3, 1880.

32. Ibid., Jan. 7, 1880, Jan. 10, 1880.

33. Thomas N. Brown, *Irish-American Nationalism, 1870–1890* (Philadelphia: J. B. Lippincott, 1966), 3; Michael Gordon, "The Labor Boycott in New York City, 1880–1886," *Labor History* 16 (Spring 1975): 184–229; Gale Christianson, "Secret Societies and Agrarian Violence in Ireland, 1750–1840," *Agricultural History* 46 (July 1972): 369–84; Galen Broecker, *Rural Disorder and Police Reform in Ireland, 1812–1836* (London: Routledge and Kegan Paul, 1970), 6–10.

34. *Chicago Tribune*, Jan. 13, 1880, Jan. 14, 1880, Jan. 15, 1880.

35. Ibid., Jan. 26, 1880, Feb. 10, 1880.

36. *Fourth Biennial Report of the Illinois Bureau of Labor Statistics*, 187; Jonathan Garlock, comp., *Guide to the Local Assemblies of the Knights of Labor* (Westport, Conn.: Greenwood, 1982), 63–92; *Progressive Age*, July 20, 1882; *Chicago Tribune*, Nov. 2, 1886.

37. *Chicago Tribune*, Feb. 23, 1880, May 15, 1880, May 20, 1880, May 1, 1881, Feb. 20, 1882; *Record of the Proceedings of the Seventh Regular Session of the General Assembly Held at Cincinnati, Ohio, Sept. 4–11, 1883*, 544, Reel 67, PHP.

38. *Second Biennial Report of the Illinois Bureau of Labor Statistics*, 272.

39. *Chicago Tribune*, Mar. 1, 1882, Mar. 2, 1882, Mar. 10, 1882; *Progressive Age*, Mar. 4, 1882.

40. *Chicago Tribune*, Mar. 7, 1882, Mar. 10, 1882 (first quote), Mar. 17, 1882; figures derived from biographies in John J. Flinn, *History of the Chicago Police from the Settlement of the Community to the Present Time* (Chicago: Police Book Fund, 1887); Ffrench, *Biographical History of the American Irish in Chicago*, 790–92 (second quote).

41. *Progressive Age*, Mar. 11, 1882, Mar. 18, 1882; *Chicago Tribune*, Mar. 17, 1882; *Second Biennial Report of the Illinois Bureau of Labor Statistics*, 262–63.

42. *Chicago Tribune*, May 16, 1882, June 3, 1882 (quotes); *Second Biennial Report of the Illinois Bureau of Labor Statistics*, 262–65.

43. *Chicago Tribune*, June 10, 1882; *Second Biennial Report of the Illinois Bureau of Labor Statistics*, 265 (quote).

44. *Chicago Tribune*, Mar. 10, 1882.

45. *Workingman's Advocate*, Apr. 28, 1866; *Chicago Tribune*, Jan. 13, 1880.

46. *Chicago Inter-Ocean,* July 26, 1877; Broecker, *Rural Disorder and Police Reform in Ireland,* 55–70. On the peelers as turncoats, see *Irish World and American Industrial Liberator,* Aug. 6, 13, 1881.

47. Flinn, *History of the Chicago Police,* 198–99; Andreas, *History of Chicago,* 3:589.

48. Sidney Harring argues that the police exercised social control in *Policing a Class Society: The Experience of American Cities, 1865–1915* (New Brunswick, N.J.: Rutgers University Press, 1983), 38–39; the lack of professionalism is argued by Mark H. Haller, "Historical Roots of Police Behavior: Chicago, 1890–1925," *Law and Society Review* 10 (Winter 1976): 303–23.

CHAPTER 5

The Irish Land League and the Knights of Labor

The transformation of the mass strike of Irish workers from a community, ethnic-based struggle to a cosmopolitan, class-aware unionism led by the Knights of Labor has thus far been treated without an in-depth discussion of Irish nationalism. That transformation cannot, however, be understood without reference to the remarkable outpouring of Irish nationalism that swept Chicago in the early 1880s. The struggles of the butchers, brickmakers, blast-furnacemen, and iron-ore shovelers had important links to Irish nationalism. Furthermore, key leaders in the Knights of this period, notably District Master Workman William Halley and officers John J. Mahoney, Leo P. Dwyer, Lars P. Nelson, and Elizabeth Rodgers, were all ardent Irish nationalists.

In recent years historians of the labor movement have reexamined Irish-American nationalism from a new perspective. They have demonstrated that the movement was not just a phase in the assimilation of "traditional" Irish immigrants into an undifferentiated "modern" American identity but also a crucial link in the complicated equation that in the 1880s produced a new working-class identity, not only among the Irish but among other workers as well.[1]

More specifically, the way in which the physical force used by mass strikers was replaced by "moral force" owed much to the popularity of the boycott, which grew out of the agitation of the Irish Land League. Just as important, the Irish Land League's struggle against landlordism imparted critical impetus to local workers' acceptance of the idea of land nationalization and Henry George's program of the single tax. Together these developments assimilated a significant segment of Chicago's Irish workers into new currents of labor radicalism that were becoming part of the mainstream of Chicago's labor movement, currents rooted in America's liberal republican and Protestant reform traditions.

The Irish Land League emerged as the fruit of a "new departure" that tentatively united three strands of Irish nationalism, hitherto at odds. The Clan na Gael (successor to the Fenians) and its chief, John Devoy, stood for independence from Britain achieved by physical force. By the late 1870s its leaders realized they could not effect a mass movement without appealing to the Irish agrarian poor. A second strand, consisting of representatives from Ireland to the British Parliament and led by Charles Parnell, were constitutional nationalists, who favored home rule but not full independence. The third element in the equation was the apolitical, antilandlord agitation that tapped the land hunger of poor tenants in Ireland and lingering discontent of Irish immigrants to the United States. When Michael Davitt organized the Land League of County Mayo, he became the leading symbol of this agrarian discontent. The new departure consisted of a complicated set of shifts in policy, agreements, and rapprochements whereby these strands united behind the Irish National Land League under the leadership of Charles Parnell. By demanding a peaceful but nonetheless revolutionary transfer of land ownership from British landlords to the Irish tenants, the Irish National Land League politicized rising peasant discontent and channeled it toward nationalist purposes.[2]

The Formation of the Land League in Chicago

The new departure was not evident in the United States until early 1880, when Parnell launched a triumphant tour across the country to raise funds for the Land League. Parnell elicited an amazing outpouring of warmhearted support from all classes of Americans wherever he spoke. In Chicago, which Parnell visited in February, the effect was twofold: it overcame longstanding divisions in the Irish-American community, and it opened the way for socialist and labor reform influence among the Irish.

First, as was apparent from the list of contributors, the Land League's cause tapped the enthusiasm and generosity of the widest range of Irish-Americans, from churchgoers, wealthy merchants, professionals, and other lace-curtain Irish to benevolent societies, machine politicians, ordinary policemen, and trade unionists as well as the nationalists.[3] Perhaps most significant was the Catholic church's new interest in the nationalist cause, for until that year the church hierarchy, with the exception of some parish priests, was quite alienated from physical force nationalism. In 1864 Bishop James Duggan officially interdicted members of his church from joining the Fenian Brotherhood. When the Clan na Gael took over from the small and declining Fenians in 1877, it organized an Irish National Day on August 15 each year, a day of public celebration that the church, together with respectable Irish, boycotted. At the height of nationalist agitation, Irish National Day rose to such importance that the Clan na Gael advocated abandoning St. Patrick's Day to concentrate efforts and funds for the Land League.[4]

In eastern cities and other parts of the United States the tensions between the Catholic church and the secular nationalists were transferred to the movement to support the Land League, but not in Chicago. At the same time that Parnell arrived in the city, Chicago's church came under the leadership of a new archbishop, Patrick Feehan, a strong Irish nationalist. Feehan not only openly endorsed the Land League but also was friendly with Alexander Sullivan, the chief of the Clan na Gael in Chicago. Under Feehan's influence the *Western Catholic,* Chicago's church paper, became virulently anti-British and even called for the burning of London. Not coincidentally, Feehan, along with another liberal archbishop, entertained few qualms about unionism.[5]

Feehan's benevolent attitude toward social movements among his Irish flock was reinforced by his approach to church building. Feehan broke up large parishes so that his pastors could become better acquainted with their parishioners. Within five years he had added 40 churches to the existing 160. The new parishes were filled with priests who tended to be "young and energetic," as one reporter called them, and capable of playing a missionary role in the tough, new working-class colonies, notably Bridgeport and the stockyards district. Among them were four priests who played major roles in the Land League: Father John Waldron, Father Thomas Pope Hodnett, Father J. M. Hagen, and Father Maurice Dorney. The last three priests served working-class parishes in and around Bridgeport. Dorney, who served as president of the Illinois Land League in 1881–82 and gave countless speeches before league meetings, was particularly important.[6]

The widespread legitimacy the Land League immediately attained among Irish citizens had another effect, which was not at first appreciated by the Irish notables who dominated the February reception for Parnell. The issue of land reform and the fact that the Land League was mobilizing a mass movement of poor tenants in Ireland opened up a pathway for different forms of American radicalism to enter the movement. The strongest American supporter of the primacy of the social question in Irish nationalism and land reform in the United States was Patrick Ford, publisher of the New York-based *Irish World and American Industrial Liberator.* Ford was a supporter of the Greenback-Labor party who believed that monopolization of land created the condition for "usury," which in turn embodied "the entire circuit of man's inhumanity to man." In Chicago the *Irish World* created a link between the Land League and radical elements in the labor movement. Lars P. Nelson, a Swedish Knights of Labor leader who was also a Greenbacker, served as Ford's Chicago correspondent. Chicago Master Workman William Halley, another Greenbacker, called the *Irish World* "our leading organ."[7]

Unlike many Greenbackers, Ford was friendly to socialism because he believed that "Socialism in Germany, Communism in France, Nihilism in Russia, Anti-Rentism in Ireland, and Greenbackism in American are all varying phases of the same movement." In Chicago the SLPers latched onto the Land League with special fervor. English-speaking Socialists, recognizing the need to Americanize socialist ideology, hoped to accomplish that task by uniting it with indigenous reform movements, such as the Greenback-Labor party. In the same vein the Land League provided an opportunity to bring socialism in the shape of land nationalization to the Irish, who had long been resistant to socialism. The SLP boldly attempted to claim the Land League movement as their own in February 1880, when they held a separate demonstration and reception for Parnell in conjunction with their support for the butchers' strike. Though it attracted few Irish workers, the English-speaking Socialists, led by one of its few Irish members, Tommy Ryan, were successful in organizing two Ford-affiliated "Spread the Light" clubs in Bridgeport and the Town of Lake. The clubs not only collected funds for the Land League but also distributed the *Irish World* and collected subscriptions to have the paper sent to relatives in Ireland.[8]

The Ford wing of the Land League did not become a mass movement in Chicago. The prominence of the socialists and the absence of support from the Chicago Clan na Gael were obstacles too great to overcome. By the end of 1881, however, the National Land League, in which the Clan na Gael played a central role, established a branch in the city. Then suddenly, within a four month period beginning in January 1881, the number of clubs shot up from two to twenty. The Land League's agitation seemed to tap into a well-spring of high-mindedness that for a moment collapsed all social, political, and religious differences into one transcendent cause. John F. Finerty, publisher of Chicago's leading Irish nationalist newspaper, the *Citizen,* remarked that "one of the best features of the Chicago movement is that . . . Protestants and Catholics unite to aid the cause of humanity and justice." Echoing Patrick Ford, another Land Leaguer asserted that the "Irish were not struggling simply for their own rights but for the rights of the downtrodden all over the world."[9]

These typical remarks, often delivered in stirring, melodramatic tones at Land League meetings, helped fuel a more general revival of the social reform ethos in the city. Land League clubs became a magnet for socialists, trade unionists, Knights, and Greenbackers. Those active included Richard Powers, president of the sailors' union; John B. Murphy, president of the tanners and curriers' union; Tim O'Meara, an Irish socialist and Knight; and O. A. Bishop, a socialist. Greenbackers included the old Fenian John F. Scanlon and Michael Haley. There was also a women's club headed by Alice May Quinn. Bridgeport, which became the banner ward of the Land League, included two flourishing clubs, one of them the precursor of the Ford-affiliated Michael Davitt Land Club, based in the rolling mills and packinghouses. By September 1881 Chicago clubs affiliated with the Land League combined to send the second highest amount of funds in the United States to the Land League and boasted the second highest number of league branches, behind New York City. What the SLPers and the Spread the Light clubs had tried and failed to accomplish in 1880—enlisting Irish nationalism to serve the cause of American labor and social reform—had become a reality in 1881 and 1882.[10]

"Captain Boycott" and the Chicago Labor Movement

Without doubt the most important contribution of the Land League to the labor movement and to class formation came in the form of the boycott. It was also over this issue that the class divisions in the movement first became unavoidable.

The term *boycott* originated in the Irish struggle then going on against the hated British land agent in the County Mayo, Captain Charles Boycott. The boycott was popular because it was a nonviolent form of the Irish peasant tradition of conducting struggle against landlords by isolating those who collaborated with them. According to Thomas N. Brown, "The League's history reveals how closely the nationalist adapted himself to the peasant world, for the Land League's essential power lay in its legitimation of old Whiteboy techniques." That the boycott was a republican alternative to peasant violence, suited to the United States as well as Ireland, was a central theme of a lecture delivered by James Redpath, the American abolitionist associate of Parnell, in Chicago in February 1881.[11]

The first indication that the boycott might be transferred to urban American conditions came in February, when Bridgeport's Michael Davitt Land Club called for a boycott of British goods and followed it up in April by resolving to boycott "any person keeping English goods for sale until England does justice to Ireland." Other clubs, led by those affiliated with Ford's *Irish World*, followed suit, and the issue was vigorously debated at the Illinois Land League's convention in May, though as a general policy it was rejected.[12]

At the height of this discussion Chicago labor leaders, many of them Irish, such as the Trades and Labor Assembly president and Knights leader George

Rodgers, adapted the boycott to their own uses. The precipitating incident came with the strike of the West Side streetcar workers. Not coincidentally, their benevolent association had a heavily Irish membership and had been organized in 1879 by the Bridgeport butchers, who were intimately involved in Irish nationalist politics. The strike of the streetcar workers began April 7 after the company had discharged a committee of conductors and drivers for requesting a 20 percent wage increase. From the start the strike had enormous public sympathy. The company was a classic case of a government-made monopoly that had abused its privilege by running overcrowded, unheated cars and had enraged West Siders by failing to run its cars on time the previous winter. On the eve of the strike workers discussed boycotting scabs, and the Trades and Labor Assembly responded by declaring a boycott and demanding municipal ownership of the streetcars. Addressing a mass meeting of streetcar workers the next day, President Rodgers said that "he did not believe there was a man or woman on the West Side but would rather walk twenty miles than ride with a scab."[13]

When the company announced its capitulation, the victorious strikers shouted themselves hoarse in exultation. Their emotion was shared by community residents, who responded by "waving their handkerchiefs" and "shouting congratulations" as the "cars hurried by." It was the first successful use of a public boycott by Chicago's labor movement.[14]

The streetcar boycott anticipated features of the boycott that developed after the turn of the century. It has been said that unskilled workers, lacking the power of skilled workers, tended to rely on the wider community for support through the boycott, supplementing a withdrawal of labor power with a withdrawal of consumption power. But boycott in the early 1880s usually retained its original Irish meaning: the shunning of scabs or the products of their labor. The word was therefore commonly used as part of the expression "boycott scabs." Instead of being a new tactic, the boycott in Ireland and the United States was a community alternative to violence in enforcing class or community cohesion. Moreover, because it relied on the support of those not directly affected by a dispute, the boycott demanded even more commitment than a strike since boycotters asked that people adhere to a boycott merely because it was issued by a labor organization rather than out of an impartial process of ascertaining which side was right. The success of a boycott thus rested on a spontaneous and unselfinterested class loyalty. The explosive implications of boycotting were not lost on respectable opinion. The *Nation* excoriated its use by the Irish as "a wild and barbarous mode of expressing" that which in "more civilized communities" would find vent in the press and the influence of the "well-to-do industrial middle class."[15]

In Chicago the success of the streetcar strike had the effect of widening interest in the boycott far beyond the Irish struggle. Richard Powers, addressing the striking iron molders two weeks after the streetcar victory, urged iron molders to "shun their fellow workmen who refused to join their movement; to refuse to associate with them; to consider them outlaws, in short to 'boycott them' in every case (cheers), not by violence." Several months later, a local leader of the Brotherhood of Carpenters and Joiners of America stated that piecework could not be abolished "without the aid of Captain Boycott. . . . Let no Union foreman give a job to a man who is known to take piecework, let no union man work with a man who takes piecework, and neither union nor non-union man should raise a hand for a boss who is known to let piecework."[16]

Within two months of the streetcar victory the gas workers, brickmakers, tin and sheet iron workers, sailors, and switchmen struck. Instead of simply contesting wages many of these strikes manifested broader class norms. The gas workers struck to protect their leaders from discharge, the sailors won a closed shop, and the cigarmakers began to hold public meetings to publicize their union label adopted in 1880. But until 1882 the enthusiasm for boycotting could not be effectively harnessed because there was no central organization strong enough to coordinate boycotts by workers from different trades. With the Trades and Labor Assembly in disarray, the Knights of Labor stepped into the vacuum in 1881–82 by effecting a juncture with the Irish and the trade union boycott and strike movement.[17]

The transformation of the Knights from a political organization of mixed assemblies devoted to greenbackism into a bona fide labor organization was largely the work of three men: William Halley, Myles McPadden, and Joseph G. O'Kelley. William Halley was a printer and journalist who came from California, where he had worked closely with Denis Kearney and had been friendly with Henry George, to Chicago via Peoria. In 1879–80 he became a leader in the Chicago branch of the National Greenback-Labor party and served as editor of the antimonopolist *Chicago Express*. In late 1881 Halley, a compelling speaker, became prominent in the Land League agitation and found himself catapulted into the position of the master workman of the Knights' District Assembly (DA) 24. O'Kelley and McPadden were both Knights organizers, sent to Chicago by the general executive board. Like Grand Master Workman Terence V. Powderly, both were Irish, and both were Clan na Gael members. Both also were part of the Pittsburgh wing of the order, which represented unskilled workers, many of Irish-Catholic origin, and were sensitive to the requirements of organizing these workers in Chicago, including the need for better relations with the Catholic church and the need to cater to neighborhood and ethnic concerns.[18]

Before 1882 the name of the Knights of Labor was still not spoken publicly, and the secrecy of the organization encouraged extravagant estimates of its strength and its ultimate aims. Though the Knights had been founded by trade unionists, union members, especially Germans, were wary of the organization. In 1882 the order made several major modifications in its mode of operations to accommodate the church and improve its appeal to the masses of workers. In 1881 the Knights' general assembly allowed the name of the order to be made public and in early 1882 abolished the oath.

The Knights in Chicago did not take advantage of these dispensations until McPadden's arrival. In December 1881 it held its first open mass meeting, and in January McPadden consented to the order's first public interview. McPadden emphasized that the order was now "open and above board," and he was eager to point out that, contrary to rumor, there had never been a Catholic pastoral issued against the Knights. A little more than a month later Master Workman Halley wrote an article in a similar vein, published on the front page of the *Progressive Age,* a trade union paper. The purpose of the article was to answer three common objections: that the Knights of Labor was a secret, oath-bound organization, that it was opposed to trade unions, and that it encouraged strikes. In answer to the first objection, Halley proclaimed, "The Knights of Labor have now become strong enough to leave their hiding places and make their professions in public." Then Halley stated that the Knights aimed "only to bind, toughen and enlarge the trade union system." He continued, "Amalgamation of different trades with a common purpose and a common fund alone has proved successful. The Knights of Labor have recognized this fact and are a grander embodiment of the principle of amalgamation." Finally, Halley reiterated the Knights' stand favoring arbitration over strikes.[19]

Perhaps the most important appeal made by the Knights to Chicago workers was their claim to offer an alternative to strikes and conflict. Labor activists were searching for a form of organization and a strategy that could win demands without bringing down on their heads undue public condemnation. The Knights' claim that perfect unity and organization could, by itself, compel employers to bargain and arbitrate seemed to offer an answer to this dilemma. But it was an abstract claim, largely empty since it had first been made in 1877. The importance of the boycott was that it seemed to concretize this promise. In his January interview McPadden, when queried about the "Irish system of boycotting," endorsed it as "one of our most potent weapons" in place of strikes. A few days later, speaking before the carpenters, McPadden pointed to the success of the Pittsburgh Knights in boycotting rat, or scab, printers. "If the union printers in this city would join hands with the Knights," the *Tribune* reported, McPadden "would guarantee that the proprietor of the [nonunion] *Times* would shortly . . . request them to name their own terms." Similarly, Joe Gruenhut, correspondent of the *Progressive Age*, argued that the formation of an "amalgamated building trades union" would enable tradespeople to "boycott" scabs on the building site.[20]

Using arguments such as these and rumors that Archbishop Feehan had urged Catholic workers to join the Knights, McPadden began a whirlwind campaign on behalf of the order among local unions. In early March McPadden had formed local assemblies among the butchers, packinghouse workers, dry-goods clerks, bricklayers, caddymakers, assortment workers, solderers, machinists and blacksmiths, brass finishers, patternmakers, sewing women, brickmakers, and iron and steel workers. Within a month the painters and the tanners and curriers had also joined, and by July there were 4,000 local members, up from 766 in October 1881, giving credence to McPadden's prophecy that by the end of the year the Knights in Chicago would have 50,000 members.[21]

The new assemblies were organized on a more liberal basis than even the new Knights rules permitted. In July Grand Master Workman Powderly sounded a note of caution: "I am afraid many of the new LA's are of mushroom growth. . . . They told me in person that they supposed that they were to be organized on the plan of the Land League. No more secrecy or formula, that is a wrong impression." Among German trade unionists the effect of the order's new openness was signaled by Joe Gruenhut's change of opinion. In February he objected to the Knights because "secrecy isn't possible when you get a large scale amalgamation." By May he concluded, "The amalgamated union of the Knights of Labor is our only salvation, industrially, politically, and socially."[22]

The Knights' new policy had its greatest impact on Irish workers, including the packinghouse workers, butchers, brickmakers, blast-furnacemen, and others with a Bridgeport connection. The painters' union, brought into the Knights as LA 1940 under their president John J. Mahoney, illustrated the Irish connection. Born in Chicago of Irish parents, Mahoney had been active from his youth in nationalist politics. In November 1881 he was an officer in the first central Land League established in Chicago, and beginning in 1883 he was an officer in the United Irish Societies, eventually becoming its president. Possibly a Clan na Gael leader, Mahoney continued as a well-known nationalist through the 1890s. Within the Knights he served as a district worthy foreman and an organizer in 1882. Another Irish nationalist leader in the Land League was John B. Murphy, who led the tanners and curriers' union into the Knights. Meanwhile, Richard Powers, both a prestigious trade union leader and an Irish nationalist, proclaimed himself a Knight.[23]

By mid-1882 the Knights of Labor appeared to be on the verge of fulfilling the promise of 1877, when it had unsuccessfully sought to take the local labor movement under its wing. The order set up citywide offices and a labor bureau to compete with corrupt private employment agencies. Not only did it hold open recruiting meetings, but it offered lecture series at local assemblies by a variety of labor reform figures, including the antimonopolist journalist O. J. Smith, the eight-hour advocate Albert Parsons, and the advocate of voluntary cooperation John R. Markle. DA 24 organized a band and glee club. The new working-women's assembly, headed by Elizabeth Rodgers, entertained its brother assemblies with songs and recitations and played an important role in raising strike funds.[24]

The Knights soon overshadowed the Trades and Labor Assembly as the city's umbrella organization, even though it had far fewer members. More so than the Trades and Labor Assembly, the Knights mediated labor disputes and sponsored picnics and balls for the benefit of strikers. There was little overt conflict between the Knights and local trade unionists even though the two labor federations sometimes openly competed for the allegiance of organized workers. This was largely because the pro-union attitude of Knights leaders attracted Trades and Labor Assembly leaders into the order, notably George Rodgers and Richard Powers. The Knights also helped fund the *Progressive Age* and adopted it as the order's official Chicago organ.[25]

The 1882 movement for solidarity and amalgamation, led by the Knights and spurred by the popularity of the Land League's boycott, reached its apex in the tanners' and curriers' strike in May. The seventy-two-day conflict was the first sympathy strike in Chicago's history, and according to the Illinois Bureau of Labor Statistics, it was "one of the most remarkable on record," a strike "conducted on the principle of the Knights of Labor which proclaims that 'an injury to one is the concern of all.'" But the strike also revealed the dilemmas and weaknesses inherent in the Knights' strategy and appeal to the city's trade unions.

The 1,500 men employed in Chicago's tanning industry were divided into two skill categories. The tanners or beamsters were all foreign-born, mostly recently arrived immigrants. They performed the most difficult, repulsive work at a dollar a week less than the pay of the more skilled, English-speaking curriers. In March 1882 the German-speaking tanners joined the Knights as LA 1801, followed by the English-speaking curriers as LA 1810. On May 15 the tanners struck for a dollar pay increase to equal the pay of the curriers. When the two largest firms in the city refused to give in, the curriers struck one plant in sympathy, and the rest joined to beat a threatened lockout. By the third week of the strike 450 men were on strike, most of them curriers.[26]

To the *Tribune* the class solidarity that had prompted the curriers to unite with the immigrant tanners was wholly unwarranted and inexplicable: "Here is a strike by a body of skilled workmen not for an increase in wages, not because any reduction in wages, not because of any disagreement about hours or rules, nor because of any grievance of their own, but because of a sentimental and sympathetic feeling for another class of workmen." The *Progressive Age*, however, hailed the strike as "something new and wonderful. We might say that nothing like it was ever known before."[27]

The strike impaled the Knights on the horns of a dilemma. Though the district assembly had not sanctioned the walkout, the Knights felt bound to back it because it symbolized their labor philosophy. Since it came in the midst of several other strikes, however, support for the strike placed the local order in the position of supporting strikes over arbitration, and it strained its resources.

How the Knights handled the dilemma revealed an emerging split in the local order and prefigured later problems. At first Richard Griffiths, the order's titular leader, discountenanced the strike. Halley, however, aware of the strike's popularity, reversed the decision, though he announced that the district assembly would not assess its assemblies and would accept only voluntary strike contributions. He then attempted to arbitrate the strike by offering to rescind the tanners' demand for a dollar pay increase in return for taking the workers back. The strikers refused to accept this, as did the large employers, who sent East for the latest "whitening" and "fleshing" machines, whose installation was expected to result in the layoff of half the firm's labor force.[28]

With the backs of the employers thus stiffened, the order, unable to arbitrate the dispute in the midst of a wave of walkouts, published on the front page of the *Progressive Age* an appeal entitled "Indiscriminate striking must be stopped." It advised workers to "wait patiently until the time comes when your just demands cannot be resisted" and to "give up this folly of isolated and futile strikes . . . at present." When arbitration failed and the Knights withdrew support, the strike withered. On July 26 the strikers capitulated, and the two largest tanning firms in the city became nonunion shops.[29]

The tanners' and curriers' strike exposed the inherent contradictions in the new departure of Halley and McPadden. In attempting to convert trade unions to the order, they had collapsed the distinction between unionism and the Knights' labor reform orientation and between strikes and peaceful arbitration by relying on the lure of labor solidarity and boycott. Many local unionists were under the misapprehension that the district assembly would support their strikes if only they would join the order. Though most strikes of 1882 had been successful, the dramatic defeat of the tanners signaled the beginning of intransigent employers' opposition and the decline of public support for labor demands. Within a year of its high point in 1882, membership in the order declined by half, a dismal conclusion to a year that began with a prediction of fifty thousand members. The deflated expectations powerfully contributed to a series of internecine disputes in the district assembly that culminated in the conviction and removal of Halley as master workman by a DA court.[30]

That year Powderly spoke of a "tidal wave of strikes that has swept over our Order," and he blamed organizers' exaggerated reports of the Knights' strength. "Such a course," he declared, "may lead men into the Order, but by a path that leads them out again, for as soon as they become convinced that they were deceived they lose confidence in the Order."[31]

In the context of decline, confusion, and disappointment DA 24 split. During the spring of 1883 half a dozen local assemblies withdrew from DA 24, now run by Griffiths's allies, to form DA 57. All were from Bridgeport or Pilsen in the southern portion of the city. The largest number were Irish-led assemblies that had supported Halley in the DA 24 dispute. DA 57 took a more militant position than did DA 24, whose motto was "Safety through Caution" and in 1880 had called on the national organization to abolish the resistance fund or use it solely for cooperation.[32]

As an organization dedicated to labor solidarity, the Knights of Labor was the best situated of any group in the labor movement to take advantage of the class implications of the Irish boycott movement. Yet the unwillingness of Powderly nationally and Griffiths locally to risk the future of the order in a series of—what they saw as dubious—strikes not only set limits on how far the boycott could be carried but also led to confusing compromises that resulted in internal disputes.

The Chicago Movement for Land Nationalization

In 1882, while the boycott was becoming popular in the city, the Chicago Land League, despite superficial unity, was a potential powder keg of factionalism. On the one hand were the followers of Patrick Ford, a group that included greenbackers, antimonopolists, English-speaking socialists, and Irish trade unionists, many of them Knights. The Ford followers believed that the Land League's nationalist and respectable leadership masked the divergent interests of tenant and poor laborer. Because they believed that landlordism was common to both Ireland and the United States, they viewed the Irish Land League as part of the international labor movement. On the other hand were the followers of the Clan na Gael, which emphasized the national over the social question and the differences between republican America and oppressed Ireland. For Irish nationalists and conservatives alike the social question was only a means of achieving home rule or independence.

Beginning in the spring of 1882 a series of events in Ireland unleashed a crisis in the Land League that made it impossible to paper over the profound social and political differences among its members in the United States. As a result, the issue of land nationalization rose to the forefront of the movement, and many partisans of the movement became open to the ideas of Henry George and other currents of radicalism in the labor movement.

Between 1880 and 1881 Parnell successfully channeled the explosive discontent of Irish tenants and the enthusiasm and funds of Irish-Americans into a constitutional struggle against landlordism. In April 1881 William Gladstone, the British prime minister, responded by offering a land reform bill in Parliament that met most of the demands of the Land League by enabling tenants to win tenure over the land. Simultaneously, Gladstone outlawed the Land League and suspended habeas corpus to dampen peasant violence. Though Parnell's differences with Gladstone were not great, he refused to accept the land bill, thereby retaining the loyalty of Michael Davitt and Ford, who wanted to destroy landlordism altogether. Parnell's refusal to support the bill led to his imprisonment in October, along with Davitt and other nationalist leaders.[33]

The imprisonment of Land League leaders set off a wave of protests in the United States. Opposition to the arrest and the British reform bill took a more leftward turn when the Land League issued a "no-rent manifesto," calling on tenant farmers to refuse to pay rent until "constitutional liberties" were restored and the imprisoned leaders freed. It was now difficult to dodge the question: was no-rent a tactic to secure the release of the imprisoned leaders or was it a step toward the revolutionary abolition of landlordism as advocated by Davitt and Ford? At the Land League's Chicago convention in November the interpretation of no-rent was contested, and again differences were papered over. Only the socialist Spread the Light clubs carried no-rent to its logical conclusion by calling for the abolition of landlordism, and for that they were excluded from the convention. The Ford partisans were content to have the question left unanswered. Debate over this question continued after the convention. It took the form of discussion among the Ford clubs whether to "boycott" W. P. Rend, a local coal operator who said what many conservatives were no doubt feeling when he criticized the no-rent manifesto as dangerous to property.[34]

Factionalism in the Land League was also fueled by controversy over Parnell's call for women's land leagues to carry on the Irish movement after the existing Land League had been outlawed for trying to implement the no-rent policy. Chicago women responded by forming the Ellen Ford, Annie Parnell, Sebena Davitt, and Sarah Curran Land League clubs. The names suggested radical land politics, and their mere existence was enough to challenge conservative ideas about women's subordination in the public sphere. With apathy besetting many of the men's clubs in 1882, the women's groups took up the slack and assumed a highly visible role in organizing parades, balls, and bazaars. The women's participation became a political issue when Cleveland's Bishop Richard Gilmour condemned their political work as unwomanly. This prompted loud defenses of the women from John Finerty's *Citizen*, which further sharpened differences.[35]

The simmering divisions in the Land League finally erupted in May 1882, when Gladstone, fearful of escalating ferment in Ireland decided to meet Parnell's objections to the land bill. In the Kilmainham Treaty Parnell agreed to support the bill, now supplemented by a special act that removed all arrears in rent accrued up to May 1, 1881, by a payment of one year's rent. The new legislation allowed evicted tenants to take advantage of the land act. Gladstone also released the imprisoned leaders. In return Parnell agreed to rescind the no-rent manifesto, implicitly admitting that the manifesto had been a tactic after all. At this point Davitt, just released from prison, dropped a bombshell. He announced his conversion to the theory of land nationalization and commenced a speaking tour in the United States.

Henry George had recently traveled to Ireland as Ford's correspondent and had written a pamphlet, *The Irish Land Question,* as a more accessible sequel to his opus *Progress and Poverty.* To George, land monopoly was the root of all class injustice and poverty. His solution, the full taxation of land rent, appealed not only to rural landless laborers but also to urban proletarians, for whom land rent explained how industrial capitalists grew wealthy off their labor. But it did little to meet the immediate land hunger of the Irish tenants, whom the Land League championed. Davitt's espousal of state ownership of the land went further than George's proposal. It also inverted the premise of the new departure, for Davitt appeared to posit international reform as the goal of Irish movement rather than as the means to popularize independence or home rule.[36]

Davitt's support for land nationalization not only wreaked havoc in the Land League but suddenly lent legitimacy to the ideas of George, Ford, and their supporters. When Davitt visited Chicago at the end of June, the old guard of the Clan na Gael was decidedly cool to him, while the SLP, Knights of Labor, and local trade unionists were positively ecstatic. The *Progressive Age,* which had earlier professed itself unable to decide on the practicability of land nationalization, editorialized that "Davitt is simply agitating for one of the cardinal principles of the universal labor movement, which happens at this time to be of paramount importance in Ireland and will soon be the leading issue in the national politics of the United States and the Canadian Dominion." The Trades and Labor Assembly joined the Irish agitation for the first time when, along with the Knights, it cohosted a formal reception for Davitt. The local Knights, too, hailed "the belief that the land must become the common heritage of all and be in reality the commonwealth of all not of a few."[37]

The socialists saw special reason to claim George and Davitt as their own. In the early 1880s George was widely viewed (mistakenly) as a land nationalist or land socialist. In England George's single-tax theories served H. M. Hyndman and George Bernard Shaw as a way station on the road to socialist thinking and the Fabian Society. In the United States English-speaking socialists viewed his ideas as a vehicle for further Americanizing socialism. Immediately after Davitt's announcement Tommy Ryan formed the Henry George Land League Club, and later in the year T. J. Morgan and George Schilling endorsed George's theories. Charles S. Wheeler, a machinist who was the financial secretary of the Socialist Labor party, even claimed that land monopoly was the basis of all monopoly.[38]

More than socialists it was the Knights who were able to assume the mantle of George and Davitt. This was largely because Powderly, who had long been concerned with land reform, announced his own conversion to Davitt's theories at the 1882 general assembly of the Knights. "The land," he said, echoing a popular formulation, "is the property of all generations including those to come." Powderly believed that "the American labor movement and . . . the Irish land movement" were "almost identical." The convergence of the two movements actually proved short-lived, for Davitt quickly retreated from his advanced position and publicly declared his willingness to subordinate the social question to the national one. The Knights, however, continued to support these ideas.[39]

The evidence for this is fragmentary but suggestive. Toward the end of 1883 the large painters' assembly of DA 24 decided to devote twenty minutes of each meeting to a reading of *Progress and Poverty.* This occurred at the same time that the Anti-Monopoly party, a coalition of Knights and socialists, advocated a program of land nationalization in the fall 1883 elections. In March 1884 DA 24 presented a document to the Trades and Labor Assembly that called "the present monopolistic ownership of the land . . . the chief cause of those social inequalities represented by the millionaires on the one hand and the tramps on the other." The Knights demanded as a solution a tax on unimproved land held for speculative purposes equal to the tax on improved land. A year later a DA 24 committee again advocated the end of private ownership of land as the condition for ending monopoly. It is noteworthy that before 1882 there is no evidence that George's ideas were discussed in the local labor movement.[40]

The popularization of the boycott and the ideas of land nationalization were not the only significant outcomes of the Irish Land League's agitation in 1882. Those nationalists opposed to the corrupt, pro-Democratic machine leadership of Clan na Gael chief Alexander Sullivan were also inspired by the events of that year. In 1880 the Republican-dominated state legislature, in the hopes of cordoning off Democratic strength in the city, created the heavily Democratic Second Congressional District, consisting of large areas of the Fifth, Sixth, Seventh, and Eighth wards. Since about two-thirds of the voters were Irish and there was no credible Republican opposition, the 1882 primary election served to air differences in the Irish nationalist movement. The Clan na Gael's leadership united behind Henry F. Sheridan and secured his nomination. Nationalists opposed to Sullivan coalesced around the independent candidacy of John F. Finerty. As a Republican and former *Tribune* correspondent, Finerty attracted lace-curtain and other Irish yearning for respectability. But Finerty also won the support of the Irish trade unionists Richard Powers, Dan Gleason of the bricklayers' union, Leo P. Dwyer of the painters' union, and the SLPer Dan Sullivan.[41]

In the election Finerty handily defeated Sheridan, clearly demonstrating the growing strength of the independent vote in Chicago. Many voters split their tickets, particularly in the Fifth Ward. Though devoid of the social content that had marked the Davitt-Ford-George movement, the Finerty campaign showed that the Land League had infused many working-class Irish with the rationale, the organization, and the leadership to break free from community loyalties that bound them to local Democratic machines, much as the leadership of the Knights had done for outdoor laborers in Bridgeport. Throughout the rest of the decade there was a large group of South Side Irish who could not be taken for granted by the Chicago Democratic party and who were a potential constituency for independent labor politics.

The Land League movement of the 1880s has been seen as a means of freeing Ireland and remaking it in the image of republican America. Yet for the followers of Patrick Ford it was also a means of reconstructing the United States in the image of the Land League's social radicalism. The Irish movement has been interpreted as a force for assimilating the Irish into an American middle-class reform culture. Yet it also played a powerful role in the creation of an American working-class political culture. In short the boycott and land nationalization had a dialectical effect on supporters of the Land League, confounding common stereotypes about "traditional" Ireland sending its peasants (and movements) to the United States, where they could be "modernized."[42]

It should not be surprising that the Knights of Labor served as the primary vehicle for the creation of a new working-class culture mediated by the

Irish Land League struggle. As an organization with one foot in the democratic reform tradition and the other in the trade union movement, the order was well placed to mediate between the Land League and labor institutions. After 1882 the Knights became a different organization, distinctly Irish in leadership and tone. Fully 40 percent of the names of all delegates and officers of Chicago's two district assemblies were Irish.[43] The order also became more militant and more in touch with Chicago's industrial working class, yet all the while retaining its prior commitment to labor reform.

Notes

1. Examples of the first view are Thomas N. Brown, *Irish-American Nationalism, 1870–1890* (Philadelphia: J. B. Lippincott, 1966); and Michael Funchion, *Chicago's Irish Nationalists, 1881–1890* (New York: Arno, 1976). On the relation of nationalism to an Irish working-class identity, see Eric Foner, "Class, Ethnicity, and Radicalism in the Gilded Age: The Irish Land League and Irish-America," in *Politics and Ideology in the Age of the Civil War* (Oxford: Oxford University Press, 1980), 150–200; Michael A. Gordon, "The Labor Boycott in New York City, 1880–1886," *Labor History* 16 (Spring 1975): 185–229; Victor Walsh, "'A Fanatic Heart': The Cause of Irish-American Nationalism in Pittsburgh during the Gilded Age," *Journal of Social History* 15 (Winter 1981): 187–204; David Brundage, "Irish Land and American Workers: Class and Ethnicity in Denver, Colorado," in *"Struggle a Hard Battle": Essays on Working-Class Immigrants*, ed. Dirk Hoerder (De Kalb: Northern Illinois University Press, 1986), 121–42; and David M. Eammons, *The Butte Irish: Class and Ethnicity in an American Mining Town, 1875–1925* (Urbana: University of Illinois Press, 1989).

2. Foner, "Class, Ethnicity, and Radicalism in the Gilded Age," 154–55; Brown, *Irish-American Nationalism*, 85–98.

3. *Chicago Tribune*, Feb. 8, 1880, Feb. 24, 1880.

4. Ruth Ann Piper, "The Irish in Chicago, 1848–1871" (Master's thesis, University of Chicago, 1936), 18; Funchion, *Chicago's Irish Nationalists*, 264; *Chicago Tribune*, Aug. 16, 1877, Aug. 26, 1877, Feb. 21, 1881.

5. *Irish World and American Industrial Liberator*, June 18, 1881; Funchion, *Chicago's Irish Nationalists*, 75–81; Robert Cross, *The Emergence of Liberal Catholicism in America* (Cambridge, Mass.: Harvard University Press, 1958), 115–20.

6. Alfred T. Andreas, *History of Chicago from the Earliest Period to the Present Time* (Chicago: A. T. Andreas, 1884–86), 3:765; *Chicago Tribune*, Oct. 9, 1881 (quote); Cornelius J. Kirkfleet, *The Life of Patrick Augustine Feehan* (Chicago: Matre, 1922), 158–60. On Waldron, see Harry C. Koenig, ed., *A History of the Parishes of the Archdiocese of Chicago* (Chicago: Archdiocese of Chicago, 1980), 1:389; 2:1656–57; and *Chicago Tribune*, July 13, 1881. On Hodnett, see Koenig, *History of the Parishes*, 1:436, 550, 552. On Hagen, see *Chicago Tribune*, May 24, 1882, Aug. 7, 1882, and Mar. 4, 1883. On Dorney, see *Chicago Tribune*, May 2, 1881, May 25, 1881, Aug. 16, 1881; and Funchion, *Chicago's Irish Nationalists*, chap. 4.

7. *Irish World and American Industrial Liberator*, Oct. 18, 1879, May 1, 1880 (first quote), Oct. 2, 1880, Oct. 16, 1880 (second quote).

8. *Irish World and American Industrial Liberator,* Dec. 29, 1879, May 22, 1880 (quote), Oct. 2, 1880; manuscript, n.d., Reel 2, Thomas J. Morgan Papers (microfilm), Illinois Historical Survey, Springfield.

9. *Chicago Tribune,* Jan. 31, 1881, Apr. 3, 1881 (first quote); *Irish World and American Industrial Liberator,* Jan. 8, 1881 (second quote).

10. *Chicago Tribune,* Jan. 17, 1880, Dec. 11, 1880, Jan. 10, 1881, Feb. 5, 1881, Dec. 11, 1881; *Irish World and American Industrial Liberator,* Apr. 9, 1881; Foner, "Class, Ethnicity, and Radicalism in the Gilded Age," 171.

11. Brown, *Irish-American Nationalism,* 102; *Chicago Tribune,* Feb. 18, 1881.

12. *Chicago Tribune,* Feb. 7, 1881; *Irish World and American Industrial Liberator,* Apr. 9, 1881.

13. *Chicago Tribune,* Apr. 8, 1881, Apr. 9, 1881 (quote); *Progressive Age,* Apr. 2, 1881.

14. *Chicago Tribune,* Apr. 9, 1881. The Trades Assembly had unsuccessfully attempted a boycott of prison labor in 1868. Bessie Louise Pierce, *A History of Chicago,* vol. 2, *From Town to City, 1848–1871* (New York: Alfred A. Knopf, 1940), 185.

15. Harry W. Laidler, *Boycotts and the Labor Struggle* (New York: John Lane, 1913), 56–68; Leo Wolman, *The Boycott in American Trade Unions* (Baltimore, Md.: Johns Hopkins University Press, 1916), 9–15, 143; Gregory R. Zieren, "The Labor Boycott and Class Consciousness in Toledo, Ohio," in *Life and Labor: Dimensions of American Working-Class History,* ed. Charles Stephenson and Robert Asher (Albany: State University of New York Press, 1986), 131–49; *Nation* 31 (Dec. 23, 1880): 437.

16. *Chicago Tribune,* Apr. 25, 1881; *Progressive Age,* Aug. 27, 1881.

17. *Progressive Age,* July 2, 1881; *Chicago Tribune,* Oct. 12, 1881; *Cigarmakers Official Journal,* Aug. 10, 1881.

18. On Halley, see U.S. House of Representatives, *Investigation by a Select Committee of the House of Representatives Relative to the Causes of the General Depression in Labor and Business; And as to Chinese Immigration,* 46th Cong., 2d sess. (Washington, D.C.: Government Printing Office, 1879), 75–84; *Record of the Proceedings of the Sixth Regular Session of the General Assembly Held at New York City, N.Y., Sept. 5–12, 1882,* 315–17, Reel 67, in *Terence Vincent Powderly Papers, 1864–1937, and John William Hayes Papers, 1880–1921: The Knights of Labor* (Glen Rock, N.J.: Microfilming Corporation of America, 1974) (hereafter PHP); and *Irish World and American Industrial Liberator,* Jan., 3, 1880. On McPadden and O'Kelley, see John W. Bennett, "The Knights of Labor and the Clan-Na-Gael" (Prepared for the Knights of Labor Centennial Symposium, May 17–19, 1979, Newberry Library, Chicago).

19. Henry J. Browne, *The Catholic Church and the Knights of Labor* (1949; reprint, New York: Arno, 1976), 62, 63; *Chicago Tribune,* Jan. 30, 1882 (first quote); *Progressive Age,* Mar. 4, 1881 (second quote).

20. *Chicago Tribune,* Jan. 30, 1882 (first quote), Feb. 11, 1882 (second quote); *Progressive Age,* Dec. 31, 1881 (Gruenhut quote), May 20, 1882.

21. *Progressive Age,* Mar. 4, 1882, Apr. 15, 1882, Apr. 29, 1882, May 20, 1882; Knights of Labor District Assembly 24, *Minute Book,* Aug. 6, 1882, George A. Schilling Papers, Regenstein Library, University of Chicago.

22. Powderly to Halley, July 5, 1882, Reel 46, PHP; *Progressive Age*, Feb. 11, 1882, May 20, 1882.

23. Charles Ffrench, *Biographical History of the American Irish in Chicago* (Chicago: American Biographical Publishing, 1897), 465–67; *Chicago Tribune*, Dec. 8, 1880, May 2, 1881, July 5, 1882; *Progressive Age*, Feb. 11, 1882, June 3, 1882.

24. *Progressive Age*, Apr. 1, 1882, June 3, 1882, June 24, 1882, July 8, 1882; *Chicago Tribune*, June 13, 1882.

25. *Progressive Age*, June 24, 1882. Halley was on the paper's board of directors, though Powderly later disallowed it. See Knights of Labor District Assembly 24, *Minute Book*, Sept. 3, 1882.

26. *Second Biennial Report of the Illinois Bureau of Labor Statistics* (Springfield: H. W. Rokker, 1882), 274; *Progressive Age*, Apr. 1, 1882, May 20, 1882, May 27, 1882; *Chicago Tribune*, May 19, 1882.

27. *Chicago Tribune*, May 21, 1882; *Progressive Age*, May 27, 1882.

28. *Chicago Tribune*, May 19, 1882, May 22, 1882, May 26, 1882; *Second Biennial Report of the Illinois Bureau of Labor Statistics*, 276–77.

29. *Progressive Age*, June 3, 1882; *Second Biennial Report of the Illinois Bureau of Labor Statistics*, 277.

30. Net membership figures are misleading, especially for 1882–83, when there was a high turnover in membership. Between 1882 and 1883 total members admitted were reported to have risen from about 1,600 to 3,600, while net membership rose only from 1,200 to over 1,400. Much evidence indicates that 1882, not 1883, was the high point in membership. For example, Richard Griffiths, speaking before DA 24 on Apr. 30, 1883, lamented that the order was making rapid strides elsewhere in the United States, "except in Chicago where there seemed to be strong retrograde movement." Knights of Labor District Assembly 24, *Minute Book*, Apr. 30, 1883. For this reason I have taken Halley's estimate of 4,000 members in July 1882 as accurate; see Halley's defense of these figures before the 1882 Knights' general assembly in *Record of the Proceedings of the Sixth Regular Session of the General Assembly Held at New York*, 315–17. For turnover figures, see *Record of the Proceedings of the Sixth Regular Session of the General Assembly Held at New York*, 383; and *Record of the Proceedings of the Seventh Regular Session of the General Assembly Held at Cincinnati, Ohio, Sept. 4–11, 1883*, 534, 544, Reel 67, PHP.

31. *Record of the Proceedings of the Sixth Regular Session of the General Assembly Held at New York*, 278–79.

32. Ibid., 315–17; *Record of the Proceedings of the Fourth Regular Session of the General Assembly held at Pittsburgh, Pa., Sept. 7–11, 1880*, 192, 247, Reel 67, PHP; *Journal of United Labor*, Apr. 1883.

33. T. W. Moody, *Davitt and the Irish Revolution, 1846–82* (Oxford: Clarendon, 1984), 416–65; Brown, *Irish-American Nationalism*, 113–15.

34. Moody, *Davitt and the Irish Revolution*, 494–99; Brown, *Irish-American Nationalism*, 120; *Chicago Tribune*, Dec. 1, 1881, Dec. 2, 1881, Dec. 29, 1881, Jan. 1, 1882, Jan. 9, 1882; *Irish World and American Industrial Liberator*, Dec. 17, 1881.

35. *Chicago Tribune*, Nov. 22, 1881, Jan. 25, 1882, June 3, 1882, June 4, 1882, Aug. 14, 1882.

36. Brown, *Irish-American Nationalism*, 117–19; Moody, *Davitt and the Irish Revolution*, 523–26; George W. Geiger, *The Philosophy of Henry George* (1933; reprint, Westport, Conn.: Hyperion, 1975), 129–32.

37. *Progressive Age*, July 1, 1882 (first quote); *Chicago Tribune*, June 20, 1882, June 22, 1882, June 25, 1882 (second quote).

38. Geiger, *Philosophy of Henry George*, 228–35; *Chicago Tribune*, June 16, 1882, Sept. 29, 1882; *Progressive Age*, July 29, 1882; newspaper article, Dec. 11, 1888, George A. Schilling Papers, Regenstein Library, University of Chicago.

39. *Record of the Proceedings of the Sixth Regular Session of the General Assembly Held at New York*, 283 (first quote); Foner, "Class, Ethnicity, and Radicalism in the Gilded Age," 196 (second quote).

40. *Chicago Tribune*, Sept. 29, 1882; *Irish World and American Industrial Liberator*, Oct. 20, 1883, Apr. 25, 1885; *Chicago Inter-Ocean*, Mar. 27, 1884 (quote).

41. *Chicago Tribune*, Sept. 15, 1882, Oct. 10, 1882, Oct. 14, 1882, Nov. 7, 1882; Andreas, *History of Chicago*, 3:707–18; Ffrench, *Biographical History of the American Irish in Chicago*, 48–50.

42. See note 1.

43. Bruce C. Nelson, *Beyond the Martyrs: A Social History of Chicago's Anarchists, 1870–1900* (New Brunswick, N.J.: Rutgers University Press, 1988), 29, 48.

CHAPTER 6

Labor's Democracy in the Age of Carter Harrison

From the mid-1860s through the early 1880s Chicago's two major parties delivered to local workers many of the same kind of material and political benefits that socialist and labor parties did in Europe and Britain.[1] They protected and nurtured labor organization in the face of employer opposition, enacted prolabor laws while declaring antilabor laws unconstitutional, and broadcast class-oriented appeals to the electorate, thereby serving to legitimate class thinking in public discourse. This chapter discusses how the Democratic party played an aggregating role for Chicago's heterogeneous working class, bringing unity where otherwise there would have been none, not only among workers but between workers and segments of other strata. Those factions whose growing political independence has been discussed in previous chapters—German socialists, Irish nationalists, Knights, and trade unionists—all found a home under the wing of Chicago's Mayor Carter Harrison. In the optimistic phrase of Joe Gruenhut, labor's pro-Harrison intellectual, Chicago was becoming a "working class democracy, the like of which had never existed before."[2]

By the mid-1880s, however, local trade unions had developed the organizational capacities to hold political parties—whether Democratic or Socialist Labor—at arms length. One indication of this newfound independence and the power it potentially conferred was that the largest and most stable unions of skilled workers formulated and began to put into practice a strategy of formal nonpartisanship and bargaining with the two parties. The new strategy justified a continuing alliance with the Harrison regime but also promised a relatively autonomous and more recognizably modern "interest group" posture for labor in an emerging liberal polity.

Carter Harrison and the Politics of Personalism

To understand Carter Harrison, his origins, his brand of politics and governing, and his relations with labor and other social groups, one must understand his relationship with the Democratic party's organizational network or "machine." Chicago's governing Democratic party, like other parties in this era, was constrained in its ability to disburse patronage, public improvements, and city services for political purposes. The settlement of the mid-1870s, wherein property owners tolerated party rule in return for a low or nonexistent property tax assessment, a low legislated debt limit, and low taxes generally, set severe limits on the revenues available for municipal spending. Between 1880 and 1902 average per capita city outlays in Chicago actually fell 8.3 percent. If debt is added, Chicago's total liabilities were still low, lower than for other large cities in 1891. The historian Bessie Pierce has concluded that the demand for increased revenues to extend government services chronically "outran the natural increase of income accruing from the greater size of the city." The stereotype, purveyed by reformers of this era, that the governing "machines" of the 1870s and 1880s wasted money in orgies of patronage and pork spending is simply not supported by the evidence.[3]

The fiscal constraints on government explain several important characteristics of local party government. First, the number of patronage jobs was limited as a source for paying off supporters. The principal governmental entity expending revenue between 1871 and 1893 was the Department of Public Works, and, as in other cities, it was under the control of business leaders. The single largest project of these years, the building of a canal to drain the reversed Chicago River, prompted leading businesspeople and reformers in the city to create an autonomous taxing and spending authority, the Sanitary District, and enter a reform electoral slate in 1889 to prevent its jobs from being distributed politically.[4]

Though patronage certainly did exist and was an important source of party financing and cohesion, its limits, in the context of the need to offer constituents incentives to vote and get out the vote, put great pressure on politicians to engage in corrupt activities, especially in granting lucrative corporate franchises. The boodle that greased these deals provided the money to fund campaigns and make politics worthwhile as a vehicle of upward mobility. Another major source of boodle came from the payoffs to politicians from faro, craps, and roulette gamblers, houses of prostitution, and other purveyors of illegal activities to avoid arrest and prosecution. In Chicago the gamblers' political representative was Mike McDonald, who came as close to being a Democratic party boss as anyone in this era through financing party campaigns and influencing nominating conventions. But McDonald could not be a boss in the manner of a Richard Crocker of New York's Tammany Hall, because Chicago, like most cities in the 1880s, lacked a centralized machine for controlling nominations and dictating policy.[5]

The fact that party politics rested on a fiscal pyramid whose building blocks were low taxes, retrenchment in spending, and franchise and gambling corruption dictated the characteristic form that local political issues assumed in this era. The taboo on government's redistributive spending—"class" legislation—meant that politics tended to be limited to the distribution of benefits and favors by political parties. During the last two-thirds of the nineteenth century the party practiced many of the functions undertaken by government in the twentieth century. The distribution of such government benefits as land, Civil War pensions, and tariff protection on the national level and franchises and tax exemptions on the local level was, suggests Richard L. McCormick, "the policy equivalent of patronage," for "it strengthened parties and helped build bridges between their voters, leaders, and representatives in office."[6]

One major form of "distributive" politics practiced by the Democratic party was granting individuals immunity from existing laws. Such practices built political support in the manner of a logrolling coalition. Open compromise was not necessary; it was only necessary that the different parties to the coalition not oppose similar immunities for others. Because laws did not have to be repealed, such an approach did not unduly offend those who supported the principle for which the law stood. Local political leaders had used this strategy of immunity since the 1860s to deal with temperance. The inability of party leaders to deal with temperance in the old, informal way, which began when Joseph Medill's Union-Fireproof party decided to enforce the law in 1873, compelled the People's party to repeal the Sunday-closing law in 1874, bringing in the state in a formal way. The fire limit was another issue over which the party system tried to retain control but which the Citizens Association made a regulatory issue. By 1880, however, the Democratic party regime had returned the issue to party control. The *Tribune* charged that the "violations of the building ordinance are frequent and flagrant and as a rule they go unpunished" because "the police and the mayor who appoints them and the aldermen who solicit their appointment are at best indifferent to the whole matter." Another distributive practice that attracted workers to local Democrats was police inaction during the Bridgeport strikes, discussed in chapters 4 and 5.[7]

The political history of the 1870s had shown party politics to be highly vulnerable, first to the interference of organized business interests and later to workers politicized by the 1877 strikes and riots. By the 1880s party leaders could no longer incorporate working people into parties by merely granting immunities; they also had to make an overt group appeal, which in turn implied a new liberal style of politics that required an expanded state capacity to regulate and even redistribute public benefits. The developing incompatibility between new social forces and these older modes of political mobilization help explain Carter Harrison's style of leadership. Harrison was able to supplement the old appeal by making a special personal appeal to organized ethnic and class groups on the basis of a limited acceptance of new social issues.

Harrison's need to practice a politics of personalism was magnified because Chicago in the late 1870s remained a Republican city, and to win office Democrats had to pitch special appeals to groups either marginally Democratic or wholly outside the party fold. By the late 1870s and early 1880s there were four such groups: upper-class mugwumps, liberal Germans (often nominal Republicans or socialists), Irish nationalists, and trade unionists.

The Citizens Association of Chicago was not the only association of business reformers with which party leaders had to contend. In 1877 many of the same businessmen formed the Commercial Club, another nonpartisan association but one restricted to the sixty outstanding leaders in the city's most important industries. The club served as a forum for political discussion and as a caucus within the Citizens Association. Businessmen were also represented by clubs within their respective parties: the Republican Union League Club formed in 1879 and the Democratic Iroquois Club formed in 1882. By the 1880s organized business leaders were a potent force in the city, a constituency that could not be taken for granted.[8]

Democratic party businessmen were of two types. The first were utility and railroad interests that needed to cultivate a relationship with the party in power to secure advantageous corporate franchise arrangements. The second group consisted of packinghouse employers and allied industries in tanning and boot and shoemaking. These men, including Cyrus McCormick, were often exporters, attracted by the party's antitariff stance nationally. Like other businessmen, they were placated by Harrison's ability to hold the line on spending and taxing. In return they left local politics to party leaders and seem to have made a conscious effort to avoid antagonizing the city's workers by not being intransigent during strikes. In 1877 and 1886 the packers quietly acceded to their employees demands to avoid a confrontation, secure in the expectation that they could renege on the agreement once strike fever died down. The exception occurred in 1885, when the young Cyrus McCormick, who had abandoned his father's support of Harrison in that year's city election, lost his police support during a strike of iron molders. When the conflict threatened to escalate into a riot, Chicago's leading packer, Phil Armour, sent a letter to McCormick advising him to settle with his men to avoid an "open war" between classes.[9]

Harrison was famous for his ability to win the support of many nominally Republican businesspeople, despite the fierce antagonism of the Republican party press. Harrison's fiscal frugality was publicly attested to by his appointment of honest professionals and respected businessmen, many of them Republicans, to top positions. This included the crucial financial posts of comptroller, the "financial czar" of the city, and the head of the Department of Public Works. Harrison also appointed Lyman De Wolf as the commissioner of Health and Joseph Bonfield as corporation counsel, both Republicans. When he dismissed the existing fire marshal upon assuming office in 1879, leading citizens expressed fears that Harrison would repoliticize the department. The mayor responded by appointing another professional to the vacated post. Such policies allowed Harrison to attract to the party respectable elements that had not been incorporated in other ways. The police department, however, remained in political hands, allowing Democrats to enforce laws selectively to accommodate a variety of other interests.[10]

Harrison's unique capacity to attract foreign-born voters perhaps derived from his background as a Kentucky gentleman-planter, which accustomed him to wielding authority and afforded him experience in patronizing the "lower orders." It may have also stemmed from his extensive travels and residence in Europe as a young man, where he acquired a sympathetic knowledge and tolerance of European customs. Harrison felt no reform compulsion to transform and uplift the city's ethnic working classes. He consequently was the city's first mayor to make a direct appeal to Chicago's ethnic working-class voters.[11]

One of the most critical groups in the new Harrison coalition were the Germans. Catholic Germans, under the leadership of General Herman Lieb, head of the Water Department, were already solidly Democratic because of the saloon issue. Harrison, who viewed Chicago as a "cosmopolitan city," made it clear he would maintain his policy of tolerating such foreign customs as Sunday drinking, but liberal Germans required a supplemental appeal. Though driven out of the Republican party over temperance in 1873, they had returned by 1876 out of revulsion at the patronage hogging by the Irish and the open corruption in the People's party. By 1879 liberal Germans themselves were split. Anton Hesing supporters followed the *Staats Zeitung* in favoring Harrison. Others had voted for the Socialist Labor party candidate, Ernst Schmidt, who had left the Republicans over their "pro-capitalist" policies. Under these circumstances Harrison needed not only to hold on to Hesing's supporters but also to win over the socialists, which he did by giving their leaders patronage jobs, defending their right to free speech and assembly, and in general legitimizing their presence in the city.[12]

A good test of the thesis that former Republican, now Socialist Labor party, voters were a key to Harrison's success came in the 1881 mayoral election, after two years of concerted Harrison attempts to woo the socialists. In the SLP stronghold of the Fourteenth Ward the party's aldermanic candidate received 837 votes, while its mayoral candidate received only 231 votes. The *Tribune* reported that many SLP voters were "pasting Harrison's name on their ticket." In the Sixteenth Ward, where the SLP elected an alderman, Harrison won handily, with only 75 of 1,359 SLP aldermanic supporters voting the straight ticket. In analyzing Harrison's reelection, the *Tribune* blamed "socialists who read foreign newspapers" as first among the causes of the Republican party's defeat.[13]

Chicago's Irish nationalists were another troublesome constituency that required Harrison's personal attention. Alexander Sullivan, leader of the Clan na Gael, had kept nationalists strongly Democratic until the Land League's agitation in 1882, when the Republican John J. Finerty had tapped sentiment associated with land nationalization and the boycott to defeat a regular Democrat in the primary election for alderman. When Harrison snubbed an early nationalist meeting, it became clear that he had underestimated the political significance of Irish nationalism. Harrison quickly made amends by undercutting the regular Democrats in Bridgeport during the 1882 election by printing two sets of tickets, one with Finerty's name on it and the other with that of Finerty's regular Democratic party opponent, thus allowing Democrats to split their tickets. Following the election, which Finerty won, Harrison appointed Finerty supporters to local government, including Finerty's campaign manager to the post of superintendent of the Water Meter Department. Realizing the continuing importance of the nationalist vote, Harrison visited Dublin the year of the mayoral election to make a celebrated speech condemning British tyranny. In the election of that year Harrison ran about a thousand votes ahead of the vote for the Democratic candidate for city treasurer, who opposed a popular nationalist running on the Republican ticket. About 22 percent of Bridgeport's Fifth Ward voters that year were ticket splitters.[14] Harrison, of course, appealed to the city's workers not merely as Irish nationalists or German socialists but also as trade unionists, the fourth special constituency of the new Democratic coalition.

THE BEGINNINGS OF TRADE UNION POLITICS, 1879–82

By December 1881 fifty trades in Chicago had unions of varying strengths, up from about fifteen earlier in the year. This newfound strength made it possible for union and Knights leaders to separate from the confining umbrella provided by political socialists, greenbackers, and antimonopolists and build a union-based labor movement. This movement and the direction it traveled owed much to two other developments: the disillusionment with independent labor politics and the reaction against state socialism.[15]

By 1881 the labor press was filled with articles expressing disappointment with the results of third-party labor politics. The *Progressive Age* argued that the history of labor parties showed that workers were continually betrayed by politicians who had been rejected by one of the two parties and had posed as labor candidates to regain office. John J. Page, a leader of the local Knights of Labor, blamed the decline of the local order on "political tricksters." In 1882 a canvass of District Assembly 24 on the question of involvement in independent politics found only seven of the sixteen assemblies in favor of "secret supporting action." Nationally, Robert Layton, the general secretary of the Knights of Labor, declared in 1882 that the order would henceforth shelve independent labor politics in favor of trying to deliver the labor vote to whichever party could make good on its promises. Locally, the ignominious defeat in 1882 of a slate of candidates endorsed by the Trades and Labor Assembly was the final straw for many unionists. Perhaps the most profound disillusionment with politics occurred among German SLPers following the unseating of Alderman Frank Stauber in 1880 because of blatant fraud. George Schilling wrote that this event "did more, perhaps than all the other things combined to destroy the faith of the Socialists in Chicago in the efficiency of the ballot."[16]

Meanwhile, state socialism, at best superficial in its hold on Chicago labor activists, evaporated following the electoral decline of the SLP. In 1881 the *Irish World* ran a long debate between a state socialist, William G. Smart from Boston, and a champion of individualism and producer cooperation, who wrote under the pseudonym "Philip." This debate, followed by the inauguration of the periodical *Liberty* by the American anarchist Benjamin Tucker, made "systematic converts" in Chicago to "the principle of voluntary association in contradistinction to State Control," according to George Schilling. Reinforced by the new distrust of independent political action, a large faction of German-speaking SLPers, together with a small number of English-speakers, seceded in 1881 to form the Revolutionary Socialist Labor party, which in 1883 merged into the International Working Peoples' Association (IWPA). Misnamed "anarchists," IWPAers were actually socialists who rejected electoral politics as a means and state control as the end of the workers' movement. In the Pittsburgh Manifesto of 1883 they adopted a proto-syndicalist program embracing revolutionary violence to establish a "free state," consisting of autonomous, self-regulating communes bound together by voluntary contracts.[17]

The same associational, antistatist resurgence was evident among trade unionists and Knights. In the *Progressive Age* John R. Markle, an apostle of Henry George and Herbert Spencer, attacked statists who ridiculed workers' efforts to free themselves by their own associations and who relied on the "paternal" state. Even William Halley, a less doctrinaire Knight who favored state ownership of monopolies and state arbitration of labor disputes, distinguished this as a stopgap measure designed to preserve a field for "self-help—co-operation . . . labor's true remedy." Beginning in 1882 the order's national publication, the *Journal of United Labor,* ran articles in almost every issue favoring productive and distributive cooperation. Far from signifying middle-class aspirations, as earlier historians of the Knights have charged, the Knights' associational discourse, like that of the IWPA, represented an alternative to the wage system. Article 2 of the Knights' Cooperative Department stated, "The objective idea of this plan is that the members of the order shall become members of a great industrial union, self-employing, self-sustaining, self-governing, and proceed at the earliest practicable moment to boycott the wage system by refusing to serve in it, refusing to buy of it, relegating it and its adherents to the status of the slaveocracy."[18]

Local unionists and Knights hardly differed in their devotion to cooperation. Together they initiated a small flurry of cooperative experiments in the early 1880s. In 1881 the Trades and Labor Assembly revived its aborted 1872 project of a cooperative-building society designed to build cheap homes for workers in the suburbs to relieve the city's housing shortage while employing out-of-work building trades unionists. In 1883 the cigarmakers' union began a cigar factory employing four hundred workers. Knights leaders founded the Mechanics and Laborers Co-operative Association, which in 1881 operated a grocery store. In the next two years the order's assemblies opened a cooperative boot and shoe factory, a cooperative tannery, a cooperative bakery, and a cooperative tin and sheet iron works; and DA 24 operated a consumer cooperative coal company. In 1885, when the Trades and Labor Assembly set up a committee to promote cooperation, it was chaired by the master workman of the shoemakers' local assembly.[19]

The turn away form independent labor politics, the distrust of statism, and the enthusiasm for self-help led naturally to a new industrial and political strategy for the labor movement. Only dimly perceived by most trade unionists before 1881, this strategy appeared in a transitional form in the writings of local labor's most articulate intellectual, Joseph Gruenhut.

The Bohemian-born, German-speaking, and American-bred Gruenhut was, like Albert Parsons and George Schilling, part of the new line of class-conscious labor thinkers who had come of age during the 1870s depression and helped bridge the gap between German socialists, American labor reformers, and trade unionists. Gruenhut had served in the Union Army as a captain and had been a socialist since the early 1870s. Though well-read in advanced socialist literature, he differed from most socialists in that he was schooled in the ways of American party politics and was quite willing to adjust socialist ideals to local political realities. By the 1880s Gruenhut was a Democrat beholden to Carter Harrison for his job as health and workshop inspector. His political affiliation, his imperviousness to categorization, and his status as an intellectual, or "brainworker" as he liked to call himself, aroused widespread suspicion among labor activists. Though he could speak to every labor faction, he was fully trusted by none. Nonetheless, for a short period during the early 1880s Gruenhut reigned as Chicago labor's chief thinker, communicating through editorials, columns, and letters in the *Progressive Age.*[20]

Gruenhut's thinking on the labor question can be summed up under three headings: his views on how to achieve labor unity, his vision of what the labor movement might achieve, and his view of the relations between unions and the Harrison regime.

To many trade unionists from San Francisco to the East Coast, the major impediment to organizing unions and to maintaining an American standard of living was the threat from immigrants willing to supply cheap labor. As a collector of local statistics, Gruenhut critiqued this view, arguing that the "American artisan . . . has vanished from the scene," retreating into white-collar occupations and leaving Chicago virtually a "European colony." Instead of being a threat to American labor, European workers were its chief source of strength. Though Gruenhut, like other labor leaders of the time, drew the line at the Chinese, he argued that virtually all other groups should be integrated into the labor movement. "The old system of isolated trades unionism is a failure in a country that may be overwhelmed by immigrants from all parts of the civilized world." He thus rejected another response to immigrant labor, one emanating from moralistic labor reformers like Cameron, who had dominated the labor movement before 1877 and were still influential in the Knights of Labor. Drawing directly on the tradition of Protestant moral reform, these advocates viewed the moral uplift of workers' cultural standards through the inculcation of proper character as the necessary precondition for class organization, including voluntary cooperation. By contrast, Gruenhut, a freethinker, emphasized collective solutions, particularly in raising the "standard of life" and in amalgamating trades.[21]

The "standard of life," a common concept borrowed from political economy and the writings of Ira Steward, encompassed "better homes, less burdensome toil, and more agreeable conditions of labor," as well as higher wages. When workers associated in unions, wrote Gruenhut, "they learn to look upon these higher enjoyments not only as desirable, but as theirs of right. Whatever the common people of any country firmly believes belongs to them, that they will eventually encompass means to attain." Only if workers took "cheap living immigrants" into unions and taught them to demand "an American standard of life" could they build a "progressive trade union movement."[22]

The natural accompaniment of a higher standard of life and the only rational response to the spread of the division of labor and the virtual destruction of apprenticeship standards was amalgamation. Only by "amalgamating all skilled and unskilled workers" in related trades could workers "hold their own against combined capitalistic corporations." In 1881 Gruenhut suggested a plan for amalgamating all trades into five industrial branches, with an "executive central council" to raise a central strike fund and direct strikes. In 1882, with the growth of the Knights, Gruenhut enthusiastically endorsed the order as the main vehicle of amalgamation and suggested its first aim should be to raise the living standards of "the lowest paid toiler," relying on the Knights' power to "boycott scabs."[23]

A third way to unite workers that Gruenhut suggested was to advocate home ownership. Addressing himself to immigrants, he predicted that "the speculative era must pass away and life come down to the ordinary level of elsewhere. . . . Whoever now imagines that his life is to be cast in and about the industries of Chicago ought to address himself at once to owning a home. . . ." For those with savings he recommended self-help, through either the Trades and Labor Assembly's Building Society or the Building and Loan Association, which had burgeoned in the early 1880s. Because the greatest short-term problems were overcrowding and high rents, Gruenhut pushed vigorously for enforcing the health and tenement-house ordinances passed by the city council, and he later endorsed a Citizens Association proposal to erect model tenements funded by the city's capitalists.[24]

Raising the standard of life, amalgamating trades, and improving housing all pointed toward a quasi-syndicalist goal, which, in contrast to state socialism, Gruenhut labeled "industrial self-government," anticipating the 1890s ideal of industrial democracy. "The era of socialistic blatherskiting is passed and the time of practical improvement has arrived." Rejecting the Lassallean socialist dictum of the iron law of wages, he argued that unions could raise and sustain wages over a long period of time. In an argument consonant with the best economic writings of the period he tried to demonstrate by statistics that workers' real wages and their standard of life were improving, though not as rapidly as the concentration of wealth was increasing. Gruenhut should not, however, be confused with a twentieth-century theorist of pure and simple trade unionism. Though he ridiculed utopian visions, he did not lack an alternative to the wage system. Strikes, he wrote, would enable workers to become "part proprietors" of factories and thereby "appropriate more and more profit ourselves and use it to establish co-operatives."[25]

Gruenhut combined his unionist vision of social change with a broader vision of a new secular civilization. Chicago was the perfect place for "the birthplace of a new humanity" because it was a "European colony" in which "no single nationality is strong enough to boss or overwhelm all the rest, nor is there any single trade in great majority over the others."[26]

Although he temporarily opposed labor parties, Gruenhut's industrial democracy was not apolitical. In 1881 he became the first and most articulate advocate in Chicago of what the historian Selig Perlman aptly called "political collective bargaining." Perlman understood that American political parties were nonideological, "political producers' gilds," led by highly flexible "political managers," who "stock up on an assortment of political goods" to please a majority of consumers. Using the strategy of nonpartisan "political collective bargaining," the leaders of organized labor bargained with and lobbied these managers over the nature of goods. Given the evenly balanced or "stalemated" party system of the 1874–92 period, labor was in a strong position to bargain with and lobby at least one of the two parties over the distribution of offices and policies.[27]

The indispensable premise of this strategy was that workingmen could be persuaded to vote according to the recommendation of their union leaders. For this reason Gruenhut became a forceful advocate of a trade union newspaper. The *Progressive Age,* however, was at first more a labor reform paper proposing to "wage relentless war on the grasping and soulless corporations and monopolies which threaten the very existence of the Republic." Of its two proprietors, Ed Irwin was the labor reformer, while Patrick H. McLogan, soon to serve as a president of the Federation of Organized Trades and Labor Unions (forerunner of the American Federation of Labor), resigned in September 1881. That same month Gruenhut called for the paper to be owned and operated by a company whose stock would be owned by local unions and labor organizations. Accordingly, Gruenhut organized the Associated Labor Press of the Progressive Age, a press club of unionists to collect and write labor news for publication. The diversity and breadth of its membership, including presidents of the unions of the iron molders, carpenters, typographers, and seamen and the chief officers of the Knights, testified to the labor foundation of the paper. More important, it was evidence that labor had generated its own brand of labor reform, one that was not less political but more firmly union-based than that of Greenbackers and SLPers.[28]

Meanwhile, the Trades and Labor Assembly endorsed the *Progressive Age* and agreed to collect stock subscriptions. Six months later the Progressive Age Publishing Company came into existence. Two hundred shares were held by trade unionists, the carpenters being the largest single group. Claiming twenty thousand subscribers in 1882, the *Progressive Age* was perhaps the nation's only major labor paper owned, operated, and controlled by a city's trade unions. By contrast, *John Swinton's Paper* in New York, J. P. O'Donnell's *Labor Standard* in Patterson, New Jersey, and Joseph Buchanan's *Labor Enquirer* in Denver, though pro-union, represented the views of their editors. Gruenhut called the paper "a new departure, the first attempt to publish a newspaper by and for trade unionists."[29]

The practical effect of Gruenhut's and the *Progressive Age*'s policies was an unofficial alliance with Harrison's Democratic party. The relationship was a reciprocal one. To labor leaders of the early 1880s the Democrats were a prolabor political party that had been raised to power by a local voter realignment stemming from the upswing in class consciousness of the late 1870s. It was only natural that the party defer to labor's most pressing demands. For example, the Trades and Labor Assembly sent delegation after delegation to the city council and the mayor to lobby for funds for factory and workshop inspectors and to seek the appointment of prolabor men. The inspectors ultimately selected were SLPers and labor reformers, not labor leaders. In 1881 unions were still too weak to command patronage offers.[30]

Labor leaders found themselves drawn further into the business of lobbying when Shelby Cullom, the Republican governor, gutted the newly created Bureau of Labor Statistics by appointing inexperienced and nonunion men as the bureau's commissioners. Chicago labor leaders responded with a storm of protests. In 1881 Gruenhut and the Trades and Labor Assembly proposed that the city government establish its own bureau of labor statistics, staffed, of course, by unionists. This proposal stemmed partly from the fact that there were hardly any full-time, paid union positions among unions. Though the city council did not set up a bureau, it did direct the factory inspectors to collect wage and cost of living data for inclusion in the Health Department's report. The city council also voted to give the Trades and Labor Assembly a plot on the lakefront for its proposed new hall.[31]

In September 1881 Gruenhut optimistically assessed labor's power in local government, arguing that "universal suffrage and trades unionism has given to [labor] the balance of power in Chicago and the workingmen's votes have elected the Democratic city ticket at the last two municipal elections."

Chicago workers, wrote Gruenhut, "were not mere voting cattle of the two political party-machines; they know too much to allow themselves to be played off against each other. . . ."[32]

Legislation, however, was not the most important way the new city administration catered to labor's voting strength. The role of the police in aiding strikers through a benevolent neutrality during Bridgeport labor disputes has already been discussed. This informal alliance at the neighborhood level was based on the common ethnicity, residence, and political sympathies of the strikers and police. But a more formal tie existed between the police and organized labor, which illustrated labor's emerging new strategy. During virtually every major strike the Trades and Labor Assembly sent delegations to city hall to procure police support. During a violent molders' strike in 1881 Police Superintendent McGarrigle received a labor delegation with great solicitude, pointing out to them how he had refused applications from the Chicago Stove Works for special police and had ordered a police contingent removed from the picket line. The labor committee reported that "the Trade and Labor Assembly is a body well recognized by the authorities, and that they are alive to the fact that it is a body representing a large numerical force of the Labor element. They showed every desire, more particularly on the part of the Superintendent of Police, to satisfy your committee in all points." Two years later the Trades and Labor Assembly convinced the police superintendent to withdraw a police detail guarding Western Union's property during a telegraphers' strike.[33]

Joe Gruenhut openly exulted at labor's political strength that prevented the West Division Railway Company from getting police support during the 1882 strike by conductors and drivers: "If 100 policemen had been furnished to man the streetcars . . . the scabs would have run the cars under police protection until the strikers would have been compelled to accept the company's terms of unconditional surrender." Instead, the strikers won a glorious victory.[34]

The close ties between labor and the Harrison administration continued through 1886, but the leadership of Gruenhut and the *Progressive Age* was cut short. Gruenhut aroused resentment and suspicion especially among Knights leaders. Harwood Hamer, a Knights leader, criticized Gruenhut for being opposed to religion. Others were repelled by his "bombast" and pretension as "the little Napoleon of the industrial world." But more than anything Gruenhut enraged those who advocated independent labor politics. Responding to one of them, Gruenhut asserted, "In Chicago the Irish workingmen can transform the Democratic party into a workingman's movement at any time they may demand it." A mixed assembly composed of Germans responded by accusing Gruenhut of propagandizing for a political party and demanded that the *Progressive Age* stop printing his writings.[35]

The *Progressive Age* was already foundering on another issue. In 1881, before the paper had become union-owned, it had championed temperance and refused to support any mayoral candidate that year because neither supported enforcement of the Sunday-closing laws. This policy changed by 1882, but the following year a new editor, S. D. Rich, ousted the trade union officers of the publishing company. When it was discovered that he had received a check from temperance people and for this reason had sided with the Republicans against Harrison, the Trades and Labor Assembly denounced the paper in June 1883. The assembly started a new union-run paper, the *Western Workman*, which died in several months.[36]

The Emergence of Political Collective Bargaining

The demise of the *Progressive Age* and the swift decline of the local Knights of Labor after 1882 left the strategy of amalgamated trade unionism, interethnic solidarity, and labor reform bereft of its most forceful advocates. This in turn left the field relatively clear in Chicago for the emergence of a trade union movement confined largely to skilled workers practicing in a more disciplined way the strategy of political collective bargaining with the two regular parties.

Following the failure of Knights-style arbitration in the tanners' and curriers' strike of 1882, DA 24 was reeling from an acrimonious split that had given rise to DA 57 and a sharp decline in membership. After 1883 net membership in Chicago stagnated at little more than 1,000 members, with a small increase to 1,900 in July 1885. The Knights thus took a secondary position to the Trades and Labor Assembly. Still, leading trade unionists remained members of the Knights' mixed assemblies and, following the brief Halley interlude, continued to shape the Knights' policies. George Rodgers, the president of the iron molders' union who served as president of the assembly from January 1882 through December 1885, also served on DA 24's executive board and as a delegate to the Knights' general assembly. Leo P. Dwyer, who followed Rodgers, was a leading officer in a Knights painters' assembly.

In spite of these ties to the Knights, after 1882 the Trades and Labor Assembly came under the influence of a small number of skilled workers' unions, in particular those of the bricklayers, cigarmakers, iron molders, and telegraphers. The year 1883 was a watershed in this shift in the balance of power within the city's labor movement, for that year two key strikes consolidated the power of the bricklayers and the cigarmakers. Though the first was dominated by the Irish and the second by the Germans, both unions traversed similar industrial terrain to arrive at the same destination.

Both cigarmaking and building contracting were trades with low capital barriers to entry, and both registered an increase in the number of small firms in the early 1880s.[37] The combination of a small, cohesive core group of skilled workers with low capital requirements enabled both these trade groups to employ the tactic of going into business for themselves to win their labor disputes of 1883. The bricklayers went into business as individual contractors with union cards, while the cigarmakers formed two dozen small union-run cooperatives. In both industries this tactic pressured the more numerous smaller firms to break ranks with the large firms and accept union demands. By mid-1883 each union could boast of a closed shop and high initiation fees, and each had full-time paid union officials, or "walking delegates," who kept track of employment opportunities, collected dues, and kept financial records. Such officials made these unions unique and afforded them a measure of independence from political parties.[38]

The bricklayers' strike was particularly noteworthy in the effect it had on the labor movement. Like the cigarmakers' union, which in 1880 had a little over a hundred members, the bricklayers' union, founded in 1879, was a fledgling union before the boom of the 1880s. In April 1883, with 2,100 members, it felt strong enough to demand a closed shop, a large pay increase, and a standard, uniform wage. After a long strike in which they refused an arbitration settlement, the bricklayers won a complete victory.[39]

The manner in which the bricklayers had won represented another loss of face for the Knights' principle of arbitration and labor solidarity. The bricklayers' subsequent actions further repudiated these principles. They withdrew from their national union to prevent union journeymen outside Chicago from competing in the local market. They also refused the plea from the carpenters' union to join in forming a building trades council. When Local 21 of the young Brotherhood of Carpenters and Joiners of America struck in 1884, they denied the brotherhood's request for a sympathy strike, which resulted in the collapse of the local. By the end of 1884 the example of the carpenters' union, which had been the strongest supporter of the *Progressive Age*, and the painters' union, which had been among the largest of the Knights' trade locals, had been eclipsed by the bricklayers' model of unionism. The bricklayers' model, however, was suited to a homogeneous group of skilled workers relatively unaffected by workplace innovation, not to groups like the carpenters and painters, whose trades had been nearly destroyed by piecework and the use of unskilled labor.[40]

The cigarmakers, too, embraced a brand of unionism that shut out lesser-skilled workers, in this case, women and children. Under the leadership of SLPers in 1879 Local 11 had successfully struck to exclude cheaply paid women bunchmakers from union cigar shops. Afterward the employment of female tenement-house labor spread in Chicago. The union responded by adopting the union label in 1881 to distinguish its cigars from those made by cheap tenement-house labor. In 1883 a small group of socialists seceded from Local 14 and the international union to form Local 15 and Knights LA 3045. The rival unions battled for supremacy in the cigar shops of Chicago throughout the fall of 1883. The Trades and Labor Assembly supported Local 14. Eventually, the two sides agreed to work side by side, and Local 15 agreed to rejoin the international union.[41]

The success of the bricklayers and the cigarmakers gave them the balance of power in the Trades and Labor Assembly. In January 1884 a survey of membership showed that the bricklayers' union was by far the largest union, with 2,500 members, followed by the sailors' union, with 1,100; the typographers' union, with 1,200; the cigarmakers' union, with 1,100; the local of the Brotherhood of Carpenters and Joiners of America, with 1,000; and the iron molders' union, with 850. No other union could claim more than 150 members. With the exception of the sailors' union and soon-to-be defunct carpenters' local the unions and local assemblies of the unskilled were notably missing from the Trades and Labor Assembly. Thus, none of the Knights assemblies for the painter, brickmaker, and shoemaker trades, or the Bohemian and German unions among the unskilled lumbershovers and boxmakers, or the decimated packinghouse workers' association belonged to the Trades and Labor Assembly.[42]

The new lineup in the Trades and Labor Assembly was reflected in the makeup of the leadership. Beginning in February 1884 it became normal practice for the bricklayers' president to serve as vice president of the assembly. Then, following Dwyer's purely honorary term, the presidency went to chief of the typographers' union, followed by the cigarmakers' union president in January 1886.[43]

Under the new leadership the Chicago labor movement began to distance itself from the Democratic party, as well as independent labor politics, and systematically practice the strategy of political collective bargaining. Before this Harrison's concessions to labor seem to have been largely the price the Democrats paid for the refusal of unionists to engage in independent labor politics under the wing of the Greenbackers or Socialist Labor party. Gruenhut argued to aldermen in 1881 that unless they funded workshop inspection, SLPers might be elected in their stead.[44] After 1881, however, the base of labor voters was far broader than it had been in the late 1870s. Harrison's concessions of the mid-1880s may be viewed as a response to trade union lobbying and unionists' threat to support the Republicans.

The first open attempt at political collective bargaining came in the fall 1883 county elections, when the Trades and Labor Assembly decided to ask the Republican and Democratic conventions to put a labor leader on their tickets: George Rodgers for the Republicans and M. J. Carroll, president of the typographers' union, for the Democrats. When the Democrats refused labor overtures but the out-of-office Republicans nominated Rodgers, a mass meeting of the Trades and Labor Assembly endorsed the Republicans. "The interests of the workingmen," argued Patrick McLogan, "lay in the concentration of their power to show whether or not they held as they claimed the balance of power in Chicago." Though the Democrats won the election on the temperance vote, Rodgers ran fifteen hundred votes ahead of the rest of the Republican ticket. So delighted were union leaders with the results that they formed the Central Labor Club. Headed by McLogan, but also including prominent Knights, the club's purpose was to endorse candidates for the city council and the Illinois legislature on a nonpartisan basis. But the club soon decided to leave city politics to those lobbying the friendly Harrison administration and to concentrate on state and national issues. In February 1884 union and Knights leaders founded the Illinois State Federation of Labor (ISFL). The ISFL started a policy of submitting its program to both party conventions, thus formalizing political collective bargaining and lobbying on the state level.[45]

It would be a mistake to view labor's new strategy as a nonclass approach to politics, for the early 1880s witnessed a new peak of labor solidarity, especially among Irish workers who normally voted Democrat. It would also be a mistake to accept uncritically the charge of vocal labor reformers and such socialists as Thomas Morgan, George Schilling, and Charles Dixon that trade union leaders were mere shills for the Democrats. Mark Crawford, leader of the typographers' union and usually considered a "conservative," answered such a charge by Dixon by arguing that "the working classes hold the cure of all their ills in the ballot. . . . But I do not believe in their running after false gods. . . . If the working classes cease rallying around cranks and stand united with their ballots in their hands, they can get from the two great parties all they ask—justice." Crawford concluded by saying that his loyalty was to his union more than to any party.[46]

The political independence of organized workers reached new heights during the July 1884 Democratic convention held in Chicago. The struggle between Grover Cleveland, the silk-stocking liberal reform candidate, and Ben Butler, the former governor of Massachusetts who was a prolabor greenbacker, seemed to epitomize the conflict between capital and labor in party politics. When Butler arrived in the city, a labor demonstration of thousands, including eight hundred Knights and virtually every other union and labor political faction in the city except the anarchists, turned out to escort him to his hotel. Each union and assembly marched as a separate contingent carrying banners with such political slogans as "Labor and Capital Can Never Vote the Same Ticket" and "No Pandering to Dudes." The crowd was wildly enthusiastic, prefiguring workers' response to the labor tickets of 1886–87.[47]

When the hated Cleveland was nominated, union leaders tried to orchestrate a wholesale defection. Many Irish unionists had been attracted to the 1882 Finerty campaign, and at that time Irish defectors had mobilized under the banner of Irish nationalism. In 1884 much of this same constituency rallied around labor issues, focusing on Cleveland's veto of the five-cent fare and eight-hour-day bills while governor of New York. According to the *Tribune,* "As a consequence of labor agitation, which has been going on for some years, the labor element is far better organized than it has ever been before. The success in many instances of unions in maintaining wages has drawn into them nearly every good workman in some of the trades, and every union has more or less been a school of political information from the labor standpoint, resulting in a general loosening of the old party ties."[48]

T. H. Ling of the Knights painters' assembly echoed this assessment. "The laboring men," he explained, "are reading more than they used to and are discussing politics constantly. Butler is their champion now and they feel encouraged at the influence they have through him." Other Irish Democratic union leaders, including William J. Gleason, president of the bricklayers' union; William H. Muldoon, master workman of the Knights coopers' assembly; and John Foley of the iron molders' union, also a Knight, repeated these sentiments.[49]

Despite these feelings there was little support for Butler's independent candidacy, which was led by local antimonopolists, notably John M. Foley of Knights mixed assembly 1307 and Charles G. Dixon of mixed assembly 522. After the election Dixon bitterly blamed the low vote of 542 on the pro-Cleveland influence exercised by Harrison on the labor movement through "city hall socialists." But a more likely explanation was that trade unionists were wary of another Greenback-Labor, third-party fling. According to the strategy of political collective bargaining, they should vote for Republican candidate James G. Blaine to register a protest against the Democrats, and this is what they did. Following the advice of Ford's *Irish World,* the local Irish politician P. T. Barry, and the Irish union leaders Richard Powers and Leo P. Dwyer, Irish voters in the Second Congressional District split their tickets in large numbers. The Irish swing vote was greatest in the normally Democratic Fifth Ward, which included Bridgeport. There Carter Harrison, running for governor, won by about 2,500 votes, while Cleveland squeaked by with about a 600-vote margin. In the city ticket splitting gave Blaine a victory over Cleveland by 2,890 votes, while Harrison won the gubernatorial contest by 4,655 votes.[50]

The increasing ability of Knights and union leaders to deliver a vote to political friends and deny it to political enemies led Harrison to defer increasingly to union strength by awarding patronage jobs. How this occurred among the Chicago Knights is instructive. In August 1883 George Rodgers, the city's most powerful labor leader, led a committee from District Assembly 24 to meet with Mayor Harrison to request a factory inspector's position for Master Workman T. E. Randall. When Harrison agreed, Randall resigned his post in the Knights, though the district assembly refused to accept his resignation. By 1886 Rodgers and J. B. Murphy, the new district master workman, both held health inspector positions at city hall. To Knights and union leaders positions in the city's health department enabled them to enforce such prolabor laws as the Factory and Workshop Inspection Act; it also provided them with a legitimate source of sinecures for their leaders—whom they did not pay. Accordingly, in February 1885 DA 24 passed a resolution that the number of sanitary inspectors be increased to eighteen.[51]

That the new patronage ties represented a labor beachhead in government, as well as a way to cement labor's tie to the Democrats, was evident in the 1885 mayoral election. The Trades and Labor Assembly refused to endorse either Harrison or his Republican challenger. Another test came when Myles McPadden, an ex-Knights organizer who had opened a saloon and had received a patronage appointment from Cleveland as an internal revenue agent, tried to influence workers not to support an election reform law, inimical to the Democratic party. He was repudiated by the Trades and Labor Assembly.[52]

The decade of the 1880s has been characterized as a "turning point" in the major parties' gradual adoption of a liberal "educational" style of politics in which nonpartisan, rational appeals to independent voters replaced spectacular party appeals to partisanship. The history of Chicago politics provides some evidence for this interpretation, but the changes were not indications of the triumph of an "elitist" liberalism as the political historian Michael McGerr argues. Rather, they stemmed from the growth of class-identified voting, mobilized first by the SLP and then by strong multiethnic craft unions using the strategy of political collective bargaining. Increasingly parties pitched their appeals to special groups among the city's workers—German socialists, Irish nationalists, and trade unionists. These appeals were not on the basis of the old party-based distribution of benefits and immunities, which reinforced partisanship, but increasingly on regulatory and redistributive grounds, which reinforced nonpartisan group identities.[53]

Because of Carter Harrison's unique ability to deploy this new brand of politics, Chicago politics experienced a profound party realignment. Between 1857 and 1877 Republicans dominated all but two city elections. But from

Harrison's election in 1879 through 1897 the Democrats won seven of the ten mayoral elections, and two of the three Republican victories were due to a split in the Democratic vote.[54] Class-identified voting had transformed the configuration of Chicago politics, not through an independent labor party but through the existing two parties.

Notes

1. For discussion of labor and the major parties, see Herbert G. Gutman, *Work, Culture, and Society in Industrializing America* (New York: Vintage Books, 1976), 234–92; Philip J. Ethington, *The Public City: The Political Construction of Urban Life in San Francisco, 1850–1900* (Cambridge: Cambridge University Press, 1994); and Iver Bernstein, *The New York City Draft Riots: Their Significance for American Society and Politics in the Age of the Civil War* (New York: Oxford University Press, 1990).

2. *Progressive Age,* Sept. 10, 1881.

3. Stephen P. Erie, *Rainbow's End: Irish-Americans and the Dilemmas of Urban Machine Politics, 1840–1985* (Berkeley: University of California Press, 1988), 46; Bessie Louise Pierce, *A History of Chicago,* vol. 3, *The Rise of a Modern City, 1871–1893* (Chicago: University of Chicago Press, 1957), 333–38 (quote on 333); C. K. Yearley, *The Money Machines: The Breakdown and Reform of Governmental and Party Finance in the North, 1860–1920* (New York: State University of New York Press, 1970), 37–118; Terrence J. McDonald, *The Parameters of Urban Fiscal Policy* (Berkeley: University of California Press, 1986), 262–82; William T. Stead, *If Christ Came to Chicago: A Plea for the Union of All Who Love in the Service of All Who Suffer* (Chicago: Laird and Lee, 1894), part 3, chaps. 1 and 3, appendix C.

4. Pierce, *History of Chicago,* 3:309–13; Jon C. Teaford, *The Unheralded Triumph: City Government in America, 1870–1900* (Baltimore, Md.: Johns Hopkins University Press, 1984), 42–82, esp. 61.

5. Erie, *Rainbow's End,* 20–21; Pierce, *History of Chicago,* 3:305–6; *Chicago Tribune,* Oct. 29, 1882, Nov. 5, 1882, Mar. 30, 1885.

6. Richard L. McCormick, *The Party Period and Public Policy: American Politics from the Age of Jackson to the Progressive Era* (New York: Oxford University Press, 1986), 209. See also Theodore J. Lowi, "American Business, Public Policy, Case-Studies, and Political Theory," *World Politics* 16 (July 1964): 677–715.

7. *Chicago Tribune,* July 9, 1882. Stead, *If Christ Came to Chicago,* 358, noted, "At present in Chicago the policemen is normally expected to enforce an endless multiplicity of ordinances which are openly set at nought by thousands of citizens everyday, and every non-executed ordinance affords an opening for official blackmail."

8. Commercial Club, *Addresses and Discussion before the Club* (Chicago: Commercial Club of Chicago, 1906); Alfred T. Andreas, *A History of Chicago from the Earliest Times to the Present Period* (Chicago: A. T. Andreas, 1884–86), 3:56–58; Pierce, *History of Chicago,* 3:484; *Chicago Tribune,* Mar. 16, 1882, Apr. 16, 1884.

9. *Chicago Tribune,* July 27, 1877, Apr. 5, 1883; John Charles Carroll, *Armour and*

His Times (New York: D. Appleton-Century, 1938), 171; Robert Ozanne, *A Century of Labor-Management Relations at McCormick and International Harvester* (Madison: University of Wisconsin Press, 1967), 16–17 (quote).

10. *Chicago Tribune,* May 14, 1879, Apr. 5, 1883; Pierce, *History of Chicago,* 3:360; Teaford, *Unheralded Triumph,* 56, 60–64; James S. McQuade, *A Synoptical History of the Chicago Fire Department* (Chicago: Benevolent Association of the Paid Fire Department, 1908).

11. Claudius O. Johnson, *Carter Harrison I: A Political Leader* (Chicago: University of Chicago Press, 1928), 39–14, 19–23, 285.

12. Ernst Schmidt, *He Chose: The Other Was a Treadmill Thing,* ed. and trans. Frederick R. Schmidt (Santa Fe: Vegara, 1968), 122. T. J. Morgan estimated that 90 percent of the votes he received in 1878 as an SLP candidate for alderman were "from the Republican Party." See *Chicago Tribune,* Oct. 15, 1887.

13. *Chicago Tribune,* Apr. 5, 1881, Apr. 6, 1881, Apr. 7, 1881 (quotes).

14. Ibid., Nov. 9, 1882, Mar. 4, 1883, Mar. 15, 1883, Apr. 4, 1883; *Irish World and American Industrial Liberator,* July 7, 1883; Michael Funchion, *Chicago's Irish Nationalists, 1881–1890* (New York: Arno, 1976), 42–52.

15. *Progressive Age,* Dec. 31, 1881.

16. Ibid., Mar. 19, 1881; *Journal of United Labor,* Aug. 15, 1881; Knights of Labor District Assembly 24, *Minute Book,* Oct. 8, 1881, George A. Schilling Papers, Regenstein Library, University of Chicago; *Chicago Tribune,* Oct. 2, 1882, Oct. 16, 1882, Dec. 15, 1882; George A. Schilling, "A History of the Labor Movement in Chicago," in *Life of Albert R. Parsons with Brief History of the Labor Movement in America, Also Sketches of the Lives of A. Spies, Geo. Engel, A. Fischer and Louis Lingg,* ed. Lucy E. Parsons (Chicago: Lucy E. Parsons, 1903), xxviii (quote).

17. *Irish World and American Industrial Liberator,* Jan.–Nov. 1880, passim; Schilling, "History of the Labor Movement," xxix (quote); Henry David, *The History of the Haymarket Affair,* 3d rev. ed. (New York: Collier Books, 1963), 92–98; Bruce C. Nelson, *Beyond the Martyrs: A Social History of Chicago's Anarchists, 1870–1900* (New Brunswick, N.J.: Rutgers University Press, 1988), 153–65; Paul Avrich, *The Haymarket Tragedy* (Princeton, N.J.: Princeton University Press, 1984), 74–78; Michael R. Johnson, "Albert R. Parsons: An American Architect of Syndicalism," *Midwest Quarterly* 9 (Winter 1968): 195–206.

18. *Progressive Age,* July 25, 1882; William Halley, "Strikes, Their Evils, and Remedies," *Second Biennial Report of the Illinois Bureau of Labor Statistics* (Springfield: H. W. Rokker, 1893), 369; *Journal of United Labor,* June 25, 1884.

19. *Progressive Age,* Apr. 23, 1881, Mar. 18, 1882; *Chicago Tribune,* July 3, 1882, Oct. 15, 1883, Aug. 3, 1885, Nov. 15, 1885; Knights of Labor District Assembly 24, *Minute Book,* Sept. 24, 1882; *Irish World and American Industrial Liberator,* Dec. 30, 1883.

20. *Chicago Tribune,* Dec. 29, 1873, Oct. 7, 1886; Andreas, *History of Chicago,* 3:231–32.

21. *Progressive Age,* Oct. 15, 1881 ("American artisan . . ." quote), Mar. 26, 1881, Apr. 2, 1881, Jan. 21, 1882 ("old system" quote) Apr. 15, 1882.

22. Ibid., Oct. 29, 1881 ("better homes" and "learn to look" quotes), Mar. 25, 1882 (remaining quotes). See also ibid., Sept. 15, 1883, Sept. 22, 1883.

23. Ibid., May 14, 1881 ("amalgamating all . . ." and "executive control" quotes), Oct. 1, 1881, Dec. 31, 1881, May 27, 1882 ("lowest paid toiler . . ." quote).

24. Ibid., Apr. 1, 1882 (quote), Apr. 29, 1882; *Western Workman,* Aug. 4, 1883.

25. *Progressive Age,* May 20, 1882 (first quote), June 3, 1882 (second quote), Sept. 17, 1882, Oct. 5, 1882; David Wells, *Recent Economic Changes* (New York: D. Appleton, 1889), 406–22; On industrial democracy, see David Montgomery, "Industrial Democracy or Democracy in Industry? The Theory and Practice of the Labor Movement, 1870–1925," in *Industrial Democracy in America: The Ambiguous Promise,* ed. Nelson Lichtenstein and Howell John Harris (Cambridge: Cambridge University Press, 1993), 20–42; on alternatives to the wage system, see H. M. Gittelman, "Adolph Strasser and the Origin of Pure and Simple Unionism," *Labor History* 6 (Winter 1965): 74–83.

26. *Progressive Age,* Sept. 17, 1881, Oct. 15, 1881.

27. Selig Perlman, *A Theory of the Labor Movement* (1928; reprint, New York: August M. Kelley, 1968), 171–76.

28. *Progressive Age,* Sept. 3, 1881, Sept. 17, 1881, Oct. 1, 1881; on McLogan, see *Progressive Age,* Feb. 24, 1882; and *Irish World and American Industrial Liberator,* Sept. 15, 1883.

29. *Progressive Age,* Jan. 21, 1882, Apr. 1, 1882, Apr. 29, 1882 (quote); Philip S. Foner, *History of the Labor Movement in the United States,* vol. 2, *From the Founding of the A.F. of L. to the Emergence of American Imperialism* (New York: International Publishers, 1955), 29–31.

30. *Chicago Tribune,* Feb. 20, 1880.

31. *Progressive Age,* May 14, 1881, July 15, 1882; *Western Workman,* Oct. 6, 1883; *Irish World and American Industrial Liberator,* Aug. 19, 1882.

32. *Progressive Age,* Sept. 10, 1881.

33. Ibid., Oct. 8, 1881 (quote); *Western Workman,* Aug. 11, 1883.

34. *Progressive Age,* Mar. 25, 1882.

35. Ibid., Feb. 4, 1882 ("bombast . . ." quote), June 10, 1882, July 15, 1882 ("In Chicago . . ." quote), July 29, 1882.

36. Ibid., Mar. 12, 1881, Mar. 26, 1881; *Western Workman,* June 30, 1883; *Chicago Tribune,* June 25, 1883.

37. Chicago was the only major city in the United States to have an increase in the number of cigarmaking firms between 1879 and 1884, and building was the city's most prosperous industry in the first half of the decade. *Cigarmakers Official Journal,* Sept. 4, 1884; *Chicago Tribune,* Jan. 1, 1885.

38. On the bricklayers, see *Chicago Tribune,* Apr. 25, 1883, Apr. 27, 1883, June 7, 1883; and *Western Workman,* June 30, 1883, July 28, 1883. On the cigarmakers, see *Cigarmakers Official Journal,* July 15, 1883; and *Irish World and American Industrial Liberator,* June 2, 1883.

39. *Chicago Tribune,* Apr. 12, 1883, Apr. 13, 1883, Apr. 24, 1883, May 31, 1883; *Western Workman,* June 30, 1883, July 28, 1883.

40. *Chicago Tribune,* May 10, 1884, May 13, 1887; *Carpenter,* Sept. 1884, Oct. 1884, Feb. 1885.

41. *Chicago Tribune,* Oct. 17, 1879, Sept. 29, 1883, Oct. 5, 1883, Nov. 26, 1883, Dec. 3, 1883, Dec. 8, 1883; *Cigarmakers Official Journal,* Sept. 15, 1879, Aug. 10, 1881, May 9, 1884; Knights of Labor District Assembly 24, *Minute Book,* Feb. 1, 1884.

42. *Chicago Tribune,* Jan. 7, 1884.

43. Ibid., Jan. 7, 1884, Jan. 5, 1885; Knights of Labor District Assembly 24, *Minute Book,* Jan. 11, 1885.

44. *Chicago Tribune,* Feb. 20, 1881.

45. Ibid., Nov. 3, 1883 (quote), Nov. 7, 1883, Nov. 28, 1883, Dec. 10, 1883, Dec. 31, 1883, Feb. 13, 1884, Feb. 27, 1884; Eugene Staley, *History of the Illinois State Federation of Labor* (Chicago: University of Chicago Press, 1930), chaps. 2, 3, and 4.

46. *Chicago Tribune,* July 24, 1884.

47. Ibid., July 6, 1884, July 8, 1884.

48. Ibid., July 6, 1884 (quote).

49. Ibid., July 13, 1884 (quote), July 19, 1884.

50. Ibid., July 27, 1884 (quote); *Irish World and American Industrial Liberator,* Nov. 6, 1884, Nov. 24, 1884; Pierce, *History of Chicago,* 3:542.

51. Knights of Labor District Assembly 24, *Minute Book,* Aug. 6, 1883, Aug. 20, 1883, Sept. 3, 1883. See also Louis Hartmann's history in *Chicago Record,* Jan. 31, 1889.

52. *Chicago Tribune,* Nov. 1, 1885, Nov. 2, 1885, Oct. 11, 1890.

53. Michael E. McGerr, *The Decline of Popular Politics: The American North, 1865–1928* (New York: Oxford University Press, 1986), 69–106, esp. 76–78.

54. Pierce, *History of Chicago,* 3:352–54, 356, 379–80, 539.

CHAPTER 7

The Decline of Harrison's Democracy and the Origins of Haymarket, 1883–86

Historians have commonly viewed the rise of the United Labor party in 1886 and 1887 as an outgrowth of the eight-hour-day strikes and as labor's political response to the repression visited on that movement following the Haymarket bomb. As we have seen, however, an essential precondition for a third party was the emergence, beginning in the late 1870s, of a mobile labor vote created and mobilized in segments, first by German socialists, later by Irish nationalists, and finally by trade unionists using the strategy of nonpartisan political collective bargaining. By 1883 these segments were structurally integrated within the Democratic party by special group appeals emanating from Carter Harrison and party managers. Three developments between 1883 and 1886 greatly loosened Harrison's hold on the labor vote. The first was the successful antisaloon and election reform movement between 1883 and 1885, spearheaded by leading business reformers. The second was the new antilabor animus of the Chicago police, which alienated a large sector of the mainline trade union movement. Finally, the rise of revolutionary politics among the anarchists heightened the fears of the city's upper class and reinforced its opposition to Mayor Harrison's tolerant labor policies. These developments led to a political crisis that rent the fabric of the local party system, opening the way for a resurgence of independent labor politics in 1886–87 and in the long run hastening the prolabor realignment in Chicago politics that would become apparent by the end of the decade.

The Political Assault on Chicago's Saloons

The antiliquor movement that had created so much havoc for business reformers in 1873 was far from being a dead issue in city politics. Though the Citizens Association and Republican party managers had successfully avoided "sumptuary nonsense" since that time in deference to the German vote, alcohol was widely deemed to be a major urban social problem. To observers of the social scene, family breakup, fallen women, delinquency among slum children, vice and criminal behavior of all sorts, poverty, and even riots and labor violence could all be traced to "the liquor influence," manifested most obviously in the alarming spread of saloons. In the 1880s a variety of church-related groups sustained the antiliquor cause, notably the Woman's Christian Temperance Union and the Citizens Law and Order League.[1]

After the 1877 strikes and riots upper-class reformers also reentered the antisaloon field. Though they abjured the explosive Sunday-closing issue, such prominent businessmen as Marshall Field, Cyrus McCormick, Franklin MacVeagh, and Henry W. King were horrified at the prevalence of young teenagers in the riots and resolved to do something about it. In addition to trying to strengthen the police and militia, they founded the Citizens League for the Prevention of the Sale of Liquor to Minors. Until 1880 the Citizens League limited its activities to prosecuting saloonkeepers for selling liquor to minors. But after 1880 the Citizens League shifted its focus to a direct attack on saloons by affiliating with the national movement for high license fees for saloons.[2]

There were three reasons, all essentially political, why the push for a high license fee became a major issue in city politics. The first was the attempt to find revenue to increase the size of the police force. Since 1877 Citizens Association leaders had been attempting to increase the number of police to contain crime and threatened riots. The sticking point was the limit on city revenue created by the state cap on property taxes, bonded debt, and the local underassessment of personal property. In 1881–82 the Citizens Association sought to increase property assessments to pay for more police and other city improvements, but the campaign elicited stiff opposition from major merchants. The failure of this campaign led Citizens leaders to turn to higher saloon license fees, not simply to contain drinking but also to raise revenue.[3]

A second reason for the movement to increase license fees was the attempt of Republican party managers to neutralize the continuing strength of prohibitionist sentiment in the party. The 1882 election had been a national disaster for the Republicans because vocal prohibitionists had frightened away liberal Germans. The issue of license fees, argued the *Tribune,* would preempt prohibitionism and co-opt the "cranks" who had split the party. Because a lower fee could be legislated for German beer gardens, the movement need not unduly alarm the party's German base. At the same time party leaders hoped to preempt the kind of criticism of men of "wealth and power" that emanated from the Sabbatarians for "neglect[ing] to educate the new comers from foreign lands" and "withhold[ing] the means needed for support of a sufficient number of missions." Republican business leaders' support of high license fees was thus intended to shore up their claim to leadership by paying their respects to the pietistic Protestant norms of the respectable middle class, thereby silencing attacks on them from clergy and temperance advocates for abdicating moral responsibility.[4]

Finally, unlike the Sunday-closing movement, the more moderate movement for high licensing fees promised to win support within the liquor camp, thereby assuring victory over the prosaloon bloc in local politics. Saloonkeepers in Chicago paid the lowest wholesale prices for their beer of any major city in the United States, thus favoring the proliferation of small saloons. The growing number of saloons also intensified competition among manufacturers for stable outlets for their product. In this climate the large brewers supported high license fees as a way of forcing saloons not already tied to them to become their outlets; in return, they would pay the saloonkeeper's license fee. In effect the reform would stabilize competition, raise prices and profits for beer and liquor manufacturers, and promote capital accumulation. Of course, antiliquor reformers had their own reasons for supporting high license fees. High license fees would force "low doggeries" out of business, reduce liquor sales, and strike a blow at Irish ward politics.[5]

The English-speaking segment of the city's labor movement did not offer resistance to the movement for high license fees, because many labor leaders viewed the labor movement as an alternative to saloons. Saloonkeepers in this era often offered their halls to unions at reduced rates, in return for the understanding that each member would purchase at least one drink. In 1882 the *Progressive Age* reprinted a *Tribune* editorial claiming that all labor unions had been run as "appendages" of saloons, and the greatest promise of the Knights was "the separation of the labor interest from the liquor interest." It was not just the Knights who shunned saloons. As union memberships stabilized, unions could afford their own halls. In 1882, when the Trades and Labor Assembly attempted to build a central hall to be used by its constituent unions, its appeal to the city council for a grant of lakefront property included the argument that it was necessary to free the labor movement from the "saloon influences." The coalition of greenbackers and socialists in the Chicago Labor Union and the American section of the Socialist Labor party supported a limit on saloons as early as 1881. German and Bohemian socialists and anarchists, however, were culturally tied to saloons. The main meeting hall of the socialist-affiliated unions at 54 West Lake Street was Grief's Saloon and Hall; Twelfth Street Turner Hall was also a saloon.[6]

Even though unions refused to back liquor interests, no union would risk division in its ranks by aligning itself with the movement for higher license fees. When high-license reformers, backed by top businessmen in both parties, formed the Citizens Union party in spring 1883 to oppose Mayor Harrison's reelection, the only labor representatives prominent in its council were the prohibitionists Charles G. Dixon and Leo P. Dwyer. Chicago's Germans, however, were far from neutral. What they objected to was not so much the concept of high license fees—which discriminated in their favor by allowing beer to be sold for $150, while a liquor license cost $500—but the mere fact that temperance reformers could refer to their national custom as something dangerous to the community. In September 1882 the city's Turners, with its many prolabor members, convened a mass meeting that was chaired by the anarchist August Spies but featured Democratic party speakers. The meeting adopted a resolution on personal liberty that was almost identical with the one adopted by the Democratic State Convention, and it endorsed Democratic candidates for state and national elections. The Turners' influence helped Mayor Harrison win reelection by a comfortable margin of 9,000 votes in 1883.[7]

Harrison's reelection doomed the chances of passing high license fees in the city council. But reform advocates immediately turned to the Republican state legislature, which in June 1883 passed a high-license bill known as the Harper Act. The bill's terms, which in Chicago were enforced grudgingly and with as much delay as possible, had several significant effects. First, within a year 780 saloons closed, although by the end of 1885 over 80 percent had reappeared under licenses paid for by large brewers. In return saloonkeepers were compelled to purchase the brewer's brand of beer at increased cost. By the turn of the century three-quarters of all Chicago saloons were tied to manufacturers, leading the *Knights of Labor* to lambaste the Harper Act in 1887 for promoting "concentration and monopolization." Meanwhile, the city used the increased license fees to expand the police force from 500 to 924 in December 1884.[8]

The most significant effect of the Harper Act was that liquor was no longer a major public issue. With Republican antisaloon advocates temporarily mollified, Democrats could no longer exploit the issue to stampede liberal Germans out of the Republican party. As long as the issue was one of public contention, Germans felt bound to stand united. But with passage of the act, liberal Germans suddenly felt free to speak out on the saloon question. As one prominent North Side German socialist put it a week after passage, "High license [now finds] favor among the Germans it certainly did not possess when it was a few weeks ago the issue in the municipal campaign." Like American labor reformers, German socialists disliked the disreputable saloons and wanted to separate the labor movement from the saloon interests. Even the *Arbeiter-Zeitung* editorialized in favor of reducing the number of saloons.[9]

There were three great issue areas in Chicago politics: those centering on personal liberty and ethnicity; class and labor; and governmental corruption and electoral reform. At any one time the prominence of one could overshadow the others. Once the looming shadow of personal liberty and ethnicity was removed after 1883, other issues took on greater importance to Germans. Suppressed class issues bobbed up to the political surface, freeing German socialists to vote their political conscience. Though this tendency was disguised for the moment by the influence of the anarchists' anti-electoral politics, it would become apparent in the 1886 elections, following the Haymarket crisis. German liberals, however, turned to one of their favorite issues, fraud and the abuse of political power. In 1873 liberal Germans had split from the Republicans to help catapult the People's party to power. Once the old Sunday-closing law had been repealed, they had turned their attention to the abuse of power by Irish-Democratic politicians and in 1876 had returned to the Republican party. This scenario recurred a decade later following passage of the Harper Act.

Throughout Harrison's administration unsubstantiated rumors and charges of voter fraud and the corrupt use of patronage had dogged him. In February 1885, a month before the mayoral election, a grand jury indicted Mike McDonald's chief lieutenant, Joseph Mackin, for voter fraud. Mackin and several associates were prosecuted by a special committee of upper-class "citizens." The resulting trial revealed a shocking degree of fraud in voter registration, ballot counting, and the final canvass of the November 1884 returns, and it momentarily galvanized public opinion. One of the most notable reactions to the trial's revelations was the Iroquois Club's abandonment of its hands-off attitude toward municipal politics. It demanded that the Democratic party allow the club the right to appoint one election judge per precinct. The ensuing mayoral campaign revolved as much around the issue of election fraud as the 1883 election had revolved around high license fees. Though on the eve of the election Harrison belatedly denounced Mackin's crimes, his margin dwindled to less than 375 votes, and there was a widespread supposition that the votes had been manufactured by party "ward bummers."[10]

Evidence confirms that the decline in Harrison's vote was largely due to the defection of the liberal Germans. In the Fourteenth Ward, which was 44 percent German and where Harrison had received 64 percent of the vote in 1883, his 1885 figure fell to less than 50 percent. In the Fifteenth Ward, 68 percent German, Harrison's share fell from 61 to 48 percent, and in the Sixteenth Ward, 73 percent German, it fell from 69 to 54 percent. By comparison, Harrison's majority in the city fell from 56 to 50 percent. Within a month of the election Harrison fired Herman Lieb, his top German political lieutenant, who had warned him that with lagging interest in the personal liberty issue he would have to distance himself from the McDonald gang.[11]

The razor-thin margin of Harrison's victory, coming on the heels of the Mackin revelations, elicited renewed charges of fraud and a chorus of demands for a recount. Two days after the election an aroused assembly of elite businessmen, including Marshall Field, the city's most prestigious man of wealth, met under the auspices of the Citizens Association to discuss the disputed election and take steps to reform the electoral process. Acting through the state legislature, business reformers devised an election law, which among other things set up a bipartisan, court-appointed board of election commissioners to redraw precinct lines, appoint registration and polling officials, and oversee the election process. Enacted as state law in June, the bill was ratified locally—with almost no opposition from organized labor—in November 1885 by more than a two-to-one margin.[12]

By the close of the year the Iroquois Club had temporarily ousted the McDonald wing of the party. William C. Goudy, a silk-stocking lawyer, replaced Mackin in the city leadership, while Charles Kern, an ex-sheriff and elite businessman who was hated by the Irish, took over as chair of the Cook County Democratic party. The bipartisan unity of the city's upper class was in evidence in January, when committees from the Iroquois Club, Union League Club, and Citizens Association met to examine ballot boxes. In the municipal elections of April 1886 the reformers and Republicans completed their "clean-up" of the city council. Democrats, who made up 20 of the 36 aldermen in 1883, were reduced to just 11. By 1886, 19 of the council's aldermen had been elected for the first time in 1885 or 1886.[13]

The defection of the liberal Germans, elite businesspeople's renewed class unity and involvement in local politics (recalling the founding of the Citizens Association), the declining influence of Chicago's ward politicians, and the resurgence of the Republican party around the reform issue all followed from the Harper Act in a complex chain of cause and effect. As had happened in the mid-1870s, the triumph of liberal business reform and the loosening of the Democratic party's grip on the different elements of its working-class constituency would, by the mid-1880s, clear the field for independent labor politics. But before this could happen the labor movement would have to be jolted out of its alliance with the Harrison administration.

Captain Bonfield and the 1885 Streetcar Strike

Before the passage of the Harper Act the Citizens Association confined itself to lobbying for an increase in the size of the police force, a reform to which all citizens could readily assent. With that goal accomplished, business reformers turned to an issue with more partisan implications: the partiality and unprofessionalism of the police during elections and labor conflicts.

Reinforcing business concerns was a severe two-year depression, which in Chicago began in November 1883 and bottomed out in mid-1884. As late as the first few months of 1885 there were new layoffs of workers and wage cuts for those who had jobs. The effect of the depression on labor was evident in a Trades and Labor Assembly survey in November 1885, which found 20 to 25 percent of the cigarmakers, harnessmakers, and printers still unemployed, though iron molders and tanners had largely returned to work. By forcing employers to retrench on labor costs, the depression also added to the volatility and intensity of labor conflict during this period and helped propel them into police reform.

In its 1885 *Annual Report* the Citizens Association, in liberal mugwump fashion, pinpointed democratic politics as the source of the problem of police conduct. The report observed that in the ten years since the advent of the People's party, "the struggle to obtain and retain office has become so active and violent that no possible factor or contingency is too great or too insignificant to be attempted for its possession, or underestimated in its importance." Politicians, the report exclaimed, thus found it easy "to calculate the probable effect of a prompt, bold, and determined attitude against a large body of defiant rioters who have ballots to cast in the early future."[14]

Three important strikes in this period—two molders' strikes and a streetcar strike—underscored the Citizens Association's point, helping to unite and mobilize upper-class political opinion, while throwing pro-Harrison labor leaders into dismay and consternation. The first strike was the five-month iron molders' strike at the Cribben and Sexton Company, which culminated in August 1884. Because of the hands-off policy of the Harrison police, the large West Side foundry decided to hire Pinkerton detectives to guard its premises and to issue revolvers to the nonunion men it employed to replace the strikers. In August the strikers began to get desperate, and, with the help of street toughs recruited in local saloons, they resorted to attacks on scabs.

On August 13 the affair climaxed in a pitched battle between union and nonunion men. Fully seventy-five to a hundred shots were exchanged within fifteen minutes, during which time no police were to be seen. One man died in the battle, which resulted in the company's being censured in police court for providing its employees with pistols.[15]

The Citizens Association's *Annual Report* called police inaction during the molders' strike "a flagrant neglect of duty." They might have added that among organized workers the largely Irish molders had the tightest city hall connections. Walter McDonald, the city sealer, was "an old, respected member of the Molders Union," boasted the *Western Workman,* and "has granted innumerable favors to organized labor." Many Irish molders and policemen were also members of the Ancient Order of Hibernians and bound by oath to render mutual assistance and sympathy. This, according to a Pinkerton detective's report during another molders' strike at McCormick's Reaper Plant in the spring of 1885, accounted for police reluctance to interfere, or, as the Citizens Association report put it, their "uncertain and apathetic attitude." When reinforced by the mayor's decidedly hostile attitude toward the younger McCormick, it is little wonder that the reaper magnate lost both his police protection and the strike itself. The most conspicuous action of the Chicago police during the conflict was the arrest of four Pinkertons for shooting into a crowd of five hundred strikers that had stopped a busload of scabs.[16]

The patent unwillingness of Harrison's police force, even with its numbers beefed up, to permit employers to retrench labor costs during the 1883–85 depression precipitated a crisis during the July 1885 streetcar strike. The trouble began when the company reduced the number of daily trips made by employees, and the West Side Streetcarmen's Benevolent Association asked for a compensating wage increase. The strike began when the company fired fifteen union leaders, including President Luke Coyne, in an attempt to break the union. This brought the entire city labor movement, plus West Side residents, to the carmen's side. In 1882 the streetcar employees had won their dispute with the aid of a popular boycott, backed by the threat of community crowd actions. In 1885 this threat became a reality as a result of the intransigent attitude of the company's Superintendent Lake. The strike mushroomed into the largest and most violent mass strike since the 1877 riots.[17]

On the first day of the strike thousands of workers patrolled the company's main tracks along West Madison Street. When Chicago police attempted to carry off prisoners, the crowd aggressively intervened to protect their brethren. Those arrested were released by the mayor the next day. Meanwhile, the Trades and Labor Assembly convened a mass meeting of seven thousand, where Alderman Frank Lawler called for the revocation of the company's charter. Knights mixed LA 1307, composed of leading labor reformers and socialists, went further by calling on the city to take over the streetcar lines.[18]

Mayor Harrison then met with Superintendent Lake and issued a remarkable statement, calling on the company to put its cars in the barns and publish a statement of its position to "let the public decide which side is right." He concluded this transparently prostriker statement by calling for arbitration. The company, however, refused to compromise its "right to hire and fire." As the situation threatened to escalate into a full-scale conflagration, a delegation of Iroquois Club men, led by the packers Sid Kent and Phil Armour and the importer John Doane, requested that Lake accept a compromise settlement. On the other side, Levi Leiter, a wealthy Democrat who was a stockholder in the streetcar company, requested that Harrison protect the company's right to run its cars. In the face of the company's obduracy Police Superintendent Austin Doyle, with Harrison's consent, turned to a little-known police captain, John Bonfield, to guard the cars.[19]

Then ensued one of the most brutal confrontations of police and strikers in the entire decade. Bonfield, described by one reporter as a "large, powerful, resolute, ruthless man," arrayed fully half the Chicago police force to man a train of ten streetcars. With the lead car jammed with twenty-five policemen, followed by a prisoner car and then police reinforcements, the procession moved at a snail's pace as it ran a gauntlet of barricades and jeering strikers and sympathizers along Madison Street. At every opportunity Bonfield urged his legions forward to club anyone congregating near the tracks. Testifying to the almost superstitious power the word *scab* had acquired, Bonfield also instructed his police to arrest anyone who shouted the word. It was a transparent attempt to overawe a crowd welded together by class solidarity and to reestablish civil authority. By the afternoon Bonfield's police had taken 150 prisoners, including 65 striking conductors and drivers. Among the arrested sympathizers was a contingent of bricklayers, who had shouted "rats" from the top of a building under construction and a group of workers who had used the word *scab* while standing in front of their factory.[20]

The affair strikingly demonstrated that new leadership under new circumstances could radically alter the role of the police in labor disputes. It also showed how acts of incredible brutality could coexist with ethnic ties and class sympathy. In the heat of battle the police completely forgot these ties and waded into the working-class crowds with gusto. A year later John J. Flinn, a police historian, wrote that at the start of the strike the police had "permitted their sentiments and prejudices to blind them. They had momentarily forgotten their allegiance to the public." Bonfield restored "their sense of duty." Leadership made all the difference.[21]

Bonfield's actions aroused outrage and indignation from a variety of interested citizens. A meeting of two hundred West Side businesspeople condemned the captain's actions. A large Trades and Labor Assembly meeting resolved in favor of the municipalization of the company. August Spies, anarchist editor of the *Arbeiter-Zeitung*, advocated revolution, and Knights LA 1307 talked of forming an anti-Harrison party. These were all portents of events to come. The immediate impact of Bonfield's actions, however, was the end of the strike, without arbitration. Under a compromise settlement the men returned to work without a wage increase. In return the company agreed to "investigate" the case of the dismissed men, and ultimately all but two were rehired. It was status quo ante.[22]

During the strike Harrison and the Iroquois Club had pursued the old policy of recommending arbitration while judiciously limiting the use of police power. After the strike Harrison abruptly changed course and embraced Bonfield and the policy implications of his actions. In October Police Superintendent Austin Doyle resigned under pressure, and Harrison replaced him with Frederick Ebersold and promoted Bonfield to inspector, the second highest post on the force. It was a political move in two senses. Ebersold was a German Republican and Bonfield an Irish Republican, both groups whose defections had figured prominently in the recent decline of Harrison's political fortunes.[23]

The new appointments also signified an attempt to propitiate business reformers in the Citizens Association, who had been flaying Harrison over voting fraud and more recently his handling of labor disputes. Bonfield was both a modernizer and professionalizer in the police department. In 1881 he had helped devise a new telegraph system that enabled policemen to make hourly reports without leaving their beats and facilitated speedy dispatch of reinforcements when disturbances threatened. The appointment of Bonfield signified a shift from Harrison's prior policy of deferring to the ethnic opinion in Chicago's ethnic working-class neighborhoods. Such an approach had been represented by his appointment of Bridgeport's Lieutenant John Byrne, who believed that too much force by police might spark a riot. Bonfield's actions in 1885 embodied a different policy, which the new inspector summarized in the phrase, "the club today saves the bullet tomorrow." In a letter to the *Tribune* Bonfield referred to the 1877 riots as a reason to avoid treating strikers too leniently. So well did Bonfield fit the needs of employers in these years that in later months rumors were rife among labor leaders that he was secretly in the pay of leading capitalists.[24]

The fruits of Bonfield's new approach to the police were first apparent in the Maxwell box factory strike undertaken by a Knights local assembly in the winter of 1885–86. During the dispute Lieutenant Archibald Darrow of the Hinman Street police station allowed strikers to attack scabs with impunity. At the urging of local businesspeople Bonfield dispatched a police spy to the scene to confirm the charge. Darrow, suspecting the man was a spy, told strikers that he was a strikebreaker, which led them to "slug" him. Claiming that Darrow knew who the spy's assailants were but refused to arrest them, Bonfield had Darrow and two officers under his command dismissed from the force. It later came out that Darrow was immensely popular in his district and was viewed as a "friend of the poor workingman." The *Tribune* reported that Darrow planned to use his community ties "for the sake of capturing the Democratic nomination for West Town Supervisor and his course during the last few months had been governed by his desire of leaving the police force and getting a more remunerative office."[25]

Within the labor movement Bonfield's appointment was met with indignation. The Trades and Labor Assembly immediately delegated a committee chaired by Leo P. Dwyer to request that Harrison dismiss Bonfield. When Harrison refused, the committee appeared before the city council, also without success. It was soon revealed that Harrison was not without labor support. At the very time that Dwyer's committee was meeting with the council, another committee from the Trades and Labor Assembly was visiting Harrison to ask for a labor appointment to city government. Harrison's price was the withdrawal of the Bonfield protest, and the second committee asked a prolabor alderman to withhold a report critical of Bonfield that he was about to present to the city council.[26]

When the facts became known at its January 1886 meeting, the Trades and Labor Assembly dissolved in pandemonium. The Bonfield dispute brought to a head the growing disagreement within the ranks of the Knights and trade unionists over the merits of the alliance with Harrison's "working-class democracy." It was also a dispute over the viability of political collective bargaining, for despite the universal outrage at Bonfield's action leaders of the Trades and Labor Assembly had refused to "bargain" with Harrison over the issue, thereby risking their city jobs. There would always be differences among union leaders over whether the delivery of labor votes was worth it. In this case labor's beachhead in the city government began to appear to some trade unionists as more of a hindrance than an aid. Chief among these segments of the labor movement were those of lesser skill and political influence, who had no stake in the strategy and favored independent politics.

Whatever the implications of the dispute, the immediate significance of the Bonfield appointment lay in the unraveling of the Harrison administration's labor alliance. The modus vivendi of the first six years of the

Harrison administration that had preserved class peace at the expense of a growing labor presence in industrial and political life was dissolving, a casualty of an aroused business elite bent on regaining political supremacy in the civic arena.

Chicago's Anarchists and the Revolutionary Alternative

The growing lack of public confidence in Harrison's democracy need not have created a crisis of the quality and magnitude it did, had it not been for the appearance, growth, and impact of the revolutionary socialists, or "anarchists," in the labor movement and the broader political system. As long as such English-speaking socialists as Thomas Morgan, George Schilling, and Charles Wheeler maintained their precarious hold on the Socialist Labor party, the differences between greenbackers, Knights, trade unionists, and German-speaking socialists, significant though they were, could be bridged often enough. But because the anarchist leadership and membership were solidly embedded in a political culture that clashed with the American political tradition in crucial ways, the Chicago labor movement fractured into two parallel class-political movements, separated by more than what united them. This split in turn exacerbated the tendencies unraveling labor's alliance with the Harrison administration, thus laying the foundation for the Haymarket crisis of 1886.

After the breakup and decline of the SLP and the formation of the International Working Peoples' Association (IWPA) in 1883 at Pittsburgh, a revolutionary socialist movement took shape in Chicago and grew rapidly during the depression of 1883–85. By 1885 there were at least 1,000 anarchists in the city; by the beginning of 1886, according to the historian Bruce C. Nelson, there were approximately 2,800 anarchists in Chicago, organized in twenty-six autonomous groups. The movement also supported seven daily newspapers that had a combined circulation of 30,000. Chicago became, in Paul Avrich's words, "the Mecca of the anarchist movement, to which adherents from all over the country looked for advice and support."[27]

But more significant than sheer numbers was the fact that the anarchists exercised leadership over a large body of German trade unionists. In June 1884 the Progressive Cigarmakers Union No. 15, which had seceded from the larger International-affiliated body and accordingly had its delegates rejected by the Trades and Labor Assembly, brought together seven other German-speaking trade unions to found the Central Labor Union (CLU). The new citywide federation initially included German-speaking branches of the metalworkers, tailors, printers, butchers, cabinetmakers and was probably smaller than the Trades and Labor Assembly. All the top offices of the new CLU were filled by members of the IWPA or the SLP. These new leaders rejected unionists' seeking office and bargaining over reform demands.[28]

Some historians have emphasized the differences between the "revolutionary" CLU and the "moderate" and "labor aristocratic" Knights of Labor and Trades and Labor Assembly.[29] Though the differences were certainly significant enough, they appear less stark and the categories far from mutually exclusive when viewed in the context of their similarities. The IWPA, together with what remained of the SLP, related to the CLU very much the way the mixed assemblies of the Knights related to the trade unions affiliated with the Trades and Labor Assembly and the Knights' own local trades assemblies. Both the IWPA and Knights mixed assemblies were overtly political associations of individual unionists, journalists, politicians, and the like who sought to "educate" the members of the trade bodies to which they also belonged. Anarchists, Knights, and trade union leaders were also largely drawn from the skilled crafts. According to Bruce C. Nelson's exhaustive survey, though there was considerable diversity among anarchists, the typical anarchist member was a German skilled worker in a small shop, not a factory. August Spies appeared to confirm this when he wrote that up to late 1884 "the revolutionary movement has been restricted to the better situated and more intellectual German, Bohemian, and Danish workingmen." That anarchist skilled workers sought to mobilize and organize unskilled workers stamps them in the same mold as the Knights of Labor. Indeed, some anarchists, including Albert Parsons and August Spies, remained members of the local order's mixed LA 1307.[30]

The ideological common ground between the Knights and the anarchists comes into clearer focus if their rhetoric is scrutinized. The anarchists, like the Knights, embraced a politics shaped by a labor-based reinterpretation of producers' republican doctrine. Both held to what Bernard Moss has termed a "republican socialism," common to skilled workers in Europe and the United States at this time.[31] Anarchist speakers often used the word *liberty* to describe their goals. Like good labor republicans, they counterposed liberty to the "slavery" of the wage system enforced by the institution of private property. Unlike American labor leaders, however, the anarchists held that private property and the statute law that upheld it violated workers' natural rights to the fruits of their labor.[32] Yet the anarchists' alternative to law and private property—a society of associated individuals in self-governing cooperatives—was almost identical with the property-based producer cooperation advocated by American radicals (though both differed in important ways from what the Marxists called "scientific socialism"). As Albert Parsons put it in 1886, "The foundation principle of socialism, or anarchy is the same as the Knights of

Labor, viz., 'The abolition of the wages system' and the substitution in its stead of an industrial system of universal cooperation."[33]

Despite these similarities there were profound differences between the anarchists and English-speaking labor activists. Though anarchist political philosophy was highly eclectic and in no sense monolithic, anarchist thinking and practice was part of a distinct political culture carried by the German language that provided the political symbols and terms that mediated workers' perceptions of social reality. Relatively acculturated Germans were therefore less prone to embrace the kinds of politics discussed here. IWPAers tended to be recently arrived immigrants from continental Europe, who had experience in workers' parties and viewed their American work as a continuation of their struggle against Bismarckian oppression. That the average anarchist had been in the United States only seven years suggests the critical importance of language and lack of acculturation.[34]

German workers' political language was freighted with the symbols and terms of the French revolutionary tradition, originating in the Jacobin phase of the French Revolution and culminating in the Paris Commune of 1871. Unlike American liberal republicanism, Jacobinism posited a sharp conflict between the self-interest generated by commercial society and the revolutionary virtue that was needed to perceive the common good. For Jacobins the great problem was how to animate, mobilize, and sustain public virtue.[35] Anarchist culture, a strain of the Jacobin culture, was essentially an attempt to create a kind of alternative (civil) religion of virtue—also part of a freethinker tradition—replete with secular martyrs and saints, anniversaries of revolutionary moments, demonstrations to unmask the hypocrisy of official American holidays, and socializing occasions, such as picnics and dances. Integral to this culture was a militant opposition to the organized church, which the anarchists identified with the state. One striking example of this anarchist counterculture was the celebration of the anniversary of the Paris Commune of 1871, which beginning in 1872 became an annual event that appropriated the French revolutionary tradition for socialist purposes. The "Communfest" featured large busts of Ferdinand Lassalle and Karl Marx, prominent red flags, plays, and the singing of the "Marseillaise," ending with the words "Vive la Commune."[36]

Far from attempting to Americanize or legitimize Jacobin revolutionary culture by integrating it with the symbols of American political culture as the SLP had, the anarchists sought to underline the differences and so unmask American hypocrisy. Anarchist demonstrations often occurred on hallowed American civil or religious holidays: the Fourth of July, Thanksgiving, and Christmas. For example, a leaflet for a Thanksgiving Day demonstration stated that while "our Lords and Masters are feasting on Turkey and champagne . . . , the wage-slaves of Chicago, the unemployed, the enforced idle, the tramps . . . will assemble . . . to mutter their curses loud and deep against the Lords who have deprived them of every blessing during the past year."[37]

American workers had their own republican civil religion (as well as a much higher level of church affiliation), but instead of being counterposed to the existing government and culture, native workers' political culture identified with the Republic and sought to save it from impending corruption. Though Jacobinism did find some echoes in the Protestant abolitionist tradition epitomized by John Brown, most assimilated organized workers still viewed the Republic as humankind's "last best hope." When the anarchist Parsons said that "America is not a free country; the economic conditions of the workers here are precisely the same as they are in Europe" and when anarchists refused to carry the American flag in parades and attacked all religion, most Americanized labor activists were repelled. They especially could not accept the open advocacy of dynamite and revolutionary violence to overthrow the U.S. government. As Andrew Cameron put it on the eve of Haymarket, "The red flag of the socialism of Europe" could never be joined "to the democratic republicanism of America."[38]

In contrast to Jacobinism's emphasis on revolutionary virtue, American political culture had a stronger liberal streak. Unlike the Jacobin republican socialists who, along with Pierre Joseph Proudhon, viewed private property as theft, American republican socialists wanted a wider access to property. American political culture was more liberal in another way. It held fast to the principle of the sovereignty of the people as exercised in associations of individuals pursuing happiness in a society protected by a constitutionally limited state.[39] Within this political culture revolutionary change was to be accomplished through evolutionary and constitutional methods. As Ed Irwin, a printer responding in 1881 to the formation of the anarchists, wrote, "Methods of doing business whether societary or industrial are . . . the result of slow and gradual growth. . . . True and healthy progress is not a hot house product." Most unionists, he wrote, "feel, in a helpless sort of way that the wage system is a great economic wrong; that it makes the workers virtual economic slaves. . . . We feel too that some time a better and more equitable industrial method will be devised." But, counseled Irwin, "we live under a system that reason tells us cannot be removed at least during our lifetime. . . . Our destination may be upon the mountain top but we shall arrive at it all the sooner, and have a more comfortable journey if we pay heed to the steps that lie in between. . . ."[40]

The differences between the anarchists and the Knights and trade unionists were not merely ideological. The continental European model of insurrection uncritically adapted to the United States led to grievous misjudgments about the mass strike. To some anarchist leaders, the mass strike and the use of violence by Irish workers in 1877 and during other mass strikes portended violent revolution. According to the recollections of one of the Haymarket martyrs, "In the approval of violence we were guided mainly by the Irish movement of that time and the occasional brutal outbreaks of the American workers." During the molders' strike of 1881 Irish workers even used dynamite. The increasingly violent strikes—chronicled in detail in the English-language weekly *Alarm*—were, according to August Spies, "storms raging through the industrial life." Like volcanoes, they would provide the energy and impetus for the revolution for which the anarchists were merely preparing workers.[41]

But Spies and other anarchist leaders misconstrued Irish violence, which after 1877 was directed against strikebreakers, not the state. Even the *Irish World*'s advocacy of a dynamite campaign against the British was directed toward the goal of republican revolution and rationalized by the example of the American revolution. Irish nationalists did not call for such violence to be practiced in republican America.[42] Of all the events of the decade it was the violence of the 1885 streetcar strike that encouraged anarchists to believe that the mass strike was a prelude to revolution. Spies and other IWPAers called on trade unionists to abandon their "hypocritical" lip service to "law and order" and begin to practice armed self-defense. Dyer Lum, editor of the *Alarm*, speculating on the possibility that a mass strike might create the condition for a revolutionary upheaval, asked rhetorically, "If the great railroad strike of 1877 were to be repeated today, would it not be such an occasion?" Lum and other anarchist leaders were approaching the Blanquist theory that conditions were ripe for a band of determined revolutionaries to lead the masses into revolutionary conflict.[43]

The growing belief in the imminence of revolution was demonstrated in the anarchist response to the eight-hour movement, which began gathering steam in the last months of 1885. Though many "intransigents" remained aloof from the struggle, which they viewed as a piddling reform, others welcomed it as an opportunity rather than a diversion of energy. Spies argued that the demand could not be won without violent conflict, and in October the CLU passed his resolution calling for an armed general strike for the eight-hour workday. Lack of concern with winning the reform itself also led the anarchists to advocate eight hours of work for ten hours of pay, instead of merely a reduction to eight hours. While the idea had much rank-and-file support, the demand stiffened resistance on the part of employers, who faced intercity competition, and subsequently divided the Eight Hour Association, many of whose leaders wanted a negotiable demand. To the anarchists, however, the more intransigent demand furthered the possibility that the eight-hour movement could precipitate an armed confrontation with apocalyptic consequences.[44]

It is easy to exaggerate the impact of the spectacular utterances of the anarchists on Chicago's political scene. But according to Henry David, "Though Chicago did not take the talk of arming the workers with oppressive seriousness, the city nevertheless didn't regard it with benign amusement." Particularly threatening were the public lakefront meetings. Between May and November 1885 there were twenty-six meetings along the lakefront, in addition to anarchist gatherings elsewhere in the city. With the advent of the eight-hour movement these meetings became weekly occurrences. Several thousand excited workers listening to speakers of the "whoop her up" school of anarchism seemed further proof of the bankruptcy of Harrison's policy of toleration toward the customs of the foreign-born working class.[45]

In 1883 many in the respectable classes refused to listen to the *Tribune* when it argued against Harrison's reelection by declaring that he had "deliberately severed the honorable connection [to the respectable classes] and placed himself at the head of the vicious classes." But events in 1884–85 culminating in the Haymarket bomb created a change of heart. There were reports of businessmen arming themselves and their clerks in early 1885, and city leaders held the National Guard in readiness as the May 1 deadline for the strike approached. The head of the Law and Order League criticized "the intelligent and cultivated people" for their division, thus allowing "the dangerous classes of the great cities to hold the balance of political power; and to obtain [their] votes [politicians] have been more than willing to sell high places of trust and profit or more frequently indulgences for the violation of particular laws. . . ." According to John J. Flinn, those who opposed Harrison's reelection in 1887 rejected "methods which had tolerated anarchistic harangues on the lakefront and elsewhere, which led to the Haymarket Riot, and the practical suspension of the ordinances against gambling and other forms of public vice which flaunted themselves with the impudence born of long immunity."[46]

The set of informal and formal compromises and accommodations that Harrison had brokered between social groups and classes, evident in government appointments, political rhetoric, municipal fiscal policy, and the immunity of gamblers, saloonkeepers, and strikers from law enforcement, was no longer viable. To Chicago's respectable leaders, Mayor Harrison and the Democratic party had granted workers a larger share of power than was compatible with sound business practice and public order. Far from avoiding a recurrence of the 1877 riots, Harrison's police-labor policies seemed now to be encouraging mass disturbances. His tolerance of vice and saloon interests also alienated respectable elements, whose support was necessary for his political rule. As in the period before 1877, when liberal mugwumps in the Republican party ascended to power, a transformed political opportunity structure in the city was conducive to a great labor upheaval.

Notes

1. *Chicago Tribune,* Jan. 17, 1881; Bessie Louise Pierce, *A History of Chicago,* vol. 3, *The Rise of a Modern City, 1871–1893* (Chicago: University of Chicago Press, 1957), 455–59.

2. *Chicago Tribune,* Jan. 12, 1881, Nov. 24, 1882, Oct. 24, 1883; Perry R. Duis, *The Saloon: Public Drinking in Chicago and Boston, 1880–1920* (Urbana: University of Illinois Press, 1983), 98–99, 179–80.

3. *Chicago Tribune,* Dec. 8, 1882, Dec. 11, 1881, Apr. 6, 1884; Citizens Association of Chicago, *Annual Reports, 1879–1901* (Chicago: Citizens Association of Chicago, 1901), 1882 Report, 15–16, 19–31. Those arguing for an increase in the police force pointed out that in 1884 Chicago had 620 policemen, while New York, with twice the population, had 2,700.

4. Chicago Tribune, Nov. 9, 1882 ("cranks" quote); Paul Kleppner, *The Third Electoral System, 1853–1892: Parties, Voters, and Political Cultures* (Chapel Hill: University of North Carolina Press, 1979); Charles Carroll Bonney, *The Present Conflict of Labor and Capital* (Chicago: Chicago Legal News, 1886), 24–25 ("wealth and power . . . neglecting . . ." quote).

5. *Chicago Tribune,* Dec. 12, 1882, Jan. 12, 1884; Perry Duis, "The Saloon in a Changing Chicago," *Chicago History* 4 (Winter 1975–76): 217–18.

6. *Chicago Tribune,* Jan. 4, 1880, June 27, 1881, Sept. 12, 1881, Nov. 12, 1881, Apr. 16, 1882; *Progressive Age,* Apr. 22, 1882 ("appendages" quote); *Irish World and American Industrial Liberator,* Aug. 19, 1882 ("saloon influences" quote); Duis, *Saloon,* 178–81.

7. *Chicago Tribune,* Mar. 13, 1881, Sept. 18, 1882, Mar. 3, 1883, Mar. 18, 1883, Apr. 4, 1883.

8. Ibid., June 9, 1883, June 16, 1883, Dec. 17, 1885; *Knights of Labor,* May 7, 1887; John J. Flinn, *History of the Chicago Police from the Settlement of the Community to the Present Time* (Chicago: Police Book Fund, 1887), 216, 221; Citizens Association, *Annual Reports,* 1885, 20–22.

9. *Chicago Tribune,* May 20, 1883, May 27, 1883 (German socialist quote); *Arbeiter-Zeitung* editorial translated in *Chicago Tribute,* Nov. 14, 1883.

10. Ibid., beginning Feb. 9, 1885, through Mar. 15, 1885 (for the Mackin trial), Feb. 28, 1885, Mar. 26, 1885, Apr. 2, 1885, Apr. 9, 1885.

11. Ibid., Apr. 4, 1883, Apr. 9, 1885, Apr. 26, 1885.

12. Ibid., Apr. 10, 1885, July 9, 1885, Oct. 30, 1885, Nov. 4, 1885; Pierce, *History of Chicago,* 3:360–61.

13. *Chicago Tribune,* Dec. 18, 1885, Dec. 23, 1885, Jan. 21, 1886. Figures were derived from biographies of aldermen in M. L. Ahern, *The Political History of Chicago* (Chicago: Donohue and Henneberry, 1886), 118–32.

14. Citizens Association, *Annual Reports,* 1885, 21.

15. *Chicago Tribune*, Aug. 13, 1884, Aug. 14, 1884, Aug. 16, 1884.

16. Citizens Association, *Annual Reports*, 1885, 20–22 (first and third quotes on 21); *Western Workman*, June 30, 1883 (second quote); Robert Ozanne, *A Century of Labor-Management Relations at McCormick and International Harvester* (Madison: University of Wisconsin, 1967), 16–17; Flinn, *History of the Chicago Police*, 340; *Chicago Tribune*, Apr. 10, 1885, Apr. 11, 1885, Apr. 12, 1885.

17. *Chicago Tribune*, June 30, 1885, July 1, 1885.

18. Ibid., July 2, 1885; *Chicago Express*, July 2, 1885.

19. *Chicago Tribune*, July 2, 1885 (first quote), July 5, 1885, July 7, 1885 (second quote); Flinn, *History of the Chicago Police*, 240–48.

20. *Chicago Tribune*, July 4, 1885; Paul Avrich, *The Haymarket Tragedy* (Princeton, N.J.: Princeton University Press, 1984), 97 (quote).

21. Flinn, *History of the Chicago Police*, 340–43.

22. *Chicago Tribune*, July 4, 1885, July 5, 1885, July 8, 1885, July 11, 1885, July 18, 1885.

23. Ibid., Oct. 16, 1885, Oct. 20, 1885.

24. Ibid., Dec. 22, 1880, Oct. 14, 1885, Jan. 31, 1886 (quote); Flinn, *History of the Chicago Police*, 403–5, 408; *Labor Enquirer*, Jan. 6, 1888; Albert Parsons, "Autobiography of Albert Parsons," in *The Autobiographies of the Haymarket Martyrs*, ed. Philip S. Foner (New York: Monad, 1969), 51–52. Though the Bonfield rumors are plausible, I have not been able to verify them from nonlabor sources.

25. *Chicago Tribune*, Feb. 20, 1886 (quotes), Feb. 21, 1886; *Chicago Herald*, Feb. 20, 1886.

26. *Chicago Tribune*, Oct. 23, 1885, Nov. 20, 1885, Jan. 4, 1886; *Chicago Herald*, Jan. 4, 1886.

27. Bruce C. Nelson, *Beyond the Martyrs: A Social History of Chicago's Anarchists, 1870–1900* (New Brunswick, N.J.: Rutgers University Press, 1988), 81; Avrich, *Haymarket Tragedy*, 85.

28. Before comprehensive surveys were taken in 1886 numbers are hard to discern, but because many of the unions affiliated with the Trades and Labor Assembly were multiethnic unions with regularized bargaining arrangements and because in October 1885 the Trades and Labor Assembly had nineteen affiliated unions, more than the CLU's thirteen unions, it is likely that in 1885 the CLU was smaller. *Chicago Tribune*, June 6, 1884, Nov. 24, 1884; Avrich, *Haymarket Tragedy*, 92; Nelson, *Beyond the Martyrs*, 40–44.

29. Eric L. Hirsch, *Urban Revolt: Ethnic Politics in the Nineteenth-Century Chicago Labor Movement* (Berkeley: University of California Press, 1990); Bruce C. Nelson, "'We Can't Get Them to Do Aggressive Work': Chicago's Anarchists and the Eight-Hour Movement," *International Labor and Working Class History* 29 (Spring 1986): 1–13.

30. Nelson, *Beyond the Martyrs*, 86–87 (quote), 88, 91, 98, 101; *Chicago Express*, July 11, 1885; *Knights of Labor*, Nov. 18, 1887. A small anarchist assembly existed in 1882 but soon lapsed.

31. B. H. Moss, "Republican Socialism and the Making of the Working Class in Britain, France, and the United States: A Critique of Thompsonian Culturalism," *Comparative Studies in Society and History* 35 (Apr. 1993): 390–413; B. H.

Moss, *The Origins of the French Labor Movement: The Socialism of Skilled Workers, 1830–1914* (Berkeley: University of California Press, 1976). The economist John Bates Clark called socialism "economic republicanism." Quoted in James Livingston, *Pragmatism and the Political Economy of Cultural Revolution, 1850–1940* (Chapel Hill: University of North Carolina Press, 1994), 53. Thomas J. Morgan, *Chicago Tribune*, Oct. 15, 1887, called the Knights' program a "kind of socialism."

32. Henry Demarest Lloyd viewed anarchism as "the fag end of the system of perfect freedom for the individual initiative which was breaking down." Quoted in Caroline Augusta Lloyd, *Henry Demarest Lloyd, 1847–1903* (New York: G. P. Putnam's Sons, 1912), 1:96. On the importance of natural rights thinking among the anarchists, see Thorstein Veblen, *The Theory of Business Enterprise* (1904; reprint, New York: Mentor Books, 1963), 219n18; Henry David, *The History of the Haymarket Affair*, 3d rev. ed. (New York: Collier Books, 1963), 101–19, esp. 109 and 115–16, 130; Carl Smith, *Urban Disorder and the Shape of Belief: The Great Chicago Fire, the Haymarket Bomb, and the Model Town of Pullman* (Chicago: University of Chicago Press, 1995), 166–68; and Hartmut Keil and Heinz Ickstadt, "Elements of German Working-Class Culture in Chicago, 1880 to 1890," in *German Workers' Culture in the United States, 1850–1920*, ed. Hartmut Keil (Washington, D.C.: Smithsonian Institution Press, 1988), 92–93.

33. Parsons quoted in David, *History of the Haymarket Affair*, 115–16. In 1875 Karl Marx had criticized a program of the German Workers party in Gotha that advocated labor's "equal right" to the "(undiminished) proceeds of [its] labor." The sanctification of the individual right to the fruits of one's labor, Marx strongly implied, was incompatible with modern industry, which required continuous reinvestment of surplus labor. In this respect both the anarchists and the Knights of Labor echoed the program of German workers. Karl Marx, *Critique of the Gotha Programme* (New York: International Publishers, 1973), 6–11.

34. Keil and Ickstadt, "Elements of German Working-Class Culture," 99–100; Nelson, *Beyond the Martyrs*, 98.

35. Judith Shklar, *Men and Citizens: A Study of Rousseau's Social Theory* (Cambridge: Cambridge University Press, 1969); Moss, "Republican Socialism and the Making of the Working Class," 403–7; K. Stephen Vincent, *Pierre Joseph Proudhon and the Rise of French Republican Socialism* (New York: Oxford University Press, 1984), 33–47; Leo A. Loubere, *Louis Blanc: His Life and His Contribution to the Rise of French Jacobin-Socialism* (Evanston, Ill.: Northwestern University Press, 1961); Patrick H. Hutton, *The Cult of the Revolutionary Tradition: The Blanquists in French Politics, 1864–1893* (Berkeley: University of California Press, 1981).

36. Dick Geary, "The German Labor Movement, 1848–1919," *European Studies Review* 6 (July 1976): 297–300; Bruce C. Nelson, "Revival and Upheaval: Religion, Irreligion, and Chicago's Working Class in 1886," *Journal of Social History* 25 (Winter 1991): 233–53; Nelson, *Beyond the Martyrs*, 144–45.

37. Quoted in Avrich, *Haymarket Tragedy*, 143–44.

38. Ibid., 115 (Parsons quote); *Chicago Tribune*, May 3, 1886 (Cameron quote).

39. Daniel T. Rodgers, *Contested Truths: Keywords in American Politics since Independence* (New York: Basic Books, 1987), 80–111; Hannah Arendt, *On Revolution* (Chicago: University of Chicago Press, 1963); Ferenc Feher, *The Frozen Revo-*

lution: An Essay on Jacobinism (Cambridge: Cambridge University Press, 1987), 128–48, 150–51.

40. *Progressive Age,* Aug. 13, 1881, Nov. 12, 1881.

41. Philip S. Foner, ed., *Friedrich A. Sorge's Labor Movement in the United States: A History of the American Working Class from Colonial Times to 1890* (Westport, Conn: Greenwood, 1977), 211 (first quote); *Chicago Tribune,* Jan. 7, 1882; Avrich, *Haymarket Tragedy,* 90–91, 125 (second quote), 162–63.

42. *Irish World and American Industrial Liberator,* Oct. 6, 1883. Richard Powers advocated dynamite in the *Chicago Tribune,* Dec. 31, 1883.

43. *Chicago Tribune,* July 6, 1885 (Spies quotes); *Alarm,* Nov. 14, 1885 (Lum quote). See also David, *Haymarket Affair,* 126, 138n6; and Avrich, *Haymarket Tragedy,* 90–91. Louis Auguste Blanqui was "the leader in the transition from neo-Jacobin militancy to proletarian revolt," according to George Lichtheim, *The Origins of Socialism* (New York: Praeger, 1969), 62.

44. *Chicago Tribune,* Oct. 12, 1885. For the best detailed account of the anarchist response to eight hours, see David, *Haymarket Affair,* esp. 151–53, 159–62.

45. David, *Haymarket Affair,* 137; Avrich, *Haymarket Tragedy,* 109.

46. *Chicago Tribune,* Apr. 2, 1883; Bonney, *Present Conflict of Labor and Capital,* 25; Flinn, *History of the Chicago Police,* 349.

CHAPTER 8

The Knights of Labor and the Great Upheaval of 1886

It has been more than three-quarters of a century since Selig Perlman first used the term *great upheaval* to give unity and meaning to the events centering on the eight-hour-day strikes of 1886.[1] Even today the surpassing importance historians attach to this period seems justified. Statistics alone suggest the significance of the story. The Knights grew from an organization of about 100,000 into a mammoth movement of 725,000 in scarcely a year; in Chicago the order increased tenfold. The numbers of strikes and workers participating in them also increased dramatically. From 1881 through 1885 an average of 6,357 Chicago workers participated in an average of 35 strikes a year. In 1886, 88,000 workers participated in 307 strikes; in 1887, 31,483 workers were part of 82 strikes. There can be little doubt that capital-labor conflict, labor organization, and the awareness of class issues assumed a far more pervasive role than ever before in Chicago.[2]

Notwithstanding the plethora of historical descriptions of the great upheaval in its center, Chicago, there are cogent reasons for traversing this seemingly familiar terrain once again. First, the political economic origins of the great upheaval need closer scrutiny. While there was an upheaval and it was great, its cause often has been relegated to such unmediated and hazy processes as industrialization and capitalism. In fact, as will be argued here, the dynamics of the great upheaval and workers' concerns were quite specific responses to a deepening late nineteenth-century socioeconomic crisis stemming from overproduction. An examination of the connections between that national crisis and the events of 1886 may lend a new perspective on the great upheaval. Second, previous studies of 1886 in Chicago have put anarchism and the Haymarket affair in the foreground, while relegating the boycott, the eight-hour movement, the Knights of Labor, and trade unionism to the background. Some accounts have told a story of revolutionary hope tragically dashed by repression and crowned with martyrdom. This quasi-mythic narrative has had a remarkable hold on the labor, socialist, and progressive imagination over the last century.[3] Whatever its sentimental or hortatory value, this approach obscures much about the organizational thrust of the upheaval.

Finally, the reconstruction in earlier chapters of the events and trends in Chicago of the early 1880s, a period that has not been explored in depth, provides a fresh and revealing perspective on the events of 1886–87. From that vantage point the events of the great upheaval, including Haymarket, appear as elements in a crisis of legitimacy resulting from the unwillingness of the local establishment to acquiesce in the Democratic party's compact with organized labor.

The Socioeconomic Origins of the Great Upheaval

The great upheaval of 1886 had its origins in the prodigious growth in the late nineteenth-century capitalist economy. In Martin Sklar's words, the 1880s witnessed the most rapid growth in the postbellum period, "as measured by per capita rate of growth of reproducible tangible wealth, especially in manufacturing and railways, by amount of savings and investment funds, and by growth of per capita income."[4] Rapid capital accumulation was accompanied by a new emphasis on intensive rather than extensive investment. In this new phase employers of labor began, fitfully and with limited success, to transform the processes of production and distribution that until then had been under the control, if not the authority, of skilled workers. One result was the burgeoning army of semiskilled machine hands, whose rebellious self-assertion was the dominant feature in both the 1877 and 1886 upheavals.

Another result, almost coterminous with the beginnings of the extensive phase of industrialization, was the advent of cutthroat market competition, inaugurating the crisis phase of proprietary competitive capitalism and along with it the era of "initial proletarianization." The year 1873 commenced a severe and extended deflationary period lasting through the 1893–98 depression in which wholesale prices, wages, interest rates, and returns on invested capital fell dramatically. Deflation was accompanied by depressions in 1873–78, 1883–85, and 1893–98 and a rate of business failures between 1883 and 1898 that exceeded that of the 1930s. Also distressing for employers was the ability of skilled workers to hold up wages, which exacerbated the chronic struggle at the workplace that was such a prominent feature of the Gilded Age. The inability of employers to adequately transform the character of production in the midst of high rates of capital formation was another feature of the crisis of proprietary competitive capitalism, which was resolved only at the turn of the century by corporate consolidation, centralization of the investment function, and the transfer of production out of the hands of skilled workers and into the hands of managers.[5]

Many features of the crisis were widely recognized by mid-1880s observers. In response a diverse group of political economists began to rethink classical political economy to take account of market malfunction and disequilibrium. One of the first was the popular economist David A. Wells in *Recent Economic Changes.* Wells pointed out that underlying the crisis of this period was what some, including U.S. Commissioner of Labor Carroll Wright and the economists Arthur Hadley and later Jeremiah Jenks, called "overproduction." Wells defined it as "an amount of production in excess of demand at remunerative prices, or what is substantially the same thing, an excess of capacity for production." Wells went on to argue that the root causes of overproduction were the new methods of production, transportation, and communication, which required increased productive capacity to raise labor productivity.[6]

Those economists who pointed to the existence of overproduction were forced to reject Say's Law, a widely accepted axiom of political economy which held that under normal market conditions supply created its own demand, making overproduction an impossibility. According to the new departure among economic observers, industrialization had transformed a mercantile economy, in which the bulk of capital was invested in variable forms, primarily in short-term trade ventures. In such an economy capital values could be easily adjusted in accordance with market fluctuations. Not so in an industrialized economy, in which capital was invested predominantly in "fixed" forms—that is, in plant and equipment—which could not be easily liquidated. Lyman Gage, a Chicago banker who was one of the most penetrating of local observers, pointed to this phenomenon as early as 1879, when he testified before a House committee that the depression had been caused by "the immense transfer of capital into fixed forms, such as ships, railroads, mines, manufactories, &c" and was manifested in "a large surplus of loanable funds in the banks."[7]

The new departure was far from being unanimous among workers, farmers, or businesspeople for it required them to believe that the source of depression and other social distortions, such as the unearned profits on the labor of producers and the maldistribution in wealth, lay not outside the market but *within* it. Like orthodox political economists, greenbackers and other critics of monopoly blamed not market society but politics and bad laws for creating favoritism and monopoly power. They pointed to the 1862 national banking law that gave private banks control over note issue, the tariff that created a privileged class of manufacturers, and the corporate franchises granted by corrupt state legislatures and city councils. William Halley, for example, a representative of the national Greenback party as well as the Knights of Labor, viewed the possibility of overproduction or underconsumption as "ridiculous." To Halley, depression arose "from no natural cause" but "alone in the scarcity of money and failure of credit." Before the Civil War antimonopolists advocated a return to laissez-faire principles of government as a cure for monopoly. By the 1880s, however, Greenbackers and other radicals began to call for aggressive government intervention, including public ownership of monopolies, to clear concentrations of market power in order to sustain a republican economy of small producers. For some such an economy would center on a partially socialized sector of producer and consumer cooperatives.[8]

Many who acknowledged overproduction recognized, however, that there was a growing incongruity between industrial society and the self-regulating competitive market. Industrial society had a social character, evident in the complex division of labor among large agglomerations of workers, the systematic application of science and technology to the process of production and distribution, and the growing concentration of capital. This was a social interdependence that the unregulated competition of the market seemed to upset. The depressions, financial panics, unemployment, widespread business failures, strikes and lockouts, and social unrest since 1873 were all manifestations of the dysfunctionality of an unregulated market society. This new thinking, with its stress on the rationality and beneficence of large-scale industrialism and the irrationality and insufficiency of the competitive market, went beyond producerism, with its faith that a self-regulating market shorn of political favoritism would guarantee to producers the fruits of their labor.

By the 1860s and 1870s prolabor thinkers developed a quite similar critique of political economy. Socialists thought depressions were the result of using machinery in the labor process, which in turn fostered overproduction. The socialist analysis found support among many trade unionists and labor reformers influenced by the writings of the Boston-based political economist and eight-hour-day advocate Ira Steward. Steward rejected Say's Law and the theory that wages were fixed by the fund of available capital. Like the socialists, he believed that exploitation of labor resided in the realm of production, not in the realm of exchange as the antimonopolists believed. Unlike the socialists, Steward and his many followers argued that shortening the hours of labor would lead workers to demand higher wages, which in turn would raise the standard of living to which workers were accustomed. Higher wages would then stimulate higher levels of employment and increased demand for production, thereby counteracting overproduction. To those influenced by Steward, the eight-hour-day demand and a unionism that would raise workers' expected standard of living were the key ingredients not only to restoring prosperity but also to ending exploitation of labor through forming workers' cooperatives.[9]

By the 1880s Steward's ideas had evolved into an analysis widely shared by labor leaders, prolabor political economists, and Republican party tariff advocates focusing on the need to maintain or raise workers' standard of living and implying an underconsumptionist analysis of crisis. The prolabor political economist George Gunton, who issued eight-hour pamphlets and established his own journal in the 1880s, wrote in 1887 that the "possibility of adopting improved methods of production finally depends upon the increased consumption of wealth by the community—by the masses—which in modern society, means increasing wages." Partly in response to the extensive growth of a consumer culture during this period, labor leaders began to abandon an older republican ideal of frugality and simplicity and publicly affirmed a new working-class personality characterized by constantly augmenting wants and desires made possible by higher wages. In this context the eight-hour workday took on a new meaning. Though still at times linked to emancipation from the wage system and revitalization of workers' citizenship, it more often was viewed as a means of decreasing unemployment, improving labor's bargaining power, increasing wages, raising the standard of living, and strengthening the labor movement itself.[10]

In Chicago such ideas as these were expounded by the Eight Hour League in 1879. Many of the same men who had been active in the Eight Hour League helped form the Eight Hour Association in October 1885. Socialist or socialist-inclined leaders included George Schilling, Joseph Gruenhut, Robert C. Owens, and Charles F. Seib. Labor reformers included Thomas E. Randall, Benjamin Goodhue, Robert Nelson, and William Gleason. They were joined by the middle-class reformers Thomas E. Hill, J. H. Randall, and D. A. Colton. All were Knights and all except Schilling and Seib were members of mixed assembly 1307.[11]

The purpose of the Eight Hour Association was to implement the little-known 1884 resolution of the Federation of Organized Trades and Labor Unions that "eight hours shall constitute a legal days labor from and after May 1, 1886." In the last three months of 1885, while the anarchists stood largely aloof, the Eight Hour Association called meetings, issued manifestos, and energetically publicized its analysis that labor-saving machinery caused overproduction and unemployment and that eight-hour workdays would "in consequence of more leisure, operate upon the habits and customs of the people, enlarging their wants, stimulating ambition, decreasing idleness and increasing wages."[12]

The 1886 report of the Illinois Bureau of Labor Statistics, written by persons close to the Eight Hour Association, noted that the arguments for eight hours decisively turned away from the labor reformers' contention in 1867 that shorter hours were necessary for more effective citizenship on the part of workers. "Within the past twenty years," noted the report, "the plane of the shorter-day demand has been shifted from that which its opponents have characterized as the 'sentimental' to the domain of political economy." The report continued:

> It is now broadly claimed . . . that a further reduction of the working day is made necessary by the over-production which has resulted from maintaining long hours while the multiplication of machinery and of labor-saving inventions has greatly increased product per hour; that this over-production is a most potent . . . cause of the great industrial depressions . . . that a reduction of 20 per cent in the time which the employed now work would create employment for 20 per cent of the entire working force . . . that the conversion of this 20 per cent from unemployed consumers . . . into self-employed consumers would increase the demand for all products and counteract the evils of over-production.

The same report, which surveyed more than 85,000 Illinois workers, noted that only 20 percent were employed forty-eight to fifty-two weeks a year, while 65 percent were employed less than forty weeks a year.[13]

The new argument had increasing appeal to the leaders of skilled workers who dominated the labor movement and had long been skeptical about eight hours. For years many of these unionists had tried to resist the introduction of labor-saving machinery. Since the failure of the 1867 general strike they also believed that growing intercity competition among manufacturers would prevent the local introduction of eight hours, because eastern competitors working their employees ten hours a day would have a cost advantage and be able to undersell eight-hour producers. Accordingly, there had been no united push for eight-hour workdays in Chicago for almost two decades.[14] By the early 1880s, however, the widespread use of de-skilling machinery and the epidemic of overproduction and unemployment had disposed trade unionists to be more receptive.

Since the early 1880s trade unionists had been involved in a series of conflicts involving machinery. The strikes in tanning, brickmaking, coalheaving, and the packinghouses discussed in chapters 4 and 5 all involved the use of machinery to replace expensive skilled labor. This tendency was intensified by the impact of the 1877 strikes on local police policy, which bolstered the ability of organized skilled workers to win strikes over wages and working conditions. According to local figures, the share of wages in manufactured products dropped sharply from 1873 to 1876; it was only in 1877 that this share leveled off and began to rise. Even during the 1883–85 downturn workers' share did not approach the low level of 1876–77. These statistics were paralleled by national trends in the 1880s, when according to James Livingston, "the share of revenue from value added that industrial capitalists could retain after covering workers' wages became relatively smaller." To put it differently, the fear of a repeat of 1877 made employers more aware of the dangers of cutting wages—though wage cuts did continue—and led many to augment labor productivity through the use of machinery.[15]

Employers' resort to labor-saving and de-skilling machinery in the course of industrial conflict, combined with the more general tendency of investment to pour into production for expanding markets, exacerbated the problem of overproduction. This in turn put increased pressure on costs and led to intensified conflict over wages. That employers and skilled workers were involved in a vicious circle is evident in brief case studies of five industries in the first half of the 1880s. Conflicts in each industry played a role in the city's great upheaval and helped dispose local labor leaders toward the eight-hour movement.[16]

In the 1880s, as the steel industry became capital intensive and adopted mass production methods, it faced a problem of overcapacity to produce both nationally and locally. In February 1883 the Union Iron and Steel Company in Bridgeport, which had been defeated in a community-aided strike by Knights blast-furnace workers in 1882, suspended operation, citing a lack of market for its products as priced. The managers also complained about constant strikes and a truculent spirit among their men that was "nearly all" due "to the contemptible conduct of the city authorities last year." It might have been this workplace power, which prevented the managers from using a nonunion foreman to cut costs, that sent the modern Bridgeport mills into bankruptcy.[17]

Overproduction was also a problem in brickmaking, an industry that by 1886 had become flooded with small to medium-sized firms. Though the industry had been using "mud machines" since before the Civil War, the introduction of the Chambers machine in the early 1880s magnified threefold the productive power of the average worker. The results were immediate: the flooding of the local market with bricks, which led to falling prices and the lowering of wages by the more backward North Side firms to meet the competition. In the absence of united action by the employers to limit production, the South and Southwest Side Knights Brickmakers' Local Assembly was faced with the choice of either lowering wages or limiting the use of machinery.[18]

The nail industry also confronted overproduction. Between 1881 and 1884 high profitability in nail manufacturing led owners to nearly double the industry's capacity. Prices soon fell to such an extent that nails sold at 10–15 percent below cost. In June 1885 the Western Nail Association attempted to impose a 19–45 percent cut in the piece rate paid to skilled nailers. This prompted a regional strike by the Nailers, Heaters, and Rollers of America. In the Chicago area the Calumet Iron and Steel Company at Cummings began operating its plant using boy nail feeders in place of the skilled men on nail machines. The strike, which featured a local riot against the "black sheep" or "scabs" and a boycott called by the Chicago Trades and Labor Assembly and the Knights, simmered through spring 1886.[19]

A related dispute over machinery occurred in boxmaking, another industry faced with overproduction. In May 1885 the skilled boxmakers, including nailers, formed Knights Local Assembly 3838. Henry B. Maxwell, a large West Side employer, was irate at this development. "The men were too arbitrary," he told the *Tribune,* "running the shops to suit themselves and allowing the proprietors no voice in the matter. They had been so pressed for business that this state of affairs had to be permitted." With a return to prosperity in December, Maxwell resolved to introduce automatic nail-feeding machines and use boys to replace the nailers. The union responded by demanding that no boys be employed and that workers receive the same price for machine as for hand labor, a demand intended to halt the spread of machinery in the industry. The result was a strike in December 1885, which lasted until March 1886.[20]

Another example of conflict stemming from the use of machinery came in agricultural implement manufacturing, where since the early 1870s productivity had increased to the point where 600 men could do the work formerly done by 2,145. Skilled unionized iron molders and a slightly larger number of skilled metal workers, however, still had a strategic hold on the production process. In 1881 the management at McCormick Harvester, following the example of the railroads, had begun cost accounting for labor expenses. This new cost-consciousness led to the first confrontation with the union in 1885, which the molders won, with the help of the Chicago police. Immediately following the victory, McCormick began weeding out union leaders. Then he replaced his skilled foundrymen with pneumatic molding machines operated by nonunion laborers. By February 1886 it became apparent that the machines were not efficient. This encouraged the remaining skilled workers, whom Myles McPadden of the Knights had organized into the United Metal Workers Union, to unite with the molders and other

McCormick workers in Knights Local Assembly 852 to proclaim a strike. In February 1886 they demanded the return of the fired molders, an advance in unskilled workers' wages, and the discharge of nonunion workers. The strike, which lingered through May, eventually triggered the Haymarket affair.[21]

These cases illustrate the complex relationship between the introduction of machinery, overproduction, cost pressures, and working-class power. The growth of workers' power in industry and in local politics in the late 1870s had held up wages, furthering the already existing incentive for employers to introduce machinery. Yet improved machinery exacerbated overproduction. An excess capacity to produce, or surplus capital, which is the same thing, induced falling profit rates, which led to further attacks on unions, with machinery sometimes the prime weapon used by employers to displace troublesome workers. The repetition and intensification of these particular struggles over the spread and effects of machinery approached a crescendo in 1886 and, in the context of the agitation by the Eight Hour Association, impelled union leaders to realize the system-wide problem of overproduction and society-wide solutions to it.

This dawning realization was evident in the growing enthusiasm within the Trades and Labor Assembly for the eight-hour demand. In October the Trades and Labor Assembly endorsed the demand and established an eight-hour committee, which overlapped with the Eight Hour Association. While the Eight Hour Association distributed thousands of tracts throughout the city and provoked a public debate between its leaders and the *Tribune*, such local unions as the carpenters held meetings on the eight-hour workday. Nonetheless, by mid-December 1885 only eleven assembly-affiliated unions, representing just two thousand Chicago workers, had endorsed the demand. Recognizing the problem of intercity competition, Eight Hour Association leaders predicted that only the building trades could win eight hours the following May. In early January the powerful bricklayers' union endorsed eight hours, but President A. C. Button argued against a mass movement. Instead, he recommended that other workers emulate the bricklayers in building up strong organizations able to control the local labor market. As late as March 1886 the preeminent conflicts in the city were those of the Calumet nailers, Maxwell boxmakers, and McCormick workers.[22]

The Knights of Labor and the Boycott

Though the concern about machinery, unemployment, and overproduction, which underlay the great upheaval, had been deeply felt before 1886, the upsurge of the unskilled, the workers' turn to the Knights of Labor, and the mass movement for eight hours were relatively late-blooming developments. What can be called the second stage of Chicago's great upheaval had two, mutually reinforcing, but nonetheless separable aspects. The first was skilled workers' turn toward the boycott and solidarity with the rest of their class. The second, which occurred on the eve of the May strikes, was the movement of unskilled workers into unions and Knights local assemblies (LAs), sparked by the demand for eight hours of work for ten hours of pay.

Given the police support unions had received from the Harrison administration and their consequent success in winning strikes and holding up wages in a deflationary environment, union leaders' refusal to make a mass appeal to the city's working people that might threaten political stability was quite understandable. In fact, in mid-February the Maxwell strikers were winning their conflict with police aid. At the same time, the McCormick workers had confidently turned down McCormick's capitulation to most of their demands in order to strike for the discharge of nonunion molders. It was at this point that the changed balance of power in the city that had led to the promotions of Frederick Ebersold and John Bonfield on the police force had its greatest impact.

When McCormick refused to accept the union's demands, he locked out his union labor and declared his intention to run the works with nonunion labor. Police Superintendent Ebersold responded by gathering a force of 350 policemen selected from every precinct in the city except Bridgeport's Third Precinct, which had proven so disloyal to employers' interests. When the plant reopened March 1, the police, under Captain Bonfield, set an example by invading the Union House saloon and brutally clubbing scores of workers who had been shouting "rats." The plant soon resumed operations with a nonunion work force.[23]

A week and a half earlier, on February 20, Bonfield had removed Lieutenant Darrow of the Hinman Street station, who had been so helpful to the Maxwell strikers. This resulted in the disintegration of the boxmakers' strike, culminating when the workers returned to their jobs on March 1. Thus on the same day two major strikes had been stymied by the Harrison administration's new police policy. At this point the Maxwell and McCormick strikers led the turn to mass action through the boycott.

In Chicago the boycott took on its modern character as a strike tactic during the 1886 upheaval. It will be remembered that in the early 1880s the boycott was generally a synonym for social ostracism of scabs by working-class communities in the city. Between 1883 and 1885 there were no major boycotts in Chicago. But in 1885 a boycotting craze had begun in the East, leading to the first national Knights boycott, known as the Deuber Watch Case Company affair. The 1885 general assembly set up a general boycotting board to rule on the feasibility of national boycotts, while leaving local boycotting policy to the district assemblies.[24]

Chicago Knights DA 24 adopted a conservative boycotting policy, probably because of their experience in the 1882 tanners' strike. John Foley, head of the DA's Boycotting Board stated that the Knights intended to "go slow" in boycotting and that "the standing of any union in organized labor would be carefully weighed before anything is done." Thus, when the nailers requested a boycott of Calumet nails in December 1885, the DA refused, though the Trades and Labor Assembly did agree to boycott. Though the DA approved a boycott against five major boot and shoe firms in mid-January for contracting work to prison labor, this did not represent a change in the Knights' policy, for it had unanimous labor support. But the DA's conservatism proved short-lived. To understand why requires an examination of Chicago's DA 57.[25]

DA 57, which had split from DA 24 in 1882, represented workers in large-scale industries on Chicago's South Side and Southwest Side and in the towns south of the city. While DA 24 membership languished throughout 1885, DA 57 took full advantage of the Knights' national victory over Jay Gould's Wabash Railroad in Missouri in August–September 1885. When the notorious "robber baron" Jay Gould was humbled by the Knights, it was the first time a large corporation had been defeated by a labor organization. All over the country normally deferential and fearful workers shed their apathy and flocked to the Knights in unprecedented numbers. In October Myles McPadden reorganized DA 57 and began to found new LAs in the industrial towns of Pullman, Kensington, Calumet, and Cummings.[26] In early 1886 the only three Knights strikes called in Chicago were authorized by DA 57. The DA also called a boycott of all Maxwell products in March, the first Knights boycott of a struck firm in Chicago. This was followed on March 20 by a DA 57 boycott of McCormick. All at once the conservative Knights policy on boycotting had been overturned.[27]

Within a span of two weeks the prison shoe and the Maxwell boycotts proved spectacular successes. March also saw a successful Knights boycott, in conjunction with the cigarmakers' union, of a scab cigar firm. Nationally, another Knights strike against Gould began March 7 and at first seemed to be another victory. At this point, in mid- to late March, Chicago workers of all trades and skill levels began to stream into the Knights. The *Tribune* reported that "the result of the two boycotts on the membership of the Knights . . . has been very marked. . . . Nearly every local assembly . . . has been looking for larger halls," because of additions of "from twenty to one hundred applicants." A week later the paper reported that the order was growing at the rate of a thousand per week.[28]

Ironically, the metamorphosis of the local order from a small, conservative organization into the prime vehicle for the mass movement of 1886–87 came almost at the moment that Terence Powderly issued his famous March 13 "go slow" circular. The edict disavowed support for the eight-hour strikes on May 1, suspended the formation of new assemblies for forty days, and counseled against strikes and boycotts. Locally, DA 24 implemented Powderly's circular by attempting to absorb its boycott-prone sister DA 57 so that it could avert "the abuse of that means of warfare, which is now perhaps the chief fear of the more level-headed leaders of the labor movement in this city." But DA 57 rebuffed the offer.[29]

Membership figures confirm that the mid-March period of boycotting mania was the great watershed in the growth of the Knights. In July 1885 Chicago's two district assemblies reported 1,906 members. By March 20, 1886, Knights leaders claimed 10,000 members, and in July the state Bureau of Labor Statistics credited the order with 18,000 members. By the fall, long after the eight-hour movement had spent its force, the Knights continued to grow, reportedly doubling its July figure, making its numbers equal to those of the trade unions affiliated with the Central Labor Union (CLU) and the Trades and Labor Assembly. Further evidence that the boycott and not the eight-hour movement was at the root of the Knights' growth is that of the ninety-four Knights assemblies organized in Illinois in the first six months of 1886, fifty-seven were located outside of Cook County, where the eight-hour movement was confined.[30]

The Mass Movement for the Eight-Hour Day

Though the boycott mania preceded the eight-hour-day strikes, the two were closely connected. Both followed in the wake of the breakdown of the alliance with the Harrison machine, and both represented powerful appeals to and vehicles for the growing class awareness and class assertiveness that had gripped the larger part of Chicago's work force. Once workers, attracted by the prospects of labor solidarity, had joined the Knights and other labor bodies, they tended to gravitate toward the eight-hour-day demand that embodied their needs in very specific ways.

The appeal of shorter hours was multilayered. It promised to reduce labor time and increase wages for those employed and to provide work for those not employed or underemployed. It therefore appealed to workers with different dissatisfactions in distinctive labor markets and work environments. It was also a potent rallying cry for union organizers. For these "agitators" eight hours was like the "loss leader" merchants used to get customers into the store. Once prospective members were part of the movement, activists could "sell" them on the entire panoply of principles, rules, and benefits offered by unionism. Finally, the words *eight hours* bore a republican reform appeal that wage demands did not. Shorter hours meant the leisure necessary to the intellectual and social elevation of workers into full citizenship, and shorter hours promised to restore to workers the stolen fruits of their labor by establishing the cooperative commonwealth.[31]

Beginning in January 1886 Eight Hour Association leaders abandoned the pessimistic forecast that only building trades workers could win shorter hours and began to build a mass movement for eight hours with no hourly pay boost (that is, eight hours of work for eight hours of pay). There were three important reasons for confining the movement to this demand. First, by asking only for shorter hours they would undermine the objection of local manufacturers who feared that decreased production combined with the same costs would leave them vulnerable to competitors outside the city. Second, by focusing solely on eight hours without the pay boost, Eight Hour Association leaders could promote their movement as a broad social reform designed to uplift workers' moral standards. This would allow them to appeal to the middle class through the arbiters of the community, the religious leaders. By mid-April not only had several heterodox religious leaders, notably William Salter of the Ethical Culture Society and the Reverend Charles F. Goss, endorsed the movement, but also expressions of support had been secured from several Baptist and Methodist ministers.

Finally, the limited demand reflected the tactics of unionized workers, who then formed the base of the movement. These workers foresaw the opportunity to win eight hours of work for ten hours of pay through a two-stage strategy that had been endorsed by no less an authority than Ira Steward. First win shorter hours, and when the demand for labor had increased, only then request a compensatory wage increase.

As the social base of the movement broadened, however, this strategy broke down and the eight-hour movement assumed a more militant, class-specific character. The membership of the Eight Hour Association changed from skilled and organized workers to predominantly unskilled and newly organized workers. Because these workers lacked the monetary resources to wait until eight hours had been won before demanding a compensatory wage increase, the main demand changed to eight hours of work for ten hours of pay. Moreover, because they lacked a skill strategic to the production process, they were compelled to use militant methods to shut down the entire industry. The change in the character of the eight-hour movement can be understood through four case studies.

The transformation was most dramatic in the building trades. Having won the eight-hour day in January, the bricklayers were the early leaders, indeed the principal protagonists, of the demand among construction unionists. Yet they disdained measures that might precipitate a mass movement for it, which the carpenters and other trades sorely needed. The carpenters trade was in partial disintegration from the effect of wood-working machinery, which made the employment of unskilled, largely immigrant pieceworkers possible. By mid-November 1885 few of the 6,500 carpenters in the city were organized; only 800 of them were in Local 21 of the Brotherhood of Carpenters and Joiners of America.[32]

With news of the boycott successes and the formation of Knights carpenters' LA 6570 in March, the unionization of carpenters began to "boom," according to James Brennock, founder of both the local brotherhood and the Knights local assembly. "Initiations of members took place at every meeting, not by ones and twos but by tens and hundreds." The March issue of the new paper the *Knights of Labor* reported that "the carpenters of Chicago are rapidly coming into the Order" and claimed that nationally there "appears to be more carpenters in the Knights of Labor than in the Brotherhood." The growth of the Knights, according to Brennock, forced the Brotherhood of Carpenters and Joiners to "prick up their ears too, and say now we must begin to do something," and both "grew on apace together."[33]

On March 22 the different factions of the carpenters met to form a federative body capable of supervising the eight-hour movement. The new United Carpenters Committee (UCC) consisted of the English Amalgamated Society of Carpenters, the Brotherhood of Carpenters and Joiners, and several CLU unions. Though the Knights of Labor was not formally affiliated because of Powderly's opposition to strikes, it generally cooperated in the movement. During a month of nightly meetings union membership shot up, including, for the first time in the 1880s, the vast majority of pieceworkers. On April 23 the UCC commenced negotiations with the Contractors Association.[34]

The process by which unskilled immigrant workers were drawn into the labor movement was repeated in the ladies' garment industry. Like carpenters, garment workers were divided into a group of skilled and semiskilled wageworkers and semiskilled immigrant pieceworkers. The major difference was that female and child pieceworkers made up the majority of the industry and worked in the "outside shops" on material supplied by the clothing manufacturers. They were unorganized, while the skilled "cutters" had a history of organization. In the last week of March six hundred clothing cutters organized Knights LA 5859 and immediately demanded eight hours of work for ten hours of pay. Within two weeks twenty-eight of thirty-one clothing houses had reduced hours to eight while allowing nine-and-a-half-hours' pay. It was at this point that the pieceworkers intervened in the story.[35]

The story of how one group of immigrant garment workers, the West Side Jews, organized during the great upheaval is described in the biography of Abraham Bisno, founder of the Chicago cloakmakers' union. Among the

Russian Jews, who did not read English or German or any daily papers, there was almost no knowledge of the eight-hour movement or boycotting. Nonetheless, recalled Bisno, "it was in the atmosphere and it seemed to have crossed the border of our settlement."[36]

Organized by their contractor bosses, one of whom was Bisno, the outside workers selected a committee to demand higher rates and a regular day's work in place of the variable, arbitrary, and often long hours they toiled. When the large clothing houses ridiculed their demands, the workers struck and then turned to the Knights for succor. On May 5, the day after the Haymarket bomb, a committee of the whole, consisting of six hundred strikers, began a march to the downtown manufacturing shops to call their employees out on strike. The police treated this march as an anarchist invasion and clubbed the Jews until they fled back to their neighborhood.[37]

Many garment strikers were women. In fact, by 1880 almost half of all wage-earning women were employed in garment making. On May 4, three to four hundred female tailors, working in some of the larger shops, formed a procession and visited the tailor shops on the North Side. Befitting a group of workers with no organization, they behaved much as the 1877 strikers. "As the procession moved along," reported the *Tribune*, "the girls shouted and sang and laughed in a whirlwind of exuberance that did not lessen with the distance traveled." That day three separate meetings of female tailors decided to seek the assistance of the Knights in winning the eight-hour day with ten-hour pay. They were joined by their boss contractors, who also organized a Knights assembly. Despite the existence of Knights women's LA 1789—founded in 1882 and practically moribund by 1885—the garment workers' walkout was the first significant strike waged by the city's women workers and inaugurated their large-scale entrance into Chicago's labor movement. By the end of the year the local order had eight LAs either partially or wholly composed of women, including five garment workers' LAs, two of female tailors, and one of female shoe hands.[38]

A third group of workers whose experiences paralleled that of the carpenters and garment workers were the railroad yardmen. Here, too, a successful strike by more skilled and organized workers triggered a walkout by unskilled hands. The switchmen, the most skilled grouping among the railroad yardmen, had been organized since 1877. In mid-April the union, comprising 1,300 switchmen, won a strike forcing the only railroad that had refused to hire union men to accede to the closed shop. On April 23 the company gave in, prodded by Philip Armour and other packinghouse magnates who feared a "railroad war."

Inspired by the switchmen's victory, on May 4, 2,000 unskilled freight handlers struck for eight-hour work for ten-hour pay. Their walkout, like that of the tailors, was marked by processions of hundreds of workers marching through the railyards. The spontaneous character of the affair was evident in the fact that only three railroads received formal demands. It was three days into the strike before the freight handlers realized the necessity of organization, after the switchmen informed them that they would not extend sympathy action unless they received a formal request from a union. Though the freight hands did organize, the switchmen did not support them, and the strikers went back to work on May 10.[39]

The actions of the carpenters, garment workers, and freight handlers all illustrate the way the influx of lesser-skilled workers into the movement transformed its character. But it was the strike of the furniture workers that had the greatest impact on the scope and strategy of the eight-hour movement. Next to meatpacking, furniture making was Chicago's fastest growing industry, with employment rising from 1,100 in 1870 to 5,400 in 1880. By 1890 the city was the nation's leading furniture producer. The majority of the new workers were machine woodworkers employed in large firms, about half of which utilized steam power. The furniture workers' union, however, was based among the skilled cabinetmakers, who generally worked in the smaller custom shops. By 1886 this predominantly German union, with perhaps the largest proportion of socialists in the city, had about 800 members. Then, in a burst of organizing in the spring, the union added over 3,000 new members, predominantly machine hands. Against the wishes of the existing socialist leadership, still cautious after its 1879 defeat, the new workers forced the union to demand eight for ten. By the third week in April the union had struck two large furniture plants. On May 1, 4,000–5,000 more furniture workers walked out for the same demand.[40]

Eight Hour Association leaders immediately voiced their strong opposition to the change in strategy. At a mass meeting of eight-hour supporters held on April 10 virtually every speaker had called for restraint in wage demands. By contrast, a large anarchist meeting on April 25 championed the demand for eight hours with no pay reduction. After the Eight Hour Association condemned the furniture workers' demands, the press blamed "foreign communists" for the shift in strategy and began identifying the eight-hour movement with anarchism and the CLU.[41]

For workers who had been outside the labor movement, the differences between the various factions blurred. All merged into one vast, undifferentiated class movement, for which eight-hour work at ten-hour pay became the most conspicuous demand and symbol. Furthermore, this burgeoning movement gravitated toward the Knights, despite its distaste for class conflict and even though it was the anarchists who championed eight for ten. It was not so much that the Knights were reaching out to workers as it was that a mass movement of workers were embracing the reluctant Knights.

Of the 116 new Knights LAs founded in 1886—constituting 53 percent of all its Chicago locals that year—the Knights had disproportionate strength among poorer laborers and semiskilled workers. The largest single category of assemblies, twenty-eight, was "mixed" and probably consisted of those without a trade. The next largest were the fourteen assemblies of tailors and other garment workers. There were ten assemblies of outdoor laborers, including lumbershovers, coal heavers, freight handlers, and salt laborers. A large percent of about fifteen thousand packinghouse workers were organized in at least eight different assemblies. Construction workers, mostly carpenters, made up five assemblies. Finally, several thousand clerks belonged to LA 1756.[42]

To the general public it seemed that the Knights were the principal advocates of the eight-hour-day movement. Even the usually reliable *Tribune* reported, "As it is now pretty generally understood, the great movement of the American Knights of Labor to secure the adoption and ultimate recognition of eight hours . . . is to take ultimate form on May 1st." Symbolic of this metamorphosis of the Knights' boycott movement into an eight-hour movement was the change of name of the Eight Hour Association's paper, the *Boycotter,* to the *Eight Hour Day* at the end of the first week of April.[43]

The Reaction against Eight for Ten and the Haymarket Bomb

The transformation in April of the eight-hour-day movement from an almost respectable reform with cross-class support to an insurgent mass movement for eight hours with no loss in overall pay checked public sympathy and greatly strengthened resistance to the movement. Though repression was a major cause of the movement's ultimate defeat, its strength has been exaggerated. Many organized workers successfully resisted its effects and retained their victories through the end of the year.

The repression following the Haymarket bomb was prefigured in late April. "Boycotts, lockouts, demands of labor organizations, and the eight hour movement," charged the *Chicago Journal* on April 22, "have checked and interrupted the prospective waves of prosperity in every direction. Every form of business and industrial enterprise has been attacked or threatened." In early April it became apparent that many manufacturers were coalescing in new or revitalized employers' associations to resist workers' demands. The furniture manufacturers reversed their conciliatory stance taken in March and strongly opposed eight for ten in late April. Chicago's boot and shoe manufacturers inaugurated an association called the Western Boot and Shoe Manufacturers to oppose the same demand. In early May a diverse group of metal manufacturers established a new employers' group to resist eight hours in any form and unionization as well. In each case the large employers led the way.[44]

Meanwhile, the movement spiraled out of the control of Eight Hour Association leaders, who had never advocated a general strike. Feeling their strength in solidarity, workers disdained arbitration and prudence as counseled by Knights and trade union leaders. The reasoning of many workers may have been captured in the crass words of one socialist: "This is a grab game. Everybody is trying to get as few hours of work and as much wages as he can. After the furor is over no one will get a thing."[45]

The eight-hour day seemed to be an unstoppable tidal force. The *Tribune* wrote that "there is every indication that the eight hour system will be generally adopted . . . soon after May 1." Already approximately 47,500, according to the Illinois Bureau of Labor Statistics, had won shorter hours, in many cases accompanied by a wage increase. On May 1, an additional 30,000 to 60,000 struck for eight hours, prominent among them the building trades workers, freight handlers, furniture workers, lumbershovers, garment workers, and cigarmakers. According to the press, industry was "paralyzed," and the city "assumed a Sabbath-like appearance." That day the International Working Peoples' Association led a parade of 80,000 up Michigan Avenue, while the National Guard waited in readiness.[46]

On May 2 it was obvious to Eight Hour Association leaders that the movement had not followed their prescribed course. In the vast majority of instances striking workers demanded a wage increase to compensate for shorter hours, and the movement was becoming publicly identified with anarchism. Perhaps most important, the movement did not have comparable strength in other cities—only about 200,000 workers struck in the nation as a whole. Combined with the spontaneous demand for no loss in pay, the lack of solidarity elsewhere greatly stiffened local employers' opposition. For these reasons eight-hour leaders were not in a mood to cooperate with the CLU. When R. C. Owens of the carpenters, one of the few trades that had built working unity among all labor factions, appealed at a Trades and Labor Assembly meeting for citywide organizational cooperation, he was rebuffed. Andrew Cameron spoke for many when he said that "the red flag of the socialism of Europe" could never be joined to "the democratic republicanism of America."[47]

A few days into the strike, eight-hour leaders were thrown into confusion and consternation by the Haymarket affair. Though the Haymarket bomb has usually been credited with killing off the eight-hour movement, the movement was actually in disarray and facing strenuous opposition before the bomb. Public hysteria following the bomb, however, was critical in turning around public opinion and demoralizing strikers.

The events at Haymarket cannot be understood in their full significance without recognizing that they were part of a larger process of business and middle-class reaction against Mayor Harrison's compact with labor. Haymarket was the culmination of a train of events dating back to the decline of Harrison's liberal Republican support and his promotion of Ebersold and Bonfield during the 1885 streetcar strike. The immediate catalyst for Haymarket occurred on May 3, when Bonfield's police assaulted McCormick strikers trying to prevent replacement workers from entering the plant. When two workers were fatally wounded by police firing indiscriminately into a crowd, August Spies, who had witnessed the incident, rushed back to the *Arbeiter-Zeitung* offices. There he wrote up a leaflet beginning with the words "Revenge! Workingmen to Arms!!!" and calling for a protest meeting. Many anarchists believed the time had come for "the war of classes."

On the evening of May 4 a relatively small crowd of two to three thousand heard anarchist speeches and had begun to dwindle, when Bonfield and a phalanx of 176 policemen appeared. Earlier, Mayor Harrison, recognizable in his trademark slouch hat, had visited the meeting and later told Bonfield that it was "tame" and did not warrant interference. Nonetheless, Bonfield's men advanced on the meeting and commanded it to disperse. After the speaker, Samuel Fielden, responded, "All right, we will go," an unknown person threw a dynamite bomb into the ranks of the police. Dozens were wounded, and seven officers ultimately died. The maddened police responded by firing their revolvers into the crowd of workers for fully two minutes, probably killing a like number. There were at least sixty-seven casualties, most of them—including at least three policemen—victims of indiscriminate police bullets.[48]

What the *Tribune* headlined as a "hellish deed" kindled a pervasive hysteria and Red scare in Chicago. Almost everyone outside of labor's ranks assumed that the bomb had resulted from a revolutionary conspiracy directed at American institutions. The next day leading businessmen called on the mayor to suppress all anarchist meetings and shut down the anarchists' press. Harrison refused, but he did issue a proclamation banning public meetings and processions. Meanwhile, his police, spurred by the ambitious Captain Michael Schaack, arrested leaders of the International Working Peoples' Association, including the printers and editors of the *Alarm* and *Arbeiter-Zeitung*. Thus began an eight-week "period of police terrorism." According to William Holmes, an IWPAer, "Socialists are hunted like wolves. . . . To proclaim oneself a Socialist in Chicago now is to invite immediate arrest." In all, police brought in over two hundred suspects or witnesses. On June 5, thirty-one anarchists were indicted, and eventually eight leaders—August Spies, Albert Parsons, Samuel Fielden, George Engel,

Adolph Fischer, Louis Lingg, Oscar Neebe, and Michael Schwab—stood trial for conspiracy to commit murder.[49]

More critical to the disposition of the great upheaval then in progress were the actions of the police. Even though crowd actions were only sporadic and relatively free of violence, the police reverted to behavior reminiscent of 1877. According to Abraham Bisno, "After May 1 [4] picketing became absolutely impossible. The police arrested all pickets, even two or three. The attitude on the part of the police was practically the same as though the city was under martial law. Labor unions were raided, broken up, their property confiscated, the police used their clubs freely. Arrests were made without cause, and the life of the workingman was not quite safe when out on strike."[50]

Yet, contrary to the myth, started by labor leaders themselves, that Haymarket destroyed the eight-hour movement, the success of the antilabor reaction was highly selective.[51] Generally those strikes that resorted to crowd actions, like Bisno's garment workers' strike, succumbed to police attack. Many other strikers, however, were well organized and could not be so easily crushed by overt coercion. To maximize their claim to respectability and thereby preserve immunity from police assault, unionists strove loudly and strenuously to disassociate themselves from the anarchist "menace." The Trades and Labor Assembly and Knights DA 24 issued a joint statement that condemned "lawbreakers" but still pledged to "continue to fight for eight hours by any and every lawful means at our disposal even if it takes all summer." The statement cautioned workers to refrain from public demonstrations and to avoid the use of "boisterous and inflammatory language." As a result, many strikers avoided direct attacks, and existing struggles continued practically unabated.[52]

The imperviousness of many labor struggles to the effects of the Haymarket reaction is evident in a cursory examination of the major groups of workers participating in the eight-hour movement. Among the largest were the 15,000 packinghouse workers, 3,000 of whom had joined the Knights in April in a whirlwind campaign directed by George Schilling. By May 3 the packers had all agreed to the eight-hour workday for ten hours of pay, which lasted through the summer. Chicago cigarmakers, machinists, many building trades workers, and a large, indeterminate number of furniture workers, retail clerks, brewers, bakers, and garment workers also retained shorter hours into mid-June.[53]

The ability of some workers to resist the Haymarket reaction is illustrated in the continuing struggle of local carpenters. One week after the bomb exploded the Carpenters Contractors Council reneged on its earlier agreement to the eight-hour day and declared its intention of restoring the ten-hour day. By early June over a thousand carpenters were locked out, and the union responded by striking.[54]

The manner in which the strike was enforced affords a revealing glimpse of the transformation in labor leadership and its tactics that resulted from events of the great upheaval. When the May strike was about to fail, Louis Henry Jackson, a former leader of a large armed Métis rebellion in western Canada in 1885, rose to the position of "strike general." Jackson concentrated his forces guerrilla fashion, so that his men outnumbered their foes. Because the incidents occurred simultaneously at different locations, there was little the police could do to interfere. The new tactics helped enforce union discipline among the unskilled pieceworkers, laying the foundation for a union victory the following year. For the first time in its history the union did not lose its base or factionalize when it did not achieve a full victory.[55]

The tactics Jackson taught set a precedent for a more militant, but nonetheless organized, approach to the problem of scabbing. In contrast to the experiences during the 1877 strikes and during the 1879–80 packinghouse workers' strike, the 1886 carpenters' strike proved that with scattered worksites and effective leadership, organized labor intimidation could work. According to Jackson, who later became known in the press as "the father of the labor sluggers," the strike "marked the first organized violence in the building trades in Chicago." Moreover, it set a precedent for slugging that spread beyond building trades unionism and was ultimately embraced at the turn of the century by other unions, most notably the teamsters' union. In this fashion the anarchist strategy of armed revolutionary struggle, instead of being completely rejected, took a subordinate place as a tactic in the labor culture of Chicago's workers.[56]

The retail clerks, like the carpenters, also were able to resist the return to longer hours. By May 1 most large dry-goods stores had conceded the clerks' demands for closing on Sundays and at 7 P.M. during the weekdays. It was the first great success for organized white-collar clerks, whose movement for early closing dated to 1855 and most recently had failed in 1883. Not long after the May bomb, when most stores restored their former hours, the clerks appealed to the clergy, the YMCA, the Citizens Association, and finally the mayor, without success. Then in the early summer clerks began to join Knights LA 1756. With the support of DA 24 the clerks mounted a boycott that had sporadic success. In 1887 they joined with clergymen and the Sabbath Association to support passage of a state law mandating Sunday closing. Because the law included saloons, it stirred up too much opposition to win passage. Nonetheless, about 15,000 of 35,000 local clerks still enjoyed a Sunday holiday in 1887.[57]

The U.S. Bureau of Labor Statistics records reveal still more about the relative success of 1886 strikers. That year 87,849 workers were involved in 307 separate strikes counted by the bureau. Though 180 were classified as failures, 72 were successes and 55 were partial successes; if the latter two categories are combined, 41 percent of all 1886 strikes achieved some success. Such gains often came in the form of wage increases. About a month after the strikes the *Knights of Labor* reported that workers still laboring ten hours had received a substantial pay increase; the *Express* estimated that the wages of unskilled labor in general had been raised from $.90 to $1.50. According to still another measure of success, it seems that for many workers the gains of 1886 were far from ephemeral. In a spring 1888 survey Joseph Gruenhut estimated that about twenty-five thousand workers—the two largest groups being construction workers and retail clerks—still held the eight-hour day.[58]

Still, most eight-hour strikers failed. At the end of May the *Knights of Labor*, speaking for leading trade unionists, spoke of "a general failure of the eight hour movement." Yet even the reason for failure lay as much in the old problem of competition from other cities as in the post-Haymarket repression.

The Lesson of Organization

Chicago's great upheaval must be understood as the product of a conjuncture of two crises, one economic and the other political. Cutthroat competition, overproduction, deflation, recurring depressions, and insistent cost pressures on firms created the conditions for an ineradicable conflict between skilled workers and their employers. Without this deepening crisis local employers and civic leaders in the Citizens Association would never have united to undermine the Harrison regime's conciliatory policy toward labor and socialism. Bonfield's rise to power in the police force represented Harrison's acquiescence in this shift in the balance of class relations, symbolized by the new police policy of "the club today saves the bullet tomorrow."

The inability of Harrison's party to deliver on its implicit promises to the unions of skilled workers led them to endorse boycotting and enter a mass movement for the eight-hour day, mainly through the Knights of Labor. Once unskilled workers employed in large-scale, intercity firms began to be mobilized, however, they pushed the movement beyond the strategy that Eight Hour Association leaders had envisioned. The demand of packinghouse, railroad, garment, and other workers for eight-hour workdays at no loss in pay—backed by the anarchists and the CLU—made local eight-hour success crucially dependent on shortening hours in other cities. Otherwise, intercity employers would have faced a debilitating cost disadvantage. George Schilling pointed this out in a report in John Swinton's New York-based paper on May 28: "We did not 'paint the town red' as we would have done if the other cities had stood by us. Chicago can lead the country, but it cannot . . . run away from it."[59]

The upheaval of the mid-1880s was also the third great moment of class formation in Chicago, building on and going beyond the 1864–67 and 1877–79 moments. The 1886–87 strikes were distinctive in several critical ways. First, in contrast to the 1877 strikes, these were primarily a trade union affair. In 1877 the strikes were undertaken by crowds that often coerced workers into leaving their jobs; the so-called riots were strikes as well. Nine years later there were few crowd actions. Workers prepared for several months before May 1 by discussing issues and building their own organizations, and they struck voluntarily and relied on such sophisticated tactics as the boycott. For example, in the 1877 strikes women participated through their neighborhoods, while in 1886 they participated through organizations at their workplace.

One measure of the extent to which workers were able to organize was the number of strikes called by a labor organization. Between 1881 and 1885 Chicago workers had participated in 176 strikes, an average of 35 per year. Of these 59 percent were called by a labor organization. In 1886 the number of strikes jumped almost ninefold, to 307. Just as significant, however, a labor organization called 254, or 83 percent, of these strikes. This jump of 24 percentage points is all the more remarkable because in 1886 so many of those in previously unorganized trades and occupations, such as the carpenters, women and other garment workers, and machine woodworkers, participated in a strike for the first time.[60]

The greater commitment to organization on the part of the 1886 participants allowed some of the strikes of May to continue far beyond the Haymarket bomb on May 4. Indeed, the great upheaval can be extended to include the struggles of 1887. By contrast, almost all the strikes of May 1867 or July 1877 had succumbed within a month or two.

Finally, unlike in 1867, the goal of restoring to workers the fruits of their labor by abolishing the wage system was clearly receding; the short-lived producers' cooperative movement that followed the strikes and boycotts of 1886–87 was the last such episode in Chicago labor history. Though producerism and antimonopolism were far from dead, the goal of raising the standard of living through shorter hours and higher wages—Samuel Gompers's "more and more"—was now a realistic alternative path for trade unionists. Both were means of diffusing or socializing the fruits of the new industrial system.

In sum, the distancing of workers from crowd violence, their reliance on unions, sympathy strikes, the boycott, and other tactics to enforce group unity, and their concern with stabilizing the new industrial system in a prolabor way all suggest that workers, like their employers, were learning that the rules of an industrial market society were not immutable and could be transmuted through organization and calculated behavior.

Notes

1. Selig Perlman, *A History of Trade Unionism in the United States* (New York: Macmillan, 1922), 81–105.

2. On Knights membership statistics, see note 30; on local strikes, see U.S. Commissioner of Labor, *Third Annual Report of the United States Commissioner of Labor, 1887: Strikes and Lockouts* (Washington, D.C.: Government Printing Office, 1887), 100–171.

3. See, for example, Paul Avrich, *The Haymarket Tragedy* (Princeton, N.J.: Princeton University Press, 1984); and David Roediger and Franklin Rosemont, eds., *Haymarket Scrapbook* (Chicago: Charles H. Kerr, 1986). For an analysis of the mythic belief structure surrounding Haymarket, see Carl Smith, *Urban Disorder and the Shape of Belief: The Great Chicago Fire, the Haymarket Bomb, and the Model Town of Pullman* (Chicago: University of Chicago Press, 1995), 101–74.

4. Martin J. Sklar, *Corporate Reconstruction of American Capitalism, 1890–1916: The Market, the Law, and Politics* (Cambridge: Cambridge University Press, 1988), 44.

5. Ibid., 20–33, 43–47; David M. Gordon, Richard Edwards, and Michael Reich, *Segmented Work, Divided Workers: The Historical Transformation of Labor in the United States* (Cambridge: Cambridge University Press, 1982), 94–99, 101–3; Rendig Fels, *American Business Cycles, 1865–1897* (Chapel Hill: University of North Carolina Press, 1959), chaps. 4–5; David Montgomery, *The Fall of the House of Labor: The Workplace, the State, and American Labor Activism, 1865–1925* (Cambridge: Cambridge University Press, 1987), 214–56; James Livingston, "Social Analysis of Economic History and Theory: Conjectures on Late-Nineteenth Century American Development," *American Historical Review* 92 (Feb. 1987): 69–95.

6. David Wells, *Recent Economic Changes* (New York: D. Appleton, 1889), 25–26; U.S. Bureau of Labor, *Industrial Depressions* (Washington, D.C.: Government Printing Office, 1866), 66; Carl P. Parrini and Martin J. Sklar, "New Thinking about the Market, 1896–1914: Some American Economists on Investment and the Theory of Surplus Capital," *Journal of Economic History* 43 (Sept. 1983): 559–78; Sidney Fine, *Laissez-Faire and the General-Welfare State: A Study of Conflict in American Thought, 1865–1901* (Ann Arbor: University of Michigan Press, 1964), 198–251.

7. Sklar, *Corporate Reconstruction of American Capitalism*, 53–61; U.S. House of Representatives, *Investigation by a Select Committee of the House of Representatives Relative to the Causes of the General Depression in Labor and Business; And as to Chinese Immigration*, 46th Cong., 2d sess. (Washington, D.C.: Government Printing Office, 1879), 5–6 (first Gage quote), 9 (second quote).

8. James L. Huston, "The American Revolutionaries, the Political Economy of Aristocracy, and the American Concept of the Distribution of Wealth, 1865–1900," *American Historical Review* 98 (Oct. 1993): 1079–1105; U.S. House of Representatives, *Investigation by a Select Committee*, 79 (Halley quote); Sklar, *Corporate Reconstruction of American Capitalism*, 54–55; Leon Fink, *Workingmen's Democracy: The Knights of Labor and American Politics* (Urbana: University of Illinois Press, 1983), 18–37; John A. Garraty, *The New Commonwealth, 1877–1890* (New York; Harper and Row, 1968), 309–35.

9. On the socialists, see testimony in Illinois House of Representatives, *Report of the Special Committee on Labor* (Springfield: Weber, Magie, 1879); on Steward, see David Montgomery, *Beyond Equality: Labor and the Radical Republicans, 1862–1872* (New York: Vintage Books, 1967), 249–60; and *Progressive Age*, Aug. 27, 1881, Nov. 5, 1881.

10. Quoted in Lawrence Bennett Glickman, "A Living Wage: Political Economy, Gender, and Consumerism in American Culture, 1880–1925" (Ph.D., diss., University of California, Berkeley, 1992), 167. See also Lawrence Glickman, "'Inventing the American Standard of Living': Gender, Race, and Working Class Identity, 1880–1925," *Labor History* 34 (Spring–Summer 1993): 221–35; Jack Blicksilver, "George Gunton: Pioneer Spokesman for a Labor–Big Business Entente," *Business History Review* 31 (Spring 1957): 1–22; and James L. Huston, "A Political Response to Industrialism: The Republican Embrace of Protectionist Labor Doctrines," *Journal of American History* 70 (June 1983): 35–57. On the maturation in the 1880s of a mass-marketing strategy among manufacturers and a consumer culture among Americans, especially urban working people, see Gunther Barth, *City People* (New York: Oxford University Press, 1980); Alfred D. Chandler Jr., *The Visible Hand: The Managerial Revolution in American Business* (Cambridge, Mass.: Belknap, 1977), 207–39; Glenn Porter and Harold C. Livesay, *Merchants and Manufacturers: Studies in the Changing Structure of Nineteenth-Century Marketing* (1971; reprint, Chicago: Ivan Dee, 1989), 214–27; and James Livingston, *Pragmatism and the Political Economy of Cultural Revolution, 1850–1910* (Chapel Hill: University of North Carolina Press, 1994), 49–52. In the 1880s bureaus of labor statistics "constructed a model of working-class consumption" that rested on pioneering statistical investigations of the working-class standard of living. Mary O. Furner, "Knowing Capitalism: Public Investigation and the Labor Question in the Long Progressive Era," in *The State and Economic Knowledge*, ed. Mary O. Furner and Barry Supple (Cambridge: Woodrow Wilson International Center for Scholars and Cambridge University Press, 1990), 247.

11. Association leaders were identified in J. M. Foley's "Labor Department," published in the *Chicago Express*, June 1885–Apr. 1886.

12. *Chicago Tribune*, Jan. 16, 1886.

13. *Fourth Biennial Report of the Illinois Bureau of Labor Statistics* (Springfield: H. W. Rokker, 1886), 318–19 (quotes), 474.

14. *Chicago Tribune*, Mar. 15, 1873.

15. Figures derived from data reported in *Industrial Chicago*, vol. 3, *The Manufacturing Interests* (Chicago: Goodspeed Publishing, 1894), 594; James Livingston, *Origins of the Federal Reserve System: Money, Class, and Corporate Capitalism, 1890–1913* (Ithaca, N.Y.: Cornell University Press, 1986), 39–40 (quote); Gregory S. Kealey and Bryan D. Palmer, *Dreaming of What Might Be: The Knights of Labor in Ontario, 1880–1900* (Cambridge: Cambridge University Press, 1982), 33. On the effects of the 1877 strikes on subsequent wages, see Robert Bruce, *1877, Year of Violence* (Chicago: Quadrangle Books, 1959), 301–2; and David Lightner, *Labor on the Illinois Central Railroad, 1852–1900: The Evolution of an Industrial Environment* (New York: Arno, 1977), 203–4.

16. For another analysis relating labor action to crises in capital accumulation,

see Shelton Stromquist, *A Generation of Boomers: The Pattern of Railroad Labor Conflict in Nineteenth-Century America* (Urbana: University of Illinois Press, 1987)

17. *Chicago Tribune,* Feb. 2, 1883 (quotes); Chandler, *Visible Hand,* 258–69.

18. *Chicago Tribune,* July 1, 1884, July 7, 1884; *Chicago Express,* July 25, 1885.

19. Wells, *Recent Economic Changes,* 79; *Chicago Tribune,* Mar. 24, 1886, Apr. 3, 1886.

20. *Chicago Tribune,* Dec. 30, 1885, Feb. 21, 1886 (quote); *Fourth Biennial Report of the Illinois Bureau of Labor Statistics,* 390.

21. Wells, *Recent Economic Changes,* 51; Robert Ozanne, *A Century of Labor-Management Relations at McCormick and International Harvester* (Madison: University of Wisconsin Press, 1967), 10–11, 9–22; *Knights of Labor,* Mar. 1886.

22. *Chicago Tribune,* Oct. 15, 1885, Dec. 7, 1885, Dec. 14, 1885, Dec. 28, 1885, Jan. 17, 1886, Feb. 2, 1886, Feb. 3, 1886; *Chicago Express,* Oct. 10, 1885, Dec. 19, 1885.

23. Ozanne, *Century of Labor-Management Relations,* 21–22; *Chicago Tribune,* Mar. 1, 1886, Mar. 2, 1886.

24. Norman J. Ware, *The Labor Movement in the United States, 1860–1895: A Study in Democracy* (New York: Vintage Books, 1929), 334–45.

25. *Chicago Tribune,* Dec. 25, 1885 (quote); *Chicago Express,* Dec. 26, 1885; Knights of Labor District Assembly 24, *Minute Book,* Jan. 15, 1886, George A. Schilling Papers, Regenstein Library, University of Chicago; *Fourth Biennial Report of the Bureau of Labor Statistics,* 453.

26. *Chicago Express,* Oct. 17, 1885; Knights of Labor District Assembly 24, *Minute Book,* Mar. 15, 1886.

27. *Chicago Tribune,* Mar. 21, 1886, Mar. 22, 1886.

28. Ibid., March 5, 1886, Mar. 20, 1886 (quotes), Mar. 27, 1886.

29. *Chicago Express,* Apr. 10, 1886; *Chicago Tribune,* Mar. 20, 1886 (quote).

30. *Record of the Proceedings of the Ninth Regular Session of the General Assembly Held at Hamilton, Ont., Oct. 5–13, 1885,* 173, Reel 67, in *Terence Vincent Powderly Papers, 1864–1937, and John William Hayes Papers, 1880–1921: The Knights of Labor* (Glen Rock, N.J.: Microfilming Corporation of America, 1974); *Fourth Biennial Report of the Illinois Bureau of Labor Statistics,* 192, 213, 221, 226. The Bureau of Labor Statistics took its enumeration in July but published its report in November, at which time it estimated that the number of Knights equaled the number of unionists.

31. *Knights of Labor,* Apr. 23, 1887; *Chicago Labor Enquirer,* Apr. 30, 1887; Robert Max Jackson, *The Formation of Craft Labor Markets* (Orlando, Fla.: Academic, 1984), 187–89.

32. *Chicago Tribune,* Nov. 23, 1885; *Carpenter,* July 1885; *Irish World and American Industrial Liberator,* Jan. 2, 1886.

33. James Brennock, "History of the Chicago District Council of Carpenters," 1902 manuscript in possession of the Chicago District Council of Carpenters (first Brennock quote); *Knights of Labor,* Mar. 1886; U.S. Industrial Commission, *Report of the U.S. Industrial Commission* (Washington, D.C.: Government Printing Office, 1901), 8:465 (second Brennock quote).

34. *Chicago Inter-Ocean,* Mar. 23, 1886; *Chicago Express,* Mar. 23, 1886; *Knights of Labor,* Apr. 24, 1886.

35. Wilfred Carsel, *A History of the Chicago Ladies Garment Workers Union* (Chi-

cago: ILGWU, 1940), 4–14; *Chicago Express,* Apr. 10, 1886; *Fourth Biennial Report of the Illinois Bureau of Labor Statistics,* 187.

36. Abraham Bisno, *Abraham Bisno: Union Pioneer* (Madison: University of Wisconsin Press, 1967), 66.

37. Ibid., 67–80.

38. *Chicago Tribune,* May 4, 1886 (quote), May 5, 1886; Lizzie M. Swank Holmes, "Women Workers of Chicago," *American Federationist* 12 (Aug. 1905): 507–10; Joanne J. Meyerowitz, *Women Adrift: Independent Wage Earners in Chicago, 1880–1930* (Chicago: University of Chicago Press, 1988), 29; Carolyn Daniel McCreesh, "On the Picket Line: Militant Women Campaign to Organize Garment Workers, 1880–1917" (Ph.D. diss., University of Maryland, 1975), chap. 1; Richard Schneirov, "The Knights of Labor in the Chicago Labor Movement and in Municipal Politics, 1877–1887" (Ph.D., diss., Northern Illinois University, 1984), 456–65. Nationally, see Susan Levine, *Labor's True Women: Carpet Weavers, Industrialization, and Labor Reform in the Gilded Age* (Philadelphia: Temple University Press, 1984).

39. *Chicago Tribune,* May 1, 1886, May 5, 1886, May 11, 1886; *Fourth Biennial Report of the Illinois Bureau of Labor Statistics,* 377.

40. *Chicago Tribune,* Apr. 16, 1886, Apr. 30, 1886, May 16, 1886, June 19, 1886; Alfred T. Andreas, *History of Chicago* (Chicago: A. T. Andreas, 1884–86), 2:733.

41. *Chicago Tribune,* Apr. 19, 1886, Apr. 20, 1886, Apr. 26, 1886, Apr. 30, 1886.

42. Jonathan Garlock, comp., *Guide to the Local Assemblies of the Knights of Labor* (Westport, Conn.: Greenwood, 1982), 63–92; *Fourth Biennial Report of Illinois Bureau of Labor Statistics,* 187; Hartmut Keil, "The Knights of Labor, the Trade Unions, and German Socialists in Chicago, 1870–1890," in *Impressions of a Gilded Age: The American Fin-de-Siècle,* ed. Marc Chenetier and Rob Kroes (Amsterdam: Universiteit van Amsterdam, 1983), 301–23.

43. *Chicago Tribune,* Mar. 21, 1886 (quote), Apr. 9, 1886. Bisno, *Abraham Bisno,* 66, also recalled the Knights as the leaders of the movement.

44. Quoted in *Public Opinion* 1 (May 1, 1886): 47; *Chicago Tribune,* Mar. 27, 1886, Apr. 28, 1886; *Knights of Labor,* May 15, 1886.

45. *Chicago Tribune,* May 2, 1886.

46. Ibid., Apr. 11, 1886; *Fourth Biennial Report of the Illinois Bureau of Labor Statistics,* 479–80, estimates 62,500 struck; Henry David, *The History of the Haymarket Affair,* 3d rev. ed. (New York: Collier Books, 1963), 163, estimates 30,000; press quotes from Philip S. Foner, *History of the Labor Movement in the United States,* vol. 2, *From the Founding of the A.F. of L. to the Emergence of American Imperialism* (New York: International Publishers, 1955), 103–4.

47. Of approximately 19,000 workers reporting, 16,000 demanded eight for ten according to the *Fourth Biennial Report of the Illinois Bureau of Labor Statistics,* 491. David *History of the Haymarket Affair,* 163, estimates that two-thirds demanded eight for ten. *Chicago Tribune,* May 2, 1886 (quote), May 3, 1886.

48. Avrich, *Haymarket Tragedy,* 190–214 (quote by Spies on 190, Harrison on 204, Fielden on 206).

49. *Chicago Tribune,* May 5, 1886; Avrich, *Haymarket Tragedy,* 215–39 (terrorism quote by Richard T. Ely on 222); David, *History of the Haymarket Affair,* 193 (Holmes quote).

50. Bisno, *Abraham Bisno,* 80–81.

51. John R. Commons, David J. Saposs, Helen L. Sumner, E. B. Mittelman, H. E. Hoagland, John B. Andrews, and Selig Perlman, *History of Labour in the United States* (1918; reprint, New York: Macmillan, 1946), 2:385; Ware, *Labor Movement in the United States,* 316. David, *History of the Haymarket Affair,* 442, was the first to dissent from labor leaders' interpretation.

52. *Knights of Labor,* May 7, 1886.

53. *Chicago Express,* May 29, 1886; *Knights of Labor,* June 19, 1886; *Fourth Biennial Report of Illinois Bureau of Labor Statistics,* 480.

54. *Chicago Inter-Ocean,* May 22, 1886, June 4, 1886; *Knights of Labor,* June 12, 1886; *Fourth Biennial Report of Illinois Bureau of Labor Statistics,* 369.

55. *Chicago Tribune,* Oct. 1, 1886, Dec. 22, 1886, Sept. 18, 1915; *Saturday Evening Post,* June 1, 1907; Donald Smith, "William Henry Jackson: Riel's Disciple," in *Pelletier-Lathin Memorial Lecture Series, Brandon University, 1979–80,* ed. A. S. Lussier (Brandon: Department of Native Studies, Brandon University, 1980); Steven Sapolsky, "The Making of Honore Jaxon," in *Haymarket Scrapbook,* ed. Roediger and Rosemont (Chicago: Charles H. Kerr, 1986), 103–5; *Knights of Labor,* Dec. 30, 1886; Richard Schneirov and Thomas J. Suhrbur, *Union Brotherhood, Union Town: The History of the Carpenters' Union of Chicago, 1863–1987* (Carbondale: Southern Illinois University Press, 1988), 21–43.

56. *Chicago Tribune,* Sept. 18, 1915 (first quote); Luke Grant, *The National Erectors' Association and the International Association of Bridge and Structural Ironworkers* (Washington, D.C.: Government Printing Office, 1915), 118 (second quote). Two years later, after a violent episode during the Burlington railroad strike, the *Knights of Labor,* July 14, 1888, editorialized that "dynamite had become so common that people cease to be afraid of it anymore." On the tie between anarchism and construction unionism, see the biography of Anton Johannsen by Hutchins Hapgood, *The Spirit of Labor* (New York: Duffield, 1907).

57. *Chicago Tribune,* Apr. 17, 1886, June 12, 1887; *Knights of Labor,* Aug. 7, 1886, Feb. 12, 1887.

58. U.S. Commissioner of Labor, *Third Annual Report of the Commissioner of Labor,* 100–171; *Knights of Labor,* June 19, 1886; *Chicago Express,* May 29, 1886; *Chicago Times,* Apr. 14, 1888.

59. *John Swinton's Paper,* May 30, 1886.

60. U.S. Commissioner of Labor, *Third Annual Report of the Commissioner of Labor,* 100–171.

CHAPTER 9

Chicago Politics and the United Labor Party, 1886–87

The resounding impact of the boycott, the eight-hour-day movement, and the extension of labor organization among unskilled working people in the first half of 1886 laid the foundation for another independent foray of Chicago's workers into electoral politics. Chicago's United Labor party (ULP) was a major component of a broad "tide of electoral initiatives" in the United States in the mid-1880s that indicated an accelerating politicization of major segments of America's working class. Leon Fink counts labor tickets in 189 towns and cities in 34 of 38 states, including the ULP effort led by Henry George in New York City, as well as in Chicago. In Illinois labor parties were conspicuous in 15 cities.[1]

The ULP's political thrust mixed older producers' republican politics with newer trade union concerns. On the one hand, as a movement opposed to the use of the police and courts against organized labor, it drew on and reinvigorated the republican belief that the state should not favor any class but should be neutral. The republican fear that government had been prostituted to create special privilege could also be detected in the ULP's call for public ownership of the street railways and other utilities and its demand for a tax assessment and land reform. On the other hand, these very same demands could be interpreted in different ways. The call for government to own utilities was viewed by some as an opening wedge for municipal socialism. More to the point, the ULP came into existence primarily to defend the labor movement rather than to reconstitute a producers' republic. Indeed, the ULP was Chicago's first party directly representative of its organized workers. Unlike the Greenback-Labor and Socialist Labor parties, which were reform parties formed by labor politicians to register the protest of workers whose organizations had been shattered or enfeebled during the depression, the ULP was a broad-based, popular expression of those parts of the working class that had been mobilized and organized during the great upheaval. This was symbolically expressed in the name of the party itself—united labor—which had been invented by the trade unions in 1882 to distinguish themselves from the socialists and antimonopolists.

The ULP's distinctive program helped embody a short-lived synthesis that subsumed the differences between trade unionists, labor reformers, and socialists and between the political cultures of American constitutionalism and European Jacobinism. With the repression of the International Working Peoples' Association, this volatile coalition found its most significant vehicle in the Knights of Labor, which served as an umbrella group and a forum for diverse strands of reform thought, ranging from anarchism and state socialism to the single tax and voluntary cooperation. For these diverse factions the Knights came the closest to embodying the outraged response of Chicago labor and reformers to the guilty verdict against the anarchists as well as to the unfair use of the courts and the police against strikers and boycotters. Before this could happen, however, a bitter internal debate grew up within the Knights, resulting in a startling transformation in local leadership that brought the socialists to power within the order by the end of 1886. Still, the party's career was short-lived. The ULP proved incapable of attracting elements outside the immigrant working class. Moreover, much of the ULP's base proved susceptible to the same Democratic party blandishments that had stymied independent labor politics since the 1870s.

Labor's Response to Haymarket and the Origins of an Independent Labor Party

The immediate impact of the explosion of the Haymarket bomb was the dissolution of whatever unity had existed in the eight-hour movement. The Eight Hour Association tried to shift the blame for the tragedy to John Bonfield, whose police had attacked without warrant a constitutionally protected assembly of workers at Haymarket Square.[2] A more typical labor response was the vituperative blast leveled by the Knights of Labor publisher George Detwiler, who disclaimed that the order had any "affiliation, association, sympathy or respect for the band of cowardly murderers, cut-throats, and robbers, known as anarchists, who sneak through the country like midnight assassins, stirring up the passions of ignorant foreigners. . . ." The anarchists, editorialized Detwiler, "were entitled to no more consideration than wild beasts."[3]

The bomb also polarized rank-and-file unionists along ethnopolitical lines. For the Irish, who had deeply resented Bonfield's brutal actions during the 1885 streetcar strike, the killing of seven, mostly Irish, policemen inverted their sympathies. One of the dead officers had been an honorary member of the iron molders' union, and over two hundred union molders attended his funeral. Patrick Ford, editor of the *Irish World,* described the Haymarket affair as an unleashing of war by Bohemian and German workers against the police and termed the police "faithful defenders of the law." When the jury condemned the defendants to death, Ford endorsed the verdict. Simultaneously, he defended the use of dynamite by Irish revolutionaries fighting for Irish independence. Unlike Ireland, he maintained, "there is no despotism on American soil except that permitted by the people themselves."[4]

Following Haymarket, leading Knights, including Detwiler, J. B. Murphy, George Rodgers, and Richard Griffiths, began a campaign to eliminate the influence of all those, particularly socialists, who fostered unrest in the order and threatened its good name by their sympathetic ties to the anarchists. In May they suspended DA 57, which had first involved the Knights in the boycott and eight-hour agitation. At the same time, the May–June special general assembly suspended all organizers' commissions, compelling prospective Knights to join established assemblies headed by nonsocialists. Upon his return from the convention George Rodgers introduced resolutions in DA 24—which were rammed through in a midnight session—expelling from local assemblies all publicly avowed anarchists.[5]

But even as the Knights' leaders sought to shore up their power within the order, a series of developments outside their control strengthened the very tendencies unraveling it. The first development concerned the political impact of labor's new emphasis on boycotting. The Illinois Bureau of Labor Statistics counted fifty boycotts in the first half of 1886; and of the thirty-one cases in which the outcome could be judged, all but one achieved at least some success. The most important boycott was a statewide boycott of contract prison labor that had the support of craft unions in shoemaking, coopering, and stonecutting. Initially deemed a success, it came out in July that many companies had retained their prison contracts. By that time, however, DA 24 had decided to restrict boycotts in the face of a series of well-publicized New York prosecutions of boycotters, which raised the fear that employers would resort to the courts. That decision set the policy of Knights leaders at odds with a powerful phalanx of unions that had been conducting a statewide boycott on prison-made shoes and encouraged labor leaders to move away from boycotting and in the direction of political action on the state level.[6]

A second development also called into question the conservative policy of Knights leaders. The switchmen of the Lake Shore and Southern Railroad resumed their strike when the company reneged on its agreement to transfer nonunion men. When the company tried to run its trains using Pinkerton detectives, the strike won the active support of large numbers of working people in and around Packingtown. In the midst of assaults on scabs and the destruction of railroad property, the railroads asked for and received a federal court injunction against the strikers for interfering with interstate commerce.[7]

Stymied in both episodes by the courts, many labor leaders thought the time had come to engage in independent political action. J. M. Foley, a Knights leader, deplored a "deep rooted conspiracy all along the line to suppress the action of workingmen," particularly when they resorted to the boycott. "It is proposed," reported Foley, "to carry the fight from the courts to the ballot box." Foley concluded that industrial emancipation could be achieved only by a "boycott by the ballot."[8] The fateful move toward independent politics occurred in July when the state general assembly of the order recommended that assemblies engage in independent political action on the issue of prison contract labor wherever feasible. Following that decision a committee of nine active members of DA 24, then boasting over twenty thousand members, began discussing the advisability of forming a labor party. By the first week of August the committee, consisting of socialists and Eight Hour Association leaders, issued a call for all labor organizations to meet on August 21. At once, the Central Labor Union and the Socialist Labor party, which had been reorganized to fill the vacuum left by the International Working Peoples' Association, reinforced the movement.[9]

Despite a consensus on the need for political action, labor's relation to the Democratic party created divisions over strategy among the Knights. George Rodgers, J. B. Murphy, and other Knights associated with the craft unions wanted the movement to confine itself to the prison labor issue and nominate only legislative candidates. That limitation would avoid undermining the strategy of political collective bargaining and labor's alliance with the local Democratic party. They were backed by a crop of political aspirants from local unions and from the two old parties who had entered the Knights in droves during the late spring. In contrast, Knights, socialists, and Eight Hour Association leaders, backed by the CLU and SLP, argued that labor should nominate candidates for county as well as state legislative offices.[10]

The question of labor's relation to the Democratic party was closely tied to the Haymarket trial. The trial of the eight indicted anarchist leaders gripped the attention of the entire city from June through August, and it gradually became clear to workers that there was no credible evidence tying them to the bomb. In early August mixed LA 522 passed a resolution, which disavowed any sympathy for anarchism but condemned Bonfield "for his uncalled for and un-American attack on a peaceable meeting in

Haymarket Square." It further charged that "it was a put up job to injure the eight-hour movement in Chicago." The *Knights of Labor,* which by this time had been taken over by the more moderate George Sceets, editorialized that there was not enough evidence to convict the men.[11]

On the day before the August 21 meeting at Greenbaum Hall to establish a labor party the jury arrived at its stunning verdict of guilty. Without a shred of evidence linking them to the commission of the crime, August Spies, Albert Parsons, Samuel Fielden, Michael Schwab, Adolph Fischer, George Engel, and Louis Lingg were sentenced to death; Oscar Neebe was given a fifteen-year sentence. Never before had the partiality of the local government been so searingly etched in the minds of local workers. The *Chicago Express,* in a front-page editorial, stated that the prosecution had not "the faintest conception of the magnitude of the tidal wave which this tragedy . . . will set in motion upon the world's great ocean of thought. There is a vast army of laborers who are of the opinion that the bomb throwing was not the work of anarchists, but of some irresponsible party," to defeat the eight-hour movement. "This belief not only exists, but is rapidly spreading through all the ranks of labor."[12]

For the first time a socialist cause had touched a sensitive political nerve among American workers: the issues of free speech, free assembly, and equal rights. In short, just as the bomb of May 4 had divided the labor movement, the verdict of August 20 helped bring many German socialists, Irish nationalists, and American labor reformers back together. The Greenbaum Hall meeting began with a standing ovation given to Hortensia Black, wife of the attorney who had defended the anarchists. Following her short talk the meeting almost unanimously endorsed the idea of fielding a full slate of candidates, against the wishes of Richard Powers and the Trades and Labor Assembly president. A small group of English-speaking former SLPers, led by Thomas J. Morgan, played a prominent role in the proceedings, but in no sense was the outcome solely a victory for the CLU as the local press implied. Unlike the old SLP, the Greenbaum Hall movement, according to R. C. Owens, emanated "distinctively from the Knights of labor and was . . . a bona fide movement of organized labor." According to one report, three-fifths of all Chicago Knights supported independent political action in late July. At the convention itself delegates from Knights LAs outnumbered those from all trade unions, 171 to 138.[13]

Within two weeks of these events the balance of power shifted markedly in DA 24. In elections for seven delegate slots for the upcoming general assembly, the district assemblies selected four socialist sympathizers who had been prime movers in the independent labor party effort. Meanwhile, Master Workman J. B. Murphy died at the end of August and was replaced by

Elizabeth Rodgers, mother of nine children and the city's leading women's labor organizer. Rodgers was an antisocialist who had close ties to Terence Powderly, but because she had less prestige than her predecessor, she was less able to dampen the rising opposition.[14]

During this time DA 57, which had been reorganized in late July but had not taken part in the Greenbaum Hall meeting, officially ratified the movement for independent politics. Unions opposed to or skeptical about the movement, notably the typographers' union, Cigarmakers Union No. 14, and the bricklayers' union, realized they could not maintain their ties with the two old parties by merely ignoring the new developments. As the September 25 convention date of the United Labor party approached, they too endorsed the movement for independent politics, seeking some influence over a phenomenon whose existence they could not prevent.[15]

The ULP and the Election of 1886

When the convention met, it was soon clear that delegates from the older and larger unions and Frank Lawler's party regulars were determined either to take over the convention, as they had in 1877, or to disrupt its proceedings. At this point, Charles G. Dixon, who had been elected chair in a two-to-one vote, adjourned the convention. It was obvious that the proponents of independent politics had a solid majority. More important, only 75 of Dixon's 301 votes had come from the CLU, an indication of the broad base of support for independent labor politics.

Two days later pro–Democratic party delegates from the typographers, bricklayers, cigarmakers, clothing cutters, and boxmakers formed the Labor League. The Labor League sought an alliance with the prolabor Irish faction of the Democrats, which since 1885 had been deprived of power by the Iroquois Club. They nominated John Dunphy, a popular Irish Democrat, for sheriff, the most prestigious prize in the upcoming elections. Dunphy had been passed over by the party in favor of an Iroquois man.

On September 25 the official ULP convention met to consider a platform and nominate candidates. On national issues the platform virtually reproduced the Knights' general program, with the exception of the prominence given to a national eight-hour law. Other planks demanded government ownership of the means of transportation and communication, land reform, and a national monetary system to replace the existing one operated through the national banks. As expected, the state platform gave priority to the abolition of prison contract labor, but it also included an eight-hour law, payment of wages in lawful money on a weekly basis, compulsory education, and the right of women to serve on school boards. The ULP county program was divided into two kinds of issues: nonpartisan demands aimed at corruption, including calls to abolish the contract system and end the division of the city into towns, and social demands, including taxation of land held for speculative purposes, the abolition of toll roads, and a call for the equality of all citizens in the courts.[16]

The backgrounds of the ULP's nominees and its delegates reflected the predominant influence of the Knights. At the top of the ULP ticket for the fall election was an Irishman and a German: for sheriff Matthew J. Butler, the master workman of DA 57; and for county treasurer the former SLPer Frank Stauber. There were thirty-four other candidates, not including the judges who were nominated from the two old parties. Of those whose affiliation could be identified thirteen were prominent Knights, while only two represented a union from the Trades and Labor Assembly or the CLU; only six of the candidates were socialists.[17] The makeup of the party's executive board, the "Committee of 21," reflected the strong influence of the Knights. Fully fifteen had their primary affiliation with Knights assemblies. Of these seven were master workmen or held leadership posts in their district assemblies. Of those LAs that could be identified, five were trade LAs, while four were mixed. But of the mixed LAs two were consisted largely of Pullman and McCormick workers. Though the press claimed, with some truth, that the Committee of 21 was socialist-dominated, only six of its members could be identified as SLPers or as prosocialist.[18]

The election, held five weeks after the convention, produced astonishing results. The ULP polled 26 percent of the city vote for countywide offices. Though the party elected no one for county office, it took enough votes away from the Democrats to hand the Republicans a sweeping electoral victory. By virtue of the cumulative voting system in Illinois, the party elected seven of its state candidates. The ULP candidate for Congress, Dan Gleason, helped by ticket peddlers from the bricklayers' union, came within sixty-four votes of defeating Frank Lawler in the Irish Second Congressional District. The ULP did particularly well in the Town of Lake, electing every local candidate on its ticket. The Labor League, however, was overwhelmed at the polls and closed its headquarters the day after the election.[19]

Because there are lists of registered voters broken down for nativity by precinct for 1886, it is possible to test contemporary ideas about the character of the ULP's constituency. The *Tribune* editorialized that the ULP's vote was concentrated in "manufacturing centers where the foreign element is strong, and is more or less tainted with Karl Marx's socialistic ideas. . . ." Notwithstanding its name, argued the paper, the party was essentially the old SLP of the late 1870s. Statistics do show that voting behavior for the old SLP and the ULP strongly correlated with the percentage of foreign-born. On the ward level in 1879 the SLP vote correlated positively with the percentage of foreign-born at 0.86, while in 1886 the same correlation at the precinct level measured 0.83. A more striking indication of the character of the party's voters can be obtained from a panoramic view of the city's 339 precincts. Only a little more than a third, 125, had native-born majorities among registered voters. The ULP did not gain a majority in any of these precincts. Of the 214 foreign-born precincts 40, or 19 percent, had ULP majorities. Two-thirds of the precincts in which the ULP had a majority came from the 104 precincts in which a single ethnic group had a majority, indicating that ULP voters tended to reside in ethnically segregated neighborhoods.[20]

But ULP strength cannot be ascribed simply to foreign-born voters. Though there is no strict quantitative measure of class available, the location of precincts with ULP majorities in proximity to the city's large-scale industries suggests that ULP voters were solidly working class. Of the top twenty-five ULP precincts seventeen were located on the South Side in the Fifth and Sixth wards near the rolling mills, stockyards, planing mills, lumberyards, and coalyards. The three precincts adjoining the packinghouses in the Town of Lake were 79, 84, and 52 percent Irish and turned out ULP majorities of 62, 67, and 77 percent, respectively.

Further analysis reveals the weight of the city's various ethnic groups in ULP voting. Though no ethnic group exceeded the variable of foreign-born in its power to explain ULP voting, the Germans came closest; its 0.43 correlation exceeded the Irish correlation of 0.25.[21] Though this tends to confirm the continuity between the SLP and the ULP, the German correlation with SLP voting was much lower than in 1879 and the Irish much higher. Indeed, if the Town of Lake could have been included in this analysis, the Irish correlation might have been as high as that of the Germans. The only ward in the city with a ULP majority was the Fifth Ward, where 55 percent of its registered voters were Irish. The willingness of a growing number of Irish voters to engage in reform and labor politics followed a trend that had begun with the Land League movement in 1881. The active participation in the ULP of these voters and Irish Knights leaders indicated that the ULP was not, as the press charged, merely a socialist attempt to save the anarchists from the gallows but was a rather broadly based protest of immigrant workers and unionists against the repression visited on the boycott and eight-hour movement.

The Packinghouse Strikes and the Transformation of the Knights

The 1886–87 great upheaval had begun in fall 1885 in labor's response to the depression and the use of labor-saving machinery. It had become a mass movement in the spring with the adoption of the boycott and the eight-hour-day demand and then had turned to political action in August and September. By November and December the upheaval, like the swelling of a stream into a mighty river, had gathered enough strength to challenge incumbents in the Trades and Labor Assembly and the Knights of Labor. Before examining the source and outcome of this challenge, however, it is necessary to survey briefly the different factions in the opposition forces.

Leading Knights trade unionists labeled their opposition "anarchist" or, at best, "socialist and communist." On closer inspection that opposition emerges as highly heterogeneous, composed of four major groups. At the core, around which all other groups revolved, were the English-speaking socialists, consisting of workers who retained links to German-speaking socialists but had escaped the taint of anarchism. Most reports suggest that socialists and their followers made up a majority in about half of all Knights local assemblies. Few socialists shared T. J. Morgan's rigor of thought or his statist bent, but they were single-minded enough to provide leadership to the Committee of 21, much like what they had done for the city's labor movement in the late 1870s. This group included Paul Ehman, Gustav Belz, Charles S. Wheeler, George Schilling, and, by February 1887, Joseph R. Buchanan, as well as Morgan.[22]

A second major group consisted of those whose political moorings lay in the antislavery and greenback traditions. Among them were the greenback publishers E. F. Norton of the *Sentinal* and B. S. Heath of the *Express* and the Greenback-Labor politicians Benjamin Goodhue, J. H. Randall, Charles Dixon, and J. M. Foley. Trade unionists, such as Matthew Butler and Robert Nelson, also had Greenbacker backgrounds and shared their political concerns.

A third group consisted of trade unionists who until 1886 had no political affiliation but were searching for a new set of prolabor principles to challenge classical economic orthodoxy. Some, such as Thomas H. Ling, a Knights painter, and Thomas Randall, an engineer, chose Henry George's single-tax theory. Others, such as Charles Seib and Ethelbert Stewart, became socialists or socialist sympathizers. Along with socialists, Greenbackers, and about twenty women, many joined LA 1307, of which Gruenhut said, "You might as well call it the English-speaking wing of the Socialistic Labor Party."[23]

A fourth group consisted of ethnic leaders allied with labor's political movement through the ethnic mixed LAs. From the Irish came a diverse group of veterans of the Land League and the fight for independence from the Democratic party, including William Gleason, L. P. Dwyer, and Dan Gleason, all members of LA 1307. Other Irish politicians, small businesspeople, and self-promoters of all stripes had joined the Knights along with packinghouse workers after the winning of the eight-hour day in May. Among the Bohemians the cabinetmaker Frank Dvorak organized several mixed assemblies and served as a master workman for one of them, a statistician for DA 57, and a delegate to the Committee of 21. The Poles contributed two important Knights organizers, Louis Koellen and Benzel Majewski.

Among the French William Henry Jackson's work was supplemented by the efforts of Felix Chartrand, who used his prestige as the president of Chicago's French National Club and a leader in the Brotherhood of Carpenters and Joiners of America to play a similar role in the ULP. Christopher Larson represented Norwegians on the Committee of 21 and served as ULP nominee for North Town supervisor. Considering their small numbers, Chicago's African Americans had a strong presence in the ULP and in the Knights in this period that centered on the colored waiter and barber assemblies. In 1886 the ULP nominated William Bruce, a barber, and in 1887 it nominated John W. Terry, a waiter, and James S. Nelson, a molder who also served on the party's executive committee.[24]

Two labor factions are notable for their absence: the trade union proponents of political bargaining with the two parties and the anarchists. The bomb had discredited the anarchists as a political force in the city. Their archenemies, trade unionists who had led the Knights since 1877 except for William Halley's brief interlude, met a similar fate following the great packinghouse workers' strike six months later. That watershed struggle utterly discredited the leadership of Powderly and his local allies and swept away the remaining barriers in the order to an all-out challenge to the local Democratic party.

Outside of the building trades workers, packinghouse workers were the last major group to retain eight-hour workdays after May 1. With large orders to fill, the packers had conceded eight-hours to their employees out of expediency and waited only for an opportune moment to resume ten hours. In the meantime Knights membership in the stockyards district had grown from 3,000 to 15,000. Through their sympathetic support of the Lake Shore switchmen's walkout in July they also demonstrated militancy and a newfound commitment to labor solidarity.[25]

On October 8 during the Knights' general assembly in Richmond, Virginia, the large packers, led by Philip Armour, informed the Knights that because of competitive pressures from other midwestern packingtowns, they would return to ten-hour workdays on October 11. Spurred on by the butchers and coopers, the packinghouse LAs took up the challenge, and 15,000 Knights walked out, though without the sanction of DA 57. At the Richmond convention Powderly was persuaded by leaders from DA 24 that the conflict could be settled by the timely intervention of an emissary, and he dispatched Thomas B. Barry to Chicago. After several days of fruitless negotiations, Barry wired back to Powderly, "The people here are fighting a losing fight. The packers set a trap for them and they fell into it. The city is in a state of siege. Eight hundred Pinkertons here. Eight of them were beaten to-day. One of them was stripped of his clothes, and to put it mild, hell was knocked out of the four of them; they are all in the hospital. No arrests. This is the hardest body of people I ever tried to control." Unable to effect a settlement, Barry ordered the men back to work on the packers' terms.[26]

Unbeknown to Powderly, Barry had promised local Knights leaders that the return to work would be only temporary. Barry's optimism was based on a secret understanding he had concluded with two large firms to break free from Armour's leadership and settle with the Knights. This set the stage for a second strike on November 3 among the beefpackers, which mushroomed into a general walkout of 20,000 workers on November 6. Barry was on the verge of a compromise settlement on November 13 when Powderly inexplicably ordered the men to return to work. It was a bitter defeat for packinghouse workers and gave rise to a flood of accusations and recriminations. Leading Knights in Chicago and spokesmen on the general executive board declared that the strike was unconstitutional and illegal because of Powderly's well-known order to refrain from contention over the eight-hour-day issue. Richard Griffiths and Richard Powers blamed Matthew Butler and DA 57's leadership for allowing George Schilling and other militants to instigate the general walkout. However, many assemblies, aided by opposition forces in the Knights, attacked Powderly for "unwarranted interference" in local affairs and declared that, but for his order, the men would have attained a decent compromise.

Amidst the welter of charge and countercharge several conclusions emerge. First, the strike represented a major step forward in organization and discipline for packinghouse workers. The 1877 and 1879–80 strikes had been predominantly neighborhood affairs in which a community-based union leadership had resorted to semi-organized intimidation. The 1886 strikes were called, if not sanctioned, by a national, classwide organization. With twenty thousand idle men in the streets and the provocative presence of Pinkertons and the militia, large-scale clashes might have been expected. Yet by all accounts there were very few incidents, largely because of squads of Knights that patrolled the town to keep the workers away from the stockyards area and out of saloons. The strength of new classwide norms and loyalties and organizational discipline was manifest in the mere fact that the men had returned to work upon the telegraphed order of a national leader.[27]

A second conclusion that emerges is that the packers had the unity, determination, and resources to take back the eight-hour concession. The packinghouse workers had shown an eagerness for striking born of immaturity.[28] Powderly was probably right in implying that even if a compromise had been achieved, it would only have temporarily staved off defeat. Yet it is also true that Powderly blundered badly in calling off the strike in the way he did. His clumsy intervention badly injured the reputation of the Knights and shook the faith of packinghouse workers in the viability of unions.

Before shock and bitterness turned to cynicism and apathy, however, packinghouse workers and observers of the affair, particularly the Irish, drew several important political conclusions. First, calling in the militia by the county sheriff, who had hitherto been allied with local labor organizations through the Irish Democratic boss "Buck" McCarthy, alienated stockyards workers from the town and county Democratic organizations, much as Bonfield's actions in 1885 had alienated labor from Harrison's regime. The killing of an innocent bystander, Terrence Begley, by a Pinkerton agent's errant shot had a similar effect. At first authorities arrested the agent, but after the November elections District Attorney Julius Grinnell, who had just finished prosecuting the anarchists, declared that he could not prosecute the Pinkerton agent because the city had no money. Grinnell released the agent, despite the Knights' donation of $300 to do the job. The Begley affair was to Irish workers what the Haymarket trial was to German and Bohemian workers. It undercut sympathy for Democrats, pointed to the class bias of the state, and seemed to confirm the need for an independent labor party to restore its impartiality. Since the aborted prosecution of Begley's murderer did not become known until after the November elections, however, its full ramifications in ULP voting among the Irish were not felt until the April 1887 election.[29]

The second and the most immediate impact of the packinghouse strike occurred within the labor movement. Powderly's back-to-work order resulted in a monumental blow to his prestige and that of his allies. Less than two weeks after the defeat Elizabeth Rodgers wrote to Powderly that "almost to a man" packinghouse workers, encouraged by local opposition leaders, believed the strike had been sold out for "boodle." Not only did this tend to discredit existing Knights leadership, but also it gave an immense boost to the radical opposition led by George Schilling, who had helped lead the strike. But what occurred was more complex. By a process of transference, anti-Powderly sentiment and the Begley affair legitimated the radicals' position that the anarchists' convictions had resulted from a capitalist political conspiracy and that an independent labor party was required to redress class bias within the state. Put differently, in the hands of the radical opposition, support for the condemned anarchists became a lightning rod attracting outrage from packinghouse workers and encouraging them to support the ULP and new leadership in the Knights.[30]

This process could be seen in several major developments that unfolded within a month of the strike's end. Immediately after the strike opposition forces tried unsuccessfully to censure Powderly, but they did succeed in passing a resolution of sympathy for the condemned anarchists. Then a joint meeting of the two Knights district assemblies passed a resolution terming the verdict "an outrage upon common justice" and "a capitalistic and judicial conspiracy." It was a complete reversal of the Knights' July 2 decision to expel the anarchists, and it led local LAs to contribute to the anarchists' defense fund.[31]

At this point Powderly responded with his famous order of December 18, categorically forbidding it. In the letter, which he directed George Rodgers to read before DA 24, Powderly argued that whether or not the trial was unfair and whether or not the police had interfered with a peaceable meeting, it would be suicide to commit the Knights to "anarchy" in any way. The letter, according to the *Knights of Labor,* produced a "sensation" in the city. LA 1307 responded with a series of resolutions condemning Powderly for asking Knights to abjure a fellow member—Albert Parsons—in distress. The final straw came when DA 57 and the seamen's DA 136 enacted a secret boycott of Armour in defiance of Powderly. Richard Griffiths wrote to Powderly that the "communists" had taken complete control of the local Knights.[32]

In the midst of this insubordination and ferment another major leadership change occurred. The *Knights of Labor,* under George Detwiler and later George Sceets, had become the largest weekly newspaper in the city. In early December Detwiler, under pressure for condemning the anarchists, abandoned the paper and purchased the *Star,* which he later merged with the *Telegram.* On December 4 the *Knights of Labor* came under the editorship of a young Knight from Decatur, Bert Stewart. A self-educated worker searching for a new labor philosophy, Stewart befriended Henry Demarest Lloyd, a *Tribune* editorial writer who had just published a seminal essay attacking monopolies in the *North American Review.* At Lloyd's urging Governor Richard Oglesby appointed Stewart to a post in the Bureau of Labor Statistics, and Stewart helped write its 1886 report. Meanwhile, Stewart launched a series of editorials denouncing the anarchist verdict as a violation of workers' rights of free speech and free assembly. On December 30 Stewart repudiated Powderly's December 18 letter. The right "to a fair trial," thundered Stewart, "is of more importance than all the organizations on earth."[33]

Even worse for local Powderly supporters, Joseph R. Buchanan brought his prosocialist weekly paper, the *Labor Enquirer,* from Denver to Chicago in February 1887. Buchanan belonged to Burnett Haskell's West Coast International Workingmen's Association, and in Chicago he joined the SLP. Chicago now had a paper for each major English-speaking labor tendency; a year earlier, it had had none. The *Star-Telegram* represented the beleaguered Knights leadership; the *Labor Enquirer* added impetus to the growth of socialism; and the *Knights of Labor* reflected the new consensus on independent labor politics.[34]

By late December 1886 the local order of the Knights was stalemated between contending factions. The Knights' trade unionists had been discredited, but the opposition, led by the socialists, lacked the legitimacy to assume power. A frustrated J. M. Foley of the *Express* protested that "organized labor in this city has come to a dead standstill. . . . It is politics till you can't rest to the exclusion of everything else." Griffiths reported to Powderly that labor was "more disorganized here than almost anywhere else. There are splits and factions working and pulling against each other." The stalemate was broken in the first week of January. In DA 24 both sides agreed to support Robert Nelson, an iron molder, in the election for master workman. Though reputedly a "radical," Nelson was a trade unionist and was deemed to be an independent thinker. Moreover, while supporting the ULP, he had taken no part in the revolt against Powderly.[35]

A similar development unfolded in the Trades and Labor Assembly, which was still dominated by unions committed to the alliance with the Democratic party. In December, however, the cigarmakers repudiated their own C. W. Rowan, then president of the Trades and Labor Assembly. A new slate of cigarmaker delegates tipped the balance to the opposition. Rather than split the Trades and Labor Assembly, Schilling nominated William Kliver, a leader of the carpenters, who was then elected president over Andrew Cameron.[36]

Kliver was a good compromise candidate for several reasons. He was part of new leadership that had taken over the local Brotherhood of Carpenters and Joiners of America. Unlike some old-timers, he steered clear of temperance reform and, while no socialist, was attuned to the new labor radicalism enough to support the defense of the anarchists and independent politics. Kliver and other brotherhood leaders supported militancy at the workplace, which the Germans and Bohemians appreciated during the long eight-hour struggle that year. As a result, the CLU-affiliated carpenter unions rejoined the Brotherhood of Carpenters and Joiners of America in the last months of 1886. An additional factor in Kliver's attractiveness was that the carpenters were set to renew their eight-hour fight in 1887, and all factions in the Trades and Labor Assembly could unite behind it. Finally, though Kliver was a member of mixed LA 1307, he had successfully resisted the inroads of the Knights' trades assemblies into the brotherhood. In short, Kliver and the carpenters seemed to have overcome at the trade level all the factionalism that the labor movement was attempting to resolve on the political level.[37]

With the opponents to independent politics and labor militancy out of power, the local labor movement could move forward again. This was evident in DA 24's open endorsement of the Armour boycott, its support for several strikes, and a strong, united push in both district assemblies for the ULP. The ousted leadership meanwhile vainly beseeched Powderly to revoke the organizers' commissions of the radical leaders and to send a secret committee to "re-organize" the Chicago Knights.[38]

Yet the new leaders of Chicago labor were political novices and figureheads, not representatives of a partisan cause. Both factions regarded Robert Nelson, later nominated by the ULP for mayor, as a weak leader. One socialist described him as "an ordinary workman without education or special ability of any kind, and if elected will be the puppet of some man or clique, nobody can tell who." Bert Stewart was honest and intelligent but lacked clear political ideas. Kliver and Matthew Butler could also be classified in this group.[39]

By any measure there were experienced and intelligent leaders among the various labor factions in the city, but none of them could muster the majority necessary to win leadership. At the most critical juncture in its short history the Chicago labor movement saddled itself with political leaders who could not command the respect and support to lead forcefully and creatively. The consequences of this inability to sustain a true political synthesis were ultimately devastating.

The ULP Mayoral Campaign of 1887

As the ULP prepared for the spring 1887 mayoral election its leaders exuded an expectation of millennial change. Some anticipated a party realignment in which the Democrats would give way to a labor party while the Republicans would remain the party of the capitalists. For this to happen, however, the Germans needed the support of the Irish. As Joseph Gruenhut put it, the Germans "had drilled and agitated" for a labor party for "twenty years in their native land, and it required no great effort to draw them into a distinct labor party in Chicago. The Irish were aroused by the agrarian movement in Ireland, and they rushed into the United Labor party in such great numbers as to frighten the Democratic politicians out of their wits." But the Irish were an ambivalent labor constituency, and survival of the ULP turned on the question of whether the Irish would remain in the ULP or whether they would return to the Democratic party in exchange for offices and other party favors. This latter prospect was not a question of sellout but a reflection of the fact than many Irish and other labor leaders simply did not believe independent working-class politics possible and hoped to use the

ULP to gain a better deal for themselves with the Democrats. Fear of this tendency toward "fusion" lurked in the minds of ULP leaders throughout the three months prior to the April election.[40]

Another major question remained to be decided. Some ULP leaders believed that even with the support of Irish workers the party could not hope to win a majority unless it could win enough legitimacy to attract elements of other classes. To do so, it would have to become a party in the American political tradition, that is, a principled or programmatic party rather than a class party, one that appealed to a multiclass constituency with broadly popular reforms.[41] To take this route meant that the ULP would have to modify its quasi-socialist program and its exclusive labor appeal. These two questions were intertwined such that the answer to the first determined the answer to the second. These answers ultimately determined the fate of the ULP.

The question of fusion first presented itself to the ULP in late November 1886. Richard Prendergast was an Irish nationalist lawyer and a rising star in the Democratic party who acted as a liaison with labor. In 1880 he had won the confidence of SLPers by defending Frank Stauber in the infamous ballot box–stuffing case. Having been elected judge as a fusion candidate on the Democratic and ULP tickets in November, he repaid his political debt by offering an election board seat to the ULP. Socialists presented a list of party stalwarts to Prendergast, but he listened to his fellow Irish nationalist William Gleason, who was about to become his chief clerk, and appointed Luke Coyne. Coyne was the ex-president of the West Side Streetcar Workers Benevolent Association, who had been fired during the 1885 strike. His appointment was less a favor to the ULP than a gesture toward healing the breach between the Democratic party and the labor movement stemming from Bonfield's actions during the streetcar strike. Coyne's appointment on December 6 set off the first major dissension in the Committee of 21.[42]

From this point until the eve of the mayoral election the fusion question dominated city politics. Realizing that the largest part of the ULP's constituency had been drawn from Democratic party ranks, both major factions of the party tried to dicker with the ULP. Iroquois Club leaders, banking on labor's interest in election reform, asked the ULP to support the mayoral candidacy of its president, Erskine Phelps. The Citizens Association had made similar overtures in late November, and the ULP's response demonstrated the large gap that remained between respectable mugwump liberal reform and labor reform. Rather than simply fight vice and corruption, the ULP proposed a seven-plank program to harmonize reformers that included the following demands: (1) honest taxation, including taxes on stocks, bonds, and other untaxed personal property; (2) the end of renting public properties to political favorites; (3) public condemnation of those who refused to pay their fair share of taxes; (4) punishment of bribe givers as well as bribe takers; (5) the prevention and punishment of bribery of public officials by railroads and other corporations; (6) enforcement of laws preventing the renting of property for immoral purposes; and (7) a prohibition against police levying tribute on prostitutes as a condition of noninterference. The first five planks, which linked political corruption with wealth and business rather than with the personal character of politicians, represented a sharp break with mugwump reform. The attack on the political privileges of the wealthy, however, was too big a stumbling block to overcome in constructing a cross-class movement for reform.[43]

During the same period, overtures came from Mayor Harrison to support his own candidacy. The apprehension that Democrats were scheming to capture the ULP convention was heightened when the press reported that Harrison had ordered party workers to join Knights assemblies and ULP ward clubs. To prevent such a maneuver, Morgan convinced the party to confine membership to Knights and trade unionists. The ULP also limited the power of ward clubs by retaining the right to select final nominees from a list submitted by each ward club. This gave the citywide party a veto over all ward nominations. Finally, the Committee of 25, which had replaced the Committee of 21, mandated that the founders of ward clubs be unionists and that prospective members be voted into the club.

The fear of a Democratic takeover, combined with the absence of the strong craft unions from the ULP, allowed the socialists to control the ULP convention. The platform, written by Morgan, reflected a socialist agenda in contrast to the Knights' agenda of 1886. The first plank demanded, as a way of fighting corruption, the municipal ownership of all utilities. Other planks, in order, demanded taxation to the limit of all unoccupied lands; the end of exempting the wealthy from taxation; the redistricting of the city's wards on the basis of population rather than registered voters to better represent noncitizens; and the end of city contract work. The eight-hour day, the foremost demand in 1886, was relegated to the end of the 1887 platform.[44] The party's nominations also reflected the fear of fusion. Though the vast majority of candidates were Knights as before, only three of the thirty-four candidates were Irish-born. Given the importance of keeping Irish votes in the ULP column, it was also surprising that the convention did not nominate a popular Irishman to head the ticket, as had been done in 1886. Instead, the ULP nominated Robert Nelson for mayor. After the convention the South Side Irish were said to be "up in arms against the candidates put up by the Socialistic Germans."[45]

Despite the unmistakable metamorphosis of the ULP into a class-based party, the different factions left the convention unified in the expectation of electoral success. Party leaders had reason to believe they would poll many more votes than in 1886, when ULP ticket peddlers and active clubs were confined to the immigrant wards. In 1887 virtually every ward had ticket peddlers and functioning clubs by early March. The ULP also had an election judge and clerk in each precinct. The ULP tried to appeal to the prevalent antipartyism and electoral reform impulses of respectable Chicagoans that had energized the rising tide of local reform since 1885. Condemnations of corrupt election practices, the spoils system, and the immunity of the rich from taxation dominated ULP campaign literature, the pages of labor papers, and Nelson's speeches. The strategy of posing as Chicago's reform party broke down, however, when the Republicans nominated John Roche for mayor. Though a relative unknown, Roche had a reputation for personal integrity and being "above party." The *Knights of Labor* admitted flatly that he was "a foe worthy of our steel."[46]

Meanwhile, the Democrats schemed until the last moment to get the ULP to drop Nelson in favor of Harrison. When this failed, Harrison refused the Democratic nomination and practically endorsed Nelson. ULPers were jubilant; Gruenhut declared that Harrison was returning the favor of labor's earlier support of his candidacies. What probably carried more weight was Harrison's fear that a Republican victory would enable them to use patronage to fortify themselves in office and his belief that the Democrats needed labor to remain a majority party. If other Democrats had followed Harrison in endorsing Nelson, the ULP might have made a more respectable showing. But, rather than fuse with the hated socialists, they fled wholesale into the Republican camp, dropping all their candidates for citywide offices, including mayor, and fusing with the Republicans in six wards. On the eve of an election that Joseph Medill called the most important since the one after the fire, the ULP thus faced the worst possible situation, a defensive merger of the two old parties.[47]

Given the grandiose expectations built up by ULP leaders, the election results were profoundly disappointing, barely mitigated by an increase of 5,000 votes in the ULP total over 1886, to 23,410. For Nelson and other defeated ULP candidates that represented a rise in the percentage of the vote, from 26 to 31 percent. In aldermanic races the ULP did almost as poorly, winning only the Fifth Ward's aldermanic seat. The ULP did take enough votes away from Democrats to allow the Republicans to sweep thirteen of eighteen aldermanic races. In the Town of Lake the ULP also went down to defeat, though labor candidates garnered between 41 percent and 46 percent of the vote.[48]

Further analysis of the vote reveals the reasons for the ULP's limited success. The correlation of the percentage of foreign-born voters with the

ULP vote was actually stronger in 1887 than in 1886, and the ULP did not win a majority in a single native-born precinct. Since party strength continued to be confined to the Fifth Ward and Sixth Ward industrial areas, it is clear that the ULP remained very much a party of Chicago's foreign-born working class. Within this framework of continuity, however, there was a major change in the character of ULP voting. The correlation between Germans and ULP vote fell from .43 to .22, while the correlation of Irish and the ULP vote rose from .25 to .51. Among the party's top 25 precincts the number with a German plurality fell from 12 in 1886 to 4 in 1887, while the number of precincts with an Irish plurality rose from 9 to 16. The ULP had changed from being a labor party with a German bias to one with an Irish bias. That shift can be largely attributed to the impact of the packinghouse workers' strike.[49]

The biggest reason the ULP failed to win local offices was that the while the ULP vote for citywide offices went up, the total ULP vote for aldermanic offices in the city remained about equal to the total citywide ULP vote for 1886. Many former Democrats—most likely Irish voters—who opted for Nelson chose a Democrat when offered a choice for alderman. The tenuousness of the Irish vote is further confirmed by the fact that Irish turnout and ULP voting correlated negatively. It may be concluded that low turnout among the Irish was a significant element in limiting the ULP vote in the 1887 election. In short, many Irish not only split their tickets but also were so confused by conflicting counsels that they stayed home.[50]

Voting statistics therefore tend to confirm what has been hypothesized. The inability of the ULP to pose as the only legitimate reform alternative in the election limited its ability to appeal to nonforeign-born voters. Its inability to attract Irish voters on the ward level prevented the ULP from winning more than one victory in aldermanic races, which contributed to the disappointment of party supporters.

The Sources of ULP Failure

Even before the shock of defeat had dissipated, the ULP divided into opposing camps in seeking to explain its cause. The socialists and their supporters among labor reformers pointed proudly to the increase in the ULP vote, while blaming the defeat on the monopolistic press and the fusion of the two old parties. They also charged that flagrant police intimidation prevented hundreds of South Side labor voters from casting ballots. One day after the election Bonfield gave credence to that analysis by boasting, "The police took a personal interest in this election to a man and did all they could consistently and honorably to help the good cause."[51]

While not exonerating the press and the police, Bert Stewart spoke for other ULP leaders in advancing a different explanation for the election results. Instead of blaming external causes, Stewart charged Morgan and the "ultra-socialists" with three major errors. First, by confining party membership to those belonging to a labor organization, the party excluded influential allies in neighborhood communities who happened to be lawyers, small shopkeepers, and artisans. Second, Stewart charged that by having the Morgan-led convention rather than the ward clubs nominate the aldermen, the ULP saddled itself with hard-to-elect candidates. Finally, Stewart joined conservatives and many moderates in the charge that the ULP leadership had given credence to press propaganda of "red flaggism" by allowing open anarchists to be associated with the party. Stewart later clarified his objections to the socialists in two important editorials. To Stewart legitimate socialism was "non-political," and its aim was simply that "trade unions should manage, own, and control for the benefit of all workers all machinery used in their particular branch of trade" under "the co-operative plan." When "class legislation and legal privileges granted to a few create unnatural economic conditions, the class legislation can be made a political issue, but economic conditions cannot." Stewart thus reaffirmed an older analysis in which the concentration of capital resulted from special privileges granted by the state. To Stewart—as well as to anarchists—the path to an alternative society was essentially the nonpolitical one of creating self-employment by voluntary cooperative production—in this case mediated by trade union action.[52]

Chicago socialists had fundamental differences with such ideas, which were strongest in the Knights. They saw them as impractical, outdated conceptions, unsuited to an era of large-scale industry that required socialization of property by the democratic state. This attitude was evident in Morgan's dismissal of the packinghouse workers' cooperative company, started after the defeat of the 1886 strike as "individual" cooperation. He contrasted it with "universal" cooperation, that is, government ownership of large-scale industry.[53]

In the interests of maintaining party unity, the Committee of 25 dismissed Stewart's arguments as a cover for fusion. There was some truth to that charge, for in the next several months the ULP split three ways. The CLU and the largest part of DA 24 stayed with the Morgan-led ULP. The largest part of the fast-declining DA 57 formed the Reformed ULP, soon rechristened by its detractors as the "Free Lunch Party," with loose ties to the Prendergast wing of the Democrats. A different alternative to the ULP, but one with no base among workers, was the Union Labor party, started by greenbackers.[54]

Notwithstanding the impact of these factional differences, it is not at all clear why the ULP should have been stillborn. Why a vote of 31 percent in

Chicago and 41 percent in the Town of Lake should be interpreted as a demoralizing defeat when the Independent Labour party in Britain and the Social Democratic party in Milwaukee were able to use less impressive results in the next decade as promising first steps to extended electoral careers arouses curiosity. The foregoing account of the Chicago ULP suggests some answers to what David Montgomery calls "the one strike and you're out quality of American labor party movements outside of Milwaukee." The case of Milwaukee is instructive, for in that city, according to Leon Fink, socialist success rested on two key ingredients: the party's ability to "close ranks with the city's craft unions" and its "adroit seizure of the municipal reform issue."[55] In Chicago, however, neither condition existed by 1887.

The powerful craft unions capable of delivering the "labor vote" over an extended period of time were at best loosely aligned with the ULP, and once the party shifted from contesting state legislative seats in 1886 to vying for municipal offices in 1887, they were susceptible to appeals that would return them to their alliance with the Democratic party. Indeed, the *Labor Enquirer* estimated that the ULP "did not receive ten per cent of the vote of the unions" in 1887.[56] Traditional party ties were especially evident among the Irish workers and the Irish leadership of these unions. Recognizing the ever-present danger of fusion, the Morgan-led socialists were forced to fall back on weak, figurehead leadership that allowed them to exercise behind-the-scenes manipulation. Overreliance on the socialists to keep the party independent led the ULP in the direction of becoming a class or ideological party rather than a multiclass reform party, which further limited its attraction to voters.

The second factor limiting the ULP's appeal was its inability to capture the municipal reform issue. Two types of multiclass reform coalitions were possible. One would have entailed an alliance of organized workers and small property holders against monopolists based on producers' republican politics. Such an attempt had been made by the Greenback party in the 1870s and been found wanting. A different possible cross-class alliance might have drawn together labor and middle-class and upper-class voters in an antiparty, anticorruption reform crusade that included social reform issues. Though this alternative was discouraged by the ULP's working-class emphasis, that is not a sufficient explanation for the ULP's failure to realize fully its reform potential. The reform forces led by the upper class in the city were adamantly opposed to combining political and social reform because it pointed to the explosive discovery that business corrupted politics. As Stewart put it in a letter to Henry Demarest Lloyd after the election, "As a matter of fact the whole fight upon the labor party of Chicago is made to save the scalp of the tax dodgers. That is all there is in it."[57] A cross-class alliance of reform forces on the basis the ULP proposed in its letter to the Citizens

Association might have appealed to enough voters to have won the election, but the conditions were not yet ripe for such a movement. Such an alliance would await the 1890s.

In addition to the two factors just discussed a third, more difficult, condition might have been necessary for labor party success: the perception among organized workers that the government was hostile to all forms of labor activity. This condition did exist in Chicago in 1886–87 because of the Haymarket trial and the repression of strikes and boycotts, but it soon dissipated. The ephemeral nature of local antilabor repression and the attendant transformation of elite liberalism are major themes of the following two chapters.

Notes

1. Leon Fink, *Workingmen's Democracy: The Knights of Labor and American Politics* (Urbana: University of Illinois Press, 1983), 23–29; Steven J. Ross, "The Politicization of the Working Class: Production, Ideology, Culture, and Politics in Late Nineteenth-Century Cincinnati," *Social History* 2 (May 1986): 171–95. See also David Scobey, "Boycotting the Politics Factory: Labor Radicalism and the New York City Mayoral Election of 1886," *Radical History Review* 28–30 (1984): 280–325; and Jama Lazerow, "'The Workingmen's Hour': The 1886 Labor Uprising in Boston," *Labor History* 21 (Spring 1980): 200–220.

2. *Chicago Express*, May 29, 1886, July 10, 1886.

3. *Knights of Labor*, May 9, 1886.

4. *Irish World and American Industrial Liberator*, May 15, 1886, May 22, 1886 (first quote), Aug. 28, 1886 (second quote).

5. *Chicago Tribune*, July 3, 1886, July 25, 1886; *Knights of Labor*, June 19, 1886; *Chicago Sun*, July 3, 1886.

6. *Chicago Tribune*, July 2, 1886, July 20, 1886; *Fourth Biennial Report of the Illinois Bureau of Labor Statistics* (Springfield: H. W. Rokker, 1886), 452–53; Michael A. Gordon, "The Labor Boycott in New York City, 1880–1886," *Labor History* 16 (Spring 1975): 219–28; *Chicago Express*, Aug. 7, 1886.

7. *Chicago Tribune*, June 24, 1886, June 27, 1886, June 29, 1886.

8. *Chicago Express*, Aug. 7, 1886 (quote); Scobey, "Boycotting the Politics Factory," 280–325.

9. *Chicago Express*, Aug. 28, 1886.

10. *Chicago Tribune*, July 2, 1886, July 30, 1886, Aug. 22, 1886; Richard Oestreicher, "Socialism and the Knights of Labor in Detroit, 1877–1886," *Labor History* 22 (Winter 1981): 5–30.

11. *Chicago Express*, Aug. 7, 1886 (quotes); *Knights of Labor*, Aug. 7, 1886.

12. *Chicago Express*, Aug. 28, 1886.

13. *Chicago Tribune*, July 30, 1886, Aug. 22, 1886; *Chicago Express*, Aug. 28, 1886, Sept. 18, 1886 (quote).

14. *Record of the Proceedings of the Special Session of the General Assembly Held at Richmond, Va., May 25–June 3, 1886*, 104–5, Reel 67, in *Terence Vincent Powderly*

Papers, 1864–1937, and John Willliam Hayes Papers, 1880–1921: The Knights of Labor (Glen Rock, N.J.: Microfilming Corporation of America, 1974) (hereafter PHP); *Chicago Tribune,* Aug. 27, 1886.

15. *Chicago Tribune,* Sept. 23, 1886.

16. *Chicago Express,* Oct. 2, 1886.

17. Figures derived from campaign biographies in ibid.

18. Ibid.

19. *Chicago Tribune,* Nov. 4, 1886.

20. Ibid.; Lars P. Nelson, *Statistics Showing by Wards and Voting Precincts [sic] the Original Nativity of the Voters in Chicago* (Chicago: Lars P. Nelson, 1887). These data, along with the election results, were analyzed using an SPSS-x program. It was not possible to gather precinct-level data to code such variables as religion or class; it should be noted, therefore, that this study is not intended to be a test of the ethnoreligious hypothesis of voting behavior. Pearsons R for 1879 based on ward totals on the nativity of registered voters by ward, reported in Bruce C. Nelson, *Beyond the Martyrs: A Social History of Chicago's Anarchists, 1870–1900* (New Brunswick, N.J.: Rutgers University Press, 1988), 64.

21. A multiple regression analysis, with ULP vote as the dependent variable and different nativities as independent variables, can be used to measure the impact of the foreign-born vote. In the 1886 election the regression coefficient was 0.45 for foreign-born voters as whole; that is, a 1.00 percent increase in the percentage of foreign-born per precinct would result in a 0.45 percent increase in the ULP vote (significance = 0.00).

22. *Chicago Tribune,* Dec. 23, 1886.

23. Ibid.

24. Biographical information from ibid., Feb. 27, 1887; and *Labor Enquirer,* Apr. 2, 1887. For other biographies of African American leaders in the Chicago Knights, see Philip S. Foner and Ronald L. Lewis, eds., *The Black Worker during the Era of the Knights of Labor* (Philadelphia: Temple University Press, 1978), 3:409–10.

25. M. J. Butler to Powderly, Jan. 3, 1887, in *Proceedings of the General Assembly of the Knights of Labor of America, Eleventh Regular Session Held at Minneapolis, Minnesota, Oct. 4–9, 1887,* 1494, Reel 67, PHP; *Knights of Labor,* July 24, 1886.

26. *Proceedings of the General Assembly Held at Minneapolis,* 1480 (quote). This account of the packinghouse strike is based on published letters in ibid., 1477–99; *Chicago Tribune,* Oct.–Nov. 1886; and *Knights of Labor,* Jan. 8, 1887. See also Louise Carroll Wade, *Chicago's Pride: The Stockyards, Packingtown, and Environs in the Nineteenth Century* (Urbana: University of Illinois Press, 1987), 218–63.

27. *Knights of Labor,* Nov. 13, 1886; *Chicago Daily News,* Nov. 15, 1886; Howard Barton Myers, "The Policing of Labor Disputes in Chicago: A Case Study" (Ph.D. diss., University of Chicago, 1929), 170, 183.

28. At a Trades and Labor Assembly meeting Powderly's order won support from trade unionists—presumably more experienced in the hazards of striking—but not Knights. *Chicago Tribune,* Nov. 14, 1886. See also Powderly to P. T. Caldwell, Dec. 19, 1886, in *Proceedings of the General Assembly Held at Minneapolis,* 170, 183.

29. *Knights of Labor,* Nov. 13, 1886, Nov. 20, 1886, Nov. 27, 1886; *Labor Enquirer,* June 4, 1887.

30. Rodgers to Powderly, Nov. 25, 1886, PHP.

31. *Knights of Labor,* Nov. 20, 1886.

32. Powderly to George Rodgers, Dec. 18, 1886, Reel 67, PHP; *Knights of Labor,* Dec. 30, 1886; *Chicago Tribune,* Jan. 5, 1887; Griffiths to Powderly, Dec. 16, 1886, Reel 67, PHP.

33. *Chicago Tribune,* June 23, 1887; *Knights of Labor,* Dec. 4, 1886; Dec. 30, 1886 (Stewart quote); Stewart to Lloyd, Sept. 15, 1884, Ethelbert Stewart Papers (microfilm), Southern Historical Collection, University of North Carolina (hereafter BSP); Lloyd to Stewart, Dec. 23, 1886, BSP; undated biographical clipping, BSP.

34. *Labor Enquirer,* Feb. 23, 1887; Joseph R. Buchanan, *Story of a Labor Agitator* (New York: Outlook, 1903), 254–344.

35. *Chicago Tribune,* Dec. 19, 1886 (Foley quote), Jan. 6, 1887 ("radical" quote); *Chicago Daily News,* Dec. 24, 1886 (Griffiths quote).

36. *Chicago Tribune,* Jan. 3, 1887, Jan. 4, 1887.

37. Ibid., Apr. 4, 1887; *Knights of Labor,* Feb. 12, 1887. Information on the dates when locals joined the brotherhood is available from the United Brotherhood of Carpenters and Joiners of America, Washington, D.C.

38. *Chicago Tribune,* Jan. 21, 1887, Feb. 20, 1887 (quote); Griffiths to Powderly, Dec. 6, 1887, Dec. 16, 1886, Reel 18, PHP; Mrs. George Rodgers to Powderly, Nov. 25, 1885, Reel 18, PHP.

39. *Chicago Tribune,* Apr. 2, 1887 (quote); Powers to Powderly, Oct. 24, 1886, Reel 18, PHP.

40. *Knights of Labor,* Sept. 24, 1887.

41. This was the argument, among others, of Carter Harrison, ibid., Mar. 5, 1887.

42. *ULP Executive Committee Minutes,* Nov. 26, 1886, Dec. 2, 1886, Dec. 9, 1886, Reel 7, Thomas J. Morgan Papers (microfilm), Illinois Historical Survey, Springfield; *Chicago Tribune,* Dec. 7, 1886.

43. For the ULP program, see *Knights of Labor,* Nov. 27, 1886; *Chicago Tribune,* Jan. 7, 1887, Jan. 8, 1887; and Richard L. McCormick, "The Discovery That Business Corrupts Politics: A Reappraisal of the Origins of Progressivism," *American Historical Review* 85 (Apr. 1981): 247–74.

44. *Labor Enquirer,* Mar. 2, 1887.

45. Nationality of candidates based on biographical data in *Chicago Tribune,* Feb. 27, 1887, Mar. 2, 1887 (quote).

46. *Knights of Labor,* Mar. 26, 1887.

47. *Chicago Tribune,* Mar. 14, 1887, Apr. 2, 1887.

48. Ibid., Apr. 6, 1887.

49. A multiple regression analysis of the vote, with the ULP vote as the independent variable, shows an increase in the regression coefficient of percentage foreign-born from 0.45 in 1886 to 0.53 in 1887 (significance = 0.00).

50. To test the relationship between ethnicity and turnout, precincts with a 50 percent ULP majority were selected, and multiple regression analysis was per-

formed with percent Irish, percent German, and percent native-born as independent variables. The only significant coefficient was a negative one of 0.32 for the Irish. In other words, a 1.00 percent increase in the number of Irish registered voters yielded a 0.32 percent decrease in turnout in strong ULP wards. This analysis was confirmed in an editorial in the *Chicago Tribune,* Apr. 10, 1887.

51. *Labor Enquirer,* Apr. 30, 1887; *Chicago Tribune,* Apr. 6, 1887 (quote).

52. *Knights of Labor,* Apr. 9, 1887 (Stewart quotes through "trade unions should . . ."), Apr. 23, 1887 ("class legislation" quote). See also editorial Dec. 4, 1886.

53. *Chicago Tribune,* Nov. 29, 1887.

54. On Gleason's Free Lunch party, see *Chicago Tribune,* Sept. 11, 1887, Oct. 23, 1887; on the ULP, see ibid., Apr. 23, 1887.

55. Montgomery quote from discussions with author; Fink, *Workingmen's Democracy,* 205. For similar conditions in San Francisco, see Michael Kazin, *Barons of Labor: The San Francisco Building Trades and Union Power in the Progressive Era* (Urbana: University of Illinois Press, 1987).

56. *Labor Enquirer,* Apr. 14, 1887.

57. Stewart to Lloyd, Apr. 15, 1887, Reel 1, Henry Demarest Lloyd Papers (microfilm), Wisconsin State Historical Society, Madison. See also Joseph R. Buchanan editorial, *Labor Enquirer,* Feb. 23, 1887.

CHAPTER 10

The Decline of the Knights and the Rise of the Trade Unions, 1887–89

In Chicago, as in other industrial cities in the United States and Canada, the failure of important strikes undertaken by the Knights of Labor, the disappointing defeat of an independent labor ticket, and the consequent crushing of millennial expectations and hopes precipitated an epochal transition in American labor history from the Knights of Labor to the American Federation of Labor (AFL). Until fairly recently this transition has been interpreted as the defeat of a utopian, antimodern, or at best unrealistic political strategy in which labor viewed itself as part of the "producer" strata and sought to escape wage labor and the stranglehold of monopolists by attaining economic independence through individual property ownership. Unlike the Knights, unionists adopted an antipolitical or voluntarist strategy in which trade unions realistically accepted wage labor and large-scale business organization and instead sought to maximize short-term gains by focusing on strikes.[1]

In the past two decades this interpretation has been successfully challenged and largely revised by the scholarship of "the new labor history." In the new accounts—taking the form of local case studies—the Knights of Labor was a far more diverse, flexible, and potentially viable organization than previous historians seem to have been aware of in their national studies. The new historians view the Knights and its ideology of labor republicanism as an integral part of the great labor upheaval of the 1880s and as a legitimate expression of labor's democratic and class aspirations. The defeat of this broad class movement was simultaneously the defeat of the Knights.[2]

The organizational and ideological history offered in this chapter builds on this new scholarship while appropriating elements of the old. In Chicago the conflict between labor republicanism or producerism and the new trade unionism was real, but it was evident as much in battles *within* the Knights as in the rivalry between the Knights and the AFL. Despite the Knights' limitations, considerable accommodation of local unions was possible within its structure and in special bodies that united diverse labor tendencies. The fatal decline of the Knights was not because of its utopianism or inflexibility but because of debilitating internal dissension compounded by crippling strike defeats in those sectors of the economy most vulnerable to employers' countermobilization.

Labor Republicanism and Trade Unionism

The interpretation that associates the Knights of Labor with an antimonopolistic politics incompatible with the trade unionism of skilled workers is based heavily on events in New York City. In that city a motley assemblage of factions, known as the Home Club, took control of District Assembly 49 and adopted policies opposed to the methods and aims of trade unions. In 1886 they instigated a jurisdictional battle between cigarmakers in the Knights and cigarmakers in the Cigar Makers International Union (CMIU) that soon spilled over into a bitter national struggle between Terence Powderly, then enmeshed in a secret alliance with the Home Club, and Samuel Gompers, representing both the CMIU and the AFL. In Chicago, however, the decline of the Knights had little to do with its opposition to trade unionism per se. As an 1882 DA 24 internal report put it, "It will be conceded by all that the Order is a trades union to all intents and purposes, and in its early days in this city it was fostered, maintained, and kept alive solely and entirely by trade unionists." By the end of 1886 the Knights had come under the control of socialist and allied forces, which, far from being anti–trade union, were more militant than most unionists and dedicated to extending labor organization into the city's large-scale factories.[3]

An understanding of the decline of the Knights in Chicago and the subsequent opposition of trade unionists must therefore focus on events occurring *within* the order, not between the order and rival trade unions. Indeed, it was the order's very attempt to embrace, incorporate, and regulate the struggles associated with the great upheaval that ultimately led to its downfall in Chicago.

The Knights of Labor as an organization is difficult to characterize precisely. At any one time it was highly diverse socially and eclectic ideologically, and over time its politics and makeup changed radically. Nonetheless, what may be called a producers' republican paradigm was embraced by most Knights leaders and provided an element of continuity and stability in the organization. The philosophical premise of this paradigm was a natural rights theory of ethical justice, given substance by a political economy in which producers ensured control of the fruits of their labor through ownership of property, either individually or associationally, and disposed of that property in a market governed by the principle of freedom of contract. The social dependence exemplified by wage labor and the social parasitism characterized by the growing disparities in wealth were anomalies in the producers' republican paradigm, and radicals believed that a thorough reconstruction of the political economy on first principles was necessary to remove these aberrations. That task is what Henry George, Alexander Campbell, and other greenbackers and the anarchists and other republican socialists, like many in the Knights of Labor, had in common.

Undertaking this reconstruction, however, forced producer radicals into mental contortions. A good example of how the Knights struggled mightily to accommodate natural rights premises and conclusions to contradictory new social experiences was their attitude toward strikes and boycotts. Because labor republicans believed that in a just political economy "every man who works is a laborer and every man who has saved something is a capitalist," as one writer in the *Knights of Labor* put it, there was "no natural conflict" between labor and capital. Only "combined capital" needed to "be restrained by combined labor." Another writer justified strikes by saying that "a right to strike" existed to resist tyranny and was necessary under the circumstances, but "the necessity should never exist; is itself a wrong, a crime, and rights based upon wrongs are best defended when destroyed by the destruction of the wrong upon which they are based." While many Knights reluctantly defended particular strikes, they always advocated arbitration and emphasized measures—both voluntary and political—of bringing about the abolition of the wage system that made strikes a necessity.[4]

As the Knights struggled to make sense of strikes within the framework of labor republicanism, they confronted another contradiction. Labor republicans commonly believed that strikes could bring no lasting improvement in wages or, in the rare cases that did, were "mere palliatives" that left the underlying injustices of the wage system untouched. As Bert Stewart put it, wages under a "competitive wage system" would "drop to the point of lowest possible sustenance." Such a belief was paralleled by the German Lassallean socialist belief that wages were subject to an "iron law" that kept them to a minimum and Henry George's belief that trade unions could do little or nothing to raise wages. Trade unionists, however, believed that thorough organization and strikes, vigorously but prudently pursued, could permanently raise workers accustomed "standards of life" and hence wages. More important, the thousands of workers who joined the Knights during the great upheaval shared the expectation that working conditions could be improved. The Bureau of Labor Statistics found that about the same percentage of Knights assemblies resorted to striking in 1886 as did trade unions, though the trade unions struck more frequently.[5]

Because the Knights could never satisfactorily resolve these dilemmas, they emphasized producer cooperation as an alternative to both strikes and wage labor. Cooperatives were formed beginning in the fall of 1886 and especially in 1887 by the clothing cutters, female garment workers, soapmakers, cigarmakers, brickyard workers, boot and shoemakers, and packinghouse workers, all encouraged by the Knights of Labor. The idea of a society based on cooperatives, known then as the "cooperative commonwealth," has been termed here *republican socialism.* The cooperative commonwealth was an attempt to abolish and socialize personal property within the confines of existing property laws and market relations—in order to sustain and revivify the Republic.

According to a draft DA 24 program in 1884, "The political rights of a people are not more sacred than their economic rights, and to prevent a class from possessing all the material advantages of progressive civilization is as much an act of tyranny as to prevent them from exercising their right of self-government. . . . Men will sacrifice their liberties for their lives and those who control the industries of people can and do control their votes." This fairly standard labor republican preamble was followed by a synthesis of trade unionism and producer cooperation. Workers' "liberty" under the wage system, said the draft, could be obtained only by "solidarity of the workers," leading to "higher wages, and better opportunities of work [until] wages shall represent the whole earnings and not the bare necessities of living of the laborer, thus taking profit upon labor out of existence and making cooperation or self-employed labor the logical step from wage-slavery to free labor." This formulation, combining an acceptance of trade unionism, and by implication strikes for higher wages, with the ideal of the harmony of labor and capital based on the right of self-employment by associated labor, was typical of the thinking of local Knights in the mid-1880s.[6]

As these examples suggest, the labor republican paradigm was being stretched to its limits by Knights leaders trying to accommodate the social innovations of workers in the great upheaval. It was only a matter of time before a paradigm shift or revolution in worldview occurred, in which a new framework constructed by new postulates would supersede the old, a framework directly responsive to what were considered anomalies in the old paradigm. Such a shift was described by Thorstein Veblen at the turn of the century, when he wrote of the decline of the "metaphysic" or "dogma" of "natural liberty" among workers that justified the ownership of property and the emergence of an "iconoclastic" and "matter of fact" habit of mind inculcated by the discipline of the machine process. The new way of thinking—which in philosophical terms translated into evolutionary positivism—and the emerging class culture that nurtured it entailed the pragmatic acceptance of large-scale industrial organization, trade unions, strikes, and boycotts, and the regulation of the marketplace by groups (e.g., corporations and unions) rather than individuals. It also treated cavalierly and with short shrift the property rights of employers, the equity dictums of courts, and the idealism and moral universality of labor republicanism.[7]

A rival paradigm or discourse based on the habit of mind described by Veblen did not emerge among unionists until the "pure and simple" trade unionist philosophy—espoused most prominently by Samuel Gompers—became prevalent in the 1890s. Virtually no one in the labor movement at this time suggested that "monopolies" could be accepted as the basis of a new political economy.[8] The growing trade union exasperation and often outright opposition to the Knights therefore did not result in the outright rejection of labor republicanism. Rather, it was manifested in criticisms of the Knights' handling of strikes.

The Knights and the Questions of Trade Autonomy and Socialism

In the same way that the Knights sought awkwardly and not always successfully to stretch its natural rights paradigm to incorporate ideas of trade union action, local Knights leaders tried to reshape the order's organizational policies to accommodate the strike behavior of their trade local assemblies. The major issue in Chicago was not *exclusive jurisdiction* (i.e., the principle of one union per trade), which led to the irremediable rift between the Knights and the CMIU and other trade unions in New York. Instead, the major issue of contention in Chicago was *trade autonomy* (i.e., the struggle of trade locals to be free from the dictates of labor officials not from their own trade). As will be seen, even on this issue many Knights leaders sought, not without success, to reconcile the order's integrity with the needs of trade unions.

The question of trade autonomy resounded throughout the local labor movement in 1886–87. In December 1886 Ed Mulroney, the Trades and Labor Assembly's delegate to the first convention of the AFL, explained his objection to the Knights: "When I have trouble as a bricklayer, I don't want a butcher, a shoemaker, and blacksmith, who do not know anything more about bricklaying than a dog does about his sidepocket for a bone, to act upon any trouble that my union becomes involved in."[9] The theme was reiterated in February 1887 by a CMIU leader to explain why workers in his union were leaving the Knights: "The Cigarmakers Union does not believe in allowing men outside of its trade, politicians, etc. to dictate what it shall do." Abraham Bisno, leader of the garment workers, came to the same conclusion in his *Autobiography* when he recalled how the Knights had obliged garment workers to negotiate with their employers through a committee appointed by its district assembly.[10]

Chicago Knights responded to these complaints with two arguments. They reiterated their belief that strikes were ultimately futile and that only a policy that would lead to the abolition of the wage system would meet the needs of workers. Concomitantly, they argued that technological changes had leveled skill distinctions in the work process and that a unified policy for the entire working class must replace the distinct policies of each trade. As the *Knights of Labor* put it, "The trade union idea of each business for itself must give way to the idea that 'an injury to one is an injury to all.'" But there were also organizational imperatives behind the Knights' attempt to subordinate the autonomy of different trades. With the enormous growth of the Knights, its leaders had to be responsible to a broad constituency that included substantial numbers of newly organized unskilled and semiskilled workers, whose enthusiasm for striking threatened to ensnare the Knights in a host of unwinnable conflicts while diverting it from its most important goal: confronting the wage system as a whole. As a result, the Knights under Powderly, Griffiths, and other old-time leaders in Chicago adopted a cautious strike policy for all its membership, thus restraining the more winnable struggles of the skilled workers and giving the order a reputation for failure in strikes.

But the Knights' belief that technology was about to level all skill distinctions and that the strikes of skilled craftworkers were futile was overdrawn. Despite the advent of skill-diluting machinery and labor-saving processes in the 1880s, such skilled workers as machinists, garment cutters, butchers, and iron molders still played a strategic role in production. Moreover, as old skills were displaced by new processes, new skilled positions were constantly created.[11] Since many skilled workers faced small-scale employers with whom it was possible to negotiate, they were often quite capable of winning strikes and improving working conditions without joining the Knights' comprehensive organization or adhering to its policy of restraining strikes in the interests of solidarity.

The Knights themselves implicitly recognized this reality by acquiescing to the craft organization of workers in large-scale industries. Skilled packinghouse workers were thus organized in twelve different assemblies of skilled and semiskilled workers. The clothing cutters organized separately from the sweated garment workers. Organized McCormick's Reaper workers were led by skilled patternmakers, blacksmiths, and iron molders in the United Metal Workers Union, while laborers joined the Knights. Despite the district assembly's ultimate control over strikes, success still depended on withdrawing skilled labor. Notwithstanding its rhetoric of amalgamation and solidarity, the Knights represented a revision, not an outright rejection, of the policy of the craft unionism. Laborers' assemblies were in practice still auxiliaries of craft assemblies. Only when skilled workers were pushed to the margins of production by mass production methods—which were not in wide use until the twentieth century—could industrial unions emerge on a large scale.[12]

The Knights' ambivalence on the question of skill dilution and its inability to give skilled, organized workers the trade autonomy they desired was evident in the dispute between the Knights and the trade unions in the carpentry trade, one of the pivotal battles in deciding the order's fate in Chicago. By the end of 1886 the Knights claimed between five and six thousand carpenters, a clear majority in the trade. In the spring of 1887 the carpenters decided to renew their struggle to win the eight-hour day. This time they founded the United Carpenters Council (UCC), a body more centralized than the old United Carpenters Committee that had led the 1886 strike.[13]

In April 1887 the UCC struck Chicago's carpenter contractors for the eight-hour day, a standard minimum wage, a large wage increase, and union recognition in the form of the closed shop. On advice from the *Labor Enquirer*'s Joseph Buchanan, the UCC decided to sign an agreement with the more numerous smaller contractors to get union members back to work and thus pressure the downtown millwork contractors. The strike—now focused on the larger contractors—dragged into the summer and was complicated by an open-shop lockout. As financial pressures mounted, the carpenters from both the Knights and the Brotherhood of Carpenters and Joiners of America appealed to their respective central bodies for strike funds. In line with their policy of minimizing strikes, the Knights' general executive board refused to appropriate any funds, while the Brotherhood of Carpenters and Joiners did so. In a letter to the Knights the organizer Ira Aylesworth predicted that denying strike funds to Knights carpenters would result in "the discouragement of our members and the absorption of the nine carpenter assemblies in that city by outside organizations." Meanwhile, the UCC, together with other building trades, had defeated the employers' open-shop movement and had won widespread adherence to the eight-hour day, though a compensatory wage increase and union recognition remained elusive. Rank-and-file carpenters credited the victory to the Brotherhood of Carpenters and Joiners, not the Knights, who were reputed to oppose the eight-hour demand.[14]

By the end of the year Aylesworth's prediction had come true. Carpenters LA 6570, the largest and most influential of the Knights assemblies, had decreased from 500 in January 1887 to 180 at the end of the year, and the German carpenters' assembly had lapsed. In mid-December a local Knights leader admitted, "A year ago the Knights and the carpenters Brotherhood were upon an equal footing as far as members were concerned. The carpenters Brotherhood have now swallowed the Knights and have more than doubled their membership. Nothing succeeds like success and nothing fails like failure."[15] In explaining the swift decline of the Knights among the carpenters, James Brennock, a leader of the Brotherhood of Carpenters and Joiners and a founder of the UCC, pinpointed the same reason that Bisno, Mulroney, and many other unionists had posited: "The district assembly did not handle [trade matters] as they ought to or perhaps could not handle them intelligently, because . . . every kind of trade and calling was in there."[16]

Yet the experience of the carpenters offers important evidence that despite the inherent weaknesses of the Knights the interests of the order and the trade unions could have been rendered compatible. The UCC's victory in 1887 proved that even though the treaty failed to take hold on the national level, Knights assemblies and the trade unions could cooperate on the local level in a consolidated organization. Indeed, the UCC would continue to coordinate union affairs in Chicago until its dissolution in 1894; the brotherhood's Chicago District Council of Carpenters played almost no policymaking role in local affairs. At least through the fall of 1887, the UCC's policy of peaceful coexistence represented a viable alternative to the idea of inevitable war between the Knights and the unions and to the emerging Gompers policy of exclusive jurisdiction of one union in each trade and industry.

The Knights' relations with trade unions during strikes was therefore not enough to explain a decline in the local order that a *Chicago Tribune* reporter wrote "was rapidly assuming the proportions of a stampede." What would ultimately convince many local labor activists and leaders to give up on the Knights was a set of collateral political issues that divided pro–trade union socialists and radicals from pro-Powderly Knights.[17]

On the heels of the Haymarket affair and the Knights' subsequent entrance into local politics, thousands of socialists and former anarchists had joined local assemblies of the Knights because they thought they could be used as a vehicle to save their indicted leaders and create a viable labor party. The legitimacy of the socialists was further enhanced by outrage at the palpable injustice of the anarchist trial and the dismay at Powderly for opposing the clemency campaign; the successful socialist leadership in the ULP fall campaign of 1886; and the disgrace of the existing Griffiths-Rodgers leadership in being associated with Powderly during the packinghouse strike. During the intense and controversial ULP campaign in early 1887 the socialists, as the faction most opposed to fusion, won even more prestige in the local labor movement. Under Bert Stewart the *Knights of Labor* had become friendly to the socialists. In the same vein DA 57's Master Workman Matthew J. Butler viewed the socialists as allies against Powderly. Joseph R. Buchanan's *Labor Enquirer* went even further in openly espousing socialist politics.

Both labor papers, as well as such leaders as Butler, reflected local Knights' dislike of Powderly, not only for his meddling in the stockyards strike but also for his circular ruling against local Knights' funding of the anarchist defense and for undermining the ULP campaign with his circular forbidding discussion of politics in the order. "In no city in the United States," commented a reporter, "is T. V. Powderly so much disliked and even despised as in Chicago." Even after Stewart had been replaced as editor by the more conservative George Detwiler, the *Knights of Labor* blamed Powderly for "coquetting with the enemy" and called him "the George McClellan of the labor movement."[18]

Leadership by the socialists and radicals offered the best hope that the local order could make the changes necessary to accommodate the specific needs of trade locals, including the energetic prosecution of strikes. Three of these men were critical in attempting to bridge the gap between trade unions and the order: Charles F. Seib, George Schilling, and Joseph R. Buchanan. Seib, a cigarmaker elected secretary of DA 24 in December 1886, was an outspoken radical with open anarchist sympathies. He was also a member of the CMIU and the Knights cigarmakers' LA 3079. The *Knights of Labor* credited Seib with "organizing more assemblies than all other organizers in Illinois put together."[19] George Schilling, a longtime local Knights leader, a supporter of the single tax, an anarcho-syndicalist, and a Democrat, had boosted his popularity through his handling of the packinghouse strike. While serving on DA 24's executive board, he had led the anarchist defense drive in 1887 and became a leader of the Powderly opposition. Though his staunch advocacy of producer cooperation, the single tax, and other reforms made him a Knight rather than a trade unionist, Schilling did not see such reform as excluding trade unionism. In 1888 as DA 24's master workman, he wrote a passionate letter to Powderly defending strikes.[20]

Joseph Buchanan, the well-liked editor, member of the Knights' general executive board, and SLP member, was another unwavering supporter of trade organization both within and outside the Knights. From his arrival in

Chicago in February 1887, the self-proclaimed "rip-roarer from the Rockies" had sided with the cigarmakers against Powderly and had run ads for their label in his paper. At the start of the carpenters' strike in 1887 Buchanan was chosen by Peter J. McGuire, the general secretary of the Brotherhood of Carpenters and Joiners of America and a member of the AFL's executive board, as his personal representative to negotiate with the contractors on behalf of the UCC. Later in the year Buchanan pioneered an attempt to form a national union composed of building trades councils, a venture that ultimately failed because of rivalry with the AFL but demonstrated his ability to reconcile craft organization with the ideals of the Knights.[21]

Because of the leadership of such men as Buchanan, Seib, and Schilling, there was no discernible support in Chicago for the New York City Home Club, which fomented the Knights' bitter jurisdictional battle with the trade unions. Throughout 1887 Knights leaders in Chicago unambiguously favored trade locals. In early 1887 DA 24 therefore agreed to a request from trades assemblies to prevent its members from transferring into mixed assemblies with lower dues and to forbid trades assemblies from turning themselves into mixed assemblies.[22]

But the ability of local Knights leaders to accommodate trade interests became more difficult as the influence of the radicals and socialists grew and as pro-Powderly forces in the Knights felt their accustomed dominance slipping from their grasp. The battle intensified as defenders of the anarchists in the Knights grew desperate to secure support for the clemency drive. Meanwhile, the painful defeat of the Henry George mayoral campaign in New York led the shaky unity among socialists, single-taxers, and trade unionists to unravel in 1887. This degeneration of "united labor" was repeated in Chicago's ULP. Both factions felt a sense of climax and finality about the fall 1887 Knights convention in Minneapolis.

On the eve of the convention there appeared to be a tidal wave of opposition to Powderly nationally and locally. In August socialists won an important victory in DA 24's delegate election. Of the seven delegates whose views were made known to the press all were anti-Powderly, six were protrade unionists, and five were socialists or prosocialist. Using its administrative powers, the Powderly camp struck back. On the first day of October fifty-one local assemblies in Chicago were suspended for nonpayment of dues and hence became ineligible to send delegates to the convention. Seib and Schilling each won long floor fights to be seated, but the influential Buchanan was less fortunate. After a raucous two-day battle the convention refused to seat him. Powderly then shored up his support among middle-of-the-road delegates by accusing his critics of being anarchist sympathizers. Powderly did rescind his order expelling CMIU members, and the general assembly did authorize greater autonomy for national trade district assemblies and encouraged the granting of charters to them, but without a change in leadership these conciliatory gestures could not reverse the general impression that the order was irremediably hostile to trade unions.[23]

Immediately following the convention thirty-five delegates from thirteen states, including Schilling, Seib, and Robert Nelson, met in Buchanan's office to form a provisional committee of opposition to Powderly. Its first circular espoused sovereignty of the trades and district assemblies, decentralization, open and free discussion in the order, and commitment to electoral action by the Knights. But as Buchanan later admitted the formation of "the provisionals" or "the kickers" was a tactical mistake. Two weeks later a socialist slate headed by George Schilling and including the *Alarm*'s editor, Dyer Lum, was elected to lead DA 24, further tightening the hold of the left and seeming to render the secession unnecessary. Meanwhile, the publicity generated by the kickers accelerated the exodus of potential supporters from the local order. By the end of 1887 the provisional committee was moribund, and both Seib and Buchanan had quit the order, leaving Schilling in charge but with a dwindling base of support.[24]

Schilling did little to dampen the conflict with the trade unions or to stem the Knights' decline. Following his installation as master workman, Schilling faced a revival of the cigarmakers' jurisdictional dispute when a Knights cooperative cigarmaking shop dropped the CMIU label in favor of the Knights label, precipitating a CMIU boycott of the cooperative's cigars and a strike of its shop. When the Trades and Labor Assembly endorsed this action, Schilling recalled the DA's delegates.[25]

At the same time, the decision of the Minneapolis convention to accelerate the formation of national trade district assemblies had several unintended deleterious effects. In 1888 the remaining carpenter, clothing cutter, machinery constructor, and packinghouse assemblies left DA 24 and DA 57 and reaffiliated with national trade district assemblies of their trade. This exacerbated tensions with existing national unions, which by now were wedded to the principle of exclusive jurisdiction as well as trade autonomy. It also significantly reduced the organizational strength of the Knights in Chicago. By April 1888 membership in the two district assemblies was down to approximately 20 percent of what it had been in 1886, and by the end of the year twenty-four of the twenty-eight mixed assemblies established in 1886 had gone out of existence. In July 1888 the *Chicago Tribune* reported that DA 24 was down to three thousand members, and DA 57 was virtually lifeless.[26]

In October 1888 another major splinter movement hit the order nationally when the charismatic Thomas Barry was expelled by the general executive board and decided to form the rival Brotherhood of United Labor (BUL).

Chicago, as the center of anti-Powderly sentiment, greeted the BUL enthusiastically. By June 1889 the BUL surfaced in the South Side under the wing of ex-DA 57 leaders, thus filling the vacuum left by the disintegration of the old DA 57. The BUL was particularly strong among packinghouse workers, coopers, and waiters.[27]

The Knights, however, were not devoid of influence in the city's labor movement. In September 1888 the order mustered over five thousand marchers in a Labor Day parade, and in October Schilling led the most important strike of the year, a walkout of streetcar workers. The Knights also continued to serve as the vehicle for organizing women workers. According to Elizabeth Rodgers, there were at least nine exclusively or largely female local assemblies, along with nine trade unions of women in 1888; according to Gruenhut they enrolled five thousand members. One of them, Annie Fitzgerald, who joined the mattress makers that year, would eventually rise to the post of DA 24's master workman. The Knights also continued their earlier campaign, in alliance with Protestant ministers, to shorten the hours of retail clerks. Schilling, and his ally John Beard, in DA 57, held power until membership reached such a low ebb that the Griffiths-Rodgers faction regained control in August 1889.[28]

Despite the Knights' dispute with the trade unions over the principle and practice of trade autonomy, the sharp decline of the Knights of Labor after Haymarket cannot be easily explained. Local Knights leaders had attempted with some success to modify the order's organizational structure and policies to enlarge the sphere of action of trade locals and trade districts. The formation of the UCC and like attempts were examples of what might have been accomplished had the Knights remained viable.[29]

Moreover, neither side wished a war to the death. Between 1886 and 1888 what competed were two models of *cooperation* between labor organizations. Based on the experience of the cigarmakers who had seen a rival organization undercut wages during strikes, trade unionists embraced the ideal of exclusive jurisdiction. These unionists were not hostile to the ideals of the Knights, as evidenced by the membership of trade union officials in Knights assemblies. Rather, they wanted to reduce the Knights to the status of an educational society and perhaps a kind of catch-basin or general union—another common metaphor was nursery—for organizing unskilled workers before they were parcelled out to existing unions.

The Knights of Labor model of the relationship was different. The Knights saw themselves and the trade unions as coexisting in the task of organizing workers and engaging in collective bargaining. The December 1886 treaty the Knights proposed to the AFL contemplated a mutual exchange of working cards and a cooperative stance in bargaining with employers. The

Knights' approach was an attempt to reproduce the British case, in which multiple unions cooperated through councils in a single trade or industry.[30]

In the end neither model won. Epochal defeats in the southwest railroad and stockyards strikes in 1886, internal squabbling in public, and the loss of faith in the Powderly administration undermined the confidence of rank-and-file workers in the order for trade union or educational purposes. With so few workers looking to the Knights for leadership all attempts to adapt creatively or cooperate with the unions were doomed. But there was another reason, just as important, to explain why Chicago workers ceased to look to the Knights of Labor. The Knights had organized disproportionately in large-scale industry and in places where technological changes had undermined the indispensability of many skilled workers. Yet it was precisely there that employer hostility to labor organization of any sort was most intense and effective. After Haymarket a successful employers' counterattack in these sectors made the Knights' attempt to adapt to new circumstances almost impossible.[31]

Labor's Retreat and Stabilization, 1887–89

The period from late 1886 through 1889 was one of employers' counterattack and decline for most of the labor movement, and the Knights bore the brunt. It would be a mistake, however, to view the period as one of unmitigated labor defeat, for in the late 1880s trade unionism attained a measure of employer acceptance in several industries. But that rapprochement occurred not in industries with national competition but in those whose firms competed in local and regional markets.

The employers' attempt to turn back the gains of the labor movement actually began with the failed strike by the Knights against Jay Gould's southwest railroad system in March through May 1886. This strike triggered the sudden growth of law and order leagues in small midwestern railroad towns. During and after the eight-hour strikes the employers movement broadened into, in the words of the historian Clarence Bonnett, "a tidal wave of formation of employers associations." As the *Chicago Tribune* put it at the time, "The Knights of Labor are responsible for the appearance on the field of the Knights of Capital."[32]

Those who joined the new associations were generally those who sold in a national market and feared that strong unions and eight-hour workdays in only one city would price them out of the market. Between late March and mid-May 1886 local employers formed branches of the Furniture Manufacturers Association, the Stove Manufacturers Association, the Association of

Manufacturers in Metal, and the Western Boot and Shoe Manufacturers. On July 28 several hundred Chicago manufacturers joined the midwestern law and order movement with the founding of the Chicago Council No. 1 of the Conservators League of America. This does not count the many temporary associations, such as the one the packinghouse employers formed in the fall of 1886.[33]

Of all the Chicago unions those in the local building trades market had been least affected by the post-Haymarket reaction. In spring 1887 the largest construction union, the carpenters' union, was poised on the brink of winning the eight-hour day. In its upcoming struggle it was widely viewed as a surrogate for the entire labor movement. As the largest union in the city, it had sent the single largest number of delegates to the United Labor party convention of 1886. By the end of the year William Kliver, leader of the carpenters, headed up the Trades and Labor Assembly, while another, James Brennock, founded the Building Trades Council.[34] On the eve of the carpenters' strike employers representing builders' exchanges in twenty-six cities gathered in Chicago to form the first national organization of construction employers, the National Association of Builders (NAB). In the NAB's declaration of principles the affirmation of "absolute personal independence of the individual to work or not to work, to employ or not to employ" was number one. On this fundamental open-shop principle, which it considered the basis of "our whole social fabric," the NAB rejected all arbitration.[35]

Controversy centered on the new institution of "the walking delegate." Later known as the business agent, the walking delegate collected dues, kept the union's books, and, most important, enforced the union's wages, hours, and working rules, including the rule that no union worker could work with a nonunion worker at the widely scattered building sites throughout the union's jurisdiction. Having the absolute power to fine either journeymen or employer or as a last resort call the workers off the job, the business agent symbolized union power over the workplace in a kind of naked, almost brutal, fashion that had few parallels in other trades or industries. The *Chicago Tribune* spoke for many employers when it observed that after the strikes and boycotts of 1886 contractors feared "that unless active measures were taken, business would be ruined and the triumph of the walking delegate would be complete."[36]

The carpenters' strike for the eight-hour day and union recognition began on April 1, 1887. Within three weeks the union had concluded an agreement with the smaller and more vulnerable contractors. Then in May the bricklayers struck too. Faced with what they deemed a frivolous demand of changing the payday to Saturday, the conflict soon assumed the character of an employers' "crusade." The mason contractors announced a lockout, joined the NAB, and declared that the "walking delegate must go." Other construction employers rushed to the aid of the mason contractors. By the end of May thirty thousand building trades workers had been locked out, and contractors had begun advertising for workers in other cities. Adding backbone to the lockout, material manufacturers pledged not to supply those who violated the lockout. Many contractors signed the NAB pledge to abjure any relations with unions in the future.[37]

By the end of June, however, both sides had pulled back from a war to the finish. New leadership in the bricklayers' union withdrew the Saturday payday demand and led the union into the Building Trades Council. Even before this mason contractors realized that their would-be crusade had fallen flat. Most building trades workers found work with small contractors or with makeshift union-run cooperatives. Opinion leaders in the clergy and the press gave only lukewarm support to the lockout since the unions now stood for the publicly approved principle of arbitration. Finally, the strike was welding together the diverse unions in solidarity action on many worksites in the city.[38]

In early July the bricklayers and master masons accepted arbitration by Judge Murray F. Tuley, who threw out the masons' open-shop principles and engineered a precedent-setting system of arbitration in which a joint committee of representatives of the union and the employers would decide all disputed issues. The walking delegates could not call strikes while the committee was in session. Unlike earlier Knights arbitration, Tuley's solution was closer to mediation between two well-organized parties and hence approximated the modern trade agreement. The carpenters' strike still dragged on, but by the end of the year the UCC could claim substantial victory on the eight-hour-day issue. Though union recognition eluded it, the UCC was stronger than ever.[39]

The contrast between the outcomes of the lockout in the packinghouses in 1886 and in the building trades in 1887 is instructive for understanding the emerging shape of the labor movement. Both were initiated by employers associations seeking to nip in the bud the drive for union organization led by skilled craftworkers. The packinghouse workers faced a tiny number of powerful industrial magnates who sold products in a competitive national market and possessed impressive resources of resistance. The defeat of the packinghouse workers had a major effect in undermining the Knights of Labor. The building trades lockout occurred in an industry still dominated by small to medium-scale firms producing for a local market, and most firms possessed limited resources of resistance. The defeat of the open shop under these circumstances not only helped stabilize the labor movement in its decline but also pointed it in new directions.

In another important strike in 1887 a local union confronted an open-shop campaign, and its result reinforced the trend deriving from the building trades conflict. The printing trade was divided into two labor markets, newspaper printers and book and job printers. Because profits for newspapers depended more on advertising than on labor costs and because strikes were extremely costly, especially in the midst of circulation wars, newspapers had considerably less incentive to oppose unionization than did book and job printers. Both sectors of the industry, however, were becoming mechanized with the introduction of the Linotype machine, thus threatening, without displacing, skilled labor. This in turn provided an incentive for all typographers to unite behind the shorter-hours movement. In 1886 the Chicago Typographical Union No. 16 with its 1,300 mostly skilled members, two-thirds of whom worked in book and job printing, had committed itself in principle to the eight-hour workday. In 1887 it decided to strike for the nine-hour day with no reduction in pay. Meanwhile, the book and job employers organized themselves into the Chicago Typothetae, which in October 1887, founded the United Typothetae of America, a militant antiunion, open-shop organization.[40]

The strike, which began November 1, involved 415 compositors and 58 apprentices in thirty-five offices doing most of the printing in the city. On November 14 the Typothetae announced the open shop, thus transforming the nine-hour-day strike into a strike over the survival of unionism. When the pressmen's union would not join the printers, No. 16 was fatally weakened and was forced to call off the strike on December 4. The Typothetae, however, would allow the men back only as individuals. Fortunately, the continued financial support of newspaper printers allowed the book and job men to hold out until the growing demand for skilled compositors compelled the employers to take most of the union men back in January 1888. Though the strike had failed, the employers' open-shop drive, like the one in construction, had been defeated.[41]

Two other, less important labor campaigns in 1887 continued this pattern. During the spring and summer of 1887 the Knights clerks' assembly, claiming a membership of 2,500, spearheaded a campaign for a state law to require retail stores to close evenings and Sundays. The campaign drew the active support of not only the Knights and the Trades and Labor Assembly but also the city's leading temperance advocates: the Sabbath Association, C. C. Bonney of the Law and Order League, and the Woman's Christian Temperance Union. The bill finally failed because of Republican concerns that it would alienate German supporters, who feared it might be used to close saloons. The clerks' campaign continued vigorously through the 1890s, drawing on its appeal to the Protestant middle class and influential segments of the city's establishment.[42]

Another important victory was won by the city's streetcar workers in September 1887, when Mayor Roche, learning from Mayor Harrison's mistake in 1885, refused to supply the company with police to act as drivers. Instead, he mediated the dispute, which resulted in the workers' winning a reduction in hours to ten and a pay increase, amounting to "two-thirds of what they asked for," according to the *Knights of Labor.*[43] In the cases of the clerks and the streetcar workers, a union had sustained its campaign or won a victory because it did not face employers who sold products in national markets and because it was able to win middle- and upper-class support for its cause in the political arena.

Overall, the number of strikes declined from 307 during the banner year of 1886 to 82 in 1887. Less drastic was the decline in the number of employees on strike: from 87,849 to 31,483. Yet the number of strike failures actually declined from 59 percent in 1886 to 46 percent in 1887. In the spring of 1888 Joseph Gruenhut estimated that more than 60 percent of those estimated to have won the eight-hour day in 1886 still retained it. The number of workers in labor organizations is more difficult to estimate. The same survey reported that the Knights had lost 75 percent of its 28,000 members at its peak, but a *Chicago Tribune* reporter estimated in September that of those who had left 75 percent had entered trade unions. He concluded that "labor had held its own" in the two years since Haymarket. Though surviving unions were reduced in membership, many were still strong enough to sustain full-time, paid "walking delegates." At the end of 1887 there were twenty-five such labor officials employed by the two Knights district assemblies, the Trades and Labor Assembly, the United Carpenters Council, and the local unions of the carpenters, bricklayers, hodcarriers, painters, lathers, slateroofers, stonecutters, cigarmakers, shoemakers, conductors and drivers, coal unloaders, barbers, and iron molders.[44]

The year 1888 continued labor's unrelenting decline, a trend exacerbated by a depressed economy and enlargement of the floating labor pool. The year began with the national strike of the railroad brotherhoods on the Chicago, Burlington and Quincy Railroad to halt a classification system and to establish a uniform pay scale. The strike, which was centered in Chicago, initially united Knights and brotherhood members, many of whom held dual memberships, and was almost 100 percent effective. But this exemplary concert of action broke down within the first month. Many Knights on the Reading Railroad, angry over the brotherhoods' abandonment of their struggle in 1887, crossed picket lines with the approval of Richard Griffiths. For their part the brotherhoods sabotaged a planned boycott they themselves had called on March 5. Even if labor solidarity had held, the strike's prospects would still not have been good because, as Shelton Stromquist has shown, the railroads' new classification system stemmed from their pressing need to meet intensifying rate competition by reducing wages. That, plus railroad managers' growing recognition of a community of interest in labor disputes and the issuance of a federal injunction, considerably stiffened their backs against any concessions.[45]

Immediately following the railroad brotherhoods' defeat the Chicago brewery workers' union lost a short, but hard fought lockout. The brewing industry in Chicago was dominated by large-scale, well-capitalized brewers, who by the late 1880s faced overcapacity and intense national competition. But they also were able to develop a significant community of interest locally in fixing prices and developing uniform methods of distributing beer to saloons. Meanwhile, the CLU-affiliated brewery workers' union organized the industry's largely unskilled workers. In 1888 the city's brewery employers, after joining a national trade association, followed the lead of their New York associates and pulled out of closed-shop collective bargaining. The unions, backed by the Trades and Labor Assembly and the CLU, responded with a neighborhood-based beer boycott. By this time, however, two-thirds of Chicago saloons had come under the ownership of the big brewers and were less amenable to pressure from ethnic working-class consumers. The boycott failed, the strike and the closed shop were lost, and 360 workers lost their jobs, though the union hung on precariously.[46]

In another notable defeat in 1888 the concentrated resources and intransigence of big business defeated labor solidarity. On October 5 the North Side streetcar workers affiliated with DA 24 struck the cable car corporation owned by Charles Yerkes from Philadelphia. Under pressure from a delegation representing the city's united labor movement, Mayor Roche reaffirmed his arbitration policy of the previous year. He refused to supply police to operate the cars and convinced Yerkes to withdraw private detectives and begin negotiations. On October 10, however, the strike was joined by the West Side carmen's union, whose members were also employed by Yerkes, and Yerkes tried to run his cars with out-of-town scabs, provoking massive public demonstrations and a violent confrontation with the scabs. Under pressure from downtown businessmen to settle the strike, Roche again called the two parties together and mediated an end to the strike on union terms. But a week later Yerkes reneged on an understanding ancillary to the bargain by refusing to hire back Knights strikers. Thumbing his nose at both labor and public opinion, he successfully broke the union.[47]

In the three defeats of 1888 labor continued its retreat from the commanding heights of the local economy and left it in the hands of corporate employers with national ties. In two out of three cases the Knights were the victims. Yet in two less important episodes labor held its own. In each case trade unions faced small employers selling in local, often ethnically defined markets.

Labor's most notable success occurred in baking, which as John Jentz has shown, was a small-scale, ethnic neighborhood–based industry. Only 20 of 280 firms in 1880 were wholesale bakeries, but even those firms did not use much machinery or engage in national competition. In April 1888 the bakers' union was able to win an agreement with the vast majority of these small-scale employers. By 1890 a multiethnic bakers' union had organized two-thirds of the city's 1,800 journeymen; only the large-scale, highly mechanized cracker bakeries resisted unionization and collective bargaining.[48]

Like baking, cigarmaking was a small-scale, fragmented industry with more than eight hundred cigar shops in 1888, the largest employing only ninety workers. The major obstacle to union control of the industry came from prison labor contracted out to tenement-house workshops. The union countered this threat with the union label, which created a protected market for employers. By 1889 the union had won the eight-hour day for its 1,500 members.[49]

The garment industry was another case in which unionists realized that the key to winning collective bargaining was to use strong labor organization to maintain market standards. The union leader Abraham Bisno was told by employers that "the union itself must . . . control the entire market and protect against the competition which makes it impossible for us to maintain the price for labor and sell our merchandise." Though the union was not strong enough in 1888 to regulate the labor market, the strategic road to success was clear. By 1890 the union had ejected contractors from its ranks, chartered itself, and engaged in sporadic collective bargaining with wholesale employers. Because of continuing competitive inroads from New York, however, the union remained weak.[50]

The few successes and the major defeats of 1888 confirmed the trend established after Haymarket. Overall, the number of strikes fell from 82 to 37, of which 65 percent failed. The number of employees on strike fell even more drastically, from 31,483 to 11,860. The year 1889 was also one of quiescence and decline for Chicago labor. The number of strikes fell from 37 in 1888 to only 24, and two-thirds were failures. The number of employees on strike fell by 74 percent, to only 3,082. On Labor Day, when the labor movement normally took stock of itself, Joe Gruenhut estimated that since Haymarket the unions and the Knights had lost 60,000 workers. Assuming there were approximately 100,000 organized workers in the city at that time, the overall loss can be put at 60 percent, a figure that suggests a major decline but not a catastrophe.[51]

In fact, the aggregate figures miss the big picture. Not only had the labor movement stabilized itself, but also a very different movement was emerging from the bloom of 1886 and the storms of the ensuing two years. Concentration of capital, increasing scale of operation, and mechanization and division of labor had affected virtually every industry in the city. Where these trends were most prevalent—the very sphere where the Knights of Labor had been strongest—unionism was weakest. But in many industries these trends had made only minor inroads, affecting only a small segment of the market. Where significant small-scale sectors of industries continued to thrive, where competition remained largely local, and where a tradition of skill, craft pride, and personal independence existed that was threatened but not destroyed by sweating and the division of labor, a new kind of worker organization was taking hold by 1887–88, evolving out of and drawing on the traditions supplied by craft unionism and the Knights of Labor. Unionism that could take advantage of the conditions and opportunities in these industries had not fully developed in the 1887–89 period but would in the 1890s. In sum, in 1886 a tidal wave of unionism had washed over broad segments of the city's industrial economy. When it receded, all was not lost, for unionism had established small but secure beachheads where it could safely thrive and develop.

Notes

1. Selig Perlman, *A Theory of the Labor Movement* (New York: Macmillan, 1928), chap. 5; Gerald N. Grob, *Workers and Utopia: A Study of Ideological Conflict in the American Labor Movement, 1865–1900* (Chicago: Quadrangle Books, 1961). For a more recent argument along similar lines, see Victoria C. Hattam, *Labor Visions and State Power: The Origins of Business Unionism in the United States* (Princeton, N.J.: Princeton University Press, 1993), chap. 3.

2. A precursor to the new accounts was Norman J. Ware, *The Labor Movement in the United States, 1860–1895: A Study in Democracy* (New York: Vintage Books, 1929). The application of the new labor history to the Knights began with the Knights of Labor Centennial Symposium held at Chicago's Newberry Library in 1979. Since then see Leon Fink, *Workingmen's Democracy: The Knights of Labor and American Politics* (Urbana: University of Illinois Press, 1983); Gregory S. Kealey and Bryan D. Palmer, *Dreaming of What Might Be: The Knights of Labor in Ontario, 1880–1900* (New York: Cambridge University Press, 1982); Peter J. Rachleff, *Black Labor in the South, 1865–1890* (Philadelphia: Temple University Press, 1984); Richard Jules Oestreicher, *Solidarity and Fragmentation: Working People and Class Consciousness in Detroit, 1875–1900* (Urbana: University of Illinois Press, 1989); and Kim Voss, *The Making of American Exceptionalism: The Knights of Labor and Class Formation in the Nineteenth Century* (Ithaca, N.Y.: Cornell University Press, 1993).

3. Robert Weir, "Powderly and the Home Club: The Knights of Labor Joust among Themselves," *Labor History* 34 (Winter 1993): 84–113; Knights of Labor

District Assembly 24, *Minute Book*, Oct. 15, 1882, George A. Schilling Papers, Regenstein Library, University of Chicago.

4. *Knights of Labor*, Oct. 16, 1886 (first quote), Jan. 22, 1887 (second quote). See also *Fourth Biennial Report of the Illinois Bureau of Labor Statistics* (Springfield: H. W. Rokker, 1886), 363; and Sarah Babb, "'A True American System of Finance': Frame Resonance in the U.S. Labor Movement, 1866–1886," *American Sociological Review* 61 (Dec. 1996): 1033–52.

5. *Knights of Labor*, Dec. 11, 1886 (Stewart quote); Henry George, *Progress and Poverty*, abridged ed. (New York: Robert Shalkenbach Foundation, 1970), 121–23; *Fourth Biennial Report of the Illinois Bureau of Labor Statistics* (Springfield: H. W. Rokker, 1886), 403–4. The trade union defense of strikes can be found in 1883 testimony before the Senate Committee. See, for example, U.S. Senate Committee on Labor and Education, *The Relations between Labor and Capital*, 47th Cong., 2d sess. (Washington, D.C.: Government Printing Office, 1885), 1:322.

6. *Chicago Inter-Ocean*, Mar. 27, 1884 (quotes). See also Richard Oestreicher, "Terence Powderly, The Knights of Labor, and Artisanal Republicanism," in *Labor Leaders in America*, ed. Melvyn Dubofsky and Warren Van Tine (Urbana: University of Illinois Press, 1987), 30–61.

7. Thomas S. Kuhn, *The Structure of Scientific Revolutions*, 2d ed. (Chicago: University of Chicago Press, 1970); Paul F. Boller Jr., *American Thought in Transition: The Impact of Evolutionary Naturalism, 1865–1900* (Chicago: Rand McNally, 1969), 47–69; Thorstein Veblen, *The Theory of Business Enterprise* (1904; reprint, New York: Mentor Books, 1963), 144–76.

8. Victoria Hattam takes a different view on the question of economic concentration in *Labor Visions and State Power*, 132.

9. *Chicago Tribune*, Dec. 13, 1886.

10. *Chicago Inter-Ocean*, Feb. 4, 1887 (first two quotes); Abraham Bisno, *Abraham Bisno: Union Pioneer* (Madison: University of Wisconsin Press, 19670, 89 (Bisno quote).

11. David Montgomery, *The Fall of the House of Labor: The Workplace, the State, and American Labor Activism, 1865–1925* (Cambridge: Cambridge University Press, 1987); John B. Jentz, "Artisan Culture and the Organization of Chicago's German Workers in the Gilded Age, 1860 to 1890," in *German Workers' Culture in the United States, 1850 to 1920*, ed. Hartmut Keil (Washington, D.C.: Smithsonian Institution Press, 1988), 59–79; Lloyd Ulman, *The Rise of the National Trade Union: The Development and Significance of Its Structure, Governing Institutions, and Economic Policies* (Cambridge, Mass.: Harvard University Press, 1955), 374–77.

12. Louise Wade, *Chicago's Pride: The Stockyards, Packingtown, and Environs in the Nineteenth Century* (Urbana: University of Illinois Press, 1987), 243–45; James R. Barrett, *Work and Community in the Jungle: Chicago's Packinghouse Workers, 1894–1922* (Urbana: University of Illinois Press, 1987), 123; Robert Ozanne, *A Century of Labor-Management Relations at McCormick and International Harvester* (Madison: University of Wisconsin Press, 1967), 21–23, 27–28; David Hounshell, *From the American System to Mass Production, 1800–1932: The Development of Manufacturing Technology in the United States* (Baltimore, Md.: Johns Hopkins University Press, 1984), 152–87. Nor was the AFL wedded at this time to craft jurisdiction. See Gerald N. Grob, *Workers and Utopia: A Study of Ideological Conflict in the Ameri-*

can Labor Movement, 1865–1900 (Chicago: Quadrangle Books, 1961), 140–42. It has sometimes been claimed that the Congress of Industrial Organizations fulfilled the promise of the Knights in organizing workers of all skills into industrial unions. It is forgotten, however, that only in the twentieth century was the withdrawal of the labor of less-skilled workers sufficient to shut down entire industries. In the 1880s skilled workers alone could accomplish that.

13. *Knights of Labor,* Dec. 30, 1886; *Chicago Inter-Ocean,* Dec. 5, 1886; *Chicago Tribune,* Oct. 26, 1886; Jan. 5, 1887; United Carpenters Council, *Minute Book,* Jan. 28, 1887, May 6, 1887, June 3, 1887, Archives of the Chicago District Council of Carpenters, Chicago. For parallel events elsewhere, see Elizabeth and Kenneth Fones-Wolf, "Knights versus Trade Unionists: The Case of the Washington, D.C. Carpenters, 1881–1886," *Labor History* 22 (Spring 1981): 192–212.

14. Ira Aylesworth to the General Executive Board, Aug. 18, 1887, in *Proceedings of the General Assembly of the Knights of Labor of America, Eleventh Regular Session Held at Minneapolis, Minnesota, Oct. 4–9, 1887,* 1423–24 (quote), Reel 67, in *Terence Vincent Powderly, 1864–1937, and John William Hayes Papers: The Knights of Labor* (Glen Rock, N.J.: Microfilming Corporation of America, 1974); *Chicago Tribune,* Apr. 20, 1887; *Knights of Labor,* Apr. 16, 1887; Joseph R. Buchanan, *The Story of a Labor Agitator* (New York: Outlook, 1903), 352–54.

15. Chicago Trades and Labor Assembly, *Ledger Book, 1887,* Chicago Historical Society; *Carpenter,* June 1887; *Chicago Tribune,* Dec. 14, 1887 (quote).

16. "Testimony of James Brennock, Treasurer of the Building Trades Council, Mar. 31, 1900," in U.S. Industrial Commission, *Report of the U.S. Industrial Commission,* (Washington, D.C.: Government Printing Office, 1901), 8:469.

17. *Chicago Tribune,* July 17, 1887.

18. Ibid. (first quote); *Knights of Labor,* May 25, 1889 (second quote).

19. *Knights of Labor,* Dec. 23, 1886, Oct. 27, 1887 (quote).

20. According to Schilling, "Is it not probable that should our Order serve notice on the public that it has abandoned strikes, every Industrial Baron and Monopolistic Tyrant will immediately 'put on the screws' and if this comes to pass, will it not force our members to join some other organization for their own protection?" Schilling to Powderly, Apr. 16, 1888, George A. Schilling Papers, Regenstein Library, University of Chicago. For biographical information on Schilling, see *Chicago Times,* Apr. 7, 1888; and Eugene Staley, *History of the Illinois State Federation of Labor* (Chicago: University of Chicago Press, 1930), 22.

21. Buchanan's efforts to heal the rift with the unions persisted into 1893. *Labor Enquirer,* Mar. 16, 1887, July 2, 1887, Sept. 3, 1887, Oct. 2, 1887; Buchanan, *Story of a Labor Agitator,* 352–53, 438–39.

22. *Chicago Tribune,* Apr. 15, 1887, Apr. 25, 1887, Dec. 14, 1887; *Labor Enquirer,* Mar. 9, 1887; *Knights of Labor,* Sept. 3, 1887. It also appears that Powderly did not favor mixed assemblies over trades assemblies. See Weir, "Powderly and the Home Club," 111.

23. Philip S. Foner, *History of the Labor Movement in the United States,* vol. 2, *From the Founding of the American Federation of Labor to the Emergence of American Imperialism* (New York: International Publishers, 1955), 162–64; Buchanan, *Story of a Labor Agitator,* 362–70; *Chicago Tribune,* Oct. 7, 1887, Oct. 8, 1887.

24. *Chicago Tribune*, Oct. 24, 1887; *Knights of Labor*, Oct. 29, 1887; *Labor Enquirer*, Oct. 29, 1887, Dec. 10, 1887; Buchanan, *Story of a Labor Agitator*, 370–72.

25. *Labor Enquirer*, Jan. 14, 1888; *Knights of Labor*, Feb. 22, 1888; *Chicago Daily News*, Feb. 14, 1888.

26. *Knights of Labor*, Feb. 29, 1888, Oct. 13, 1888; *Chicago Tribune*, Apr. 17, 1888, July 29, 1888; Jonathan Garlock, comp., *Guide to the Local Assemblies of the Knights of Labor* (Westport, Conn.: Greenwood, 1982).

27. *Knights of Labor*, Oct. 20, 1888, Dec. 8, 1888, June 22, 1889, Sept. 14, 1889; *Rights of Labor*, Jan. 18, 1890.

28. *Knights of Labor*, Sept. 8, 1888, Aug. 10, 1889; *Chicago Tribune*, Feb. 19, 1888; *Union Labor Advocate*, Feb. 1908.

29. The Marine Trade Council was another attempt, like that of the UCC, to forge cooperative relations between the Knights and the trade unions. See *Chicago Times*, Feb. 15, 1888. According to William C. Birdsall, "The Problem of Structure in the Knights of Labor," *Industrial and Labor Relations Review* 6 (July 1953): 540, "The course of its development illustrates a characteristic of the Knights wherever found: whenever the formal structure did not meet their needs, the members improvised and asked for authorization later, if at all."

30. Ulman, *Rise of the National Trade Union*, 359–68.

31. On this theme in other cities, see Fink, *Workingmen's Democracy;* and Voss, *Making of American Exceptionalism.*

32. Clarence Bonnett, *History of Employers' Associations in the United States* (New York: Vantage, 1956), 321; *Chicago Tribune*, Apr. 2, 1886.

33. *Chicago Tribune*, Mar. 27, 1886, Apr. 28, 1886, Apr. 30, 1886; *Knights of Labor*, May 15, 1886; Bonnett, *History of Employers' Associations*, 252.

34. *Chicago Tribune*, Jan. 4, 1887, Apr. 5, 1887.

35. James Beeks, *30,000 Locked Out! The Great Strike of the Building Trades in Chicago* (Chicago: F. Gindele Printing, 1887), 9 (quotes); Robert Max Jackson, *The Formation of Craft Labor Markets* (Orlando, Fla.: Academic, 1984), 213–42.

36. Robert Christie, *Empire in Wood: A History of the Carpenters' Union* (Ithaca, N. Y.: Cornell University Press, 1956), 62–67; Mark Erlich, *With Our Hands: The Story of Carpenters in Massachusetts* (Philadelphia: Temple University Press, 1986), 78–84; *Chicago Tribune*, Sept. 4, 1887, May 16, 1887 (quote).

37. *Chicago Tribune*, May 13, 1887 (quote), May 14, 1887, May 15, 1887, May 25, 1887, May 26, 1887, May 30, 1887.

38. Ibid., June 22, 1887, June 24, 1887; *Labor Enquirer*, June 4, 1887, July 2, 1887.

39. *Chicago Tribune*, July 9, 1887, July 19, 1887, July 26, 1887, Aug. 3, 1887, Aug. 6, 1887; Josephine Shaw Lowell, *Industrial Arbitration and Conciliation* (New York: G. P. Putnam's Sons, 1894), 81–89. Selig Perlman, *A History of Trade Unionism in the United States* (New York: Macmillan, 1922), 142, referred to the Chicago bricklayers' settlement as "one of the earliest stable trade agreements in a conspicuous trade covering a local field."

40. Emily Clark Brown, *Book and Job Printing in Chicago: A Study of Organizations of Employers and Their Relations with Labor* (Chicago: University of Chicago Press, 1931), 35–42; Jackson, *Formation of Craft Labor Markets*, chaps. 11 and 12.

41. *Labor Enquirer*, Dec. 17, 1887; Brown, *Book and Job Printing*, 43–49.

42. *Knights of Labor,* Feb. 12, 1887, Mar. 5, 1887, Nov. 9, 1889; *Chicago Tribune,* June 12, 1887.

43. *Chicago Tribune,* Sept. 22, 1887; *Knights of Labor,* Sept. 24, 1887.

44. Strike figures derived from reports in U.S. Commissioner of Labor, *Tenth Annual Report of the United States Commissioner of Labor, 1894: Strikes and Lockouts* (Washington, D.C.: Government Printing Office, 1894), 162–250; *Fourth Biennial Report of the Illinois Bureau of Labor Statistics,* 479–80; *Chicago Times,* Apr. 14, 1888; *Chicago Tribune,* Sept. 4, 1887, Sept. 3, 1888 (quote).

45. Donald McMurray, *The Great Burlington Strike of 1888: A Case Study in Labor Relations* (Cambridge, Mass.: Harvard University Press, 1956); Nick Salvatore, *Eugene V. Debs: Citizen and Socialist* (Urbana: University of Illinois Press, 1982), 73–81; Shelton Stromquist, *A Generation of Boomers: The Pattern of Railroad Labor Conflict in Nineteenth-Century America* (Urbana: University of Illinois Press, 1987), 59–61, 211–14, 250–51.

46. *Chicago Times,* May 15, 1889; *Chicago Tribune,* Apr. 13, 1888, Apr. 21, 1888; Perry R. Duis, *The Saloon: Public Drinking in Chicago and Boston, 1880–1920* (Urbana: University of Illinois Press, 1983), 18–20.

47. *Knights of Labor,* Oct. 13, 1888, Oct. 20, 1888. The strike can be followed in the *Chicago Tribune,* Oct. 1–23, 1888.

48. *Chicago Tribune,* Apr. 22, 1888, Apr. 25, 1888; *Chicago Times,* May 13, 1889; John B. Jentz, "Bread and Labor: Chicago's German Bakers Organize," *Chicago History* 12 (Summer 1983): 24–35.

49. *Chicago Times,* Apr. 23, 1888, May 8, 1889.

50. Bisno, *Abraham Bisno,* 105–8 (quote on 105).

51. *Chicago Tribune,* June 10, 1888; U.S. Commissioner of Labor, *Tenth Annual Report,* 162–250; *Rights of Labor,* Sept. 14, 1889 (Gruenhut); *Chicago Times,* Apr. 14, 1888 (100,000 workers). The *Tribune,* Sept. 1, 1888, estimated that the city's unions had 30,000 members.

CHAPTER 11

Labor and Modern Liberalism in Chicago Politics, 1887–91

Historians of late nineteenth-century urban politics have commonly dated the beginnings of modern urban liberalism and progressive reform to the 1893–97 depression, when a recognition of poverty and destitution and the impact of renewed social unrest generated a new social reform driven by a democratic mass politics. They have also viewed reformers from the business and professional classes as the primary agents of this political shift. In doing so they have tended to neglect the impact that class formation, the rise of the labor movement, and, more generally, "the labor question" had on the revision of the public agenda and the legitimation of organized interest groups in the polity during the late nineteenth century.[1]

If the labor question is admitted as important, then the origins of new liberalism and the progressive reform movement must be backdated and reperiodized, for the formal recognition of the working class in urban politics and society dates at least to the great upheaval of the mid-1880s, not the 1890s depression. In Chicago the transformation of the political outlook and the politics associated with "mugwump-reform liberalism" into a recognizably modern liberalism associated with progressive reform was a direct response to, and may be viewed as an integral part of, the great upheaval.[2] As the Citizens Association's reaction in November 1886 to the United Labor party's letter proposing a reform alliance indicated, however, the old liberalism had great difficulty finding common ground with the new reform movements rising from below in this period. Leading mugwumps initially adopted an elitist and aloof stance for three reasons.

First, to many mugwump liberals liberty was closely associated with the prevalent dogma of laissez-faire. To Gilded Age opinion leaders laissez-faire connoted a series of propositions having the force of natural law that governed the workings of the economy. Simply put, left alone, humans competed with each other in the market out of self-interest, and as long as the government did not interfere in the workings of the competitive market, commodity prices resulting from the laws of supply and demand ensured a self-regulating market that generated constantly augmenting wealth, social harmony, and society's best interest. The belief in laissez-faire was reinforced in this period by the popular interpretation of Darwin's theory of natural selection, according to which the natural law of survival of the fittest resulted in the dominance of those best adapted to the business world.[3]

Faith in the self-regulating market logically led to two political beliefs that Karl Polanyi identified as being at the core of nineteenth-century classical liberalism: (1) opposition to the tariff and the espousal of free trade, and (2) opposition to government attempts to regulate the value of money through the coinage of silver and the issuance of greenbacks (paper money) and steadfast support for a unitary gold standard to ensure the constancy of market values. Laissez-faire advocates, however, were not merely shills for business interests, for many also opposed the growth of corporations, trusts, and cartels and attempts to monopolize the competitive market, as well as government land grants to railroads and other subsidies to business.[4]

Yet the outlook of the mugwump liberals rested only partly on classical political economy. The second pillar of their vein of liberalism was the belief that the state should not grant special privileges to the few, whether those few were workers or wealthy capitalists, for any grant of privilege would both deprive citizens of the fruits of their labor and invite strife and corruption into the classless commonwealth. The republican belief in a limited, neutral state therefore reinforced the laissez-faire opposition to the tariff, government-issued greenbacks and coinage of silver, special subsidies or grants of monopoly, and any legislation aiding special interests, including legislation in the interest of workers, such as that establishing shorter hours and factory inspection. Special state privileges aiding the lower classes were viewed as class legislation and as "paternalistic" at best and "socialistic" at worst. Because local governments influenced by party machines potentially engaged in redistributive fiscal and patronage policies, liberals viewed party machines as some of the worst offenders of their principles. Under pressure from liberals, as well as antitax business interests, urban politics tended to remain distributive, but rarely redistributive. Yet because liberal reformers were strong republicans, they often advocated increased regulations and the expansion of state capacities to administer them where there was a clear general interest. Examples included boards of charities and public health, bureaus of labor statistics, state national guards, and a professionalized civil service.[5]

A third reason why mugwump liberals remained alienated and aloof from emergent labor politics was moral and stemmed from their commitment to the country's dominant Protestant work ethic. To liberals the beneficent working of the market was crucially dependent on individuals' good character. When workers indulged in excessive drink or for other reasons failed to exercise the virtues of industriousness, frugality, perseverance, self-restraint, and other tenets of the work ethic that guaranteed personal independence, they not only became responsible, in the eyes of liberals, for their own impoverishment but also invited the paternalistic intervention of the state. For this reason liberals who ran the Relief and Aid Society opposed "outdoor" charity, except with intensive investigation by "visitors," and advocated limiting relief to poorhouses under conditions of the utmost rigor. Concomitantly, they supported moral reform missions to the poor and stringent laws designed to reduce opportunities for intemperance. Mugwumps rarely failed to mention that unions met in saloons, and they counseled building up personal character as a surer path to prosperity than combining to violate the immutable laws of the market.[6]

Mugwump liberals blamed the redistributive actions of the state and the corruption of party and government officials on the poor character of the lower-class voters who elected them. In his founding address to the Citizens Association Franklin MacVeagh called universal suffrage an "eccentric freedom," which "in our great cities" has hamstrung "the best part of the community" and placed "political power in the hands of the baser element of the people." MacVeagh's solutions to the problem—better education of the masses, limitation of suffrage, and the transfer of power to the educated few through civil service reform and voluntary associations of the "best men," such as those in the Citizens Association—epitomized a mugwump analysis in which the evils threatening the Republic and the self-adjusting market emanated from the political influence of the lower orders, whether they were freed slaves in the South or urban immigrant workers. Though many mugwumps, like MacVeagh, liked to think of themselves as "gentlemen," liberals were not a displaced elite revolting against industrialism. Many leading liberals were modern professionals, who allied themselves with progress and social efficiency, and were members of the American Social Science Association.[7]

During the great upheaval mugwump liberalism faced a crisis, both intellectually and as a coherent reform movement. The ineradicable growth of monopolies and labor organizations seemed to threaten individual liberty in a competitive market, while labor agitation for such demands as the eight-hour day and higher wages challenged the idea that the workings of that market were beneficent and that a morality of individual character was sufficient to guarantee personal independence. Just as important, the growth of the labor vote and the implosion of the two party system led some liberals to recognize the incompatibility of elitist liberal attitudes and viable antiparty reform. Reform might win victory *with* labor support, and because of labor's strength it was doomed to failure without it. In such a situation the very idea of reform would have to undergo a renovation. Though that process took several generations and did not flower until the mid-1890s, three new elements of liberal reform first appeared in the thinking of key reformers and in the form of political developments in the period during and after Haymarket. These were (1) a revised conception of social ethics, (2) a revived republicanism and new citizenship that began the acceptance of what had previously been called class legislation, and (3) the limited public acceptance of regulation of the market by associations of capital and labor.

A New Conscience and New Cross-Class Alignments

In 1886–87 both Republican and Democratic silk-stocking reformers had fused in a citywide coalition that left labor in a weak minority position. Under these circumstances ULP leaders had two choices: try to maintain a labor party with little hope of achieving majority status or abandon independent labor politics and seek a renewed alliance within the Democratic party. If they chose the latter, on what basis and with which Democratic faction should they ally? Meanwhile, key leaders among silk-stocking reformers began to ask themselves a similar question: could a political basis be found to annex the labor vote to the reform cause in an antimachine reform coalition? The answers to these questions hinged first and foremost on whether a new ethical basis could be found for reform, for morality was and remains the surest, most durable, and most comprehensive basis for transcending class and other social and political differences and cementing multi-interest coalitions. The protagonists of this new social sympathy and new coalition were none other than the aforementioned liberals.

In the immediate aftermath of Haymarket there seemed little prospect of such a moral transformation. Historians have painted a bleak picture of police repression and class hostility to social reform in the late 1880s. Richard Sennett has described how middle-class residents of Union Park on Chicago's West Side interpreted the Haymarket affair, the city's continuing labor strife, and a series of local burglaries as elements in "a reign of terror." These residents responded by turning to increased police surveillance to enforce a "separatism," to protect against "the threatening 'otherness' of the populace outside the community." According to Paul Avrich, "a vicious circle had taken shape" after Haymarket in which "the terrorized city whipped the police to greater effort, while the police, in turn, kept public fear at a high pitch" with recurring revelations of anarchist conspiracies. As late as June 1887 a judicial ticket headed by the Haymarket prosecutor Julius B. Grinnell crushed a coalition of ULP and reform Democrats with 71 percent of the vote.[8]

Though there is no lack of evidence for these generalizations, they obscure less dramatic but no less important developments occurring at the same time. Important respectable liberals overcame fear and social isolation in the city and began to reach out to members of the putatively dangerous classes. It is notable that many of the famous 1890s and turn-of-the-century reformers of middle- and upper-class origins—John Peter Altgeld, Henry Demarest Lloyd, Clarence Darrow, Lyman Gage, Bertha Palmer, Jane Addams, and Franklin MacVeagh—were enlightened about the labor question by personal contacts with working-class reformers and socialists formed in the Haymarket period. Several reformers became "new intellectuals" by voluntarily relinquishing their social status to identify openly with oppressed workers.[9] By the same process labor leaders were able to pierce Haymarket's iron curtain of repression that might have hardened class hostility into a castelike barrier.

One important example of this occurred during the eight-hour agitation of 1886. In 1885 John Peter Altgeld, a wealthy real estate speculator, builder, and young lawyer, had written a book, *Our Penal Machinery and Its Victims,* indicting police brutality and supporting the rehabilitation of criminals, and had sent it to George Schilling. When the two met over lunch, Altgeld offered to buy a bottle of wine of rare vintage, but Schilling refused "because a labor leader must not accept luxuries from a representative of the upper classes." Notwithstanding their social differences, the two became fast friends because their German-born and American-bred backgrounds gave them much in common, because Altgeld wanted to cultivate Schilling to further his political career, and because Schilling hoped to influence the up-and-coming Altgeld.[10]

Under Schilling's tutelage Altgeld converted to the eight-hour cause and in April 1886 wrote a newspaper article advocating arbitration. Schilling, for his part, brought Altgeld into labor circles and convinced him to run for a judgeship under joint Democratic-ULP sponsorship. Altgeld, meanwhile, helped turn Clarence Darrow, a fellow Ohioan who had recently arrived in Chicago, into a new liberal and patronized his career within the Democratic party. It was Darrow who had the "fantastic" idea to "take a man like Judge

Altgeld, first elect him mayor of Chicago, then governor of Illinois." When Altgeld did become governor in 1892, riding what Morton Keller called "the first wave of urban Democratic liberalism," he pardoned the three remaining jailed Haymarket anarchists, signed into law a raft of landmark progressive legislation, and appointed Schilling as the head of the Illinois Bureau of Labor Statistics.[11]

Henry Demarest Lloyd was a leading example of the "better sort" of mugwump intellectuals who surmounted class boundaries. In the 1860s the Columbia University–educated Lloyd was a zealous young liberal reformer, who served as an organizer for the American Free Trade League. In 1872 he moved to Chicago to work for the free trade *Chicago Tribune,* and by the early 1880s he had become its financial editor and chief editorial writer. By then he was independently wealthy and moved easily in the circles of Chicago's elite. In the early 1880s he published four major articles in leading liberal periodicals criticizing the doctrine of laissez-faire formalism and establishing himself as the nation's first "muckraker" of corrupt, unethical, and predatory business practices.[12]

Lloyd's pioneering work was part of a new dialogue involving classical liberal thought and socialism that began during these years. A small group of economists who founded the American Economics Association in 1886, including Henry Carter Adams, John Bates Clark, and Richard T. Ely, sought to adapt German socialism to Anglo-American individualism by drawing on Christian ideals of cooperation and perfectionism, American republicanism, and modern evolutionary positivist thought. Few reformers made the jump to socialism or Marxism as occurred in Europe, but most accepted the criticisms of laissez-faire and incorporated socialist proposals into their thinking in diluted form.[13]

Though Lloyd, who corresponded regularly with Adams, Ely, and the University of Chicago professor Edward Bemis, was now on the path toward socialism, he was still aloof from working people and unions, which he classed along with monopolies as enemies of the market. In 1884, however, he began a correspondence with an unemployed factory worker from Decatur, Illinois, Ethelbert Stewart. Lloyd used his influence with the governor and personal encouragement to get Stewart to write on the labor question, and by 1886 Stewart had become editor of the *Knights of Labor.* In an anguished letter to Lloyd after Haymarket Stewart wrote of a soul-searching inner struggle between his "fiery, vindictive, passionate" side, symbolized by the figure of Martin Luther, and the wise reformer side of himself, symbolized by Erasmus. Under Lloyd's mentorship Stewart's *Knights of Labor* charted a middle road between unionists and socialists. After the ULP died Stewart cooled his outrage and eventually won a position with the U.S.

Bureau of Labor. Though his conclusions, he wrote, would still be "radical," his "manner of stating them" would henceforth be "mild."[14]

Meanwhile, Lloyd suffered a breakdown and left the *Tribune,* returning from a European recovery a month after Haymarket. Convinced of the trial's injustice, Lloyd unreservedly threw himself into the clemency campaign, thereby earning the respect of labor leaders and socialists. Resuming his friendship with Stewart, Lloyd toured Chicago's slums, met labor leaders, and grasped the logic connecting the appearance of monopolies and the need for unions. Three months after the execution of the four Haymarket anarchists Lloyd returned to print for the first time since his breakdown by writing a passionate defense of trade unionism. After the Trades and Labor Assembly printed fifty thousand copies of his article, his well-to-do friends refused to see him, he was dropped from clubs, and he was snubbed on the street. Under the influence of William Salter of the Chicago Ethical Culture Society Lloyd began to reconcile his Emersonian individualism with his new political economic beliefs. In 1888 he delivered an influential talk entitled "The New Conscience or the Religion of Labor."[15]

Lloyd had begun a personality transformation from an aloof patrician to a relaxed, sympathetic "universal reformer" and a partisan of working people. In 1888 he and his wife, Jesse, turned their suburban Winnetka home into a "social mecca of transoceanic reform," a kind of reform salon open to all classes, one in which such labor leaders as Stewart, Abraham Bisno, Thomas J. Morgan, and Eugene V. Debs could mingle with men and women of the respectable classes who were undergoing personal evolutions similar to Lloyd's. This latter group included Altgeld, Professor Bemis, Clarence Darrow, and the remarkable group of women around Jane Addams and Florence Kelley at Hull-House.[16]

Well before the advent of Hull-House in 1889 cross-class association was flowering among female reformers. Despite lacking the right to vote or hold office, women during the Gilded Age wielded moral authority in public life based on the ideology of separate spheres, which yielded to them special prerogatives in the management of home and family. Women of different classes could unite as women and exercise a limited public power under the rationale of protecting their assigned sphere from external threats. Under the banner of "home protection" the Woman's Christian Temperance Union (WCTU), the nation's largest grass-roots organization of women, and its president, Frances Willard, revived the temperance movement in the 1870s. Still concerned with pursuing women's special tasks as municipal housekeepers, Willard convinced the WCTU in the 1880s to endorse woman suffrage and address such social problems as prison reform and the conditions of working women. According to Ruth Bordin, the great upheaval led Willard to reverse her position that drink caused poverty and recognize that a social environment of poverty helped lead to drink. In 1886 she became friends with Terence Powderly and sent a WCTU representative to the Knights convention. In Chicago she joined the local order and worked with Elizabeth Rodgers to organize working women. Her growing belief that the individual's moral development was influenced by social environment and her longstanding willingness to rely on the state to promote moral change led her publicly to espouse Bellamy nationalism and Christian socialism by 1889.[17]

Even more critical as a foundation for 1890s social reform was the thriving of what Kathryn Kish Sklar calls "women's public culture," which allowed women activists with different backgrounds to work together in a way that most men found difficult. By the mid-1880s the Chicago Woman's Club discussed social and labor issues and united such upper-class philanthropists as Bertha Palmer (in the 1890s a leader in the Civic Federation of Chicago) and Ellen Henrotin (later the national president of the Women's Trade Union League) with such professional reformers as Willard and Jane Addams and such working-class socialists as Corrine M. Brown. In 1888 an even broader assemblage of women from fifty-six different labor, socialist, and philanthropic associations and clubs formed the Chicago Women's League. That year a similarly heterogeneous collection formed the Illinois Women's Alliance (IWA). Called by Meredith Tax a "crossroads" in women's history, the IWA eschewed traditional charity work and for the first time made the interests of working women a women's issue, stamping the IWA as a forerunner of Hull-House and the Women's Trade Union League.[18]

Hull-House, the best-known women's reform effort of the era, was a settlement house founded in 1889 in the heart of the sweatshop district on the near West Side by the well-to-do reformer Jane Addams. Known for its pioneering attempt to create an educational community devoted to cultural uplift and the revitalization of civic obligation, Hull-House succeeded partly because its respectable progenitors consciously sought to transcend their class and status. Addams and her friends Julia Lathrop and Ellen Gates Starr had few or no labor contacts before Hull-House. Three other women—Mary Kenney, Florence Kelley, and Alzina Stevens—educated Adams, Lathrop, and Starr much the same way Schilling did Altgeld and Stewart did Lloyd.

Mary Kenney was a young Irish bindery worker, a natural organizer, and a fierce champion of working women. Kenney found Addams a welcome contrast to patronizing "club women" and was astonished when she offered Hull-House as a headquarters for Kenney's union, which had been meeting above a saloon. By 1891, when Kenney became an organizer for the AFL, she could point with pride to two women's unions that had been organized at Hull-House and four that met there regularly. Florence Kelley had an overseas background in socialism and, according to Allen F. Davis, "more than any other person" made Hull-House "a center for social reform," supplementing its original liberal goal of uplift and service. Alzina Stevens, who had worked since age thirteen and was a veteran of many women's organizing campaigns in the city, was another Hull-House regular who influenced Addams. Hull-House, like Lloyd's Winnetka home, became a meeting place and staging ground for cross-class social reform in the 1890s.[19]

Not all of those who underwent political transformations during these years were reform intellectuals. Several of the city's leading mugwump liberals entered the path of social liberalism. In early November 1887, on the eve of the anarchists' executions, key opinion leaders among silk-stocking Democrats broke ranks with the antilabor fusionist front. Judges Murray F. Tuley and Thomas Moran; Lyman Trumbull and William C. Goudy, both lawyers; and Lyman Gage, a leading banker, all signed petitions to the governor for clemency. The highly respected Judge Tuley made a personal plea to the governor, not on the grounds of mercy or the unjust trial—the two most common grounds—but on the basis of "public policy." Recognizing that many workers believed that the anarchists were being hanged for their advocacy of labor, Tuley, who had recently devised the arbitration settlement for the bricklayers' lockout, supported commutation out of concern that the executions would strain labor-capital relations in the city. Lyman Gage made the same argument to fifty leading patrons of his bank at a meeting. Only the opposition of Marshall Field prevented many who agreed with Gage from supporting him. Both Gage and Franklin MacVeagh were former liberal Republicans who had joined the Cleveland wing of the Democratic party. Both became figures of national repute and served as U.S. treasury secretaries under presidents McKinley and Taft. MacVeagh, a leader in the Civic Federation of Chicago, became an officer in the National Civic Federation.[20]

Developments among silk-stocking Democrats were paralleled by those in the ULP. During the fall 1887 campaign for superior court judge and county commissioners the ULP split. The single-taxers and the socialists took the name Radical Labor party. The antisocialists called themselves the Reformed ULP but were christened by the press the "Free Lunch Party" because of the office-seeking proclivities of those, like William Gleason, who had been advocating fusion with the Democrats since the fall of 1886. Not all Reformed ULPers were motivated by crass ambition, though. Moderate Knights, led by Albert Christello, the president of the Knights' cooperative soap company, and Charles R. Temple, a leader of the paperhangers, would leave the Reformed ULP after fusion. Another faction of moderate trade unionists, led by William Kliver, wanted a "straight labor party" without socialists or Democrats. "I know there are many honest men in this movement," said one, "but the leaders are not honest and I know it. . . ."[21]

The core group of the Reformed ULP came from DA 57, whose Irish executive board members clustered around Judge Richard Prendergast. Like Frank Lawler, the Democrats' earlier intermediary with labor, Prendergast was a prolabor, Irish-born nationalist, but in other respects he was quite different from Lawler. Not only had Prendergast represented Frank Stauber in the ballot box–stuffing case of 1880, but after Haymarket he had been one of the few Irish politicians who explained the bombing as a response to the Stauber case. In 1886 he had joined the Knights and been elected to DA 57's executive board, a position he still held in 1888. In 1886, with the ULP's support, he had been elected county judge. Meanwhile Lawler had alienated himself from the party's labor constituency by opposing Robert Nelson and had been "kicked upstairs" by the party in 1887 with a congressional nomination. Because of Prendergast's background and because he was not closely identified with the party's leadership, he could cast himself plausibly as a reformer of corrupt party politics.[22]

With the Prendergast-led split and the softening of the silk-stockings' stand on the executions the stage was set for a rapprochement between the Democrats and the labor movement. But instead of the old alliance with the McDonald machine (under the aegis of Carter Harrison), the Prendergast forces opted for direct negotiations with the Goudy-led silk-stockings. The deal, which was consummated on the eve of the election, did not lead to victory because labor's political constituency was still demobilized. But it laid the groundwork for not identifying upper-class citizen movements with antilabor, antivice reform.

The ferment that had created the rapprochement of November 1887 surfaced again in February 1888, when Lloyd gave his public address "The New Conscience or the Religion of Labor" before the Ethical Culture Society. Lloyd not only criticized economic individualism but also made the radical assertion that the labor movement was now synonymous with suffering humanity and Christ. Two months later the Ethical Culture Society instituted the first of an annual series of economic conferences, a new kind of civic forum in which labor leaders, reformers, and businesspeople could speak to each other without rancor about issues and causes considered beyond the pale of public discussion. The first series enabled Thomas J. Morgan, Andrew Cameron, George Schilling, and Joseph Buchanan to sit down with Benjamin P. Hutchinson of the Chicago Board of Trade, Lyman Gage, and Franklin MacVeagh.

Most significant were the words and sentiments of Gage and MacVeagh, each of whom in public addresses questioned laissez-faire doctrine. Though neither went as far as Lloyd, who had become a socialist, both endorsed the principle that private wealth had public responsibilities. By this time Gage was spending hours in conversation with Schilling and William Henry Jackson on the labor question. Gage even helped inaugurate the conferences, and his home was the meeting place of the first few sessions before they became public. In his address Gage reflected orthodox views in arguing for the futility of both monopolistic and trade union control over the market. But he spoke intelligently and sympathetically of industrial protest, and he endorsed "a maturing of our individualism" and "a more generous sympathy across society as a whole." MacVeagh went further in breaking with elitist liberalism. He accepted that big business did "social damage," in the form of uncertain employment, maldistribution of wealth, excessive hours, and child labor. Admitting that "the rush of our great industrial system has somewhat outstripped our less stimulated ethical system," MacVeagh, while rejecting socialism, articulated a full-blown vision of the new liberalism, optimistically linking the emerging new economy with social reform:

> The crudeness of our individualism shows unmistakable signs of the mellowing influence of the right social instinct; so that what with such correctives as the voluntary acknowledgements of private property, the limitations of the law of competition, the concessions to organized labor, the division of capital in joint stock companies and its organization in co-operative forms, the reduced and reducing returns of capital as new worlds cease to offer themselves to the conqueror, the reduction of all men's labor, the spread of education, and finally, the ever-growing harmony of the people under the reign of a victorious democracy,—all is tending toward the reduction of the inequalities of life to the measure of the justifications of nature.[23]

In 1888 Gage's economic conferences, like Lloyd's work on behalf of the anarchists, elicited "suspicion and contempt" among his associates. According to Gage, "The first audiences were composed of "the lower bourgeoisie," while "the well-to-do were feebly represented." But in March 1889 the economic conferences were supplemented by a new upper-class association that welcomed the new reform ethos, the Sunset Club. Male and female reformers, trade unionists, and intellectuals mingled with the wealthy and discussed such topics as Bellamy nationalism, land taxation, municipal ownership, criminal justice reform, and the acceptance of trade unions and strikes. Referring to the economic conferences and the Sunset Club, the *Knights of Labor* in 1890 claimed to discern in the city "a new spirit of inquiry into an ethical basis for industrial relations."[24]

Press Sensationalism and the Popularization of the New Politics

It took more than public discussions to popularize the new ethical critique of unfettered economic individualism. The reform spirit first began to grip the imaginations of a popular urban audience in two press campaigns of the *Chicago Times*. Three years after the death of Wilbur Story, its conservative publisher and editor, the *Times* came under the editorship of James J. West, aided by the brilliant humorist Finley Peter Dunne. Seeking to rescue the paper from decline, they embarked on a sensationalistic exposé of sweatshop labor, much in the manner of William Randolph Hearst and Joseph Pulitzer, both pioneers of sensationalist journalism in these years.[25] Conducted by an undercover "lady reporter" in July 1888, the series catapulted the *Times* to the city's largest morning daily. The series began on July 29 with the entire front page festooned with such lurid headlines as "Life among the Slave Girls in Chicago," "Shocking Revelations," and "Organized Hells on Earth." Nell Nelson, the reporter, began her exposés as a seamstress in the sweatshops of the clothing industry, but by the middle of the month she had extended her work to shoe, box, mattress, and pillow factories and dry-goods stores. Nelson's firsthand accounts painted a shocking picture of how women and children were exploited economically and even sexually by cruel and heartless bosses. The dominant theme was a comparison of the condition of African American slaves in the antebellum South with that of female and child labor in urban sweatshops and factories, a theme underlined by repetition of the phrase "white slave girls of Chicago."[26]

The series continued daily on page one for over a month, and within a few days had captured the attention of Chicagoans. "Not since it was founded," editorialized the paper on August 3, "has the *Times* undertaken work which has aroused so much interest or met with such a hearty and spontaneous approval as that in which it is now engaged." Within a week hundreds of letters had poured into the paper, and in two weeks letters were printed from readers all over the United States. After three weeks the Trades and Labor Assembly endorsed "the *Times* crusade."[27] By the end of the month the paper opened its editorial pages to possible solutions, including stricter sanitary laws and compulsory schooling, themes it pursued the rest of the year.

As *Uncle Tom's Cabin* had done with slavery in the 1850s, the series and the response it generated crystallized on a more limited urban scale a new public mood and set of concerns that had deep cultural and political resonance. The focus on the exploitation of women and children touched a Victorian nerve of sympathy as few strikes or exposés of working conditions of men could. The resulting outrage allowed for a new common ground on which reformers from different backgrounds could view "the social question." In previous years the respectable classes had viewed this question from the perspective of drink or Catholicism or labor violence, all perspectives that painted workers as threats to American institutions. The new common ground incorporated a recognition of exploitation and a straightforward sympathy with underdog workers. But the impact went further, for just as the Victorian sensibility evoked by Harriet Beecher Stowe had proven congenial to women's activism in the abolitionist and antislavery movement, the new emphasis on the exploitation of women and children by heartless industrialism cleared a path in which middle-class women might, as the special guardians of Victorian morality, play a similar role as political activists in the industrial era. The opening for women to pursue these issues was all the greater because few men of this era were willing to commit themselves to action on them.

In the aftermath of the success of its exposé the *Times* deepened its commitment to reform and labor issues. It printed regular Sunday columns by Joe Gruenhut advocating socialism. Gruenhut in turn lauded the *Times* as "the first daily newspaper in this city which undertook to investigate certain grievances and to champion the cause of oppressed labor at the risk of losing advertising patronage. . . ." The following year the paper printed a daily survey over three weeks detailing how trade unionism and eight-hour workdays had affected local industry, easily the most in-depth and comprehensive such study ever published in the city.[28] By the fall of 1888 the *Chicago Tribune* paid the *Times* the ultimate compliment of imitation. Hiring its own undercover "lady reporter," the *Tribune* ran a regular Sunday series of exposés of working conditions of women and the poor, though it omitted an editorial judgment.[29]

All the while, the activities of a host of women were percolating barely beneath the surface of politics as usual. The critical group of women were working-class women and socialists. While the rest of the labor movement was on the downgrade, women's organizing in the Knights of Labor and in independent unions was flourishing. Among them was the AFL-affiliated Ladies Federal Union (LFU), founded by Elizabeth Morgan, T. J. Morgan's wife.[30] With the appearance of the *Times* series the LFU sprang into action. In October it organized the Illinois Women's Alliance (IWA), consisting of twenty-five women's church, suffragist reform, and self-improvement clubs. Among these groups was the Woodlawn chapter of the WCTU, whose Chicago-based national journal commented during the *Times* series that the city government "seems to be just as indifferent to the enforcement of its own sanitary regulations as it is to the execution of the dram shop ordinance." The IWA's goal was the prevention of "the moral, mental, and physical degradation of women and children as wage-workers," specifically relying on the enforcement of existing factory and compulsory education laws. The IWA's leadership was diverse, but its core group were prolabor socialists: Morgan, Corrine Brown, and Fanny Kavanaugh.[31]

The first major issue the IWA pursued was the lack of enforcement of the 1883 compulsory education law, requiring children from ages eight through fourteen to be in school at least twelve weeks a year. Estimating that at least fifty thousand children between these ages were not in school, the women, with the support of the Trades and Labor Assembly, members of the Chicago

Board of Education, and prominent citizens, lobbied the city and the Board of Education for more truant officers and successfully pushed for a new state compulsory education law. The Edwards law, which passed the Illinois General Assembly in July 1889, lowered the minimum age to seven, increased the number of required weeks of education to sixteen (the IWA had asked for forty), and, most important, mandated fines for lack of compliance. Emboldened by its success, the IWA next turned its attention to the enforcement of factory and tenement-house laws, which had been largely unenforced since 1880, and the passage of a new, more effective child labor law to replace the worthless 1881 law. In enforcing these laws, the IWA asked that committed women be appointed as school truant officers and factory inspectors and to the Board of Education.[32]

The *Times* revelations and the IWA's attempt to enforce new laws raised two related issues that, like the new moral sensitivity to working people, would be central in renovating the old liberalism. First, the attempt to legislatively protect women and children challenged the liberal opposition to class legislation, an issue that would become more critical when in 1895 a Florence Kelley–drafted law creating the state's Department of Factory Inspection was declared unconstitutional by the state supreme court.[33] More urgent was the question of how to create and sustain the administrative capacities on the municipal level that would be effective in enforcing prolabor regulations. The stumbling block lay in party machines' control of much of local government. According to Louis Hartmann, the Trades and Labor Assembly representative to the IWA, when labor organizations sought to have "inspectors chosen from our membership and friends" to "see that the law was enforced," the result was "that union after union was brought under [Democratic party] control." Patronage power thus ensured that the very responsiveness of politics to labor as a new interest group would undercut both the independence of that interest group and the effectiveness of state action in its behalf. The IWA tried to get around this dilemma by asking that city factory and school inspectors not be paid so that "a class of professional officeholders" would not be created. Much to the embarrassment of such socialists as Elizabeth Morgan, however, this did not prevent other IWA women from accepting the positions offered to them by the city and Board of Education.[34]

The IWA's agitation had shifted the ground that underlay the internal debate in the city's labor movement, from how to ensure the independence of labor leaders to how to build a more effective state. Ironically, the most advanced labor and socialist thinkers shared with the advocates of laissez-faire the same realistic assessment of the danger of extending government action: a party-dominated state could not be trusted to serve the public interest. In the past this dilemma was not a major problem because organized male workers leavened their support for positive state action with a commitment to self-help through their unions and benevolent societies. But women (and the children they spoke for), because of their presumed timidity, their identification with home and family, and the intense competition they faced in the labor market, were thought to be a special "dependent" class less capable of self-help. After a decade of organizing that failed because of this structural situation, women trade union organizers began to rely on alliances with middle-class women and on the state for protection. The IWA's call for enforcement of social welfare laws thus created a far stronger impetus for state-building in the form of an autonomous administrative mechanism than the local labor movement had ever effected.[35]

The movement for an expanded state to serve social welfare needs was not the only development of 1888 pointing toward a new politics. That year also saw the stirrings of a mass antimonopoly movement in the city. The spring 1887 United Labor party campaign and the spring 1888 Radical Labor party campaign were the first to lay out a complete program of municipal reform, anticipating liberal progressive reform of the 1890s. Both platforms called for public ownership of all municipal utilities, a reduction in streetcar fares and gas and electricity rates, and the equitable assessment of property based on the law rather than on "profitable personal agreements between the assessor and large property owners." Implementing these reforms, said the Radical Labor party, would end "the principal source of corruption that purchases our common council and administrative officers."[36]

Throughout the 1880s there had been sporadic press exposés and citizen complaints about poor streetcar service, high utility rates, and franchise giveaways by the city council. But there was nothing to compare with the protest, mostly directed against Yerkes's cable cars, that began in 1888. Between April and August there were twenty-one accidents resulting in serious injuries on Yerkes's North Side cable cars. In the wake of a citizens movement of irate North Siders, the *Chicago Tribune* argued that reform of the street railway system should take precedence over the eight-hour demand, because the Yerkes corporation, "enjoying valuable franchises attained from elected representatives of the people without compensation as far as the people know . . . has been steadily and stealthily adding an hour each day to the period of toil of thousands and tens of thousands of workingmen and women, youths and young girls."[37]

The Knights' strike against "Baron" Yerkes in October brought these issues to a boil. Crowds of up to ten thousand people, including middle-class clerks, set up barricades on the North Side and the West Side to block scab railroad cars from moving. On the West Side a mass meeting of fifteen hundred small businessowners aired their grievances against Yerkes and endorsed the strike. With business all over the city prostrated from lack of transportation, the prominent lawyer Leonard Swett wrote an open letter to Mayor Roche asking him to put the Yerkes corporation in public hands.[38]

The events of 1888 not only fueled antimonopolism but also opened up a remarkable public discussion over public ownership of utilities. The *Chicago Daily News* had for some time supported the concept, but now the rest of the press joined the discussion. In February, referring to the *Chicago Tribune*'s call for municipal ownership of the gas trust, the *Knights of Labor* wrote that "the people have much to encourage them in the present attitude of the press toward monopolies in general and trusts in particular."[39]

Another sign of broadening social reform beyond the boundaries of labor was the formation of the Chicago branch of the Personal Rights League (PRL). The PRL enabled socialists in the German-speaking trade unions and turnverein (gymnastic societies) to form a nonpartisan united front with businesspeople and professionals opposed to Prohibition. The PRL was active in a variety of causes, including amnesty for the imprisoned anarchists, support for strikes, ballot reform, antimonopolism, anti–political corruption, and municipal ownership, as well as defending against nativism and Prohibition. Its leaders, the attorney Charles Bary and later the prominent Board of Trade broker Robert Lindblom, served as cofounders—together with the nationalists and single-taxers—of the Ballot Reform League, several labor parties, citizens reform movements, and the amnesty movement. The PRL had its own newspaper and claimed to represent thirty thousand German voters and hold the balance of power in Chicago politics.[40]

The period from the execution of the anarchists in November 1887 to the *Times*'s sensationalist exposés of female and child labor in 1888 had witnessed the beginnings of a new ethical sensibility among liberal reformers in the city, together with new kinds of cross-class alignments in the form of the accord between silk-stocking reformers and the Reformed ULP, the economic conferences, the IWA's agitation for state enforcement of what had formerly been construed as class legislation, and an antimonopolist movement that pondered public ownership of the streetcars. By the end of 1888 the local political system had also begun to respond to the newfound strength and legitimacy that the new reform politics had created for labor and labor issues.

The Revival of Political Collective Bargaining

Public recognition of the importance of the labor vote made it possible for segments of organized labor to return to the strategy of political collective bargaining. By 1888 Richard Prendergast, using the Irish remnants of the ULP, had built a new labor Democratic machine. He not only had made the union leader Luke Coyne an election judge but also had appointed Bill Gleason his chief clerk. Approximately half of Prendergast's appointments had gone to former ULP leaders.[41] Coyne was particularly important as a new labor politician. He used his ties to Prendergast and De Witt Cregier, the West Side streetcar superintendent, to win jobs for his own supporters in the union or new ones with the county if they were discharged. In the summer of 1888, with the Burlington railroad strike dragging out, Coyne and leaders of the unions of the switchmen, engineers, and brakemen formed the state Independent Club of Railroad Employees to punish the state for its use of Pinkerton detectives.

The *Chicago Tribune* recognized that the club's plan was "to hold over both parties the threat of a combined opposition vote unless influence is brought to bear upon the Chicago, Burlington and Quincy Company. It is, in fact, the threat of a political boycott." Since the Republicans were unwilling to meet labor's demands, the club soon became a potent force in convincing the skilled railroad brotherhood workers, many of whom were Republicans, to support the gubernatorial campaign of the Democratic challenger, John Palmer.[42]

In October the streetcar strike against Yerkes highlighted the partisan jockeying for the labor vote. The *Tribune* accused Coyne of an elaborate scheme to build a citywide federation of railway unions under the control of him and his Democratic party confederates, with the goal of damaging Mayor Roche's reelection chances and boosting Palmer's fortunes. But Mayor Roche appealed to the labor vote just as clearly by refusing to introduce police into the strike and ruling out private detectives. A week before the November election for governor Palmer stumped the stockyards district emphasizing his opposition to the use of Pinkertons in the 1886 stockyards strike and the 1888 Burlington strike. By this time even the Republicans were unabashedly appealing to the labor vote by trying to explain away the legislature's passage of the Cole antiboycott law and the Merritt Conspiracy Act.[43]

In the election, which the *Knights of Labor* called "the most remarkable that has occurred for the apparent interest that was displayed by both parties for the welfare of the working classes," city turnout was up dramatically over the previous three elections, even exceeding the mayoral election of 1887 by 65 percent. Palmer narrowly lost the state but won a smashing victory over Republican governor Joseph W. Fifer in Chicago by 6,000 votes, outpolling President Cleveland. Only 4,000 voters had selected the Radical Labor party, now an overtly socialist party.[44] The *Tribune* blamed Palmer's good showing on "the unnatural and shameful coalition" of labor and the Democrats and frankly admitted that since the mayoral election of 1887 the combined labor and Democratic vote was a majority in the city; that only the existence of an independent labor party had allowed Republicans to win; and that with the Radical Labor party in shambles the Republican cause was lost. The Democratic *Chicago Times* concluded, "It is obvious that any acceptable candidate who can unite the Democratic and labor vote can win against any candidate running merely as a partisan." Joe Gruenhut noted that German socialists throughout the city had voted Democratic on the free trade issue. Identifying himself as a Democrat, Gruenhut wrote, "Chicago can be made overwhelmingly Democratic if the labor vote is carefully looked after."[45]

The shift in public mood that had afforded organized labor formal recognition in the political arena was still threatened by lingering fears of anarchism. Long months of sensational trial testimony about desperate conspiracies had terrorized the public and prepared respectable opinion for Roche's law and order ticket. Evidence given in later years made clear how contrived much of this hysteria really was. Police chief Frederick Ebersold admitted in 1889 that during Roche's administration Captain Michael Schaack, the police detective in charge of investigating the anarchists, had tried to "work the people's fears" by inciting violence or the threat of it and, then after suppressing it, had posed as the savior of the wealthy. Schaack himself boasted that for eighteen months after Haymarket the police, through informers, had maintained constant surveillance of virtually every anarchist meeting and presumably were aware in advance of any dangers to the public. In the days following the Haymarket bomb three hundred leading Chicago capitalists had subscribed to a secret fund, averaging between $50,000 and $140,000 annually, to pay police for protection against anarchism. Continued anarchist raids by the police kept the money flowing.[46]

In July 1888, eight months after the hanging, during which time the Red scare seemed to have subsided, Schaack and John Bonfield rekindled it with the arrest of three Bohemian anarchists, who were charged with plotting the assassination of Bonfield; Judge Joseph E. Gary, who presided over the Haymarket trial; and Julius Grinnell, the prosecuting attorney. The story was amplified by further revelations over a two-week period. With the start of the trial on November 27, public fears reached a new pitch. After Bonfield gave an interview on December 3, claiming that the anarchists were reorganizing, overt police repression resumed with a public ban on all anarchist gatherings. When the anarchists defied the order, police closed down a meeting of the Arbeiter Bund on December 23.[47]

Anarchism was, of course, hardly the public threat the press portrayed it to be. No more than a handful of physical-force anarchists—as distinct from the "individualist" anarchist followers of Benjamin Tucker, such as George Schilling—were left in the city. Few outside the colorful Lucy Parsons, the woman the press loved to hate, were ready to offer bloodthirsty quotes. The fears of anarchism did, however, serve to shunt aside the growing impetus for social reform and unite many Democrats and Republicans behind the administration of John Roche, who was running for reelection in April 1889. In sum, law and order, fusion politics, and public fears of anarchism, on the one hand, and the new social reform politics, on the other, represented two complexes of issues that reflected competing stances of segments of the city's respectable classes.[48]

In January 1889 the local concert of reaction was dealt a crushing blow in a surprising series of events. The new year began when Master in Chancery Thomas G. Windes of a local police court voided the police prohibition on anarchist meetings. Two weeks later this decision was ratified at a higher level when Judge Tuley ruled on behalf of the Arbeiter Bund and against the police, vindicating the principle that treasonable intentions unaccompanied by deeds were not punishable by law. The most critical development in a dramatic turnaround of public opinion came with another exposé by the *Times,* this time of the activities of Bonfield, Schaack, and a patrolman named Jacob Lowenstein. In January the *Times* reprinted charges, originally aired in the *Arbeiter-Zeitung,* that Captain Schaack had stolen considerable property and used it to amass a personal fortune.[49]

Bonfield's response was to arrest the editors of both papers for libel. The *Times* counterattacked with a vigorous editorial campaign discrediting and heaping contempt on the two detectives and their confederate. Following the pattern of its exposé of "slave girls," the *Times* kept up sensational daily revelations and attacks on Bonfield and Schaack. Headlines called Bonfield an "evil genius" and "a despot," and editorials demanded his dismissal. The paper recalled Bonfield's brutality in the 1885 streetcar strike and his indiscriminate use of the term *anarchist,* such as when he described the printers' union as anarchist for asking for a repeal of the Merritt Conspiracy Act. The *Times* also exposed the ways Bonfield had trumped up the anarchist menace for political purposes. As one editorial put it, "To create the impression that Roche and his favored police officials alone stand between the city and destruction, and that to defeat his re-election is to encourage an uprising of anarchists, the department has resorted to extremes with the satisfaction of finding that its inventions are swallowed in certain credulous quarters as momentous facts." In doing this the editorial accused Roche of breaking his promise "to protect the rights of the workingman as sacredly as the rights of the capitalists."[50]

On February 6 Roche relented by suspending Bonfield and Schaack. It was a dramatic surrender to the *Times*'s crusade, ratifying a stunning turnaround in public opinion. During its assault on the police the *Times* had also exposed police inaction on gambling and had placed the police attack on anarchism in the context of a general pattern of unwillingness to enforce the law. Once the police were viewed in the light of these mugwump concerns, they were turned from heroes to villains: along with corrupt politicians and local monopolies they were enemies of public morality and free speech. In contrast workers and labor organizations were to be counted on the side of morality and justice.[51]

In exposing the politics of fear the *Times* acted as a midwife to the new social reform politics, which built on older elements of mugwumpism, such as Victorian moralism and antimonopolism, but jettisoned much of its elitism and fear of the dangerous classes. Entrepreneurial reporters, using the techniques of exposé-sensationalist journalism, had in effect "manufactured" the news and helped to create a new politics, in much the same way that the police and the mugwump press had manufactured the anarchist hysteria and law and order politics.

The power of class-bridging reform was evident when a committee of twenty-one trade unionists and labor reformers announced in February that it sought a mayoral candidate to lead a nonpartisan "peoples ticket" against both monopolies and political despotism. Led by James Brennock of the carpenters' union and delegates from other politically unaffiliated trade unionists, the committee excluded both socialists and labor Democrats and repudiated the ULP's idea of a class party. In the words of John Lavine, an officer in the cigarmakers' union and spokesman of the committee, "We are nearly all agreed that it isn't good policy for the labor party to draw the class line. . . ." Leaders openly courted Judge Tuley and Franklin MacVeagh.[52]

On February 22, the day of a rally to kick off the American Federation of Labor's eight-hour-day campaign, a candidate seemed to fall into the laps of the labor movement. Sam E. Gross, a popular builder of houses for working people who could buy them on the easy payment plan, wrote a letter to the Eight Hour Association endorsing eight hours as a nonpolitical reform that interested all classes. At this point George Detwiler and George Schilling of the Knights of Labor also boosted labor's political movement in the hopes of reestablishing a labor party. On March 14 the newly formed Joint Labor party held a convention that nominated Gross for mayor and W. P. Rend, a pro-union coal operator, for city treasurer. The platform supported eight hours and repudiated anarchist fear-mongering and the use of Pinkertons, but it primarily emphasized social reform issues that would appeal to a broad constituency. It endorsed municipal ownership, enforcement of child labor laws, Sunday closing of all businesses to give workers a day's rest, the application of single-tax principles to local taxation, and the adoption of the Australian ballot. A few days later the party put out a communication stating that it was neither a red flag nor a class party but a party of principle.[53]

But the new labor party had too many obstacles in its path. The primary one was that so many trade unionists were tied to the Democratic party. At the Democratic convention, two days after the Joint Labor party convention, the machine elements of the party united to back De Witt Cregier, an associate of the Prendergast-Coyne machine. Rend and Gross, realizing that labor would not be united behind their candidacies, both refused their nominations within the week. The Joint Labor party then collapsed, leaving the field to candidates of the two old parties.[54] In the ensuing campaign, issues stemming from ethnic identity gained strength. Both Roche and Cregier were accused of being members of the United Order of Deputies, a virulently anti-Catholic association. The issues the parties articulated in public, however, were labor and civic reform. The Democrats audaciously turned over the writing of their platform to Joe Gruenhut, who produced one virtually identical with that of the Joint Labor party. Roche supporters boasted about the mayor's mediation of the streetcar strike and his dismissal of Bonfield and Schaack. Each side tried to identify Yerkes with their opponents, each distorted the record of the other in the streetcar strike, and each claimed the other party was run by "a machine."[55]

Prominent reformers and the reform press, including the *Times* and the *Knights of Labor* but not the *Daily News*, supported Roche. Cregier, however, won the election handily by 10,000 votes. A chagrined *Tribune* pointed to two factors in the defeat. First, it thought that trade unionists wanted to punish Roche for defeating Robert Nelson in 1887. The paper also admitted that many were attracted by the Democrat's "semi-socialistic program." But, also important, claimed the paper, was "the anti-machine ticket," a contrivance of John Peter Altgeld, a little-known Democratic judge, in which a nonpartisan ballot that had Cregier's and other Democrats names at the top was mailed to thousands of Republican voters. Detwiler concurred, writing that Roche was defeated by "the old time, dyed-in-the-wool Republicans who went to the polls with their votes in their vest pockets or did not go at all." This was another way of saying that it was the strength of reform that defeated Roche, for Republicans had split their tickets because Roche was now identified with the Republican machine.[56]

Despite its advanced platform Cregier's Democratic administration disappointed municipal reformers. It did, however, implement the interest group politics of political collective bargaining, going far beyond Carter Harrison's personalism. Within the labor movement before the election, advocates of such a policy were at least as powerful as those promoting the Joint Labor party, and they gained in stature under Cregier. Michael V. Britzius, a socialist and an official in the cigarmakers' union who then became president of the Trades and Labor Assembly, argued that "if we put up the right sort of a man from the employer class, we might as well go into one of the old parties and try to control its action in the same direction from the inside. My judgment is that we can gain more by casting our votes for the man who comes nearest filling our requirements on whatever ticket we find him."[57] Once in office Cregier demonstrated that he recognized labor's importance in his victory. When it seemed as if his administration would emasculate an eight-hour ordinance applying to contractors passed under Roche's administration, he quickly withdrew the attempt after the Trades and Labor Assembly protested. In June Cregier signed a landmark ordinance granting the eight-hour day with time-and-a-half for overtime to all city employees except police and fire fighters.[58]

Cregier's embrace of labor went far beyond Carter Harrison's arms-length wooing. A month into his administration Detwiler noted that Cregier had hired every member of the old Committee of 21 and that "there is no question as to the honesty of his purpose to fully recognize what he considers to be a respectable element of the Labor Party." The Democratic party planned to recapture the state legislature in 1890, and Detwiler noted that "it is safe to say there is nothing within the gift of the Democratic party of Chicago that the labor people cannot have by asking for it." Among the appointments Gruenhut returned to his old post in the Health Department as tenement inspector; Charles G. Dixon was given the position as assistant health commissioner; Captain John McCarthy, the head of the sailors' union, was appointed harbormaster; and Robert Cowdry, a leader of the single-tax movement, received a position in the Water Department. Gruenhut estimated that by 1890 eight hundred labor leaders had received appointments at the city, county, and state levels. Admitting the enormous impact of Democratic patronage, Morgan argued, "The worst thing that ever happened in this county was the election of Frank Lawler to Congress. It fired the ambition of workingmen, and there's not one of them now who hasn't a picture of Lawler pasted on the footboard of his bed and who doesn't hope someday to follow in his footsteps."[59]

Such appointments did not necessarily create loyal party hacks. Those who took jobs can be divided into four groups: loyal trade unionists who were also loyal Democrats; labor reformers who, in the absence of a viable labor party, sought to use the Democratic party as a base for their reforms; trade unionists who practiced political collective bargaining in the interests of labor; and those who seem to have fit the stereotype of ambitious office-seekers. To all these labor groups, however, Cregier offered very real policy inducements, ranging from the customary hands-off police policy during the critical strikes of 1890 to eight-hour legislation to an unprecedented secret order that at least some city hiring be done through union hiring halls. As a result, a new expression, "labor-Democrats," entered the political lexicon of Chicagoans in 1889. The *Tribune* went so far as to call the Democratic party a "social-democratic" party, later estimating that approximately 80 percent of its voters were workers.[60]

As the Cregier election revealed, labor's exercise of its new clout within the party system bore an ambivalent relationship to the new politics of social reform. Though labor's bargaining with the Democratic machine entailed the sordidness commonly associated with the era's party politics, many labor leaders, as well as labor voters, shared the prevalent antiparty reform mood and were willing to work with reformers. This became evident when the reform constituency achieved an important new impetus in June 1889 with the annexation of outlying suburbs to the north and south of the city, including the important stockyards district in the Town of Lake. Overnight, the city quadrupled its area and gained 220,000 new citizens and ten new wards. Living in these suburbs were large numbers of the "new middle class," a rapidly increasing stratum of nonmanual workers, educated professionals, business clerks and salespeople, and others associated with the rising service, government, and sales segments of the economy. This rather amorphous class—and doubtless many respectable skilled workers—provided a major source of antimachine sentiment. Not only were many, such as in the Town of Lake, opposed to local machines, but suburbanites, including those who had organized in Lake View against Yerkes the previous year, were highly dependent on public transportation and were weary of the dangers, delays, and inconveniences associated with monopoly. In his study of Chicago progressive reform in the mid-1890s Michael P. McCarthy found that aldermen from these wards were the staunchest supporters of the Municipal Voters League, which championed a "new citizenship" transcending class and ethnicity.[61]

The new reform ethos in the city and the legitimization of labor interests reached new levels in the election campaign that fall. Preparing for the election of county board members and a recorder, the Democratic convention, dominated by Mike McDonald and the Irish, nominated the union leader Mark Crawford for recorder. Gruenhut once more wrote the party platform, which included a plank calling on the county board to investigate unequal assessments of taxable property, especially taxable securities. When the results came in, the Democratic slate had been swept into power, but Crawford had suffered an embarrassing defeat. The mugwump *Daily News* explained that "he was regarded as a Democratic politician who masqueraded as a labor man for the sake of office and it was a pleasure to many workingmen to cast their votes against him."[62]

Reform issues continued to be important as the different political interests prepared for the December election of commissioners for the new Sanitary District. Before the parties made their nominations, the Trades and Labor Assembly put itself on record as favoring the Single Tax Club's proposal that funds for the new canal be raised by a tax on land values, excluding buildings or improvements, and that the construction work be done by day labor rather than by contract, thus eliminating the incentive for corruption and ensuring that the appropriated funds go to labor. The next week a gathering of labor-Democrats, single-taxers, Knights, and socialists endorsed slightly different proposals and decided to bargain with each of the parties. Prominent citizens, led by Lyman Gage, were next in turn. Observing that never before had such an enormous sum of money been controlled by one governmental body, leaders expressed concern that the interest be paid into the sanitary board's treasury rather than appropriated for personal use by the treasurer, as was the custom. They called for a mass meeting to nominate independent candidates.[63]

On November 27 a coalition of citizens and prominent labor Democrats, including Richard Prendergast, met to voice their concern that "ward bummers" not control the drainage ditch. When the Democratic convention nominations proved a disappointment, leading citizens united on a nonpartisan ticket of six, including the Board of Trade millionaire Murray Nelson. The most novel feature was the addition of the ex-SLP German alderman J. J. Altpeter and the head of the labor-Democrats, Richard Prendergast. The platform included the eight-hour day and the performance of all labor by U.S. citizens, but its major thrust was antimachine. Both SLPers and Democrats railed against the citizen-labor alliance. Gruenhut declared, "Politics makes strange bedfellows. The bankers . . . who once posed as deadly enemies of self-styled anarchists and socialists, now enter into a political conspiracy with self-appointed labor leaders to outvote the local democracy which stands for all the practicable labor reforms in municipal administration." On December 12 a coalition of socialist German and Republican voters elected every citizen-candidate. Evidently, the much vaunted labor vote could not be wielded so easily by the Democrat party.[64]

The alliance of Republican and Democratic party patrician antimachine reformers with labor leaders and socialists was a breakthrough in Chicago politics. During the critical 1887 campaign the Citizens Association had refused a similar offer of an alliance from the United Labor party. The first break in the elitism of mugwump reformers had occurred with the conciliatory stance taken by silk-stocking Democrats during the clemency drive for the condemned anarchists. The 1888 and 1889 victories of Democratic candidates relying on the labor vote also had demonstrated conclusively that the reform movement could defeat the machine only by depriving it of labor votes. The citizen-labor alliance was thus the culmination of two years of developments in local politics. The political alliance over the drainage ditch construction did not last, but it did set an important precedent for the 1890s.

Viewed through the eyes of Thomas J. Morgan and other advocates of a labor party, the years 1887 and 1888 were ones of disappointment, demoralization, and failure. Both the labor and socialist movements and especially the Knights of Labor had seen the new institutions they had founded in 1886 destroyed or greatly reduced in influence. Yet by 1888 it was clear that the forces of reaction had proven to be almost as fragile. Two weeks after the Sanitary District elections Detwiler looked back on the events of the previous two years as "one of the most startling revolutions in public opinion that it would be possible to conceive of." After referring to the election alliance as "revolutionary," he mentioned the Sunset Club and the economic conferences as "milestones on the road to progress and the ultimate solution of economic and social problems." Detwiler also lauded the city's press for opening its columns to prolabor communications, such as those coming from Henry Demarest Lloyd. It "marks such a revolution in the attitude of the newspapers toward the working classes as would hardly have been deemed within the reasonable bounds of probability a few years ago."[65]

From Political Collective Bargaining to Collective Bargaining

Throughout the 1880s stable unions had increasingly relied on political collective bargaining to maintain a policy of noninterference on the part of city police in order to win strikes. The growth and broadening of labor organizations and labor's new legitimacy among respectable reformers helped make possible the beginnings of collective bargaining, with minimal political interference. At first such bargaining required the mediation of sympathetic and influential private figures, such as Judge Tuley. It was Tuley, backed by the strong force of public opinion, who mediated the building trades lockout of 1887. In August 1889 Tuley arbitrated a strike of Knights brickmakers. Though he found for the employers, he concluded by enunciating the principle that "it is only by employers and employees dealing justly and fairly with one another and carrying out their contracts in good faith that any harmonious relations can exist between them." He also arbitrated a wage demand by a small group of women workers connected with Hull-House, thereby winning the respect and admiration of Jane Addams.[66]

Labor was basking in its newfound legitimacy that year when civic leaders presented to the U.S. Congress its request that the 1892 World's Columbian Exposition be held in Chicago. The fair was conceived in the atmosphere of civic pride and social reform that had emerged in the city after the great upheaval. Willis J. Abbot, editor of the *Chicago Times,* recalled that "the days leading up to the Columbian Exposition" presented "a picture of extreme intellectual activity. . . . Men and women were talking and planning great things. Clubs for discussion, for study, for political reform, were springing up on every side."[67]

To labor the fair presented an unprecedented opportunity and a grave threat. By attracting unemployed skilled and especially unskilled labor to the city from all around the nation, the fair threatened to undermine local unions when surplus labor flooded the market. If, however, the fair's governing board would accept collective bargaining and other planks in labor's program, the fair could legitimize unionism in the city. In 1889 the fair badly needed popular support, and labor was in a position to provide it by lobbying before the state legislature and Congress and by subscribing to stock shares. Labor leaders agreed to do this, and in return the fair entered into an understanding that it would employ only union labor and arbitrate all disputes.[68] The prolabor tilt of the fair's leadership became evident when at a mass meeting in April 1890 the fair's executive council recommended that the new fair board include two labor representatives, while freezing out representatives of the city's ethnic groups. The new president of the board was Lyman Gage, who by this time called himself a "progressive conservative," subscribing to the Knights of Labor's ethical principle that "an injury to one is the concern of all." The *Tribune* casually called him "a champion of workers rights."[69]

The revolution in the public attitude toward the labor question was soon put to a test. In 1889 the American Federation of Labor had proclaimed another eight-hour strike for May 1, 1890. Though the strike was soon narrowed to the carpenters, it became an opportunity for other unions to revive or redouble organizing efforts in local industry. The carpenters' strike, scheduled for April 5, therefore threatened not only another shutdown of building operations but also a major labor-capital conflagration on the order of the one in 1886. City leaders had good reason to want to avoid a generalized upheaval. Another bitter strike would threaten the quid pro quo between capital and labor on building at the World's Fair. The carpenters' strike was thus a major test for the new civic consciousness, cross-class social reform, and the legitimacy of unionism.[70]

Since the city's carpenter contractors were resisting union recognition, city opinion leaders vigorously intervened on the eve of the strike. In a public petition they called on the contractors to submit their dispute to an arbitration committee, with a disinterested party to cast the deciding vote in case of deadlock. The petition was signed by most of the city's newspaper publishers, including Joseph Medill of the *Chicago Tribune;* twelve leading judges, including Judges Prendergast, Tuley, and Altgeld; and five top bankers, including E. G. Keith and Lyman Gage. Victor Lawson of the *Daily News* went furthest editorializing in favor of collective bargaining: "In other great industries employers recognized unions. Experience has proven to workingmen that united action is the best for them. Therefore they are not likely to go back to the old pauperizing system of individual competition unless they are driven to it by actual suffering." The Board of Trade millionaire and president of the Personal Rights League Robert Lindblom openly supported the carpenters, arguing that their strike was "in conformity with the recognized rules of business."[71]

It is noteworthy that business and civic leadership was being assumed not by large employers of labor but by bankers, judges, and newspaper editors, who were at the pinnacle of the local economy and society and who in their everyday business dealings were required to view industrial and civic life as an integrated whole and from a long-term perspective.[72]

When the union accepted arbitration and the contractors rejected it, the union was able to occupy the high ground in public opinion. Within weeks the union won a settlement from the smaller contractors, though the larger millwork contractors, as before, resisted a settlement until the following year. In the meantime the *Rights of Labor,* formerly the *Knights of Labor,* congratulated the carpenters for being the first union to win public opinion over to its side during a strike, noting that the list of contributors to the strike fund included "many of the most prominent Citizens of Chicago."[73]

Leading businessmen's support for the eight-hour day, union recognition, and arbitration in the planning for the World's Fair and during the carpenters' strike of 1890–91 represented another milestone in the emergence of a cross-class social reform movement in the three years following the Haymarket executions. But as the spring 1891 mayoral campaign approached, labor's budding alliance with patrician and respectable reformers was on the rocks. The first important issue of contention arose when a prime contractor for the actual building of the fair, McArthur Brothers, announced it would hire a thousand nonunion men for dredging work. At the very time that the carpenters were about to win the most significant collective bargaining contract in the city's history, the fair's resort to nonunion construction labor threatened to undo that triumph.

In early February James O'Connell, president of the United Carpenters Council, spoke defiantly before the Trades and Labor Assembly, asserting that "the day is passed when organized labor can be ignored in a great public enterprise of this kind." The *Rights of Labor* accused the fair of violating specific promises that it had made to get labor's support in 1889 when it was lobbying for the fair. On February 20 a joint committee representing labor organizations in the city approached the fair's directors with demands for preference for local union labor and U.S. citizens; the eight-hour day for all employees; a minimum wage of $1.50 a day for unskilled and unorganized labor; and arbitration of all labor disputes.[74]

Both Lyman Gage and Mayor Cregier were conciliatory and soothing, but on March 5 the fair's board of directors decided that while it could mandate arbitration and the eight-hour day, it could not dictate to contractors whom they should employ or what wages they should pay. Gage said he was not opposed to the principle of the closed shop but rather was concerned about the prospect of the construction unions' being unable to supply enough labor to complete the fair on time. He wrote Schilling confidentially that he had supported the minimum wage principle at board meetings, but he thought that its precedent should first be established by bargaining in the private sector. The fair's public reply was unacceptable to the joint labor committee, and from March through the rest of the year a series of strikes and skirmishes between labor and the fair and its contractors marred the building of the "White City." Still another sign of discord in the alliance of elite reformers and labor came in Springfield, where labor lobbyists joined representatives of capital in defeating a bill that provided for compulsory arbitration, with stiff penalties for noncompliance. The bill had been supported by the prolabor judges Altgeld and Prendergast.[75]

It was under these circumstances that some labor-Democrats, led by Charles Dixon and George Schilling, came together with representatives of the Personal Rights League, the Sunday Rest Association, and antimachine Republicans, including the publisher of the *Daily News*, Melville Stone, to reconstitute the citizen-labor alliance. On March 7 leaders nominated the business reformer Franklin MacVeagh for mayor. When MacVeagh formally refused to run three days later, they turned to Elmer Washburn, and the budding coalition quickly came apart. Washburne had been Mayor Medill's chief of police in 1873 when he tried to enforce the Sunday-closing law, and as superintendent of the stockyards in 1886 he had not endeared himself to unions. Washburn stood for clean government and strict enforcement of the laws, including Sunday closing, antigambling, and the Edwards law on mandatory education, but his politics bore little sign of the new progressive agenda. Almost immediately the PRL withdrew, dooming any chance of mass support from Germans.[76]

The citizens movement never included direct participation by trade union leaders. Some unionists continued to support the shell of the United Trade and Labor party, which had been formed the previous year by the carpenters and cigarmakers in an attempt to resuscitate the United Labor party, but most labor leaders were disposed to support Cregier's reelection campaign. The *Rights of Labor* credited him not only with abolishing police interference in strikes and winning the eight-hour day for city employees and World's Fair workers but also with seeking enabling legislation from the state for municipal ownership. As earlier elections had demonstrated, however, organized workers, like other elements of the city's voting population, were increasingly disquieted by machine politics and the corrupting ties engendered by the patronage that Democrats dispensed to the unions. Many unionists, the powerful carpenters in particular, had become alienated from the Trades and Labor Assembly and the United Trade and Labor party, both of which had fallen into the hands of a corrupt group led by William C. Pomeroy.[77]

As the Democratic primaries approached, dissatisfaction with Cregier found a lightning rod in the resurrection of the candidacy of Carter Harrison. On March 16 the PRL nominated Harrison for mayor on its own ticket. Going into the primaries, Harrison, with support from the *Illinois Staats Zeitung*, solidified his hold on the German-speaking voters of the city by pitching an appeal to ethnic workers on the issue of "personal rights," which meant opposition to the use of the police force to break up anarchist and socialist meetings and the threatened enforcement of the Sunday-closing law. Backed by the party's infrastructure, Cregier narrowly won the primaries and was nominated for mayor by the Democratic convention. But Harrison pressed on with his candidacy, portraying himself as the antimachine candidate, as Prendergast had done a year earlier.[78]

On the eve of the election five candidates were involved in a political free-for-all. The Irish and machine Democrats united behind their discredited friend Cregier. The Personal Rights League and ethnic workers rallied to Harrison, while the clergy and mugwump moralists held fast to Elmer Washburn. Republicans nominated Hempstead Washburne, a good government reformer who had the imprimatur of the Citizens Association. The fifth candidate, the socialist Thomas J. Morgan, ran on a municipal reform ticket. The election resulted in narrow victory for the Republican Hempstead Washburne, who with 46,957 votes outpolled Cregier by only 369 votes and Harrison by 4,026 votes. Elmer Washburn received 24,027 and Morgan only 2,376.[79]

The 1891 mayoral election represented a revival of ethnocultural issues and Harrison's old appeal to the city's ethnic community, but the appeals of all candidates except Cregier to antiparty reform also reflected the intensifying dissatisfaction with machine politics. Labor issues and the new prolabor progressive reform coalition and agenda played a minor role in the campaign, suggesting the limits of the ability of this movement to become a dominant force in the local electoral arena.

Elements of Diversity and Continuity

Beginning in 1887, not the depression of the 1890s, Gilded Age liberalism began to undergo a renovation of its prime postulates. Under the unsettling impact of labor's great upheaval—which dramatized the profound consequences of the growth of large-scale industry, the dysfunctionality of the competitive market, and the intractable social problems associated with wage work—key opinion leaders in Chicago began to question, rethink, or revise their belief in the self-regulating market, laissez-faire, and the isolation of individual character development from social influences, as well as their political distrust of the masses. A fertile environment for this process to ripen was created by the sensationalist exposés of the *Chicago Times*, which dispelled the public hysteria and antilabor reaction stemming from Haymarket and allowed respectable citizens to contemplate new ideas. The crucibles for this process were the personal relationships forged within groups that bridged class differences and allowed a more progressive liberalism to emerge in the post-Haymarket period, a liberalism championed by a new type of reform intellectual allied with working people in the name of social harmony and social justice. Because of their extraordinary ability to cross class boundaries, women, such as Elizabeth Morgan, played a crucial part in this process.

As Karl Polanyi has argued, the new liberalism was part of a reaction in the late nineteenth-century within and among all classes against the self-regulating market regime: "Not single groups or classes were the source of the so-called collectivist movement, though the outcome was decisively influenced by the character of the class interests involved." In Martin J. Sklar's formulation of the same process, "class conflicts and changing class relations, corresponding with developing modes of production, *generate* conditions and pressures for changes of profound effect, but emergent cross-class alignments *transact* them." The new urban liberalism was in essence an evolving political and ideological construction of a heterogeneous group of intellectuals, civic leaders, reformers, and spokespeople for capital and labor rather than a class-specific belief system, whether hegemonic or insurgent.[80]

Still, the emphasis on what new liberals had in common and how that differed from earlier liberalism should not obscure important elements of diversity and continuity. For one thing class differences prevented the new liberalism from constituting anything like a universal consensus. As evidenced by the dispute over the building of the World's Fair, few new liberals accepted the idea that unions had the right to prevent nonunion workers from working. Despite their support for arbitration and collective agreements, they could not endorse the closed shop or union hiring hall, a central principle of craft unionism. Put differently, though respectable liberals could countenance group regulation of the market, few were collectivists or corporatists. Because they viewed group membership as voluntary and group action as supplementing not displacing individualism, the term *liberal* is still applicable to these reformers.[81]

The same unwillingness to countenance collectivism was evident in different approaches to state involvement. Liberals like Franklin MacVeagh and Lyman Gage could accept voluntary associational regulation of market activities through corporations, trusts, employers' associations, and unions as the price for stabilizing the market, but they were loath to view the state as the terrain of society's course toward "cooperation." Intellectuals like Henry Demarest Lloyd, Clarence Darrow, and Jane Addams were willing to accept a larger degree of state initiative, but they too bridled at statism, that is, total state command of the economy. Whatever their differences, new liberals wanted to dilute individualism and competition with a large dose of socialism or cooperation, while retaining as much scope for individual initiative as possible. An influential solution offered by Henry Carter Adams in his 1886 essay "The State in Relation to Industrial Action" argued that government regulation could raise the ethical plane on which competition occurred without abolishing the market and that government should own public utilities and other natural monopolies but leave the rest of the economy in private hands.[82]

In the same way that the new liberals retained and carried forward their concern for individualism and property as a way of obviating state dictation, they also revived and built on republican themes dating to the eighteenth century. The belief that city monopolies granted by municipal franchises caused government corruption replicated a longstanding republican belief that cabals and conspiracies in government threatened or corrupted liberty. The willingness of a variety of civic leaders to seriously consider public ownership of municipal utilities no doubt drew on the antebellum belief that city government was a commonwealth.[83] Finally, devotion to a republican common good dictated that reform intellectuals not endorse industrial conflict as the means of change. Though such thinkers as Lloyd and Addams accepted strikes as a fact of social life, they sought as much as possible to mitigate conflict in the republic's social fabric through arbitration. Arbitration commissions, on which the public held a deciding vote, affirmed the republican principle that the general interest should have precedence over special interests, captured in Jane Addams's ideal of "organic democracy" as well as the social gospel principle of "social love." Though trade unionists remained wary of compulsory arbitration that might strip them of their right to strike, they and the new liberals found common ground in the principle of collective agreements.[84]

Another major element the new liberals retained and amplified was the 1870s faith in social science, expertise, and professionalism. Despite the democratization implicit in their broadened moral compass, they often proposed solutions with an elitist thrust. This was evident in their support for new state agencies of regulation and investigation staffed by social science experts such as themselves and the tendency to treat workers as "fallen souls" in need of moral uplift, even while moral suasion and Protestant crusading were being replaced by environmental solutions.[85]

Notwithstanding these continuities, it is evident that after 1886 a profound rethinking was taking place in the political economic thought of Gilded Age opinion leaders. It was the latest phase in the ongoing accommodation of liberty to equality in American history. By the late 1880s enough common ground existed among respectable reformers, progressive business leaders, trade unionists, and civic leaders to support joint action in the political sphere and to reshape the terrain of political possibility for labor action in the city.

Notes

1. See, for example, Melvin G. Holli, *Reform in Detroit: Hazen S. Pingree and Urban Politics* (New York: Oxford University Press, 1969); David P. Thelen, *The New Citizenship: Origins of Progressivism in Wisconsin, 1885–1900* (Columbia: University of Missouri Press, 1972); David Paul Nord, *Newspapers and New Politics: Midwestern Municipal Reform, 1890–1900*, Studies in American History and Culture, No. 27 (Madison, Wis.: UMI Research Press, 1981); Harold U. Faulkner, *Politics, Reform, and Expansion, 1890–1900* (New York: Harper and Row, 1959); and Paul Boyer, *Urban Masses and Moral Order in America, 1820–1920* (Cambridge, Mass.: Harvard University Press, 1978). For a different view, see J. Joseph Huthmacher, "Urban Liberalism in the Age of Reform," *Mississippi Valley Historical Review* 44 (Sept. 1962): 321–41.

2. Dorothy Ross argues that Haymarket repression largely aborted labor's socialistic influence on social science intellectuals. See Dorothy Ross, "Socialism and American Liberalism: Academic Social Thought in the 1880s," *Perspectives in American History* 9 (1977–78): 7–79; and Dorothy Ross, *The Origins of American Social Science* (Cambridge: Cambridge University Press, 1991), 98–140. For a different view, more in keeping with the one argued here, see Mary O. Furner, "The Republican Tradition and the New Liberalism: Social Investigation, State Building, and Social Learning in the Gilded Age," in *The State and Social Investigation in Britain and the United States*, ed. Michael J. Lacey and Mary O. Furner (Cambridge: Cambridge University Press, 1993), 197–218.

3. Sidney Fine, *Laissez-Faire and the General-Welfare State: A Study of Conflict in American Thought, 1865–1901* (Ann Arbor: University of Michigan Press, 1964), 47–95; Hebert Hovenkamp, *Enterprise and American Law, 1836–1917* (Cambridge, Mass.: Harvard University Press, chaps. 1–8.

4. Karl Polanyi, *The Great Transformation: The Political and Economic Origins of Our Times* (1944; reprint, Boston: Beacon, 1967), 3; John G. Sproat, *"The Best Men": Liberal Reformers in the Gilded Age* (1968; reprint, Chicago: University of Chicago Press, 1982), 142–203.

5. Michael Les Benedict, "Laissez-Faire and Liberty: A Re-Evaluation of the Meaning and Origins of Laissez-Faire Constitutionalism," *Law and History Review* 3 (Fall 1985): 293–331; William R. Brock, *Investigation and Responsibility: Public Responsibility in the United States, 1865–1900* (Cambridge: Cambridge University Press, 1984); Stephen Skowronek, *Building a New American State: The Expansion of National Administrative Capacities, 1877–1920* (Cambridge: Cambridge University Press, 1982), 47–68.

6. Charles Carroll Bonney, *The Present Conflict of Labor and Capital* (Chicago: Chicago Legal News, 1886); Carl Smith, *Urban Disorder and the Shape of Belief: The Great Chicago Fire, the Haymarket Bomb, and the Model Town of Pullman* (Chicago: University of Chicago Press, 1995), 64–87; Karen Sawislak, *Smoldering City: Chicagoans and the Great Fire, 1871–1874* (Chicago: University of Chicago Press, 1995), 88–100; Michael B. Katz, *Poverty and Policy in American History* (New York: Academic, 1983); Boyer, *Urban Masses and Moral Order,* 143–55.

7. Sproat, *"Best Men,"* 253–71; Citizens Association of Chicago, *Annual Reports, 1874–1901* (Chicago: Citizens Association of Chicago, 1901), 1874 report, 4–5 (quote); Gerald W. McFarland, *Mugwumps, Morals, and Politics, 1884–1920* (Amherst: University of Massachusetts Press, 1975), 38–52, 107, 120–21; *Chicago Tribune,* Mar. 24, 1874; Skowronek, *Building a New American State,* 52–55. Compare Richard Hofstadter, *The Age of Reform: From Bryan to F.D.R.* (New York: Vintage Books, 1955), 135–43.

8. *Chicago Tribune,* June 5, 1887; *Labor Enquirer,* June 4, 1887; Richard Sennett, "Middle-Class Families and Urban Violence: The Experience of a Chicago Community in the Nineteenth Century," in *Anonymous Americans: Explorations in Nineteenth-Century Social History,* ed. Tamara K. Harevan, (Englewood Cliffs, N.J.: Prentice-Hall, 1971), 288; Paul Avrich, *The Haymarket Tragedy* (Princeton, N.J.: Princeton University Press, 1984), 224; Bessie Louise Pierce, *A History of Chicago,* vol. 3, *The Rise of a Modern City, 1871–1893* (Chicago: University of Chicago Press, 1957), 284–93.

9. Christopher Lasch, *The New Radicalism in America, 1889–1963: The Intellectual as a Social Type* (New York: W. W. Norton, 1965), xiv–xvii.

10. Harry Barnard, *Eagle Forgotten: The Life of John Peter Altgeld* (1938; reprint, Secaucus, N.J.: Lyle Stuart, 1966), 88–93 (Shilling quote on 91).

11. Ibid., 121 (Darrow quote); Ray Ginger, *Altgeld's America, 1890–1905: The Lincoln Ideal versus Changing Realities* (Chicago: Quadrangle Books, 1958), 67–68, 71; Morton Keller, *Affairs of State: Public Life in Late Nineteenth Century America* (Cambridge, Mass.: Belknap, 1977), 581.

12. Chester McArthur Destler, *Henry Demarest Lloyd and the Empire of Reform* (Philadelphia: University of Pennsylvania Press, 1963), 1–144; Henry Demarest Lloyd, "The Story of a Great Monopoly," *Atlantic Monthly* 47 (Mar. 1881): 317–34; Henry Demarest Lloyd, "The Political Economy of $73,000,000," *Atlantic Monthly* 48 (July 1882): 69–81; Henry Demarest Lloyd, "Making Bread Dear,"

North American Review 86 (Aug. 1883): 118–36; Henry Demarest Lloyd, "Lords of Industry," *North American Review* 87 (June 1884): 535–53; E. Jay Jerrigan, *Henry Demarest Lloyd* (Boston: Twayne, 1976), 40–62.

13. Ross, "Socialism and American Liberalism"; Mary O. Furner, *Advocacy and Objectivity: A Crisis in the Professionalization of American Social Science, 1865–1905* (Lexington: University Press of Kentucky, 1975); Fine, *Laissez-Faire and the General-Welfare State,* 198–251; Edward W. Bemis, "Socialism and State Action," *Journal of Social Science* 21 (Sept. 1886): 33–68.

14. Stewart to Lloyd, Jan. 14, 1887 (first quote), Reel 1, Henry Demarest Lloyd Papers (microfilm), Wisconsin State Historical Society, Madison (hereafter HDLP); Stewart to Lloyd, Aug. 21, 1893, HDLP (second quote); Richard Schneirov, "The Friendship of Bert Stewart and Henry Demarest Lloyd: A Personal Vignette," in *Haymarket Scrapbook,* ed. Dave Roediger and Franklin Rosemont (Chicago: Charles H. Kerr, 1986), 157–59.

15. Destler, *Lloyd and the Empire of Reform,* 176; Henry Demarest Lloyd, "The New Conscience or the Religion of Labor," *North American Review* 91 (Sept. 1888): 325–39.

16. Destler, *Lloyd and the Empire of Reform,* 155–222 (quote on 216); John L. Thomas, *Alternative America: Henry George, Edward Bellamy, Henry Demarest Lloyd and the Adversary Tradition* (Cambridge, Mass.: Belknap, 1983), 80–81.

17. Paula Baker, "The Domestication of Politics: Women and American Political Society, 1780–1920," *American Historical Review* 89 (June 1984): 620–47; Ruth Bordin, *Women and Temperance: The Quest for Power and Liberty, 1873–1900* (Philadelphia: Temple University Press, 1981), 95–139; Ruth Bordin, *Frances Willard: A Biography* (Chapel Hill: University of North Carolina Press, 1986), 137–52.

18. Kathryn Kish Sklar, *Florence Kelley and the Nation's Work: The Rise of Women's Political Culture, 1890–1900* (New Haven, Conn.: Yale University Press, 1995), xii–xvi, 177, 370nn12, 13; Bordin, *Frances Willard,* 151–52; Kathleen D. McCarthy, *Noblesse Oblige: Charity and Cultural Philanthropy in Chicago, 1849–1929* (Chicago: University of Chicago Press, 1982), 46; Meredith Tax, *The Rising of the Women: Feminist Solidarity and Class Conflict, 1880–1917* (New York: Monthly Review, 1980), 291.

19. Mary Kenney O'Sullivan, "Autobiography," Papers of the Women's Trade Union League and Its Principal Leaders, Arthur and Elizabeth Schlesinger Library, Radcliffe College, Cambridge, Mass.; Jane Addams, *Twenty Years at Hull-House* (1910; reprint, New York: New American Library, 1981), 157; Jane Addams, "Hull-House: An Effort toward Social Democracy," *Forum* 14 (Sept. 1892–Feb. 1893): 238; Jane Addams, "The Settlement as a Factor in the Labor Movement," in *Hull-House Maps and Papers: A Presentation of Nationalities and Wages in a Congested District of Chicago by Residents of Hull-House* (New York: Thomas Y. Crowell, 1895), 183–204, 214–17; Tax, *Rising of the Women,* 56–61; Allen F. Davis, *American Heroine: The Life and Legend of Jane Addams* (New York: Oxford University Press, 1973), 77–80, 110–12 (quote about Kelley on 77).

20. *Chicago Tribune,* Nov. 5, 1887 (Tuley quote); Henry David, *The History of the Haymarket Affair,* 3d rev. ed. (New York: Collier Books, 1963), 356–76; Destler, *Lloyd and the Empire of Reform,* 161–63.

21. *Chicago Times,* Oct. 26, 1887, Oct. 30, 1887.

22. Ibid., Apr. 23, 1889, June 3, 1889, June 24, 1889; *Chicago Tribune,* Dec. 12, 1889, Mar. 10, 1891.

23. *Chicago Times,* Apr. 16, 1888; *Knights of Labor,* Jan. 4, 1890; *Chicago Tribune,* May 1, 1890; Lyman J. Gage, *Memoirs of Lyman J. Gage* (New York: House of Field, 1937), 69; MacVeagh's talk reprinted in *Leader,* Dec. 29, 1888, 18. On Gage's relationship with Schilling, see unpublished draft of Barnard's *Eagle Forgotten,* chap. 22, section "s," Harry Barnard Papers, Illinois State Historical Society, Springfield; his relationship with Jackson is discussed in Willis J. Abbot, *Watching the World Go By* (Boston: Little, Brown, 1933), 83–84.

24. Gage, *Memoirs,* 70–71 (first quote); W. W. Catlin, comp., *Echoes of the Sunset Club* (Chicago: Howard, Bartels, 1891); *Knights of Labor,* Mar. 1, 1890 (second quote). Speaking of the economic conferences, Jane Addams, "Hull-House: An Effort toward Social Democracy," 240, wrote, "Many thoughtful men in Chicago are convinced that if these conferences had been established earlier the Haymarket riot and all its sensational results might have avoided. The Sunset Club is at present performing much the same function."

25. Pierce, *History of Chicago,* 3:413–14. The new *Times* editors also allowed its employees to be unionized for the first time. See *The Rights of Labor,* June 18, 1892. By 1890 the *Times* was out of West's hands, ceased its exposés, and adopted a much more partisan and conservative editorial position. On the close tie between sensationalist journalism and nonpartisan, liberal interest group politics, see Philip J. Ethington, *The Public City: The Political Construction of Urban Life in San Francisco, 1850–1900* (Cambridge: Cambridge University Press, 1994), 308–19. On the link between a nonpartisan press and an "educational" style of politics, see Michael E. McGerr, *The Decline of Popular Politics: American North, 1865–1928* (New York: Oxford University Press, 1986), 107–83.

26. *Chicago Times,* July 29, 1888.

27. Cited in ibid., Aug. 20, 1888.

28. Ibid., Jan. 27, 1889. The series lasted from Apr. 29 through May 24, 1889.

29. For example, see *Chicago Tribune,* Nov. 18, 1888. The series lasted two months

30. Ibid., Feb. 19, 1888.

31. *Union Signal,* Aug. 23, 1888 ("seems to be" quote), Sept. 6, 1888; Ralph Scharnau, "Elizabeth Morgan, Crusader for Labor Reform," *Labor History* 14 (Summer 1973): 340–51 (IWA goal quote); Tax, *Rising of the Women,* 66–89; *Chicago Tribune,* Jan. 12, 1891; *Eight-Hour Herald,* Sept. 29, 1896; Carl S. Smith, *Chicago and the American Literary Imagination, 1880–1820* (Chicago: University of Chicago Press, 1984), 40–56.

32. Tax, *Rising of the Women,* 73–79.

33. Sklar, *Florence Kelley and the Nation's Work,* 216–23, 280–84.

34. On this dilemma, see esp. the *Chicago Record,* Jan. 31, 1889 (quotes), Mar. 7, 1889; *Knights of Labor,* Jan. 26, 1889.

35. Kathryn Kish Sklar, "Hull House in the 1890s: A Community of Women Reformers," *Signs* 10 (Summer 1985): 658–77; Skowronek, *Building a New American State,* chaps. 1–5.

36. *Knights of Labor,* Mar. 5, 1887; *Labor Enquirer,* Mar. 24, 1888 (quotes).

37. *Chicago Tribune,* Aug. 3, 1888, Aug. 12, 1888, Sept. 1, 1888 (quote).

38. Ibid., Oct. 10, 1888, Oct. 11, 1888, Oct. 12, 1888, Oct. 14, 1888.

39. Ibid., July 19, 1888; *Knights of Labor,* Feb. 22, 1888 (quote). On the *Daily News,* see Nord, *Newspapers and New Politics,* 41–42.

40. *Chicago Tribune,* Feb. 6, 1890, Mar. 5, 1890, Jan. 3, 1891, Feb. 21, 1891, Mar. 9, 1891, May 13, 1892; Destler, *Lloyd and the Empire of Reform,* 232; Ralf Wagner, "Turner Societies and the Socialist Tradition," in *German Workers' Culture in the United States, 1850–1920,* ed. Hartmut Keil (Washington, D.C.: Smithsonian Institution Press, 1988), 221–39.

41. *Knights of Labor,* May 18, 1889.

42. *Chicago Tribune,* July 23, 1888 (quote), Sept. 20, 1888, Oct. 15, 1888, Oct. 19, 1888, Oct. 24, 1888.

43. Ibid., Oct. 11, 1888, Oct. 18, 1888, Oct. 23, 1888, Nov. 7, 1888; Earl R. Beckner, *A History of Labor Legislation in Illinois* (Chicago: University of Chicago Press, 1929), 13–16, 34–37.

44. *Knights of Labor,* Nov. 10, 1888; *Chicago Tribune,* Oct. 11, 1888, Oct. 18, 1888, Oct. 23, 1888; *Chicago Times,* Nov. 8, 1888.

45. *Chicago Tribune,* Nov. 7, 1888; *Chicago Times,* Nov. 8, 1888; *Knights of Labor,* Nov. 10, 1888 (Gruenhut quote and Gruenhut's detailed analysis of the vote).

46. *Chicago Times,* May 11, 1889 (quote); *Chicago Tribune,* July 18, 1888, July 19, 1888, July 29, 1888; Bruce C. Nelson, *Beyond the Martyrs: A Social History of Chicago's Anarchists, 1870–1900* (New Brunswick, N.J.: Rutgers University Press, 1988), 194. On the secret fund, see *Chicago Herald,* Jan. 4, 1892.

47. *Chicago Tribune,* Nov. 17, 1888, Nov. 28, 1888, Nov. 30, 1888, Dec. 3, 1888, Dec. 9, 1888, Dec. 24, 1888.

48. Ibid., Aug. 12, 1888; Carolyn Ashbaugh, *Lucy Parsons: American Revolutionary* (Chicago: Charles H. Kerr, 1976), 126–66.

49. *Chicago Times,* Jan. 1, 1889, Jan. 5, 1889, Jan. 6, 1889.

50. Ibid., Jan. 20, 1889.

51. Ibid., Jan. 2, 1889, Jan. 6, 1889, Jan. 16, 1889.

52. Ibid., Feb. 24, 1889.

53. Ibid., Feb. 24, 1889, Mar. 15, 1889; *Knights of Labor,* Feb. 23, 1889, Mar. 16, 1889, Mar. 23, 1889.

54. *Chicago Tribune,* Mar. 17, 1889; *Knights of Labor,* Mar. 23, 1889.

55. *Knights of Labor,* Mar. 23, 1889; *Chicago Tribune,* Mar. 27, 1889, Mar. 28, 1889, Mar. 29, 1889.

56. *Chicago Tribune,* Mar. 27, 1889 (first and second quotes), Apr. 3, 1889; *Knights of Labor,* Apr. 6, 1889 (third quote). The origins of the antimachine ticket is discussed in depth in Barnard, *Eagle Forgotten,* 135–43.

57. Royal J. Schmidt, "The Chicago Daily News and Traction Politics, 1876–1920," *Journal of the Illinois State Historical Society* 64 (Autumn 1971): 315; *Chicago Times,* Feb. 24, 1889 (quote).

58. *Knights of Labor,* May 4, 1889, July 20, 1889.

59. Ibid., May 18, 1889 (first quote), Mar. 14, 1891 (second quote); *Chicago Times,* May, 7, 1889, June 25, 1889; Chester McArthur Destler, "The People's Party in

Illinois, 1888–1896: A Phase of the Populist Revolt," (Ph.D. diss., University of Chicago, 1932), 100n2 (Gruenhut estimate); *Chicago Tribune*, Nov. 11, 1889 (Morgan quote). On the effect of city hall hiring on the painters and tin workers, see *Chicago Tribune*, Mar. 6, 1893.

60. *Chicago Tribune*, Feb. 5, 1889 (quote), Nov. 1, 1890.

61. Michael P. McCarthy, "The New Metropolis: Chicago, the Annexation Movement, and Progressive Reform," in *The Age of Urban Reform: New Perspectives on the Progressive Era*, ed. Michael H. Ebner and Eugene M. Tobin (Port Washington, N.Y.: Kennikat, 1977), 43–54. On the annexation in the Town of Lake, see Louise Carroll Wade, *Chicago's Pride: The Stockyards, Packingtown, and Environs in the Nineteenth Century* (Urbana: University of Illinois Press, 1987), 331–51. On the new middle class, see James Gilbert, *Perfect Cities: Chicago's Utopias of 1893* (Chicago: University of Chicago Press, 1993), 4–11.

62. *Chicago Tribune*, Oct. 30, 1889, Oct. 31, 1889, Nov. 6, 1889; *Knights of Labor*, Nov. 9, 1889 (*Daily News* quote).

63. *Chicago Tribune*, Nov. 18, 1889, Nov. 20, 1889, Nov. 24, 1889.

64. Ibid., Nov. 28, 1889, Dec. 5, 1889; *Chicago Times*, Dec. 6, 1889 (Gruenhut quote).

65. *Knights of Labor*, Dec. 28, 1889.

66. *Chicago Tribune*, July 23, 1889, Aug. 3, 1889 (quote); Jane Addams, *The Excellent Becomes the Permanent* (New York.: Macmillan, 1932), 73–75.

67. Abbot, *Watching the World Go By*, 93.

68. *Rights of Labor*, Mar. 7, 1891.

69. *Chicago Tribune*, May 1, 1890. On Gage, see his address to the first economic conference in ibid., Jan. 4, 1890.

70. *Knights of Labor*, Mar. 2, 1889, Jan. 18, 1890, Jan. 25, 1890; *Chicago Tribune*, Mar. 5, 1889.

71. *Chicago Tribune*, Mar. 27, 1890; *Rights of Labor*, Apr. 5, 1890 (quotes).

72. Ginger, *Altgeld's America*, 280, emphasizes the role of bankers in the genesis of respectable reform, while David Paul Nord, "The Business Values of American Newspapers: The Nineteenth-Century Watershed in Chicago," *Journalism Quarterly* 61 (Summer 1984): 265–73, emphasizes the press.

73. *Rights of Labor*, May 10, 1890 (quote), June 7, 1890.

74. *Chicago Tribune*, Feb. 9, 1891 (quote), Feb. 13, 1891; *Rights of Labor*, Mar. 7, 1891.

75. *Chicago Tribune*, Feb. 6, 1891, Feb. 7, 1891; *Rights of Labor*, Feb. 14, 1891, Feb. 21, 1891, Feb. 28, 1891; Gage to Schilling, June 8, 1891, George A. Schilling Papers, Illinois State Historical Society, Springfield. On the carpenters' dispute with the World's Fair, see Richard Schneirov and Thomas J. Suhrbur, *Union Brotherhood, Union Town: The History of the Carpenters' Union of Chicago, 1863–1987* (Carbondale: Southern Illinois University Press, 1988), 48–53.

76. *Chicago Tribune*, Feb. 22, 1891, Mar. 1, 1891, Mar. 8, 1891, Mar. 11, 1891.

77. *Rights of Labor*, Mar. 14, 1891; *Chicago Tribune*, Mar. 18, 1891.

78. *Chicago Tribune*, Mar. 17, 1891.

79. *Rights of Labor*, Mar. 7, 1891, Mar. 21, 1891; *Chicago Tribune*, Apr. 8, 1891; Pierce, *History of Chicago*, 3:539.

80. Polanyi, *Great Transformation*, 161–62; Martin J. Sklar, *The United States as a Developing Country: Studies in U.S. History in the Progressive Era and the 1920s* (Cambridge, Cambridge University Press, 1992), 19. See also Martin J. Sklar, *Corporate Reconstruction of American Capitalism, 1890–1916: The Market, the Law, and Politics* (Cambridge: Cambridge University Press, 1988), 36–40, 434–41; David P. Thelen, "Social Tensions and the Origins of Progressivism," *Journal of American History* 56 (Sept. 1969): 323–41; and Stuart Hall, "Variants of Liberalism," in *Politics and Ideology*, ed. James Donald and Stuart Hall (Philadelphia: Open University Press, 1986), 67–68.

81. Martin Sklar, *Corporate Reconstruction of American Capitalism*, 437–38.

82. Henry Carter Adams, "The State in Relation to Industrial Action," in *Two Essays by Henry Carter Adams*, ed. Joseph Dorfman (New York: Columbia University Press, 1954), 57–133. See also Clarence Darrow, I. K. Boyeson, and George A. Schilling, "The State: Its Functions and Its Duties," in *Echoes of the Sunset Club*, comp. Catlin, 155–64; Martin Sklar, *Corporate Reconstruction of American Capitalism*, 437–38; Sidney Fine, *Laissez-Faire and the General-Welfare State*, 167–68, 335, 376.

83. Jon Teaford, *The Municipal Revolution in America: Origins of Modern Urban Government, 1650–1825* (Chicago: University of Chicago Press, 1975). As late as 1858 two transportation franchises retained the option of public ownership. See Robert David Weber, "Chicago Local Transportation in the Nineteenth Century" (Ph.D. diss., University of Wisconsin, 1971), 114.

84. Addams, *Twenty Years at Hull-House*, 100; Jane Addams, "The Present Crisis in Trades-Union Morals," *North American Review* 179 (Aug. 1904): 178–93.

85. Boyer, *Urban Masses and Moral Order*, 220–32; Smith, *Urban Disorder*, 209–31.

CHAPTER 12

Consolidating the New Unionism

The momentous events of the mid-1880s concentrated the implications of the industrial and social developments since the Civil War and presented them in the form of a political crisis for labor republicanism, the dominant ideology of organized Chicago workers, just as it did for mugwump liberalism, the ideology of respectable reformers. Labor republicanism (what antebellum workers called "equal rights republicanism") was a static philosophy ill-suited to make sense of and respond to rapid change. The juxtaposition of a golden age situated in a state of nature or a mythical America outside of history—in which workers owned and controlled the wealth produced by their labor and in which government was neutral and monopolies nonexistent—and real-life events could be used with devastating effect to highlight the deficiencies of existing social arrangements. Although natural rights thinking justified outrage at infringements on liberty and counseled subversive action, it provided no guide to identifying conditions in existing social life that had the potential for transformative change.[1] Natural rights republicanism posited an ideal republic whose health—equated with the citizenry's civic virtue—was ever at risk from corruption stemming from the growth of commerce or centralized power in the state. Republican thinking was, in the words of J. G. A. Pocock, in a perpetual "quarrel with history."[2]

Nowhere was the historical and social change feared by American republican thinkers more sudden, discontinuous, and stunning than in Chicago. Between 1880 and 1890 the city had more than doubled in size, from 503,000 to 1,100,000; since 1860 the population had increased by a factor of ten. Meanwhile, what had been a regional commercial entrepôt had become the nation's second largest industrial city, with a higher percentage of its population in manufacturing than any other large American city. Manufacturing workers were highly concentrated in a few large firms. According to 1890 Board of Health statistics, 3,000 large firms employed 125,000 of the city's 360,000 wage earners. Sixty-six of these firms, each averaging over 500, employed approximately 75,000 of these workers. Chicago's largest "monopoly," however, was chartered by city government, the so-called gas trust founded in 1887. By 1890 the city also boasted over two hundred homegrown millionaires, six of whom owned over 10 million dollars in assets, while Marshall Field led with 25 million.[3]

Confronted by unprecedented social change, the concentration of wealth and power, and attendant industrial warfare, thinkers influenced by natural rights republicanism responded with a burst of apocalyptic writings. The American republican fabric woven of agrarian simplicity, Protestant moral virtues, propertied independence, and small-town harmony appeared to be on the brink of a cataclysm, produced by a kind of "social dynamite" in its urban centers. The source of destruction might be, depending on the background and proclivities of the writer, grasping monopolists, demagogic and corrupt machine politicians, ignorant and infidel foreign-born anarchists, a desperate and impoverished proletariat, or combination of any of them. Often the same writings warning of cataclysm depicted an alternative utopia or, if warnings were not heeded, a dystopia. Henry George's *Progress and Poverty* (1879), Edward Bellamy's *Looking Backward* (1888), William Dean Howell's *Traveller from Altruria,* Mark Twain's *Connecticut Yankee in King Arthur's Court* (1889), and Ignatius Donnelly's *Caesar's Column* (1890) were among the most popular and influential works in this genre. According to Kenneth Roemer in a study of 160 utopian novels published in the twelve years beginning in 1888, the writings reflected a perception that America was "coming apart" and sitting on top of an urban "volcano." To these writers utopias were final opportunities to put the Republic back together again and renew it for all time. The United States was "the great experiment on which the last hopes of the race depends . . . ," wrote Bellamy, "if it be a failure, it will be a final failure."[4]

In Chicago this apocalyptic discourse was not limited to the middle and upper classes. A variety of labor leaders after Haymarket expressed a deep sense of foreboding about the direction of change. The *Knights of Labor* printed a seer's prophecy that a tremendous upheaval would give the monopolists' the power to reinstitute a "monarchy," which would spark a mighty contest that "would sound the death knell of monopoly." An editorial compared the times to those of ancient Rome when the Gracchi brothers waged a battle against the privileged classes for the soul of the republic. References in the paper to the urban poor and tramps as "huns and vandals" echoed Henry George, who wrote, "Whence shall come the new barbarians? Go through the squalid quarters of our great cities and you may see even now their gathering hordes."[5]

During the violent Homestead Steel strike of 1892, George Detwiler editorialized that to perpetuate "American institutions on the line laid down by the founders . . . may require a social earthquake, compared with which the Homestead Affair will be but a slight ripple. . . . The volcano under the social strata is burning with a hundred times more intensity today than it did six years ago." These thoughts seem to have been common currency among Chicago labor leaders. "It would surprise the wealthy to know," wrote Detwiler, "how often violent revolution is discussed [by labor leaders] without any expressions of disapproval. They think they are on a railroad train hurtling toward a chasm." In 1894 the city's most influential labor leader, the notorious William C. Pomeroy, published a cataclysmic, dystopian novel—in answer to labor-Populists—in which a 1910 revolution against "the rule of mammon" resulted in a Marxist "social republic," making men "slaves to the state."[6]

Among the very same people who were voicing fears that the Republic was on the verge of irreparable corruption, however, a very different labor philosophy was arising. It may even be that the very intensity with which the fear of social catastrophe gripped the imaginations of labor leaders impelled them all the more to recoil from its consequences and seek alternatives to the antihistorical equal rights republicanism. At its base the new thinking was resolutely evolutionary and historicist. Unlike the subversive metaphysic of natural liberty, it accommodated to evolving conditions but nonetheless viewed the direction of that evolution as compatible with some of the most idealistic labor goals. It also treated individual rights as capable of being supplemented by or even merged into group interests.

On the national level the new discourse has been traced in the thought of Samuel Gompers. It is evident as well in the extant labor papers in Chicago following the end of the great upheaval, particularly in the writings of two influential figures, the *Knights of Labor* editor George Detwiler and the former *Alarm* editor Dyer Lum. Of the three European, at times conflicting, at times mutually reinforcing, intellectual sources of the new discourse—Herbert Spencer, August Comte, and Karl Marx—by far the most influential among such American-born thinkers as Detwiler and Lum was Herbert Spencer. Spencer's thought has been mistakenly conflated with a social Darwinism that rationalized the amoral business methods of Gilded Age robber barons. In fact, Darwinian thought—popularized by Spencer—constituted the intellectual sea in which late nineteenth-century Americans swam. As a kind of national common sense, Spencer's thinking could be and was interpreted in a number of different ways. While Andrew Carnegie used Spencer's struggle for survival doctrine to justify large accumulations of capital, labor leaders and journalists drew on Spencer's warm support of "voluntary cooperation" among freely contracting individuals to justify their dreams of a cooperative commonwealth. In the course of this selective appropriation of Spencer some also imbibed Spencer's evolutionary naturalism, which was used to predict and justify the coming age of social cooperation. Laurence Gronlund relied heavily on Spencer in his book predicting socialism, entitled *The Cooperative Commonwealth* (1886), as did the feminist socialist Charlotte Perkins Gilman and the utopian nationalist Edward Bellamy.[7]

Spencerian evolutionism was also at the core of a remarkable transformation in the thought of George Detwiler. A pro–Republican party labor editor who originally had called for hanging the anarchists and had staunchly supported Powderly and his local allies, Detwiler exhibited a remarkable capacity for change. He visited the anarchists in their cells to deliver a personal apology and supported the United Labor party. By 1888 he was disillusioned with Powderly and opened the columns of the *Knights of Labor* to the socialist Joe Gruenhut and the ex-anarchist Dyer Lum. Then, beginning with the AFL's eight-hour campaign in 1889, Detwiler repudiated Powderly, endorsed Samuel Gompers and the principle of trade autonomy, and changed the name of the paper to the *Rights of Labor.* Trade unions "are here to stay," wrote Detwiler. "The trade union movement is a natural movement in the line of evolution." Rejecting such "absolute philosophies" as greenbackism and state socialism, Detwiler wrote, "These theorists and dreamers have had their day in court, now let us see what can be done by the other side, by the Trade Unionist who believes in compromises, by the intelligent employer of labor who believes in arbitration, by the men who are managing the great eight hour movement, and by the men who are conservative as to measures and radical as to results." Seeking to square his belief in individual rights with trade unionism, Detwiler argued, "In a state of society wherein voluntary co-operation has succeeded the militant regime such as Herbert Spencer has characterized as the 'industrial type' and toward which all sociologists admit we are tending," trade unionists had the same right to coerce strikebreakers as a country "invaded by an aggressive and warlike power" did to defend itself.[8]

The major mechanism for evolution was the collective struggle for an improved standard of living in the form of higher wages and shorter hours. "Increased leisure with the maintenance of present standards of comfort and decency knowing that these will thereby increase," wrote Detwiler, "is the cry of the new spirit. The growing desire for solidarity between toilers . . . and increased comfort will give an impetus to the demand of labor to gratify still higher wants, and with increased intelligence necessarily result[s] the ability to gratify them." Detwiler contended that "[labor] organization had directly affected wages." There was an "inexhaustible storehouse of unacquired wealth" produced by modern society from which workers could draw. Hence, Detwiler jettisoned the Knights' opposition to strikes and lauded AFL unionists for being "radical labor men. They believe in strikes; it may be as a dernier resort, but when they strike they believe in striking hard."[9]

Dyer Lum, the firebrand revolutionary of 1886, was another who adapted his beliefs in free association and individualism to the era of trade unionism. In 1892 the AFL published his *Philosophy of Trade Unions,* in which he argued, citing Herbert Spencer, that in the new age that would succeed "militancy," trade unions would embody the new ethical spirit of industrialism. Like Peter J. McGuire, the socialist leader of the Brotherhood of Carpenters and Joiners of America, Lum saw the highest stage of unionism as the time "in which labor will no longer contest on the old grounds, but step into the market and contract for itself, and under its own guidance, furnish the required labor supply without asking the aid of an intermediate boss." This evolution toward free association was proceeding slowly but inexorably, like "the vine [that] unconsciously creeps along the ground and up a stone wall." Lum's agent of evolution, the trade union, embodied the values of self-reliance and mutualism, thus enabling it to eschew dependence on state paternalism. Such views endeared Lum to George Detwiler, who predicted in the wake of the successful 1890 carpenters' strike that "within a life time 'the strike' will change its character, and instead of being merely a demand for wages will consist in discharging the 'boss' and undertaking the job under contract."[10]

The ideas of Lum and Detwiler suggest that while AFL advocates abandoned the goal of immediately asserting workers' natural rights to the product of their labor through producers' cooperatives or revolution, they retained it as the end point of a natural evolution of industrial society whose direction and impetus was produced by trade union solidarity and tactics. In 1890 Samuel Gompers, long tutored in Marxism and still a socialist, reproduced this formulation, asserting that trade unions "pure and simple" were "the natural organization of the wage workers to secure their present material and practical improvements and to achieve their emancipation." The yoking of long-term aims to trade unionism and natural evolution was therefore not a repudiation of socialism or theory but rather anticipated a fin de siècle transformation—popular among many craft unionists—of socialism into a "revisionist" or Fabian socialism, in which ultimate ends were seen at first as imminent in the short-term reforms generated by working-class action and later as part of an evolution without end.[11] As the German "revisionist" socialist Eduard Bernstein put it, "The movement means everything for me and what is 'usually' called the final aim of socialism is nothing." The views of the evolutionist trade unionists echoed those of Ed Irwin, a typographer and the editor of the *Progressive Age,* who in objecting to anarchist revolution, wrote, "We live under a system that reason tells us cannot be removed at least during our lifetime. . . . Our destination may be upon the mountain top but we shall arrive at it all the sooner, and have a more comfortable journey if we pay heed to the steps that lie in between. . . ." Both evolutionary trade unionism and "revisionist" socialism may be viewed as part of the era's intellectual revolt against formalism that "paradoxically" resulted in relocating America's state-of-nature, mythical "Adam" in a utopian future toward which industrial evolution was (apparently) inevitably progressing.[12]

In placing so much faith in the power of self-reliant labor organizations, the new trade union philosophy was in significant ways voluntarist. Still, it normally acknowledged an important role for government action, especially on the local and state levels.[13] Ex-anarchists like Lum notwithstanding, most Chicago labor leaders implicitly distinguished between statism, or what they called "paternalism" or "tyranny," and positive state action, which could include regulatory and redistributive laws. George Detwiler rejected Bellamy's and the Socialist Labor party's state socialism but nonetheless endorsed federal ownership of the railroads and telegraphs and, like the platforms of labor parties and the Democratic party, supported state action to regulate sweatshops, shorten the hours of labor, and take over municipal utilities. A survey in 1890 suggests that rank-and-file skilled workers backed their leaders. "In general, they seem to have a leaning toward socialism," reported the *Tribune,* by which the paper meant government ownership of trusts. Labor's most popular political leader in the early 1890s, John Peter Altgeld, closely mirrored labor's attitude toward state action. He opposed labor injunctions, specifically the one used to bring federal troops to Chicago in the 1894 Pullman strike, and spoke out against centralization on the federal level, yet he also supported a raft of progressive legislation that expanded government's role in regulating the economy. On the national level the AFL also supported state action as a supplement to trade unionism. Although the AFL steered clear of independent labor or socialist parties and a socialist plank that would federalize all means of production largely out of fear that trade unions would become subordinated to the Socialist Labor party and to a Leviathan state, it sanctioned federal ownership of the railroads, local ownership of utilities, a federal income tax, and state sweatshop regulations, among other things.

It did, however, oppose state action that might compete with the goods that might be won by unions through collective bargaining or supplied by them as benefits.[14]

The AFL and the Eight-Hour Campaign of 1890

It was in 1889 that the AFL first exerted undisputed organizational and ideological hegemony over the Chicago labor movement. Drawing on labor's experience during the great upheaval, the AFL's national convention in 1888 called for a strike for the eight-hour day on May 1, 1890, and authorized the agitation to begin in 1889. As Gompers well knew, the eight-hour movement had the potential of uniting the warring internal factions of labor in a single phalanx and mobilizing the rank and file behind the cause of unionism. Strong unions in turn were the surest route to the acceptance of the "trade agreement," which may have been the single most important labor achievement of the 1890s.[15]

With approximately 60 percent fewer members at the end of 1889 than at the end of 1886, the labor movement in Chicago was in "a dead calm," and few unions were ready to strike. Those unions actively committed to the eight-hour movement, principally the carpenters' union, agitated for legislation and government action to establish shorter hours. The city passed an eight-hour ordinance—which reaffirmed Mayor Cregier's prolabor credentials and allowed him to speak at the Fourth of July picnic. Soon after, the county and the Chicago Board of Education followed with similar action. But there was little serious organizing—with the small exception of Tom Barry's Brotherhood of United Labor (BUL) in the packinghouse region—until two months before the great day.[16]

In March 1890 the AFL executive council decided to forego a general strike and instead selected the Brotherhood of Carpenters and Joiners of America—recognized as the most likely trade union to succeed in winning the shorter workday—to carry the banner for the other unions. Over the previous four years the carpenters' union had emerged as Chicago's largest union and the prime source of vitality for local labor. In 1889, as the union prepared for the 1890 strike, it had overcome longstanding ethnic and political divisions. Former German anarchist locals 240 through 244, the independent Progressive Carpenters Union, plus prominent Knights leaders of the old LA 6570 merged into Local 1. The new local of twelve hundred members comprised over half of the brotherhood's membership in the city and was the most politically active and militant as well. By July 1890 Local 1's president, James O'Connell, was also president of the Trades and Labor Assembly; another carpenter official headed the city's Building Trades Council; and still another had risen to secretary treasurer of the Central Labor Union. On the national level Chicagoan William Kliver was president of the brotherhood.[17]

For the carpenters the prime issue was not the winning of shorter hours but union recognition in the form of a joint arbitration committee, for the union realized that only a stable trade agreement would enable them to generalize throughout the industry a demand that been won and then lost twice since 1886. On the eve of the April 7 strike date the United Carpenters Council controlled 70–90 percent of the carpenters. Recognizing the strength afforded the union by the World's Fair building boom and the widespread fear of another upheaval on the order of the one in May 1886, city leaders intervened to urge arbitration. Though a strike did occur, never before had labor and the principle of collective bargaining basked in so much respectability and public sympathy.[18]

In the week before the strike two union victories by the cigarmakers and plumbers intensified the mood of anticipation among workers. "Almost every trade is awakening," reported the *Rights of Labor.* Organizing efforts were particularly strong among the waiters and machine woodworkers and to a lesser extent among the painters, hardwood-floor finishers, shoemakers, machinists, and the coopers in the packinghouses. On the eve of the great strike the carpenter contractors accepted arbitration with the union, though the large millwork contractors refused to participate. On April 23, 30,000 workers heard Samuel Gompers, Henry Demarest Lloyd, and Samuel Gross laud the need for shorter hours; on May 1, 10,000 workers attended a May Day parade, and a total of 25,000 heard speeches on the lakefront by the mayor and labor leaders. The next day 4,000 machine woodworkers in the door, sash, and blind mills walked out for the eight-hour day.[19]

The number on strike was a tiny fraction of the 100,000 hoped for by some and dreaded by others in the city. The *Chicago Tribune* observed that the mood was quite different from that of 1886: "While enthusiasm is not lacking, it is not like that effervescent sentiment of four years ago. It is more subdued." Several factors explain the difference. Many of the strikers of 1886, notably the cigarmakers and those in the building trades, had already won eight hours. Another large segment, those in the packinghouses, were largely quiescent in 1890. After the 1886 strike many of the Irish, who had dominated not only the skilled butcher and cooper trades but also the floating mass of laborers, had been replaced by recent immigrants. These workers were divided by nationality and were less responsive to the leadership provided by the Irish Knights, formerly of DA 57, now of the BUL.[20]

The lack of enthusiasm and millennial expectation was far from disappointing to labor leaders, though. It meant that the anarchists, who in 1886 had sought to link eight hours with violent revolution, were no longer present to spook the public and give employers a pretext to stand firm against union demands. It also signified that fewer newly organized workers were prone to the naive expectation that they could win their demands against the intransigence of large firms simply by relying on the promises of solidarity from the Knights of Labor. Four years of experience had left veteran labor leaders affiliated with the AFL at the helm of local labor. These officials "represented a strong nucleus of well-disciplined [union] men who know what they want and are trained at estimating the chances of success," reported the *Tribune.* Rank-and-file workers were responsive to the pleas of these leaders to avoid striking out of the enthusiasm of the moment. The strikes of 1890 were therefore fewer in number but more deliberate, and they were part of ongoing organizing campaigns. Unlike in 1886, the eight-hour day demand was less a goal in itself than a means to union recognition.[21]

If May 1, 1890, had been something of an anticlimax, events during the ensuing twelve months went a long way toward fulfilling early spring's high expectations. The storms of labor conflict continued to roil the atmosphere of the city as the carpenters sought to consolidate their April victory by signing up the millwork contractors. In September 1890 over eight thousand carpenters struck, but they were again stymied in their quest for union recognition. Because of the pressure from the World's Fair directors, the millwork contractors finally accepted a trade agreement the following March. Meanwhile, the cornicemakers, bakers, and Illinois Central workers aggressively organized and struck for union recognition and shorter hours. Organizing revived among the Yerkes streetcar workers and among the shoemakers, painters, machinists and blacksmiths, cloakmakers, and architectural ironworkers, the key trade in the construction of the city's new skyscrapers. Especially energetic were the continuing efforts of the machine woodworkers and the waiters, including African American waiters, to sign up restaurants on a closed-shop contract. In September railway switchmen in the stockyards threatened a shutdown of the packinghouses. As late as October the steamfitters fought for union recognition and the eight-hour day.[22]

Altogether, in 1890 the number of strikers in Chicago rose over tenfold, to 34,220 from 3,082 the previous year, and slightly exceeded the total in 1887. Of the 83 strikes, 56, or 67 percent, were called by a labor organization, and a slight majority of these resulted in partial or complete successes. Unlike in 1886, when the vast majority of strikes had been over hours, the strikes in 1890 contested a variety of issues: 36 were for higher wages, 21 were over hours, 16 were over control of employment, and 8 were over union rules. By fall 1890 approximately 65,000 workers were organized in unions in the city, 90 percent of the peak during the Haymarket era.[23]

The impetus from the AFL's 1890 movement continued into 1891. The number of strikers fell to 11,226, but 68 percent of the strikes were successful. In February the *Rights of Labor* reported that "within the past three or four weeks more than thirty organizations have been perfected. . . ." By Labor Day a *Chicago Tribune* reporter estimated that the city had as many as 150,000 union members organized in 300 unions, an incredible 42 percent of the city's work force. This figure was probably exaggerated, since the same paper reported only 90,000 organized in 146 unions a year later. Still, there can be no doubt that in the first years of the 1890s union organization had exceeded the peak achieved during the Haymarket era.[24]

The New Unionism of the 1890s

According to a widely accepted view, AFL craft unionism was an institution that served the narrow interests of skilled craftworkers and excluded those unskilled and semiskilled workers, women, African Americans, and new immigrants previously organized by the Knights of Labor. Drawing fodder from the new unionism's contemporary socialist (later Industrial Workers of the World—IWW) critics, many have characterized the AFL approach as business unionism or pure and simple unionism, one that prudentially eschewed lofty goals as unwinnable and pragmatically accepted the wage system or capitalism. In pursuing narrower bread-and-butter goals, the new unions sought to contain contagious mass strikes, including sympathy walkouts, and marginalized recent immigrants, women, and African Americans, especially after the mid-1890s.[25] Whatever its merits for characterizing a later period, the thesis that craft unionism was largely conservative or even reactionary is seriously misleading if applied to the 1887–95 period. A survey of craft unionism in this period that looks at how much wine was *in* the bottle rather than how much of the bottle was empty reveals not only the progressive accomplishments of the new unionism but also important elements of continuity with the culture of the Knights of Labor, as well as accommodationist tendencies. The major institutional features of the new unionism can be summarized in four points.

First, the impetus from the great upheaval for solidarity and broad-gauged organization to incorporate less-skilled workers remained powerful in the early 1890s. The 1890s was an integral part of an ongoing transition that had begun in the late 1870s and had been accelerated by the Knights of Labor, from the ethnic community-based mass strike, accompanied by contagious enthusiasm and explosive confrontations with authorities, to the more calculating union-sanctioned strike oriented toward establishing stable trade agreements with employers.

During this period unions experimented with a variety of organizational forms not only to unite ethnopolitical factions but also to overcome jurisdictional animosities and rivalries and to unite workers of different skill levels. Because many formerly skilled and privileged trades were confronted with an intensified division of labor and the consequent employment of less-skilled, lower-paid workers, they had long since lost the option of walling themselves off from competitors. One way to attract less-skilled workers was to demand a uniform minimum wage for all workers, regardless of ability; another was to fight for shorter hours. In such trades as carpentry and painting, in which two-thirds of all journeymen were greenhorn workers employed by the piece under the subcontracting system, such demands attracted less-skilled workers as satellites around the loyal core of skilled journeymen. Something similar was going on among unions in other sweated trades, such as cigarmaking, baking, cloakmaking, and the service trades in the restaurant and hotel businesses. In some industries activists formed true industrial unions. In Chicago the most prominent ones of the early 1890s were the Machine Woodworkers International Union (1890), which, unlike the International Furniture Workers Union, organized machine woodworkers, and the American Railway Union (1893), which united railroad workers of different skill levels. Two other important local unions founded on an industrial basis—the brickmakers and brewery workers—also included large numbers of machine tenders.[26]

Another common approach to incorporating unskilled workers was the formation of separate unions. The steamfitters' helpers organized separately from the journeymen, as did the vessel unloaders' union and most women workers. Once formed, these unions often united in councils for purposes of resolving jurisdictional disputes, coordinating strike activities, and making agreements with employers. The tendency to form councils originated with the Knights of Labor. The first building trades council was formed by the Knights, as was the first marine trades council, both in 1887. Reflecting the newfound power of the national and international unions, these councils began to usurp functions earlier performed by the Trades and Labor Assembly, Knights district assemblies, and the Central Labor Union in ordering boycotts and coordinating sympathy strikes.

The most important exemplar of the trades council movement was the Building Trades Council (BTC). Formed in October 1890 in the midst of the struggle against the refusal of the World's Fair to grant a union wage and composed of twenty-four unions, the BTC was the first enduring council of building trades unions in the city's history. A constitution vested authority in a house of delegates, but real power lay in the hands of the Board of Business Agents, or walking delegates, which at a moment's notice could call out all union labor working on a particular building. The idea of many trades' "sympathy striking" one building at a time to prevent the use of nonunion labor, instead of each trade's striking many buildings, won general acceptance after two strikes in 1891 united the stronger trades that had trade agreements, such as the bricklayers, with the weaker trades, such as the painters. The forging of a centralized BTC was a turning point in the ability of building trades workers in Chicago to win their strikes. Between 1886 and 1890 only 43 percent of strikes were successful; in the next three years the percentage of successful strikes rose steadily, reaching 85 percent in 1894.[27]

Alongside the BTC came other new councils serving the same purpose. Perhaps second in importance was the Allied Printing Trades Council, which consisted of the type founders, lithographic engravers, English, German, Scandinavian, and Bohemian printers, electrotypers, stereotypers, press feeders, and binders and boasted twenty unions by 1895. Seven unions of the machine woodworkers plus skilled cabinetmakers and hardwood-floor finishers came together in the United Mill Trades Council. The Marine Trades Council united skilled ship carpenters and unskilled lumber, coal, and salt unloaders. Waiters and cooks of different skill levels and ethnic and racial backgrounds, many of them former Knights, organized the Culinary Alliance. The Machinery Trades Council consisted of the blacksmiths, brassworkers, boilermakers, patternmakers, machinists, and iron molders. The Clothing Trades Council consisted of over a dozen skilled and unskilled trades unions, including women. On both the local and the national level, the skilled trades of conductors, firemen, switchmen, and trainmen cooperated in the Supreme Council of Federated Order of Railway Employees.[28]

In short the search by craft unionists for forms to include new groups of workers, so characteristic of the Knights during the great upheaval, remained an important feature of early 1890s unionism. Though not identical with industrial unionism, the attempts of craft unions to amalgamate prefigured an early twentieth-century "craft industrialism" that sought to reconcile craft organization with industrial organization within the AFL on the national level.[29]

A second element of unionism of this period was the tendency to rely on high enough dues to supply benefits, thereby enabling members to enjoy a measure of personal security and independence. Dues also paid full-time professionals on both the local and national levels to administer benefit systems and strike funds. No less important, benefits promoted a spirit of interdependence and fraternity and to union leaders provided an incentive for loyalty to the organization through hard times. For dues of $.30 a week the cigarmakers' union, an exemplar of the new unionism designed by Samuel Gompers and Adolph Strasser, offered sick benefits of $5.00 per week for up to thirteen weeks in a year, out-of-work benefits of $3.00 a week for up to eighteen weeks, and death benefits up to $550. In 1891 the union bragged that in ten years its members' pay had doubled and hours had decreased 25–40 percent; during their recent walkout strikers had received $8.00 a week for six weeks from the national strike fund. By 1893 twenty thousand Chicago unionists were receiving unemployment benefits from their unions, prominent among them were the cigarmakers, typographers, carpenters, and bricklayers.[30]

The tendency to run unions as businesses dedicated to advancing members' short-term interests while abandoning the long-term goal of emancipating workers from the wage system has been called business unionism. The term is accurate in its implication that unionists sought efficiency and expertise in the conduct of their unions through paid professionals at the local and national level and that they boasted that strikes, union label boycotts, and collective bargaining agreements were paying propositions for their members. But rather than view labor leaders as rejecting the ideal in favor of the practical, it makes more sense to understand them as attempting to put real foundations under the castles in the sky constructed by the movements of the mid-1880s, that is, to fashion more realistic means to advance the same ends.[31]

For one thing a significant number of 1890s union leaders had lived through the period of the great upheaval, which had been indelibly stamped with the Knights' and socialist ideals of inclusiveness, solidarity, and emancipation from the wage system. According to the biographies of twenty-nine union leaders printed in the *Eight-Hour Herald,* a labor paper, from 1896 to 1897 only half had joined the labor movement recently enough to have missed the 1880s great upheaval, and this sample omitted the socialist and radical wing of labor leaders.

A perusal of the *Eight-Hour Herald* in the mid-1890s suggests that many of the more conservative trade unionists viewed trade unionism much as George Detwiler and Dyer Lum did. Chicago's James O'Connell, president of the International Association of Machinists, averred that "the object of trade unions" was "the absolute emancipation of the wage workers from that form of slavery—working for wages. . . . The Trade-union movement of today has no thought of limiting, moderating or modifying the most advanced ideals of the most advanced (so-called) radical thinkers." He differed only in rejecting "revolutionary spasms" in favor of gradual evolution. O. E. Woodbury, president of the United Carpenters Council, speaking before the Sunset Club, said that one of the goals of the carpenters' unions was to do "what lies within their power to educate the masses up to where they will get out from the thralldom of the wage slave system. . . ." The British visitor Charles Spahr concluded his observations of the Chicago labor movement at the end of the decade by prophesying that "the time is coming when the unions may be able to manage business co-operatively. . . . The men may seem commonplace and the measures petty, but it is through just such instrumentalities that the great designs for human advancement are always worked out." In short, business unionism mixed opportunism and idealism and short- and long-term outlooks; which pole would predominate depended on circumstance.[32]

A third and critical feature of trade unionism in this period was the drive toward control of employment, that is, regulation of the labor market. Arbitration, the catchphrase of the Knights of Labor, was increasingly replaced by the more practical demands necessary for implementing it—union recognition in the form of the closed shop and the trade agreement—and the strike, which gave workers the power to enforce these demands. The highest form of control that a union could exercise would be to get employers to agree to hire only from the union hiring hall, a privilege enjoyed by the bricklayers. Less entrenched unions, such as the carpenters' union, could still rely on a closed-shop agreement. In both cases the negotiated benefits enjoyed by the workers derived from a worker's membership in his or her particular trade rather than the rights attached to the job at the worksite. Craft unions offered workers employment security within the trade as a whole but not security at a particular job, as later industrial unions did.[33]

During this formative period many of the goals pursued by unions were shaped by the larger organizational aspirations of winning control of employment. The demand for the eight-hour day stimulated union loyalty among nonunion workers, thus improving bargaining strength; apprenticeship limitations prevented employers from increasing the supply of labor beyond expected demand; federal restrictions on immigration, lobbied for by the AFL, limited the supply of cheap competitors of American labor; and the restrictions on women and child labor were justified along the same lines. Membership in national unions that issued a working card allowed unions to regulate intercity labor mobility.

To achieve control of employment required more than a variety of barriers to entry into the labor market. For one thing it required that the union be able to guarantee to employers that the labor supplied by the union would be productive and reliable. The apprenticeship program served this purpose, as did the provisions in many union constitutions that members be of good moral character. Controlling the labor market also required solidarity among different trades, manifested in its highest form by the sympathy strike and the refusal to work with nonunion workers. The period from 1887 through 1894, especially 1890–91, was the high-water mark for sympathy strikes in the country.[34]

Regulating the labor market allowed unions to limit the division of labor and the introduction of new machinery and hence ensured employment security for their members. The imperative to control the labor market and the concern with employment security for the most part preceded the ferocious struggle over workplace control triggered at the turn of the century by the attempted introduction of scientific management.[35]

Closely related to the drive to regulate the labor market was a fourth feature of the new unionism: the union label and the attempt to insulate the Chicago market against out-of-town competition. Controlling the labor market required limiting and regulating competition in the product market, and this in turn necessitated cooperation with employers.[36] Notwithstanding their protestations, the Knights of Labor never approached the level of cooperation with employers that the AFL unions in Chicago attained. The major difference was that for the Knights cooperation or arbitration was an alternative to strikes, while for the AFL-affiliated unions cooperation grew in tandem with, and often resulted from, strikes, boycotts, and other coercive tactics. As Norman Ware so aptly put it, the post-Knights principle was that "'good' employers are the product of 'bad' labor unions."[37]

For unions of this period the major instrument of union-employer cooperation was the union label movement. The idea of using the label to promote enduring bargaining relations with employers was first adopted by the Cigar Makers International Union in 1881, but it remained for the Knights of Labor to popularize the idea as an adjunct to its goal of replacing strikes with consumer boycotts. Of the nine national unions that used labels in the decade of the 1880s, all but the cigarmakers' union adopted the label between 1885 and 1887, at the height of the Knights' power. After a hiatus of three years the label emerged in the early 1890s to become a leading weapon in the arsenal of trade unionism. Between 1890 and 1895 thirteen national unions adopted labels, followed by eighteen more by the end of the decade.[38]

The label movement of the 1890s differed from earlier efforts in two important ways. First, the label replaced the boycott, which was falling into disuse because of court injunctions and general ineffectiveness. With the decline of the boycott, unions gave up a generalized appeal to the public and relied instead on their own membership, which in the interim had grown considerably in numbers and stability. Second, by the 1890s the label was viewed not merely as an alternative to the boycott and strike in bringing employers to the bargaining table but also as a device to forge an institutionalized alliance with employers in controlling the labor and product markets.

In this respect the union label acted as a kind of license, like that for doctors but without government sanction.

The new features of the union label became evident in Chicago during the 1890 upsurge in efforts for the eight-hour day. On the eve of their strike the coopers argued (unsuccessfully) to the packers that by adopting their label they could in effect use the union to boycott cheaper prison-made barrels. Label leadership soon passed to the cigarmakers. Because of their intense lobbying, in 1891 the state enacted a law registering the label and providing criminal penalties for counterfeiting it. By then two hustling local business agents and one international label agitator worked full time prosecuting dealers in cigars for displaying counterfeit labels. The union also had a "label custodian," who kept track of manufacturers using the label, their revenue district, the number of workers, total labels used each week, and the like. Labels were issued solely to shops that hired union members and followed union rules. The union also tried to set a firm floor under competition by setting a minimum price that cigar manufacturers could charge. Violations of union rules resulted in the employer's forfeiting a $100 bond; a second infraction resulted in forfeiting the union label itself for six months. In return for abiding by label rules, manufacturers and dealers received free union advertising and a protected market for their goods, which were largely bought by workers.[39]

In July 1892 the label received more impetus with the start of M. J. Carroll's *Eight-Hour Herald,* a labor paper whose express purpose was to advertise the label. By Labor Day the next year a *Tribune* labor reporter wrote that twelve local unions used the union label, including the Clothing Trades Council and the Allied Printing Trades Council, both of which were formed to facilitate use of the union label. "In this way a quiet, effective, non-prosecutable boycott has been inaugurated all along the line," reported the *Tribune,* "to drive employers, firms, or corporations into the ranks of the union or into handling only union labeled goods or out of business."[40]

In 1894 the cigarmakers won a signal victory when they obtained the consent of the First District Liquor Dealers Association to use only union-label cigars. In 1896 and 1897 the Republican party's national committee and the city of Chicago both agreed to putting the label of the Allied Printing Trades Council on their publications. By 1895 nine unions were members of a local trade union label league. The next year virtually all unions with labels belonged to the league, which the *Eight-Hour Herald* reported was "fast becoming one of the most powerful central organizations of trade unionists in the city."[41]

The union label movement was not the only means by which unions sought to control the product and labor markets. In the early 1890s the building trades unions helped inaugurate the three-cornered "exclusive agreement" among the unions, associations of contractors, and material suppliers. Both groups of employers agreed to employ only union labor, in return for which the union agreed to work only for employers who joined contractors' associations and used materials supplied by its members. For their part, material manufacturers agreed to sell only to union contractors. That enabled contractors to shut out low-wage competitors; it permitted manufacturers to boycott cheaper materials, generally those sold by out-of-town manufacturers; and it empowered unions to shut out nonunion workers. By the end of the 1890s the bricklayers, steamfitters, plumbers, carpenters, painters, hod carriers, brickmakers, and other unions had exclusive agreements requiring them to boycott out-of-town materials. Referring to the material boycott, one observer marveled that "Chicago unionists were ready to use the boycott in favor of Chicago union labour to the detriment of out-of-town union labour. . . . yet in this peculiarly anti-social struggle the Chicago unions had the support instead of the hostility of their employers." When the construction unions finally repudiated these agreements in 1900, the contractors inaugurated a bitter thirteen-month lockout.[42]

Where unions had less bargaining power and could not offer employers relief from competition, they often turned to the government. The city's leading labor federations, for example, lobbied for excluding out-of-town, noncitizen labor from the construction of both the drainage ditch (successfully) and the World's Fair (unsuccessfully).

The power exercised by some labor unions over local markets makes it clear that although craft unionism might have originated as a defensive movement of those in the traditional crafts, it became a progressive force in its own right. For one thing unionism often collaborated with new technological developments. Though technological change has usually been associated with de-skilling, skill was often a *product* of technological innovation, as with the steam and gas fitters and architectural iron workers in construction and the electrotypers in the printing industry. The word *craft* in craft unionism thus should not be confused with an older meaning of the term in which a craft was the traditional knowledge and customary practices associated with the artisan. As Dorothy Sue Cobble argues, employment control unionism could become a powerful force for creating skill. An unskilled group, such as waitresses, creatively used the craft union to attain the kind of workplace control, pride, respectability, access to benefits, and alliance with employers that males in the building, printing, cigar, and other trades enjoyed. The same could be said of African American waiters organized by craft unions and unskilled pieceworkers organized by skilled general carpenters in this period. It therefore seems a gross oversimplification to equate craft unionism with elite white males clinging to an outmoded organizing approach.[43]

Still, employment control unions of the late 1880s and early 1890s had clear limits. For the most part they thrived in a particular kind of market and firm structure. The most important characteristics of such structures were (1) a relative inability of employers to substitute capital and machinery for labor inputs, (2) extensive capital at risk per worker, (3) vulnerability of capital to damage or short-term disruption by workers, and (4) a secure market for a firm's products. Put differently, these unions thrived in those sectors of the local economy that were immune from tendencies toward mass production and corporate ownership. While such sectors were usually subject to an advancing division of labor that created threats and fears among workers, these tendencies generally did not advance far enough to destroy skill (or the possibility of creating a new skill) and the strategic position of these workers. Nor were employers in this sector strong enough to resist determined unions. At the end of the decade Abraham Bisno testified, "There is no show for an organization [of labor] where a man has a lot of capital. . . . [Unions] have gained in smaller concerns where the boss was not so strong and was not able to crush them out quite so easily as these large concerns; but these large concerns . . . employ more than one half the entire number of people employed in the factories of this city."[44]

Still another drawback—already apparent to some observers by the mid-1890s—stemmed from the disturbing tendency of the union label and other devices for joint regulation of markets to exclude cheaper, lower-paid labor competitors. Charles Spahr called it "protectionism pure and simple." In the very process of consolidating their gains from the great upheaval, many unions began, in George Detwiler words, to take a "laissez-faire" attitude "toward their weaker brethren." Detwiler deplored the prevalent belief that there could be "no affiliation between the man who gets a dollar and a half a day and the man that gets four dollars a day."[45]

A similar portent of exclusivity was labor's hostility to those who were used by employers to undermine "the American standard of living" and family wage to which white male wageworkers felt entitled. Labor was particularly fearful of African Americans, whose numbers in Chicago had doubled to 30,000 in the decade after 1890. In 1894 employers brought up from the South hundreds of black strikebreakers to replace the butchers in the packinghouses, thereby incurring the racist wrath of white workers. Some unions, such as the machinists' union and the American Railway Union, barred blacks from membership. The alternative policy, practiced by the waiters, of preventing the use of black strikebreakers by organizing and uniting with them, had only sporadic success. One major reason for the defeat of the Pullman workers in 1894 was their refusal to enroll the company's two thousand African American porters. In 1895 Gompers and the AFL acquiesced in the national trend toward racial exclusion when they admitted the machinists' union with its color bar.[46]

Certainly the unionism that took hold in the 1890s was very different from the industrial unionism that triumphed in mass-production industry in the 1930s. But it was neither backward looking nor outmoded, and it was as much a product of technological innovation as the Knights of Labor and the American Railway Union were. Its tendency to rely on regulation of the local market made it a forerunner of what Barbara Newell termed the "metropolitan unionism" that dominated the city's labor movement during the first third of the twentieth century. Moreover, despite the growing number of breaches of solidarity in the mid-1890s its organizational forms, its aims, and its strategies proved capable—under the right industrial circumstances—of accommodating the less-skilled, female, and African American workers to which the Knights of Labor had appealed. At the turn of the century this unionism was capable of penetrating, albeit temporarily, the packinghouses and other corporate-dominated industries.[47]

In 1905, after the old animosities with the Knights had faded, Ed Nockles, secretary of the Chicago Federation of Labor, expressed the high regard AFL union activists had for the Knights: "The truths expounded by the Knights of Labor and adopted by the American Federation of Labor, in effect that the 'Injury of one is the concern of all,' seems more true today than when first announced, and upon this principle rests all the progress of our upward, forward march, and if the self-sacrificing men and women of our country did not accept and place all their hopes and aspirations upon this principle, slavery would still be extant in this country, not alone among the blacks, but among the whites."[48]

The New Labor Culture

The network of unions, trade councils, and the four trades assemblies of unions constituted the organizational framework for Chicago's labor movement. Adding stability to this framework were the unions' own rules and benefits, plus its trade agreements and the union label that bound employers as well as workers to these unions. Full-time, paid walking delegates and national officers administered the framework. But Chicago's labor infrastructure could not have endured without being part of a rich and vibrant labor culture. By labor culture is meant a set of everyday habits, customs, beliefs, and attitudes of labor activists and rank-and-file unionists that revolved around the trade union.

Much has been written about the "movement culture" or "sub-culture of opposition" of the Farmers Alliance and the Knights of Labor during this period. In Chicago as elsewhere the Knights played a pioneering role in creating a culture of labor solidarity transcending workers' immediate workplace interests through their mixed local and district assemblies, consumer boycotts, sympathy strikes, producer cooperatives, and labor parties. Yet the Knights were unable to create the enduring organizational and bargaining framework to sustain such a culture. The labor culture that emerged in the early 1890s drew on the innovations of the Knights but focused more on organization and material achievement, and because it was able to cement alliances with employers, it was less vulnerable to temporary setbacks.[49]

Perhaps the first journalistic recognition that such a culture existed was George Detwiler's evocation of "labor row," the street within a stone's throw of city hall on which most local union halls and their full-time officials were located. On labor row the leaders of labor quickly developed a collegial relationship with a new breed of newspaper reporters: the labor reporter. By the early 1890s, in addition to the trade journals associated with national unions, there were more than a half dozen labor papers in the city—including the *Rights of Labor;* the *Eight-Hour Herald,* edited by M. J. Carroll and eventually endorsed by the bricklayers; and the *Union Record,* a short-lived organ of the Trades and Labor Assembly—and the press of the foreign-language socialists and anarchists, also representing unionists in the Central Labor Union. In 1892 railroad workers devoted to industrial unionism read the *Age of Labor,* edited by L. W. Rogers (the paper went out of business when Rogers helped found the American Railway Union); reform-oriented activists read the *Union Workman,* founded in 1894 by W. S. Timblin of the typographers' union to succeed the *Illinois Trade Unionist.*[50]

Just as impressive was the emergence of a group of labor reporters employed by the regular press. If the daily commercial press had not accommodated to growing prolabor sentiment after Haymarket, the English-language labor press might have spawned a vigorous daily newspaper—the *Eight-Hour Herald* came closest in the mid-1890s—to complement the *Arbeiter-Zeitung.* But the regular press began to hire reporters who specialized in labor news, hung out on labor row, and developed friendships with labor leaders. They reported labor news accurately and respectfully, without the derogatory terms that had previously laced news stories on labor. In 1893 the Trades and Labor Assembly decided to encourage this trend by awarding a gold star on Labor Day for the best labor reporting in the city, which produced a noticeable rise in the literary quality of labor news, especially around Labor Day. S. P. McLean became the regular labor reporter for the *Chicago Tribune,* and William C. Roberts, a socialist, edited labor news for the *Chicago Dispatch.* The prolabor trend reached its high point when Carter Harrison hired the Populist Willis J. Abbot in 1891 to edit the *Chicago Times.* From then until the paper was sold in 1894 the *Times* was as avid in its advocacy of the labor and reform causes as any labor paper.[51]

Two images and symbols central to the larger culture were also widely used in the labor culture in Chicago during this period. One image was religious and ethical in character. "With a majority of [labor leaders]," wrote George Detwiler, "the labor movement is their religion with various creeds and sects almost as numerous as that other religion instituted by the carpenters' son nineteen hundred years ago." But, he added, "however much they may disagree on tactics, they stand together on the great ethical proposition that society as it is presently constituted is corrupt and vicious, and that its only salvation is a complete reconstruction. . . . In the minds of the men of labor row great changes are impending throughout the world." The emphasis on salvation and the coming of a new day drew on Protestant millennialism and infused the still strong belief that labor's ultimate goal should be its emancipation from wage labor.[52]

A closely related facet of the religious impulse was labor's attempt to reconstruct the church. Workers' lack of interest in Protestant formal religion was a widely accepted, if lamented, fact among 1880s clergy. Social gospel advocates, such as George C. Lorimer, Jenkin Lloyd Jones, and Charles F. Goss, wanted to restore the church to social advocacy. Other advocates of spiritual renewal without ties to the churches, most notably Henry Demarest Lloyd, Graham Taylor, and William T. Stead, entertained lofty hopes that the labor movement itself would become a new church and modern religion, one more suited to an urban industrialism than an older Protestantism rooted in small-town America was.

By the early 1890s a significant group of labor leaders, from George Detwiler to William C. Pomeroy, had aligned themselves with social gospel religion and protoprogressivism, especially in the movement against the sweating system, even while disagreeing with the bulk of Chicago's clergy over Sunday closing of the World's Fair. In 1894 the Unitarian minister Jenkin Lloyd Jones agreed to be pastor of a new "labor church," formally sponsored and supported by the city's trade unions. The church had its greatest support from L. T. O'Brien, president of the retail clerks' union, which earlier had created the alliance with local clergy to close retail stores on Sundays. The church would have no dogma or pew rentals and would be ethical in character.

Labor leaders had far less incentive to criticize the Catholic church, which openly supported unionism though rejected socialism. The Catholic *New World,* established with the support of Archbishop Patrick Feehan in 1892, endorsed a role for labor in railroad management and actually defended Eugene Debs after his indictment during the Pullman strike.[53]

The religious pretensions and oft-used symbology of labor were more than counterbalanced by a far more widespread image utilized by labor leaders: labor patriotism and militant defense of the labor community. The idea of labor as an established community inspiring loyalty stemmed from the increasingly successful fight for the closed shop and the union label. Labor patriotism gained force from new ideas about how to treat the nonmember or scab. The image of scabs and the practice of ostracizing them through the boycott dated to the early 1880s. By the 1890s, however, the defense of this ostracism had become subordinated to the defense of an established institution—the trade union. The image of labor as a revolutionary movement was being replaced by the image of the labor patriot.

In explaining why unions had the right to ostracize nonunionists, Detwiler, citing Herbert Spencer, editorialized that labor was in the midst of "an industrial war," in which workers were being "invaded" by "industrial combinations," and was justified in self-defense: "the industrial scab is a social traitor." In another editorial Detwiler compared the logic of trade unionism to the logic of warfare: "he that is not with us is against us." For the first time labor found champions of this right before the bar of public opinion when Henry Demarest Lloyd compared walking delegates to lawyers and defended the trade unions' antiscab stance before the Sunset Club. At Hull-House Mary Kenney and other members of "the Jane Club" caught the spirit and would check the hats and cigars of their male dance partners for union labels.[54]

Labor patriotism was more than an image and an ideological justification; it was a set of cultural practices. For labor patriots Labor Day, with its marching ranks of loyal unionists in uniform carrying trade banners and officered by labor officials, was a counterpart to the country's Fourth of July celebration or the Grand Army of the Republic marching on Decoration Day. The union label became a venerated symbol, much like the American flag. The labor community even had its own heroes emerging from its strikes, the counterpart of an army's battle campaigns. The Haymarket martyrs were heroes to many German-speaking workers, but to mainstream unionists, the first use of the term *labor hero*—meaning steadfast adherence to a recognized code of labor conduct during strikes—dated to the 1888 Burlington railroad strike. Its use by railroad workers may have paved the way for the appellation to be applied to Debs and his American Railway Union sympathy strikers in 1894–95. During the carpenters' strike of 1890 the *Rights of Labor* lauded the strikers for greater "heroism than any body of strikers have displayed in the history of the labor movement." Finally, like the soaring Washington

Monument or the skyscrapers sprouting in the city, the ten-story Labor Temple, built to complement the architectural wonders of the World's Fair, was a proud symbol for labor.[55]

But labor patriotism, like nationalism, which at this time was entering its imperial era, had its dark side. Patriotic and military images reinforced a tendency for labor's morality to become subordinated to the material success of trade unionism, labor's version of "my country right or wrong." The workers on labor row, wrote Detwiler, "rarely take others into their confidence. They are suspicious of outsiders." Sometimes such symbols as the union label became tools to bash political opponents. The cigarmakers and musicians were often involved in fractious disputes over other unions' alleged unwillingness to respect their label and their jurisdiction.[56]

Labor patriotism was not closely associated with the ethic of business unionism before 1895. The major alternative to both the movement idealist and the labor patriot was the labor hustler, labor's counterpart to the era's robber baron. The foremost exemplar of this type was the leader of the waiters' union, William C. Pomeroy. Pomeroy was a strange blend of the idealist and the cynical manipulator speaking in the name of both religion and labor patriotism and, later, antisocialist business unionism. Pomeroy had been converted to the labor cause after hearing a speech by Peter J. McGuire, had joined a Knights local assembly of waiters, and had become an outstanding orator and organizer. Pomeroy was genial, easy-going, glib, and generous, all the qualities of a successful ward boss. But he was also classically educated, a brilliant speaker, and a dispenser of romantic bombast. In Pomeroy's 1894 novel, *The Lords of Misrule,* the protagonist, like Pomeroy himself, was a man with two souls in one body.[57]

By 1891 Pomeroy had risen, on the strength of his ability to unite the opposition to T. J. Morgan, to become the behind-the-scenes manipulator of the Trades and Labor Assembly, displacing the socialists' long dominance. His secret was his ability to unite his followers in a sordid grab game. More than anyone who had gone before him, Pomeroy raised to a high art the practice of ensuring labor votes for the Democratic party in exchange for government jobs and payoffs, an art he undertook with a shameless gusto. At the same time, Pomeroy and his gang, known as "labor skates," looted the Trades and Labor Assembly's treasury and profited handsomely from a scheme in which advertisements for *Labor Gazettes* sold on Labor Day were extorted from businessmen. By 1892 many unions were leaving the Trades and Labor Assembly in disgust at Pomeroy's cynical manipulations. To counter the racketeering of the labor skates, Detwiler aligned the *Rights of Labor* with the socialists and even endorsed Morgan for mayor.[58]

Observers linked labor corruption with the corruption in Chicago's machine politics. George Detwiler noted that "in Chicago power has been wrested from the workers and vested in the hands of freebooters perpetuating themselves by the tricks of politicians." The greatest detriment to labor organizations, explained Detwiler, was the "dishonesty" of their leaders, a trait he attributed to "the introduction of the methods of the ward heeler into the union." T. J. Morgan was just as critical, writing to Lloyd that the labor leaders in the great cities were "confidence men. Only spasmodically can they be moved by lofty ideals." The British moral critic and social reformer William T. Stead rooted the dishonesty of the leaders in the culture of Chicago labor. "[Chicago union members] distrust each other," he wrote in 1894, "malign their leaders, and are more singularly lacking in enthusiastic devotion to their chiefs than any body of men I have ever met." According to Stead, "the great bar to progress [toward the "brotherhood of labor"] is the belief that all men are thieves."[59]

In December 1892 Detwiler lamented that "very little headway is being made in the labor movement. Why? . . . Labor was never so well organized as now. It is the lack of moral force which is the precursor to success in any movement." Labor's festering corruption and its reliance on intimidation to enforce class norms on individuals helped deprive it of the public legitimacy that might have accrued from its organizational strength. Combined with the simultaneous appearance of a new social reform movement and the benefits that machine politics offered labor, this weakness helps explain labor's inability to generate an independent labor, pro-reform politics in the early 1890s and its reliance on either the informal machine politics epitomized by a Luke Coyne or formal political collective bargaining.[60]

More important for the long run, labor had generated a durable organizational culture and ideology that represented not the antithesis of the Knights of Labor but a fruitful synthesis of the Knights and an older craft unionism. Simultaneously craft-based and inclusive of new groups, drawing on the Knights of Labor yet breaking from its equal rights republicanism, intensely moral in its own way yet practical and often cynical, and resolutely reform-minded but refusing to eschew fundamental change, Chicago labor's culture had become consolidated and stabilized.[61] Labor's institutionalization of new forms of collective action—the strike, the label boycott, the trades council, and the trade agreement—allowed it to regulate labor (and sometimes product) market competition in a select sector of the local economy. Such market regulation enabled unions, according to outside observers, to maintain and raise pay rates in the face of falling prices.[62] Its sanctioning of group interests partly over and against individual rights and partly as a supplement to them helped generate a reformed liberalism. In doing so, organized Chicago workers in the 1890s began to go beyond the informal presence they had enjoyed from the late 1870s through most of the 1880s to become formally recognized players in a new politics that will be explored in more depth in the next chapter.

Notes

1. Daniel T. Rodgers, *Contested Truths: Keywords in American Politics since Independence* (New York: Basic Books, 1987), 45–79; Staughton Lynd, *Intellectual Origins of American Radicalism* (New York: Random House, 1968).

2. J. G. A. Pocock, *The Machiavellian Moment: Florentine Political Thought and the Atlantic Republican Tradition* (Princeton, N.J.: Princeton University Press, 1975), 545.

3. Allen R. Pred, *The Spatial Dynamics of U.S. Urban-Industrial Growth, 1800–1914* (Cambridge, Mass: M.I.T. Press, 1966), 20; Bessie Louise Pierce, *A History of Chicago*, vol. 3, *The Rise of a Modern City, 1871–1893* (Chicago: University of Chicago Press, 1957), appendix; *Chicago Tribune*, May 7, 1890, Aug. 30, 1891.

4. Carl Smith, *Urban Disorder and the Shape of Belief: The Great Chicago Fire, the Haymarket Bomb, and the Model Town of Pullman* (Chicago: University of Chicago Press, 1995), 210–31; Matthew Schneirov, *The Dream of a New Social Order: Popular Magazines in America, 1893–1914* (New York: Columbia University Press, 1994), 162–201; Frederic Cople Jaher, *Doubters and Dissenters: Cataclysmic Thought in America, 1885–1918* (Glencoe, Ill.: Free Press, 1964), 19–32; Dorothy Ross, "The Liberal Tradition Revisited and the Republican Tradition Addressed," in *New Directions in American Intellectual History*, ed. John Higham and Paul K. Conklin (Baltimore, Md.: Johns Hopkins University Press, 1979); Neil Harris, *The Land of Contrasts, 1880–1901* (New York: George Braziller, 1970), 17; Kenneth M. Roemer, *The Obsolete Necessity: America in Utopian Writings, 1888–1900* (Kent, Ohio: Kent State University Press, 1976), 22–24 ("volcano" quote), 171–78 ("coming apart" and Bellamy quote on 172).

5. *Knights of Labor*, Oct. 19, 1886, Nov. 13, 1886, Dec. 19, 1887; Henry George, *Progress and Poverty*, abridged ed. (New York: Robert Shalkenbach Foundation, 1970), 203.

6. *Rights of Labor*, July 16, 1892, Nov. 29, 1890; William C. Pomeroy, *Lords of Misrule: A Tale of Gods and Men* (Chicago: Laird and Lee, 1894).

7. George B. Cotkin, "The Spencerian and Comtian Nexus in Gompers' Labor Philosophy: The Impact of Non-Marxian Evolutionary Thought," *Labor History* 20 (Fall 1979): 510–23; J. D. Y. Peel, *Herbert Spencer: The Evolution of a Sociologist* (New York: Basic Books, 1971), 214–23; Robert C. Bannister, *Social Darwinism: Science and Myth in Anglo-American Thought* (Philadelphia: Temple University Press, 1979); Mark Pittinger, *American Socialists and Evolutionary Thought, 1870–1920* (Madison: University of Wisconsin, 1993), 15–87. Compare Richard Hofstadter, *Social Darwinism in American Thought* (Boston: Beacon, 1955).

8. *Labor Enquirer*, Apr. 16, 1887 (Detwiler's past); *Rights of Labor*, Jan. 18, 1890 (pro-Gompers), Apr. 18, 1891 ("here to stay" quote), July 27, 1889 ("theorists and dreamers" quote), Apr. 26, 1890 ("state of society" quote).

9. *Rights of Labor,* Mar. 1, 1890 ("increased leisure" quote), Apr. 5, 1890 ("storehouse" quote), Jan. 18, 1890 ("radical labor men" quote).

10. Dyer Lum, *Philosophy of Trade Unions* (New York: American Federation of Labor, 1892), 17–18 (Lum quotes); Mark Erlich, "Peter J. McGuire's Trade Unionism: Socialism of a Trade Union Kind," *Labor History* 24 (Spring 1983): 165–97; *Rights of Labor,* Apr. 26, 1890 ("within a life time" quote).

11. Gompers quoted in William Dick, *Labor and Socialism in America: The Gompers Era* (Port Washington, N.Y.: Kennikat, 1972), 38. See also Dick's chapter entitled "American Revisionist Socialism"; and Stuart B. Kaufman, *Samuel Gompers and the Origins of the American Federation of Labor* (Westport, Conn.: Greenwood, 1973), 190–222. For a labor version of evolutionary socialism, see Michael Kazin, *Barons of Labor: The San Francisco Building Trades and Union Power in the Progressive Era* (Urbana: University of Illinois Press, 1987), 149–50; H. M. Gittelman, "Adolph Strasser and the Origins of Pure and Simple Trade Unionism," *Labor History* 6 (Winter 1965): 71–82; and James T. Kloppenberg, *Uncertain Victory: Social Democracy and Progressivism in European and American Thought, 1870–1920* (New York: Oxford University Press, 1986) 199–246.

12. Eduard Bernstein, *Evolutionary Socialism* (1899; reprint, New York: Schocken Books, 1961), xxix; *Progressive Age,* Nov. 12, 1881; Morton White, *Social Thought in America: The Revolt against Formalism* (Boston: Beacon, 1957); David W. Noble, *The Paradox of Progressive Thought* (Minneapolis: University of Minnesota Press, 1958).

13. Georg Leidenberger, "'The Public Is the Labor Union': Working-Class Progressivism in Turn-of-the-Century Chicago," *Labor History* 36 (Spring 1995): 187–210; Kazin, *Barons of Labor,* 152, 283–84; Gary M. Fink, "The Rejection of Voluntarism," *Industrial and Labor Relations Review* 26 (Jan. 1973): 805–19. For a different view, see Victoria C. Hattam, *Labor Visions and State Power: The Origins of Business Unionism in the United States* (Princeton, N.J.: Princeton University Press, 1993), 164–65.

14. *Knights of Labor,* Apr. 26, 1889; *Rights of Labor,* Apr. 12, 1990; *Chicago Tribune,* Dec. 28, 1890 (quote); Harry Barnard, *Eagle Forgotten: The Life of John Peter Altgeld* (1938; reprint, Secaucus, N.J.: Lyle Stuart, 1966), esp. chaps. 7, 19, and 35; Dick, *Labor and Socialism in America,* 38–48.

15. Sidney Fine, "The Eight-Hour Day Movement in the United States, 1888–1891," *Mississippi Valley Historical Review* 40 (Dec. 1953): 441–62; Selig Perlman, *A History of Trade Unionism in the United States* (New York: Macmillan, 1922), 145; David Montgomery, "Industrial Democracy or Democracy in Industry? The Theory and Practice of the Labor Movement, 1870–1925," in *Industrial Democracy in America: The Ambiguous Promise,* ed. Nelson Lichtenstein and Howell John Harris (Cambridge: Cambridge University Press, 1993), 28–34.

16. *Knights of Labor,* May 4, 1889 (quote), May 25, 1889, June 29, 1889, Sept. 14, 1889, Jan. 18, 1890.

17. Ibid., Feb. 9, 1889; Richard Schneirov and Thomas J. Suhrbur, *Union Brotherhood, Union Town: The History of the Chicago Carpenters' Union of Chicago, 1863–1987* (Carbondale: Southern Illinois University Press, 1988), 48.

18. *Knights of Labor,* Mar. 8, 1890; *Chicago Tribune,* Mar. 5, 1890, Apr. 7, 1890.

19. *Knights of Labor,* Apr. 5, 1890; *Chicago Tribune,* Apr. 3, 1890, Apr. 23, 1890, Apr. 27, 1890, May 2, 1890, May 3, 1890.

20. *Chicago Tribune,* Apr. 29, 1890, May 5, 1890 (quote).

21. Ibid., Apr. 27, 1890, May 5, 1890 (quote).

22. Ibid., June 28, 1890, July 3, 1890, Aug. 7, 1890, Aug. 14, 1890, Aug. 23, 1890, Aug. 29, 1890, Oct. 28, 1890; *Rights of Labor,* Aug. 9, 1890.

23. Figures derived from the U.S. Commissioner of Labor, *Tenth Annual Report of the United States Commissioner of Labor, 1894: Strikes and Lockouts* (Washington, D.C.: Government Printing Office, 1894), 162–250; and *Rights of Labor,* Oct. 18, 1890.

24. Figures derived from U.S. Commissioner of Labor, *Tenth Annual Report,* 162–250; *Rights of Labor,* Feb. 28, 1891; and *Chicago Tribune,* Aug. 30, 1891, Sept. 5, 1892. The 42 percent figure was derived from a base of 360,000 wageworkers, estimated by Gruenhut in *Chicago Tribune,* May 7, 1890.

25. Bruce Laurie, *Artisans into Workers: Labor in Nineteenth-Century America* (New York: Noonday, 1989), 198–99.

26. John B. Jentz, "Bread and Labor: Chicago's German Bakers Organize," *Chicago History* 12 (Summer 1983): 24–35; Schneirov and Suhrbur, *Union Brotherhood, Union Town,* 21–43; Lloyd Ulman, *The Rise of the National Union: The Development and Significance of Its Structure, Governing Institutions, and Economic Policies* (Cambridge, Mass.: Harvard University Press, 1955); Frederick Diebler, *The Amalgamated Woodworkers' International Union of America: A Historical Study of Trade Unionism in Its Relation to the Development of an Industry* (Madison: University of Wisconsin Press, 1912), chap. 1; *The Labor Directory of Chicago and Vicinity, 1891* (Chicago: William C. Hollister and Bro., 1891).

27. *Chicago Tribune,* Mar. 8, 1891; S. V. Lindholm, "Analysis of the Building Trades Conflict in Chicago, from the Trades-Union Standpoint," *Journal of Political Economy* 28 (June 1900): 328–33; *Constitution and By-Laws of the Building Trades Council of Chicago and Vicinity* (Chicago: Eight-Hour Herald, n.d.); Ernest Bogart, "The Chicago Building Trades Dispute," in *Trade Unionism and Labor Problems,* ed. John R. Commons (New York: Ginn, 1921), 88–92. On the origins of sympathy strikes, see John Mangan, *History of the Steamfitters' Protective Association of Chicago* (Chicago: Steamfitters Protective Association of Chicago, 1930), 23–24; and *Tribune,* June 21, 1891. Statistics derived from U.S. Commissioner of Labor, *Tenth Annual Report,* 162–250.

28. *Chicago Tribune,* Apr. 27, 1891, Oct. 5, 1891, Apr. 11, 1892, Apr. 16, 1892, Mar. 19, 1894; *Labor Directory of Chicago and Vicinity, 1891.*

29. The term *craft industrialism* is Selig Perlman's in *History of Trade Unionism,* 221–25. See also Charles F. Sabel, *The Second Industrial Divide* (New York: Basic Books, 1984), 115–20. On trades councils as stepping-stones toward or alternatives to industrial unionism, see Bruno Ramirez, *When Workers Fight: The Politics of Industrial Relations in the Progressive Era, 1898–1916* (Westport, Conn.: Greenwood, 1978), 104–22, esp. 119–20.

30. On the cigarmakers, see Charles B. Spahr, *America's Working People* (New York: Longmans, Green, 1900), 186–88; and *Rights of Labor,* June 20, 1891. On unemployment benefits, see *Chicago Record,* Sept. 4, 1893.

31. Philip S. Foner, *History of the Labor Movement in the United State*, vol. 2, *From the Founding of the American Federation of Labor to the Emergence of American Imperialism* (New York: International Publishers, 1955), 174–78; Warren R. Van Tine, *The Making of the Labor Bureaucrat: Union Leadership in the United States, 1870–1920* (Amherst: University of Massachusetts Press, 1973), 1–31; Stuart Bruce Kaufman, *Samuel Gompers and the Origins of the A. F. of L., 1848–1896* (Westport, Conn.: Greenwood, 1973).

32. *Eight-Hour Herald*, May 21, 1897 (O'Connell quote); Sunset Club, *Yearbook, 1899–1901* (Chicago: Sunset Club, 1901), 58 (Woodbury quote); Spahr, *America's Working People*, 190. See also the letter of W. D. Mahon, president of the Amalgamated Street Railway Employees' Association, *Eight-Hour Herald*, July 9, 1897.

33. On the distinction between these two kinds of unionism, see Dorothy Sue Cobble, "Organizing the Postindustrial Work Force: Lessons from the History of Waitress Unionism," *Industrial and Labor Relations Review* 44 (Apr. 1991): 419–36, esp. 424–25.

34. For an example of attempts to ensure productive and reliable labor, see the constitution of the women's cloakmakers' union, which called for fostering "a spirit of dignified independence, which cannot fail to elevate her moral character as an individual and stimulate her to a more conscientious discharge of her duties as an employe." Hull-House Association Records, Reel 53, Jane Addams Papers, University of Illinois, Chicago. On sympathy strikes, see David Montgomery, *Workers' Control in America: Studies in the History of Work, Technology, and Labor Struggles* (Cambridge: Cambridge University Press, 1979), 20–25.

35. David Montgomery, *Fall of the House of Labor: The Workplace, the State, and American Labor Activism, 1865–1925* (Cambridge: Cambridge University Press), 214–56. The distinction between worker control and market control is developed in Robert Max Jackson, *The Formation of Craft Labor Markets* (Orlando, Fla.: Academic, 1984), 7–14, 323–24.

36. The growing literature on labor's cooperation with employers in regulating the market in the 1890s includes Jackson, *Formation of Craft Labor Markets;* Marc Jeffrey Stern, *The Pottery Industry of Trenton: A Skilled Trade in Transition, 1850–1929* (New Brunswick, N.J.: Rutgers University Press, 1994); and Ron Mendel, "Cooperative Unionism and the Development of Job Control in New York's Printing Trades, 1888–1898," *Labor History* 32 (Summer 1991): 354–75. See also Colin Gordon, *New Deals: Business, Labor, and Politics in America, 1920–1935* (Cambridge: Cambridge University Press, 1994), 87–88.

37. Norman J. Ware, *The Labor Movement in the United States, 1860–1895: A Study in Democracy* (New York: Vintage Books, 1929), 125.

38. Ernest R. Spedden, *The Trade Union Label*, Studies in Historical and Political Science, Series 28, No. 2 (Baltimore, Md.: Johns Hopkins University Press, 1910), 9–22.

39. *Rights of Labor*, Apr. 12, 1890; *Chicago Tribune*, July 18, 1891, July 28, 1891; on the Illinois label act, see John Graham Brooks, "The Trade Union Label," in *The Making of America*, vol. 8, *Labor* (1906; reprint, New York: Arno, 1969), 195–98; Spedden, *Trade Union Label*, 35, 36, 39, 40, 45, 57–61, 76.

40. *Chicago Tribune*, Sept. 4, 1893.

41. *Eight-Hour Herald,* Dec. 7, 1895, June 25, 1896 (quote), Aug. 27, 1896, May 25, 1897.

42. Lindholm, "Analysis of the Building Trades Conflict," 333–36; Bogart, "Chicago Building Trades Dispute," 94–96; Royal E. Montgomery, *Industrial Relations in the Chicago Building Trades* (Chicago: University of Chicago Press, 1927), 21–22; 188–89; Spahr, *America's Working People,* 181 (quote). For an example of the exclusive agreement in this period, see the testimony of John S. Kelley, the national president of the plumbers, steam and gas fitters' union, in U.S. Industrial Commission, *Report of the U.S. Industrial Commission* (Washington, D.C.: Government Printing Office, 1901), 7:966–73; and Martin Segal, *The Rise of the United Association: National Unionism in the Pipe Trades, 1884–1924* (Cambridge, Mass.: Wertheim Committee, Harvard University, 1970), 140–44.

43. Cobble, "Organizing the Postindustrial Work Force," 429–32. See also Jackson, *Formation of Craft Labor Markets,* 23–29, 313–23. Charles Tilly, "Solidary Logics," *Theory and Society* 17 (May 1988): 453, has written that skill was "a social product, a negotiated identity."

44. Tilly, "Solidary Logics," 454–55 (characteristics); U.S. Industrial Commission, *Report,* 8:49 (Bisno quote). See also Spahr, *America's Working People,* 171, 179–80, 188–89.

45. Spahr, *America's Working People,* 181; *Rights of Labor,* June 3, 1893 (Detwiler quotes); Mary H. Blewett, *Men, Women, and Work: Class, Gender, and Protest in the New England Shoe Industry, 1780–1910* (Urbana: University of Illinois Press, 1990), 290–92.

46. Alma Herbst, *The Negro in the Slaughtering and Meatpacking Industry in Chicago* (1932; reprint, New York: Arno, 1971), 16–20; Susan E. Hirsch, "The Search for Unity among Railroad Workers: The Pullman Strike in Perspective," in *The Pullman Strike and the Crisis of the 1890s: Essays on Labor and Politics,* ed. Richard Schneirov, Shelton Stromquist, and Nick Salvatore (Urbana: University of Illinois Press, forthcoming); Foner, *History of the Labor Movement in the United States,* 2:348–49.

47. Barbara Warne Newell, *Chicago and the Labor Movement: Metropolitan Unionism in the 1930s* (Urbana: University of Illinois Press, 1961), 209–22; C. Lawrence Christenson, "Chicago Service Trades," in *How Collective Bargaining Works,* ed. Harry A. Millis (New York: Twentieth Century Fund, 1942), 806–68; James R. Barrett, *Work and Community in the Jungle: Chicago's Packinghouse Workers, 1894–1922* (Urbana: University of Illinois Press, 1990).

48. *Daily Labor Bulletin,* May 26, 1905, John Fitzpatrick Papers, Chicago Historical Society.

49. On "movement culture," see Lawrence Goodwyn, *The Populist Moment: A Short History of the Agrarian Revolt in America* (Oxford: Oxford University Press, 1978); for its application to the Knights, see Peter J. Rachleff, *Black Labor in the South, 1865–1890* (Philadelphia: Temple University Press, 1984), chap. 8; and Laurie, *Artisans into Workers* 74–112. On the "sub-culture of opposition," see Gregory S. Kealey and Bryan D. Palmer, *Dreaming of What Might Be: The Knights of Labor in Ontario, 1880–1900* (New York: Cambridge University Press, 1982), chaps. 1 and 8; Richard Jules Oestreicher, *Solidarity and Fragmentation: Working*

People and Class Consciousness in Detroit, 1875–1900 (Urbana: University of Illinois Press, 1989), chap. 3; and Robert E. Weir, *Beyond Labor's Veil: The Culture of the Knights of Labor* (University Park: Pennsylvania State University Press, 1996).

50. *Rights of Labor,* Nov. 29, 1890; *Chicago Tribune,* May 14, 1894; *Eight-Hour Herald,* Nov. 9, 1895; Bruce C. Nelson, *Beyond the Martyrs: A Social History of Chicago's Anarchists* (New Brunswick, N.J.: Rutgers University Press, 1988), 115–26; Shelton Stromquist, *A Generation of Boomers: The Pattern of Railroad Labor Conflict in Nineteenth-Century America* (Urbana: University of Illinois Press, 1987), 77–79.

51. *Chicago Tribune,* Sept. 4, 1893; *Eight-Hour Herald,* Nov. 9, 1895, Oct. 14, 1897; Willis J. Abbot, *Watching the World Go By* (Boston: Little, Brown, 1933), 104–31; Willis J. Abbot, "Chicago Newspapers and Their Makers," *Review of Reviews* 11 (June 1895): 646–65.

52. *Rights of Labor,* Nov. 29, 1890.

53. On support for social gospel and reform, see the *Eight-Hour Herald,* 1895–96, passim. On the relations between labor and the churches, see William T. Stead, *If Christ Came to Chicago: A Plea for the Union of All Who Love in the Service of All Who Suffer* (Chicago: Laird and Lee, 1894), 389, 394–98; Pierce, *History of Chicago,* 3:437–40; *Chicago Tribune,* Feb. 20, 1893, Jan. 23, 1894, Feb. 9, 1894, Feb. 12, 1894; and Matthew C. Lee, "Onward Christian Soldiers: The Social Gospel and the Pullman Strike," *Chicago History* 20 (Spring–Summer 1991): 5–21.

54. *Rights of Labor,* Apr. 5, 1890 ("he that is not" quote), June 28, 1890 ("industrial war . . ." quote), July 19, 1890; *Chicago Tribune,* Nov. 7, 1890, Dec. 7, 1890; Van Tine, *Making of the Labor Bureaucrat,* 48–50; Mary Kenny O'Sullivan, "Autobiography," 71–72, Papers of the Women's Trade Union League and Its Principal Leaders, Arthur and Elizabeth Schlesinger Library, Radcliffe College, Cambridge, Mass. I am indebted to Seven Sapolsky for suggesting the metaphor of labor patriotism. Clarence Darrow utilized the same martial and patriotic imagery. See U.S. Industrial Commission, *Report,* 8:71–72. See also Frank K. Foster, "Strikes and the Philosophy of the Strikers," in *Making of America,* 8:157.

55. Donald L. McMurry, *The Great Burlington Strike of 1888: A Case History of Labor Relations* (Cambridge, Mass.: Harvard University Press, 1956), 175, 277–78; *Rights of Labor,* Apr. 26, 1890, May 10, 1890, Aug. 29, 1891.

56. *Rights of Labor,* Nov. 29, 1890.

57. On the relative lack of business unionism before 1895, see Van Tine, *Making of the Labor Bureaucrat,* 50–51. On Pomeroy, see Matthew Josephson, *Union House, Union Bar: The History of the Hotel and Restaurant Employees and Bartenders International Union AFL-CIO* (New York: Random House, 1956), 8–9; Eugene Staley, *History of the Illinois State Federation of Labor* (Chicago: University of Chicago Press, 1930), 89–90; and Stead, *If Christ Came to Chicago,* 399.

58. *Rights of Labor,* Apr. 4, 1891, Nov. 28, 1891.

59. *Rights of Labor,* Dec. 17, 1892 (Detwiler quotes); Morgan to Lloyd, Dec. 19, 1893, Reel 5, Henry Demarest Lloyd Papers (microfilm), Wisconsin State Historical Society, Madison; Stead, *If Christ Came to Chicago,* 390, 392. Stead was echoed by another British observer, Charles Spahr. In *America's Working People,* 167–68, Spahr wrote disparagingly of the character of Chicago trade union leaders

compared with their British counterparts but attributed this to greater social mobility in the United States. Pomeroy's first appearance on the Chicago labor scene is discussed in the *Rights of Labor,* May 9, 1891; see also ibid., Sept. 9, 1892, Apr. 29, 1893.

60. *Rights of Labor,* Dec. 17, 1892; Jane Addams, "The Present Crisis in Trades-Union Morals," *North American Review* 179 (Aug. 1904): 178–93.

61. It was only after this chapter was written that I noticed that "Stabilization, 1888–1897" was the title of chapter 6 in Perlman, *History of Trade Unionism in the United States.*

62. In 1892 the British consulate noted that "labor organizations have had a powerful influence in keeping up the rate of pay . . . and in some employments wages have even risen despite falling prices." *Report on the Earnings of Labour and Cost of Living in the Consular District of Chicago,* Misc. Series No. 235 (London: British Foreign Office, 1892).

CHAPTER 13

Creating a New Urban Agenda in the Depression Era

During the 1893–98 depression cross-class social reform finally flowered into a mass movement capable of appealing to a majority of Chicago voters. The Civic Federation of Chicago and later the Municipal Voters League sought to bridge the city's class rift and create a new urban agenda by drawing in representatives of unions, arbitrating labor disputes, and joining the wave of urban antimonopolism. The mobilization of reform forces reshaped Chicago's political terrain in the 1890s. A progressive alliance of organized labor and the respectable reform element might have taken over one of the two parties or created a new one. But in the end a large segment of the labor movement joined a labor-Populist coalition and, when that failed, returned to the Democratic party.

The emergence of a new type of liberal reform grew in tandem with changes underway in American society. Under the impact of an organizational and technological revolution that had created a culture dedicated to continuous and accelerating change and development, the individual proprietor-patriarch-producer-citizen was receding as the central figure in the polity. Nowhere was modernizing society more evident than in Chicago, which had felt the explosive growth of a population enmeshed in market relations, the centralizing and homogenizing effects of new technologies in transportation and manufacturing, the vertical and horizontal integration of business in major sectors of the economy, the growing differentiation and specialization of urban space, and the assumption of new and expanded responsibilities by local government. What historians call "the crisis of the

1890s" had much of its source in the disjuncture between on one hand this complex and interdependent industrial society's need for stability and on the other the destabilizing tendencies inherent in a regime of a self-adjusting market system.

The deepening "labor question" manifested in the rise of class feeling, trade unions, disruptive and violent strikes, and labor politics was only one example of this widely recognized "crisis." Another was the so-called trust question that became evident in the provision of city services—gas and light, electricity, telephone service, and local transportation. The creation of new technologies—for example, electricity-powered cable cars—and the simultaneous need to service vast new populations meant that utilities were required to make massive capital investments in new plant and equipment. To make these investments profitable, utilities extended their infrastructural investments beyond small enclaves and sought longer-term franchises from the city. To Chicagoans such business expansion spelled "monopoly."[1]

The rise of consolidated utility industries as an integral part of the urban-industrial economy occurred slightly later but was as significant as the rise of the railroad and telegraph corporations in national markets. These industries were, in the new phrase of the day, "natural monopolies," part of an emerging segment of the economy manifestly "clothed in the public interest." Because the health of the rest of the economy depended on such monopolies, their regulation for the common good could not be safely relegated either to the invisible hand of the market or to unregulated "trust."

There were many other issues testifying to the fact that the free use of property was often dysfunctional in the new interdependent society. Among them were the numerous deaths at railroad crossings, continuing epidemics of cholera and typhoid, the "smoke nuisance" arising from coal-powered steam engines, the ever-present stink from the stockyards and the soap, glue, and fertilizer factories, the sale of adulterated or spoiled meat and milk, the existence of garbage-strewn and congested streets, and the conditions of working-class families, especially women and children, in sweatshops and tenements. These issues were different from such old moral evils as intemperance that could be equated with individual character defects and had attracted mugwump concerns. Like the issues of public utility regulation and education, they were manifestly social in nature in that they revealed the interdependence of all citizens. In the two decades before 1890 Chicagoans had responded to these public issues with a gradual increase in democratic regulation. The city enacted a wide array of ordinances governing private behavior, ranging from garbage disposal and smoke emissions to the length of women's hatpins in crowded streets. Except in the area of public health, however, much of this regulation was sporadic, ineffective, and subject to the inefficiencies attributable to patronage politics; many new ills escaped public scrutiny altogether.[2]

The greatly accelerated pace of change in the 1880s convinced many middle-class leaders that reform could no longer be piecemeal or entrusted to party hacks. There would have to be a rethinking of the principles of laissez-faire and the general relation of society to government. As much as anything it was the ethical theory of socialism that contributed to this rethinking and came to symbolize it. Since 1887 socialism had become detached from the revolutionary working-class socialism represented by anarchism. Speaking in part from personal experience, George Detwiler wrote in 1890 that Chicagoans had "ceased to regard socialists as wild animals." They "have been studying socialism for the past four years and have become very much enlightened on the subject." The new socialism was not partisan political socialism but the utopian evolutionary socialism of Edward Bellamy, the ethical socialism of Henry Demarest Lloyd, and the proposals by Richard T. Ely and Henry Carter Adams for government ownership. Far from being an alternative system to "capitalism," a word rarely used, it was viewed as a leaven for excessive individualism.[3]

When the socialist Florence Kelley arrived in Chicago in December 1891, she found the city's intellectual environs fertile ground for socialist ideas. Writing to Friedrich Engels in 1892, she reported, "The increased discussion of socialism here is very marked, though the study of books and requests for lectures come almost exclusively from people of the prosperous middle classes. Thus, I have been asked to speak twice before the Secular Union and five times in churches in Chicago and its suburbs, and the more radically I speak the more vigorous the discussion in all these meetings."[4]

Bellamy's advocacy of a state-owned and operated economy and a "religion of solidarity" that would overcome social inequality and class conflict found considerable resonance among the Protestant middle class. Followers in Chicago founded Nationalist Club No. 2 in September 1889, and by the beginning of the next year, when another club composed primarily of women was formed, the *Tribune* published a series of editorials and letters attacking the new fad. Detwiler estimated in 1891 that under the influence of Bellamy "half" of local ministers had become "socialists," and as early as 1890 there was a Society of Christian Socialists in the city.[5]

Certainly nothing close to a majority of ministers made the change. But more significant than the number of conversions was the simple fact that socialist thought was legitimate enough to enter into a constructive dialogue with Christian moral thought, with which it shared much. In a talk on nationalism before the Sunset Club, Lloyd observed that under nationalism's influence discussion of the social problem was going on in "the parlor, the club, on the sidewalk, in the lecture-room, and even in the pulpit." Just as the political economic side of this dialogue spawned the new liberalism, the ethical side of it resulted in what came to be known as "social gospel" Christianity. According to the new theology as articulated by Washington Gladden, "salvation can no more come to the man apart from the community than life can come to the branch when separated from the vine." Recognizing the inability to banish social strife by simply reasserting the authority of existing institutions, progressive or social gospel Protestants sought a vague middle ground between individual regeneration and social justice. They supported such proposals as strike arbitration, sweatshop regulation, and a cautious public ownership of utility monopolies.[6]

The utopian social possibilities toward which industrial evolution apparently was heading was dramatized in the early 1890s by the World's Columbian Exposition. Despite the labor disputes marring its construction and what some criticized as vulgar display and architectural backwardness, the completed World's Fair offered a concrete example of what an ideal city planned by experts taking advantage of the latest in technology could offer. The sociologist Charles Zueblin said that the White City "was a miniature of an ideal city; a symbol of urban regeneration." The *Chicago Tribune* caught the impact of the White City when it ended, bidding farewell "to a little ideal world, a realization of utopia . . . in which for the time all thoughts of the great world of toil, of injustice, of cruelty, and of oppression outside its gates disappeared, and in which this splendid fantasy of the artist and architect seemed to foreshadow some far-away time when all the earth should be as pure, as beautiful and as joyous as the White City itself."[7]

By seeming to bring utopia directly into the experience of Chicagoans, the World's Fair unleashed a tremendous civic optimism that until then had been linked with the motive of acquisitiveness, private ambition, and material achievement. "Visions of what Chicago could become," wrote the reformer Graham Taylor, "hovered over it like a mirage in the desert. Pioneering spirits caught higher glimpses of civic ideals and new incentives to realize."[8]

Then in a short space of time, three seemingly unrelated but portentous events—the depression, the sudden demise of Carter Harrison, and the arrival of the reformer William Stead—highlighted the contrast between ideal and reality, possibility and actuality, and spurred reformers to put foundations under the castles they had built in the air rising from the White City.

The end of the fair's construction, which had induced a feverish artificial prosperity in the city, brought Chicago back into line with the rest of the nation, which was entering a five-year depression that began with a financial panic in the spring of 1893. Even as the fair opened, thousands of unemployed fair laborers, joined by hundreds more arriving by rail each day from the West, swelled the ranks of those desperate for work. On August 19 the *Tribune* estimated that ten thousand idle men had asked for work at the packinghouses the previous morning. Throughout August the carpenters' union and other unions mobilized the unemployed in weekly mass meetings on the lakefront. Some ended in marches on city hall, reminding downtown businessmen of the anarchist demonstrations of 1886. Mayor Harrison met with the march leaders and negotiated an end to the parades in return for setting up a committee to coordinate relief and to employ men on the drainage ditch, but the crisis worsened. In September half of all building trades workers were out of work, and the police reported that employment in twenty-two hundred large firms had declined 40 percent. The contrast with the harmony, gaiety, and perfection of the World's Fair was inescapable.[9]

Heightening the sense that optimistic utopia had given way to what the novelist Ernest Poole called the "chaos and grime of the Black Winter of '94" was the assassination of Carter Harrison, who had been elected in 1893 for a fifth term as mayor, on the last special day of the World's Fair, October 28, 1893. The end of the Harrison years symbolized the end of an era when Chicago was a "wide open" town and "defied" "the moral and respectable classes" with open gambling and vice. It was an era in which the episodically explosive tensions between labor and capital could be regulated only by party machine politics, in part because prevailing liberal doctrine would not allow open bargaining and compromise between social groups.[10]

On the day of Harrison's assassination William T. Stead, the English social gospel reformer and journalist, landed in New York. When he arrived in Chicago the next week, he found over 100,000 unemployed, including over 1,000 men, packed like sardines, sleeping on newspapers in the corridors of city hall. "Like the frogs in the Egyptian plague, you could not escape from the tramps, go where you could," he wrote. What Stead found most remarkable, however, was the attitude of Chicagoans toward the unemployed. Despite the fact that by Stead's own survey two-thirds had a skill and virtually all had recently held jobs, they were viewed by the "respectable" classes as "only bums." Playing the role of the muckraker determined to bring to light the hypocrisy rife in the city, Stead undertook a two-week immersion in the underworld of tramps, the unemployed, prostitutes, gamblers, and ward heelers. Then he surfaced and reported to women's clubs, to clergy, to newspapers, and to labor unions what he had found, challenging them to put into practice the social gospel.[11]

Encouraged by leaders of the Trades and Labor Assembly, Stead called a mass meeting at the Central Music Hall on November 12 to bring together labor and the Protestant churches in a new "civic church." The result was the Civic Federation of Chicago (CFC), a centralized federation of civic, reform, charity, and other influential associations whose purpose was to focus the new ideals of social cooperation and social efficiency on the task of renovating Chicago society. In the words of its energetic secretary, Ralph Easley, a former "politico-economic" editor of the *Chicago Inter-Ocean* who would soon be transformed into a "professional reformer" during the Pullman strike, the CFC was "an evolution of the modern progressive combination spirit of this age."[12]

A social analysis of the leaders of the CFC would find that many were or had been members of the Citizens Association. Moreover, many mugwump concerns animated the CFC, notably the eradication of vice and the promotion of civic economy and efficiency through civil service and charter reform. There were, however, major differences. The CFC embodied a new definition of society as composed of interest and reform groups and classes rather than a moral hierarchy of individuals topped by the best men.[13] Like the cross-class reform associations that preceded it in the late 1880s, the CFC sought to "serve as a medium of sympathy and acquaintance between persons and societies who pursue various and differing vocations and objects, who differ in nationality, creed, and surrounding [and] who are unknown to each other." According to Easley its "favorite method" of "promoting any important local movement" was to "call a conference to which are invited representatives of all leading clubs and organizations thus securing all the strength possible. . . ."[14]

Five types of groups and their leaders were represented in the Civic Federation: representatives of major business and labor organizations, notably Franklin MacVeagh, Lyman Gage, and M. J. Carroll, editor of the *Eight-Hour Herald;* social gospel clergy, such as Graham Taylor; women philanthropists and reformers, such as Bertha Palmer and Jane Addams; social science experts, such as Edward Bemis; and leaders of such respectable reform societies as the Union League Club. Labor representation was more than pro forma. Fully one-sixth of the CFC's first members were "men associated with a labor organization," and M. J. Carroll was chairman of the Committee on Organization.[15]

The Civic Federation's new approach was predicated on three principles. First, Stead trumpeted his belief that the city's sin and corruption were rooted not in the bad character of the dangerous classes but in the greed, hardheartedness, and idleness of respectable businessmen, clubwomen, and churchgoers. In his hard-hitting book entitled *If Christ Came to Chicago: A Plea for the Union of All Who Love in the Service of All Who Suffer* Stead described how he had found that saloonkeepers who provided patrons with a free lunch did more for the poor than did all the city's charities combined; he drew the connection between working women's rock-bottom wages and the lure of prostitution; he voiced the open secret that the refusal of the rich to pay their taxes had led politicians into corrupt property assessment and extortionate corporate franchises; and he likened the Protestant churches to "Chinese opium joints" for isolating well-to-do parishioners from workers and the poor. Stead's new moral realism thus helped popularize among Chicago liberal reformers the principle that Richard L. McCormick has argued was at the core of progressive era reform: the idea that "business corrupted politics."[16]

With this as a foundation two other principles followed. First, labor could be expected to be at least as reliable an ally of reform as the respectable classes. Second, reformers rejected merely individual salvation and endorsed the social gospel belief that changing the social environment could help reform individual moral character. This in turn allowed the CFC to build on the optimistic, idealistic, cooperative civic spirit that had motivated the World's Columbian Exposition and the utopian writings popular in the period. The discovery that corruption, both political and personal, had social sources, whose amelioration required more than the good character that the "best men" could offer, allowed this idealism to move out of the realm of utopia and become the driving force in civic and industrial reform.[17]

The Pullman Strike and the New Liberalism

With the formation of the Civic Federation in 1893–94 local politics was poised on the brink between an older mugwump liberalism and a new liberalism; between accepting the untrammeled exercise of the right to dispose of individual property in the market, subject only to the policing of that market, and the new idea that individual rights could be limited or folded into group rights and that the market could be regulated by these groups and the government. Labor, too, was on the threshold of major change, from relying only on police noninterference to win strikes to regularized trade agreements. As during the great upheaval, the collective actions of workers provided an important impetus for this transformation.

The Pullman strike and boycott originated in a walkout by several thousand workers in the Pullman factories, which manufactured railroad sleeping cars. Founded by George Pullman in 1880, the Pullman works provided the nucleus of a planned company town ten miles south of Chicago. By the mid-1880s such social experts as Carroll Wright viewed the town of Pullman as an exemplary blend of industrial efficiency, corporate paternalism, and personal benevolence, a laudatory utopian experiment. Employees lived in the beautiful, tree-lined, six-hundred-acre town designed by the world famous architect Solon Bemen. They rented clean and tidy Pullman homes, shopped at Pullman stores in an arcade, and sent their children to Pullman schools. Though they enjoyed such amenities as indoor plumbing and clean streets and air that most Chicago workers could only dream of, they also were subject to humiliating periodic inspections of their homes, were forced to contend with a ban on saloons—then an essential part of working-class daily life—and were without union protection against the favoritism and other arbitrary actions of their supervisors. One of the few observers to recognize Pullman's shadow side before the strike was Richard T. Ely. After visiting the town in 1884, he wrote an article calling it "a benevolent well-wishing feudalism, which desires the happiness of the people, but in such a way as shall please authorities." It was a criticism that was echoed in Jane Addams's poststrike portrayal of George Pullman as a "modern Lear."[18]

The panic and depression of 1893 revealed starkly the potential incompatibility between the desire for efficiency and profit and the idealism in Pullman's experiment. Faced with declining revenues and determined to win business even while operating below cost, Pullman drastically reduced the size of his work force and then cut the wages of his remaining employees an average of 33 percent. He did not, however, lower the rents he charged the tenants in his houses or the prices he charged at his stores. Faced with a drastic decline in their standard of living, even many of those working faced destitution.

Not surprising, Pullman workers watched the meteoric rise of the American Railway Union (ARU) with fascination and hope. Organized by the charismatic thirty-eight-year-old Eugene V. Debs from Terre Haute, Indiana, a former official in the Brotherhood of Locomotive Fireman, the ARU went beyond the most advanced policies of the craft unions. Rather than a federation of existing craft brotherhoods—the structure of the Supreme Council of the United Orders of Railway Employees, founded in 1889—the ARU was an industrial union that united different crafts and the unskilled yardmen and laborers in one union. After a victory over the Great Northern Railroad, railroad workers in the West flocked into the new organization, much as they had done with the Knights of Labor following the Gould strike of 1885. By 1894 the ARU had 150,000 members, making it the largest union in the United States and threatening to displace the railroad craft brotherhoods.[19]

Beginning in late March about 35 percent of Pullman workers—mostly skilled craftworkers—joined ARU locals. On May 7 a union committee met with the company's vice president, Thomas Wickes, to request a restoration of pay cuts or a reduction in rents. When the company not only refused the request but also fired three members of the committee, Pullman workers walked out on May 11.[20]

At this early stage of the strike the Civic Federation, led by its president, Lyman Gage, attempted to conciliate the dispute. Gage asked Jane Addams to propose to the company an arbitration of the rents, but Pullman refused. In June the company rejected an ARU attempt to mediate the dispute. On June 26, in a move designed to force Pullman to bargain, the ARU declared a sympathy boycott of all railroads carrying leased Pullman sleeping cars.

The boycott nationalized what had been a local dispute involving several thousand workers into an all-out test of strength between the fledgling ARU and the nation's railroads. Since 1886 the general managers of the railroads centering in Chicago had cooperated in setting uniform policies in matters of common interest. By 1893 the General Managers Association (GMA) determined railroad labor policies by setting standard classifications and wages, recruiting strikebreakers, and reapportioning differential revenue losses because of strikes. A major reason for the formation of the ARU was to meet the GMA on equal ground. As notes of its secret meetings indicate, the GMA viewed the Pullman boycott as an opportunity to crush the ARU before it reached maturity. Accordingly it summarily rejected demands to operate without Pullman cars and made plans to discharge and blacklist strikers, recruit replacement workers, and draw the federal government into the fray to make the overriding issue one of law and order. In response ARU members struck, and within a week all freight traffic had ceased in and out of Chicago and numerous towns and railroad junctions throughout twenty-seven states and territories.[21]

As the nation's commercial arteries from the Midwest to the Pacific Coast closed down, the local and national press responded as if the nation were on the brink of anarchy or revolution. It referred repeatedly to "Dictator Debs" and reported incidents of violence and disorder that a federal strike commission subsequently proved were chimerical. The one paper sympathetic to the strike, the *Chicago Times,* which Carter Harrison had bought just before his death, denied the existence of any rioting and exposed the press for attempting to bring into Chicago "deputies, militia, and federal troops to shoot down unarmed and undisciplined men." Realizing the threat of federal intervention, the ARU had instructed its members to avoid violence or involvement in mob actions.[22]

Despite press inaccuracy, public opinion in favor of the strikers extended across class lines. Florence Kelley, writing immediately after the strike, reported, "No other strike has ever found the same amount of approval and interest from so many different sections of the society of our great community. Businessmen, among them some of the most distinguished ones from Chicago, rich ladies, philanthropists of both sexes made a request to Mr. Pullman to grant the demands of the workers after the appointment of a court of arbitration." On returning to the city in the midst of the strike, Jane

Addams remembered "almost everyone on Halsted Street wearing a white ribbon, the emblem of the strikers' side." Even policemen donned the prostrike symbol.[23]

Throughout the strike workers enjoyed the support of local and state authorities. Mayor John Hopkins, who had been elected in December, continued the policies of mayors Harrison, Roche, and Cregier of limiting the support police would provide to employers in the midst of labor disputes. During the strike Hopkins's police refused to provoke disputes or defend strikebreakers, forcing the railroad to rely on private detectives. Hopkins, himself strongly anti-Pullman because his store was forced out of Pullman's Arcade, tried to mediate the strike and contributed $1,500 to the strikers' cause. On the state level Governor John Peter Altgeld, elected with labor votes, was similarly sympathetic. But in a dispute of national proportions the policy of the federal government was crucial, and almost from the beginning U.S. Attorney General Richard Olney, a former railroad attorney who believed that the ARU had brought the country "to the ragged edge of anarchy," worked closely with the GMA to defeat the strike. On June 30 he appointed GMA counsel Edwin Walker as special U.S. attorney for Chicago. The next day, after a minor incident at Blue Island, Walker applied for and received an injunction from the U.S. District Court in Chicago preventing ARU leaders from using any method, including peaceful persuasion, to induce railroad workers not to perform their work duties.[24]

The legal foundation for the injunction was one of the things that made the strike so important in the movement toward new liberalism. In the early 1890s American legal thinking was in the initial stages of a historic transformation as it sought to accommodate and promote the transition from proprietary competitive capitalism to corporate-administered capitalism. Changes proceeded along two lines. First, beginning in 1886 and continuing through the 1890s the Supreme Court in a series of cases redefined property and contractual liberty to include earning value, that is, the right not to be deprived improperly by government of a reasonable return on investment in intangible as well as tangible assets. Corporations were now legal persons entitled to the due process guaranteed by the Fifth and Fourteenth amendments. The new definition facilitated the issuance of securities and, by the turn of the century, a corporate reorganization of major sectors of the U.S. economy.[25]

With regard to law regulating the market federal courts continued to assert, as they had throughout the nineteenth-century, a public interest in preventing restraints of trade from hindering the public welfare or legitimate public policy, but neither law protecting freedom of contract nor law limiting restraint of trade forbade business combinations as such. The combinations of workers, however, received different treatment under the law. With some exceptions the courts treated the collective actions of workers—whether they were strikes for closed shops, boycotts, or secondary/sympathy boycotts—as an interference in the natural right of laborers to the free exercise of property in their own labor, which included their right to work on such terms as they chose to accept. Unlike capital, workers could not escape the common law by incorporating, without inviting judicial supervision of internal union activities.[26]

Meanwhile, the Sherman Act and judges' increased invocation of the interstate commerce clause of the U.S. Constitution resulted in a growing federalization of law regulating the market, thus bringing federal courts increasingly into labor relations beginning in the late 1880s. Later, when the 1897 Trans-Missouri decision of the U.S. Supreme Court applied the Sherman Act to all restraints of trade, including those business combinations previously judged reasonable under the common law, a legal crisis developed, whose resolution would be central for the acceptance of organized bodies of both labor and capital during the Progressive Era.[27] But in the early 1890s the federal courts severely restricted, often declared illegal, and punished group action by strikers and boycotters, while reserving the freedom to regulate the market activity of such business combinations as railroad corporations.

Invoking the Sherman Act, the federal district court of Chicago issued an injunction on July 1 that fundamentally changed the course of the strike. Until that juncture the city and environs had been quiet, and Debs and ARU leaders felt justified in ignoring the injunction. But, as minor riots south of the city continued, Olney convinced President Cleveland to dispatch federal troops to the city to enforce the injunction. In two public telegrams Governor Altgeld protested that the sending of troops without his request and over his opposition amounted to an unconstitutional centralization of power in the hands of a "military government." Altgeld's action lent new weight to an older labor republicanism that disposed workers to suspect an oligarchy of wealth had corrupted the Republic through centralization of power. Like the Haymarket trial and conviction eight years earlier, the injunction and the use of federal troops seemed to demonstrate that instead of serving the public interest the government was partial to class interests. That these actions had been taken by a Democratic president against the wishes of a Democratic governor and mayor and in violation of the anticentralization tradition of the Democratic party only magnified workers' sense of betrayal.[28]

Under these circumstances federal troops served as a symbol of unconstitutional usurpation of political power and transformed a strike into an open political protest of the most profound sort. With the threat of federal troops looming, Martin Madden, a leader in the Building Trades Council, declared, "If the situation assumes the attitude of a war of corporations against labor, every department of [Chicago] labor will be called out" and "industry shall cease until our rights are adjusted and justice takes precedence of public convenience." The next day he stated that "we are on the eve of a great political uprising bordering upon a revolution." On July 4 the *Chicago Times* printed a cartoon portraying the ARU as the patriots of 1776 and the next day accused railroad managers of favoring "the re-establishment of slavery."[29]

Meanwhile, the arrival of troops had sparked widespread rioting and the killing of strike sympathizers attempting to stop trains run by replacement workers. Sympathy and support from the respectable classes quickly evaporated with the onset of violence. Though ARU members were not part of the disturbances, crowds of thousands of young boys, strike supporters, and spectators thronged the stockyards district and the railroad yards in other industrial areas. On July 7 the Building Trades Council, then the most powerful central body in the city, called for a nationwide general strike if Pullman did not consent to arbitration. The next day, after a forty-eight-hour closed-door meeting, the Trades and Labor Assembly called a general strike for July 10. But because influential unions enjoyed trade agreements they were loath to break with a sympathy strike, because national union leaders had come to Chicago to lobby their locals not to strike, and perhaps because the ARU effort seemed on the verge of failure, only about 25,000 Chicago workers actually walked out.[30]

On July 13 the AFL executive council, meeting at Briggs House in Chicago, issued a statement expressing admiration for the ARU but counseling against a nationwide sympathy strike. Not only did Gompers as head of a labor federation have no power to call such a strike, but a direct confrontation with the federal government and the 14,000 troops and militia in the city was sure to be defeated. Since the strike's prospects for success were now greatly diminished, Debs's address to the Briggs House gathering asked mainly that the AFL mediate an end to the dispute so that ARU members could return to work. But the GMA was taking no prisoners. It refused to consider a communication from any labor organization. With Debs in jail for contempt of court and trains starting to move, the boycott had no hope of success, and on August 2 the ARU all but declared it over. That did not prevent a GMA-sponsored blacklist of all strikers. Pullman strikers were accepted back, but they had to sign a yellow-dog contract promising never to join a labor organization.[31]

Ironically, the defeat of the strike almost miraculously restored the prolabor thrust of public opinion that had dissolved so quickly with the issuance of the federal injunction. The political atmosphere suddenly reverberated with calls for legislated alternatives to the court injunction as a method of settling labor disputes. Attorney General Richard Olney himself expressed the emerging view when privately he advised a federal judge, "Whatever else may remain for the future to determine, it must now be regarded as substantially settled that the mass of wage-earners can no longer be dealt with by capital as so many isolated units. . . . Organized labor now confronts organized capital . . . and the burning question of modern times is how shall the ever-recurring controversies between them be adjusted and terminated."[32]

Within a decade Olney's view would become part of a new liberal jurisprudence that would argue that labor combinations as well as business combinations should be accorded legal recognition.[33] But in the mid-1890s those who believed that group organization was required to supplement or supersede individual action in the market were forced to turn to legislative alternatives. One view, proposed by Debs, ARU leaders, socialists, and some Populists, favored federal ownership of the railroads as a supplement to collective bargaining. The U.S. Bureau of Labor commissioner Carroll Wright agreed that the country needed to reexamine "socialist" propositions and "if expedient apply some of the features involved in them" to railroad labor relations. By far the most common new liberal approach, however, was the advocacy of some form of government-facilitated collective bargaining. On July 19 the CFC's industrial committee, which was chaired by M. J. Carroll and included Bertha Palmer, Jane Addams, and prominent trade unionists, decided to call a national conference of capital and labor to propose state and national means for the conciliation and arbitration of labor disputes. Two days later the *Tribune* editorialized that Congress should require that interstate railroads make contracts with their employees in return for no-strike agreements. Meanwhile, President Cleveland established the U.S. Strike Commission to investigate the strike's causes and recommend means for adjusting labor disputes.[34]

In mid-November the Pullman Strike Commission, chaired by Wright, issued a report that was a ringing manifesto of the new liberalism. It declared, "Our railroads were chartered upon the theory that their competition would amply protect shippers as to rates, etc., and employees as to wages and other conditions. Combination has largely destroyed this theory and has seriously disturbed the natural working of the laws of supply and demand." It castigated the GMA's refusal to deal with the ARU as "arrogant and absurd." It not only endorsed collective bargaining but also called for the establishment of a permanent federal strike commission modeled on the Interstate Commerce Commission, with powers of conciliation and arbitration enforced by the courts. It called for yellow-dog contracts to be banned, and it recommended that government ownership of the railroads be seriously considered in the form of an experiment.[35]

During the same week that the strike commission's report was released the Civic Federation held its national conference on conciliation and arbitration. Retreating from the advocacy of compulsory state arbitration that had been popular in the weeks following the strike, most speakers still favored collective bargaining and voluntary arbitration as an alternative to strikes. One of the few advocates of compulsory arbitration was Judge Murray F. Tuley. Tuley firmly criticized the federal court's reliance on labor injunctions and proposed a legislative remedy in which workers and employers would be enrolled in publicly licensed bodies that would be compelled to bargain collectively.[36] Following the conference craft unionists in the Civic Federation submitted to the state legislature a bill creating an arbitration board, though without compulsory powers. Chief among its advocates were M. J. Carroll, editor of the *Eight-Hour Herald,* and officers of the bricklayers' union, but the bill drew broad labor support, especially from unions with trade agreements. Labor leaders lobbied vigorously for the bill, which passed in July 1895.[37]

From one perspective the crushing defeat of the Pullman strike, coming barely two years after a similar defeat at Homestead, amounted to a dispiriting and debilitating setback for the plans to organize industrial unions in such companies as Carnegie Steel or the combined railroad corporations. In the wake of these defeats AFL leaders hunkered down in their secure niches in small-scale industry, prudently forbearing the mass sympathy action that might trigger the deadly combination of corporate intransigence and federal repression.[38]

Labor leaders in Chicago, however, were not willing to accept defeat so easily, especially with the prospect of new liberal allies. The Pullman Strike Commission's report and the Civic Federation conference were part of a string of congressional investigatory efforts in the 1890s that mobilized new liberals in the fight to establish the legitimacy of collective bargaining and to limit the power of federal judges to issue antistrike injunctions. In 1898, after three years of legislative wrangling, Congress passed the Olney-sponsored Erdman Act, which banned yellow-dog contracts, recognized railway brotherhood–type unions in interstate commerce, and established a federal voluntary arbitration board. That same year President William McKinley signed a bill establishing the U.S. Industrial Commission, an investigatory commission on labor-capital relations. Two years later the Civic Federation established a national body known as the National Civic Federation to further its efforts at union recognition in the context of labor-capital conciliation. The Pullman strike was therefore far from an unalloyed defeat; it was a powerful spur to the growing realization among reformers that if collective regulation of the market by trusts or corporations was not complemented by some form of industrial democracy—Henry Demarest Lloyd's new term for extending political democracy into industrial relations through trade agreements—neither social peace nor social justice could be guaranteed in America's evolving new corporate order.[39]

The Rise and Fall of Labor Populism in Chicago, 1894–95

New liberal reform did not yet dominate the political agenda in Chicago, though. The social distress during the early years of the depression and the blatant partiality of the federal government in crushing a peaceful strike fueled an outrage on the part of workers that found a ready outlet in the insurgent national alternative to the two old parties in the form of the People's (or Populist) party. In Chicago advocates of a labor party, led by T. J. Morgan and Henry Demarest Lloyd, worked tirelessly to use populism as a vehicle for launching a counterpart to Britain's Independent Labour party.

In December 1893, at the instigation of its socialist delegates, the AFL decided to canvass its members nationally on whether to conduct an independent campaign based on a program that advocated in plank 10 collective ownership of the means of production. At the Illinois State Federation of Labor convention in July 1894 Lloyd effected a historic compromise between state Populists, single-taxers, and labor advocates of independent political action. The compromise involved an alternative to plank 10 that affirmed the principle of collective ownership but applied it only in cases where a popular majority could be mustered. The socialist collectivism of the compromise, however, rested in an uneasy balance with an older principle derived from labor republicanism. Lloyd's recently published book, *Wealth against Commonwealth,* had argued that giantism and concentration of capital resulted not from an inevitable evolutionary process but from fraud and political favoritism. Lloyd portrayed his movement as a "counterrevolution of the people" against corporate combinations and other trusts and appealed to workers to regain ownership and control of the product of their labor through a cooperative commonwealth. Yet at the same time Lloyd championed many of the same proposals that socialists with an evolutionary orientation advocated. Instead of suggesting the break up of trusts and a reversion to small-scale firms operating within a competitive market, Lloyd, as a British Fabian socialist, proposed the democratic socialization of large industry through stringent government regulation and public ownership. In this way Lloyd could bridge the gap between populists, single-taxers, socialists, and trade unionists.[40]

The new Illinois People's party formed in July found the bulk of its support in Chicago. There Lloyd's historic compromise and his own ideological ambivalence allowed Morgan to persuade German-speaking socialists to break from the sectarian revolutionary leadership of Daniel DeLeon, the Socialist Labor party chief, and merge their identity with the People's party. It also enabled local single-taxers to enter into coalition with the Socialists, which in turn, required a break with the single-taxers' national leader, Henry George. Finally, Lloyd's leadership persuaded a majority of local unionists to sidestep Samuel Gompers's opposition to third parties, a position that in Chicago was championed by William Pomeroy's labor skates. The result was a precarious coalition on the local level that was vulnerable to the pressures from national leaderships based in New York City.[41]

Chicago's unions dominated the People's party, making it virtually a labor party, though a coterie of Populists led by Henry S. Taylor played an important minority role. The party enjoyed the support of an impressive array of newspapers, including two labor papers, the *Railway Times* and the *Chicago Workman*, and a Populist paper, the *Searchlight*, edited by Henry Vincent. The party's most important media friend was the *Chicago Times*, which boasted the city's largest circulation because of its support of the ARU during the Pullman strike. That fall the party conducted a vigorous campaign relying on ward-level clubs of unionists and reformers to organize rallies and torchlight parades, and it packed mass meetings in downtown auditoriums with rousing speeches. In party organization and in its mobilization of active union members the campaign was at least the equal of any labor or socialist electoral effort in the city's history.[42]

With the number of organized workers at least as large as that of the Haymarket period, party leaders were optimistic and expected to poll at least 50,000 votes in November. They were sorely disappointed. The 30,000 votes received by Populist candidates left the party with only 12 percent of the vote, far below the 31 percent the United Labor party received in 1887, and cast a pall over the hopes of Lloyd and his allies that they would be able to parlay local success into a national labor-Populist alliance on the model of Britain's Independent Labour party.[43]

Party leaders and activists publicly wrung their hands and debated the reasons for labor's failure to turn out for the People's party. Even in retrospect the reasons for the failure of the People's party are not at all clear. One possible reason for labor's unexpected weakness may have been the effect of unemployment on union membership. With unemployment in the city's large firms, which employed 38 percent of the work force, at over 40 percent, one local union leader estimated that of the 110,000 members claimed by the unions in 1893 not more than 50,000 remained in 1894. A year and a half later

T. J. Morgan wrote that "economically the industrial class is on the rocks." Historically, however, unemployment and trade union weakness had been inversely proportional to the strength of labor protest at the polls. Both the Socialist Labor party in 1877–79 and the United Labor party in 1886–87 emerged as rivals to the two major parties during times of high unemployment or union strike defeats or both.[44]

A different explanation for the labor-Populist failure centers on the deep and persistent rift between socialists and nonsocialists within the labor movement and among potential labor voters. Even though the principle and sentiment of socialism had grown in popularity and the topic had become acceptable in respectable circles, opposition to socialist *ideology* remained unalterable among the small property owners and middle-class professionals, who were potential allies of the party, and among Catholic workers, who constituted perhaps half of the city's work force. When Chester McArthur Destler researched his unsurpassed history of Chicago's labor-Populists in the 1930s, Clarence Darrow and an ex-Knights leader told him that the party was hurt by "the reluctance of Catholic wage-earners to support an independent movement in which Socialism figured so prominently."[45]

Ideological tensions in the People's party over socialism were evident as early as October 1894, when Henry George, speaking in Chicago, repudiated the local club's alliance with the Socialist Labor party. This encouraged single-taxers to support Pomeroy in his successful attempt to seize control of the Illinois State Federation of Labor and replace Lloyd's modified plank on collective ownership with a single-tax plank. In November the defeat of the party compounded these internal strains and led Lloyd and like-minded reformers to create a Fabian socialist forum, the Radical Club, independent from the party apparatus. When the December convention of the national AFL repudiated the plank on collective ownership and independent political action, Chicago unions supporting the People's party withdrew from the Trades and Labor Assembly and formed the Chicago Labor Congress. Dominated by German-speaking socialists, the Labor Congress endorsed advanced democratic reforms and affirmed the cooperative commonwealth.[46]

Although dissent over socialism clearly divided members of the local labor-Populist coalition, there is little evidence that it was a major factor in limiting the Populist vote in the electorate. In 1887 the split of nonsocialists from socialists in the United Labor party did nothing to create a bloc of nonsocialist, prolabor party voters among workers in Chicago (or in New York for that matter). Likewise, the eventual takeover in 1895 by the nonsocialist Populists of the local People's party did not enable the party to pick up any additional votes. In fact, deprived of its socialist voting bloc, the party's electoral strength quickly evaporated, just as in 1887–88.

To explain the People's party defeat, we may return to the three factors used in chapter 9 to explain the ULP's defeat. First, the benefits trade unionists received from the major parties, in the form of not only immunity from police interference but also support for arbitration, continued to attract labor to the two regular parties. In virtually every union that supported the People's party there were strong factions opposed to an independent labor party. T. J. Morgan wrote that during the depression union leaders vastly overestimated their membership to "keep up a false prestige" for purposes of bargaining with the parties and were demoralizing the Populist effort by selling themselves "for the smallest job in the gift of the politician." There is considerable anecdotal evidence that trade unionists did not deliver a strong labor vote for the party. Henry Vincent of the *Searchlight* observed that wards with a heavy union membership did not poll more Populist votes than did wards with few unionists. In a *Searchlight* forum union leaders agreed, admitting that members who wanted revenge on President Cleveland probably supported Republican rather than Populist candidates. Such an explanation is made more persuasive because 1894 was a national election year in which voters tended to ignore third parties and choose between the two regular parties. To make matters worse, by running Populist candidates for local offices against Democrats, the party hurt most by Populist votes, the new party ensured itself of virulent Democratic opposition.[47]

Two other factors combined to limit the party's attractiveness: the growing strength of nonpartisan social reform, which made it impossible for the labor-Populists to monopolize the reform mantle; and the willingness of major political and civic leaders to stand against federal antilabor repression, which minimized the incentive to look for protection outside the existing parties. These two developments occurred *outside* the labor movement and constituted labor's political opportunity structure. Lloyd caught sight of this in January 1895, when he was interviewed in Boston. Lloyd admitted his grave disappointment with Chicago workers for failing to support the party in November: "It is amazing that workingmen are not more radical than they are. In Chicago the workingmen are mystified, troubled, apprehensive, and scarcely know which way to turn." Standing in contrast to working-class disarray was middle-class vigor, according to Lloyd: "The most striking effect [of recent events and decisions of the courts] is the spread of radicalism among the middle classes." Lloyd was referring to "the demand for municipal or state control of public functions," which he viewed as "but an intermediate step toward public ownership."[48]

Lloyd then took steps to bring the People's party into line with his updated evaluation of the middle class. In his February 22 draft program for the Populist spring mayoral campaign Lloyd revised the party's emphasis on immediate municipal ownership, instead stating that as a step toward that goal no further franchises should be granted except on condition that the city secure "an adequate portion of the annual gross earnings and that the franchise revert absolutely to the city after twenty years." Rather than attack the Civic Federation's reform efforts, as had been done in the first campaign, Lloyd commended them. The convention then nominated the physician Bayard Holmes, an obvious appeal to reform-oriented urban professionals. During the mayoral campaign Lloyd, Darrow, and others dropped their rhetorical advocacy of the cooperative commonwealth in favor of focusing on the link between city corruption and franchise steals, a popular cross-class issue.[49]

Lloyd's reworking of the Populist program in the direction of cross-class progressivism was based on a profound transformation of the political terrain in the city from the mid-1880s. Since 1887, especially since the annexation of surrounding suburbs in 1889, the city included large numbers of reform voters not only hostile to corrupt machines but also sensitive to such social issues as inequitable taxation, the regulation of sweatshops, Yerkes's monopoly of public transportation, and the arbitration of labor disputes.[50] During the 1880s the independent labor vote composed of German socialists, Irish nationalists, and trade unionists had been the swing vote between the two regular parties. But beginning in 1889 a much larger independent reform vote held the potential balance of power in the city. Something of the strength of the independent reform vote was evident in 1897, when John Maynard Harlan, a Municipal Voters League reformer, ran as an independent for mayor against Democratic and Republican candidates. Harlan received 69,730 votes, or 22.5 percent of the total, but 30.5 percent of the vote in the newly annexed suburban Twenty-fifth through Thirty-four wards. By contrast, at the height of the People's party strength in 1894, the labor vote for sheriff produced 30,724 votes, or 12 percent of the total, and 12 percent in the suburban wards. These changed electoral conditions implied that the labor vote could have clout only as part of a reform coalition with the middle class rather than as part of the Democratic party or as an independent party.[51]

Two other political developments further strengthened the reform vote and inhibited labor-Populist prospects: press sensationalism and the growing openness of some business leaders to reform. Like the "educational" politics of the old liberals, press sensationalism was above partisanship and was issue-oriented, but in contrast to mugwump elitism the new press campaigns sought to mobilize a mass constituency. In the mid- to late 1890s Chicago's newspapers united in a nonpartisan reform campaign full of sensational exposés of the vote-buying machinations of the traction magnate

Charles Yerkes. Building on the tactics and politics of William Stead, the press further popularized a new politics that condemned business for corrupting municipal government. Doing so enabled new liberals to link two of the three major issue complexes of Gilded Age urban politics—reform of party corruption and the righting of the injustices to labor (dropping the issue of temperance reform)—to create a new political agenda.[52]

By the mid-1890s Chicago's downtown businessmen had turned against franchise buccaneers like the streetcar promoter Charles Yerkes and were becoming open to reform issues with mass appeal, such as tax reform. At the same time they were adamantly opposed to the People's party subtreasury program and free silver, both of which obstructed the kind of banking reform such local and national leaders as Chicago's Lyman Gage, the leading new liberal heading up the Civic Federation, were advocating. Chicago differed from other midwestern cities where the upper class was split over the issue of silver, thus opening up a fissure through which urban populism might flow. By contrast, Chicago business leaders lent their support to middle-class municipal reform at the very time that they stiffened opposition to the local People's party for its national stands.[53]

The continuing vigor of labor's ties to the Democratic party, the growing support among respectable voters for a new liberal political agenda sponsored by the press, and the united opposition of business leaders to populism all contributed to the faltering of the local People's party at a time when progressive reform was gaining momentum. These factors were strongly present in the spring mayoral campaign. Popular wrath was aroused by a press exposé of nine blatant franchise giveaways by the city council, notably one to the Ogden Gas Company. When Mayor Hopkins, who secretly owned shares in Ogden Gas, signed the ordinance, voters were outraged. Seeking to punish the Democrats, they gave the Republican George B. Swift a landslide victory. The Populist Holmes received less than 5 percent of the vote, which was a crushing blow for the labor-Populist alliance. Just before the election Henry S. Taylor had executed an antisocialist coup in the party. After the election the socialists reconstituted themselves as an independent body and returned to DeLeon's Socialist Labor party and his revolutionary strategy, which involved the formation of a dual union federation, the Socialist Trade and Labor Alliance. Simultaneously, Henry Vincent adopted an antisocialist and prosilver policy for the *Searchlight*. Nationally, the defeat emboldened prosilver forces in the People's party, foreshadowing their success in fusing with the Bryan-led Democrats in 1896. As a result, the ardent hope of Lloyd and Morgan that the old antimonopolist-socialist-trade unionist coalition dating from 1879 could be used to fashion an American labor party under the auspices of the People's party was effectively dashed.[54]

Labor and the Municipal Voters League

The disintegration of the labor-Populist alliance was only the start of a remarkable flowering of nonpartisan municipal reform under the wing of the Municipal Voters League. Before this occurred, however, George Swift, the newly elected mayor and an erstwhile mugwump, emerged as an unlikely but nonetheless genuine reformer of a new type. Swift left temperance and antivice reform alone and instead broke with his party's machine by supporting state-level reform legislation and strictly implementing the new civil service act in Illinois. He also fell in lockstep behind the new reform emphasis on franchise giveaways by vetoing the city council's ordinances. Most remarkably, Swift took the lead in popularizing tax reform.

Forced into action by the city's revenue crisis, Swift argued that revenues could be increased by making assessments more equitable and by bringing wealthy tax dodgers to justice. Since the 1870s the unstated agreement between machine politicians and large propertyholders to underassess property had limited the scope of the reform program and the base of the reform forces' support. Only a few years earlier Marshall Field and downtown businessmen had threatened the *Times* with an advertising boycott for exposing wealthy tax cheats. But in 1895 the Chicago Real Estate Board joined the agitation for assessment reform in the belief that "the gang's" tax assessments unfairly milked downtown propertyholders. In November the Civic Federation began to mobilize different reform groups to formulate a new tax system. In February Swift appointed a business investigatory commission, whose report demonstrated the glaring inequities in assessment. In 1898 a CFC-sponsored bill passed the state legislature that reformed the assessment process and stipulated that property be assessed at one-fifth of its value. The result was a 35 percent increase in assessment, which in turn allowed revenues and spending to expand. By 1896 the old adherence to low-tax government—espoused and practiced by both mugwump reformers and machine politicians—was being challenged and to some degree replaced by the view that ending tax dodging would increase revenues and resolve the city's fiscal crisis.[55]

Meanwhile, the reform movement entered a new phase when in January 1896 the city council gang mustered the two-thirds majority to pass a boodle franchise ordinance over Mayor Swift's veto. It appeared that a reform mayor was not enough; something would have to be done to clean out the city council. On January 11 a multiclass array of leaders from respectable clubs, reform associations, and labor unions came together under the auspices of the Civic Federation to form the Municipal Voters League (MVL).

Its first president was Judge Tuley, who the previous year had refused the Democratic party's mayoral nomination. In the April elections the MVL boasted a "rout of the gang." Voters returned to office only five of the twenty-four aldermen who had been openly denounced by the MVL, and only four boodlers defeated MVL candidates.[56]

Early accounts of the MVL accepted at face value its rhetoric that it was putting reputable professionals and businessmen in office in place of disreputable ward politicians. Revisionist scholars on progressivism seized on this rhetoric to brand MVL leaders anti-immigrant, anti-working-class elitists. Whatever the accuracy of this characterization for other urban centers, it was not the case in Chicago during the mid-1890s. The MVL was not run by the city's leading business magnates but by their sons and by much less substantial businessmen, notably George Cole. The MVL did not seek to remove power from working-class wards by sponsoring at-large (as opposed to ward) elections or commission government. Such activists as Cole, William Kent, Walter Fischer, and Charles Merriam had faith in a public opinion educated and directed by reformers and the press. The reform journalist Lincoln Steffens distinguished Chicago's reform movement from "reform waves that wash the 'best people' into office to make fools of themselves and subside leaving the machine stronger than ever." MVL reform was "slow, sure, political democratic reform, by the people, for the people."[57]

Viewed in historical perspective, the official program of the Municipal Voters League and its criteria for endorsing candidates were quite distinct from those of the old mugwumps. The MVL's stated goal was "to wrest the city away from the clutches of men who brazenly barter away the people's rights to corporations." It called for utility franchises that would expire in twenty years and "provide for the opportunity of public ownership on fair and reasonable terms." The goal of possible municipal ownership and franchise reform as a means of remedying political corruption was close to the draft program Lloyd crafted for the People's party a year earlier to appeal to the reform middle class. The MVL's acceptance of this goal helped legitimize public ownership and place it first on the public agenda during the next decade.[58]

There were three keys to the MVL's ability to forge a popular majority. One was its ability to rise above class interests instead of simply mediating and conciliating between them as the Civic Federation had done. George "King" Cole was the MVL's "dictator" and was not beholden to the respectable clubs, whose members composed much of the Civic Federation's leadership. This allowed Cole, for example, to refuse to endorse for office a friend of Lyman Gage, despite a personal appeal from Gage. Cole even went before the Union League Club to echo Stead in declaring that the worst enemies of good government were the "members of what we are pleased to call good society" and that "the franchise buyers, the jury packers and bribers of assessors" were "worse than the boodler." As a result of its independence, the MVL abjured mugwump moralism and pragmatically adopted many of the same methods of the machine it fought.[59]

A second reason for the MVL's success was that it had almost unanimous editorial support. Victor Lawson of the *Daily News* actually helped finance the MVL, assigned employees to work for it, and served as an adviser. In exposing and delegitimizing the activities of Yerkes and in mobilizing an issue-oriented mass constituency for civic reform, the press helped create what has been called "advertising politics" and played an "agenda-setting" role in local politics.[60]

A third key was the MVL's attempt to court support from the labor movement, resulting in partial reciprocation from a segment of labor leadership. Though most Chicago unions were either too discouraged by the dissolution of the People's party or too suspicious of business leadership to be actively involved in progressive reform, the MVL won avid support from the bricklayers' union, which had close ties with Judge Tuley. John J. McGrath, an ex-president of the bricklayer's union and the Trades and Labor Assembly, was heavily involved in the Civic Federation and the MVL. Other active labor leaders included J. J. Ryan (gasfitters), J. J. Elderkin (seamen), P. J. Minter (bricklayers), J. J. Linehan (carpenters), and V. B. Williams (painters). M. J. Carroll, a longtime leader of the typographers' union, was labor's most forceful spokesman for an alliance with progressive reformers and employers. As editor-proprietor of the *Eight-Hour Herald*, which was funded by the bricklayers' union, Carroll supported Gompers's opposition to third parties and published biting attacks on "faddists, rainbow chasers" and advocates of a cooperative commonwealth. Carroll distinguished trusts or monopolies from corporations, which he saw as valuable and impossible to eradicate. He consistently favored arbitration and endorsed the idea that the building trades should pull back from sympathy strikes in order to facilitate stable agreements with employers. Carroll served on the CFC's executive board and the MVL's Committee of 15. During the spring campaign he was tapped by Cole to be on the Committee of 7 that governed the daily activities of the MVL.[61]

An analysis of the sources of MVL voting strength reveals its ability to draw on both the labor-Populist and progressive reform constituencies. When the MVLer John Harlan ran as an independent mayoral candidate in 1897, six of his top ten wards (in absolute vote) had also been among the top ten wards of People's party in 1894. Every one of these wards ranked among the top ten in the percentage of German-born registered voters. In subsequent years these German wards continued to provide a base for the MVL.[62]

Notwithstanding the proclivities of the Germans, most labor-Populists refused to participate in a labor-reform alliance. The *Union Workman*, the paper of the Chicago Labor Congress, championed immediate municipal ownership and sought to unmask Mayor Swift, the Civic Federation, and the MVL as probusiness, antilabor reformers. The paper ridiculed the idea of a "businessmen's council" because businesspeople were the source of municipal corruption. The *Union Workman* was distressed that Jane Addams, prolabor ministers, and women's unions based at Hull-House cooperated actively with the MVL, and it attacked labor leaders who at MVL meetings endorsed reforms that often had been decided in advance.[63]

There was some truth to these criticisms. Most respectable reformers were ambivalent about whether electing good men was enough to clean up municipal government. Moreover, with the exceptions of Carroll and McGrath, labor leaders were followers rather than leaders in mid-1890s progressive reform. Yet it is hard to argue that the MVL program endorsing tax reform and the principle of municipal ownership differed fundamentally from that of Lloyd's in 1895. Alzina Stevens, leader of the women's labor movement based at Hull-House, recognized that cross-class progressivism was the only viable social reform in Chicago when she wrote Lloyd, "We see reason for tolerating the Civic Federation, while we must regret that the opposition [to Yerkes] was not initiated by a really representative, clean-handed body of citizens."[64]

Business progressives, far from being shills for business interests, were far in advance of most city employers. When Lincoln Steffens arrived in the city in 1903, he found that all but one of the great business leaders he interviewed were opposed to the MVL. "They rose up, purple in the face," wrote Steffens, "and cursed reform. They said it had hurt business; it had hurt the town."[65] The gulf between reform leaders and employers was nowhere more evident than when it came to engaging in collective bargaining. During the MVL's campaign in 1896 a major strike of garment workers put the labor question on the front burner of reform for the first time since the Pullman strike. The strike began with a lockout of 900 union clothing cutters by large garment employers. When the Civic Federation asked employers to accept state arbitration, they refused, just as Pullman had done a year and a half earlier. Like the Pullman sympathy boycott, the strike soon expanded when 20,000 unskilled and sweated tailors walked out, both in sympathy with the cutters and for recognition of their own union. At the behest of Addams, Civic Federation leaders signed a letter supporting union recognition and sought to arbitrate the strike themselves. In their meeting with employers Civic Federation leaders backed its new president, the Board of Trade chief William T. Baker, in his statement "that all through the building trades, the printing trades, iron trades in almost every line of skilled labor, trades unions were recognized without any demoralization of business." Baker's pronouncement indicated that the term *arbitration* was becoming almost synonymous with voluntary collective bargaining without a third-party arbiter, a practice that would later be sanctioned by the National Civic Federation. Still, garment employers were intransigent, forcing the strike's defeat.[66]

The defeat pointed up flaws in the state's new system of voluntary arbitration, and it underlined the gap between the support for collective bargaining by progressive reformers and the practices of employers facing a weak group of workers in a fiercely competitive market.[67] The inability of reformers to deliver meaningful collective bargaining beyond such trades as construction explained as much as anything the continued resistance among the broader ranks of labor to cooperation with the Civic Federation and the MVL.

Throughout the rest of the year until the election of November 1896 the differences between the leaders of the Trades and Labor Assembly and the Labor Congress persisted and even worsened. The two factions held separate Labor Day parades and carried on a rancorous exchange in their respective papers over trade union philosophy and support for progressive reform initiatives. The political gulf deepened when the Labor Congress, along with most Chicago union leaders and rank-and-file Democrats, endorsed free silver, while the Trades and Labor Assembly criticized it. The election on November 3 was a disaster for the silver forces in Chicago. William Jennings Bryan suffered a 57 to 41 percent thumping. Of 20 wards "inhabited almost exclusively by workingmen," according to M. J. Carroll, "only 8 returned free silver majorities." Governor Altgeld also went down to defeat, garnering only 45 percent of the vote.[68]

It was also a watershed for the late nineteenth-century labor movement. Disillusioned with independent politics, the Labor Congress finally merged with the Trades and Labor Assembly on November 10 to form the Chicago Federation of Labor (CFL). The CFL acceded to the wishes of the Labor Congress to bar those not working at their trade, a slap at William C. Pomeroy and his corrupt cronies. But it also adopted a provision preventing it from endorsing any political party, a slap at the Labor Congress and the silverites. The program was hardly pure and simple trade unionist, for while it expressly repudiated free silver, it favored federal ownership of the railroads and telegraphs and municipal ownership of all utilities, as the Labor Congress did.[69]

Chicago labor's support for reform was part of a new tide of cross-class urban progressivism that began to restir the political waters of Chicago during the late nineteenth century. In the spring of 1897 the city's reform forces, including the CFL, united to oppose the Humphrey bill in the state legislature, which would have extended the Yerkes streetcar franchises for ninety-nine years, eliminating any possibility for municipal ownership. But antimachine reform unity could not be sustained. Carter Harrison II, the young son of the five-time mayor, gathered up his old coalition of ethnic groups, added organized labor, and was elected mayor in a landslide. This was not simply a return to the old machine politics, though. Just as in 1895, when voters had turned en masse to the Republicans when the Democrats nominated an anti-reform candidate, so they voted Democrat in 1897, when the Republicans threw sand in the face of reformers by nominating their own machine candidate. The Republican candidate finished third, behind John Harlan.[70]

Though the new mayor deferred to his party base by openly tolerating gambling and refusing to implement the new civil service law, Harrison demonstrated his reform credentials by assuming leadership of the fight in the state legislature against the Allen bill, a revised version of the Humphrey bill, thereby winning the MVL's endorsement. The mass movement against franchise corruption reached a crescendo in December 1898, when the MVL, the CFL, the former governor Altgeld, Mayor Harrison, and a united press mobilized a series of mass public meetings that prevented the city council from extending the Yerkes franchises. Egged on by strident editorial comment, respectable citizens attended rallies wearing nooses in their buttonholes to symbolize what would happen if boodle aldermen voted with Yerkes. The council relented, and a defeated Yerkes left town. Meanwhile, Harrison continued the Democratic machine's policy of police neutrality during strikes and one-upped progressive reformers' support of arbitration by endorsing the closed shop for the building trades, something elite new liberals would not do. According to one observer in 1904, Harrison had assembled his own version of a progressive coalition consisting of "the regular Democratic machine; the more or less independent Democrats, whose public consciences had been soothed by gradual improvements in the city hall; the regular radicals, whose social consciences had been soothed by insinuations about municipal ownership; and the reformers, who, possessing consciences of both the public and the social kind, halted between two opinions, but finally inclined to the latter." Harrison's new politics demonstrated that if old mugwump reformers could become new progressives, machine politicians could keep pace with the new agenda just as well.[71]

Harrison's opportunistic politics preempted and forestalled the possibility of a third party or a nonpartisan antimachine coalition between labor-Populists and MVL reformers. In 1899 the anti-Yerkes coalition split into two camps: one, led by the CFL, in favor of immediate municipal ownership; the other, a more moderate one led by the MVL and Harrison, for stringent franchise regulation with an option for public ownership. In the spring of 1899 the immediatist wing united behind the mayoral candidacy of John Peter Altgeld. In the election Harrison swamped Altgeld, proving once again a third-party movement that appealed exclusively to the working class could not gain a majority in the city. The restoration of the labor-Harrison alliance limited progressives' ability to control the CFL during this period. With the CFL under the control of Martin "Skinny" Madden racketeering and corruption returned to the labor movement. Only when John Fitzpatrick won the CFL's presidency in 1905 did labor progressives consolidate their hold on the labor movement.[72]

The mixed local success of the progressive movement should not be confused with the outcome of the new liberalism, which achieved a more significant triumph on the national level. In 1900 Ralph Easley, the secretary of the Civic Federation of Chicago, founded the National Civic Federation, with key members of the Chicago Civic Federation as its nucleus. Bringing together such corporate and banking leaders as Andrew Carnegie, George Perkins, and George Corleyou and such national labor leaders as Samuel Gompers and John Mitchell of the United Mine Workers, the National Civic Federation proposed a labor-capital bargain in which unions would receive recognition in the form of trade agreements and the eight-hour day in return for abandoning limitations on production and assuring business leaders that there would be no strikes during the life of the contract. Franklin MacVeagh, who had done so much to facilitate the transformation of liberal political thought in Chicago, was a prominent member of the executive board.[73]

In 1897, looking back on twenty-five years of involvement in liberal reform, MacVeagh openly rejected his earlier antilabor "toryism." He had come to see that democracy was no longer incompatible with property, for "the truth is that democracy, as it has turned out, rather unexpectedly to the world, is not radical even, and certainly not lawless." Like Carroll Wright, he admitted that though he disagreed with socialism, "the world is taking some hints from socialist thought and agitation—and applying them." MacVeagh believed that with the end of the frontier "it is practically certain that combination in some form and measure is a permanent factor of modern industrial life." Consequently, "competition has not only to be moderated for the protection of capital; but it has to be moderated for the protection of labor. . . . the only conceivable way to raise wages—and wages must be constantly raised and the hours of work must be constantly lowered—is with the help of labor unions." During the 1898–1905 period the budding rapprochement between capital and labor blossomed into what one historian has called "the golden age of the trade agreement"—though cross-class support for the National Civic Federation and the trade agreement would later falter.[74]

We may conclude with three points. First, the on-again, off-again alliance of labor and middle- and upper-class progressives suggests that by the last half of the 1890s these two powerful reform forces had moved close enough to each other to create a new public agenda, linking reform of corruption with greater public control over business and more equity in taxation and in the market relations between organized capital and organized labor. That agenda was often as powerful within the major parties as outside of them. Second, despite important differences, labor populism and new liberalism or progressivism were not mutually exclusive alternatives, the former radical and insurgent and the latter antidemocratic and hegemonic. Progressivism was capable of containing, including, and transcending labor populism as well as opposing it. The Pullman strike, the emergence of strong unions with a presence in local politics, the popularization of urban socialism, the nationwide Populist insurgency, but also the newly mobilized middle class, a new liberal business leadership, the growth among all classes of evolutionary, utopian, optimistic thinking, and the discovery that business corrupted politics shaped the content of the new liberal reform.

Finally, the Chicago story confounds the commonly accepted categories dividing those in the labor movement into pure and simple trade unionists who eschewed political involvement and socialists and Populists who favored third-party involvement. Chicago labor was politicized to its core. Though leaders of the most effective local unions believed that the trade union would be the major force for industrial evolution, this did not prevent them from supporting their own version of progressive reform. Weaker and newly organized segments of labor supported a more state-centered version of progressivism after 1898. By the end of the Progressive Era many advocates of labor acted as left-wing progressives, balancing their commitment to associational regulation of the market through collective bargaining with support of a greater role for the state in providing for the public welfare and guaranteeing unionism.[75]

Notes

1. A notable example was the gas and light industry in which four companies competed against one another to expand markets. Following a brief rate war the rivals agreed to consolidate to form the Chicago Gas Trust in 1887. With a monopolized market and a capital dwarfing that of all local businesses, the trust immediately increased its gas prices to raise the revenue required to justify stock issued in its name. The ensuing press-supported outcry led the Citizens Association to file a suit against the trust that resulted in its dissolution in 1889, although seven years later the Illinois Bureau of Labor Statistics found that the monopoly was still flourishing. See Bessie Louise Pierce, *A History of Chicago,* vol.

3, *The Rise of a Modern City, 1871–1893* (Chicago: University of Chicago Press, 1957), 221–24.

2. Perry Duis, "Whose City? Public and Private Spaces in Nineteenth-Century Chicago, Part Two," *Chicago History* 12 (Summer 1983): 2–23; Pierce, *History of Chicago*, 3:320–23.

3. *Rights of Labor*, Nov. 15, 1890.

4. Florence Kelley, *The Autobiography of Florence Kelley: Notes of Sixty Years*, ed. Kathryn Kish Sklar (Chicago: Charles H. Kerr, 1986), 11.

5. *Chicago Tribune*, Jan. 4, 1889, Jan. 19, 1889, Sept. 10, 1889, Dec. 8, 1889; *Knights of Labor*, Dec. 28, 1889, June 7, 1890, Feb. 7, 1891 (quote); Mari Jo Buhle, *Women and American Socialism, 1870–1920* (Urbana: University of Illinois Press, 1983), 77.

6. Chester McArthur Destler, *Henry Demarest Lloyd and the Empire of Reform* (Philadelphia: University of Pennsylvania Press, 1963), 247–48 (Lloyd quote); William G. McLoughlin, *Revivals, Awakenings, and Reform* (Chicago: University of Chicago Press, 1978), 173 (Gladden quote); Henry F. May, *Protestant Churches and Industrial America* (New York: Harper and Bros., 1949), 171–203.

7. Donald David Marks, "Polishing the Gem of the Prairie: The Evolution of Civic Reform Consciousness in Chicago, 1874–1900" (Ph.D. diss., University of Wisconsin, 1974), 104–6 (quotes). See also Matthew Schneirov, *The Dream of a New Social Order: Popular Magazines in America, 1893–1914* (New York: Columbia University Press, 1994), 162–201.

8. Graham Taylor, *Pioneering in Social Frontiers* (Chicago: University of Chicago Press, 1930), 5.

9. *Chicago Tribune*, Aug. 1, 1893, Aug. 19, 1893, Aug. 29, 1893, Aug. 30, 1893, Sept. 24, 1893, Dec. 18, 1893; Carlos C. Closson, "The Unemployed in American Cities," *Quarterly Journal of Economics* 8 (Jan. 1894): 189–95.

10. James Gilbert, *Perfect Cities: Chicago's Utopias of 1893* (Chicago: University of Chicago Press, 1991), 210 (Poole quote); interview with Joseph Medill, *Chicago Tribune*, Nov. 8, 1893 (quotes on Harrison years).

11. William T. Stead, *If Christ Came to Chicago: A Plea for the Union of All Who Love in the Service of All Who Suffer* (Chicago: Laird and Lee, 1894), 17 ("frog" quote), 24 ("bum" quote).

12. Frederic Whyte, *The Life of W. T. Stead* (New York: Houghton Mifflin, 1925), 2:39–53; Marks, "Polishing the Gem of the Prairie," 136–38; Gordon Maurice Jensen, "The National Civic Federation: American Business in an Age of Social Change and Social Reform, 1900–1910" (Ph.D. diss., Princeton University, 1956), 24–25 (last quotes).

13. Though interest or pressure groups were active in the polity during the "party period" in the nineteenth century, they began to be recognized in the late Gilded Age and especially during the Progressive Era as ineradicable and increasingly legitimate forms of public representation. See Richard L. McCormick, *The Party Period and Public Policy* (New York: Oxford University Press, 1986), 223–27; Arthur S. Link and Richard L. McCormick, *Progressivism* (Arlington Heights, Ill.: Harlan Davidson, 1983), 48, 56–59, 66; David P. Thelen, *The New Citizenship: Origins of Progressivism in Wisconsin, 1885–1900* (Columbia, Mo.: University of Missouri Press, 1972), chaps. 1 and 2; Philip J. Ethington, *The Public City: The Politi-*

cal Construction of Urban Life in San Francisco, 1850–1900 (Cambridge: Cambridge University Press, 1994), 299–308, 319–26, 408–11; Ballard Campbell, *Representative Democracy: Public Policy and Midwestern Legislatures in the Late Nineteenth Century* (Cambridge, Mass.,: Harvard University Press, 1980), 150–57.

14. Civic Federation of Chicago, *First Annual Report of the Central Council* (Chicago: R. R. Donnelley and Sons, 1895), 7 (first quote), 9; *Chicago Tribune*, Feb. 6, 1894; Ralph Easley, *The Civic Federation of Chicago: What It Has Accomplished* (Chicago: Hollister Bros., 1899), 14 (Easley quote).

15. Civic Federation, *First Annual Report*, 9.

16. Stead, *If Christ Came to Chicago;* Richard L. McCormick, "The Discovery That Business Corrupts Politics: A Reappraisal of the Origins of Progressivism," *American Historical Review* 85 (Apr. 1981): 247–74.

17. Henry Demarest Lloyd, "No Mean City," in *Mazzini and Other Essays*, ed. Henry Demarest Lloyd (New York: Doubleday, Page, 1910), 201–32.

18. Stanley Buder, *Pullman: An Experiment in Industrial Order and Community Planning, 1880–1930* (New York: Oxford University Press, 1967), 49–104; Carl Smith, *Urban Disorder and the Shape of Belief* (Chicago: University of Chicago Press, 1995), 177–208; Richard T. Ely, "Pullman, a Social Study," *Harper's Weekly* 70 (Feb. 1885): 465; Jane Addams, "A Modern Lear," *Survey* 29 (Nov. 2, 1912): 131–37.

19. Shelton Stromquist, *A Generation of Boomers: The Pattern of Railroad Labor Conflict in Nineteenth-Century America* (Urbana: University of Illinois, 1987), 69–84.

20. Buder, *Pullman*, 147–62; Almont Lindsey, *The Pullman Strike: The Story of a Unique Experiment and of a Great Labor Upheaval* (1942; reprint, Chicago: University of Chicago Press, 1967), 90–105, 122–25.

21. Donald L. McMurry, "Labor Policies of the General Managers' Association of Chicago, 1886–1894," *Journal of Economic History* 13 (Spring 1953): 160–78; Lindsey, *Pullman Strike*, 239.

22. *Chicago Times*, July 3, 1894.

23. Florence Kelley, "Ein Ruckblick auf den Pullman-Strike" ("Looking Back on the Pullman Strike"), *Sozial-politisches Centralblatt* 4, no. 5 (1895), 55 (trans. Kathryn Kish Sklar); Jane Addams, *Twenty Years at Hull-House* (1910; reprint, New York: New American Library, 1981), 160; U.S. Industrial Commission, *Report of the U.S. Industrial Commission* (Washington, D.C.: Government Printing Office, 1901), 8:81.

24. Lindsey, *Pullman Strike*, 80–81, 130, 184, 197, 153–62, 245 (quote).

25. Martin J. Sklar, *The Corporate Reconstruction of American Capitalism, 1890—1906: The Market, the Law, and Politics* (Cambridge: Cambridge University Press, 1988), 47–53; Scott R. Bowman, *The Modern Corporation and American Political Thought: Law, Power, and Ideology* (University Park: Pennsylvania State University Press, 1996), chaps. 1 and 2.

26. Haggai Hurvitz, "American Labor Law and the Doctrine of Entrepreneurial Property Rights: Boycott, Courts, and the Juridical Reorientation of 1886–1895," *Industrial Relations Law Journal* 8, no. 3 (1986): 307–61; Herbert Hovenkamp, *Enterprise and American Law, 1836–1937* (Cambridge, Mass.: Harvard University Press, 1991), 226–38; Melvyn Dubofsky, *The State and Labor in Modern America* (Chapel Hill: University of North Carolina, 1994), 20–21, 24–27, 31–32.

27. Sklar, *Corporate Reconstruction of American Capitalism*, 179–332; Daniel R. Ernst, *Lawyers against Labor: From Individual Rights to Corporate Liberalism* (Urbana: University of Illinois Press, 1995).

28. Harry Barnard, *Eagle Forgotten: The Life of John Peter Altgeld* (1938; reprint, Secaucus, N.J.: Lyle Stuart, 1966), 290–98, 302–7 (quote on 306); Lindsey, *Pullman Strike*, 185–90.

29. *Chicago Tribune*, July 3, 1894 (first Madden quote), July 4, 1894 (second Madden quote); *Chicago Times*, July 4, 1894, July 5, 1894.

30. *Chicago Times*, July 4–11, 1894; *Chicago Tribune*, July 9, 1894, July 10, 1894.

31. *Chicago Tribune*, July 13, 1894, July 14, 1894; Lindsey, *Pullman Strike*, 226–35; Nick Salvatore, *Eugene V. Debs: Citizen and Socialist* (Urbana: University of Illinois Press, 1982), 136.

32. Olney to Judge George M. Dallas, quoted in Gerald G. Eggert, *Richard Olney: Evolution of a Statesman* (University Park: Pennsylvania State University, 1974), 157–58.

33. Ernst, *Lawyers against Labor.*

34. *Chicago Tribune*, July 21, 1894; Carroll Wright, "The Chicago Strike," *Publications of the American Economic Association* 9 (Oct. and Dec. 1894): 36 (quote); Civic Federation of Chicago, *First Annual Report*, 75–81; U.S. Strike Commission, *Report of the Chicago Strike of June–July, 1894 by the United States Strike Commission* (Washington, D.C.: Government Printing Office, 1894), xv–xvi.

35. U.S. Strike Commission, *Report of the Chicago Strike*, xxxi, xlvi–liv. For local reactions, see *Chicago Tribune*, Nov. 14, 1894, Nov. 17, 1894; and *Chicago Times*, Nov. 13, 1894, Nov. 14, 1894.

36. *Congress on Industrial Conciliation and Arbitration Arranged under the Auspices of the Industrial Committee of the Civic Federation of Chicago, Nov. 13–14, 1894* (Chicago: Civic Federation of Chicago, 1895); *Chicago Times*, Nov. 11, 1894, Nov. 14, 1894. Tuley was said by Jane Addams to have been the originator of the term *government by injunction*. See Jane Addams, *The Permanent Becomes Excellent* (New York: Macmillan, 1932), 77.

37. *Chicago Times-Herald*, May 20, 1895, June 29, 1895, Aug. 3, 1895; Earl Beckner, *A History of Labor Legislation in Illinois* (Chicago: University of Chicago Press, 1929), 77–79. That the arbitration bill enjoyed wide and active support among Chicago trade union leaders is evident in interviews in the *Chicago Times-Herald*, Aug. 3, 1895. Like other reformers in this period, labor leaders affirmed the power of voluntary association and an educated public opinion to shape political behavior with minimal state administrative intervention. See Alexander Yard, "Coercive Government within a Minimal State: The Idea of Public Opinion in Gilded Age Labor Reform Culture," *Labor History* 34 (Fall 1993): 443–56.

38. Bruce Laurie, *Artisans into Workers: Labor in Nineteenth-Century America* (New York: Noonday, 1989), 203–10.

39. Mary Furner, "The Republican Tradition and the New Liberalism: Social Investigation, State Building, and Social Learning in the Gilded Age," in *The State and Social Investigation in Britain and the United States*, ed. Michael J. Lacey and Mary O. Furner (Cambridge: Cambridge University Press, 1993), 171–241;

Dubofsky, *State and Labor*, 32–33; on industrial democracy, see Lloyd's address before the 1893 AFL convention in *Chicago Tribune*, Dec. 12, 1893.

40. Henry Demarest Lloyd, *Wealth against Commonwealth* (New York: Harper and Bros., 1894); Henry Demarest Lloyd, "Revolution," in Chester McArthur Destler, *American Radicalism, 1865–1901: Essays and Documents* (New London: Connecticut College, 1946), 217 (quote); John L. Thomas, *Alternative America: Henry George, Edward Bellamy, Henry Demarest Lloyd and the Adversary Tradition* (Cambridge, Mass.: Belknap, 1983), 288–308. Lloyd explicitly argued against the idea that trusts were an organic, unavoidable development in a review of Ernest Von Halle's *Trusts and Industrial Combinations in the United States* published in the *Chicago Times-Herald*, Apr. 14, 1895.

41. The best history of the labor-Populist alliance in Chicago is still Destler, *American Radicalism*, 162–254. On the making of the coalition, see 200, 224–25.

42. *Chicago Times*, Aug. 19, 1894, Aug. 20, 1894, Aug. 26, 1894; *Union Workman*, Feb. 1, 1896; Destler, *American Radicalism*, 190–209; Willis J. Abbot, "The Chicago Populist Campaign," *Arena* 62 (Feb. 1895): 190–205.

43. *Chicago Times*, Nov. 6, 1894, Nov. 8, 1894; *Searchlight*, Jan. 9, 1895.

44. *Chicago Tribune*, Dec. 18, 1893; *Searchlight*, Jan. 9, 1895; Morgan to Lloyd, Feb. 2, 1896, Reel 7, Henry Demarest Lloyd Papers (microfilm), Wisconsin State Historical Society, Madison (hereafter HDLP). Bureau of Labor Statistics of the State of Illinois, *Twelfth Biennial Report, 1902* (Springfield: Phillips Bros., 1904), 314, listed 44,193 unionists in Chicago in 1897.

45. Destler, *American Radicalism*, 190 (Destler's words).

46. *Chicago Times-Herald*, Feb. 18, 1895; Destler, *American Radicalism*, 200–204. *Union Workman*, Jan. 6, 1895, contains platforms of affiliated unions and officers of the Labor Congress.

47. Morgan to Lloyd, Feb. 2, 1896, HDLP; *Searchlight*, Jan. 9, 1895; Terence J. McDonald, *The Parameters of Urban Fiscal Policy: Socioeconomic Change and Political Culture in San Francisco, 1860–1910* (Berkeley: University of California Press, 1986). McDonald found that when municipal elections were held separately from national and state elections, significantly higher numbers of voters voted independent.

48. *Searchlight*, Jan. 17, 1895.

49. Ibid., Feb. 28, 1895. That Lloyd and the People's Party turned toward the middle classes and the political center during the winter and spring of 1895 is argued in Destler, *American Radicalism*, 236–51.

50. Michael P. McCarthy, "The New Metropolis: Chicago, the Annexation Movement, and Progressive Reform," in *The Age of Reform: New Perspectives on the Progressive Era*, ed. Michael H. Ebner and Eugene M. Tobin (Port Washington, N.Y.: Kennikat, 1977), 43–54; Michael P. McCarthy, "On Bosses, Reformers, and Urban Growth: Some Suggestions for a Political Typology of American Cities," *Journal of Urban History* 4 (Nov. 1977): 29–38.

51. Election results reported in *Chicago Daily News Almanac and Political Register* (Chicago: Chicago Daily News, 1895 and 1898).

52. David Paul Nord, "The Politics of Urban Agenda Setting in Late Nineteenth-Century Cities," *Journalism Quarterly* 58 (Winter 1981): 565–74; David Paul

Nord, *Newspapers and New Politics: Midwestern Municipal Reform, 1890–1900*, Studies in American History and Culture, No. 27 (Madison, Wis.: UMI Research Press, 1981), 16–18, and passim. Compare Michael E. McGerr, *The Decline of Popular Politics: The American North, 1865–1928* (New York: Oxford University Press, 1986), 107–83.

53. The strength of antisilver forces in the respectable wing of the Democratic Party is evident in the struggle for the presidency of the Iroquois Club. See *Chicago Times-Herald*, Apr. 18, 1895, Apr. 20, 1895, Apr. 24, 1895. In St. Louis the controversy over silver overwhelmed municipal reform, while in Chicago the unity over municipal reform in the middle and upper classes was reinforced by unity over the silver question. See Nord, *Newspapers and New Politics*, 81–82, 98–100.

54. Destler, *American Radicalism*, 251–53; Thomas J. Morgan to Lloyd, June 9, 1896, Reel 7, HDLP. Local socialists invited DeLeon to speak in Chicago to promote his dual union. See *Chicago Record*, May 1, 1896.

55. *Chicago Times-Herald*, June 10, 1895, Sept. 24, 1895, Nov. 10, 1895, Dec. 5, 1895, Dec. 9, 1895, Dec. 29, 1895, Feb. 8, 1896, Mar. 6, 1896; Bennett Stark, "Political Economy of State Public Finance: Illinois, 1830–1970" (Ph.D. diss., University of Wisconsin, Madison, 1982), 75–81, 95, 103, 113; Willis J. Abbot, *Watching the World Go By* (New York: Little, Brown, 1933), 105–7 (on boycott); Douglas Sutherland, *Fifty Years on the Civic Front: A History of the Civic Federation's Dynamic Activities* (Chicago: Civic Federation, 1943), 18–19. For similar developments in Milwaukee, see Thelen, *New Citizenship*, 203–11.

56. *Chicago Times-Herald*, Jan. 12, 1896, Jan. 26, 1896, Mar. 7, 1896, Apr. 6, 1896, Apr. 8, 1896; Michael Patrick McCarthy, "Businessmen and Professionals in Municipal Reform: The Chicago Experience, 1887–1920" (Ph.D. diss., Northwestern University, 1970), 33.

57. For an early account, see Sidney I. Roberts, "The Municipal Voters' League and Chicago's Boodlers," *Journal of the Illinois State Historical Society* 53 (Summer 1960): 117–48; Steffens, *The Shame of the Cities* (1903; reprint, New York: Hill and Wong 1992), 164 (first quote), 184 (second quote). Revisionist scholars include Samuel P. Hays, "Political Parties and the Community-Society Continuum," in *The American Party Systems: Stages in Political Development*, ed. William Nisbet Chambers and Walter Dean Burnham (New York: Oxford University Press, 1975), 152–81; and the much-cited Joan S. Miller, "The Politics of Municipal Reform in Chicago during the Progressive Era" (M.A. thesis, Roosevelt University, 1966). For different views, see McCarthy, "Businessmen and Professionals in Municipal Reform," 34–39; Nord, *Newspapers and New Politics*, 115; and Gerald W. McFarland, *Mugwumps, Morals, and Politics, 1884–1920* (Amherst: University of Massachusetts Press, 1975), 125–48.

58. *Chicago Times-Herald*, Feb. 26, 1896 (first quote), Mar. 5, 1896 (second quote); Roberts, "Municipal Voters' League," 139. The final set of principles the People's party adopted for the mayoral campaign was an amalgam of progressive reform and socialism. Its first four principles called for "good government and civil service reform; Non-partisan administration of the city government; Municipal control of the city railways, gas works, natural monopolies and municipal construction; ownership and control of the down-town loop; Franchises not to be

squandered, but controlled for the benefit of the municipality." "Principles Advocated by the Peoples Party of the Twenty-Sixth Ward for the Municipal Campaign," Reel 23, HDLP.

59. *Union Workman*, Apr. 25, 1896.

60. Roberts, "Municipal Voters' League," 142–43; McGerr, *Decline of Popular Politics*, 107–83; Nord, *Newspapers and New Politics*, 16–18.

61. *Eight-Hour Herald*, Oct. 26, 1895 (quote), Nov. 2, 1895, Nov. 9, 1895, May 21, 1896, Aug. 6, 1896, Sept. 15, 1896; *Union Workman*, Jan. 8, 1896.

62. Election results reported in *Chicago Daily News Almanac and Political Register*, 1895 and 1898; percentage elected in each ward of aldermanic candidates acceptable to the MVL reported in McCarthy, "New Metropolis," 51.

63. *Union Workman*, Dec. 28, 1895, Jan. 4, 1896, Jan. 18, 1896, Jan. 25, 1896, Apr. 25, 1896. See also Morgan's attack on the Civic Federation in *Chicago Times-Herald*, Dec. 15, 1895.

64. Stevens to Lloyd, Mar. 15, 1897, Reel 8, HDLP.

65. Steffens, *Shame of the Cities*, 188–89. Most Chicago businesspeople, including Marshall Field, still preferred "government by purchase," according to the MVL leader William Kent. Quoted in Robert L. Woodbury, "William Kent: Progressive Gadfly, 1864–1928" (Ph.D. diss., Yale University, 1967), 118.

66. *Chicago Times-Herald*, Feb. 20, 1896, Feb. 23, 1896, Mar. 9, 1896, Mar. 14, 1896, Mar. 22, 1896 (Baker quote).

67. For a mixed evaluation of the results of the state arbitration board, see Beckner, *History of Labor Legislation*, 79–101.

68. *Union Workman*, Jan. 18, 1896, Feb. 8, 1896, Apr. 25, 1896; *Eight-Hour Herald*, Aug. 20, 1896, Oct. 13, 1896, Nov. 10, 1896 (quote).

69. *Chicago Times-Herald*, Nov. 11, 1896, Nov. 23, 1896; *Eight-Hour Herald*, Nov. 10, 1896, Nov. 24, 1896.

70. *Chicago Times-Herald*, Apr. 7, 1897, Apr. 8, 1897.

71. Ibid., Apr. 8, 1897, Apr. 19, 1897, May 11, 1897, May 23, 1897, Aug. 15, 1897; Nord, *Newspapers and New Politics*, 103–8; "Why Municipal Reform Succeeds in Chicago and Fails in New York," *Independent* 56 (Apr. 14, 1904): 833 (quote); John Buenker, *Urban Liberalism and Progressive Reform* (New York: W. W. Norton, 1973), 27–31.

72. Kenneth Finegold, *Experts and Politicians: Reform Challenges to Machine Politics in New York, Cleveland, and Chicago* (Princeton, N.J.: Princeton University Press, 1995), 119–37; Georg Leidenberger, "'The Public Is the Labor Union': Working-Class Progressivism in Turn-of-the-Century Chicago," *Labor History* 36 (Spring 1995): 187–210; Ray Ginger, *Altgeld's America, 1890–1905: The Lincoln Ideal versus Changing Realities* (1958; reprint, Chicago: Quadrangle Books, 1965), 253–303; Barbara Warne Newell, *Chicago and the Labor Movement: Metropolitan Unionism in the 1930s* (Urbana: University of Illinois Press, 1961), 24–26, 252–53.

73. James Weinstein, *The Corporate Ideal in the Liberal State, 1900–1908* (Boston: Beacon, 1968), 6–29; Jensen, "National Civic Federation," 30; McFarland, *Mugwumps, Morals, and Politics*, 144–46, 157; James Weinstein, "Gompers and the New Liberalism, 1900–1909," *Studies on the Left* 5 (Fall 1965): 101–14; David Montgom-

ery, *Workers' Control in America: Studies in the History of Work, Technology, and Labor Struggles* (Cambridge: Cambridge University Press, 1979), 48–90.

74. Franklin MacVeagh, *The Values of Certain Social and Economic Facts: Address before the Chicago and Cook County High School Association, Mar. 6, 1897* (Chicago: Chicago and Cook County High School Association, 1899); Bruno Ramirez, *When Workers Fight: The Politics of Industrial Relations in the Progressive Era, 1898–1916* (Westport, Conn.: Greenwood, 1978), 11–12 ("golden age" quote), 129–41; Selig Perlman, *A History of Trade Unionism in the United States* (New York: Macmillan, 1922), 163–90; Montgomery, *Workers' Control in America*, 48–90; Howell John Harris, "Industrial Democracy and Liberal Capitalism, 1890–1925," in *Industrial Democracy in America: The Ambiguous Promise*, ed. Nelson Lichtenstein and Howell John Harris (Cambridge: Cambridge University Press, 1993), 51–55; Jeffrey Haydu, "Trade Agreement vs. Open Shop: Employers' Choices before WWI," *Industrial Relations* 28 (Spring 1989), 159–73.

75. Mary O. Furner, "Knowing Capitalism: Public Investigation and the Labor Question in the Long Progressive Era," in *The State and Economic Knowledge: The American and British Experience*, ed. Mary O. Furner and Barry Supple (Cambridge: Woodrow Wilson International Center for Scholars and Cambridge University Press, 1992); Dubofsky, *State and Labor*, chap. 2; Gary M. Fink, "The Rejection of Voluntarism," *Industrial and Labor Relations Review* 26 (Jan. 1973): 805–19.

Conclusion

In 1895 Henry Demarest Lloyd tried to explain to readers in Great Britain why the United States had no labor party. No doubt drawing on his experiences in Chicago, Lloyd observed that union officials, who were given "appointive places" in government by party leaders, "play the bellwether to prevent the body of working men from leaving them." The "capitalistic parties" bolstered their hold on working people by having police "favor" unions during strikes, thus making it "impossible for the employers to introduce 'scabs.'" When "independent political action is broached in the lodges of a union which has thus been favored," those members who have government berths "are quick to point out that the union cannot expect police favors in the next strike if they wander from the old political fold." To Lloyd, an ardent advocate of an independent labor party, this practice by the two major parties "operates to diminish not to add to the political power of the working people."[1]

Historians of American labor politics have, for the most part, affirmed the judgment of Lloyd and others that to the extent the major parties accommodated the labor movement in this fashion, they undermined, diverted, and stymied—in a word co-opted—class-conscious political action. The premise of this belief—the identification of working-class politics with labor or socialist parties—has contributed, wittingly or not, to the formulation of labor history as a response to that hoary exceptionalist query and lament, "Why no socialism in America"? Viewed through this lens, successful labor political action becomes limited to periodic flashes of light in the long night of Gilded Age politics, in the case of Chicago: the Eight Hour League of 1866, the Socialist Labor party of 1877–79, the United Labor party of 1886–87, and the People's party of 1894–95.

In this book I have shifted the focus of analysis from the rise and decline, appearance and disappearance, of labor or socialist parties to a deeper, more inclusive, more persistent phenomenon: the formation, augmentation, and increasing influence, in both the regular parties and governmental policy-making, of working-class political power. Working-class political power evolved in the context of the interaction between the two major parties and the various independent labor parties. Each of the city's four great upheavals generated dissatisfaction with the existing informal and formal accommodations and bargains between political representatives of the labor movement and local party and governmental officials. In each case newly mobilized worker-citizens precipitated a rupture in the tie between labor leadership and the two major parties. The independent labor forays that issued from these ruptures very quickly redounded to the benefit of labor-machine politics by strengthening labor representatives' bargaining position with major party leaders. New bargains were then struck that expanded the resources, privileges, and immunities these leaders could offer their labor constituents and draw on personally themselves. Such benefits were, in effect, the price political leaders paid to labor representatives for resisting or disowning independent labor politics. The resulting material incentives for labor leaders to maintain party loyalties enhanced the potential for corruption and tended to limit their scope of action. These conditions then helped set the stage for a reaction against this informal "regime" in the form of a labor upheaval and a corresponding bout of independent labor politics. In short, the ebb and flow of independent labor parties and the making and breaking of bargains between labor representatives and major party politicians were closely related to each other, with each drawing strength from the other's failures.

As Lloyd indicated, the ability of labor to win benefits from one or both of the two major parties was a major reason for the failure of an independent labor or socialist party to endure. It would be a mistake, however, to reduce this complex phenomenon to a case of "bourgeois ideological hegemony." American political parties were (and are) fundamentally different from European parliamentary parties, though their policy results—in the shape of the welfare state—have not differed substantially. In systems with proportional representation, as in Europe, parties tend to be ideological, and the cross-class compromises and coalition making necessary to govern occur after elections. In the United States (and Britain) the "winner take all, single member district" system means a vote for a losing candidate is a wasted vote; voters are thus encouraged to extend their support to one of two parties that have a chance to win. U.S. parties are therefore encouraged to assemble their multiclass coalitions before, not after, elections. For this reason they must go before the electorate not as ideological parties but as (at best) principled and programmatic parties, whose social basis is nearly always multiclass. Instead of representing classes and interests as they do in proportional systems, parties in winner-take-all-systems aggregate them.[2] It follows that labor influence in U.S. political history must be explored not just or mainly in the terms of independent labor parties or single class appeals but more in terms of preelection coalition making, in postelection appointments, and in party policies. Taking account of this distinction makes it possible to appreciate that while the U.S. political system may generally obscure class and socialist characteristics, its practices reveal an important place for them, if we examine all the relevant points in the political process.

In Chicago local parties were first compelled to take account of the labor question and the potential labor vote as a consequence of the formation of the Trades Assembly in 1864 and the Eight Hour League in 1866. Beginning with Andrew Cameron, politicians and union leaders created and mobilized a labor vote at least potentially independent of the two parties. This process was an integral part of the recurrent crises of proprietary, competitive capitalism manifested in overproduction, falling prices, financial panics, extended depressions, and the increasing resort by businesses and workers to organization and collective action to regulate the competitive market. It was also a segmented process, that is, one in which ethnic leaders mobilized ethnic workers in their neighborhoods on the basis of different working-class versions of republican ideology. In the latter stages of the 1873–79 depression German-speaking socialists successfully pitched a class appeal to German workers and reformers in the Republican party, eventually leading many into the Democratic party. During the early 1880s Irish Land League nationalists and Irish Knights of Labor politicians won significant numbers of working-class Irish Democrats to independent politics. By 1879 the rise of the class-identified labor vote had enabled the Democratic mayor, Carter Harrison, to accomplish an electoral realignment in local politics, making prolabor Democrats the dominant party.

In transacting this realignment Mayor Harrison pioneered a new brand of politics by pitching special appeals to social groups that had organized independent of the major parties in the midst of the 1870s depression. To wealthy businessmen seeking to limit their tax liabilities he offered fiscal retrenchment; to obviate opposition from liberal reformers in the Citizens Association, he appointed honest professionals to key positions in government; to win the support of German socialists, he protected their right to free speech and assembly and wooed them with appointments; to the trade unions, which had become strong enough to engage in nonpartisan political collective bargaining, he offered police neutrality during strikes.

The critical turning point in the creation of a new liberal politics occurred in 1886–87. In the context of a renewed industrial crisis, the mix of informal accommodations through distributive politics and the increasingly formal group appeals and government policies, which had enabled Mayor Harrison to broker between social groups and classes, was no longer viable. Most important, beginning in the 1885 streetcar strike, employer pressure prevented Harrison from utilizing the police as he had in the past to accommodate trade unions politically. During four labor disputes in which skilled workers' unions were resisting the effects of machinery introduced by employers facing cost pressures because of overproduction in their industries, Harrison's police sided with employers. Faced with defeat, the city's trade unions abandoned their Democratic party alliance. They turned en masse to the Knights of Labor and its promise of labor solidarity with the unskilled through the boycott and the demand of the eight-hour day, which was trumpeted as a class answer to the effects of overproduction.

Though Chicago's third great upheaval had limited success in winning shorter hours, its deeper significance lay in a fundamental reorientation of the goals of the labor movement. Organized workers distanced themselves from community-based mass strikes and, like their employers, embraced the idea that the competitive market required regulation by the visible hand of group organization. To the degree they were organized, workers deemphasized the goal of regaining ownership of the means of production or the conditions of their labor by establishing producers' cooperatives and instead began to emphasize raising the standard of living in the form of higher wages and more certain employment. Concomitantly, the Knights of Labor underwent a major internal transformation in which anti-Powderly, pro-unionist, prosocialist leaders took power. Not only did this enable the labor movement to unite in the city's first true labor party, but also it opened the way for that party to adopt a socialist-initiated reform program that exposed the way business corrupted local politics through inequitable tax assessments and corporate franchise bribery and championed municipal ownership as an alternative.

The immediate post-Haymarket years in Chicago have been remembered in popular myth, and by some historians as well, as a period of antisocialist repression and labor retreat. Repression and retreat there was. But the outstanding feature of this period was the defeat of that short-lived repression; the more formal recognition by the two parties, especially the Democrats, of organized labor as the voice of the city's working people; and the first flowering of a new liberal, cross-class political coalition that prefigured progressive reform. In the late 1880s leading mugwump liberals began to shed their distrust of working people, their reflexive faith in the immutable laws of the market, their opposition to "class" legislation, and their understanding of society as composed of a moral hierarchy of individuals topped by the "best men." In addition, such new liberal thinkers and reform leaders as Henry Demarest Lloyd and John Peter Altgeld, such women as Jane Addams and Ellen Henrotin on the "left," and Franklin MacVeagh, Murray Tuley, and Lyman Gage altered their thinking as a result of personal relationships with labor activists. To one extent or another, they cultivated a new sympathy for the plight of working people, provisionally accepted what had been previously viewed as "class legislation" (for example, sweatshop regulation), and began to view society as composed of associations that might legitimately regulate market activity.

The growing public acceptance of capital-labor collective bargaining was a key to the post-Haymarket rapprochement between segments of capital and labor. In 1887 Judge Tuley arbitrated a dispute in the mason industry, forestalling the open shop; and during the building of the World's Fair, city leaders intervened in a carpenters' dispute to compel contractors to recognize the union. Labor leaders in turn accepted new liberal businessmen as candidates of labor parties. Meanwhile, after a period of retreat, the organized labor movement revived and reformed in the early 1890s, raising its membership to a level higher than during the upheaval of the mid-1880s. A new unionism emerged, utilizing union label boycotts and exclusive agreements to regulate the labor market. Like the new trusts forming in the business world, unions appeared more than ever to be an ineradicable development in an inexorable evolution with which liberals would have to deal.

New thinking about the market and the character of reform matured still further with the World's Fair and the 1890s depression. Although the 1880s had been characterized by the major parties' acceptance of social groups, the 1890s witnessed a revival of the ideal of a public interest outweighing selfish private interests and a "new citizenship." The revised conception of the public was greatly influenced by new conceptions of socialism. Among both labor activists and respectable reformers, the older republican socialism and revolutionary socialism began to give way to an evolutionary socialism that abandoned natural-rights premises and affirmed the evolution of industrial society as both unavoidable and beneficently tending toward socialism. Shorn of its insurrectionary and class warfare features, socialism became part of reform discourse in the 1890s and contributed to the rethinking of liberalism. One way this occurred was through a wider, though still conditional, acceptance of organizational regulation of market competition by both corporations and unions, with the proviso that the public interest be represented by third-party arbitration, a solution proposed by the newly formed Civic

Federation during the Pullman strike. Applied to municipal reform, the new thinking translated into a recognition that respectable business monopolists, such as Charles Yerkes, more than men of low origins and bad character, were at the root of municipal corruption. The new civic consciousness helped reformers challenge the low tax and low public spending fiscal policies that underlay the political settlement of the 1870s. Drawing on the program socialists had been advocating since 1887, the Municipal Voters League supported shorter franchises with an option for municipal ownership as a solution to party corruption. Meanwhile, the press used sensationalist and advertising methods to mobilize the reform constituency as a mass public rather than as a congeries of groups. By the late 1890s the new liberal reform vote overshadowed "the independent labor vote" by more than two-to-one, implying that to act as the swing vote between the two parties, labor must align itself with a broader reform sentiment.

The relationship between new liberal politics and labor politics mixed elements of conflict and cooperation. As late as 1895 Henry Demarest Lloyd hoped that a new cross-class reform constituency might find a vehicle in the People's party. But labor leadership's ability to rely on Democratic politicians and some civic leaders for alternatives to antilabor repression and labor's reputation for corruption, coercive boycotts, and strike violence forestalled a labor-reform alliance within the People's party. The vacuum created by the failure of labor-Populists was filled by the Municipal Voters League, which sought—with partial success—to create a synthesis between labor populism and new liberal reform. When divided labor reunited in the Chicago Federation of Labor and the end of the 1893–1898 depression allowed a resurgence of labor organizing, most labor voters returned to the Democratic party. But the alliance was on a new basis, for Democrats accommodated the new labor and progressive reform agenda just as they had done in the 1870s and 1880s.

The most important impact of the new liberalism came on the national level when the leaders of the Civic Federation of Chicago founded the National Civic Federation, with its commitment to the trade agreement and reform of the Sherman Act. The new liberalism did not "triumph" in this period, but it did begin its long transformation into what we think of as twentieth-century liberalism.

Notes

1. Henry Demarest Lloyd, "The American Labour Movement," *Labour Leader*, Nov. 5, 1895, Reel 23, Henry Demarest Lloyd Papers (microfilm), Wisconsin State Historical Society, Madison.

2. Leon D. Epstein, *Political Parties in Western Democracies* (New Brunswick, N.J.: Transaction Books, 1980), 73–76; Maurice Duverger, *Political Parties: Their Organization and Activity in the Modern State* (London: Methuen, 1969), 206–55; Arend Lijphart and Barnard Grofman, eds., *Choosing an Electoral System* (New York: Praeger, 1984). See also Robert H. Wiebe, *The Segmented Society: An Introduction to the Meaning of America* (New York: Oxford University Press, 1975), 136–46.

Index

Richard Schneirov received his Ph.D. from Northern Illinois University in 1984 and taught in Germany under a Fulbright junior lectureship in 1985–86 and at Ohio State University from 1986 to 1989. For the last decade he has taught U.S. history at Indiana State University in Terre Haute. He is the coauthor (with Thomas J. Suhrbur) of *Union Brotherhood, Union Town: The History of the Carpenters' Union of Chicago, 1863–1987* (1988) and the author of *Pride and Solidarity: A History of the Plumbers and Pipefitters of Columbus, Ohio, 1889–1989* (1993) and has written numerous journal articles on labor and politics.

BOOKS IN THE SERIES
THE WORKING CLASS IN AMERICAN HISTORY

Worker City, Company Town: Iron and Cotton-Worker Protest in Troy and Cohoes, New York, 1855–84 *Daniel J. Walkowitz*

Life, Work, and Rebellion in the Coal Fields: The Southern West Virginia Miners, 1880–1922 *David Alan Corbin*

Women and American Socialism, 1870–1920 *Mari Jo Buhle*

Lives of Their Own: Blacks, Italians, and Poles in Pittsburgh, 1900–1960 *John Bodnar, Roger Simon, and Michael P. Weber*

Working-Class America: Essays on Labor, Community, and American Society *Edited by Michael H. Frisch and Daniel J. Walkowitz*

Eugene V. Debs: Citizen and Socialist *Nick Salvatore*

American Labor and Immigration History, 1877–1920s: Recent European Research *Edited by Dirk Hoerder*

Workingmen's Democracy: The Knights of Labor and American Politics *Leon Fink*

The Electrical Workers: A History of Labor at General Electric and Westinghouse, 1923–60 *Ronald W. Schatz*

The Mechanics of Baltimore: Workers and Politics in the Age of Revolution, 1763–1812 *Charles G. Steffen*

The Practice of Solidarity: American Hat Finishers in the Nineteenth Century *David Bensman*

The Labor History Reader *Edited by Daniel J. Leab*

Solidarity and Fragmentation: Working People and Class Consciousness in Detroit, 1875–1900 *Richard Oestreicher*

Counter Cultures: Saleswomen, Managers, and Customers in American Department Stores, 1890–1940 *Susan Porter Benson*

The New England Working Class and the New Labor History *Edited by Herbert G. Gutman and Donald H. Bell*

Labor Leaders in America *Edited by Melvyn Dubofsky and Warren Van Tine*

Barons of Labor: The San Francisco Building Trades and Union Power in the Progressive Era *Michael Kazin*

Gender at Work: The Dynamics of Job Segregation by Sex during World War II *Ruth Milkman*

Once a Cigar Maker: Men, Women, and Work Culture in American Cigar Factories, 1900–1919 *Patricia A. Cooper*

A Generation of Boomers: The Pattern of Railroad Labor Conflict in Nineteenth-Century America *Shelton Stromquist*

Work and Community in the Jungle: Chicago's Packinghouse Workers, 1894–1922 *James R. Barrett*

Workers, Managers, and Welfare Capitalism: The Shoeworkers and Tanners of Endicott Johnson, 1890–1950 *Gerald Zahavi*
Men, Women, and Work: Class, Gender, and Protest in the New England Shoe Industry, 1780–1910 *Mary Blewett*
Workers on the Waterfront: Seamen, Longshoremen, and Unionism in the 1930s *Bruce Nelson*
German Workers in Chicago: A Documentary History of Working-Class Culture from 1850 to World War I *Edited by Hartmut Keil and John B. Jentz*
On the Line: Essays in the History of Auto Work *Edited by Nelson Lichtenstein and Stephen Meyer III*
Upheaval in the Quiet Zone: A History of Hospital Workers' Union, Local 1199 *Leon Fink and Brian Greenberg*
Labor's Flaming Youth: Telephone Operators and Worker Militancy, 1878–1923 *Stephen H. Norwood*
Another Civil War: Labor, Capital, and the State in the Anthracite Regions of Pennsylvania, 1840–68 *Grace Palladino*
Coal, Class, and Color: Blacks in Southern West Virginia, 1915–32 *Joe William Trotter, Jr.*
For Democracy, Workers, and God: Labor Song-Poems and Labor Protest, 1865–95 *Clark D. Halker*
Dishing It Out: Waitresses and Their Unions in the Twentieth Century *Dorothy Sue Cobble*
The Spirit of 1848: German Immigrants, Labor Conflict, and the Coming of the Civil War *Bruce Levine*
Working Women of Collar City: Gender, Class, and Community in Troy, New York, 1864–86 *Carole Turbin*
Southern Labor and Black Civil Rights: Organizing Memphis Workers *Michael K. Honey*
Radicals of the Worst Sort: Laboring Women in Lawrence, Massachusetts, 1860–1912 *Ardis Cameron*
Producers, Proletarians, and Politicians: Workers and Party Politics in Evansville and New Albany, Indiana, 1850–87 *Lawrence M. Lipin*
The New Left and Labor in the 1960s *Peter B. Levy*
The Making of Western Labor Radicalism: Denver's Organized Workers, 1878–1905 *David Brundage*
In Search of the Working Class: Essays in American Labor History and Political Culture *Leon Fink*
Lawyers against Labor: From Individual Rights to Corporate Liberalism *Daniel R. Ernst*
"We Are All Leaders": The Alternative Unionism of the Early 1930s *Edited by Staughton Lynd*

The Female Economy: The Millinery and Dressmaking Trades, 1860–1930 *Wendy Gamber*

"Negro and White, Unite and Fight!": A Social History of Industrial Unionism in Meatpacking, 1930–90 *Roger Horowitz*

Power at Odds: The 1922 National Railroad Shopmen's Strike *Colin J. Davis*

The Common Ground of Womanhood: Class, Gender, and Working Girls' Clubs, 1884–1928 *Priscilla Murolo*

Marching Together: Women of the Brotherhood of Sleeping Car Porters *Melinda Chateauvert*

Down on the Killing Floor: Black and White Workers in Chicago's Packinghouses, 1904–54 *Rick Halpern*

Labor and Urban Politics: Class Conflict and the Origins of Modern Liberalism in Chicago, 1864–97 *Richard Schneirov*